THE MAGILL BIBLIOGRAPHIES

The American Presidents, by Norman S. Cohen, 1989
Black American Women Novelists, by Craig Werner, 1989
Classical Greek and Roman Drama, by Robert J. Forman, 1989
Contemporary Latin American Fiction, by Keith H. Brower, 1989
Masters of Mystery and Detective Fiction, by J. Randolph Cox, 1989
Nineteenth Century American Poetry, by Philip K. Jason, 1989
Restoration Drama, by Thomas J. Taylor, 1989
Twentieth Century European Short Story, by Charles E. May, 1989
The Victorian Novel, by Laurence W. Mazzeno, 1989
Women's Issues, by Laura Stempel Mumford, 1989
America in Space, by Russell R. Tobias, 1991
The American Constitution, by Robert J. Janosik, 1991
The Classic Epic, by Thomas J. Sienkewicz, 1991
English Romantic Poetry, by Brian Aubrey, 1991
Ethics, by John K. Roth, 1991
The Immigrant Experience, by Paul D. Mageli, 1991
The Modern American Novel, by Steven G. Kellman, 1991
Native Americans, by Frederick E. Hoxie and Harvey Markowitz, 1991
American Drama: 1918-1960, by R. Baird Shuman, 1992
American Ethnic Literatures, by David R. Peck, 1992
American Theater History, by Thomas J. Taylor, 1992
The Atomic Bomb, by Hans G. Graetzer and Larry M. Browning, 1992
Biography, by Carl Rollyson, 1992
The History of Science, by Gordon L. Miller, 1992
The Origin and Evolution of Life on Earth, by David W. Hollar, Jr., 1992
Pan-Africanism, by Michael W. Williams, 1992
Resources for Writers, by R. Baird Shuman, 1992
Shakespeare, by Joseph Rosenblum, 1992
The Vietnam War in Literature, by Philip K. Jason, 1992
Contemporary Southern Women Fiction Writers, by Rosemary M. Canfield Reisman and Christopher J. Canfield, 1994
Cycles in Humans and Nature, by John T. Burns, 1994
Environmental Studies, by Diane M. Fortner, 1994
Poverty in America, by Steven Pressman, 1994
The Short Story in English: Britain and North America, by Dean

Baldwin and Gregory L. Morris, 1994
Victorian Poetry, by Laurence W. Mazzeno, 1995
Human Rights in Theory and Practice, by Gregory J. Walters, 1995
Energy, by Joseph R. Rudolph, Jr., 1995
The History of the Book, by Joseph Rosenblum, 1995
Psychology, by The Editors of Salem Press, 1996
The Search for Economics as a Science, by The Editors of Salem Press, 1996

Psychology

An Introductory Bibliography

The Editors of Salem Press

Consulting Editor: Susan E. Beers

Magill Bibliographies

The Scarecrow Press, Inc.
Lanham, Md., & London
and
Salem Press
Pasadena, Calif. & Englewood Cliffs, N.J.
1996

SCARECROW PRESS, INC.

Published in the United States of America
by Scarecrow Press, Inc.
4720 Boston Way
Lanham, Maryland 20706

4 Pleydell Gardens, Folkestone
Kent CT20 2DN, England

British Cataloguing-in-Publication Information Available

Library of Congress Cataloging-in-Publication Data

Psychology: an introductory bibliography / the editors of Salem Press;
consulting editor, Susan E. Beers.
p. cm. — (The Magill bibliographies)
Includes indexes.
1. Psychology—Bibliography. I. Beers, Susan E. II. Salem Press. III. Series.
Z7201.P79 1996 [BF121]   016.15—dc20   95-48933   CIP

ISBN 0–8108–3119-8 (cloth : alk. paper)

⊖™ The paper used in this publication meets the minimum requirements of
American National Standard for Information Sciences—Permanence of
Paper for Printed Library Materials, ANSI Z39.48–1984.
Manufactured in the United States of America.

CONTENTS

page

Introduction 1

History, Definition, and Careers 3

Methodologies 11
  Descriptive and Correlational 11
  Experimental 15
  Methodological Issues 17

Biological Bases of Behavior 25
  Endocrine System 25
  Nervous System 31

Sensation and Perception 45
  General Constructs and Issues 45
  Auditory, Chemical, Cutaneous, and Body Senses 49
  Vision 56

Emotion 67

Motivation 77
  Theory 77
  Social Motives 83
  Physical Motives 90
  Animal Behavior 97

Learning 102
  General Concepts 102
  Biological Influences on Learning 106
  Cognitive Learning 110
  Aversion Conditioning 113
  Instrumental Conditioning 114
  Pavlovian Conditioning 118

Cognition 122

Consciousness 134
   States, Functions, and Levels 134
   Sleep and Dreams 140

Memory 145

Language 155

Developmental Psychology 169
   Theory and Methodology 169
   Infancy and Childhood: Cognitive Development 171
   Infancy and Childhood: Social and Personality Development . . 173
   Infancy and Childhood: Physical Development 181
   Adolescence 187
   Adulthood 194
   Aging 201

Social Psychology 210
   Aggression 210
   Attitudes and Behavior 213
   Group Processes 217
   Interpersonal Relations 222
   Prejudice and Discrimination 227
   Prosocial Behavior 236
   Social Perception and Cognition 238

Psychological Assessment 250
   Intelligence and Intelligence Testing 250
   Personality Testing Techniques 262
   Mental Illness Assessment 268

Personality 272
   General Concepts 272
   Behavioral and Cognitive Models 274
   Psychodynamic and Neoanalytic Models 279
   Humanistic-Phenomenological Models 290

Stress 295
   Biology 295
   Coping 298
   Stress and Illness 310

CONTENTS

Psychopathology 317
   Models of Abnormality 317
   Childhood and Adolescent Disorders 324
   Anxiety, Somatoform, and Dissociative Disorders 330
   Depression 338
   Organic Disorders 344
   Personality Disorders 346
   Schizophrenia 348
   Sexual Disorders 350
   Substance Abuse 352

Psychotherapy 358
   Historical Approaches 358
   Behavioral Therapies 359
   Biological Treatments 364
   Cognitive Therapies 368
   Group and Family Therapies 371
   Humanistic Therapies 376
   Psychodynamic Therapies 379
   Evaluating Psychotherapy 383
   Community Mental Health 385

Author Index 389

Subject Index 429

INTRODUCTION

Since its beginning in the mid-1800's, psychology has developed into a rich and complex field. Taking as its subject the behavior and mental life of humans and animals, the study of psychology is related to, and overlaps with, biology, sociology, health, education, business, and public policy. Thus it is not surprising that psychology is of great interest both to students and to the public at large. Psychology is a popular major among college and university students and is widely offered as an elective in high school. The abundance of information about psychology in the popular press and on television testifies to the public's interest in this field.

Increasingly, the study of psychology has become specialized, some would even say fragmented. As in any scientific discipline, research methods and topics become highly focused as the questions and problems in an area become more refined. In addition, practitioners such as clinicians, industrial/organizational psychologists, and educational psychologists have different immediate goals from psychologists engaged in "pure" research. Information about the various areas of psychology, both pure and applied, is widely scattered, published in books, monographs, and hundreds of specialized journals. The task of keeping up with the field of psychology is therefore daunting, even for the professional. For the nonspecialist, the task is further complicated by the wealth of "popular psychology" books, which vary greatly in quality and accuracy.

Psychology: An Introductory Bibliography is intended to place significant bibliographic material from the entire field of psychology under one cover and to provide annotations that can assist the reader in evaluating possible reading. Here the high school or college student will be able to find appropriate material for study, and the general reader can find readings on topics of interest. The instructor of psychology may even find help in planning class readings.

The bibliography is arranged in chapters corresponding to the organization of many introductory psychology texts. Each of the major subdisciplines of psychology is presented: biological psychology, sensation and perception, emotion, motivation, learning, cognition, consciousness, memory, language, developmental psychology, social psychology, assessment, personality, stress, psychopathology, and psychotherapy. The larger chapters are subdivided into major topic areas. For example, the chapter "Psychopathology" includes nine subtopics reflecting major types of psychological disorders, such as depression, childhood and adolescent disorders, schizophrenia, and sexual disorders. The "Psychotherapy" chapter also has nine subtopics, ranging from behavioral therapies to psychodynamic therapies to community mental health. Entries within each section are organized alphabetically by author's last name. Two indexes at the end of the volume provide additional guidance. The subject index helps the reader find specialized topics, topics which are touched upon in several chapters, and works discussing particular psychologists and theorists. The author index provides a listing of all authors whose works are included.

Entries include books, chapters of books, and articles appropriate to an interested nonspecialist. A few are popular psychology books of high quality; most are books geared toward the serious reader. Entries are largely from the 1970's to early 1990's, but significant historical works in psychology—including the major works of such pioneers as Sigmund Freud, John B. Watson, and B. F. Skinner—are also included. Topics on which entries may be found, then, range from works on, and by, the founders of the discipline to such topics of current interest as feminist psychotherapy, substance abuse, and careers in psychology. Most entries in the bibliography will be available at college and university libraries, and many may be found in public libraries. Annotations include a brief description of the entry, in enough detail for the reader to judge its appropriateness for further study. Often, evaluative comments place the entry in the context of the field, and the appropriate audience for the work is indicated. Through the annotations, the reader can easily get a sense of the "lay of the land" regarding a given topic.

Susan E. Beers

HISTORY, DEFINITION, AND CAREERS

Adler, Helmut E., and Robert W. Rieber, eds. *Aspects of the History of Psychology in America: 1892-1992*. Washington, D.C.: American Psychological Association, 1995. Includes essays on the history of psychology from eleven contributors. Social, political, and ideological forces that influenced the development of psychology are described. For college-level readers and above.

American Psychological Association. *Getting In: A Step-by-Step Plan for Gaining Admission to Graduate School in Psychology*. Washington, D.C.: American Psychological Association, 1993. Acceptance into graduate study in psychology is very competitive. This relatively brief (221-page) book outlines a strategy that undergraduate students can use to maximize their chances of gaining admissions. The needs of special populations (women, ethnic minorities, gays and lesbians) are addressed. Highly recommended for those seeking a career in psychology.

_____. *Graduate Study in Psychology and Associated Fields*. Washington, D.C.: Author, 1990. Presents more than five hundred programs of graduate study in psychology in the United States and abroad that lead to a master's or doctorate degree in any field of psychology. Lists the requirements for admission for each school, financial assistance available, degree requirements, and the procedures for submitting applications. Most helpful to any student considering graduate study in psychology.

_____. *Psychology as a Health Care Profession*. Washington, D.C.: Author, 1979. A seventeen-page pamphlet covering psychology in its professional role. Discusses how psychological methods are applied to the health care profession; what psychologists do in various settings; the question of how cost-effective their contributions are; and ways that psychologists have affected public policy in health care issues. Single issues of this pamphlet are available at no cost from the American Psychological Association.

Boakes, Robert A. *From Darwin to Behaviorism*. New York: Cambridge University Press, 1984. The evolution of the scientific consideration of the minds of animals, including man, is described, along with a look at the people involved.

Boring, Edwin Garrigues. *A History of Experimental Psychology*. New York: Century, 1929. Few historians have undertaken a history of psychology. One of the finest early psychologists, Edwin Boring, came the closest to being a true and creative historian of the new science. An enduring and incisive work, scholarly but readable. Boring's contribution to historiography was his brilliant explication of how the intellectual climate of the times, the *Zeitgeist*, was responsible for the development of new and even great ideas.

Brennan, James F. *History and Systems of Psychology*. 3d ed. Englewood Cliffs, N.J.: Prentice-Hall, 1991. Chapter 12 presents a good overview of the rise of functionalism. Particularly useful is the list of primary sources at the end of the chapter.

Bringmann, Wolfgang G., and Ryan D. Tweney, eds. *Wundt Studies*. Toronto, Canada: C. J. Hogrefe, 1980. This volume brings together a number of key articles that represent a renaissance of interest in the legacy of Wundt and structuralism. Until the time around the publication of this work, Wundt was often seen as responsible only for the misbegotten attempt to use introspective reductionism that prompted the later "workable" systems. Here one may see both the problems with and the considerable positive influence of Wundt's contribution.

Carr, Harvey A. *Psychology: A Study of Mental Activity*. New York: Longmans, Green, 1925. Presents a clear picture of the functionalist view of psychology. Carr was one of the American psychologists who formalized functionalism.

Chaplin, James Patrick, and T. S. Krawiec. *Systems and Theories of Psychology*. New York: Holt, Rinehart and Winston, 1960. Chaplin and Krawiec's survey of psychology, its history, major theories, and experimental research is an interesting, lively account of the subject. They discuss classical and contemporary approaches to psychological research and the principal contributions of leading psychologists of the twentieth century. They also address famous experiments in human and animal behavior.

Fancher, Raymond E. *Pioneers of Psychology*. New York: W. W. Norton, 1979. This book provides biographies of several prominent psychologists who have had an impact on the field.

Gilgen, Albert R. *American Psychology Since World War II: A Profile of the Discipline*. Westport, Conn.: Greenwood Press, 1982. Presents an overview of the major developments and trends in American psychology during World War II, which ended in 1945, and from the postwar period through the 1970's.

_____. "The Psychological Level of Organization in Nature and Interdependencies Among Major Psychological Concepts." In *Annals of Theoretical Psychology*. Vol. 5, edited by Arthur W. Staats and Leendert P. Mos. New York: Plenum Press, 1987. Presents a detailed rationale for defining psychology as the systematic study of the information available to each person that allows each individual to move with direction and control.

Giorgi, Amedeo. *Psychology as a Human Science*. New York: Harper & Row, 1970. This scholarly book provides a fine summary of a human science approach to psychology and carefully distinguishes it from a natural science approach. Giorgi also describes a phenomenological foundation for human science psychology.

Hearst, Eliot, ed. *The First Century of Experimental Psychology*. Hillsdale, N.J.: Lawrence Erlbaum, 1979. Primarily for the student interested in the history of experimental psychology. This is a 693-page book; while most of the fourteen chapters are devoted to specific topics in psychology such as emotion, development, and psychopathology, the final chapter by William Estes provides an excellent overview of experimental psychology and considers some broad, profound issues.

Heidbreder, Edna. *Seven Psychologies*. New York: Century, 1933. Heidbreder's book remains the most readable introduction to the major "schools" of psychology up to and including behaviorism. Although the book is dated, the insight, humanity, and beauty of her narrative writing make this a classic. One can read this work as one would a novel. The discussion of structuralism is particularly fine.

Hilgard, Ernest Ropiequet. *Psychology in America: A Historical Survey*. San Diego: Harcourt Brace Jovanovich, 1987. Chapter 19, "Industrial and Organizational Psychology," is a definitive review of about eighty years of the field's advancement from a promising application of the new "scientific psychology" to a major subdiscipline of contemporary psychology. An energetic reader could use material in several of Hilgard's other chapters (for example, those on intelligence, on motivation, and on social psychology) to place industrial and organizational psychology in the context of its parent discipline.

Hunt, Morton M. *The Universe Within*. New York: Simon & Schuster, 1982. Hunt's book discusses the findings of the scientific specialty called cognitive science, arguing for a greater appreciation for the humanity of the human mind than detractors have allowed.

Ishaq, Waris, ed. *Human Behavior in Today's World*. New York: Praeger, 1991. Chapters written by different behaviorists indicate how a behavioral analysis is generated, what some basic principles are, and how they can be applied to cultural and social, as well as individual, actions.

James, William. *Principles of Psychology*. 2 vols. New York: Dove, 1890. Although more than a hundred years old, James's classic text on psychological issues remains both readable and illuminating. His functionalistic thinking is evident.

Kendler, Howard H. *Historical Foundations of Modern Psychology*. Chicago: Dorsey Press, 1987. A well-written account of the emergence of cognitive psychology and the contributions of other disciplines such as linguistics, engineering, and computer science. Approachable for the layperson; provides a fine historical backdrop. It is of limited use, beyond review, for the upper-level college student.

Kennedy, Eugene C. *On Becoming a Counselor*. New York: Seabury Press, 1977. A reference source for paraprofessionals and professionals alike. Provides insight into the many problems experienced by human beings. This work causes the reader to deal with his or her own issues prior to attempting to help others confront theirs. It is logically progressive in moving from the interview process to the different types of people one will encounter in counseling situations.

Kinget, G. Marian. *On Becoming Human*. New York: Harcourt Brace Jovanovich, 1975. This readable book answers the question "What is human about a human being?" by describing seventeen key characteristics of uniquely human existence. Topics include time, death, symbols, reflective consciousness, creativity, ethics, freedom, and beauty.

Lapointe, François H. "Who Originated the Term 'Psychology'?" *Journal of the History of the Behavioral Sciences* 8, no. 3 (1972): 328-335. The most thorough analysis of the origination of the term "psychology." An essential reference for anyone interested in the history of the concept.

Leahey, Thomas H. *A History of Modern Psychology*. Englewood Cliffs, N.J.: Prentice-Hall, 1991. A very readable textbook that contains two chapters (4 and 5) specifically related to functionalism and its antecedents. Also discusses some European functional ideas.

Lee, Vicki L. *Beyond Behaviorism*. Hillsdale, N.J.: Lawrence Erlbaum, 1988. This book describes the differences between the positions of Watson and other "behaviorists," as well as the radical behaviorism of B. F. Skinner.

Lundin, Robert William. *Theories and Systems of Psychology*. 4th ed. Lexington, Mass.: D. C. Heath, 1991. Lundin handles the mind-body problem in detail, showing both the philosophical origins and relevant psychological perspectives in this textbook on the intellectual history of psychology.

May, Rollo. *Psychology and the Human Dilemma*. Princeton, N.J.: Van Nostrand, 1967. May's accessible yet probing analysis of humans' paradoxical capacity to experience themselves as both subject and object. Topics include meaning, anxiety, freedom, responsibility, values, psychotherapy, science, and the social responsibilities of psychologists.

Murphy, Gardner. *Historical Introduction to Modern Psychology*. Rev. ed. New York: Harcourt Brace, 1950. In a concise way, presents the major differences between the schools of structuralism and functionalism.

Murray, David J. *A History of Western Psychology*. 2d ed. Englewood Cliffs, N.J.: Prentice-Hall, 1988. Includes clear discussions of the origins of the term "psychology" and the meaning of the concept for the act psychologists, the structuralists, the functionalists, and the behaviorists.

Patnoe, Shelley. *A Narrative History of Experimental Social Psychology: The Lewin Tradition*. New York: Springer-Verlag, 1988. This volume contains a series of interviews with modern social psychologists and discusses the impact of Lewin on their research and theories.

Petrinovich, Lewis. "Darwin and the Representative Expression of Reality." In *Darwin and Facial Expression: A Century of Research in*

Review, edited by Paul Ekman. New York: Academic Press, 1973. The author traces the far-reaching influence of Darwin's theory of evolution on the development of various psychological theories and approaches including animal psychology, structuralism, functionalism, learning theory, social psychology, and ethology.

Pollio, Howard R. *Behavior and Existence: An Introduction to Empirical Humanistic Psychology*. Monterey, Calif.: Brooks/Cole, 1982. This book is the most coherent introductory textbook on general psychology from a humanistic standpoint. It covers the usual survey of psychology topics (such as learning, thinking, perceiving, and remembering) from a humanistic approach.

Rachlin, Howard. *Introduction to Modern Behaviorism*. 2d ed. San Francisco: W. H. Freeman, 1976. This dated but excellent text reviews the development of behavioral thinking and reviews how behaviorism is translated into action.

Robinson, Daniel N. *An Intellectual History of Psychology*. Rev. ed. New York: Macmillan, 1981. Although mental illness as such occupies a small part of this book, it is a genuinely important book in helping to understand the philosophical and intellectual currents which have played such a major role in the psychological and scientific understanding of mental illness. A sometimes demanding book to read, it is well worth the intellectual energy for one who wants to understand how various intellectual disciplines interact together.

Sahakian, William S., ed. *History of Psychology: A Source Book in Systematic Psychology*. Itasca, Ill.: F. E. Peacock, 1968. Contains samples of the writings of people whose thinking developed psychology. Includes some of William James's most influential works as well as those of others important to functionalism such as Dewey, Angell, and Carr.

Schultz, Duane P., and Sydney Ellen Schultz. *A History of Modern Psychology*. 4th ed. San Diego: Harcourt Brace Jovanovich, 1987. Refined, readable, and biographically based, this is one of the best introductions to the history of psychology available. It has narrative flow rather than definitions and enumerations, and includes key passages from original sources. The structuralism chapter has a particularly felicitous excerpt (more than ten pages) from Titchener's 1909 work, *A Text-Book of Psychology*.

Siegel, Michael H., and H. Philip Zeigler, eds. *Psychological Research: The Inside Story*. New York: Harper & Row, 1976. Personal accounts of their research by prominent psychologists. Chapters provide a good overview of the variety of types of studies and designs used by developmental researchers and other psychologists. Includes insiders' insights into how hypotheses emerge and how research plans grow, change, and mature. Readable and at times humorous.

Skinner, B. F. *About Behaviorism*. New York: Alfred A. Knopf, 1974. This book is Skinner's attempt to explain his philosophy of behaviorism in terms of questions and behavioral answers.

_____. *Science and Human Behavior*. New York: Macmillan, 1953. This early work sets forth the basics of radical behaviorism and discusses its application to many kinds of behavioral questions.

Sommer, Barbara B., and Robert Sommer. *A Practical Guide to Behavioral Research: Tools and Techniques*. 3d ed. New York: Oxford University Press, 1991. A jargon-free, understandable first introduction to behavioral research. Further describes observational, self-report, and experimental research methods, and descriptive, correlational, and experimental data analyses.

Stevens, Leonard A. *Explorers of the Brain*. New York: Alfred A. Knopf, 1971. A history of the explanation of brain function. Chapters are devoted to those researchers who mapped out the areas of the brain. A good overview of how research in the past was carried out, written at the level of the nonexpert.

Titchener, Edward Bradford. *A Primer of Psychology*. Rev. ed. New York: Macmillan, 1913. Presents a clear and detailed analysis of psychology from the structuralist perspective, and in the process identifies many of the challenges involved in attempting to decipher the structure of mind and consciousness.

Valle, Ronald S., and Steen Halling, eds. *Existential-Phenomenological Perspectives in Psychology: Exploring the Breadth of Human Experience*. New York: Plenum Press, 1989. A widely ranging collection of topics, many centrally important to psychology, each approached phenomenologically in original and creative ways. Topics include social psychology, assessment, perception, learning, child development, emotion, and many others, including transpersonal psychology.

Van den Berg, Jan Hendrik. *A Different Existence*. Pittsburgh: Duquesne University Press, 1972. A remarkably easy introduction to some major themes of phenomenological psychology. Within the framework of a case study of a disturbed patient, van den Berg examines such forms of experiencing as "world," "others," "time," and "body."

Watson, John Broadus. *Behaviorism*. New York: W. W. Norton, 1925. This is the ultimate statement of behaviorism as intended and presented by the father of this approach to psychology.

Watson, Robert Irving, Sr., and Rand B. Evans. *The Great Psychologists*. 5th ed. New York: HarperCollins, 1991. Watson was one of the best proponents of the biographical approach to the history of psychology. He argues forcefully for the recognition of the individual genius that often characterized the pioneering efforts of the psychologists of his title. His great writing, zeal, and intimate knowledge of the material bring it alive. The discussion is fascinating and easily readable. One learns much about philosophy as well.

Wertheimer, Michael. *A Brief History of Psychology*. New York: Holt, Rinehart and Winston, 1970. Provides a brief historical overview of various approaches to psychological study including gestalt, behavioral, and psychodynamic. The facts regarding the history of each movement are concise and interesting.

METHODOLOGIES

Descriptive and Correlational

Baker, Therese L. *Doing Social Research*. New York: McGraw-Hill, 1988. Gives the reader a general introduction to field research, observational studies, data collection methods, survey research, and sampling techniques, as well as other topics which will help the reader evaluate "good" field studies from those that are poorly constructed.

Berdie, Douglas R., and John F. Anderson. *Questionnaires: Design and Use*. Metuchen, N.J.: Scarecrow Press, 1974. Provides extensive, detailed information that guides the reader through the process of questionnaire creation. Also helps the novice learn how to administer a questionnaire correctly.

Berg, Bruce Lawrence. *Qualitative Research Methods for the Social Sciences*. Boston: Allyn & Bacon, 1989. Discusses a field strategy used by anthropologists and sociologists to study groups of people. In addition, discusses the ethical issues that arise while conducting such research. The dangers of covert research are discussed; the book also provides the guidelines established by the National Research Act.

Bordens, Kenneth S., and Bruce B. Abbott. *Research Design and Methods: A Process Approach*. 2d ed. Mountain View, Calif.: Mayfield, 1988. Presents a discussion of how to develop and use various types of observational methods in psychology. Emphasis is placed on tailoring the methods to fit the investigators' purpose. The relationship between these methods and the statistical analysis of obtained results is also discussed conceptually. The book has an extensive reference section and can be understood by high school or college students.

Converse, Jean M., and Stanley Presser. *Survey Questions: Handcrafting the Standardized Questionnaire*. Beverly Hills, Calif.: Sage, 1986. Provides explicit, practical details which would be of use to a person who needs to put together a questionnaire for any of a variety of reasons. Stresses the art of questionnaire creation.

Cozby, Paul C. *Methods in Behavioral Research*. 4th ed. Mountain View, Calif.: Mayfield, 1989. Examines the importance of survey research in the context of conducting experiments and doing research in psychology in general. Allows the reader to understand the research process from a broad perspective.

Dudycha, Arthur L., and Linda W. Dudycha. "Behavioral Statistics: An Historical Perspective." In *Statistical Issues: A Reader for the Behavioral Sciences*, edited by Roger E. Kirk. Monterey, Calif.: Brooks/Cole, 1972. This highly readable article relates the history of descriptive and inferential statistics and their use by psychologists. Most textbooks on statistics for the social and behavioral sciences neglect this important topic.

Gluck, J. P., and A. J. Beauchamp. *Research in Psychology: Ethics, Learning, and Cognitive Psychology*. Lexington, Mass.: Ginn, 1987. The authors present a discussion, along with examples and laboratory exercises, of the various observational techniques used in psychology. For example, students are presented with an exercise that provides step-by-step instructions on how to develop a functional behavioral taxonomy. The authors also discuss descriptive statistics and bias. Can be understood by high school students.

Griffin, John H. *Black Like Me*. New York: American Library, 1962. This excellent book is a narrative of the author's experiences traveling around the United States observing how people react to him after he takes on the appearance of a black man. This monumental field study, which contributed to an understanding of social prejudice, provides the reader with an excellent example of the significance of and need for conducting field research.

Jessen, Raymond James. *Statistical Survey Techniques*. New York: John Wiley & Sons, 1978. Provides a clear introduction to statistical sampling. The examples are clear and relevant, and they illustrate the points made on sampling technique. Although this book is not written for mathematicians, each chapter contains mathematical notes that demonstrate points made in the chapter.

Kidder, Louise H., and Charles M. Judd. *Research Methods in Social Relations*. 5th ed. New York: Holt, Rinehart and Winston, 1986. A popular book whose writing style is exceptionally clear. Offers thorough information that introduces the reader to the process of doing research in psychology, including how to get an idea for a research topic, how to collect the information, how to be ethical with subjects, and how to report the results. Detailed information is provided on questionnaires and interviews.

Kish, Leslie. *Survey Sampling*. New York: John Wiley & Sons, 1965. This book is the definitive work on sampling in social research; the coverage ranges from the simplest matters to the most complex and mathematical. Somewhat difficult reading, but Kish manages to be both highly theoretical and extremely practical.

Langer, Walter Charles. *The Mind of Adolf Hitler*. New York: Basic Books, 1972. A fascinating account of a World War II archival research project that attempted to generate a psychiatric profile of the German leader.

Leahey, Thomas Hardy. *A History of Psychology: Main Currents in Psychological Thought*. 2d ed. Englewood Cliffs, N.J.: Prentice-Hall, 1987. Leahey summarizes the evolution of observational methods in psychology. Philosophical underpinnings are discussed, along with the logic behind the observational strategies selected for use in psychology. Can be understood by beginning college students.

McCall, G. J., and J. L. Simmons. *Issues in Participant Observation: A Text and Reader*. Reading, Mass.: Addison-Wesley, 1969. This text provides an in-depth discussion on how to get inside a group as a participant observer and conduct observational field research. Also provides a number of examples from the literature to help understand how this research is conducted.

Phillips, John L., Jr. *How to Think About Statistics*. 3d ed. New York: W. H. Freeman, 1988. A very readable presentation of statistics that emphasizes the role of error in inference. Figures are interesting and elucidate the concepts. Sample research applications are provided for education, political science, social work, sociology, and psychology, as are answers designed to help readers think critically.

Rosenblum, Leonard A. "The Creation of a Behavioral Taxonomy." In *Data Collection and Analysis Methods*. Vol. 2 in *Observing Behavior*, edited by Gene P. Sackett. Baltimore: University Park Press, 1978. Provides an introductory discussion of how to develop functional behavioral taxonomies. Establishing the conditions of observation, informal observation, and how to describe behavior are presented in a comprehensible format. The chapter can be understood by high school students.

Rosenhan, David Leonard. "On Being Sane in Insane Places." *Science* 179 (January 19, 1973): 250-258. Rosenhan describes his research on psychiatric facilities after he and his associates assumed the identity of psychiatric patients. An interesting and provocative example of field research, this paper also raises the question of the dangers of conducting covert research and the dangers inherent in psychological labels.

Rowntree, Derek. *Statistics Without Tears: A Primer for Non-Mathematicians.* New York: Charles Scribner's Sons, 1981. Explains the essential concepts in statistics without having the reader perform calculations.

Sackett, Gene P. "Measurement in Observational Research." In *Data Collection and Analysis Methods.* Vol. 2 in *Observing Behavior*, edited by Gene P. Sackett. Baltimore: University Park Press, 1978. The author discusses in detail the many issues involved with the development and use of behavioral taxonomies. The strengths and weaknesses of the various quantitative approaches are discussed as are issues of reliability, validity, and bias effects. Although the article is targeted for the serious student of observational methods, it can be understood by high school and college students.

Selltiz, Claire, Marie Johoda, Morton Deutsch, and S. Cook. *Research Methods in Social Relations.* New York: Holt, 1959. Still a rich source of information related to research, this book's ninth chapter, "The Use of Available Data as Source Material," offers excellent detail on the use of archival data. Three other chapters describe in detail other research methods, and one chapter discusses problems of data accuracy. The book should be available in most college and university libraries.

Singleton, Royce, Jr., et al. *Approaches to Social Research.* New York: Oxford University Press, 1988. This well-written text discusses various aspects of field experimentation such as how to select a research setting and gather information, how to get into the field, and when a field study should be adopted. The chapter on "experimentation" can be used to contrast "true" experiments with field studies.

Stewart, Charles J., and William B. Cash, Jr. *Interviewing Principles and Practices.* 3d ed. Dubuque, Iowa: Wm. C. Brown, 1982. A "hands-on" introduction to interviewing which provides practical suggestions and tips along with background information.

Yin, Robert K. *Case Study Research: Design and Methods.* Beverly Hills, Calif.: Sage Publications, 1984. This rare volume is perhaps the finest single source on case-study methods in print. Yin shows the reader exactly how to design, conduct, analyze, and even write up a case study. Approximately forty examples of case studies are cited with brief explanations. The book is written for an audience that is not highly technical.

Experimental

Campbell, Donald Thomas, and Julian C. Stanley. *Experimental and Quasi-Experimental Designs for Research.* Chicago: Rand McNally, 1966. The clearest and most accessible presentation of the principles of quasi-experimental design. Includes many excellent examples and a description of sixteen experimental and quasi-experimental designs, each evaluated for twelve threats to validity. Many examples are from educational research. Includes illustrations of designs.

Cook, Thomas D., and Donald T. Campbell. "The Design and Conduct of Quasi-Experiments and True Experiments in Field Settings." In *Handbook of Industrial and Organizational Psychology,* edited by Marvin D. Dunnette. Chicago: Rand McNally, 1976. An excellent overview of the principles of quasi- experimentation as applied in industrial and organizational settings. Written for the educated nonprofessional, this article includes the revamped validity scheme developed completely in Cook and Campbell's 1979 book.

_____. *Quasi-Experimentation: Design and Analysis Issues for Field Settings.* Chicago: Rand McNally, 1979. A large book built on the foundations of Campbell and Stanley (1966). It has a much more complete consideration of the philosophical analysis of cause and effect, a reorganized conception of validity issues, detailed statistical analysis methods for quasi-experiments, and a discussion on the conduct of randomized experiments in field settings. By recasting validity into statistical conclusion validity, construct validity, internal validity, and external validity, a more comprehensive view is presented. The complex statistical information may make parts of the book incomprehensible to the nonprofessional, but it is worth reading for the parts one can understand. Illustrations of designs and statistical analyses.

Cronbach, Lee Joseph. *Designing Evaluations of Educational and Social Programs.* San Francisco: Jossey-Bass, 1982. Cronbach disagrees with the Campbell, Stanley, and Cook approach to quasi-experimentation in that he thinks they overemphasize internal validity and the importance of unequivocal causal conclusions. Cronbach argues that the major issue shaping any quasi-experimentation should be the application that the study is designed to inform. He develops a different typology of issues based on this criterion of value.

Edwards, Allen Louis. *Experimental Design in Psychological Research.* 4th ed. New York: Holt, Rinehart and Winston, 1972. Presents discussions of interactions and complex experimental designs through the use of concrete examples. More than most other statistics books, Edwards' is concerned with presenting the probabilistic basis for the concepts discussed, especially the probabilities of finding differences between groups as a result of accident or chance.

Elmes, David G., Barry H. Kantowitz, and Henry L. Roediger III. *Research Methods in Psychology.* 4th ed. St. Paul, Minn.: West, 1992. A standard textbook on all aspects of research in psychology. Chapters 6 and 7 focus on experimental design and detail methods of counterbalancing. Chapter 8 discusses several small-n designs besides the reversal design. Can be understood by college students and sophisticated high school students.

Gravetter, Frederick J., and Larry B. Wallnau. *Essentials of Statistics for the Behavioral Sciences.* St. Paul, Minn.: West, 1991. This accessible statistics text shows the strength of within-subject designs. The authors do not assume that the reader has a sophisticated mathematical background, but understanding the statistical analysis of within-subject designs may require some effort.

Martin, David W. *Doing Psychology Experiments.* 3d ed. Pacific Grove, Calif.: Brooks/Cole, 1990. An important book about the design, execution, interpretation, and reporting of psychological research, written in a clear and engaging manner. Does not provide instructions for making statistical calculations; more for helping the reader or consumer of psychological research understand what was done and what it means. Exceptional sections on theory and on research ethics.

Myers, Jerome L. *Fundamentals of Experimental Design.* 2d ed. Boston: Allyn & Bacon, 1972. Provides excellent examples of graphing higher-order interactions and of calculational methods. Contains discussions of designing an experiment and interpreting statistics. Has an important section on the further data analyses for simple main effects which should be performed after an interaction has been found.

Sidman, Murray. *Tactics of Scientific Research.* New York: Basic Books, 1960. This sophisticated book is the standard reference for the logic and methods of small-*n* research. Sidman presents a strong case for developing a high degree of experimental control so that small numbers of subjects can be used in within-subject designs.

Sprinthall, Richard C. *Basic Statistical Analysis.* 3d ed. Englewood Cliffs, N.J.: Prentice-Hall, 1990. Offers a comprehensive introduction to a wide variety of experimental and statistical procedures at the beginning university level. Notable for its discussions of cause and effect, non-parametrics, and computers in research. Better than average for its treatment of drawing and evaluating graphical representations of data.

Trochim, William M. K., ed. *Advances in Quasi-Experimental Design and Analysis.* San Francisco: Jossey-Bass, 1986. A series of articles by various experts on quasi-experimental design. Some of the issues are rather technical, but most of the articles are understandable. Chapter 3, "Validity Topologies and the Logic and Practice of Quasi-Experimentation," by Melvin M. Mark, is an excellent overview, review, and discussion of different approaches to quasi-experimentation.

Winer, B. J. *Statistical Principles in Experimental Design.* 2d ed. New York: McGraw-Hill, 1971. A widely recognized standard in the field of experimental design and statistical analysis. May be overly technical in spots for some readers, but also has very readable explanations of the meaning of interactions and how they can be understood. May be useful for understanding some of the methods and conclusions of research articles.

Methodological Issues

American Psychological Association Council of Representatives. "Ethical Principles of Psychologists." *American Psychologist* 36, no. 6 (1981): 633-638. This is the actual text of the ten ethical principles of the American Psychological Association. Number nine is on research with human participants. An annotated casebook is also available from the APA, but unfortunately it does not give examples for principle number nine.

Babbie, Earl R. *The Practice of Social Research*. 4th ed. Belmont, Calif.: Wadsworth, 1986. Written in clear, easy-to-understand language with many illustrations, Babbie discusses both the logic and the skills necessary to understand sampling and randomization. Contains appendices, a bibliography, an index, and an excellent glossary.

Baker, Therese L. *Doing Social Research*. New York: McGraw-Hill, 1988. This is a complete and understandable treatment of all areas of social research. There are thorough discussions of bias created from faulty sampling and obstacles to the validity of an experiment.

Barber, Theodore Xenophon. *Pitfalls in Human Research*. New York: Pergamon Press, 1976. It is useful to learn from the mistakes of others, and Barber provides the opportunity by describing ten categories of likely errors in designing and conducting research. This is not a long book (117 pages), and it is enjoyable reading, especially the specific accounts of flawed research.

Beauchamp, Tom L., Ruth R. Faden, R. Jay Wallace, Jr., and Le Roy Walters, eds. *Ethical Issues in Social Science Research*. Baltimore: The Johns Hopkins University Press, 1982. This excellent four-hundred-page book delves into the controversies surrounding the costs and benefits of social science research (macroallocation issues are covered in parts 1 and 2), as well as the more concrete issues of informed consent, deception, and confidentiality (parts 3 and 4). Part 5 addresses controversies over government regulation of research. A select bibliography is provided for each chapter. In-depth and thorough, yet very readable.

Blalock, Hubert M., Jr. *Social Statistics*. New York: McGraw-Hill, 1979. Provides an extensive section on sampling that pays particular attention to random sampling, systematic sampling, stratified sampling, and cluster sampling. Although there are some formulas and computations, the majority of the discussion is not technical, and the explanations are clear.

Bower, Robert T., and Priscilla de Gasparis. *Ethics in Social Research: Protecting the Interests of Human Subjects*. New York: Praeger, 1978. Provides a fairly technical, seventy-page synopsis of ethical issues in research; a ten-page appendix summarizing the ethical codes of the major social science professional organizations (does not give actual texts or full citations); a five-page appendix listing public-interest groups active in the protection of subject rights; and a lengthy annotated bibliography.

Campbell, Donald Thomas, and Julian C. Stanley. *Experimental and Quasi-experimental Design for Research.* Chicago: Rand McNally, 1966. Considered a classic in the field of experimental design in the social sciences. Campbell and Stanley originated the key concepts of internal and external validity, which have become the standards for use in analyzing research validity. This book is somewhat technical, but most advanced high school or college students should have no problem with it.

Carlson, Neil R. *Psychology: The Science of Behavior.* 3d ed. Boston: Allyn & Bacon, 1990. The second chapter of this introductory psychology text entitled "The Ways and Means of Psychology," provides a brief introductory overview of the scientific method, experimental and correlational research, and basic statistics; it is well suited for the novice. Colorful graphics, a concluding summary, and a list of key terms are all helpful.

Committee on the Use of Animals in Research Staff of the National Academy of Sciences and the Institute of Medicine Staff. *Science, Medicine, and Animals.* Washington, D.C.: National Academy Press, 1991. This thirty-page pamphlet answers commonly asked questions about the use of animals in biomedical research. Although not focusing specifically on psychology, it does address research in psychomedical areas such as brain research and drug addiction.

Cowles, M., and C. Davis. "On the Origins of the .05 Level of Statistical Significance." *American Psychologist* 37, no. 5 (1982): 553-558. Traces the historical development of the .05 criterion for statistical significance. It discusses many of the earlier standards that were applied informally by statisticians and researchers and discusses Fisher's role in formalizing and popularizing the .05 level.

Fox, Michael Allen. *The Case for Animal Experimentation.* Berkeley: University of California Press, 1986. Although the author is philosophically in favor of most animal experimentation, he gives a clear and thorough discussion of the entire context of animal experimentation from both sides. Includes sections on animal rights, similarities and differences between human and nonhuman subjects, the role of methodological considerations and replicability in scientific progress, and alternatives to animal testing.

Giere, Ronald N. *Understanding Scientific Reasoning*. New York: Holt, Rinehart and Winston, 1979. This readable book presents scientific reasoning from the point of view of a philosopher of science, with many examples from all areas of science, including psychology. Chapter 6, on testing theoretical hypotheses, and chapter 12, on causal hypotheses, provide several detailed examples of evaluating data.

Gigerenzer, Gerd, et al. *The Empire of Chance: How Probability Changed Science and Everyday Life*. Cambridge, England: Cambridge University Press, 1989. A narrative history of the ideas of chance in the nineteenth and twentieth centuries, including the influence of probability on the brain's cognitive processing. Especially relevant are the chapters "The Inference Experts" and "Statistics of the Mind." Formulas are mostly absent. Excellent conclusions are provided for each of the lengthy chapters.

Gigerenzer, Gerd, and David J. Murray. *Cognition as Intuitive Statistics*. Hillsdale, N.J.: Lawrence Erlbaum, 1987. A somewhat technical but readable account of the emergence of statistical inference in psychological research. The first chapter not only chronicles the important events in this revolution but also gives a very clear discussion of the misinterpretation and misuse of statistical significance tests.

Goldstein, Martin, and Inge F. Goldstein. *How We Know: An Exploration of the Scientific Process*. New York: Plenum Press, 1978. A book on the philosophy of science, intended for the reader who is neither scientist nor philosopher. Explains the scientific approach using historical examples in the fields of medicine, physics, and clinical psychology. Compares scientific to nonscientific approaches to knowing. Easy to browse through if so desired.

Hayslett, H. T., Jr. *Statistics Made Simple*. Garden City, N.Y.: Doubleday, 1968. Chapters 5 to 12 provide a standard approach to understanding and calculating basic inferential statistics. Exercises and answers are provided for each chapter.

Henry, Gary T. *Practical Sampling*. Newbury Park, Calif.: Sage Publications, 1990. Provides detailed examples of selecting alternatives in actual sampling practice. Not heavily theoretical or mathematical, although the material is based on the theoretical and mathematical sampling work that has preceded it. Provides references for those interested in proceeding deeper into the literature.

Howell, David C. *Fundamental Statistics for the Behavioral Sciences.* Boston: PWS-Kent, 1989. An excellent text designed for an introductory statistics course in the behavioral sciences. It does not require a mathematics background beyond high school algebra, and it emphasizes the logic of statistical procedures rather than their mathematical derivation.

Katz, Jay. *Experimentation with Human Beings.* New York: Russell Sage Foundation, 1972. Although this volume was inspired by abuses in medical research, it is extremely thorough in coverage of social and psychological issues in human experimentation, and includes many examples of psychological studies. Follows the format of a law school text, but remains accessible to the general reader.

Levine, Carol, and Robert M. Veatch, eds. *Cases in Bioethics.* Hastings-on-Hudson, N.Y.: The Hastings Center, 1982. This casebook includes a chapter on human-subjects research. Although the casebook is primarily on biomedical issues, three of the four cases presented in chapter 5 concern psychological research. Commentaries illustrate the complexity of the issues and encourage readers to make their own evaluations.

Martin, David W. *Doing Psychology Experiments.* 2d ed. Monterey, Calif.: Brooks/Cole, 1985. Martin writes with a humorous style, and this book is excellent as a first exposure to experimental methods. Light-hearted illustrations convey technical points in ways that are easily remembered.

Milgram, Stanley, and Thomas H. Murray. "Can Deception in Research Be Justified?" In *Taking Sides: Clashing Views on Controversial Psychological Issues,* edited by Joseph Rubinstein and Brent Slife. 5th ed. Guilford, Conn.: Dushkin, 1988. Each chapter includes two commentaries from different sides of controversial issues. Chapter 1 addresses the issue of deception. Milgram gives his side of the story of his controversial experiment. Murray addresses the example of studies on helping behavior.

Miller, Neal E. "The Value of Behavioral Research on Animals." *American Psychologist* 40 (April, 1985): 423-440. Good discussion of advances in the behavioral sciences that came from animal studies, including studies on effects of early experience on the brain and behavior, drug effects, eating disorders, and diseases of aging. Also includes some discussion of applied studies which benefit nonhuman species.

Moore, K. D. *A Field Guide to Inductive Arguments.* 2d ed. Dubuque, Iowa: Kendall-Hunt, 1989. An excellent workbook for learning how to analyze arguments and evaluate evidence. Chapter 4, on hypothetical evidence, provides several interesting exercises on how to generate and test hypotheses.

Nielsen, Joyce McCarl, ed. *Feminist Research Methods: Exemplary Readings in the Social Sciences.* Boulder, Colo.: Westview Press, 1990. Challenges the traditional scientific method, including traditional developmental methodologies. Argues that Western cultural and masculine biases are pervasive in research assumptions and process, and provides alternative methodologies. Hyde's critique of developmental research into cognitive sex differences is particularly relevant. Advanced reading level.

Phillips, John L. *How to Think About Statistics.* 3d ed. New York: W. H. Freeman, 1988. An excellent introduction to the statistical principles underlying the logic of experimental design. Phillips stresses the kind of problem-solving skills necessary to become a good consumer of science information as well as to evaluate advertising claims, polls, economic forecasts, and other common issues.

Platt, John R. "Strong Inference." *Science* 146 (October, 1964): 347-353. This classic article presents the philosophy of scientific falsification, whereby scientists rule out different hypotheses one by one, leaving the strongest, presumably correct hypothesis as the sole survivor of rigorous attempts at disproof. Platt, along with many others, believes that psychology will remain a "soft" science until this approach is used on a more regular basis.

Plutchik, Robert. *Foundations of Experimental Research.* 3d ed. New York: Harper & Row, 1983. This standard psychology research methods text includes many examples in historical context, and thus might be more interesting for the generalist than most other methods texts. Focus is on definitional issues, scientific reasoning, and problem solving rather than research design.

Pyke, Sandra W., and Neil M. Agnew. *The Science Game.* 5th ed. Englewood Cliffs, N.J.: Prentice-Hall, 1991. A well-written and popular introduction to all aspects of social science research. There is an extensive section on validity, with one of the most complete descriptions on threats to external validity that one will find. Also includes an in-depth discussion of sexual bias in social research.

Pyrczak, Fred. *Statistics with a Sense of Humor.* Los Angeles: F. Pyrczak, 1989. This is a workbook that provides an excellent supplement to any statistics text. The author has a real gift for presenting statistical concepts in a clear manner, and his humorous examples and riddle format tend to make the principles easier to understand.

Rowan, Andrew N. *Of Mice, Models, and Men: A Critical Evaluation of Animal Research.* Albany, N.Y.: State University of New York Press, 1984. The author is a supporter of the use of animals in scientific research; he addresses the history of animal research and the controversies surrounding it. In addition to psychological research, he covers the use of animals in medical and industrial testing.

Rowntree, Derek. *Statistics Without Tears.* New York: Charles Scribner's Sons, 1981. An excellent introduction to the main concepts and terminology of statistics. Concepts are presented through words and diagrams rather than by means of formulas and equations, which tends to reduce the impact of "math phobia."

Runyon, Richard P., and Audrey Haber. *Fundamentals of Behavioral Statistics.* 7th ed. New York: McGraw-Hill, 1991. Typical of the many textbooks written for the student studying statistics in the social and behavioral sciences. The formulas for the various descriptive statistics are presented, as are explanations of their utility. The authors do an excellent job of presenting the material clearly and as simply as possible.

Shaughnessy, John J., and Eugene B. Zechmeister. *Research Methods in Psychology.* 2d ed. New York: McGraw-Hill, 1990. This is one of a number of textbooks that discusses psychological research in the light of the scientific method. It is fairly accessible, has a thorough and competent description of experimentation, and, as a bonus, considers some ethical issues. Glossary, index, and references are all provided.

Siegel, Michael H., and H. Philip Zeigler, eds. *Psychological Research: The Inside Story.* New York: Harper & Row, 1976. A collection of articles by famous psychologists, each describing not only their research results but also the process, problems, accidents, and insights that occurred along the way. A wide diversity of research topics and a very personal approach make this book a good read for professionals and psychology newcomers alike.

Stanovich, Keith E. *How to Think Straight About Psychology.* 2d ed. Glenview, Ill.: Scott, Foresman, 1989. Stanovich tries to undermine the misconceptions that many people have about the contributions of psychology to the scientific study of human behavior. Examples of hypothesis testing abound throughout the book.

Stern, Paul C. *Evaluating Social Science Research.* New York: Oxford University Press, 1979. This is a clearly written, nonthreatening book for the early to middle-level college student. The focus of the author is on encouraging the critical analysis of research; to this end, case-research examples are presented for examination. End-of-chapter exercises are included to aid the student in integrating information.

Sudman, Seymour. *Applied Sampling.* New York: Academic Press, 1976. Intended for the majority of survey users who have only limited statistical backgrounds, this book is more readable and less technical than Kish's book. Takes a pragmatic approach to sampling, and provides excellent examples and illustrations.

U.S. Congress Office of Technology Assessment. *Alternatives to Animal Use in Research, Testing, and Education.* Washington, D.C.: Author, 1986. This 441-page document provides much more than its title indicates. In addition to alternate methodologies, the report discusses government use of animals, economic and ethical considerations, statistics and patterns of animal use, and federal policy.

Witte, Robert S. "Inferential Statistics: Generalizing Beyond Data." In *Statistics.* 3d ed. New York: Holt, Rinehart and Winston, 1989. A text designed for "mathematically unsophisticated" students who may have some fear of statistics.

BIOLOGICAL BASES OF BEHAVIOR

Endocrine System

Alberts, Bruce, et al. *Molecular Biology of the Cell*. New York: Garland, 1983. This outstanding introduction to molecular biology, written by leading scientists in the field, is of great value both to the layperson and to the research scientist. Chapter 13, "Chemical Signaling Between Cells," is a clear, exhaustive survey of hormone structure, function, and physiology in terms of production sites and target tissues. A list of major human hormones and their effects is provided.

Beck, William S., Karel F. Liem, and George Gaylord Simpson. *Life: An Introduction to Biology*. 3d ed. New York: HarperCollins, 1991. This introduction to basic biology for the beginning student is an exhaustive survey of all avenues of the subject. The book is beautifully illustrated and very well organized. Chapter 28, "Chemical Coordination," describes the principal human hormones and their effects upon the body. Chapter 32, "Behavior," describes various mechanisms of animal behavior, including the role of hormones in influencing behavior.

Beyer, Carlos, ed. *Endocrine Control of Sexual Behavior*. New York: Raven Press, 1979. This is a superb collection of review articles concerning hormonal influences on the sexual behavior of mammals. Particularly helpful in describing the methodology of such analysis.

Bioscience 33 (October, 1983). The entire issue is devoted to the effects of hormones on behavior. Includes an article on invertebrates in general, followed by articles on fish through primates. Written in nonesoteric language.

Carlson, Neil R. *Physiology of Behavior*. 4th ed. Boston: Allyn & Bacon, 1991. A college-level text that provides a good foundation of information on the nervous system and examines behavior from its underlying physiological bases. Includes chapters on methodology, sensation and perception, biological rhythms, reproduction, ingestion, and mental illness.

Connell, Elizabeth B. *Hormones, Sex, and Happiness*. Chicago: Cowles, 1971. Presents basics of endocrinology in a less than academic manner, including the role of glands and stress in relation to types of behavior. Humans are presented as sexual beings from adolescence on, while the role of the pituitary is emphasized as directly or indirectly related to this fact.

Cotman, Carl W., and James L. McGaugh. *Behavioral Neuroscience*. New York: Academic Press, 1980. Originally developed as part of a course in neuroscience. The authors provide a broad overview of the topic without becoming bogged down in detail. Several chapters deal specifically with the endocrine system and associated clinical disorders.

Donovan, Bernard T. *Hormones and Human Behavior*. Cambridge, England: Cambridge University Press, 1985. An excellent compilation of the information available on hormones and behavior up to 1985. Uses technical language, but one who reads on a high school level and has had some exposure to science will find the book informative and interesting. Focuses on the pituitary, the gonads, and the adrenals, and their effect of human behavior.

Fox, Stuart I. "The Endocrine System." In *Perspectives on Human Biology*. Dubuque, Iowa: Wm. C. Brown, 1991. This textbook is an excellent source for introductory biology information. Student aids such as chapter outlines, lists of objectives, and keys to pronunciation are included as well as clinical and practical applications of the material presented. Illustrations are outstanding.

Graham, Robert B. *Physiological Psychology*. Belmont, Calif.: Wadsworth, 1990. A comprehensive presentation of the major aspects of the physiological determination of behavior in all mammalian species. The chapter devoted to sexuality and reproduction covers most of the effects of gonadal hormones in detail.

Guillemin, Roger, and Roger Burgus. "The Hormones of the Hypothalamus." *Scientific American* 227 (November, 1972): 24-33. An excellent article that deals primarily with the regulation of the pituitary gland. The methods by which hormones of the neurohypophysis have been isolated and studied are highlighted. Particularly useful are the clear diagrams. Description of experimental approaches is minimized.

Highnam, Kenneth Charles, and Leonard Hill. *The Comparative Endocrinology of the Invertebrates*. New York: American Elsevier, 1969. The various types of invertebrate endocrine systems are described in this book. Although the book was published in 1969, it is a valuable source of information, especially on the insect and crustacean hormones. Technical language is used but is clearly explained in layperson's terms. Drawings and charts contribute to the understanding of the material.

Hole, John. "The Endocrine System." In *Human Anatomy and Physiology.* 3d ed. Dubuque, Iowa: Wm. C. Brown, 1984. Presents a well-organized discussion of the endocrine glands, including pertinent information on clinical aspects (such as pathological disorders) and laboratory techniques associated with each gland. The text is suitable for high school and college students, as the writing style is easy to read and rather informal.

Holmes, Clarissa S., ed. *Psychoneuroendocrinology: Brain, Behavior, and Hormonal Interactions.* New York: Springer-Verlag, 1990. Presents a thorough discussion of the interdependence of hormonal and psychological factors. Includes discussion of endocrine disease on growth disorders, academic development, and social interactions in children. A section also discusses effects of replacement hormone treatment.

Holmes, R. L., and J. N. Ball. *The Pituitary Gland: A Comparative Account.* Cambridge, England: Cambridge University Press, 1974. A detailed text on the structure and function of the pituitary gland in a variety of vertebrates. Though not written for the casual reader, the text is profusely illustrated and contains an extensive bibliography.

Hrdina, Pavel D., and Radhey L. Singhal, eds. *Neuroendocrine Regulation and Altered Behaviour.* New York: Plenum Press, 1981. While including articles on learning and memory, sexual behavior, and the brain's endorphin system, this volume focuses on the involvement of the neuroendocrine system in depression, anorexia, mania, and schizophrenia.

Janowsky, David S., M. Khaled El-Yousef, John M. Davis, and H. Joseph Sekerke. "A Cholinergic-Adrenergic Hypothesis of Mania and Depression." *The Lancet* 2 (September, 1972): 632-635. This landmark article recognizes the importance of the several systems of nerve-impulse transmission and proposes that the affective state represents balance between nonadrenergic and cholinergic activity. Depression and mania are viewed as attributable to relative cholinergic and adrenergic predominance, respectively. Manic-depression is seen as overreaction by part of the nervous system.

Janowsky, David S., Robert N. Golden, Mark Rapaport, John Cain, and J. Christian Gillian. "Neurochemistry of Depression and Mania." In *Depression and Mania*, edited by Anastasios Georgotas and Robert Cancro. New York: Elsevier, 1988. Reviews development of modern concepts of the neurochemistry of these mental diseases, including norepinephrine and the catecholamine hypothesis; acetylcholine and the cholinergic-adrenergic hypothesis; and serotonin, dopamine, neuropeptides, and other neurotransmitters. Throughout, interaction of these systems is stressed. More than 160 references are included.

Komisaruk, Barry R., H. I. Siegel, M. F. Cheng, and H. H. Feder, eds. *Reproduction: A Behavioral and Neuroendocrine Perspective.* New York: New York Academy of Sciences, 1986. A collection of articles that examine the two-way relationship between neuroendocrine processes and behavior. Behavioral to molecular levels of analysis are included in examining sexual and maternal behavior, sexual differentiation, puberty, biological rhythms, and energy balance in a variety of species.

Krieger, Dorothy T., and Joan C. Hughes, eds. *Neuroendocrinology.* Sunderland, Mass.: Sinauer Associates, 1980. Contains thirty-four highly readable and clearly illustrated articles on basic neuroendocrinology and its relationship with biological rhythms, feeding and drinking, stress, learning, many aspects of reproduction, and associated disease states.

Larson, David E., ed. *Mayo Clinic Family Health Book.* New York: William Morrow, 1990. Excellent text on human diseases and disorders; includes symptoms, diagnosis, treatment, and medication. The authors explain concepts clearly. Can be readily understood by high school and college students.

Lehninger, Albert L. *Principles of Biochemistry.* New York: Worth, 1982. Chapter 25 of this college textbook presents an introductory survey of the steroid hormones and related chemicals. Includes their structures, their biochemistry, their biological properties, and their interactions with receptors. Description is simple and scholarly, with several useful references included.

Lehrman, Daniel S. "The Reproductive Behavior of Ring Doves." *Scientific American* 211 (November, 1964): 48-54. An excellent example of the relationship between behavior and neuroendocrinology as revealed by a series of experiments.

Lidz, Theodore. "Emotions and Mentation." In *The Thyroid: A Fundamental and Clinical Text*, edited by Sidney C. Werner and Sidney H. Ingbar. 3d ed. New York: Harper & Row, 1971. Compiles information regarding the thyroid from many diverse sources. The book is designed for clinical use as well as the basic science laboratory. The text is thorough and detailed and is most suitable for college students. Extensive reference sections are provided at the end of each chapter.

Meites, Joseph, Bernard T. Donovan, and Samuel M. McCann, eds. *Pioneers in Neuroendocrinology*. New York: Plenum Press, 1975. Twenty-one scientists in the field of neuroendocrinology were asked for autobiographical accounts of how they became involved in their research and their own views on the development of the field.

Money, John, and Anke A. Ehrhardt. *Man and Woman, Boy and Girl*. Baltimore: The Johns Hopkins University Press, 1972. A comprehensive account of sexual differentiation, hormones, the effects of hormones on the brain and behavior, gender identity formation, puberty, and societal influences. Research on animals and humans is viewed from psychological and biological perspectives.

O'Malley, Bert W., and William T. Schrader. "The Receptors of Steroid Hormones." *Scientific American* 234, no. 20 (1976): 32-43. This succinct article describes many aspects of the hormone-receptor concept. These include some of its history, receptor interaction with target cells, molecular biology involvements in the process, and uses of the concept in medicine. Some nice graphics clarify many issues and several important references are provided.

Pinel, John P. J. *Biopsychology*. Boston: Allyn & Bacon, 1990. A textbook intended for use by the undergraduate college student. There are two chapters of particular interest. Chapter 1 defines the position of biopsychology within the larger field of psychology, delineates the subdivisions of biopsychology, and describes the type of research carried out in each area. An account of research involving the human reproductive hormones and their effects is found in chapter 10. Both chapters are interesting and well written. The author makes use of good examples, drawings, and charts.

Raven, Peter H., and George B. Johnson. *Biology*. St. Louis: Times Mirror/Mosby, 1989. Raven and Johnson's book is an introductory survey of biology for the beginning student. It contains beautiful illustrations and photographs. Chapter 48, "Hormones," describes the endocrine systems of human and mammals, the major hormones produced by each endocrine gland, and the effects of these hormones upon the body. Chapter 56, "Behavior," describes various aspects of animal behavior, including the control of some of these behaviors by hormones.

Schildkraut, Joseph J. "The Catecholamine Hypothesis of Affective Disorders: A Review of Supporting Evidence." *American Journal of Psychiatry* 122, no. 5 (1965): 509-522. Schildkraut describes the clinical basis for the catecholamine (norepinephrine) hypothesis of affective disorders. It is pointed out that depression and elation are associated with "catecholamine" deficiency and excess, respectively, at crucial brain sites. Evidence for the hypothesis is cited.

Spence, Alexander P., and Elliott B. Mason. "The Endocrine System." In *Human Anatomy and Physiology*. 3d ed. Menlo Park, Calif.: Benjamin/ Cummings, 1987. The authors describe the glands of the endocrine system in this chapter of their introductory anatomy and physiology textbook. Discussions are thorough and written at a level suitable for high school and college students. Illustrations are excellent.

Spencer, Roberta Todd. *Patient Care in Endocrine Problems*. Philadelphia: W. B. Saunders, 1973. Provides basic knowledge in the health sciences and introduces the reader to the complexities of the endocrine system. Each chapter is devoted to a discussion of the anatomy and physiology of a particular gland and is complete with charts and photographs of individuals suffering from various disorders.

Stryer, Lubert. *Biochemistry*. 2d ed. San Francisco: W. H. Freeman, 1981. Stryer's outstanding introductory biochemistry book is aimed at advanced students, although much of it is easily understandable to the layperson, with its excellent diagrams and illustrations. Chapter 35, "Hormone Action," represents a thorough study of human and mammalian hormones, their sites of production, their target tissues, their mechanisms of action, and their effects upon the body.

Unger, Rhoda Kesler. *Female and Male: Psychological Perspectives*. New York: Harper & Row, 1979. This classic text concerning the psychology of sex differences has two chapters which focus on the interaction between sex hormones and the development of gender identity, both prenatally and at puberty.

Wallace, Robert A., Gerald P. Sanders, and Robert J. Ferl. *Biology: The Science of Life*. 3d ed. New York: HarperCollins, 1991. Wallace, Sanders, and Ferl's introduction to biology for the beginning student provides a wealth of information, constructive diagrams, and beautiful photographs. Chapter 37, "Hormonal Control," discusses human hormones and their effects upon the body. Chapters 44, "The Development and Structure of Animal Behavior," and 45, "Adaptiveness of Behavior," describe various animal behaviors and hormonal/pheromonal effects upon some of these behaviors.

Zubay, Geoffrey L. *Biochemistry*. Reading, Mass.: Addison-Wesley, 1983. Zubay's introduction to biochemistry is intended for advanced biology students, although portions of it are understandable to the layperson. Chapter 29, "Hormone Action," contains a lengthy discussion of major mammalian hormones and their effects upon the body. Molecular structures and clarifying diagrams highlight much of the text.

Nervous System

Adelman, George, ed. *Encyclopedia of Neuroscience*. 2 vols. Boston: Birkhäuser, 1987. A very comprehensive source of information on neuroscience. Eleven topics cover the synapse specifically.

Bach-y-Rita, Paul, ed. *Recovery of Function: Theoretical Considerations for Brain Injury Rehabilitation*. Baltimore: University Park Press, 1980. Attempts to take areas of basic scientific research and show how that information can be used in the rehabilitation of individuals with neurological damage.

Beaumont, J. Graham. *Introduction to Neuropsychology*. New York: Guilford Press, 1983. A very accessible reference for the student who is new to the field. Particularly helpful in describing the methods used to investigate experimental neuropsychological phenomena.

Bloom, Floyd E., and Arlyne Lazerson. *Brain, Mind, and Behavior*. 2d ed. New York: W. H. Freeman, 1988. Deals with the entire brain including behavioral rhythms, emotions, and motivational behavior. Clearly written; contains some beautiful and informative illustrations.

Bradshaw, John L., and Norman C. Nettleton. *Human Cerebral Asymmetry*. Englewood Cliffs, N.J.: Prentice-Hall, 1983. Bradshaw and Nettleton examine hemispheric asymmetries in split-brain and normal subjects, focusing particular attention on differences in cognitive processes and information-processing capacities between the two hemispheres. This book is moderately difficult to read and is recommended for college students and advanced high school students.

Brown, Alan G. *Nerve Cells and Nervous Systems*. London: Springer-Verlag, 1991. A thorough text dealing with general principles of neuroscience. Begins at the level of the neuron and develops the plan of the nervous system. Included are chapters on the relationship of ionic movement and action potentials, functional and structural organization, and interaction of the nervous system with the environment.

Bryden, M. P. *Laterality: Functional Asymmetry in the Intact Brain*. New York: Academic Press, 1982. A comprehensive book on laterality research and methods for each sensory modality. In addition, such specialized topics as the genetics and development of laterality, sex differences in laterality, and individual differences in laterality are reviewed. Although very comprehensive, the book is highly technical and would be appropriate only for advanced students.

Campbell, Neil A. *Biology*. Menlo Park, Calif.: Benjamin/Cummings, 1987. A biology textbook written for college students that is easily understood even by those with less scientific background. Background information describes the general concepts of the nervous system, chemical messengers, and the autonomic nervous system.

Carlson, Neil R. *Physiology of Behavior*. 3d ed. Boston: Allyn & Bacon, 1986. A very well-written introductory text in physiological psychology. Describes the function and structure of the entire brain, and includes subsections detailing the role of the brain stem in human behavior. Appropriate for college or high school students.

Chadwick, David, Niall Cartlidge, and David Bates. *Medical Neurology*. Edinburgh: Churchill Livingstone, 1989. This medical resource discusses disorders of the nervous system and problems associated with them. Chapter 6 includes disorders of awareness and mental function, often caused by damage to areas of the cerebral cortex. Chapter 19 covers functional and psychiatric disorders. Clinical features and the causes of these disorders, diagrams of affected brain areas, and numerous tables are included. References.

Changeux, Jean-Pierre. *Neuronal Man: The Biology of Mind.* Translated by Laurence Garey. New York: Panetheon Books, 1985. This book was very popular when originally published in France, and the translated version shows this was deserved. The author reviews the history of human investigation of the nervous system and how ideas about mind and body have changed as a result of greater knowledge. It is written for the layperson. Educates about a wide range of current neurological and biochemical discoveries and philosophical issues.

Corballis, Michael C. *Human Laterality.* New York: Academic Press, 1983. Corballis draws on evidence for laterality from split-brain and normal subjects, examining laterality from comparative, developmental, evolutionary, and genetic perspectives. Examines the relationship between hemispheric asymmetries and such language disorders as dyslexia and stuttering. Well-written and moderately easy to read; highly recommended for college students and high school students.

Corballis, Michael C., and Ivan L. Beale. *The Ambivalent Mind: The Neuropsychology of Left and Right.* Chicago: Nelson-Hall, 1983. Corballis and Beale examine the concepts of left and right and the nature of handedness as it relates to behavior. In addition, they address practical applications of hemispheric asymmetry research for dyslexia, stuttering, and the development of academic skills. This book is moderately difficult and is recommended for college students and advanced high school students.

Cotman, Carl W., and James L. McGaugh. *Behavioral Neuroscience: An Introduction.* New York: Academic Press, 1980. A textbook for undergraduates; an excellent introduction to the subject. Chapters include general introductions to the nervous system, followed by more complete analyses of specific regions of the brain and of the regulation of behaviors by these regions.

Curtis, Helena. *Biology.* 3d ed. New York: Worth, 1979. Curtis' outstanding introductory biology text describes all aspects of life on Earth in very clear detail. The development of organisms is described in evolutionary sequence. Chapter 34, "Integration and Control," is a thorough but basic introduction to the mammalian nervous and endocrine systems. Other chapters demonstrate the interrelatedness of the nervous and endocrine systems with other body tissues.

Darnell, James E., Harvey F. Lodish, and David Baltimore. *Molecular Cell Biology.* 2d ed. New York: W. H. Freeman, 1990. A textbook of molecular biology that provides an excellent section with detailed descriptions of neuronal function. Especially useful are the outstanding illustrations which accompany the text. An excellent bibliography is also provided.

Durham, Ross M. *Human Physiology: Functions of the Human Body.* Dubuque, Iowa: Wm. C. Brown, 1989. An easily read textbook of general physiology that is illustrated with clear diagrams and colorful pictures. Understandable even by the novice with little background information.

Ellis, Andrew W., and Andrew W. Young. *Human Cognitive Neuropsychology.* Hove, England: Lawrence Erlbaum, 1988. Presents ideas and research on the integrated workings of the brain from the mid-1980's. Particularly helpful in establishing a theoretical framework that assists the student in integrating the often divergent research findings in a more holistic manner.

Feldman, Robert Simon, and Linda F. Quenzer. *Fundamentals of Neuropsychopharmacology.* Sunderland, Mass.: Sinauer Associates, 1984. This is a popular text addressing much information related to drugs and behavior. It covers major neurochemical systems in terms of how the synthesis, release, and fate of each neurotransmitter may be controlled by various neuroactive compounds, and it looks at the ensuing behavioral changes.

Fromm, Gerhard H., Carl L. Faingold, Ronald A. Browning, and W. M. Burnham, eds. *Epilepsy and the Reticular Formation: The Role of the Reticular Core in Convulsive Seizures.* New York: Liss, 1987. This collection of short articles supports the proposal of the first author that all epileptic convulsions are caused by the interaction of areas of the cerebral cortex with the reticular formation. The reticular core is thought to be the activating structure producing the electrical discharges of the cortex. Many references.

Gardner, Howard. *The Shattered Mind: The Person After Brain Damage.* New York: Alfred A. Knopf, 1975. A very readable account of how brain damage to various regions and connections of the brain changes a person. Excellent clinical descriptions of symptoms and how these interact with the person. Teaches the anatomy of the cerebral hemispheres in a painless and accurate way.

Geschwind, Norman. "Specializations of the Human Brain." *Scientific American* 241 (September, 1979): 180-182+. An excellent discussion of the roles played by specific regions of the brain in behavior. Emphasis is placed on the role of the forebrain. This particular issue was completely devoted to the development and function of the brain.

Getting, Peter A. "Emerging Principles Governing the Operation of Neural Networks." In *Annual Review of Neuroscience* 12. Palo Alto, Calif.: Annual Reviews, 1989. A summary of the organization and operation of neuronal networks. Highlighted are emerging principles which govern the operation of these networks. The author uses a reductionist approach in which principles are defined by cells and synapses, the "nuts and bolts" of the operation as defined by the author.

Goldberg, Jeff. *Anatomy of a Scientific Discovery*. New York: Bantam Books, 1988. An examination of the scientific rivalry that occurred between the scientists who were trying to isolate the first endogenous opiates. Contains some scientific discussions, but focuses on the personal relationships of the scientists. Enlightening to anyone interested in the endorphins and enkephalins or the workings of the scientific community.

Gottleib, Gilbert, ed. *Neural and Behavioral Specificity*. New York: Academic Press, 1976. A good historical discussion of the nervous system and its role in the development of behavior. Emphasis is on perceptual development as related to behavioral specificity. A bit dated, but a useful introduction to the topic.

Gray, Henry. *Gray's Anatomy: Descriptive and Surgical*. Edited by T. Pickering Pick and Robert Howden. New York: Bounty Books, 1977. This updated classic describes human anatomy and physiology, especially anatomy, in exquisite detail. Numerous diagrams and a clear, descriptive text make this book a tremendous reference for the student of medicine or anatomy. More than 200 pages are devoted to the structure and functioning of the human central and peripheral nervous systems.

Gregory, Richard L., ed. *The Oxford Companion to the Mind*. Oxford, England: Oxford University Press, 1987. A long article, "Neurotransmitters and Neuromodulators," contains a discussion of different chemicals and their actions. A table, numerous illustrations, and several references accompany the text. Also includes other individual articles on specific psychoactive chemicals.

Gross, Charles G., and H. Philip Zeigler, eds. *Motivation*. Vol. 2 in *Readings in Physiological Psychology*. New York: Harper & Row, 1969. Although there are dozens of newer collections of articles in the area of physiological psychology, this one does a particularly good job of covering the broad diversity of topics in the field. In addition, all the work represented in this particular collection came from animal studies. This or a similar collection can be consulted for illustration of many specific methodologies utilized in research with animals.

Hobson, J. Allan, and Mary A. B. Brazier, eds. *The Reticular Formation Revisited: Specifying Function for a Nonspecific System*. New York: Raven Press, 1980. A compilation of papers presented at an international symposium in 1978. Separate sections cover historical aspects, methods of study, arousal, motor control of the body from the brain stem, chemical regulatory processes and neurotransmitters, and mechanisms of behavioral state control, including sleep. References accompany each paper.

Hucho, Ferdinand. *Neurochemistry Fundamentals and Concepts*. Deerfield Beach, Fla.: VCH Publishers, 1986. A basic book of neurochemistry that can be understood by anyone who has had high school chemistry. The chemical formula of the opiate peptides and the role of receptors is described.

Janov, Arthur. *Prisoners of Pain*. Garden City, N. Y.: Anchor Press, 1980. This discussion of pain does not include extensive information about the endorphins, but it describes the importance of pain in determining the behavior of animals, and the extent to which pain can be alleviated by substances such as opiates. Written for the layperson; accessible to all.

Julien, Robert M. *A Primer of Drug Action*. 4th ed. New York: W. H. Freeman, 1985. This paperback book describes how synaptic transmission can be manipulated by drugs to affect physiological and psychological responses. Historical episodes about drugs and coverage of various "street" compounds make this interesting reading.

Kalat, James. *Biological Psychology*. 3d ed. Belmont, Calif.: Wadsworth, 1984. Kalat's textbook provides a relatively easy-to-read summary of the field of biological psychology. The chapter on daily rhythms of activity and sleep provides a good summary of how the hindbrain influences forebrain structures in regulating activity levels.

Kaplan, Harold I., and Benjamin J. Sadock, eds. *Comprehensive Textbook of Psychiatry.* 5th ed. Vol. 1. Baltimore: Williams & Wilkins, 1989. The functional neuroanatomy of the brain stem and reticular formation are covered in chapter 1 of this text for medical students. A later portion of the chapter also covers the physiology of sleep.

Kirshner, Howard S. *Behavioral Neurology: A Practical Approach.* New York: Churchill Livingstone, 1986. Discusses various disorders of behavior that have their source in dysfunction of the brain, particularly the cerebral cortex. Areas covered include language, reading and writing, learned movement, recognition, memory, dementias, and epilepsy. Specific disorders of the right cerebral hemisphere and the frontal lobes are also considered. References accompany each chapter.

Klemm, W. R., and Robert P. Vertes, eds. *Brainstem Mechanisms of Behavior.* New York: John Wiley & Sons, 1990. Provides a modern synthesis of the knowledge of this area of psychology, the actions of the medulla, pons, and midbrain. Articles in the first part of the book cover general information on how the brain stem, including the reticular formation, is involved in behavior. The larger second section discusses special research topics. The last article covers brain-stem functions in sleep control. Numerous references.

Kolb, Bryan, and Ian Q. Whishaw. *Fundamentals of Human Neuropsychology.* 3d ed. New York: W. H. Freeman, 1990. An excellent text. This book logically guides the reader through the fundamentals of brain and neuron function to detailed descriptions of research on the purposes of all major brain areas. Provides a general model to understand the brain and functional systems like memory or language. The material is designed to be understood at different levels.

Kuffler, Stephen W., John G. Nicholls, and A. Robert Martin. *From Neuron to Brain.* 2d ed. Sunderland, Mass.: Sinauer Associates, 1984. The authors are well-known researchers; Kuffler was a respected teacher in neurophysiology from Harvard University. This widely used neuroscience text covers historical and modern approaches to neurophysiology in general and synaptic transmission in particular.

Levin, Harvey S., Jordan Grafman, and Howard M. Eisenberg. *Neurobehavioral Recovery from Head Injury.* New York: Oxford University Press, 1987. Reviews findings related to neuropsychological assessment, neurobehavioral outcome, and memory and attention deficits.

Also presents information about common psychiatric sequelae experienced by brain-injured individuals.

Levitan, Irwin B., and Leonard K. Kaczmarek. *The Neuron: Cell and Molecular Biology*. New York: Oxford University Press, 1991. Designed to incorporate neurophysiology into an undergraduate curriculum, this text is very thorough on the concepts of cellular and molecular function of the neuron. Several chapters are devoted to the generation of the action potential, ion channels, and other aspects of intercellular communication. Excellent coverage of research techniques used to study excitation and inhibition. Includes a large bibliography and many diagrams.

Luria, Aleksandr R. "The Functional Organization of the Brain." *Scientific American* 196 (March, 1970): 66-78. Luria was a dominant force in Russian neuropsychology. He worked extensively with brain damaged soldiers and developed a neurodiagnostic approach that has had a tremendous impact on American diagnostic techniques. In this classic article he presents a simple but profound model of the organization of the human brain. The frontal lobes involve action and planning, the hind parts of the cortex involve memory and sensation, and lower brain areas organize motivation, emotion, and reflex.

_____. *Restoration of Function After Brain Injury*. New York: Macmillan, 1963. Necessary reading for anyone wanting a solid foundation in the field. Contains considerable complex material, but it is presented in an orderly, logical manner.

_____. *The Working Brain*. London: Allen Lane, 1973. One of the most cohesive and integrative descriptions of the inner workings of the brain in the field. Brain-stem mechanisms are primarily discussed as they contribute to attention and concentration abilities. Includes sections dealing with the various symptoms seen in patients with brain damage.

MacLean, P. "The Triune Brain." *American Scientist* 66 (1978): 101-113. Complex and detailed account of the brain stem's role in emotional experience. For advanced students.

Martin, Martha B., Cynthia M. Owen, and John M. Morihisa. "An Overview of Neurotransmitters and Neuroreceptors." In *The American Psychiatric Textbook of Neuropsychiatry*, edited by Robert E. Hales and Stuart C. Yudofsky. Washington, D.C.: The Press, 1987. Written for medical students and professionals, this article gives a very thorough discussion of numerous putative neurotransmitters in the central nervous system. Discusses the historical development of treatments related to neurotransmission. Covers the actions of several neurotransmitters and psychotropic drugs in schizophrenia, affective disorders, anxiety disorders, and Alzheimer's disease.

Miller, Edgar. *Recovery and Management of Neuropsychological Impairments*. New York: John Wiley & Sons, 1984. A very basic, readable account of the major theories of recovery. Also deals with the numerous factors that influence recovery of function and how they may or may not be attributed to normal spontaneous recovery and adaptation.

Nauta, Walle, and Michael Feirtag. "The Organization of the Brain." *Scientific American* 241 (September, 1979): 88-90+. An excellent, though technical, discussion of the major regions of the brain. Emphasis is placed on the role played by the cerebral cortex. The role of neuronal networks is outlined in some depth.

The Nervous System: Circuits of Communication. New York: Torstar Books, 1985. An informative and well-illustrated book for the layperson. It clearly describes the autonomic nervous system and its role in behavior. Very readable. Includes a history of the subject and supportive information relevant to the topic.

Ommaya, A. K., and T. A. Gennarelli. "Cerebral Concussion and Traumatic Unconsciousness." *Brain* 97, no. 4 (1974): 633-654. A classic article dealing with the physical aspects of brain injury and subsequent recovery. Presents technical material at a level that can be understood by the general reader.

Ornstein, Robert Evan, and Richard F. Thompson. *The Amazing Brain*. Boston: Houghton Mifflin, 1984. This is a clearly written and well-illustrated book for the nonscientist, presented as a tour of the brain. It discusses the architecture of the brain and how it receives sensory impulses, with emphasis on those for vision. Memory and the effects of separating the two cerebral hemispheres are also covered.

Parker, Rolland S. *Traumatic Brain Injury and Neuropsychological Impairment*. New York: Springer-Verlag, 1990. Deals with the sensorimotor, cognitive, and emotional adjustment problems experienced by both adults and children with traumatic brain injuries.

Prigatano, George P. *Neuropsychological Rehabilitation After Brain Injury.* Baltimore: The Johns Hopkins University Press, 1986. Presents information about cognitive deficits related to head injury and about common emotional and psychosocial adjustment problems. Also deals with rehabilitation issues and the type of brain-injured patients likely to benefit from psychotherapy.

Raven, Peter H., and George B. Johnson. *Biology.* St. Louis: Times Mirror/ Mosby, 1989. Raven and Johnson's *Biology* is a beautifully illustrated and diagrammed introduction. Major topics in biology and evolution are discussed, including mammalian anatomy and physiology. Several chapters are devoted to the functioning of the human nervous and endocrine systems.

Restak, Richard M. *The Brain.* New York: Bantam Books, 1984. Describes the brain and its functions. The experience of pain is described in some detail, and the role of the endorphins is included in this discussion. Written for the layperson.

_____. *The Mind.* Toronto: Bantam Books, 1988. Published to accompany the Public Broadcasting Service television series of the same title, this well-illustrated book discusses behavior as affected by neurotransmitters in chapters on aging, addiction, and depression.

Romero-Sierra, C. *Neuroanatomy: A Conceptual Approach.* New York: Churchill Livingstone, 1986. This review book for medical students discusses the reticular formation in several sections, with anatomical structure, motor function, and visceral control. Diagrams and lists of functions present the material in an easily understood format. Suggested readings are included.

Rosenzweig, Mark R., and Arnold L. Leiman. *Physiological Psychology.* 2d ed. New York: Random House, 1989. This textbook provides a fourfold approach for studying physiological psychology: descriptive, comparative/evolutionary, developmental, and biologically mechanistic. The chapters on brain development and the cranial nerve nuclei should contribute to the reader's understanding of the hindbrain's involvement in behavior.

Sacks, Oliver. *An Anthropologist on Mars: Seven Paradoxical Tales.* New York: Alfred A. Knopf, 1995. The author describes seven case histories, including that of a surgeon with Tourette's syndrome, an autistic design engineer, and a painter who only paints the town in which he lived as a child. Sacks is a neurologist with a gift for describing such cases with compassion and discussing the wider implications of their experience for our understanding of humankind. For a general audience.

_____. *The Man Who Mistook His Wife for a Hat and Other Clinical Tales.* New York: Simon and Schuster, 1987. A splendidly written memoir of treating patients with various disorders. Sacks is both entertaining and informative. The man of the book's title, "Dr. P.," was suffering from a tumor in the right occipital lobe of the brain.

Sagan, Carl. *The Dragons of Eden: Speculations on the Evolution of Human Intelligence.* New York: Random House, 1977. Written by a well-known astronomer, the book provides an easily understood description of the development of the brain through the course of evolution. The connection between development of forebrain structures and various behaviors is presented in the informal manner associated with this popular speaker.

Schneider, Allen M., and Barry Tarshis. *An Introduction to Physiological Psychology.* 3d ed. New York: Random House, 1986. This undergraduate textbook gives a thorough coverage of the neural impulse and the synapse in chapters 7 and 8. Several diagrams aid the discussion of the impulse cycle. Neural transmission is tied to adaptive behavior.

Scientific American 241 (September, 1979). This entire issue of the journal deals with the topic of the brain. Articles are somewhat technical, but they are well written and nicely illustrated.

Scientific American 267 (September, 1992). The 1990's was declared the "decade of the brain," and this entire issue of *Scientific American* is devoted to topics on mind and brain. Article topics include brain development, brain and language, memory, sex differences, and consciousness, among others. Articles are sophisticated, but accessible to the educated general reader.

Segalowitz, Sidney J. *Two Sides of the Brain: Brain Lateralization Explored.* Englewood Cliffs, N.J.: Prentice-Hall, 1983. A basic book on hemispheric asymmetries found in split-brain and normal subjects. In addition, Segalowitz addresses developmental issues, individual differences, and implications of brain lateralization for human behavior. Highly accessible to the student and lay reader.

42 *Psychology*

Selkoe, Dennis J. "Amyloid Protein and Alzheimer's Disease." *Scientific American* 265 (November, 1991): 68-78. A summary of the pathology and possible cause of the most common form of aging dementia. Written for the person with at least college-level knowledge of science, but well illustrated. Diagrams are at a basic level.

Shepherd, Gordon M. *Neurobiology.* 2d ed. New York: Oxford University Press, 1988. The author is an authority in the sensory physiology at Yale University. The text covers the nervous system from molecular to system levels, with synaptic transmission regarded as a major link.

Siegel, George J., Bernard W. Agranoff, R. Wayne Albers, and Perry B. Molinoff, eds. *Basic Neurochemistry.* 4th ed. New York: Raven Press, 1989. The book covers forty-eight topics, each discussed by one or more authoritative researchers in the respective fields. Thirteen topics are under "Synaptic Function," covering the major neurotransmitter systems. Useful as a text or reference source; it has a helpful glossary and an index.

Springer, Sally P., and Georg Deutsch. *Left Brain, Right Brain.* 3d ed. New York: W. H. Freeman, 1989. Springer and Deutsch have written a comprehensive introductory book on laterality. They address research with split-brain and normal subjects in considerable detail, and provide thorough coverage of potential practical applications of laterality research. The book is very readable and is highly recommended for high school students, college students, and adult readers.

Stein, Donald G. "Recovery from Brain Damage." In *Clinical Neuropsychology and Brain Function: Research, Measurement, and Practice,* edited by Thomas Boll and Brenda K. Bryant. Washington, D.C.: American Psychological Association, 1988. Debates the issues of localization of function, pointing out perceived weaknesses of the theory. Addresses numerous problems with the understanding of recovery of function after neural damage.

Steriade, Mircea, and Robert W. McCarley. *Brainstem Control of Wakefulness and Sleep.* New York: Plenum Press, 1990. This comprehensive text provides a unity of viewpoint on the topic not found in edited collections. References to the different areas of the reticular formation are found throughout the book, in discussions of the sensory information entering the brain stem and the motor control carrying instructions to muscles, among others. Brain waves in sleep and waking are discussed as originating from the reticular area. Extensive references.

Stryer, Lubert. *Biochemistry*. 3d ed. New York: W. H. Freeman, 1988. Discusses acetylcholine, its structure, its actions as a neurotransmitter, its receptor, and its breakdown and inhibition in chapter 39. Other neurotransmitters covered include epinephrine, dopamine, glycine, and GABA. Treatment of these topics is mainly chemical, including the research methods used to examine how receptor channels function. Several references are included at the end of the chapter.

Surwillo, Walter W. *Psychophysiology for Clinical Psychologists*. Norwood, N.J.: Ablex, 1990. This text provides basic knowledge of psychophysiology and highlights some areas of application. Surwillo also incorporates helpful diagrams and relevant references for research in the area.

Symposium on the Neural Basis of Behavior. *The Neural Basis of Behavior*. Edited by Alexander L. Beckman. New York: SP Medical & Scientific Books, 1982. Based on a 1979 symposium devoted to the neural basis of behavior. A specialized publication; provides a good background and history of various neural problems.

Thompson, Richard F. *The Brain: An Introduction to Neuroscience*. New York: W. H. Freeman, 1985. A particularly good introduction to the workings of the nervous system. Contains chapters about the basic brain mechanisms, sensory and motor systems, and changes that occur in the brain throughout an individual's life.

Tortora, Gerard J., and Nicholas P. Anagnostakos. *Principles of Anatomy and Physiology*. 6th ed. New York: Harper & Row, 1990. Chapter 14 of this undergraduate college text covers the brain, and chapter 15 is about the sensory, motor, and integrative systems that are contained within the cerebral cortex. Numerous photographs and diagrams help the reader visualize the area under discussion. Excellent as introductory coverage of this material. Selected readings at the end of each chapter refer to easily accessible material.

Van De Graaff, Kent Marshall, and Stuart Ira Fox. *Concepts of Human Anatomy and Physiology*. 2d ed. Dubuque, Iowa: Wm. C. Brown, 1989. An undergraduate text that covers introductory information on the brain clearly and succinctly. Extensive discussion of synaptic transmission and the chemicals and receptors involved is included in chapter 14 of this college textbook. Discusses acetylcholine, catecholamines, amino acids, and polypeptides as neurotransmitters. Also covers Parkinson's and Alzheimer's diseases. The cerebrum is discussed in chapter 15, accompanied by numerous diagrams and tables. References are given at the end of the book.

Vander, Arthur J., James H. Sherman, and Dorothy S. Luciano. *Human Physiology: The Mechanisms of Body Function.* 5th ed. New York: McGraw-Hill, 1990. This general physiology text for the college student can be easily read by the high school student. The chapter on homeostatic mechanisms, which includes a section on receptors, will shed much light on the study of the autonomic nervous system. Well illustrated and contains a wealth of knowledge in an easy-to-understand format. References are provided for further reading.

Van Toller, C. *The Nervous Body.* New York: John Wiley & Sons, 1979. Primarily a discussion of the autonomic nervous system and its effects on behavior. Sections are included that deal with psychophysiology and its effects as defined by the polygraph test, with psychosomatic disease, and with control of emotions using biofeedback.

Villee, Claude Alvin, et al. *Biology.* 2d ed. Philadelphia: Saunders College Publishing, 1989. Chapter 46 of this freshman college text covers neurons, including a lengthy discussion of transmission of a neural impulse. The effects of neurotransmitters in exciting and inhibiting depolarization of the membrane are also covered.

Wallace, Robert A., Gerald P. Sanders, and Robert J. Ferl. *Biology: The Science of Life.* 3d ed. New York: HarperCollins, 1991. A general biology text with excellent chapters outlining the structure and function of the brain. Though this is a college text, the material is written in a manner that can be easily understood by the nonexpert. Illustrations are plentiful and clear.

Ylvisaker, Mark, and Eva Marie R. Gobble, eds. *Community Re-Entry for Head Injured Adults.* Boston: Little, Brown, 1987. A practical reference presenting valuable information about cognitive and physical rehabilitation issues, family issues, personality changes, neuropsychological deficits, and outcome.

SENSATION AND PERCEPTION

General Constructs and Issues

Bridgeman, Bruce. *The Biology of Behavior and Mind.* New York: John Wiley & Sons, 1988. Chapter 5 explores the physiological mechanisms of perception, while chapter 6 treats perception as an active process—something one does rather than something that happens to one.

Brown, Evan L., and Kenneth Deffenbacher. *Perception and the Senses.* New York: Oxford University Press, 1979. This text differs from most textbooks on sensation in that it integrates ethological, cross-species information with the traditional coverage of human sensory physiology and psychophysics. Although technical, the book is user-friendly. Each chapter has its own outline, glossary, and set of suggested readings.

Buddenbrock, Wolfgang von. *The Senses.* Ann Arbor: University of Michigan Press, 1958. Easy-to-read descriptions of different *Umwelts*, with many fascinating examples. Since the focus is almost entirely on ultimate explanations rather than sensory mechanisms, new technologies have not made this book outdated.

Burkhardt, Dietrich, Wolfgang Schleidt, and Helmut Altner. *Signals in the Animal World.* New York: McGraw-Hill, 1967. Thirty-two very readable essays on the sensory systems of a wide variety of animals, including senses not shared by humans. Each essay is accompanied by at least one high-quality photograph and several drawings. Text provides a delightful combination of proximate and ultimate descriptions of different sensory *Umwelts.*

Commons, Michael L., John A. Nevin, and Michael C. Davison, eds. *Signal Detection: Mechanisms, Models, and Applications.* Hillsdale, N.J.: Lawrence Erlbaum, 1991. A collection of scholarly papers based on the tenth annual Harvard Symposium for the Quantitative Analysis of Behavior. The chapters, quantitative and theoretical in approach, illustrate sensitivity and bias as independent parameters in signal detection theory. The final three chapters give clear articulation to major applications and are of interest in themselves.

Geldard, Frank Arthur. *The Human Senses*. 2d ed. New York: John Wiley & Sons, 1972. In this excellent general review of what is known about the human senses, Geldard discusses psychophysical scaling (and psychophysics generally) in an introductory chapter. In various chapters, he describes scales derived by Stevens' method of magnitude estimation, including the "gust" scale of taste, the "dol" scale of pain, and psychophysical scaling of estimates of lifted weights and loudness of tones of varying frequencies. Discussion also includes the anatomy and physiology of the senses.

Geschieder, George A. *Psychophysics: Method and Theory*. Hillsdale, N.J.: Lawrence Erlbaum, 1976. Geschieder presents a balanced view of the whole of psychophysics, including signal detection theory. This is an excellent source for the reader seeking more advanced information.

Goldstein, E. Bruce. *Sensation and Perception*. 3d ed. Belmont, Calif.: Wadsworth, 1989. An excellent overview of the field of sensation and perception. Chapters focus on typical subjects dealing with vision, hearing, and touch, but Goldstein also adds interesting chapters on perceived speech and the chemical senses.

Green, David Martin, and John A. Swets. *Signal Detection Theory and Psychophysics*. Huntington, N.Y.: R. E. Krieger, 1974. A quantitative presentation of the general theory of signal detection and early experiments applying the theory to sensory and to decision processes for the serious reader. The final chapter contains applications of signal detection theory to ongoing problems in psychology: vigilance, attention, psychophysics, reaction time, and memory.

Gregory, R. L. *Eye and Brain: The Psychology of Seeing*. 3d ed. New York: World University Library, 1978. A broad book on vision for the general reader. Beneficial for students in the areas of psychology, biology, and physiology. Includes many illustrations that help to explain complex matters in an understandable fashion.

Hall, Edward Twitchell. *The Hidden Dimension*. Garden City, N.Y.: Anchor Books, 1969. Written by an anthropologist, this book on cross-cultural differences in use of space includes three chapters (4, 5, and 6) on the perception of space as influenced by each sensory modality. These provide good examples of using human factors and environmental psychology to address real-world problems, particularly problems in architecture and interpersonal communication.

Levine, Michael W., and Jeremy M. Shefner. *Fundamentals of Sensation and Perception.* 2d ed. Pacific Grove, Calif.: Brooks/Cole, 1991. A college textbook for students of sensation and perception, this proceeds from an introductory chapter to a clear and well-illustrated discussion of psychophysics. The pages on signal detection theory are replete with figures and diagrams, and the theory is described in historical and theoretical context. A short, enjoyable, and highly readable introduction.

Lowenstein, Otto. *The Senses.* Baltimore: Penguin Books, 1966. This book focuses on proximate, rather than ultimate, explanations of sensation. Approximately half of the book is devoted to electromagnetic senses, with most of the rest devoted to mechanoreception, especially the skin senses; includes only a small portion on chemical sensation.

Ludel, Jacqueline. *Introduction to Sensory Processes.* San Francisco: W. H. Freeman, 1978. Requires no prior study of sensory processes, anatomy, physiology, or perception. More than an introduction, Ludel gradually and clearly explores topics in depth. Conversational in tone, the book also contains mnemonics and pronunciation guides.

Mackworth, Jane F. *Vigilance and Attention: A Signal Detection Approach.* Harmondsworth, Middlesex, England: Penguin Books, 1970. Mackworth demonstrates how signal detection methods may contribute to understanding attention, vigilance, and other cognitive processes. The focus is on monitoring displays and on situations demanding continuous attention rather than on theory. Clearly shows how method contributes to research in a particular area. This is not introductory, but is well written and accessible.

Matlin, M. W. *Sensation and Perception.* 2d ed. Boston: Allyn & Bacon, 1988. Matlin's book is an introductory text covering all general areas of sensation and perception. Themes carried throughout the text are intended to provide additional structure for the material; these themes reflect the author's eclectic theoretical orientation.

Rock, Irvin. *Perception.* New York: Scientific American Library, 1984. Rock deals particularly with perception and pays little attention to sensation other than vision. The text is designed to be an introductory work to motivate the reader to future studies. The book essentially explores the perception of the properties, distance, and motion of objects.

Scharf, Bertram, ed. *Experimental Sensory Psychology*. Glenview, Ill.:
   Scott, Foresman, 1975. Includes an introduction, a chapter on psychophysics, chapters on each sensory modality, and a postscript on the
   direction of modern studies. Provides excellent detailed descriptions
   of sensory mechanisms and psychophysical laws. Includes many diagrams, formulas, and technical terms but is still very readable.

Schiff, William. *Perception: An Applied Approach*. Boston: Houghton
   Mifflin, 1980. Schiff's book is concerned with how people can, and
   do, use their senses to comprehend their world and their relation to it.
   Interesting chapters cover such topics as social-event perception, personal perception, and individual differences in perception.

Sekuler, Robert, and Robert R. Blake. *Perception*. New York: Alfred A.
   Knopf, 1985. Sekuler and Blake attempt to explain seeing, hearing,
   smelling, and tasting to students of perception. Extensive use of
   illustrations allows the reader to understand materials more fully. A
   series of short illustrations is also utilized by the authors to depict
   additional concepts.

Stevens, Stanley Smith. *Psychophysics*. New York: John Wiley & Sons,
   1975. This is Stevens' last, and likely best, exposition of his views on
   psychophysics in general, with a major emphasis on magnitude estimation and cross-modality matching. One especially appealing aspect
   of the book is that it presents many anecdotes about the development
   of the ideas, and thus illustrates the scientist at work rather than simply
   presenting the results of that work.

Stevens, Stanley Smith, Fred Warshofsky, and the editors of *Life*. *Sound
   and Hearing*. New York: Time, 1965. This presents a nontechnical and
   highly readable discussion of psychophysics in general and Stevens'
   power law in particular, with emphasis on studies using magnitude
   estimation. The impact of psychophysical scaling on the practice of
   acoustical engineering is also discussed. There is an entertaining look
   at the early psychophysics of Fechner.

Stone, Herbert, and Joel L. Sidel. *Sensory Evaluation Practices*. Orlando,
   Fla.: Academic Press, 1985. Although written for professionals, this
   text can provide the layperson with insight into the world of product
   research. Mostly describes techniques for designing studies of the
   sensory evaluation of food products, but most of the principles are
   generalizable to other products and industries.

Wickens, Christopher D. *Engineering Psychology and Human Performance*. Columbus, Ohio: Charles E. Merrill, 1984. Wickens provides a general survey of engineering psychology, or the application of knowledge from experimental psychology to engineering objects and systems for human use. Treats perception extensively and illustrates the impact of psychophysics and perceptual measurement on practical problems.

Auditory, Chemical, Cutaneous, and Body Senses

Ballantyne, John Chalmers, and J. A. M. Martin. *Deafness*. 4th ed. Edinburgh: Churchill Livingstone, 1984. This book attempts "a general account couched in simple terms, of the disability of deafness and its relief." Coverage includes description of the auditory system, diagnosis of deafness and explanation of its causes, description of hearing aids, exploration of psychological aspects, and rehabilitation of the deaf.

Berne, Robert M., and Matthew N. Levy, eds. *Physiology*. 2d ed. St. Louis: C. V. Mosby, 1988. Chapter 9, "The Somatosensory System," in this standard college physiology text outlines the anatomy and physiology of the cells and nerve tracts in the spinal column and brain involved in the sensation of temperature and other body sensations. Chapter 12, "Chemical Senses," outlines the anatomy and physiology of the systems integrated in the senses of taste and smell. Includes a discussion of the neural connections and regions of the brain involved in the perception of taste and smell. Although the text is intended for students at the college level, it is clearly written and should be accessible to high school readers.

Bess, Fred H., and Larry E. Humes. *Audiology: The Fundamentals*. Baltimore: Williams & Wilkins, 1990. A valuable book designed for students of audiology. Notable for its clear, simple language, abundant related vignettes, and many literature references. Topics of major interest include the nature of sound, the structure and function of the auditory system, the assessment of auditory function, and useful management strategies for the hearing impaired.

Bolton, Brian, ed. *Psychology of Deafness for Rehabilitation Counselors*. Baltimore: University Park Press, 1976. Provides useful information on problems associated with deafness and their treatment. A good counterpoint to the aspects of the normal auditory system. Included are aspects of intellectual and vocational development, academic achievement, psychiatry of deafness, and intervention and rehabilitation programs.

Bradford, Larry J., and William G. Hardy. *Hearing and Hearing Impairment*. New York: Grune & Stratton, 1979. Covers hearing impairment, the sciences of hearing and hearing impairment, programs and practices with the hearing impaired, mental health and hearing impairment, the hearing impaired and society, and aid delivery systems. Many valuable references and diagrams are also included.

Bridgeman, Bruce. *The Biology of Behavior and Mind*. New York: John Wiley & Sons, 1988. Includes a discussion of kinesthesis within the context of the control of movement, rather than its perception, which places it within a larger context. Also includes a particularly good discussion of vestibular sensitivity which emphasizes the experience of vestibular signals, rather than only the biology.

Coren, Stanley. *Sensation and Perception*. 3d ed. San Diego: Harcourt Brace Jovanovich, 1989. A particularly comprehensive and well-written survey of sensory processes. The section on audition contains many examples that make a complex topic accessible. Other chapters place the study of sound waves and hearing into a valuable general perspective.

Daniloff, Raymond, Gordon Schuckers, and Lawrence Feth. *The Physiology of Speech and Hearing: An Introduction*. Englewood Cliffs, N.J.: Prentice-Hall, 1980. This introductory book does a thorough job, using clear, simple language. The chapter entitled "Audition: The Sense of Hearing" is important. In addition, chapters providing overviews of speech and hearing, basic neuroscience, and acoustics are quite useful.

Deutsch, Diana, ed. *The Psychology of Music*. New York: Academic Press, 1982. A unique collection of monographs written by experts in their respective fields. Extremely comprehensive in terms of physics, psychoacoustics, and psychology of music, both its structure and performance. Intended for the professional, but much is readable by the nonexpert.

Dickinson, John. *Proprioceptive Control of Human Movement*. Princeton, N.J.: Princeton Book Company, 1974. Proprioception is an umbrella term encompassing perception of movement based on muscle, joint, and tendon receptors, as well as vestibular input. Dickinson presents an unusually good discussion of all these senses, within the context of their role in the control and learning of human movement.

Eimas, Peter D. "The Perception of Speech in Early Infancy." *Scientific American* 252 (January, 1985): 46-52. Discusses the human infant's ability to detect phonemic categories long before the age at which speech production has begun. This clearly presented article explains some of the speech perception research techniques that can be used with infants. The results suggest that at least some speech perception mechanisms are innate.

Feldman, Alan S., and Charles T. Grimes, eds. *Hearing Conservation in Industry*. Baltimore: Williams & Wilkins, 1985. Covers many useful topics including the effects of noise on hearing, federal noise regulations, hearing protection devices, workers compensation, legal issues, and noise exposure standards. The persistent reader will get an excellent overview, obtain many technical details, and find an abundant source of references on many issues.

Fodor, Jerry A. *The Modularity of Mind*. Cambridge, Mass.: MIT Press, 1983. Although this is a philosophical presentation of Fodor's theory of mind, much of the text is concerned with speech and language. The discussions may be difficult for high school students, but they are valuable lessons in an alternate approach to what may seem to be a topic restricted to scientists.

Graham, Robert B. *Physiological Psychology*. Belmont, Calif.: Wadsworth, 1990. A sound introductory college textbook with a chapter on the somatic senses, including pain. Integrates pain physiology with clinical phenomena such as the placebo effect, phantom limb, conversion reaction, neurotic pain, and acupuncture, and examines the role of fear, stress, sex, social interaction, and pain in eliciting analgesia. Other chapters provide a foundation in neuroanatomy, neurophysiology, and basic research techniques, as well as an understanding of the role of the brain in diverse phenomena: sleep, attention, eating, drinking, sexuality, learning, memory, hearing, seeing, tasting, movement, and disordered human behavior. Includes graphics and a glossary.

Gulick, W. Lawrence. *Hearing: Physiology and Psychophysics*. New York: Oxford University Press, 1971. A classic. Beautifully written so as to present difficult topics comprehensively but accessibly. All topics basic to the sense of hearing are included.

Guyton, Arthur C. *Textbook of Medical Physiology*. 7th ed. Philadelphia: W. B. Saunders, 1986. Chapter 48, "Sensory Receptors and Their Basic Mechanisms of Action," in this readable and clearly written text outlines the fundamental activities of sensory receptors. Chapter 50, "Somatic Sensations II: Pain, Visceral Pain, Headache, and Thermal Sensations," in this readable and clearly written text includes an excellent discussion of thermoreceptors, the role of the hypothalamus in regulation of body temperature, and medical implications of fever, hyperthermia, and hypothermia. Chapter 62, "The Chemical Senses— Taste and Smell," presents more detailed information on the chemo-receptors active in detection of taste and smell, and the connec-tions between these receptors and the brain. Intended for college and medical students, but easily understood by readers at the high school level.

Hamilton, Leonard W., and C. Robin Timmons. *Principles of Behavioral Pharmacology: A Biopsychological Perspective*. Englewood Cliffs, N.J.: Prentice-Hall, 1990. Provides a not-too-technical understanding of the effects of drugs on the brain and behavior (from depression to drug abuse). Includes a chapter on pain and other stressors that exam-ines the opiate and nonopiate analgesia systems, and the relationship between the immune system and pain and stress. Intended for an adult or introductory college student. Includes an extensive bibliography, index, glossary, and good illustrations.

Keidel, Wolf Dieter, S. Kallert, and M. Korth. *The Physiological Basis of Hearing*. New York: Thieme-Stratton, 1983. This expert, technical text comprehensively reviews the physiology and operation of the auditory system. Well worth examining, it includes excellent descriptions of the anatomy, physiology, and operation of the auditory system, as well as theories of its operation, with experimental and theoretical explana-tions. Almost thirteen hundred references are included.

Kelly, D. D. "Central Representations of Pain and Analgesia." In *Princi-ples of Neural Science*, edited by Eric R. Kandel and James H. Schwartz. 2d ed. New York: Elsevier, 1985. An excellent but high-level basic neuroscience text geared toward the upper-level undergraduate, graduate student, or professional, with detailed chapters on neuro-anatomy, neurophysiology, and cutaneous senses (touch), in addition to the well-written and clear pain chapter. Extensive bibliography and pictures and diagrams, as well as subject and name indices, bring the reader quickly to seminal research in the field.

Lake, Max. *Scents and Sensuality*. London: John Murray, 1989. An excellent discussion of the association of smells and taste with behavior. The influence of odor on human behavior from childhood to the adult years is described in a tongue-in-cheek manner that makes for relaxing reading. The basic premise is that the body is under the control of a variety of chemical messengers, from cell messengers to pheromones.

Lane, Harlan. *The Mask of Benevolence: Disabling the Deaf Community*. New York: Alfred A. Knopf, 1992. Lane is critical of the medicalization of deafness, particularly in cases such as the use of cochlear implants with deaf children. He argues for an appreciation of deaf culture and respect for American Sign Language as the native language of the deaf.

Lee, David N., and Eric Aronson. "Visual Proprioceptive Control of Standing in Human Infants." *Perception and Psychophysics* 15 (June, 1974): 529-532. Although this article appears in a usually daunting scientific journal, it is an easily readable account of research on the role of vision in kinesthesis. The "swinging room" demonstrates nicely that vision and kinesthesis are usually tightly linked in everyday life. An easily readable scientific article.

Liberman, Alvin M. "On Finding That Speech Is Special." *American Psychologist* 37, no. 2 (1982): 148-167. The author is the chief developer of the motor theory of speech perception. This explanation of the theory and critical experimental results that support it includes many good figures, but most references are to articles in specialized journals. Good for advanced high school and college-level readers.

Matthei, Edward, and Thomas Roeper. *Understanding and Producing Speech*. New York: Universe Books, 1985. Recommended for high school and college readers, this text about psycholinguistics contains clearly written chapters about both human speech production and perception. Includes a good index and suggestions for further reading.

Matthews, P. B. "Where Does Sherrington's 'Muscular Sense' Originate? Muscles, Joints, Corollary Discharges?" In *Annual Review of Neuroscience* 5. Palo Alto, Calif.: Annual Reviews, 1982. Reviews the history and recent evidence concerning the source of a sense of limb position and movement, focusing on whether the joint receptor or muscle spindle organ is the better candidate. Concludes that joint receptors contribute little, and that voluntary effort must also be taken into account (especially for perception of heaviness of lifted objects).

Melzack, Ronald, and Patrick D. Wall. *The Challenge of Pain.* 2d ed. New York: Viking Penguin, 1988. A detailed and thorough treatment of the subject for a nontechnical audience, written by major theorists in the field. Discusses types of clinical pain, physiological mechanisms, the evolution of pain theories, and pain control techniques. Contains references, glossary, index, and illustrations.

Middlebrooks, John C., and David M. Green. "Sound Localization by Human Listeners." In *Annual Review of Psychology* 42. Stanford, Calif.: Annual Reviews, 1991. As the title implies, this easy-to-read review concerns studies of human listeners. The subject is divided into sections dealing with two-dimensional sound localization, horizontal localization, vertical localization, monaural localization, distance perception, motion detection, dynamic cues for localization, and simulating external sources over headphones.

Milne, Lorus Johnson, and Margery Milne. *The Senses of Animals and Men.* New York: Atheneum, 1962. A simple and entertaining survey of the senses and their importance in humans and other animals, written for a popular audience. Provides interesting and thought-provoking comparisons between the sensory systems of humans and of other animals.

Neal, Helen. *The Politics of Pain.* New York: McGraw-Hill, 1978. Discusses pain from the patient's rather than the scientist's point of view. Explores the religious, psychological, and cultural aspects of pain; neglect of pain in children; the cancer industry; patient activism in the face of medical ignorance and unwillingness to respond to patients' pain; and the role of pharmaceutical companies. Dated in some respects, but places pain research and clinical practice in their proper political, social, and economic contexts.

Perkins, William H., and Raymond D. Kent. *Functional Anatomy of Speech, Language, and Hearing.* San Diego, Calif.: College-Hill Press, 1986. An excellent text for the serious high school or college student. One chapter is dedicated to speech acoustics, while three chapters treat the neurology of speech (input processing, central processing, and output processing). Good appendices are included for anatomical terminology and selected readings.

Phillips, Dennis P., and John F. Brugge. "Progress in Neurophysiology of Sound Localization." In *Annual Review of Psychology* 36. Stanford, Calif.: Annual Reviews, 1985. This comprehensive review of the scientific literature is surprisingly easy to read for the college student, considering the technical nature of the subject. There is no glossary of terms, which requires the reader to look elsewhere for help with the anatomy. The biological mechanisms used in sound localization are covered quite well.

Schiffman, Harvey Richard. *Sensation and Perception.* 2d ed. New York: John Wiley & Sons, 1982. Reviews sensation and perception generally, including particularly clear descriptions and illustrations of the vestibular apparatus, though his discussion of kinesthesis and the issue of the contribution of the muscle spindle organs is less adequate.

Schmidt-Nielsen, Knut. *Animal Physiology, Adaptation, and Environment.* 4th ed. New York: Cambridge University Press, 1990. A standard college text by one of the greatest animal physiologists. Provides a deeply perceptive comparison of sensory systems in humans and other animals. The text is remarkable for its lucid and entertaining description of animal physiology.

Smith, Karl U. "Human Hearing." In *McGraw-Hill Encyclopedia of Science and Technology.* 6th ed. New York: McGraw-Hill, 1987. This detailed review article on the human auditory system touches many bases. Examples are sound properties; detection and discrimination; and the basis for hearing, including theory and experimental aspects, neurological function, and integration with other body senses. Several useful cross-references are also included.

Stebbins, William C. *The Acoustic Sense of Animals.* Cambridge, Mass.: Harvard University Press, 1983. Excellent for the general high school or higher-level reader. Discusses insects, fish, birds, reptiles, amphibians, and all sorts of mammals. Introductory background information is combined with explanations of important experimental methods and discussions of the results. Sound localization is nicely discussed throughout the text.

_____, ed. *Animal Psychophysics: The Design and Conduct of Sensory Experiments.* New York: Appleton-Century-Crofts, 1970. A very useful book for those interested in conducting experiments of their own. High school and college readers will learn much about the correct design and execution of animal experiments.

Tobias, Jerry V., ed. *Foundations of Modern Auditory Theory.* 2 vols. New York: Academic Press, 1972. Although not primarily intended for the general reader, this is an extremely valuable reference work. Edited intensively so that most chapters are accessible to the nonspecialist.

Van Bergeijk, Willem André Maria, John R. Pierce, and Edward E. David, Jr. *Waves and the Ear*. Garden City, N.Y.: Anchor Press, 1960. Specifically written for the general reader and high school student. A very good introduction to wave theory and hearing. Key research is simply and clearly presented with excellent figures and examples. Physiology and applications are also covered.

Vision

Ackerman, Diane. *A Natural History of the Senses*. New York: Random House, 1990. Provides a subjective look at the senses. The elegant descriptions of the experience of vision include interesting facts and comparisons which heighten an understanding of what it really means to see.

Albers, Josef. *Interaction of Color*. New Haven, Conn.: Yale University Press, 1963. Albers, an artist and teacher, presents commentary on form and color in addition to his paintings. Many of his works illustrate simultaneous contrast, successive contrast, assimilation, and other brightness effects. They are especially intriguing in that they were not designed to support psychological theories but to be viewed as art.

Barlow, H. B., and J. D. Mollon, eds. *The Senses*. Cambridge, England: Cambridge University Press, 1982. Clearly written yet somewhat technical, this text was designed for medical, psychology, education, and art students and may effectively be read in sections. Chapter 8 gives a good description of spatial frequency resolution in vision. Suggested reading even if only to glimpse the figures and graphs in this section.

Berne, Robert M., and Matthew N. Levy, eds. *Physiology*. 2d ed. St. Louis: C. V. Mosby, 1988. Chapter 8, "The Visual System," in this standard college physiology text outlines the anatomy and physiology of the human organ systems integrated in the detection and perception of vision, including the eye, the optic lobes of the brain, and the nerve tracts connecting them. Intended for students at the college level, but clearly written; should be accessible to readers at the high school level.

Block, J. Richard, and Harold Yuker. *Can You Believe Your Eyes?* Klamath Falls, Oreg.: Gardner Press, 1989. A popular book for the layperson, this enjoyable work presents and describes excellent examples of hundreds of different illusions. Does not focus on the theories describing why illusions are seen; however, it does give the reader much to think about.

Bloomer, Carolyn M. *Principles of Visual Perception.* New York: Van Nostrand Reinhold, 1976. Bloomer interweaves visual perception and art theory in an easily comprehensible explanation of perceptual principles complete with illustrations from the fine arts. She includes a full chapter on color, including illustrations of contrast, and suggestions for making one's own demonstrations. Annotated bibliography.

Bornstein, M. H. "Chromatic Vision in Infancy." In *Advances in Child Development and Behavior*, edited by H. W. Reese and L. P. Lipsitt. New York: Academic Press, 1978. Bornstein argues against the view that the division of wavelengths into colors is determined by the culture in which one lives. Instead, he reviews research with infants indicating that biological makeup plays a critical role in the way people perceive colors.

Bridgeman, Bruce. *The Biology of Behavior and Mind.* New York: John Wiley & Sons, 1988. The first chapter describes the history and approach of physiological psychology, and the following two chapters give an overview of how the brain functions. Chapters 4 to 6 explain the physiology of the sensory systems, emphasizing vision.

Campbell, Neil A. *Biology.* 2d ed. Redwood City, Calif.: Benjamin/Cummings, 1990. A very easy-to-read college text which gives the basics of vision. Has two good chapters on genetics and human genetics with examples.

Coren, Stanley, and Joan Stern Girgus. *Seeing Is Deceiving: The Psychology of Visual Illusions.* Hillsdale, N.J.: Lawrence Erlbaum, 1978. Presents the history of people's interest in illusions, including the early research in the area, and provides a very complete summary of the theories and research on illusions through the late 1970's. Written for psychologists but can be appreciated by the layperson.

Crooks, Robert L., and Jean Stein. "Sensation and Perception." In *Psychology.* New York: Holt, Rinehart and Winston, 1988. A good review of the structure of the eye and the visual process. Has helpful pictures and examples of color blindness.

De Valois, Russell L., and Karen K. De Valois. *Spatial Vision*. New York: Oxford University Press, 1988. Receptive fields are reviewed at all levels as they relate to pattern recognition, using a modern spatial-frequency approach. The first few chapters provide an excellent intro-duction to the subject.

Epstein, William, ed. *Stability and Constancy in Visual Perception: Mechanisms and Processes*. New York: Wiley-Interscience, 1977. A collection of scholarly articles for the reader wishing to gain some appreciation of experimental procedures in constancy research or to pursue some aspect in greater depth. Epstein has written the initial and final chapters, which give perspective and a clear historical intro-duction.

Ericsson, K. A., and H. A. Simon. "Sources of Evidence on Cognition: A Historical Overview." In *Cognitive Assessment*, edited by Thomas V. Merluzzi, Carol R. Glass, and Myles Genest. New York: Guilford Press, 1981. Examines the role of Gestalt theory in the development of modern cognitive science, set against the contributions of other schools of psychological thought. Accessible primarily to advanced students or those with some background in perceptual or cognitive psychology.

Feldman, Robert S. "Sensation." In *Understanding Psychology*. 2d ed. New York: McGraw-Hill, 1990. This chapter gives a brief review of vision and color vision; however, it lacks a more detailed account of color blindness. Easily accessible to the high school student.

Gibson, James Jerome. *The Ecological Approach to Visual Perception*. Hillsdale, N.J.: Lawrence Erlbaum, 1986. Easily readable and consid-erably thought-provoking. Gibson presents a new level of description and a fresh approach to visual perception. Although not specifically focused on perceptual constancy, this theory will challenge the reader to consider alternatives to the classic approaches.

Goldstein, E. Bruce. *Sensation and Perception*. 3d ed. Belmont, Calif.: Wadsworth, 1989. Goldstein's book is an advanced introduction to the field of sensation and perception, with more than half the chapters concerned with vision. An interesting chapter entitled "What Can Go Wrong with Your Eyes" contains information not commonly found in sensation and perception books. May be somewhat difficult reading for the layperson or high school student.

Graham, Clarence Henry. "Visual Space Perception." In *Vision and Visual Perception*, edited by Clarence Henry Graham. New York: John Wiley & Sons, 1965. Primarily a summary of all the possible monocular and binocular cues for depth perception, and of experimental understanding of their relative importance. Since the vast majority of psychophysical experiments on visual depth acuity were performed prior to this publication, it may be relied upon as an accurate summary of how such experiments were performed and their findings, the results of which are still cited in more current publications.

Granrud, C. E., ed. *Visual Perception and Cognition in Infancy*. Hillsdale, N.J.: Lawrence Erlbaum, 1991. A collection of chapters by leading researchers in the field, this book covers a wide range of topics in visual development. The authors review their own research findings and consider the theoretical implications of their work. The writing is mostly nontechnical but challenging.

Gregory, Richard L. *Eye and Brain*. 4th ed. Princeton, N. J.: Princeton University Press, 1990. This inexpensive paperback is considered a classic in the field of visual perception. The book is written in a style that is easily accessible to the lay reader. Gregory's book contains many excellent illustrations. If one were to read one book on vision, this would be the book.

_____. *The Intelligent Eye*. New York: McGraw-Hill, 1970. Deals mainly with the issues involved in representing a three-dimensional world using two-dimensional images. Includes 3-D stereo illustrations (including 3-D glasses) and numerous examples of "impossible figures" and illusions. Often used as a supplementary text in college art courses.

Guyton, Arthur C. *Textbook of Medical Physiology*. 7th ed. Philadelphia: W. B. Saunders, 1986. Supplies the fundamental information necessary for an understanding of the mechanism of vision. Chapter 58, "The Optics of Vision," in this clearly written text provides a discussion of basic optics and considers the eye as an optical device in an understandable and readable fashion. Chapter 59, "Receptor and Neural Function of the Retina," discusses sensory cells of the retina, the chemistry of vision, and the organization of nerve cells in the eye.

Intended for college and medical students yet accessible to readers at the high school level.

Haith, Marshall M. *Rules That Babies Look By*. Hillsdale, N.J.: Lawrence Erlbaum, 1980. This book presents an entertaining description of how infants choose where to look and how their eye movements change with age. Easily the most readable summary of eye-movement research.

Hochberg, Julian E. *Perception*. 2d ed. Englewood Cliffs, N.J.: Prentice-Hall, 1978. Gives a comprehensive treatment of Gestalt principles and other areas of perceptual psychology. Explores the contributions of Gestalt theory and principles to modern theories in perception. Accessible to the college student or advanced high school student.

Hubel, David H. "Exploration of the Primary Visual Cortex." *Nature* 299 (October 7, 1982): 515-524. This article in a nonspecialized journal reviews Hubel and Wiesel's Nobel Prize-winning research on feature detectors in the cat. Though the text becomes technical in spots, the figures give an impression of what cortical receptive fields look like and how they are measured.

_____. *Eye, Brain and Vision*. New York: W. H. Freeman, 1988. An outstanding discussion of eye and brain interaction. Written in a technical manner, but provides an excellent overview of the subject. Illustrations are numerous, and include dramatic photographs. Particularly useful for the nonexpert are the introductory and closing chapters.

Hubel, David H., and Torsten N. Wiesel. "Brain Mechanisms of Vision." *Scientific American* 241 (September, 1979): 14, 18, 150-162. Part of an issue devoted entirely to brain function. An excellent discussion of mechanisms by which the brain processes visual data. Written in a technical manner, but contains excellent diagrams and photographs.

Humphreys, G. W., and M. J. Riddoch. *To See But Not to See: A Case Study of Visual Agnosia*. London: Lawrence Erlbaum, 1987. The mysterious symptoms of a patient who could see everything but recognize nothing are analyzed with intelligence and compassion. From such patients, it is possible to learn about pattern vision in normal people.

Julesz, Bela. *The Foundations of Cyclopean Perception*. Chicago: University of Chicago Press, 1971. Detailed and somewhat technical review of investigations of stereopsis, or what the author refers to as cyclopean perception, using random-dot stereograms. The stereograms represent a tremendous advance in experimental technique in that they permit the study of retinal disparity cues in total isolation. The text is supplemented with numerous examples of random dot stereograms (includes 3-D glasses).

Kaufman, Lloyd. *Sight and Mind: An Introduction to Visual Perception.* New York: Oxford University Press, 1974. This beautifully written volume reviews the methods that the brain uses to make sense of visual input patterns. Includes work on thresholds, illusions, and color.

Keller, Helen. *The Story of My Life.* New York: Airmont, 1965. For anyone who has wondered what life would be like without a functioning visual system, this is a fascinating book to read. Presents the intriguing and courageous story of Keller's own triumph over adversity. The psychological consequences of visual disability are particularly notable.

Koffka, Kurt. *Principles of Gestalt Psychology.* New York: Harcourt, Brace, 1935. Exhaustive account of Gestalt theory and experiments on perception by one of the school's confounders. Extremely comprehensive, and useful for an understanding of Gestalt methodology as well as theory and findings. Accessible to the serious college student or other advanced reader.

Köhler, Wolfgang. *Gestalt Psychology.* New York: New American Library, 1947. The classic popular exposition of Gestalt theory, written by one of the school's cofounders. Provides an accessible, comprehensive treatment of the theory and the laws of organization.

Kuffler, Stephen W. "Discharge Patterns and Functional Organization of Mammalian Retina." *Journal of Neurophysiology* (January 16, 1953): 37-68. A seminal article, this was the first to describe the receptive fields of the cells whose fibers exit the eye. Using 1950's technology, the article's methods are more accessible than those of more recent computer-controlled studies. The antagonistic center-surround organization of retinal neurons is described here for the first time.

Levinthal, Charles F. "Visual Perception." In *Introduction to Physiological Psychology.* 3d ed. Englewood Cliffs, N.J.: Prentice-Hall, 1990. A very good chapter on visual perception; extremely detailed. Nice detail on color vision and the different types of color blindness.

MacKay, Donald MacCrimmon. *Behind the Eye*. Cambridge, Mass.: Basil Blackwell, 1991. Based on the Gifford lectures, given at the University of Glasgow by an expert in the field of visual processing in the brain. MacKay's book uniquely combines an understanding of neurophysiology and philosophy to approach not only the question of how the mind perceives but also the more fundamental question of what the mind is. Suitable for advanced undergraduates, but also accessible to the nonspecialist.

Masland, Richard H. "The Functional Architecture of the Retina." *Scientific American* 255 (December, 1986): 102-111. This clearly written article describes the types of cells in the retina and how they are arranged and organized into a system functioning in light absorption and the transmission of nerve impulses. Outlines the author's research in tracing the shapes of individual retinal nerve cells, and shows how his and other techniques will eventually lead to a complete three-dimensional reconstruction of the organization of the retina. Many diagrams and photos, including both light and electron microscope pictures, illustrate the text.

Matlin, Margaret W. *Perception*. 2d ed. Boston: Allyn & Bacon, 1988. Presents a general introduction to the field of perception. The chapters concerning vision are written in a scholarly style, but with more wit and style than most texts in the field. Accessible to the layperson or high school student.

Maurer, Daphne, and Charles Maurer. *The World of the Newborn*. New York: Basic Books, 1988. This book won the American Psychological Association book award for 1988. The award was well deserved, because the book is both readable and informative in describing how newborns see as well as hear, feel, and think.

Maxson, Linda, and Charles Daugherty. *Genetics: A Human Perspective*. 2d ed. Dubuque, Iowa: Wm. C. Brown, 1988. An excellent book on human genetics. It explains inheritance very well and describes how color blindness is passed on. Very easy to read, and suitable for the high school student.

Mehler, Jacques, and Robin Fox, eds. *Neonate Cognition: Beyond the Blooming, Buzzing, Confusion*. Hillsdale, N.J.: Lawrence Erlbaum, 1985. This is a collection of chapters by leading researchers in the field. Presents many intriguing examples of the capabilities possessed by infants in the first eight months after birth.

Montgomery, Geoffrey. "The Mind's Eye." *Discover* 12 (May, 1991): 50-56. This article is written for the nontechnical reader. Presents an excellent discussion of the formation of visual maps in the function of the visual cortex. Comparison is made among reptiles, primitive mammals, and primates in how they perceive visual stimuli.

Mueller, Conrad George, and Mae Rudolph. *Light and Vision*. New York: Time, 1966. A commonly available book which uses striking photography and illustrations to present basic information about light and vision.

Nathans, Jeremy. "The Genes for Color Vision." *Scientific American* 260 (February, 1989): 42-49. A description of the research of the author and his colleagues in isolating the genes encoding the light-absorbing pigments of cones. Also describes the basics of color vision and discusses the implications of the author's work for color blindness and the evolution of color vision. Clearly written, and profusely illustrated with full-color illustrations that amplify and expand the text.

Neisser, Ulric. "The Process of Vision." *Scientific American* 259 (September, 1988): 204-214. Analyzes the interaction between the retinal image and the brain in the perception of visual images, including factors that affect visual perception such as memory and attention. Clearly and simply written; includes interesting illustrative examples. Demonstrates that what is perceived in vision is vastly more complex than the initial image projected on the retina.

Petry, Susan, and Glenn E. Meyer. *The Perception of Illusory Contours*. New York: Springer-Verlag, 1987. A collection of reports that was not written for the layperson; however, its examples of different illusory contour figures, such as the illusory triangle, can be very valuable to the nonexpert reader. Written by leading researchers; highly technical.

Pettigrew, John D. "The Neurophysiology of Binocular Vision." *Scientific American* 227 (August, 1972): 84-95. Review of how information from two eyes is "fused" in the brain and retinal disparity cues extracted. Describes experiments performed by David Hubel and Torsten Wiesel, and other neuroscientists, which revealed cortical neurons that only respond to binocular input.

Rock, Irvin. *Perception*. New York: Scientific American Library, 1984. A carefully written and beautifully illustrated book. Rock describes characteristics of object perception, subjective contours, movement, and illusions. His treatment of contrast is in relation to illusions, color, and the intelligence of perception. A major focus is on how constancy is achieved in vision in relation to an ever-changing, two-dimensional retinal image. For the general reader.

_____, ed. *The Perceptual World*. New York: W. H. Freeman, 1990. A collection of articles that originally appeared in *Scientific American*. Two deal specifically with theories of why people see illusions or illusory contour figures such as the illusory triangle. The remaining articles, while not specifically on illusions, provide a context for the study of illusions.

Rushton, William A. H. "Visual Pigments and Color Blindness." *Scientific American* 232 (March, 1975): 64-74. Lucidly outlines the visual pigments, the basic theory of color vision, and characteristics of the color blindness produced by defects in the visual pigments. Includes a description of the experiments first establishing that three pigments determine color vision, including the author's own work with light reflected from the retina.

Schnapf, Julie L., and Denis A. Baylor. "How Photoreceptor Cells Respond to Light." *Scientific American* 256 (April, 1987): 40-47. Explains the techniques used to detect and record the responses to stimulation by single rods and cones in the retina, and the patterns in which the photoreceptors respond to light absorption. Describes the differences between rods and cones, and outlines the roles of cones in color vision. Clearly and simply written, with a wealth of illustrations, some in full color.

Smith, Jillyn. *Senses and Sensibilities*. New York: John Wiley & Sons, 1989. This interesting and readable book on the senses includes a good description of the visual spectrum as well as a number of interesting historical facts about early explorers in the vision field.

Solso, Robert L. *Cognitive Psychology*. 3d ed. Boston: Allyn & Bacon, 1991. Various schemes of pattern recognition are described simply and powerfully. The chapter on pattern recognition reviews all the major theories, with extensive illustrations.

Stevens, Leonard A. *Explorers of the Brain*. New York: Alfred A. Knopf, 1971. A popular account of how scientists over several centuries devel-

oped the knowledge of brain structure and function. Written in a nontechnical fashion and easily understandable by those not in the science
field. Also presents the experimental basis for scientific knowledge.

Stine, Gerald James. *The New Human Genetics*. Dubuque, Iowa: Wm. C.
Brown, 1988. An advanced textbook on human genetics; it has a small
section on color blindness that is easy to read. It also covers the basics
of genetics.

Stryer, Lubert. "The Molecules of Visual Excitation." *Scientific American*
257 (July, 1987): 42-50. A description of the development of nerve
signals among the rods of the eye (cells which respond to light). Not
as highly technical as some articles in the publication. Particularly
impressive is the collection of microscopic photographs included in
the article. Diagrams are clear and informative.

Walk, Richard D., and Elenor J. Gibson. "A Comparative and Analytical
Study of Visual Depth Perception." *Psychological Monographs* 75,
no. 15 (1961): 1-44. A very accessible description of experimental
investigations with eleven different animal species (including human
infants as young as six months) using the visual-cliff apparatus.
Authors discuss the possible visual depth cues upon which the subjects
appeared to rely, as well as nature-nurture issues of depth perception.

Waltz, David L. "Artificial Intelligence." *Scientific American* 247 (October, 1982): 118-133. Several computer programs are reviewed in a
relatively nontechnical way. Among them are programs that find the
three-dimensional structure in line drawings.

Watson, Philip. *Light Fantastic*. New York: Lothrop, Lee & Shepard,
1982. Written for children, but useful for anyone attempting to understand the visual spectrum. Provides simple instructions for the creation
of demonstrations of the effects of light and color. The visual spectrum
must be experienced to be appreciated.

Wertheimer, Michael. "Gestalt Psychology." In *A Brief History of Psychology*. 3d ed. New York: Holt, Rinehart, and Winston, 1987. Wertheimer provides a concise but clearly written overview of the basic
principles of Gestalt psychology, the intellectual antecedents of the
theory, and its place within experimental psychology. A superb work
on the subject, easily understood by the college student and quite
accessible to the high school student.

Wolfe, Jeremy M., ed. *The Mind's Eye: Readings from Scientific American*. New York: W. H. Freeman, 1986. Twelve articles from *Scientific American* concerned with vision are featured in this book. The articles are divided into three sections: "Eyes," "Pathways to the Mind's Eye," and "In the Mind's Eye." The original writings of researchers in the field may sometimes be challenging reading for the nonspecialist, but the book is a valuable resource.

Yonas, A., and C. E. Granrud. "The Development of Sensitivity to Kinetic, Binocular, and Pictorial Depth Information in Human Infants." In *Brain Mechanisms and Spatial Vision*, edited by David J. Ingle, David N. Lee, and Marc Jeannerod. Boston: Nijhoff, 1985. Describes a program of research that shows that infants begin to use the three types of depth cues at different ages. Summarizes many experiments and includes useful illustrations that make it easy to understand how infants' depth perception is studied.

EMOTION

Andrew, Richard John, and Ernst Huber. *Evolution of Facial Expression.* New York: Arno Press, 1972. A re-publication of Andrew's study of primate calls and facial expressions, and Huber's well-illustrated anatomical study of the primate facial musculature.

Arnold, Madga B., ed. *The Nature of Emotion.* Harmondsworth, Middlesex, England: Penguin Books, 1968. Reprints a number of classic articles published before 1960. Valuable for gaining insight into the historical sweep of the topic of emotion. Some chapters are largely philosophical or theoretical, yet not too difficult to understand. Other chapters require some knowledge of physiology. This volume is not an introductory treatment of theories of emotion, and thus should be consulted only after gaining a knowledge base of the field.

Atkinson, R. L., R. C. Atkinson, E. E. Smith, and D. J. Bem. *Introduction to Psychology.* 10th ed. New York: Harcourt Brace Jovanovich, 1990. An introductory psychology text, aimed at the college-level student; includes a very good discussion of the field of emotion, clear examples of critical issues, and interesting and stimulating discussions of some controversial areas.

Barlow, David H. *Anxiety and Its Disorders.* New York: Guilford Press, 1988. In the early part of the book, the author reviews basic aspects of emotion. His theorizing relies heavily on the work of learning theorists, particularly with respect to the development of negative emotions. The latter chapters explain the development of anxiety disorders from the perspective of learning theories.

Bernstein, Douglas A., E. Roy, T. Srull, and C. Wickens. *Psychology.* 2d ed. Boston: Houghton Mifflin, 1991. Well-organized text written for college students. Defines emotions, tracing research history and integrating different theories. Discusses the sympathetic nervous system and the brain. Also presents a section on the disadvantages of not talking about emotions.

Bloom, Floyd E., and Arlyne Lazerson. *Brain, Mind, and Behavior.* 2d ed. New York: W. H. Freeman, 1988. The chapter entitled "Emotions: The

Highs and Lows of the Brain" has several wonderful diagrams of the brain structures involved in emotion. The first edition of this beauti-fully illustrated and readable text was written to accompany the excel-lent eight-part television series *The Brain* (1985), produced by WNET in New York and seen on the Public Broadcasting Service. That, and a later series, *The Mind* (1988), are highly recommended.

Bower, T. G. R. *A Primer of Infant Development*. San Francisco: W. H. Freeman, 1977. Describes the process and features of development during the first two years of life. Presents basic information regarding infant emotional, social, motor, language, perceptual, and cognitive development. Provides a basis for placing emotional development in the context of other areas of development.

Brehm, Sharon S., and Saul M. Kassin. *Social Psychology*. Boston: Houghton Mifflin, 1989. Chapter on aggression addresses the negative affect theory, the model of incompatible responses, and the arousal-affect theory—theories that address how thoughts and bodily arousal affect anger and aggressive actions. Chapter on interpersonal attraction addresses the excitation transfer hypothesis, showing how arousal from one source can affect unrelated emotions.

Buck, Ross. *The Communication of Emotion*. New York: Guilford Press, 1984. Presents the views of a critic of facial feedback theories and argues that facial expression is simply the automatic and unavoidable output from emotional experience. Intended for advanced college students, graduate students, and professionals.

_____. *Human Motivation and Emotion*. 2d ed. New York: John Wiley & Sons, 1988. This is a comprehensive textbook on emotion that places emotion within a model that also includes motivation and cognition.

Burns, David D. *Feeling Good*. New York: William Morrow, 1980. Self-help book, accepted by the psychological community, that shows how irrational thoughts can lead to unnecessary feelings and gives suggestions for changing. Chapters on perfectionism, self-esteem, guilt, depression, suicide, and love.

Christianson, Sven-Åke, ed. *The Handbook of Emotion and Memory Research and Theory*. Hillsdale, N.J.: Lawrence Erlbaum, 1992. A collec-tion of nineteen articles describing the relationship between emotion and memory. Methodological and biological issues are discussed, as are clinical observations. Includes articles on amnesia, multiple personality disorder, and eyewitness testimony. For the sophisticated reader.

Collins, W. Andrew, and S. A. Kuczaj II. *Developmental Psychology: Childhood and Adolescence*. New York: Macmillan, 1991. Discusses developmental psychology and addresses emotional experiences from a theoretical and practical perspective.

Cousins, Norman. *Anatomy of an Illness*. New York: W. W. Norton, 1979. This popular book was written for the layperson and discusses the role of cognitions and emotions in illness. Emphasis is on the protective properties of having a sense of humor, a positive outlook, and a strong will to live.

Darwin, Charles. *The Expression of the Emotions in Man and Animals*. London: J. Murray, 1872. Reprint. Chicago: University of Chicago Press, 1965. A true classic; the departure point for any serious exploration of the evolution of emotion. Vocalization, facial expression, complex emotions, and the general principles governing the evolution of expression are all lucidly treated.

Eibl-Eibesfeldt, Irenaus. "Strategies of Social Interaction." In *Emotion: Theory, Research, and Experience*, edited by Robert Plutchik and Henry Kellerman. Vol. 1. New York: Academic Press, 1980. The famous ethologist examines the function of expressions in the development of basic social strategies involved in sharing, giving, taking, friendly encounters, and so on.

Ekman, Paul, ed. *Darwin and Facial Expression: A Century of Research in Review*. New York: Academic Press, 1973. This book was published to commemorate the centennial of Darwin's classic book on emotional expression. Comprehensive, detailed chapters by Suzanne Chevalier-Skolnikoff on facial expression in nonhuman primates, and by Paul Ekman on the cross-cultural universality of facial expressions, demonstrate the continuing relevance of Darwin's ideas. Includes an in-depth discussion of Darwin's theory of emotional expression and presents evidence to support his theory.

_____. *Telling Lies: Clues to Deceit in the Marketplace, Politics, and Marriage*. New York: W. W. Norton, 1985. A highly readable treatment of some of Ekman's research on the expression and physiology of emotion that explains the practical significance of this research.

Ekman, Paul, Wallace Friesen, and Phoebe Ellsworth. *Emotion in the Human Face*. New York: Pergamon Press, 1972. This book reviews and discusses a variety of issues related to emotion and human facial expression. Includes a review of Ekman's work on the universality of emotional expression.

Emde, Robert N., T. J. Gaensbauer, and R. J. Harmon. *Emotional Expression in Infancy: A Biobehavioral Study*. New York: International Universities Press, 1976. In this research monograph in the "Psychological Issues" series, Emde and his colleagues report on their study of normal infant development during the first year of life. Their research involves the longitudinal study of emotional expression in sixteen infants using a variety of investigative techniques.

Fiske, Susan T., and Shelley E. Taylor. *Social Cognition*. 2d ed. New York: McGraw-Hill, 1991. A comprehensive textbook on social cognition that contains a brief but excellent summary of research and theory related to the facial feedback hypothesis. Reviews a number of the formulations of theories related to emotion and facial expression, including Robert Zajone and his colleagues' vascular theory of facial efference.

Frijda, Nico H. *The Emotions*. Cambridge, England: Cambridge University Press, 1986. Frijda discusses emotion in terms of expressive behaviors, physiology, experience, regulation, and other topics in a detailed yet readable account. At the same time, he develops a model of motivation and emotion, emphasizing their function.

Hughes, Jennifer. *Cancer and Emotion*. New York: John Wiley & Sons, 1987. A sensitive account of the relationship between cancer and emotions. Addresses the predisposing factors, responses to the diagnosis, and the terminal phases. Concludes with patients' accounts of their experiences with breast cancer.

Izard, Carroll E. "Emotions in Personality and Culture." *Ethos* 11, no. 4 (1983): 305-312. Discusses contemporary research on emotions and socialization. Also addresses cultural differences in standards for emotional expression.

_____. *The Face of Emotion*. New York: Appleton-Century-Crofts, 1971. An excellent presentation of the history of the field of emotion in psychology. Includes a detailed discussion of the evidence regarding the heritability and universality of emotional expression. Presents a general theoretical framework relating neural activity, facial patterning, and subjective experience as the principal components of emotion.

_____. "Facial Expressions and the Regulation of Emotions." *Journal of Personality and Social Psychology* 58, no. 3 (1990): 487-498.
_____. *Patterns of Emotion: A New Analysis of Anxiety and Depression.* New York: Academic Press, 1972. The book and journal article above present Izard's approach to the facial feedback hypothesis and his application of facial feedback principles to clinical therapy. Offering detailed and broad overviews and reviews of topics related to emotion and to facial feedback theories, these works describe major theories and research in detail and provide a useful context with which to understand the importance of emotion and facial expression in everyday life.

_____. *Human Emotions.* New York: Plenum Press, 1977. A full presentation of Izard's differential emotions theory as well as a detailed discussion of the discrete emotions and their accompanying facial expression.

_____. *Measuring Emotions in Infants and Children.* New York: Cambridge University Press, 1982. A presentation of the measurement procedures commonly used to assess emotional experiences in infants and children. Discusses several important topics regarding the development of emotions and the study of emotions in a developmental context.

James, William. "William James on Emotion." In *Emotion: Bodily Change*, edited by Douglas K. Candland. Princeton, N.J.: Van Nostrand, 1962. This book provides a reprinting of some of the original statements by James defining emotion as well as several other seminal articles on bodily aspects of emotion.

Kalat, James W. *Biological Psychology.* 2d ed. Belmont, Calif.: Wadsworth, 1988. In this introductory textbook, Kalat reviews the biological basis of emotion-related issues such as pleasure centers in the brain, aggression, and drugs that mediate emotion.

Kemper, Theodore D. "How Many Emotions Are There? Wedding the Social and the Autonomic Components." *American Journal of Soci-*

ology 93, no. 2 (1987): 263-289. Discusses physiological similarities and cultural variations in emotion. Reviews primary and secondary emotions.

_____. "Power, Status, and Emotions: A Sociological Contribution to a Psychophysiological Domain." In *Approaches to Emotion*, edited by Klaus R. Scherer and Paul Ekman. Hillsdale, N.J.: Lawrence Erlbaum, 1984. Kemper takes a sociological approach to what is often thought to be a psychological domain. He argues that strong emotions often arise when there are changes in a group or in a group member's power and status as compared to the larger social surround.

Lazarus, Richard S. "The Trivialization of Distress." In *Psychology and Health*, edited by Barbara L. Hammonds and C. James Scheirer. Washington, D.C.: American Psychological Association, 1984. Addresses a much-neglected area of emotional responses to illness. Focuses on how, by telling patients that the distress they feel when something bad happens to them is inappropriate, doctors undermine its legitimacy and indirectly tell them it is wrong to be upset at losing one of life's most precious possessions, health—or even life itself. Trivialization is neither realistic nor in the best interest of the patient.

Lewis, Michael, and Leonard A. Rosenblum, eds. *The Development of Affect*. New York: Plenum Press, 1978. Presents the work of more than twenty-five contributors, including Harry Harlow, Jerome Kagan, L. Alan Sroufe, and Robert Emde. It is the first volume in a series edited by Michael Lewis and Leonard rosenblum entitled "Genesis of Behavior." Surveys advances in methodology and theory which have promoted understanding of the meaning and development of affect.

Lewis, Michael, and Linda Michalson. *Children' Emotions and Moods: Developmental Theory and Measurement*. New York: Plenum Press, 1983. Examines emotional development from its theoretical perspective and, through a structural analysis of the meaning of emotion, outlines a theory of emotional development. Presents a measurement system for assessing emotional development in young children that is based on situation-specific assessments of children's emotional behaviors.

McNaughton, Neil. *Biology and Emotion*. New York: Cambridge University Press, 1989. Part of the *Problems in the Behavioral Sciences* series, this book provides an excellent, comprehensive overview of the physiological components of emotions. Covers early theorists such as

Charles Darwin, Walter B. Cannon, and William James through the more modern discoveries of neuroscientists.

Markus, Hazel R., and Shinobu Kitayama. "Culture and the Self: Implications for Cognition, Emotion, and Motivation." *Psychological Review* 98, no. 2 (1991): 224-253. Focuses on cultural differences between people's sense of self and others, and how this impacts on personal experiences such as emotions. Addresses emotions as a product of social life.

Myers, D. G. *Psychology*. 3d ed. New York: Worth, 1992. A general introductory psychology textbook. Contains a good discussion of many aspects of emotion; provides many examples and discusses important issues.

Myers, David G. *The Pursuit of Happiness: Who Is Happy and Why.* New York: William Morrow, 1992. A social psychologist describes evidence about what makes people happy. Describes personality and cognitive factors related to happiness, as well as the roles of friendship, love, and faith. Very well documented and a delight to read. Accessible to the general reader.

Plutchik, Robert. "A General Psychoevolutionary Theory of Emotion." In *Emotion: Theory, Research, and Experience*, edited by Robert Plutchik and Henry Kellerman. Vol. 1. New York: Academic Press, 1980. Plutchik summarizes his theory of emotion, placing it within evolutionary theory and discussing various theoretical and methodological problems encountered in the study of emotion.

Plutchik, Robert, and Henry Kellerman, eds. *Emotion: Theory, Research, and Experience*. Vol. 3 in *Biological Foundations of Emotion*. New York: Academic Press, 1986. The third volume of a five-volume set by these editors, published between 1980 and 1990. Offers detailed information on the role of the nervous system in emotional expression. Important chapters include Detlev Ploog on the neurobiology of vocal expression, Paul MacLean on affect and its cerebral substrate, Edmund Rolls on the neural systems involved in primate emotion, and two chapters on the amygdala.

Redican, William. "An Evolutionary Perspective on Human Facial Displays." In *Emotions in the Human Face*, edited by Paul Ekman. 2d ed. New York: Cambridge University Press, 1982. An engaging scientific account of the facial expression of emotion by nonhuman primates that discusses homologies with human facial expression.

Schachter, Stanley. *Emotion, Obesity, and Crime*. New York: Academic Press, 1971. This book provides an excellent account of Schachter's extension of the James-Lange theory of emotion. It includes the results of numerous experiments in support of his arguments.

_____. "The Interaction of Cognitive and Physiological Determinants of Emotional State." In *Advances in Experimental Social Psychology*, edited by Leonard Berkowitz. Vol. 1. New York: Academic Press, 1964. Reviews author's previous work on emotions and provides a detailed presentation of his theory of emotions and the research it had generated by 1964. Should be the starting point for any further investigation of emotion and attribution theory.

Scherer, Klaus R. "On the Nature and Function of Emotion: A Component Process Approach." In *Approaches to Emotions*, edited by Klaus R. Scherer and Paul Ekman. Hillsdale, N.J.: Lawrence Erlbaum, 1984. Scherer proposes a theory of emotion that examines the function of emotion as a component in a behavioral regulation process.

Staats, A. W. *Social Behaviorism*. Homewood, Ill.: Dorsey Press, 1975. The author proposes a behavioristic theory to explain a broad range of behavioral phenomena, including social behavior, language, abnormal behavior, attitudes, and personality development. Chapter 4 offers Staats's behavioral theory of emotion, which relies heavily on Pavlov's work as well as other learning theorists. Written at an intermediate level and should be consulted after one has studied the rudiments of learning theory.

Storms, Michael D., and Kevin D. McCaul. "Attribution Processes and Emotional Exacerbation of Dysfunctional Behavior." In *New Directions in Attribution Research*, edited by John H. Harvey, William John Ickes, and Robert F. Kidd. Vol. 1. Hillsdale, N.J.: Lawrence Erlbaum, 1976. Summary of early research on the use of placebos to study misattribution of arousal. Chapter focuses on how misattribution may be applied to the understanding and treatment of dysfunctional behaviors such as insomnia.

Thompson, Jack George. *The Psychobiology of Emotions*. New York: Plenum Press, 1988. Reviews the topic of psychobiology, the relationships between mind and body during emotions, discussing physiological activity during emotional states. Also covers major materialistic, mentalistic, and interactionist models.

Tomkins, Silvan Solomon. *The Positive Affects.* Vol. 1 in *Affect, Imagery, Consciousness.* New York: Springer, 1962. This book presents possibly the most radical variant of the facial feedback theories. Tomkins argues that facial expression itself *is* emotional experience. Suitable for advanced college students and graduate students.

Valenstein, Elliot S. *Great and Desperate Cures: The Rise and Decline of Psychosurgery and Other Radical Treatments for Mental Illness.* New York: Basic Books, 1986. This book, along with other works by this experimental psychologist, including *Brain Control* (1973), chronicles the sometimes horrifying history of research and treatment of mental disorders. Although much has been learned about the physiological and anatomical bases of emotion, this book is a good example of the limitations of human understanding and of an all-too-common practice: seeking cures based on weak theories. A careful and well-documented book.

Valins, Stuart, and Richard E. Nisbett. "Attribution Processes in the Development and Treatment of Emotional Disorders." In *Attribution: Perceiving the Causes of Behavior,* edited by Edward E. Jones et al. Morristown, N.J.: General Learning Press, 1972. This chapter concerns the role of causal attributions in both the development and the treatment of emotional disorders such as phobias. Also includes a review of research on the effects of both misattribution of arousal and false biofeedback of arousal. Clinical applications of the author's suggestions for treatment have not been particularly successful.

Valzelli, Luigi. *Psychobiology of Aggression and Violence.* New York: Raven Press, 1981. This thorough and scholarly work contains a good review of emotional behavior in general and aggressive behavior in particular. A good book to consult in order to understand the logic of trying to relate physiological processes and anatomical structures to behavioral functions. Most of the basic research on the role of the limbic system in emotion has been based on the aggression research reviewed in this book.

Watson, John B. *Behaviorism.* Chicago: University of Chicago Press, 1959. This is a reprint of the book that "initiated a revolution in its attempt to make psychology an objective science." Watson provides a very readable account of the early work in the conditioning of emotional responses in infants (chapters 7 and 8). Unlike most psychology books written in the 1920's, this gem can be easily understood by the beginning student.

Wortman, Camille B., and Elizabeth F. Loftus. *Psychology*. 4th ed. New York: McGraw-Hill, 1992. A college-level introductory text with a clear presentation of the field of emotion; makes effective use of examples.

Zillmann, Dolf. *Connections Between Sex and Aggression*. Hillsdale, N.J.: Lawrence Erlbaum, 1984. Reviews considerable evidence concerning the relationship between sex and aggression, with a particular emphasis on sexual violence and pornography. Describes excitation transfer theory and relevant research, and discusses implications of this work for understanding the relationship between sex and aggression.

_____. *Hostility and Aggression*. Hillsdale, N.J.: Lawrence Erlbaum, 1979. Thorough examination of the role of negative emotions in aggressive behavior. Reviews a wide range of research on emotion and aggression, and presents the author's excitation transfer theory. Discusses theoretical and practical implications of the theory for understanding and controlling aggression.

_____. "Transfer of Excitation in Emotional Behavior." In *Social Psychophysiology: A Sourcebook*, edited by John T. Cacioppo and Richard E. Petty. New York: Guilford Press, 1983. Presentation of Zillmann's excitation transfer theory and the existing research relevant to the theory. It is an excellent source for understanding Zillmann's theory and the research generated by the theory.

MOTIVATION

Theory

Apter, Michael J., David Fontana, and Stephen J. Murgatroyd. *Reversal Theory: Applications and Developments*. Cardiff, England: University College Cardiff Press, 1985. Reviews Apter's theory, applicable research results, applications to individual and social phenomena, and theoretical developments.

Berlyne, D. E. *Conflict, Arousal, and Curiosity*. New York: McGraw-Hill, 1960. Berlyne presents his theoretical propositions for the motivation of perceptual and intellectual activities, including his notions about intermediate/optimal arousal levels.

Birney, Robert Charles, and Richard C. Teevan. *Instinct: An Enduring Problem in Psychology*. Princeton, N.J.: Van Nostrand, 1961. A collection of readings intended for college students. Contains fourteen articles, ranging from William James's 1887 discussion of instinct to Frank Beach's 1955 "The Descent of Instinct," in which Beach traces the idea of instinct from the time of the ancient Greeks up to the 1950's and concludes that "the instinct concept has survived in almost complete absence of empirical validation."

Bolles, Robert C. *Theory of Motivation*. 2d ed. New York: Harper & Row, 1975. This standard text in motivation reviews the concepts of motivation and drive and presents pros and cons of the drive concept. The author is a contemporary psychological theoretician.

Boring, Edwin G., and Gardner Lindzey, eds. *A History of Psychology in Autobiography*. Vol. 5. New York: Appleton-Century-Crofts, 1967. In an autobiographical essay in volume 5 of this survey, Murray presents a detailed view of his concepts and the influence of his work.

Breland, Keller, and Marian Breland. "The Misbehavior of Organisms." *American Psychologist* 16 (November, 1961): 681-684. In the process of training performing animals, the Brelands were forced to contend with inherited behaviors of their pupils. This article alerted a generation of psychologists to the possibility that instinct had been inappropriately eliminated from their thinking. The writing is clear and amusing.

Cofer, Charles Norval, and M. H. Appley. *Motivation: Theory and Research*. New York: John Wiley & Sons, 1964. Long regarded as a classic on the topic of motivation, this book includes (in chapter 2, "Motivation in Historical Perspective") thirty-two pages of material that traces instinct through the centuries. Chapter 3, "The Concept of Instinct: Ethological Position," discusses ways the once discredited concept was returning to psychology in the early 1960's.

Crespi, Leo P. "Quantitative Variation of Incentive and Performance in the White Rat." *American Journal of Psychology* 55, no. 4 (1942): 467-517. The anticipatory nature of incentive motivation was first demonstrated in this paper. It is termed the Crespi effect, which includes the elation and depression effects following the incentive contrast.

Evans, Phil. *Motivation and Emotion*. New York: Routledge, 1989. Includes an excellent overall review and explanation of opponent process theory. Also covers the development of arousal theory, critiques the theory, notes its strengths and weaknesses, summarizes the findings of related research, and concludes with an assessment of Apter's latter-day reversal theory.

Eysenck, Hans Jurgen. *Personality, Genetics, and Behavior*. New York: Praeger, 1982. Eysenck presents selected papers dealing with his arousal-based theory of personality—especially extroversion. The opening chapter provides an excellent review of the development of his theory and its basis in arousal.

Fisher, Arthur. "Sociobiology: A New Synthesis Comes of Age." *Mosaic* 22 (Spring, 1991): 2-9. This review article provides a comprehensive overview of the biological basis of behavior and the sociobiology controversy. Includes a thorough historical perspective. A well-written summary of major research in the field between 1965 and 1990.

Franken, Robert E. *Human Motivation*. 2d ed. Pacific Grove, Calif.: Brooks/Cole, 1988. This text on motivation offers a good historical introduction to the field of motivation, summarizing the major theories and influences.

Freud, Sigmund. *New Introductory Lectures on Psychoanalysis*. New York: W. W. Norton, 1933. Freud explains his theory of the workings of the id, ego, and superego. His concept of behavioral energy is described in this book.

Geen, Russell G. "Human Motivation: New Perspectives on Old Problems." In *The G. Stanley Hall Lecture Series.* Vol. 4, edited by Anne M. Rogers and C. James Scheirer. Washington, D.C.: American Psychological Association, 1984. Surveys the state of various motivational theories, including the opponent process theory.

Hall, Calvin Springer, and Gardner Lindzey. *Theories of Personality.* 3d ed. New York: John Wiley & Sons, 1978. A definitive reference for information on most personality theorists. A thorough book that gives a detailed explanation of most of Murray's concepts. Not recommended for the casual reader.

Harvey, J. H., W. J. Ickes, and F. F. Kidd, eds. *New Directions in Attribution Research.* Hillsdale, N.J.: Lawrence Erlbaum, 1978. A collection of articles reporting empirical studies of attribution theory over a range of behaviors. The level is advanced.

Hellriegel, Don, John W. Slocum, Jr., and Richard W. Woodman. *Organizational Behavior.* 5th ed. St. Paul, Minn.: West, 1989. A popular text in industrial psychology and personnel management. How to motivate workers with various incentive systems is explained with examples; incentive motivation can be applied in industry to promote productivity.

Hilgard, Ernest Ropiequet. *Psychology in America: A Historical Survey.* San Diego: Harcourt Brace Jovanovich, 1987. The material Hilgard covers is often complex, but his clear organization and writing make it accessible to most readers. Material related to instinct in several chapters (for example, those on motivation, comparative psychology, and social psychology) can help a reader gain further background on instinct's place in psychology.

Hull, Clark Leonard. *Principles of Behavior.* New York: Appleton-Century, 1943. This classic of the Hullian neobehavioristic theory delineates the concepts of Drive and Habit and the philosophical bases of behavioral study. The theory has excited many students into studying psychology; it has gone through many revisions and additions.

Jones, Edward E. "How Do People Perceive the Causes of Behavior?" *American Scientist* 64, no. 3 (1976): 300-305. Well-written overview of attribution theory and research. Good examples illustrating many aspects of motivation in the social context. Ideal for a general but sophisticated audience.

Konner, Melvin. *The Tangled Wing: Biological Constraints on the Human Spirit*. New York: Holt, Rinehart and Winston, 1982. An informal discussion dealing with the biological basis for a variety of human behaviors and emotions, such as love, lust, and fear. Included are sections that discuss modifications of behavior and effects of differences in sex.

Liebman, Jeffrey M., and Steven J. Cooper, eds. *The Neuropharmacological Basis of Reward*. Oxford, England: Oxford University Press, 1989. Summarizes studies in the area of brain mechanisms of rewarding effects, an area of great interest to many studying incentive motivation.

Logan, Frank A., and Douglas P. Ferraro. *Systematic Analyses of Learning and Motivation*. New York: John Wiley & Sons, 1978. Logan is a well-known researcher in the area of incentive. This book summarizes the relationship between learning and motivation.

McClelland, David Clarence. *Human Motivation*. Glenview, Ill.: Scott, Foresman, 1985. McClelland's textbook on human motivation primarily attempts to develop a theoretical synthesis of the author's own view on human motivation rather than to present a broad-based approach to motivation. Particular emphasis is placed on the social motives of achievement, power, affiliation, and avoidance. Such practical issues in motivation as motivational training and relationships to societal trends set this book apart from most motivational textbooks.

Maslow, Abraham Harold. *Motivation and Personality*. New York: Harper & Row, 1954. A classic book in which the foundations of humanistic psychology are presented. Important concepts such as self-actualization and Maslow's theory of the hierarchy of needs are described in an accessible, easily read style. The book relates an optimistic view of human nature.

Mook, Douglas G. *Motivation: The Organization of Action*. New York: W. W. Norton, 1987. This book provides a comprehensive look at motivation that effectively integrates animal research with an understanding of human motivation. Written primarily for a college audience. Strengths of the book include an evenhanded presentation of divergent theories and exceptional coverage of diverse research and disciplines.

Myers, H. H., and P. S. Siegel. "The Motivation to Breastfeed: A Fit to the Opponent Process." *Journal of Personality and Social Psychology* 49, no. 1 (1985): 188-193. Describes how the affective course of breast-feeding mothers fits the opponent process theory.

Naylor, James C., Robert D. Pritchard, and Daniel R. Ilgen. *A Theory of Behavior in Organizations.* New York: Academic Press, 1980. Sophis-ticated and detailed version of a motivation theory based on cognitive processes, especially judgment and choice. The presentation is supple-mented with figures.

Olds, James, and Peter Milner. "Positive Reinforcement Produced by Electrical Stimulation of Septal Area and Other Regions of Rat Brain." *Journal of Comparative and Physiological Psychology* 47 (1954): 419-427. Reports a breakthrough in the area of studying the brain mechanisms involved in rewarding.

Petri, Herbert L. *Motivation: Theory, Research, and Application.* 3d ed. Belmont, Calif.: Wadsworth, 1990. Divides the study of motivation into three sections: biological, behavioral, and cognitive approaches. Good coverage of various motivational perspectives in their historical context is presented.

Pfaff, Donald W., ed. *The Physiological Mechanisms of Motivation.* New York: Springer-Verlag, 1982. Various authors describe the physiologi-cal substrates of different sources of drive and motivation in terms of the nervous system, hormones, and body fluid parameters.

Schultz, Duane P. *Theories of Personality.* 4th ed. Belmont, Calif.: Brooks/Cole, 1990. A review of the major aspects of Murray's theory in an easy-to-read format. Provides substantial biographical informa-tion about Murray and how this influenced his theory.

Skinner, B. F. *Beyond Freedom and Dignity.* New York: Alfred A. Knopf, 1971. A controversial, at times shocking, view of human nature from the most influential behaviorist of the twentieth century. Argues for the external control of humans and changing society through the tech-niques of behaviorism. As the title suggests, many of the cherished ideals of humanity are considered illusory and a hindrance to the improvement of society. Skinner's radical behaviorism is discussed in a style that is accessible to the general reader.

Smith, M. B., and J. W. Anderson. "Henry A. Murray (1893-1988)." *American Psychologist* 44 (1989): 1153-1154. This obituary is a personal account of Murray's career and his impact on his students as well as psychology. Covers not only the facts of Murray's work, but also his perceptions of his work.

Solomon, Richard L. "The Opponent Process Theory of Acquired Motivation." *American Psychologist* 35, no. 8 (1980): 691-712. Describes the opponent process theory and discusses research pertaining to it. Attempts to account for such diverse acquired motivations as drug addiction, love, jogging, parachuting, and sauna bathing.

Solomon, Richard L., and J. D. Corbit. "An Opponent Process Theory of Motivation: Temporal Dynamics of Affect." *Psychological Review* 8 (1974): 119-145. The original formal theoretical proposition, thoroughly detailing hypotheses and examples, both fictitious and experimental.

Stellar, James R., and Eliot Stellar. *The Neurobiology of Motivation and Reward.* New York: Springer-Verlag, 1985. Eliot Stellar, one of the best known theorists in biopsychology of motivation, along with his son, describes how biological antecedents of motivation can be found to explain various behavior.

Vroom, Victor. *Work and Motivation.* New York: John Wiley & Sons, 1964. A presentation of the rationale for choice theories of motivation, including a historical perspective. Good blend of theory and research.

Warden, Carl John. *Animal Motivation: Experimental Studies on the Albino Rat.* New York: Columbia University Press, 1931. This was the first research attempting to compare different sources of drive using various reward substances.

Watson, John Broadus. *Behaviorism.* Rev. ed. Chicago: University of Chicago Press, 1930. The fifth chapter of Watson's popular presentation of the new psychology he was sponsoring ("Are There Any Human Instincts?") nicely illustrates how behaviorism handled instinct. This chapter contains Watson's famous declaration, "Give me a dozen healthy infants, well-formed, and my own specified world to bring them up in and I'll guarantee to take any one at random and train him to become any type of specialist I might select. . . ." Watson's writing is still charming, but his position is today mainly a curiosity.

Weiner, Bernard. *Theories of Motivation*. Chicago: Markham, 1972. A textbook that provides a detailed summary of Lewin's field theory and compares it with other theories of motivation.

Weiten, Wayne. *Psychology: Themes and Variations*. 2d ed. Pacific Grove, Calif.: Brooks/Cole, 1991. Introductory psychology texts all have some coverage of instinct's return to psychology and, more important, describe how several other concepts have been introduced to deal with topics with which instinct was once inappropriately linked. Weiten's text is one of the best: easy and interesting to read, yet strong in its coverage of scientific psychology.

Wilson, E. O. *Naturalist*. Washington, D.C.: Island Press, 1994. An auto-biography by an entomologist who specializes in the study of ants and who is the major spokesperson for sociobiology, the controversial theory that argues that social attitudes are in large part a product of human evolutionary history. Entertainingly written, with many anec-dotes from Wilson's remarkable life. For the general reader.

Wilson, Edward Osbourne. *Sociobiology: The New Synthesis*. Cambridge, Mass.: The Belknap Press of Harvard University Press, 1975. A very strong presentation of the controversial theory of sociobiology, which maintains that animal behavior is a driving force in animal species evolution. Wilson contends that genetic influences play the major role in human motivation. He goes so far as to conclude that the patterns of human social behavior, including altruism, conformity, homosexuality, and gender differences, are under genetic control. A lengthy integration of motivational and evolutionary theory that the casual reader may find difficult reading.

Social Motives

Alschuler, Alfred S., Diane Tabor, and James McIntyre. *Teaching Achieve-ment Motivation: Theory and Practice in Psychological Education*. Middletown, Conn.: Education Ventures, 1970. An immensely practi-cal book that briefly discusses achievement motivation and psycho-logical growth, and then describes in considerable detail ten sessions of an achievement motivation workshop for teachers. The final chapter discusses achievement motivation training for students as well. Can easily be read by individuals at the high school level.

Atkinson, John William, and D. Birch. *An Introduction to Motivation.* 2d ed. New York: Van Nostrand, 1978. Very readable; does an effective job of discussing motivational concepts in general. Because of the first author's interest and research, a heavy emphasis is placed on achievement motivation, focusing particularly on elaborations of the expectancy value model.

Atkinson, John William, and Joel O. Raynor, eds. *Motivation and Achievement.* New York: Halsted Press, 1974. Reprints some of the most important research on achievement motivation. Many of the articles are too technical for the nonprofessional, but chapters 1, 2, 15, 19, and 20 are readable for the college student and are outstanding reviews of prior theory and application to academic achievement and career striving.

Bandura, Albert. *Aggression: A Social Learning Analysis.* Englewood Cliffs, N.J.: Prentice-Hall, 1973. Presents the social learning explanation for aggression and reveals the surprising complexity of the effects of observing models' behavior. The chapters on the prevention and control of aggression are especially interesting.

_____. *Social Learning Theory.* Englewood Cliffs, N.J.: Prentice-Hall, 1977. Describes the ways people learn by observing others' behavior, thus describing the conditions under which modeling is an effective training technique. Social learning theory is one of the most widely studied theories in psychology.

Baron, Robert A., and D. R. Richardson. *Human Aggression.* 2d ed. New York: Plenum Press, 1991. A comprehensive overview of theory and research on the biological, environmental, and interpersonal determinants of aggression. Uses negative affect theory to integrate a variety of diverse causes of aggression.

Branscombe, Nyla R., and Daniel L. Wann. "The Positive Social and Self-Concept Consequences of Sports Team Identification." *Journal of Sport and Social Issues* 15, no. 2 (1991): 115-127. This paper reports on the consequences of sports-team identification for spectators. Specifically, the importance of self-esteem, feelings of belonging, and the team's record as motivating factors are reviewed. Other emotional consequences for sports spectators such as depression and alienation are considered.

Campbell, J. P., and R. D. Pritchard. "Motivation Theory in Industrial and Organizational Psychology." In *Handbook of Industrial and Organizational Psychology*, edited by Marvin D. Dunnette. Chicago: Rand McNally, 1976. This chapter presents an overview of work motivation theories and research. Dunnette's handbook is a very useful reference for individuals interested in a wide variety of topics related to human behavior in the workplace.

Cialdini, Robert, et al. "Basking in Reflected Glory: Three (Football) Field Studies." *Journal of Personality and Social Psychology* 34 (September, 1976): 366-375. This interesting article investigates the self-esteem protecting and enhancing technique of basking in reflected glory. The authors discuss their own research on college students and point out the implications of that work for self-esteem maintenance via affiliation.

Clark, L. V. "Effect of Mental Practice on the Development of a Certain Motor Skill." *Research Quarterly* 31 (1960): 560-569. This easy-to-read journal article provides an excellent example of the effects of mental imagery on athletic performance, in addition to reviewing the methodology employed in this type of research. Much of the early work on imagery is cited and discussed.

Cox, Richard H. *Sport Psychology: Concepts and Applications*. Dubuque, Iowa: Wm. C. Brown, 1985. This book examines sport psychology primarily from a social psychological perspective. While many interesting topics within sport psychology are reviewed, the informative discussion of attributional biases adds substantially to this volume.

Craig, Robert L., ed. *Training and Development Handbook: A Guide to Human Resource Development*. 3d ed. New York: McGraw-Hill, 1987. Well-respected authors in training and development contribute chapters. This book is useful for both academics and practitioners.

Cratty, Bryant J. *Psychology in Contemporary Sport*. 3d ed. Englewood Cliffs, N.J.: Prentice-Hall, 1989. This well-written text is a "must read" for persons interested in sport psychology, especially issues related to motivation. The author provides a comprehensive discussion of the literature by reviewing the impact of motivational variables at various life stages. Topics include genetic influences, social influences, and the need for stress.

DeCharms, Richard. *Enhancing Motivation in the Classroom.* New York: Irvington, 1976. Designed primarily for teachers, with applications at all levels. Nicely incorporates prior research on achievement motivation. More than a "how-to" book; provides a challenge to the reader to think about factors involved in differing levels of achievement motivation in students.

Deci, E. L. "Intrinsic Motivation: Theory and Application." In *Psychology of Motor Behavior and Sport,* edited by Daniel M. Landers and Robert W. Christina. Champaign, Ill.: Human Kinetics, 1977. Deci conducted many of the early experiments examining the detrimental effects of extrinsic rewards on intrinsic motivation. This chapter applies the research to the sports world in addition to reviewing past research in the area of intrinsic motivation.

Dollard, John, Leonard W. Doob, Neal E. Miller, O. Hobart Mowrer, and Robert R. Sears. *Frustration and Aggression.* New Haven, Conn.: Yale University Press, 1939. A classic book detailing the role of frustration in producing aggression. It is historically very interesting, because it reveals how behaviorists attempted to recast Freudian notions into stimulus-response terms.

Freud, Sigmund. "Civilization and Its Discontents." In *The Standard Edition of the Complete Psychological Works of Sigmund Freud,* edited by James Strachey. Vol. 21. London: Hogarth Press, 1961. Expresses Freud's pessimism about the human condition, as seen in his later work. Includes Freud's notion of the death instinct and its role in aggression.

Groebel, Jo, and Robert A. Hinde, eds. *Aggression and War: Their Biological and Social Bases.* 2d ed. Cambridge, England: Cambridge University Press, 1991. Authors from diverse disciplines contribute to this volume dealing with the causes of aggression and conflict at the interpersonal, group, and societal levels. Illustrates that principles explaining conflict at one level may not be applicable at other levels.

Hall, Edward T. *The Hidden Dimension.* Garden City, N.Y.: Doubleday, 1966. Hall's insightful work is an anthropological and psychological analysis of human individual and group interactions, primarily in modern technological societies. Concentrates primarily on personal and private distance levels between individuals in individual-individual and group-group encounters. Chapter 10, "Distances in Man," describes such levels and their significance upon individual behavior. From these studies, Hall draws important conclusions and recommendations for improving human society.

Hammond, Peter B. *An Introduction to Cultural and Social Anthropology*. New York: Macmillan, 1978. Hammond's excellent introduction to anthropology for the beginning student and layperson is a comprehensive survey of relevant research and theory concerning the development and maintenance of human cultures throughout the world. Chapter 8, "Associations," compares social groups in various human societies and the motivations by which individuals enter these groups.

Herzberg, Frederick. "One More Time: How Do You Motivate Employees?" *Harvard Business Review* 46, no. 1 (1968): 53-62. One of the most frequently cited articles on work motivation. Herzberg presents his controversial motivation-hygiene theory and describes the basics of job enrichment. Herzberg provides a compelling argument in a readable form.

Landy, Frank J., and Don A. Trumbo. "Personnel Training and Development: Concepts, Models, and Techniques." In *Psychology of Work Behavior*. Pacific Grove, Calif.: Brooks/Cole, 1989. This chapter provides a good overview of training and development programs. Similar textbooks on either industrial/organizational psychology or human resource management will also have chapters on training and development.

Latham, Gary P. "Human Resource Training and Development." In *Annual Review of Psychology* 39. Stanford, Calif.: Annual Reviews, 1988. A review of academic research on training and development. Topics include training history, identifying training needs, evaluating training programs, training programs in other cultures, and leadership training. New updates are published every few years.

Locke, Edwin A., and Gary P. Latham. *Goal Setting: A Motivational Technique That Works*. Englewood Cliffs, N.J.: Prentice-Hall, 1984. Locke and Latham present a no-nonsense technique for increasing motivation and improving worker performance. The author's research suggests that a manager can improve an employee's performance through goal setting.

McClelland, David Clarence. *The Achieving Society*. Princeton, N.J.: Van Nostrand, 1961. Considered by many a classic. Applies the methods of the behavioral sciences to provide a psychological basis for evaluating economic, historical, and sociological explanations of the rise and fall of civilizations. The achievement motive is a key to McClelland's theory. Readable by the general reader at the college level and beyond. Highly recommended.

Manning, Aubrey. *An Introduction to Animal Behavior*. 3d ed. Reading, Mass.: Addison-Wesley, 1979. Manning's work is a concise, thorough survey of important animal behavior research. He cites numerous research studies on many different animal species, and he compares competing theories and models aimed at describing these behaviors. Chapter 4, "Motivation," is a detailed analysis of animal drives based upon biological principles, including group cohesiveness, aggressiveness, sexual and feeding needs of the individual, and hormonal influences. An extensive reference list is provided for further research.

Maslow, Abraham H. *Toward a Psychology of Being*. 2d ed. New York: Van Nostrand Reinhold, 1968. Maslow describes his needs hierarchy model of motivation and presents an interesting discussion of self-actualization.

Pinder, Craig C. *Work Motivation: Theory, Issues, and Applications*. Glenview, Ill.: Scott, Foresman, 1984. A well-written, college-level textbook on motivation in the workplace. Detailed discussions of theories and research are included.

Porter, Lyman W., and Edward E. Lawler. *Managerial Attitudes and Performance*. Homewood, Ill.: Richard D. Irwin, 1968. This book presents an overview of the history of expectancy theory research and development. The authors present a useful version of the theory that incorporates both intrinsic and extrinsic motivation and integrates a number of popular models of motivation.

Schneider, David J., Albert H. Hastorf, and Phoebe C. Ellsworth. *Person Perception*. 2d ed. Reading, Mass.: Addison-Wesley, 1979. Interesting chapter on self-attributions. Discusses several relevant attributional theories, including one that explains how a person can come to enjoy a task less after receiving a reward for engaging in the task.

Skinner, B. F. *Science and Human Behavior*. New York: Macmillan, 1953. This outstanding discussion of human behavior, written by one of the great psychologists/behavioral scientists of the twentieth century, thoroughly and clearly presents all principal aspects of human behavior to a general audience. Chapter 15, "Self-Control," is a study of the behavioral and physiological mechanisms by which an individual regulates conduct. Chapter 27, "Culture and Control," analyzes sociocultural restraints upon human impulses and drives.

Sloan, L. R. "The Function and Impact of Sports for Fans: A Review of Theory and Contemporary Research." In *Sports, Games, and Play: Social and Psychological Viewpoints*, edited by Jeffrey H. Goldstein. Hillsdale, N.J.: Lawrence Erlbaum, 1979. Explores the rewards that sports provide for spectators. Many motivational issues are discussed, including basking in reflected glory, stimulus seeking (eustress), and sports aggression. The author provides numerous real-life examples to illustrate the concepts.

Spence, Janet T., ed. *Achievement and Achievement Motives: Psychological and Sociological Approaches*. San Francisco: W. H. Freeman, 1983. Applies theoretical developments in achievement motivation to topics such as gender differences, children from one-parent households, social mobility, and cultural differences. Though scholarly and thorough, this excellent book is readable by the general audience at a college level, but not without effort.

Taylor, Frederick Winslow. *The Principles of Scientific Management*. New York: W. W. Norton, 1967. This management classic, originally published in 1911, describes Taylor's studies at the Midvale Steel Mill. Taylor was one of the first authors to discuss such concepts as wage incentives, time and motion studies, employee selection, and planning.

Wexley, K. N., and Gary P. Latham. *Developing and Training Human Resources in Organizations*. New York: HarperCollins, 1991. Provides an overview of training methods. The book is well written and includes many examples of actual training programs. A useful tool for students, educators, and trainers.

Wilson, Edward O. *Sociobiology: The New Synthesis*. Cambridge, Mass.: Harvard University Press, 1975. The authoritative text explaining the principles of sociobiology and its account of the evolution of social behavior. Shows how evolutionary pressures can lead not only to antisocial, aggressive behavior, but also to prosocial, cooperative behavior.

Zimbardo, Philip G., ed. *The Cognitive Control of Motivation: The Consequences of Choice and Dissonance.* Glenview, Ill.: Scott, Foresman, 1969. This informative collection of research papers by leading psychologists and behavioral scientists focuses upon experiments with individuals to test various types of individual motivation and the factors which influence variations in motivation. Essay 10, "Dissonance and the Need to Avoid Failure," by A. R. Cohen and Zimbardo, discusses social pressures as individual motivators. Other essays by Zimbardo, his colleagues, and his students illustrate the principal human motivations and drives.

Physical Motives

Arenson, Gloria. *A Substance Called Food.* 2d ed. Blue Ridge Summit, Pa.: Tab Books, 1989. Presents a variety of perspectives on eating: the psychological, the physiological, and the transpersonal. Particularly useful in providing self-help advice and treatment modalities. Examines the compulsiveness of food addiction and sees behavior modification as a means of addressing the addictive behavior.

Austin, Colin Russell, and Roger Valentine Short, eds. *Reproductive Patterns.* Cambridge, England: Cambridge University Press, 1972. This is a delightful and relatively short book covering a variety of species, including detailed descriptions of sexual patterns in marsupials and elephants. In addition, it provides information on the immunological issues of reproduction and on the effects of aging.

Bell, Alan P., and Martin Weinberg. *Homosexualities: A Study of Diversity Among Men and Women.* New York: Simon & Schuster, 1978. This official Kinsey Institute publication presents the methods and results of the most extensive sex survey to focus specifically on homosexual behavior. Presents descriptions of homosexual feelings, partnerships, and lifestyles, based on intensive interviews with more than fifteen hundred men and women.

Bell, Alan P., Martin S. Weinberg, and Sue Kiefer Hammersmith. *Sexual Preference: Its Development in Men and Women.* Bloomington: Indiana University Press, 1981. In a follow-up to Bell and Weinberg's first book, this volume compares the childhood and adolescent experiences of male and female homosexual and heterosexual adults. Organized in a question-and-answer format, this book explores possible explanations for homosexual versus heterosexual development.

Bernstein, Ilene L., and Soo Borson. "Learning Food Aversion: A Component of Anorexia Syndromes." *Psychological Review* 93, no. 4 (1986): 462-472. A review of some of the issues relevant to development of clinically significant food aversions in humans. The authors discuss tumor anorexia, cancer anorexia, anorexia nervosa, and anorexia following intestinal surgery. Technical, but interesting and important.

Blumstein, Philip W., and Pepper Schwartz. *American Couples: Money, Work, Sex.* New York: William Morrow, 1983. Part 1 presents statistical data on the lifestyles and interpersonal relationships of more than five thousand married, heterosexual cohabiting, homosexual, and lesbian couples. Part 2 presents interviews with selected couples from each of the four groups, along with a follow-up study on each several years later. Many user-friendly charts for comparison.

Bruch, Hilde. *The Golden Cage: The Enigma of Anorexia Nervosa.* New York: Vintage Books, 1979. The author is one of the best-known practitioners treating anorexia nervosa. A valuable book, based on detailed case histories from her practice, that give insight into the disease's possible causes, its effects, and the methods of treatment that have worked. Helpful in understanding the external cues involved with hunger regulation.

Carlson, Neil R. *Foundations of Physiological Psychology.* Boston: Allyn & Bacon, 1988. One of the standard texts on the physiological basis of human and animal behavior. The importance of sex hormones in development and motivation is emphasized throughout the chapter on reproductive behavior (chapter 9).

Chafetz, Michael D. *Nutrition and Neurotransmitters: The Nutrient Bases of Behavior.* Englewood Cliffs, N.J.: Prentice-Hall, 1990. Shows how neurotransmitters and nutrients interact to control food behavior. The means by which other "nonfood" behaviors (for example, learning and memory) are impacted by nutrients are also considered. The reader can safely skip the chapter and sections on neuroanatomy while focusing on the behavioral control of nutrients.

Crews, David, ed. *Psychobiology of Reproductive Behavior: An Evolutionary Perspective*. Englewood Cliffs, N.J.: Prentice-Hall, 1987. Twelve articles cover a wide range of species, including humans. The emphasis in this book is on ultimate and proximate causation of reproductive behavior, and the articles are written by experts in their fields.

Crisp, A. H. *Anorexia Nervosa: Let Me Be*. London: Academic Press, 1980. A comprehensive and readable account of a major eating disorder by an important writer in the field. Includes both biological and psychological components of the illness, and has insightful discussions of patients' behavior, psychological status, and families.

Crooks, Robert L., and Jean Stein. "Motivation and Emotion." In *Psychology*. New York: Holt, Rinehart and Winston, 1988. This chapter reviews the process of motivation and drives, and it has a good section on hunger. The chapter may be a little advanced for the high school student, but it is nevertheless worth exploring.

Denton, Derek A. *The Hunger for Salt*. New York: Springer-Verlag, 1982. This comprehensive book provides an anthropological, physiological, and medical analysis of the control of a single nutrient. Much of the historical and case data will provide fascinating reading for the general reader. The medical and scientific data is also accessible to the motivated reader.

Feldman, Robert S. "Motivation and Emotion." In *Understanding Psychology*. 2d ed. New York: McGraw-Hill, 1989. This easy-to-read chapter reviews motivation and has a good section on hunger, but it lacks a detailed account of thirst. Good simplified diagrams and figures.

Hirschmann, Jane R., and Carol H. Munter. *Overcoming Overeating: Living Free in a World of Food*. Reading, Mass.: Addison-Wesley, 1988. Reviews the psychological bases for compulsive eating and provides alternative strategies for persons who have an addictive relationship with food. Especially useful for the compulsive dieter, because it examines whether dieting actually produces the desired goal of slimness, attractiveness, and happiness.

Hutchison, John Bower, ed. *Biological Determinants of Sexual Behaviour*. New York: John Wiley & Sons, 1978. A collection of twenty-four articles covering the role of development and experience, physiological mechanisms, sensory stimulation, evolutionary concerns, and reproductive strategies in the sexual behavior of animals. Included are several readings pertaining to humans and other primates.

Jorgensen, Caryl Dow, and John E. Lewis. *The ABCs of Diabetes*. New York: Crown, 1979. An informative book on diabetes in the form of a dictionary. Contains clear explanations and is very easy to read.

Kalat, James W. *Introduction to Psychology*. 2d ed. Belmont, Calif.: Wadsworth, 1986. The sections on hunger and motivation were written by an author (Kalat) whose own work in the field provided many important contributions. His writing style is readable.

Katchadourian, Herant A. *Fundamentals of Human Sexuality*. 5th ed. Fort Worth, Tex.: Holt, Rinehart and Winston, 1989. One of the best and most readable books on human sexuality. The discussion of sex hormones in chapter 4 is thorough and clear; psychological and cultural influences on sexual motivation are covered in chapters 8, 9, 20, and 21. The presentation is accessible to high school and college students.

Koertge, Noretta, ed. *Nature and Causes of Homosexuality: A Philosophic and Scientific Inquiry*. New York: Haworth Press, 1981. This volume is the third in an ongoing monograph series entitled "Research on Homosexuality," each volume of which was originally published as an issue of the *Journal of Homosexuality*. All volumes are valuable, although somewhat technical. This one is a good place to start; others cover law, psychotherapy, literature, alcoholism, anthropology, historical perspectives, social sex roles, bisexuality, and homophobia.

Komisaruk, Barry R., et al., eds. *Reproduction: A Behavioral and Neuro-endocrine Perspective*. New York: New York Academy of Sciences, 1986. More than forty articles, all written by individuals who were or are associated with the Institute of Animal Behavior at Rutgers University, a program that emphasizes evolutionary physiological issues in the study of reproduction.

LeBow, Michael D. *Weight Control: The Behavioural Strategies*. New York: John Wiley & Sons, 1981. Exhaustive compendium of behavioral control methods used to control eating and weight. Contains the facts about weight and dieting by describing various research studies and their conclusions. The book is aimed at the long-term, repeated pattern dieter as well as the binge eater.

Lehrman, Daniel S. "The Reproductive Behavior of Ring Doves." *Scientific American* 211 (November, 1964): 48-54. This article presents a classic example of the relationships between and among the mating partners, internal physiological mechanisms, and the environment.

Levinthal, Charles F. "Chemical Senses and the Mechanisms for Eating and Drinking." In *Introduction to Physiological Psychology*. 3d ed. Englewood Cliffs, N.J.: Prentice-Hall, 1990. A very good chapter on the thirst drive. It is quite detailed, but the clarity of the writing makes it easy to read.

McNaught, Brian. *A Disturbed Peace: Selected Writings of an Irish Catholic Homosexual*. Washington, D.C.: Dignity, 1981. A very personal viewpoint from an advocate of gay rights. The publisher, Dignity, is an organization of gay Catholics (and their friends and relatives) who feel rejected by their church but who still feel a need to exercise both their religion and their sexual feelings.

Mader, Sylvia S. *Biology*. 3d ed. Dubuque, Iowa: Wm. C. Brown, 1990. An easy-to-read introductory textbook on biology that provides a good background on hormones, water regulation, and kidney function, with many fine diagrams and figures. A good basis for understanding physiological psychology.

Marmor, Judd, ed. *Homosexual Behavior: A Modern Appraisal*. New York: Basic Books, 1980. For those interested in a clinical perspective on homosexuality, this is the book. It puts the early twentieth century psychoanalytic viewpoint in context after presenting late twentieth century information from both the biological and social sciences. Collectively, the contributors' expertise is quite vast.

Masters, William H., Virginia E. Johnson, and Robert C. Kolodny. *Human Sexuality*. 3d ed. Glenview, Ill.: Scott, Foresman, 1988. An overview of human sexuality by some of the world's foremost sex researchers. Although the coverage of sex hormones is limited, the material on the other determinants of human sexual motivation is thorough, detailed, and understandable.

Mayer, Jean. *Overweight: Causes, Cost, and Control*. Englewood Cliffs, N. J.: Prentice-Hall, 1968. Addressed to the general public. Deals with the physiology of hunger and satiety, as well as the genetic and psychological aspects of obesity. Also discusses the effects of obesity on health and the effectiveness of diets. Includes an index, some references, and a long table detailing the composition of various foods.

Millman, Marcia. *Such a Pretty Face: Being Fat in America.* New York: W. W. Norton, 1980. One of the two main parts covers the social world of fat people; the second deals with living with oneself as a fat person, including means to control overeating. The language is nontechnical and accessible to the layperson. Includes a few references, an index, and photographic illustrations.

Nisbett, Richard E. "Hunger, Obesity, and the Ventromedial Hypothalamus." *Psychological Review* 79, no. 6 (1972): 433-453. Based on research which differentiated the two areas of the hypothalamus that involve hunger: the "start eating" and "stop eating" mechanisms. Explains the idea of "set point," or the body mechanism which regulates homeostasis. This article is a classic in the field of hunger because it explains the physiological location of hunger and the important role of the hypothalamus.

Pinel, John P. J. *Biopsychology.* Boston: Allyn & Bacon, 1990. Good introductory text to the physiology of human and animal behavior. The chapter "Hormones and Sex" is detailed and clearly presented; several good case studies are offered to illustrate how hormonal problems can affect human sexual development.

Schachter, Stanley, and Larry P. Gross. "Manipulated Time and Eating Behavior." *Journal of Personality and Social Psychology* 10, no. 2 (1968): 98-106. Schachter's experiments provide the basis for attention to, and recognition of the importance of, external, nonphysiological factors affecting hunger. This article was one of the first to address the psychological components of hunger by examining the external triggers to eating.

Schwartz, Hillel. *Never Satisfied.* New York: Collier-Macmillan, 1986. Presents a cultural history of diets, fantasies, and fat by explaining the cultural fit between shared fictions about the body and the reducing methods of each era, beginning with the first American weight watchers in the early 1800's. Particularly helpful in examining hunger from a sociological perspective.

Schwartz, Robert. *Diets Don't Work.* Oakland, Calif.: Breakthru Publishing, 1982. Practical "how-to" guide to dismantling the diet mentality.

This book is a good, basic, and sensible guide for taking stock of the self-defeating weight-loss attitudes and behaviors prevalent in temporary diets versus long-term attitudinal and behavior strategies for permanent weight control.

Strien, Tatjana van. *Eating Behaviour, Personality Traits, and Body Mass.* Berwyn, Pa.: Swets North America, 1986. The first part provides, in somewhat technical language, an overview of the theories explaining the determinants of eating behavior. The second part is a highly technical report of psychometric studies which does not seem relevant to the subject itself. Includes some references, but no index or illustrations.

Stuart, Richard B. *Act Thin, Stay Thin.* New York: W. W. Norton, 1977. Particularly useful in examining the moods behind the urge to eat. Written by the psychological director of Weight Watchers, an international weight-loss program. Written for those who are chronic dieters; contains ways to lose the preoccupation with food that many compulsive eaters have.

Tripp, C. A. *The Homosexual Matrix.* New York: McGraw-Hill, 1975. For those who want to sit down and read for pleasure as well as for information. Tripp covers fact, culture, and mythology, both historical and modern. A good representative of the "gay liberation" era books on homosexuality, most of the text is as valid as when it was written (though it clearly does not cover post-AIDS changes in homosexual culture and behavior).

Whitham, Frederick L. "Culturally Invariable Properties of Male Homosexuality: Tentative Conclusions from Cross-Cultural Research." *Archives of Sexual Behavior* 12 (1983): 40. Unlike much of the cross-cultural literature on homosexuality, this article focuses specifically on cross-cultural prevalence and attributes of those with a homosexual orientation, rather than on the institutionalized and ritual forms of homosexual behavior found in many non-Western cultures.

Wilson, Nancy, ed. *Obesity.* Philadelphia: F. A. Davis, 1969. Covers the subject of obesity thoroughly in a style accessible to college graduates. Deals mainly with three topics: the development of the condition, its consequences, and its management. Includes line drawings, a good index, and references at the end of each chapter.

Wise, Jonathan, and Susan Kierr Wise. *The Overeaters: Eating Styles and Personality.* New York: Human Sciences, 1979. A medical view of the overeater. Discusses the regulatory physiology of appetite, diseases leading to obesity, disorders of metabolism, psychological causes of overeating, adolescent and adult onset of obesity, and methods of treatment of the condition. Has no illustrations but includes an index and good bibliography. Not too technical; accessible to readers with a high school education.

Wolman, Benjamin B., ed. *Psychological Aspects of Obesity.* New York: Van Nostrand Reinhold, 1982. A collection of articles by fourteen authors. Provides a good account of the etiology (causation) and symptomatology of obesity, including the biology of obesity, its behavioral correlates, and its development in adolescents. Also deals with the treatment of obesity using psychological methods such as psychoanalysis, hypnotherapy, interactional psychotherapy, and multimodal behavioral therapy. A college-level book containing two indexes, one of authors and one of subjects, as well as lists of references at the end of each chapter.

Woodman, Marion. *The Owl Was a Baker's Daughter: Obesity, Anorexia Nervosa, and the Repressed Feminine.* Toronto: Inner City Books, 1980. A Jungian approach to obesity. Discusses primary and secondary obesity, body metabolism, the influences of stress on obesity, and some contemporary views on the condition. Contains an index and a bibliography.

Wurtman, Judith. *The Carbohydrate Craver's Diet.* New York: Ballantine, 1983. Translates the scientific data on carbohydrate regulation from the Wurtman laboratory into a readable presentation. The diet-book format also provides useful advice for those who need to implement this information. Especially helpful for getting a feel for the impact of science on daily life.

Animal Behavior

Alcock, John. *Animal Behavior: An Evolutionary Approach.* 4th ed. Sunderland, Mass.: Sinauer Associates, 1989. A clearly written, well-illustrated volume covering both the proximate mechanisms and the evolutionary basis of behavior. Two chapters deal with the sociobiology controversy and the evolution of human reproductive behavior. Especially helpful as an introduction to behavioral ecology.

Andrewartha, Herbert George. *Introduction to the Study of Animal Populations.* London: Methuen, 1961. This tremendous resource book for ecologists and animal behaviorists was written by one of the foremost authorities in animal behavior research. Andrewartha defines the parameters of animal population growth, including predator-prey interactions and species defense mechanisms, in the first part of the book. He devotes the second portion of the book to experimental methods and set-ups for gathering research data on animal populations. Describes all concepts with great clarity, even the mathematics and graphing of data.

Drickamer, Lee C., and Stephen H. Vessey. *Animal Behavior: Concepts, Processes, and Methods.* 2d ed. Boston: Prindle, Weber and Schmidt, 1986. An excellent, detailed text that describes the various physiological determinants of animal behavior. Includes chapters on sexual, reproductive, and aggressive behaviors.

Fichtelius, Karl Erik, and Sverre Sjolander. *Smarter than Man? Intelligence in Whales, Dolphins, and Humans.* Translated by Thomas Teal. New York: Pantheon Books, 1972. Fichtelius, a Swedish physician, and Sjolander, a Swedish ethologist, examine the comparative intelligences of cetaceans and humans in this interesting, simple book. They argue that larger brain size and other behavioral characteristics indicate that whales and dolphins have higher intellectual potential than do humans. They also state the case for human conservation of nature, including the intelligent cetaceans.

Goodall, Jane. *In the Shadow of Man.* Boston: Houghton Mifflin, 1971. Goodall examines the chimpanzees in Gombe, Tanzania. Her work is based on intensive field observation of the colony there. Describes their use of tools and employment of other symbolic devices.

Gordon, Malcolm S., George A. Bartholomew, et al. *Animal Physiology: Principles and Adaptations.* 4th ed. New York: Macmillan, 1982. The physiology of various types of animals is examined. The role of the endocrine system in lower vertebrates is included in this easily readable text. This book is well written and covers a broader scope than most books.

Gould, James L. *Ethology: The Mechanisms and Evolution of Behavior.* New York: W. W. Norton, 1982. A well-illustrated text offering a complete introduction to the basic concepts of ethology. Early chapters include a complete review of the history of ethology and the debate between ethologists and psychologists. Provides detailed descriptions of various ethological experiments; three chapters are devoted entirely to human ethology.

Grier, James W. *Biology of Animal Behavior*. St. Louis: Times Mirror/Mosby, 1984. A college-level text providing an excellent treatment of the study of animal behavior. Clearly written, well illustrated; a good introduction for the layperson. Integrates information from a variety of disciplines including ethology, behavioral ecology, psychology, and neurobiology.

Griffin, Donald Redfield. *The Question of Animal Awareness*. New York: Rockefeller University Press, 1981. This book discusses animal communication, from the honeybee to the chimpanzee. Discusses issues of animal and insect awareness and the relationships between animal language and its human counterpart.

Halliday, T. R., and P. J. Slater. *Communication: Animal Behavior*. New York: W. H. Freeman, 1983. A very comprehensive text that includes an emphasis on social processes and groups, environmental influences, and evolutionary explanations. This is a clear introductory book that can be easily read by the novice. Informative and well-written.

Klopfer, Peter H., and Jack P. Hailman. *An Introduction to Animal Behavior: Ethology's First Century*. Englewood Cliffs, N.J.: Prentice-Hall, 1967. An excellent and well-organized introduction to the history of animal behavior research. Presents major themes and models, and cites many important studies. Extremely well written and referenced.

Krebs, Charles J. *Ecology: The Experimental Analysis of Distribution and Abundance*. 2d ed. New York: Harper & Row, 1978. This well-organized, information-packed introduction to ecology was written by a leading ecologist and represents an outstanding reference for both scientist and layperson. Numerous factors that influence animal and plant populations are described, including predator-prey interactions and defense mechanisms. Hundreds of species interactions are cited with clearly explained mathematical models.

Krebs, J. R., and N. B. Davies. *An Introduction to Behavioral Ecology*. 2d ed. Oxford, England: Blackwell Scientific Publications, 1991. Intended as a basic overview of behavioral ecology for individuals outside the profession. Covers many aspects of foraging ecology, social behavior, and predator avoidance from an evolutionary perspective. Well referenced; includes many diagrams and data figures.

McFarland, David, ed. *The Oxford Companion to Animal Behavior*. Rev.
and enl. ed. New York: Oxford University Press, 1987. Intended as a
reference guide for both nonspecialists and people in the field. A comprehensive survey of behavior, written by a team of internationally known
biologists, psychologists, and neurobiologists. Contains more than two
hundred entries covering a variety of behavioral topics. A detailed index
provides cross-references organized by both subject and species lists.

Manning, Aubrey. *An Introduction to Animal Behavior*. 3d ed. London:
Edward Arnold, 1979. A concise introduction to many general aspects
of animal behavior. Topics covered include learning, evolution and
behavior, development of behavior, communication, conflict behavior,
and social organization. Well researched, clearly written, and effectively illustrated.

Marler, Peter, and William J. Hamilton III. *Mechanisms of Animal Behavior*. New York: John Wiley & Sons, 1966. Marler and Hamilton's work
is a thorough survey of animal behavior research that incorporates the
detailed experiments of hundreds of scientists. They clearly present all
major types of behaviors, in organisms from insects to humans. Chapter 3, "Reproduction: Hormones and Behavior," discusses the roles of
the sex steroid hormones in courtship, mating, and territoriality for
many diverse species. Other chapters emphasize the roles of hormones
in many types of animal behaviors.

Raven, Peter H. *Biology*. St. Louis: Times Mirror/Mosby, 1989. Chapter 56 of this general text on the science of biology offers an excellent
introduction to the general concepts of ethology and animal behavior,
with a strong emphasis on many basic ethological concepts in addition
to the learning-versus-instinct debate and the sociobiology controversy. A concise summary, suggestions for additional reading, and
review questions appear at the end of the chapter.

Rosenblum, Leonard A., ed. *Primate Behavior: Developments in Field
and Laboratory Research*. Vol. 4. New York: Academic Press, 1975. A
collection of monographs that includes an extensive descriptive account of the facial expressions of nonhuman primates by William
Redican, and one hundred pages devoted to the analysis of Japanese
monkey vocalizations by Steven Green.

Snowdon, Charles T., Charles H. Brown, and Michael R. Petersen, eds.
Primate Communication. New York: Cambridge University Press,

1982. Sixteen chapters on nonhuman primate communication summarize the field up to about 1980. Readable throughout. Chapters by Robert Seyfarth and Suzanne Chevalier-Skolnikoff provide excellent summaries of their research. Especially valuable is Uwe Jürgens' contribution on the vocal repertoire of the squirrel monkey, which offers a concise, readable introduction to his extensive research with this species.

Todt, Dietmar, Philipp Goedeking, and David Symmes, eds. *Primate Vocal Communication*. New York: Springer-Verlag, 1988. A good sampling of approaches to the study of vocalization. Includes articles by Detlev Ploog and an accessible summary of Klaus Scherer's component patterning theory of vocal affect expression.

Wright, Robert. *The Moral Animal*. New York: Pantheon, 1994. A controversial book discussing the relevance of sociobiology to everyday life. Aggression and sex differences in attitudes and jealousy are among the topics considered.

LEARNING

General Concepts

Baldwin, John D., and Janice I. Baldwin. *Behavior Principles in Everyday Life*. 2d ed. Englewood Cliffs, N.J.: Prentice-Hall, 1986. Uses hundreds of examples from ordinary human behavior to illustrate the basic principles of conditioning, including special considerations of generalization and discrimination. Detailed, yet easy to follow, this is one of the best introductions available.

Bell-Gredler, Margaret E. *Learning and Instruction*. New York: Macmillan, 1986. Bell-Gredler discusses the functions of learning theory as it applies to instruction, the history of the development of educational psychology, and six contemporary views on learning and instruction. The presentation is concise, informative, and appropriate for secondary and college students.

Biehler, Robert Frederick, and Jack Snowman. *Psychology Applied to Teaching*. 6th ed. Boston: Houghton Mifflin, 1990. A well-researched and timely look at classroom learning, this text emphasizes practical applications with real classroom situations. Especially useful for future teachers in secondary or college levels.

Chance, Paul. *Learning and Behavior*. Belmont, Calif.: Wadsworth, 1988. This is an introductory text intended for the first course in learning. It is easy to understand and very accessible to the novice. Chance's purpose is to present the basic principles of learning theory, not to review current research. His bibliography reflects this and is not as complete as in many texts.

Domjan, Michael, and Barbara Burkhard. *Principles of Learning and Behavior*. Monterey, Calif.: Brooks/Cole, 1982. Provides a complete treatment of the psychological basis and mechanisms of learning. Includes many original data tables and graphs, and a thorough review of the literature.

Estes, W. K. "Learning." In *Fifty Years of Psychology: Essays in Honor of Floyd Ruch*, edited by Ernest R. Hilgard. Glenview, Ill.: Scott,

Foresman, 1988. Estes' chapter in this book is rather short (eighteen pages), and this is truly unfortunate. It is an excellent review of the field, written by one of the pioneers of learning theory. As a participant in the field, he offers an informative and insightful perspective. Though this essay will be understandable by anyone who has taken an introductory psychology course, sophisticated readers will find more to appreciate. Estes' bibliography includes the most important and influential works in learning.

Gagné, Robert Mills, and Marcy Perkins Driscoll. *Essentials of Learning for Instruction*. Englewood Cliffs, N.J.: Prentice-Hall, 1988. Offers an in-depth look at Gagné's conditions for learning and the outcomes of learning as well as instructional applications. Written at the undergraduate/graduate level, the book is important reading for future professionals.

Grier, James W. *Biology of Animal Behavior*. St. Louis: Times Mirror/ Mosby, 1984. This college-level text provides comprehensive treatment of the study of animal behavior. Clearly written and well illustrated; should provide a good introduction for the layperson. Integrates information from a variety of disciplines including ethology, behavioral ecology, psychology, and neurobiology. Six chapters are devoted to the physiological control of behavior, and one chapter deals entirely with learning and memory.

Hebb, Donald Olding. *The Organization of Behavior*. New York: John Wiley & Sons, 1949. Hebb was one of the first to theorize about the relationship between brain mechanisms and learning. This book was one of the first (and is still one of the best) efforts to explain what happens in the brain between the stimulus and the response. Hebb intended the book for professionals in psychology, biology, and medicine; therefore, it is rather advanced.

Hergenhahn, B. R. *An Introduction to the Theories of Learning*. 3d ed. Englewood Cliffs, N.J.: Prentice-Hall, 1988. As a text for undergraduate psychology of learning classes, Hergenhahn's book is unusual. Instead of organizing the text into traditional chapters on conditioning, reinforcement, memory, and so on, he arranges by theory. Thus, there are chapters describing Thorndike's theory, Skinner's, Pavlov's, Toleman's, Jean Piaget's, Hebb's, and so on. Similar theories are placed in units with descriptions about their historical and theoretical relationships. The text assumes only an introductory course as background.

Because of the theoretical nature of the book, the bibliography includes many of the most important early works in psychology.

Herrnstein, Richard J. "Objects, Categories, and Discriminative Stimuli." In *Animal Cognition*, edited by H. L. Roitblat, T. G. Bever, and H. S. Terrace. Hillsdale, N.J.: Lawrence Erlbaum, 1984. A review of some of the work of Herrnstein and others on operant discrimination, including concept learning. Highly recommended for serious students of operant behavior.

Liddell, Howard S. "Conditioning and Emotions." *Scientific American* 190 (January, 1954): 48-57. Liddell describes his research with conditioned neurosis in goats and sheep and discusses behavioral as well as physiological effects of this procedure. The implications for human behavior are made clear in this fascinating article.

McFarland, David, ed. *The Oxford Companion to Animal Behavior*. Rev. and enl. ed. New York: Oxford University Press, 1987. Intended as a reference guide, this comprehensive survey of behavior was written by a team of internationally known biologists, psychologists, and neurobiologists, and contains more than two hundred entries covering a variety of topics. Provides a detailed summary of various forms of learning, including habituation and sensitization. The index provides cross-references organized by both subject and species lists.

Mackintosh, N. J. *The Psychology of Animal Learning*. New York: Academic Press, 1974. This book reviews the principles of learning in animals in the context of classical and operant conditioning as well as more recent accounts of learning theories. Not suitable for light reading, but an excellent source for reference material.

Manning, Aubrey. *An Introduction to Animal Behavior*. 3d ed. Reading, Mass.: Addison-Wesley, 1979. A concise handbook offering a light introduction to many general aspects of animal behavior and learning. Provides a discussion on stimulus filtering, an entire chapter on the physiological basis of behavior and motivation, and a complete summary of various forms of learning. Well researched, clearly written, and effectively illustrated.

Martin, Garry, and Joseph Pear. *Behavior Modification: What It Is and How to Do It*. 3d ed. Englewood Cliffs, N.J.: Prentice-Hall, 1988. This introduction to behavior modification offers clear explanations of the principles underlying operant behavior change, including changes based on generalization and discrimination. Discusses techniques for intentionally producing generalization and discrimination in human beings.

Miller, L. Keith. *Principles of Everyday Behavior Analysis.* 2d ed. Monterey, Calif.: Brooks/Cole, 1980. An excellent introduction to behavior analysis for the high school or college student. Material is presented in a modified programmed-instruction format. There are chapters dealing specifically with generalization and discrimination.

Raven, Peter H. *Biology.* St. Louis: Times Mirror/Mosby, 1989. Chapter 56 of this general text on the science of biology offers an excellent first introduction to the general concepts of ethology and animal behavior. Includes a brief summary of learning and detailed coverage of habituation, sensitization, and conditioning in *Aplysia.* A concise summary, suggestions for additional reading, and review questions appear at the end of the chapter.

Schmeck, Ronald R., ed. *Learning Strategies and Learning Styles.* New York: Plenum Press, 1988. Offers a timely selection of current thinking on student learning styles based on a variety of methodologies. Included are neuropsychological, cognitive, and affective perspectives. Well-suited for college students as well as professionals.

Schwartz, Barry. *Psychology of Learning and Behavior.* New York: W. W. Norton, 1984. Schwartz presents a philosophical and empirical review of learning theory. Though the book is intended for students with only an introductory course background, it is probably more advanced. A very thorough book, it reviews considerable literature. The bibliography reflects this detail.

Shepherd, Gordon Murray. *Neurobiology.* Oxford, England: Oxford University Press, 1983. This somewhat advanced college-level volume on neurobiology offers an in-depth account of the physiological basis of learning and memory. A portion of chapter 30 is devoted specifically to the neurological changes associated with habituation and sensitization. Detailed diagrams, data summaries, and complete literature reviews are provided.

Skinner, B. F. *About Behaviorism.* New York: Alfred A. Knopf, 1974. Skinner intended this book for the layperson. It is extremely well written and is understandable even by those with no background in psychology. The book presents Skinner's ideas about the philosophy of behaviorism and argues that this approach is a productive and objective method for explaining and analyzing human behavior.

_____. "How to Teach Animals." *Scientific American* 185 (December, 1951): 26-29. Describes operant conditioning, including the conditioning of discrimination, in clear and readable terms accessible to a wide audience.

Slavin, Robert E. *Educational Psychology.* 3d ed. Englewood Cliffs, N.J.: Prentice-Hall, 1991. Slavin offers a practical look at effective classroom practice based on recent research findings. The college-level text, which includes references to the author's own research, illustrates how research may directly affect classroom practice.

Staddon, J. R. "Learning as Adaptation." In *Handbook of Learning and Cognitive Processes,* edited by W. K. Estes. Hillsdale, N.J.: Lawrence Erlbaum, 1975. This review of laboratory procedures focuses on learning studies with animals. It also is concerned with the natural habitat of the animal. Clear and precise; presents an informative psychological perspective.

Verhave, Thom. "The Pigeon as a Quality Control Inspector." *American Psychologist* 21 (1966): 109-115. In this fascinating report, Verhave describes his research on using pigeons trained to discriminate good from defective pills as quality control agents. The article is lively and easy to read, as it is written largely in a nontechnical style.

Watson, John B. *Behaviorism.* New York: W. W. Norton, 1925. This book introduced the school of behaviorism and, as such, is one of the most important and influential works in all of psychology. One can still learn much from it, though in the many years since its publication, considerable thought and research have eclipsed some of Watson's theses.

Biological Influences on Learning

Beck, William S., Karel F. Liem, and George Gaylord Simpson. *Life: An Introduction to Biology.* 3d ed. New York: HarperCollins, 1991. Introduction to biology for the beginning student. Contains a clear text, many strong diagrams and illustrations, and beautiful photographs. Contains a thorough discussion of animal behavior, famous experiments, and various types of animal learning, including imprinting, and describes the studies of Konrad Lorenz and others.

Bolles, Robert C. *Learning Theory*. New York: Holt, Rinehart and Winston, 1975. One of the most concise and readable textbooks on learning theory, it reads almost like a mystery story in places. Includes a discussion of learning in its evolutionary context.

Bolles, Robert C., and Michael D. Beecher, eds. *Evolution and Learning*. Hillsdale, N.J.: Lawrence Erlbaum, 1988. Presents a dozen essays describing how learning capacities and processes reflect an organism's evolutionary history. An essay by Bolles on the nativist-empiricist issue provides a philosophical context. This readable volume illustrates how concern with biological constraints on learning has developed into a productive interchange of ideas between the long-separated traditions of learning theory and ethology.

Braveman, Norman S., and Paul Bronstein, eds. *Experimental Assessments and Clinical Applications of Conditioned Food Aversions*. New York: New York Academy of Sciences, 1985. This is volume 443 in the Annals of the New York Academy of Sciences, and it reprints papers presented at a 1984 conference. Many of the articles, by experts in the field, deal with the medical relevance of food aversions in humans. Many of the articles are quite technical, but some are accessible to the general reader with some background.

Brower, Lincoln Pierson. "Ecological Chemistry." *Scientific American* 220 (February, 1969): 22-29. An excellent and enjoyable description of taste-aversion learning in nature. Brower describes how birds become averted to insects, such as monarch butterflies, that feed on plants containing chemical toxins. Some of the evolutionary implications of this phenomenon are discussed.

Gustavson, Carl R., and John Garcia. "Pulling a Gag on the Wily Coyote." *Psychology Today* 8 (August, 1974): 68-72. Very entertaining article describing the research on averting wild predators to sheep as a way of limiting predation on ranchers' herds without destroying the predators themselves. The authors convincingly show that shooting and poisoning coyotes are unnecessary and undesirable.

Klein, Stephen B., and Robert R. Mowrer, eds. *Contemporary Learning Theories: Instrumental Conditioning Theory and the Impact of Bio-*

logical Constraints on Learning. Hillsdale, N.J.: Lawrence Erlbaum, 1989. Contains a number of relevant essays dealing with issues such as phobias and taste aversion. Includes some unusual applications of the preparedness concept.

Lorenz, Konrad. *On Aggression*. Translated by Marjorie Kerr Wilson. New York: Harcourt, Brace & World, 1966. This excellent survey of aggressive animal behavior, written by a Nobel laureate and pioneer in behavior research, is aimed at the layperson. Lorenz clearly outlines the evolution of animal behavior and the adaptiveness of aggressive behavior. He cites several species interactions, illustrating both offensive and defensive animal behaviors. Also addresses aggression within the context of human behavior, stressing the need for human control of aggressive behaviors for our own survival.

McNally, Richard. "Preparedness and Phobias: A Review." *Psychological Bulletin* 101, no. 2 (1987): 283-303. Summarizes and skeptically evaluates the evidence for the preparedness theory of phobia. Although difficult to read at points, the general reader should still be able to identify McNally's major points. The bibliography is extensive, if not definitive.

Manning, Aubrey. *An Introduction to Animal Behavior*. 3d ed. Reading, Mass.: Addison-Wesley, 1979. A concise presentation of theory and experimentation in animal behavior research. Describes major behavior theories and relevant experimental work from the biological research. Describes animal species' responses and adaptations to environmental stimuli, including displays, mimicry, and other responses to danger. "Conflict Behavior," describes various offensive and defensive mechanisms used by different species in both competition and predator-prey interactions. Includes a good discussion of imprinting studies, particularly with reference to maternal imprinting, and describes the biological bases behind imprinting and other behaviors.

Öhman, Arne, Ulf Dimberg, and Lars-Göran Öst. "Animal and Social Phobias: Biological Constraints on Learned Fear Responses." In *Theoretical Issues in Behavior Therapy*, edited by Steven Reiss and Richard R. Bootzin. Orlando, Fla.: Academic Press, 1985. A summary and refinement of the position that phobias are examples of prepared conditioning. Clearly summarizes dozens of published studies, many of which are difficult to read in their original form.

Raven, Peter H., and George B. Johnson. *Biology*. 2d ed. St. Louis: Times Mirror/Mosby, 1989. A strong presentation of all aspects of biology for the beginning student. Includes excellent diagrams and illustrations. Summarizes the major theories and classic experiments of animal behavior research, including imprinting studies.

Seligman, Martin E. P. "On the Generality of the Laws of Learning." *Psychological Review* 77 (September, 1970): 406-418. A well-written and exceptionally clear presentation of the concept of preparedness. Seligman's critique of general process learning theory remains a classic. In addition to its topical coverage, it provides a good example of a creative psychological synthesis.

Seligman, Martin E. P., and Joanne L. Hager, eds. *Biological Boundaries of Learning*. New York: Appleton-Century-Crofts, 1972. The single most important source of preparedness, this book collects all the important early literature under one cover. Includes the taste-aversion studies by Garcia; classic experiments by Brown and Jenkins, Hineline and Rachlin, Bolles, and many others on preparedness and operant conditioning; Breland and Breland's "The Misbehavior of Organisms"; and Seligman's "Phobias and Preparedness." Although some of the thirty-five papers are technical, many are well within the reach of general readers. Since the editors summarize and critique the technical reports, this collection is convenient to use.

Wallace, Robert A., Gerald P. Sanders, and Robert J. Ferl. *Biology: The Science of Life*. 3d ed. New York: HarperCollins, 1991. An outstanding book for beginning students that describes all major concepts in biology with great clarity, using numerous examples, good illustrations, and beautiful photographs. Discusses behavioral research, including studies of maternal imprinting.

Wilson, Edward Osborne. *Sociobiology: The New Synthesis*. Cambridge, Mass.: The Belknap Press of Harvard University Press, 1975. An incredibly comprehensive study of sociobiology, a perspective which maintains that animal behavior is a driving force in animal species evolution. The author, a prominent entomologist, is the leading proponent of this controversial theory, which he defends with hundreds of case studies. Describes the biological basis of behavior during all stages of animal development.

Cognitive Learning

Applebee, Arthur N. *The Child's Concept of Story, Ages Two to Seventeen.* Chicago: University of Chicago Press, 1978. An innovative approach and eight thought-provoking chapters give this book an edge on some of the classics in this field. The author examines the use of language and how perceptions can be influenced by it. Demonstrates an adult's and child's sense of story, as well as the responses of adolescents. The author shows how perceptions are easily manipulated by skillful use of phrasing. There are three appendices: a collection of analysis and data, elements of response, and a thorough supplementary table.

Baldwin, John D., and Janice I. Baldwin. "Modeling and Observational Learning." In *Behavior Principles in Everyday Life.* 2d ed. Englewood Cliffs, N.J.: Prentice-Hall, 1986. An easy-to-read textbook that applies operant conditioning, observational learning, and other theories to daily life. The chapter on observational learning includes a discussion of how emotional responses can be learned through modeling, and why people sometimes perform behaviors that are the opposite of what they observed. Technical terms are used, but are first defined.

Bandura, Albert. *Principles of Behavior Modification.* New York: Holt, Rinehart and Winston, 1969. An older, college-level textbook with a strong empirical orientation that is surprisingly easy to read. Especially interesting from a historical perspective, because Bandura presents some of the studies that moved him from the ranks of traditional learning theorists to become one of the major innovators in the field of social learning theory. Observational or vicarious learning and vicarious reinforcement and punishment are discussed in detail.

_____. *Social Foundations of Thought and Action.* Englewood Cliffs, N.J.: Prentice-Hall, 1986. Includes a complete chapter on observational learning and the factors that affect it. The rest of the book concerns the way in which social learning affects personality, covering issues such as free will, personal efficacy, personal change, and cognitive development in children. Difficult but informative reading.

Bransford, John D., and Barry S. Stein. *The IDEAL Problem Solver: A Guide to Improving Thinking, Learning, and Creativity.* New York: W. H. Freeman, 1984. This is a how-to book for students to improve their academic skills, problem-solving techniques, and strategy use. Gives many examples of problems and how to attack them and improve one's abilities. Easy to read and will benefit the reader in better performance.

Chomsky, Noam. *Language and Mind*. New York: Harcourt Brace Jovanovich, 1972. The influential inventor of transformational grammar presents his views on the relationship of language and mind, as well as presenting another extension of Edward C. Tolman's concepts.

Crain, William C. "Bandura's Social Learning Theory." In *Theories of Development: Concepts and Applications*. 2d ed. Englewood Cliffs, N.J.: Prentice-Hall, 1985. Social learning theory is presented from a developmental perspective. Although the theory is not covered in depth, the author provides a flavor of the ideas of the theory, including its origins, concepts, and some of its practical applications. Reviews the use of this theory in studies of aggression.

Labov, William. *The Social Stratification of English in New York City*. Washington, D.C.: Center for Applied Linguistics, 1982. Persuasive argument that in appropriate circumstances, the assumed inarticulateness of young African-American men disappears. Example of latent learning forming the basis for adequate performance in a setting that elicits appropriate behavior.

Menzel, Emil W. "Cognitive Mapping in Chimpanzees." In *Cognitive Processes in Animal Behavior*, edited by Stewart H. Hulse, Harry Fowler, and Werner K. Honig. Hillsdale, N.J.: Lawrence Erlbaum, 1978. Adds significantly to the research on cognitive mapping through reporting on Menzel's carefully controlled experiment with chimpanzees and hidden food.

Olton, David S., and Robert J. Samuelson. "Remembrance of Places Passed: Spatial Memory in Rats." *Journal of Experimental Psychology: Animal Behavior Process* 2, no. 2 (1976): 97-116. Research that reports on rats in a radial maze, further establishing the validity of cognitive maps and strengthening their place in learning theory.

Ormrod, Jeanne E. "Social Learning Theory." In *Human Learning*. Columbus, Ohio: Charles E. Merrill, 1990. Interesting reading for anyone interested in how humans learn. The writing is simple and straightforward, and the author shares many personal and humorous examples from her own experiences. Discusses aggression, morality, and the relevance of modeling to classroom learning.

Roberts, William A., and Nelly Van Veldhuizen. "Spatial Memory in Rats on the Radial Maze." *Journal of Experimental Psychology: Animal Behavior Processes* 11, no. 2 (1985): 241-260. Extends earlier findings of cognitive maps in rats on the radial maze to pigeons. Careful attention to method, allowing psychologists to extend their findings beyond confines of the research.

Ryckman, Richard M. "Bandura: Social and Cognitive Theory." In *Theories of Personality*. 4th ed. Pacific Grove, Calif.: Brooks\Cole, 1989. Discusses Bandura's theory of personality, social cognitive theory, which addresses how social and cognitive factors, including modeling, shape personality. Includes a brief biography of Bandura, a discussion of aggression, and a discussion of how modeling effects can be used in therapy to help a client deal with fear or anxiety.

Schwartz, Barry, and Dan Reisberg. *Learning and Memory*. New York: W. W. Norton, 1991. This book is a comprehensive outline of all aspects of psychology that pertain to learning and memory. Includes 1980's research and historical review. An excellent reference book.

Seligman, Martin E. P. *Helplessness: On Depression, Development, and Death*. San Francisco: W. H. Freeman, 1975. This easily read and understood book was written by the master researcher in the field of learned helplessness. Covers such areas as anxiety and unpredictability, education's role in emotional development, experimental studies, and how perception influences everyday life. Excellent references. This book is a must for anyone interested in the topic.

Smith, Frank. *Comprehension and Learning: A Conceptual Framework for Teachers*. New York: Holt, Rinehart and Winston, 1975. A cognitive textbook on the principles of learning in children; has both an information-processing format and a psycholinguistic perspective for a comprehensive presentation of research. It is easily read by student or teacher and includes the areas of comprehension, language, and concept development.

Thomas, R. Murray. *Comparing Theories of Child Development*. 2d ed. Belmont, Calif.: Wadsworth, 1985. Provides an overview of the origins of social learning theory, including how it fits into the behaviorist tradition. A description of key aspects of social learning theory is also presented.

Tolman, Edward Chace. "Cognitive Maps in Rats and Men." *Psychological Review* 55 (1948): 189-209. Summarizes Tolman's earlier experiments with rats in a clear and comprehensive manner. Applies the theory of cognitive maps to humans and suggests applications of the theory.

_____. *Purposive Behavior in Animals and Men.* New York: Century, 1932. The first book to report Tolman's finding regarding cognitive maps. Serves as the initial source for understanding cognitive maps.

Vygotsky, Lev Semenovich. *Problems of General Psychology, Including the Volume "Thinking and Speech."* Vol. 1 of *The Collected Works of L. S. Vygotsky,* edited by Robert W. Rieber and Aaron S. Carton. New York: Plenum Press, 1988. *Thinking and Speech* is a recent translation of the theory of concept development, based on Jean Piaget's work and given a cultural perspective. It is one of the most comprehensive theories in psychology and is complete with concrete examples for each point. Clear and easily followed by the novice.

Aversion Conditioning

Burgess, Anthony. *A Clockwork Orange.* London: Heinemann, 1962. A fictional account of an antisocial personality whose behavior is modified through the use of aversive conditioning techniques. Burgess opposes the use of such aversive conditioning techniques, and the book is an indictment of behavior modification. The behavior modifiers are described in the least favorable possible light, the techniques (although described fairly accurately) are the most shocking ones available, and the treatment is carried to an unreasonable extreme and executed for the wrong reasons. It is, however, an interesting, entertaining, and informative novel.

Dinsmoor, J. "Escape from Shock as a Conditioning Technique." In *Aversive Stimulation,* edited by Marshall R. Jones. Coral Gables, Fla.: University of Miami Press, 1968. This paper was presented at the Miami Symposium on the Prediction of Behavior, 1967. Presents an excellent description of the development of basic escape research in the laboratory and of the major variables involved.

Flaherty, Charles F. *Animal Learning and Cognition.* New York: Alfred A. Knopf, 1985. Provides a thorough, clearly written review of the experimental and theoretical foundations of learning theory. Contains references to and discussions of all major contributions to the study of avoidance learning.

Hamilton, Leonard W., and C. Robin Timmons. *Principles of Behavioral Pharmacology*. Englewood Cliffs, N.J.: Prentice-Hall, 1990. Although the emphasis of this textbook is on pharmacology, three chapters are devoted to the effects of aversive control of behavior. Topics include anxiety, fear, pain, and depression.

Klein, Stephen B. *Learning*. 2d ed. New York: McGraw-Hill, 1991. General learning text with a section on escape and the critical factors involved. Also points out the ubiquitousness of adversity in people's lives and how this often leads to inappropriate escape behavior.

Seligman, Martin E. P. *Helplessness: On Depression, Development, and Death*. San Francisco: W. H. Freeman, 1975. An easy-to-read account of the role of aversive conditioning in the cause and treatment of clinical disorders in humans.

Sidman, Murray. *Coercion and Its Fallout*. Boston: Authors Cooperative, 1989. Points out that coercion is everywhere in society and that the side effects of so much unpleasantness are disastrous. Also indicates how people can increase the use of noncoercive techniques of behavior management.

Solomon, Richard L. "The Opponent-Process Theory of Acquired Motivation: The Costs of Pleasure and the Benefits of Pain." *American Psychologist* 35 (1980): 691-712. Provides an excellent summary of opponent-process theory, which is a modern extension of the two-process theory of avoidance learning. Includes speculation on a variety of disorders, including addictive behaviors.

Staddon, J. E. R., and R. H. Ettinger. *Learning*. San Diego: Harcourt Brace Jovanovich, 1989. Behavioral-oriented text discusses escape and aversive control. Places escape conditioning within the context of all operant behavior and illustrates how general principles of conditioning apply in this situation.

Instrumental Conditioning

Baldwin, John D., and Janice I. Baldwin. *Behavior Principles in Everyday Life*. 2d ed. Englewood Cliffs, N.J.: Prentice-Hall, 1986. Uses hundreds of examples from ordinary human behavior to illustrate the basic principles of operant behavior theory. Detailed yet easy to follow; one of the best introductions available.

Catania, A. Charles. *Learning.* 2d ed. Englewood Cliffs, N.J.: Prentice-Hall, 1984. Chapter 9 of this book deals with an operant approach to language. On pp. 238-240, Catania presents an excellent brief summary of rule-governed behavior.

Ferster, Charles B., and B. F. Skinner. *Schedules of Reinforcement.* New York: Appleton-Century-Crofts, 1957. Describes the original animal studies conducted by the authors; still required reading for anyone who desires a complete knowledge of reinforcement schedules. The amount of detail presented is tremendous, but adequate background is given to make it accessible to the nonspecialist reader.

Ferster, Charles B., Stuart Culbertson, and Mary Carol Perrot Boren. *Behavior Principles.* 2d ed. Englewood Cliffs, N.J.: Prentice-Hall, 1982. A book on operant behavior that describes animal experiments and then applies behavior principles to human behavior, including verbal behavior and depression. Much of the book deals with reinforcement schedules. The authors assume no prior knowledge of psychology on the part of the reader.

Hayes, Steven C., ed. *Rule-Governed Behavior: Cognitions, Contingencies, and Instructional Control.* New York: Plenum Press, 1989. A compendium of ten chapters written by eminent behaviorists who present an in-depth analysis of different aspects of rule-governed behavior. Some of the chapters are very difficult to understand, but others are more accessible. Chapter 2, by B. F. Skinner; chapter 3, by Margaret Vaughan; chapter 9, by Roger L. Poppen; and chapter 10, by Steven C. Hayes et al. are highly recommended.

Miller, L. Keith. *Principles of Everyday Behavior Analysis.* 2d ed. Pacific Grove, Calif.: Brooks/Cole, 1980. An excellent introduction to behavior analysis for the high school or college student. Material is presented in a modified programmed instruction format. Short lessons are accompanied by quizzes and problems demonstrating real-life applications.

Ormrod, Jeanne E. *Human Learning: Principles, Theories, and Educational Applications.* Columbus, Ohio: Charles E. Merrill, 1990. A very

enjoyable and readable presentation of instrumental-operant conditioning, with specific applications to the classroom.

Schoenfeld, William N., ed. *The Theory of Reinforcement Schedules.* New
York: Appleton-Century-Crofts, 1970. A collection of technical articles
that can be understood by a nonspecialist. Particularly interesting are
"Schedules as Fundamental Determinants of Behavior" and "Reinforcement Schedules and Stimulus Control."

Skinner, B. F. *About Behaviorism.* New York: Alfred A. Knopf, 1974.
Many criticisms of Skinnerian behaviorism have been based on misunderstandings of his position. Skinner addresses these criticisms in this
book. Written in a nontechnical style; however, an elementary knowledge of behavior analysis would be helpful to readers of this book.

_____. *Beyond Freedom and Dignity.* New York: Alfred A.
Knopf, 1971. A controversial book analyzing the structure and ills of
American society. Argues that people have been ineffective in dealing
with social problems because they have ignored the causes of human
behavior. Nontechnical and highly recommended.

_____. "A Case History in Scientific Method." *American Psycholo-
gist* 11 (1956): 221-233. Reprinted in B. F. Skinner, *Cumulative Record: A Selection of Papers.* 3d ed. New York: Appleton-Century-Crofts,
1972. This often-reprinted article is a Skinner classic. He describes the
discovery of and some of the original research on reinforcement
schedules in a light, personable style with more than a touch of humor.

_____. *Cumulative Record: A Selection of Papers.* 3d ed. New
York: Appleton-Century-Crofts, 1972. A varied selection of important
papers on instrumental/operant conditioning by the most important and
influential psychologist in this area. Presents both theoretical and
applied papers.

_____. "An Operant Analysis of Problem Solving." In *Problem-
Solving: Research, Method, and Theory,* edited by Benjamin Kleinmuntz. New York: John Wiley & Sons, 1966. Although Skinner clearly
differentiated between two types of operant behavior as early as 1947,
when he gave the William James lectures at Harvard University, it was
not until 1966 that he published a paper exclusively on this topic.
Skinner's paper is recommended to familiarize the student with the
original source of the topic.

_____. "Operant Behavior." In *Operant Behavior: Areas of Research and Application*, edited by Werner K. Honig. Englewood Cliffs, N.J.: Prentice-Hall, 1966. A clearly written treatment by the foremost behaviorist of recent times. Surveys the theoretical foundations of instrumental conditioning and points out major pitfalls in analyzing experimental results. Includes a bibliography.

_____. *Science and Human Behavior*. New York: Macmillan, 1953. A thoughtful and thought-provoking discussion of instrumental/operant conditioning from the perspective of its usefulness in improving life on the individual and societal levels. Principles of reinforcement are applied to a wide variety of topics, including self-control, thinking, government, religion, economics, and education, in this accessible introduction to operant behavior theory.

Thompson, Travis, and John G. Grabowski. *Reinforcement Schedules and Multioperant Analysis*. New York: Appleton-Century-Crofts, 1972. An introduction to reinforcement schedules for the lay reader that uses a programmed instruction format. Material is presented in small units, and the student is tested on the material before proceeding to the next unit. The book provides a clear explanation of the way in which schedules exert control over rates and patterns of response.

Ullmann, Leonard P., and Leonard Krasner. *Case Studies in Behavior Modification*. New York: Holt, Rinehart and Winston, 1965. A thorough treatment of the application of instrumental/operant conditioning to the understanding and treatment of mental disorders.

Watson, David L., and Roland G. Tharp. *Self-Directed Behavior: Self-Modification for Personal Adjustment*. 5th ed. Pacific Grove, Calif.: Books/Cole, 1989. A do-it-yourself guide to behavior change. Makes extensive use of principles of reinforcement to help the lay reader improve behaviors in areas such as time management, smoking, overeating, assertiveness, insomnia, budgeting, and social behavior.

Zettle, Robert D., and Steven C. Hayes. "Rule-Governed Behavior: A Potential Theoretical Framework for Cognitive-Behavioral Therapy." In *Advances in Cognitive-Behavioral Research and Therapy*, edited by Philip C. Kendall. Vol. 1. New York: Academic Press, 1982. This chapter presents one of the most widely cited explanations of rule governance. The authors were the first to draw attention to the dual set of contingencies surrounding rules. The chapter also examines the role of self-rules and presents a compelling analysis of various cognitive therapies in terms of rule-governed behavior.

Pavlovian Conditioning

Angermeier, Wilhelm F. *The Evolution of Operant Learning and Memory: A Comparative Etho-Psychology.* New York: Karger, 1984. A critical evaluation of instrumental conditioning by a prominent European psychologist. Provides insight into the general European suspicion of reductionist approaches. Includes tables, graphs, a bibliography, and an index.

Babkin, Boris Petrovich. *Pavlov: A Biography.* Chicago: University of Illinois Press, 1949. An excellent primary source that includes otherwise inaccessible personal and professional information on Pavlov. Poorly organized but comprehensive in scope. Illustrated, with notes, a bibliography, and an index.

Brush, F. Robert, and J. Bruce Overmier, eds. *Affect, Conditioning, and Cognition: Essays on the Determinants of Behavior.* Hillsdale, N.J.: Lawrence Erlbaum, 1985. A valuable collection of articles that point out recent directions taken by operant and classical conditioning research. Includes graphs, tables, illustrations, bibliographies, and subject and author indexes.

Davey, G. C., and I. McKenna. "The Effects of Postconditioning Revaluation of CS_1 and UCS Following Pavlovian Second-Order Electrodermal Conditioning in Humans." *Quarterly Journal of Experimental Comparative and Physiological Psychology* 35B (May, 1983): 125-133. A very interesting study dealing with higher-order conditioning with human subjects. Using two different strategies, the study illustrates possible cognitive influences in the phenomenon.

Domjan, Michael, and Barbara Burkhard. *The Principles of Learning and Behavior.* 2d ed. Monterey, Calif.: Brooks/Cole, 1986. A particularly well-written text that manages to pack a stunning amount of important information, including very clear everyday examples, into a relatively small book. Primarily covers animal research but has numerous sections dealing with human applications.

Frolov, Y. P. *Pavlov and His School.* New York: Oxford University Press, 1937. Published just after Pavlov's death, this book contains a touching personal foreword about him. The reader comes to see how Pavlov was influenced by his predecessors, such as René Descartes and Charles Darwin, and how he came to his ideas about higher nervous system activity.

Gantt, W. Horsley. "Russian Physiology and Pathology." In *Soviet Science*, edited by Ruth C. Christman. Washington, D.C.: American Association for the Advancement of Science, 1952. An old but still valuable work by one of Pavlov's American students. Treats the influence of Pavlov's school on Soviet scientific and educational thought. Heavily footnoted.

Graham, Loren R. *Science, Philosophy, and Human Behavior in the Soviet Union*. New York: Columbia University Press, 1987. Offers an excellent treatment of Pavlov's contributions to Russian physiology and psychology. Includes chapters on the nature-nurture debate, biology and human beings, and cybernetics and computers. Notes, an extensive bibliography, and an index.

Gray, Jeffrey A. *Ivan Pavlov*. New York: Viking Press, 1979. An excellent biography. Particularly strong on Pavlov's intellectual background and research methodology; contains diagrams, graphs, and an index.

Hergenhahn, B. R. *An Introduction to Theories of Learning*. 3d ed. Englewood Cliffs, N.J.: Prentice-Hall, 1988. Provides an easily understood overview of the major learning theories of the twentieth century. No prior knowledge of psychology is assumed. The chapter on Pavlov's work is an excellent summary of his theoretical position and experimental work.

Hilgard, Ernest Ropiequet. *Hilgard and Marquis' Conditioning and Learning*. Revised by Gregory A. Kimble. 2d ed. New York: Appleton-Century-Crofts, 1961. Considered one of the classics in the field of learning theory. Excellent discussions of higher-order conditioning and secondary reinforcement in the context of demonstrating an important similarity between Pavlovian and operant conditioning.

Kimble, Gregory A. "Conditioning and Learning." In *Topics in the History of Psychology*, edited by Gregory A. Kimble and Kurt Schlesinger. Vol 1. Hillsdale, N.J.: Lawrence Erlbaum, 1985. An excellent orientation article that surveys Pavlovian and operant conditioning from their origins to the behaviorism of B. F. Skinner. With tables, illustrations, graphs, and a bibliography.

Klein, Stephen B., and Robert R. Mowrer, eds. *Contemporary Learning Theories: Pavlovian Conditioning and the Status of Traditional Learning Theory*. Hillsdale, N.J.: Lawrence Erlbaum, 1989. An extremely useful set of articles indicating applications of Pavlovian conditioning to learning problems. Tables, graphs, bibliographies, and subject and author indexes.

Mackintosh, N. J., and M. M. Cotton. "Conditioned Inhibition from Reinforcement Reduction." In *Information Processing in Animals: Conditioned Inhibition*, edited by Ralph R. Miller and Norman E. Spear. Hillsdale, N.J.: Lawrence Erlbaum, 1985. Many of the chapters in this book are demanding for the nonspecialist, but Mackintosh presents a crucial, alternative but complementary approach to conditioning to that of Rescorla. A full understanding of conditioning requires the effort this chapter demands.

Martin, Irene, and A. B. Levey. "Learning What Will Happen Next: Conditioning, Evaluation, and Cognitive Processes." In *Cognitive Processes and Pavlovian Conditioning in Humans*, edited by Graham Davey. New York: John Wiley & Sons, 1987. An important and provocative article, particularly useful for readers interested in information processing. Martin and Levey's twenty-one-page article traces Pavlov's historical impact on behaviorism and outlines new directions in research. A bibliography is provided.

Pavlov, Ivan Petrovich. *Conditioned Reflexes*. Oxford, England: Oxford University Press, 1927. Surprisingly, the original Pavlov monograph is readable by the patient nonspecialist. Much is of interest here, not the least of which is the quality of Pavlov's scientific dedication, brilliance, and personal humanity. It is revealing to compare Pavlov's philosophical commitment to brain theory with the contemporary emphasis on cognitive process.

_____. *Experimental Psychology and Other Essays*. New York: Philosophical Library, 1957. A useful source, some 650 pages long, that includes Pavlov's autobiography and the first public references to his conditioning theory. Includes notes, but has no index.

_____. *Lectures on Conditioned Reflexes*. Translated by W. Horsley Gantt. New York: International Publishers, 1928. An important historical treatise providing an excellent survey of the many experiments, with the actual data, that Pavlov and his associates conducted

on conditioned reflexes. Photographs and a biographical sketch are
also included.

Rescorla, R. A. "Conditioned Inhibition and Extinction." In *Mechanisms
of Learning and Motivation*, edited by Anthony Dickinson and Robert
A. Boakes. Hillsdale, N.J.: Lawrence Erlbaum, 1979. Although many
of the articles in this collection are demanding for the nonspecialist,
the Rescorla chapter is important enough to warrant the effort. There
is information in this book that is difficult to find elsewhere.

Reynolds, George Stanley. *A Primer of Operant Conditioning*. Rev. ed.
Glenview, Ill.: Scott, Foresman, 1975. This introductory-level book
describes the basic processes and methods of operant psychology,
explaining shaping, reinforcers and punishers, discrimination, and
schedules of reinforcement.

Schlesinger, Kurt. "A Brief Introduction to a History of Psychology." In
Topics in the History of Psychology, edited by Gregory A. Kimble and
Kurt Schlesinger. Vol. 1. Hillsdale, N.J.: Lawrence Erlbaum, 1985.
A well-written article placing Pavlov and the behaviorists in a wide-
ranging historical context; suffers somewhat, however, from a ten-
dency toward hero worship. Contains a bibliography.

Schwartz, Barry, and Dan Reisberg. *Learning and Memory*. New York:
W. W. Norton, 1991. Verbose and occasionally rambling, yet one of the
most down-to-earth but accurate descriptions of difficult material
around. An important benefit of this text is that it relates conditioned
to higher cognitive processes.

Vucinich, Alexander S. *Science in Russian Culture, 1861-1917*. Stanford,
Calif.: Stanford University Press, 1970. Presents Pavlov's school as
part of a wide, uniquely Russian current in experimental biology. With
notes, an extensive bibliography, and an index.

COGNITION

Allman, William F. *Apprentices of Wonder: Inside the Neural Network Revolution*. New York: Bantam Books, 1989. Readable, nontechnical discussion of neural networks that presents their various aspects and features interviews with several key researchers in this field.

Anderson, Barry F., et al. *Concepts in Judgment and Decision Research*. New York: Praeger, 1981. A reference guide to the language of judgment and decision making. Many terms are formally defined and cross-referenced. Examples are generally clear and useful.

Anderson, John R. *Cognitive Psychology and Its Implications*. 3d ed. New York: W. H. Freeman, 1990. This text is a long-standing leader in the field of cognitive psychology. Containing a chapter on problem solving, it is both scholarly and thorough. Much of the emphasis in the problem-solving chapter is on computer applications and their importance in the problem-solving field.

Andriole, Stephen J. *Handbook of Problem Solving*. Princeton, N.J.: Petrocelli Books, 1983. This book is designed to reach people of all disciplines who are interested in strengthening their problem-solving skills. It contains methods and techniques which can be used to solve problems of all kinds.

Ashcraft, Mark H. *Human Memory and Cognition*. Glenview, Ill.: Scott, Foresman, 1989. A cognitive psychology textbook that heavily emphasizes the human information-processing metaphor. It provides good coverage of all the basic areas of cognitive psychology.

Baddeley, Alan D. "The Cognitive Psychology of Everyday Life." *British Journal of Psychology* 72, no. 2 (1981): 257-269. An interesting journal article in which Baddeley describes his research conducted outside the laboratory environment. Considers such practical topics as absentmindedness, alcohol effects, and the effectiveness of saturation advertising. A must for those who question the real-life applicability of cognitive research.

Baron, Jonathan. *Thinking and Deciding*. New York: Cambridge University Press, 1988. An excellent book that emphasizes the factors that keep people from thinking effectively and provides information to help the reader improve thinking and decision-making skills. The book is clearly written, but many of the ideas are complex. The author describes the role that thinking plays in relationship to learning, intelligence, and creativity.

Baron, Robert J. *The Cerebral Computer: An Introduction to the Computational Structure of the Human Brain.* Hillsdale, N.J.: Lawrence Erlbaum, 1987. Compelling argument for viewing the human nervous system as a computer. The first chapters provide a good discussion of the relationship between neurophysiology and computers.

Benjamin, Ludy T., J. Roy Hopkins, and Jack R. Nation. *Psychology.* New York: Macmillan, 1990. In a section on problem solving, describes in detail the stages involved. The authors also list many of the procedures used to find solutions. A discussion on hindrances or obstacles to problem solving follows the section.

Berger, Dale E., Kathy Pezdek, and William P. Banks, eds. *Applications of Cognitive Psychology.* Hillsdale, N.J.: Lawrence Erlbaum, 1987. Five chapters each on three topics: educational applications, teaching of thinking and problem solving, and human-computer interactions. The chapters range in sophistication and accessibility, so this book should appeal to readers of diverse backgrounds. There are helpful name and subject indexes.

Bettman, James R. *An Information Processing Theory of Consumer Choice.* Reading, Mass.: Addison-Wesley, 1979. A scholarly presentation of an integrated theory of consumer choice from an information-processing perspective. Numerous propositions are formulated, with frequent reference to empirical research.

Biederman, Irving. "Perceiving Real World Scenes." *Science* 177 (July 7, 1972): 77-80. This article in a nonspecialized journal introduces Biederman's experiments on the role of context in recognizing patterns, with illustrations of expected and unexpected contexts.

Boden, Margaret A. *Computer Models of the Mind.* New York: Cambridge University Press, 1988. Examines attempts to simulate human cognition on computers and use humans as models for building intelligent machines. The author examines computer models in a wide range of areas, including vision, language, and reasoning.

Boring, Edwin G. *A History of Experimental Psychology*. 2d ed. Englewood Cliffs, N.J.: Prentice-Hall, 1950. This text is the foremost authority on the development and history of psychology up until 1950. Contains detailed accounts of the work of early philosophers and astronomers who contributed to the study of thought, and even contains an entire chapter devoted to the personal equation. This can be a difficult text to read, but it is the authoritative overview of the early history of psychology.

Born, Rainer, ed. *Artificial Intelligence: The Case Against*. New York: St. Martin's Press, 1987. This collection of essays presents the views of a variety of philosophers, psychologists, and computer scientists on the nature and future of artificial intelligence.

Bourne, Lyle E., Jr. *Human Conceptual Behavior*. Boston, Mass.: Allyn & Bacon, 1966. A short book of definite historical importance that summarizes the work on concept formation up to 1966. The writing style is enjoyable, and the book is clearly written, although the ideas it expresses are complex.

Bourne, Lyle E., Jr., Roger L. Dominowski, and Elizabeth Loftus. *Cognitive Processes*. 2d ed. Englewood Cliffs, N.J.: Prentice-Hall, 1986. A thorough textbook on the psychology of thinking. The chapter on concept formation is insightful and clear. The reading level is appropriate for psychologists and nonpsychologists alike.

Bransford, John, and Barry S. Stein. *The IDEAL Problem Solver*. New York: W. H. Freeman, 1984. Chapter 2 presents a simple but powerful approach to problem solving based on the five components that make up the IDEAL approach. This book is easy to read, abundant in examples, clear, and concise. Excellent for anyone who needs help in solving problems.

Brown, Roger. "Language and Thought." In *Social Psychology: The Second Edition*. New York: Free Press, 1986. Sophisticated but readable treatment of the relationship between language and thought. A thorough discussion of the ways thought may constrain language. Contains related chapters on "The Origins of Language" and "Nonverbal Communication and Speech Registers." References provided.

Bruner, Jerome S., Jacqueline J. Goodnow, and George A. Austin. *A Study of Thinking*. New York: John Wiley & Sons, 1956. This book is a classic. The first three chapters provide an insightful introduction to concepts and concept formation in general. The latter chapters describe research and provide a methodological analysis of performance, beginning a tradition in concept formation that has now been discarded as a result of new findings and updated theoretical views. A pioneering book in the area of concept formation.

Caudill, Maureen, and Charles Butler. *Naturally Intelligent Systems.* Cambridge, Mass.: MIT Press, 1990. Provides a thorough introduction to neural networks—the different types and their uses. Among the applications discussed are those for the vectorcardiograph and for the Multiple Neural Network Learning System.

Crick, Francis H. C. "Thinking About the Brain." *Scientific American* 241 (September, 1979): 219-230. Crick, 1962 Nobel laureate in physiology or medicine for his codiscovery (with James D. Watson) of the structure of DNA, discusses knowledge about brain functioning and techniques which are being used to decipher cognitive processes within the brain in this survey article. He devotes considerable attention to neural plasticity and network patterning in the encoding of information.

Dawes, Robyn M. *Rational Choice in an Uncertain World.* San Diego: Harcourt Brace Jovanovich, 1988. A social-psychological perspective on judgment and decision processes. Highly interesting content and style for all audiences. Includes thoughtful discussions of controversial applications. Nontechnical and concise. Chapters can be read individually or out of order.

Downs, Roger M., and David Stea, eds. *Image and Environment: Cognitive Mapping and Spatial Behavior.* Chicago: Aldine, 1973. A landmark book in environmental psychology. Drawing on Kenneth Boulding's 1956 *The Image: Knowledge in Life and Society* (the image refers to a person's known or believed universe), these researchers focus on that part of the image called a "cognitive map," defined as an internal representation of the spatial organization of the external world. Provides the reader with a valuable backdrop for the field's extensive work on cognitive maps.

D'Zurilla, Thomas J., and Arthur M. Nezu. "Social Problem-Solving in Adults." In *Advances in Cognitive-Behavioral Research and Therapy*, edited by Philip C. Kendall. Vol. 1. New York: Academic Press, 1982. An excellent summary of problem-solving therapy. As indicated by its title, the Kendall book in which this article appears also contains other informative articles dealing with cognitive behavior therapy.

Eccles, John C., and Daniel N. Robinson. "Language, Thought, and Brain." In *The Wonder of Being Human*. New York: Free Press, 1984. Relatively sophisticated discussion of the relationship among language, thinking, and neurophysiology from philosophical, psychological, and physiological standpoints. Places the development of language in an evolutionary perspective. Contains suggestions for additional reading.

Evans, Jonathan St. B. T. *Bias in Human Reasoning: Causes and Consequences*. Hillsdale, N.J.: Lawrence Erlbaum, 1989. Almost everyone interested in inferential thought should find this short book (slightly more than a hundred pages) a pleasure to read. The book is in an extended essay form. Classifies the types of bias and puts them in a general theoretical framework, while considering practical applications. Suggestions, based on research, are provided to help the reasoner avoid bias as much as possible. There are also suggestions for educators.

_____. *The Psychology of Deductive Reasoning*. Boston: Routledge & Kegan Paul, 1982. The author reviews the available research in the area. He has published numerous journal articles on reasoning and is one of the top experts in the area of the psychology of reasoning. It is a thorough book, and the sections that address especially theoretical concerns can be skimmed over, if desired.

_____, ed. *Thinking and Reasoning: Psychological Approaches*. Boston: Routledge & Kegan Paul, 1983. Contains eight chapters by a variety of experts in the area of inference. The chapters provide in-depth material on numerous aspects of inference, such as key logical rules, the influence of realistic content on reasoning, and thinking in general as a skill that involves the ability to draw inferences.

Eysenck, Michael W. *A Handbook of Cognitive Psychology*. London: Lawrence Erlbaum, 1984. A textbook that covers the full range of topics in cognitive psychology. Provides a readable introduction to the entire area of thinking, of which concept formation is one part. The section on categorization provides an overall perspective and succinctly summarizes the research. The chapter on problem solving and reasoning is particularly good.

Fenwick, Ian, and John A. Quelch, eds. *Consumer Behavior for Marketing Managers*. Boston: Allyn & Bacon, 1984. Reviews of the consumer-behavior research literature on issues concerning current applications. Of special interest is chapter 3, on the consumer decision-making process. Topics covered are the information overload controversy, low-involvement consumer information processing, and the view that consumer behavior involves the making of decisions.

Flanagan, Owen J., Jr. *The Science of the Mind.* Cambridge, Mass.: MIT Press, 1991. The chapter "Cognitive Psychology and Artificial Intelligence" is a readable introduction to the central philosophical issues addressed by cognitive psychology. Discusses mental representation in terms of propositions; language per se is not addressed in detail. The ambitions and criticisms of artificial intelligence are reviewed. Consciousness is discussed in a separate chapter.

Gardner, Howard. *The Mind's New Science: A History of the Cognitive Revolution.* New York: Basic Books, 1985. An excellent review of the central issues, research, and criticisms of cognitive science. Parts 1 and 2 provide a historical account of cognitive science, including contributions from psychology, artificial intelligence, linguistics, anthropology, and neuroscience. Mental imagery and natural concepts are included in part 3.

George, F. H. *Problem Solving.* London: Duckworth, 1980. Attempts to deal with problem solving in a realistic manner and tries to help people in a variety of settings who are faced with the need for plans and answers to problems. Emphasizes that whatever the problem, the would-be solver needs to go through the same sort of analysis. Meant as an introductory text.

Glass, A. L., and K. J. Holyoak. *Cognition.* 2d ed. New York: Random House, 1986. A well-written textbook covering the broad range of cognitive psychology, including problem solving. Scholarly in approach yet very readable; the examples used are superb.

Halpern, Diane F. *Thought and Knowledge: An Introduction to Critical Thinking.* 2d ed. Hillsdale, N.J.: Lawrence Erlbaum, 1989. Presents a brief overview of memory and language, then presents data and theory on performance with different types of deductive arguments, analyzing arguments, fallacies, reasoning with probabilities, and hypothesis testing. The author provides numerous examples and exercises, and the text can be understood by high school or college students.

Hanson, Stephen J., and David J. Burr. "What Connectionist Models Learn: Learning and Representation in Connectionist Networks." *Be-*

havioral and Brain Sciences 13, no. 3 (1990): 471-518. The first several pages provide good background on cognitive psychology's use of computer analogues of the mind and their relationship to neural networks.

Haugeland, John. *Artificial Intelligence: The Very Idea.* Cambridge, Mass.: MIT Press, 1985. A very readable accounting of the nature of formal systems and some of the central issues and definitions of artificial intelligence.

Hayes, John R. *The Complete Problem Solver.* 2d ed. Hillsdale, N.J.: Lawrence Erlbaum, 1989. Attempts to teach general problem-solving skills. This book is written for the general public and offers help to anyone interested in solving problems.

Holland, John H., et al. *Induction: Processes of Inference, Learning, and Discovery.* Cambridge, Mass.: MIT Press, 1986. Presents a broad cross-disciplinary account of induction and examines the role of inferential rules in induction, people's mental models of the world, concept formation, problem solving, and the role of induction in discovery. The authors provide an extensive bibliography of scholarly research on induction.

Huffman, Karen, et al. *Psychology in Action.* New York: John Wiley & Sons, 1991. In a section on problem solving, the authors describe the stages as well as the barriers in problem solving. Examples are given; key words are explained. A good source for high school seniors and college freshmen.

Hunt, Earl B. *Concept Learning: An Information Processing Problem.* New York: John Wiley & Sons, 1962. Another historically relevant book that emphasizes the mathematical and probabilistic process of concept acquisition. Hunt's view of concept formation provided a theoretical breakthrough at the time. A substantial section of the book discusses concept acquisition as it relates to the area of artificial intelligence, which was a very new field of inquiry when the book was written.

Hunt, Morton M. *The Universe Within.* New York: Simon & Schuster, 1982. A very readable introduction to cognitive science; good for the beginning student. Chapter 3 discusses how information is stored in memory, chapter 5 discusses concepts, and chapter 9 discusses artificial intelligence.

Johnson-Laird, Philip Nicholas. *Mental Models*. Cambridge, Mass.: Harvard University Press, 1983. Presents an extensive review of data and theory on syllogistic reasoning. The author presents a unified theory of the mind based on recursive procedures, propositional representations, and mental models. The text is very thorough and detailed, and many readers may find it daunting.

Kahneman, Daniel, Paul Slovic, and Amos Tversky, eds. *Judgment Under Uncertainty: Heuristics and Biases*. New York: Cambridge University Press, 1982. Presents a collection of many of the important papers on heuristics, including several papers each on representativeness, availability, causality and attribution, and corrective procedures. Many of the papers are thorough and present detailed information on experiments or theory.

Kalat, J. W. *Introduction to Psychology*. 2d ed. Belmont, Calif.: Wadsworth, 1990. This general psychology textbook presents an excellent introduction to problem solving in the cognition chapter, as well as related topics in other chapters (such as learning, memory, and intelligence). This text is easy to read, with good examples. Includes a comprehensive reference section if the reader desires more information.

Lachman, Roy, Janet L. Lachman, and Earl C. Butterfield. *Cognitive Psychology and Information Processing: An Introduction*. Hillsdale, N.J.: Lawrence Erlbaum, 1979. One of the earliest texts that adequately captures the coming importance and influence of cognitive psychology. There are outstanding chapters that trace the influences of other disciplines and traditions on what is now known as cognitive psychology. Topic areas within the field are discussed as well.

Lilly, John C. *Communication Between Man and Dolphin: The Possibilities of Talking with Other Species*. New York: Crown, 1978. Lilly, a controversial neurophysiologist and dolphin researcher, presents compelling evidence supporting the view that dolphins and other cetaceans may be more intelligent than humans. He bases his arguments upon the dolphin's larger cerebral cortex, dolphin behavior, and an elaborate dolphin communication system. Chapter 16, "The Possible Existence of Non-Human Languages," explores humans' naïveté in interpreting the behaviors of other creatures.

McClelland, J. L., and D. E. Rumelhart, eds. *Parallel Distributed Processing: Explorations in the Microstructure of Cognition*. Vol. 2.

Cambridge, Mass.: MIT Press, 1986. Provides examples of PDP models of schemata, speech perception, and reading, and discusses other potential applications of the PDP approach. The chapters are long and detailed, and readers may find the text daunting.

Marr, David. *Vision.* New York: W. H. Freeman, 1982. Presents Marr's philosophical approach to artificial intelligence and discusses his programs for the perception of surfaces. The book is well illustrated, but once Marr finishes his discussion of the philosophical approach, some readers may get lost in the mathematics and technicalities of his ideas.

Matlin, Margaret W. *Cognition.* 2d ed. New York: Holt, Rinehart and Winston, 1989. One of the most accessible general cognitive textbooks on the market. A clear writing style, along with phonetic tips to help the reader pronounce difficult words, assists the novice in understanding complex cognitive principles. Includes a number of experiments that the reader can perform to help grasp concepts.

Mayer, R. E. *Thinking, Problem Solving, and Cognition.* New York: W. H. Freeman, 1983. A book primarily dedicated to the topic of problem solving. The format of the text is interesting and creative, covering the historical perspective of problem solving, basic thinking tasks, an information-processing analysis, and implications and applications.

Neisser, Ulric. "From Direct Perception to Conceptual Structure." In *Concepts and Conceptual Development: Ecological and Intellectual Factors in Categorization.* Cambridge, England: Cambridge University Press, 1987. Contains a number of sophisticated articles on concepts, following the Rosch model. This article, by the "father" of cognitive psychology, describes the development of concepts in children from the ecological perspective, arguing for the importance of the environment in specifying the concepts that a person develops.

Nickerson, Raymond S. *Reflections on Reasoning.* Hillsdale, N.J.: Lawrence Erlbaum, 1986. This brief book is an adaptation of a report that the author prepared under a project sponsored by the National Institute of Education. It clearly describes reasoning and factors that can impede reasoning, and it provides practical chapters on how to improve one's own reasoning ability and how to use reasoning to win disputes of all kinds.

Palmer, Frank Robert. "The Non-Linguistic Context." In *Semantics: A New Outline.* London: Cambridge University Press, 1976. Discussions of behaviorism and the linguistic relativity hypothesis from the perspective of a specialist in linguistics. Relatively sophisticated treatment. A useful complement to the psychological perspectives of Anderson, Brown, and Gardner.

Penrose, Roger. *The Emperor's New Mind: Concerning Computers, Minds, and the Laws of Physics.* New York: Oxford University Press, 1989. Presents a somewhat different slant on the relationship between the brain and cognition, and the human mind as a computer; the author is a physicist.

Pylyshyn, Z. W. *Computation and Cognition.* Cambridge, Mass.: MIT Press, 1984. Pylyshyn presents the case that cognition is a form of computation and that human mental representations can be encoded in the same way that computer representations are encoded. Explains how a computational view can provide a foundation and framework for both cognitive psychology and artificial intelligence.

Rich, Elaine, and Kevin Knight. *Artificial Intelligence.* 2d ed. New York: McGraw-Hill, 1991. In this detailed introduction to the science of artificial intelligence, Rich and Knight describe models of intelligent behavior in humans and other species. They discuss neural networks and their functioning, logic, game playing, knowledge representation, understanding, and semantic analysis in a very thought-provoking work. Computer program simulations of artificial intelligence also are presented.

Rosch, Eleanor H. "Classification of Real-World Objects: Origins and Representation in Cognition." In *Thinking: Readings in Cognitive Science,* edited by P. N. Johnson-Laird and P. C. Wason. Cambridge, England: Cambridge University Press, 1975. The chapter by Eleanor Rosch is important reading; she was one of the first people to break away from research using artificial concepts and begin to explore natural ones. The chapter is quite understandable.

Russo, J. Edward, and Paul J. H. Shoemaker. *Decision Traps.* New York: Doubleday, 1989. Superb and colorful coverage of cognitive processes in decision making. Balance of research and applications. Examples are well-chosen, memorable illustrations of major concepts. Particularly relevant to the business person but will appeal to all.

Sacks, Oliver W. *The Man Who Mistook His Wife for a Hat and Other Clinical Tales.* New York: Perennial Library, 1987. This is a fascinating look behind neurological deficits that reveals the humanistic side of medicine. Sacks reviews not only the symptoms of the patients but also their adaptations to their problems.

Schank, Roger C. *The Cognitive Computer*. Reading, Mass.: Addison-Wesley, 1984. A readable introduction to the issues, promises, and problems of artificial intelligence. Describes the difficulties involved in writing programs that enable computers to understand natural language.

Schneider, Walter. "Connectionism: Is It a Paradigm Shift for Psychology?" *Behavior, Research Methods, Instruments, and Computers* 19, no. 2 (1987): 73-83. Schneider's presidential address to the Psychonomic Society. Presents a good introduction to neural networks and the impact they can expect to have on cognitive psychology.

Searle, John R. *Minds, Brains, and Science*. Cambridge, Mass.: Harvard University Press, 1984. In a very readable style, Searle summarizes his argument that computers do not possess an understanding of semantics, addresses the larger mind-body problem, and discusses the implications of his views for the social and cognitive sciences.

Slovic, Paul, Sarah Lichtenstein, and Baruch Fischhoff. "Decision Making." In *Steven's Handbook of Experimental Psychology*, edited by Richard C. Atkinson et al. 2d ed. New York: John Wiley & Sons, 1988. A comprehensive review of the field of decision making. Traces the origins of subjective expected utility theory as well as other decision theories. Brief and well-written explanations of different perspectives in the field. Ties decision making to other areas of experimental psychology.

Solso, Robert L. *Cognitive Psychology*. 3d ed. Boston: Allyn & Bacon, 1991. Various schemes of pattern recognition are described simply and powerfully. The chapter on pattern recognition reviews all the major theories, with extensive illustrations.

Sternberg, Robert J., and Edward E. Smith, eds. *The Psychology of Human Thought*. New York: Cambridge University Press, 1988. Contains chapters on concepts and thought, induction, understanding causality, deduction, judgment, and decision making. Each chapter is written by an expert on the topic and contains an extensive bibliography.

Stillings, Neil A., et al. *Cognitive Science: An Introduction*. Cambridge, Mass.: MIT Press, 1987. A standard textbook on cognitive psychology, with emphasis on neurophysiology. Also features one of the first presentations on neural networks and cognition to appear in a textbook.

Tversky, Amos, and Daniel Kahneman. "Judgment Under Uncertainty: Heuristics and Biases." *Science* 185 (1974): 1124-1131. A classic paper written for the general scientific and lay communities. The authors illustrate various judgment heuristics in thought-provoking fashion. This article is not intended to be a balanced view of human "rationality"; it emphasizes the cognitive limitations of human decision makers.

Weizenbaum, Joseph. *Computer Power and Human Reason.* New York: W. H. Freeman, 1976. The creator of the ELIZA program argues that some aspects of the human mind cannot be understood in information-processing (computational) terms. Weizenbaum also claims that there are many tasks for which computers should not be used, particularly those requiring human reason, wisdom, or morality. Written in an easy and engaging style.

Wertheimer, Max. *Productive Thinking.* Chicago: University of Chicago Press, 1982. Classic account of Max Wertheimer's original studies and observations of problem solving. Beautifully written, this book is easily read by college or high school students and contains accounts of Gestalt approaches to problems ranging from simple geometry to Einstein's development of the theory of relativity.

Wilkie, William L. *Consumer Behavior.* New York: John Wiley & Sons, 1986. A textbook stressing concepts, findings, and applications in the broad area of consumer psychology. Balanced and informative treatment of research, theory, and practice. Good coverage of the cognitive aspects of consumer behavior, including learning, information processing, perception, and decision making.

Yates, J. Frank. *Judgment and Decision Making.* Englewood Cliffs, N.J.: Prentice-Hall, 1990. A careful and detailed explanation of procedures for examining human judgment and decision making. Includes numerous examples and thoughtful discussion, with special appeal to students. The casual reader will find many graphs to be too technical. Extensive references to original journal articles.

CONSCIOUSNESS

States, Functions, and Levels

Alexander, Charles N., and Ellen J. Langer, eds. *Higher Stages of Human Development: Perspectives on Adult Growth.* New York: Oxford University Press, 1990. Explores major dimensions of adult growth, including cognitive and moral development, and development of consciousness, with a thorough discussion of Maharishi Mahesh Yogi's Vedic psychology of human development.

Boff, Kenneth R., Lloyd Kaufman, and James P. Thomas, eds. *Handbook of Perception and Human Performance.* 2 vols. New York: John Wiley & Sons, 1986. Includes three chapters relevant to attention: chapter 2, on information processing; chapter 26, on auditory information processing; and chapter 43, on vigilance.

Bowers, Kenneth S. *Hypnosis for the Seriously Curious.* Monterey, Calif.: Brooks/Cole, 1976. Explores the full range of hypnotic theories and phenomena, as well as practical applications of hypnosis research. Does a thorough job of exploring the controversy surrounding the true nature of hypnosis, providing convincing empirical support for the trance theory. Bowers has provided the most comprehensible treatment of hypnosis for high school and college students.

Dennett, Daniel C. *Consciousness Explained.* Boston: Little, Brown, 1991. Although one might question whether it fulfills its ambitious title, this is a fascinating book by one of the leading philosophers of mind of our time. Dennett argues that consciousness is a process of ongoing neural activity, not the end product of that activity. Written in an engaging fashion but at a level primarily suitable for advanced students.

Eccles, John Carew, and Daniel N. Robinson. *The Wonder of Being Human.* New York: Free Press, 1984. An interesting short book that explains the connection between language, thought, and the brain. Discusses processes that range from unconscious to conscious levels. Although the book is somewhat technical, introductory psychology students will find it interesting and helpful.

Flanagan, Owen J., Jr. "Naturalizing the Mind: The Philosophical Psychology of William James." In *The Science of the Mind.* Cambridge, Mass.: MIT Press, 1984. A readable introduction, written by a philosopher, to the central philosophical and psychological issues of consciousness. Discusses criteria and functions for conscious mental life. A good introduction to reading William James. Further information relevant to consciousness may be found in the chapter in the same volume entitled "Cognitive Psychology and Artificial Intelligence: Philosophical Assumptions and Implications."

Gackenbach, Jayne, Harry Hunt, and Charles N. Alexander, eds. *Higher States of Consciousness: Theoretical and Experimental Perspectives.* New York: Plenum Press, 1992. This collection of original essays by leading researchers on higher states of consciousness and meditation spans a variety of theoretical perspectives.

Gazzaniga, Michael S. *The Social Brain.* New York: Basic Books, 1985. A readable, interesting account of Gazaniga's development as a physiological psychologist. Written for a general audience. Describes research on the brain, including research with split-brain patients. Discusses Gazzaniga's own speculative theory about the modular organization of the mind, which argues for the central role of language in consciousness.

Hilgard, Ernest Ropiequet. *Divided Consciousness: Multiple Controls in Human Thought and Action.* New York: Wiley-Interscience, 1977. A discussion of consciousness by one of the most respected experimental psychologists. Included are discussions on the hidden observer phenomenon in hypnosis and on other dissociation phenomena such as multiple personality, amnesia, and fugue states.

Hilgard, Ernest Ropiequet, and Josephine Rohrs Hilgard. *Hypnosis in the Relief of Pain.* Rev. ed. Los Altos, Calif.: William Kaufmann, 1983. Provides a comprehensive review of the Hilgards' own research on hypnotic anesthesia and analgesia, as well as the research of others. Examines the physiological and psychological bases of pain, and explores laboratory and clinical methods of controlling pain with hypnosis. Highly recommended for college students and advanced high school students.

Hilgard, Josephine Rohrs. *Personality and Hypnosis: A Study of Imaginative Involvement.* 2d ed. Chicago: University of Chicago Press,

1979. Josephine Hilgard reviews her own extensive research on the role of imaginative involvement in hypnotic susceptibility and in the personality development of both hypnotizable and nonhypnotizable people. Written in nontechnical language; recommended for junior high, high school, and college students, as well as interested adults.

Jacobson, Edmund. *You Must Relax.* 4th ed. New York: McGraw-Hill, 1957. First published in 1934, this book presents Jacobson's views on the need for relaxation and the technique of progressive relaxation which he developed.

James, William. "Consciousness." In *Psychology: The Briefer Course.* 1892. Reprint. New York: Harper & Row, 1961. Describes the nature and functions of consciousness from the perspective of the historically important functionalist school of psychology. Significant historically, but also relevant to contemporary psychology. Delightfully written for a relatively sophisticated audience. A fuller treatment of the topic of consciousness may be found in James's *The Principles of Psychology* (1890).

Jaynes, Julian. *The Origins of Consciousness in the Breakdown of the Bicameral Mind.* Harmondsworth, Middlesex, England: Pelican Books, 1976. A fascinating but highly speculative account of the origins of consciousness; not widely accepted by psychologists. Initial chapters provide a good review of the nature and functions of consciousness. Later chapters synthesize information from anthropology, history, and physiological and abnormal psychology into Jaynes's own unique theory.

Kahneman, Daniel. *Attention and Effort.* Englewood Cliffs, N.J.: Prentice-Hall, 1973. This book first made the resource notion of attention widely popular among psychologists. It details many experiments that lend support to that view. Although written for an audience of psychologists, it is readable by a wider audience and provides the contextual background in which the ideas of automaticity were developed.

Klein, David B. "The Functions of Consciousness." In The Concept of Consciousness: A Survey. Lincoln: University of Nebraska Press, 1884. A thorough and readable account of consciousness, excellent for getting an overview on the topic. The cited chapter provides an overview of the functions of consciousness, as considered historically in psychology, and discusses contemporary biological and psychological evidence. Written for a college audience.

Langer, Ellen J. *Mindfulness*. Reading, Mass.: Addison-Wesley, 1990. Reviews research showing the lack of consciousness, termed "mindlessness," in everyday life and argues for the importance of becoming more conscious ("mindful") for a healthy and adaptive life. Offers suggestions on how to increase mindfulness. Written for a general audience. A somewhat speculative presentation of the implications of Langer's social psychological research.

Lichstein, Kenneth L. *Clinical Relaxation Strategies*. New York: John Wiley & Sons, 1988. Contains an extensive review and bibliography of relaxation techniques. In his commentary, Lichstein tends to discount any differences in effects that may exist among different forms of practice.

Mahesh Yogi, Maharishi. *On the Bhagavad-Gita: A New Translation and Commentary*. New York: Penguin Books, 1986. This classic text from the Vedic literature describes the steps of growth of higher states of consciousness. The accompanying commentary clarifies many misunderstandings about meditation and discusses the relevance of meditation to modern life.

Murphy, Michael, and Steven Donovan. *The Physical and Psychological Effects of Meditation*. San Rafael, Calif.: Esalen Institute, 1988. A review of research on a variety of meditation techniques, with a comprehensive bibliography covering the years from 1931 to 1988.

Ornstein, Robert Evan, ed. *The Nature of Human Consciousness*. New York: Viking Press, 1973. A scholarly and useful book that presents original writings by some of the pioneer thinkers in levels of consciousness. Covers a wide range of topics from understanding humans to altered states of consciousness. The writing is technical and geared for a fairly advanced college audience.

_____. *The Psychology of Consciousness*. 2d rev. ed. New York: Penguin Books, 1986. This is considered a classic text on altered states of consciousness. It provides in-depth discussions of the psychology of meditation and the relationship of altered states to hemispheric differences in the brain.

Parasuraman, R., and D. R. Davies, eds. *Varieties of Attention*. Orlando, Fla.: Academic Press, 1984. Includes articles by a variety of contributors. Many topics are covered, such as search, vigilance, levels of processing, and applications to industrial settings.

Pelletier, Kenneth R. *Toward a Science of Consciousness.* New York: Delacorte, 1978. Covers theories of consciousness from metaphysical, scientific, and self-help perspectives. Appropriate for high school or college students, or a general audience. Although some of the chapters are not quite mainstream, the overall effect is successful.

Posner, Michael I., and O. S. M. Marin, eds. *Attention and Performance XI.* Hillsdale, N.J.: Lawrence Erlbaum, 1985. A collection of thirty-five chapters from a conference on attention, covering topics such as the biological aspects of attention, covert attention, and divided attention.

Schneider, Walter. "Training High-Performance Skills: Fallacies and Guidelines." *Human Factors* 27 (1985): 285-300. This paper provides an excellent overview of what is known about the practical application of knowledge concerning automaticity to the training of high-level skills. The emphasis is on practice, rather than theory; the discussion is aimed at correcting some common errors made in training skilled personnel, including a tendency to ignore drill even when it is essential to learning.

Shapiro, Deane H., Jr., and Roger N. Walsh, eds. *Meditation: Classic and Contemporary Perspectives.* New York: Aldine, 1984. An extensive collection of descriptive, research, and commentary papers on various types of meditation practiced in the West.

Sheehan, Peter W., and Kevin M. McConkey. *Hypnosis and Experience: The Exploration of Phenomena and Process.* Hillsdale, N.J.: Lawrence Erlbaum, 1982. An advanced treatise on hypnosis, focusing on the experiential analysis of hypnotic phenomena, such as ideomotor responses, age regression, hypnotic dreams and hallucinations, and posthypnotic amnesia. Because of its technical nature, recommended only for serious, advanced students.

Smith, Barry D., and Harold J. Vetter. *Theories of Personality.* 2d ed. Englewood Cliffs, N.J.: Prentice-Hall, 1990. Although this is a college-level textbook, the writing is straightforward and easy to understand. Presents perhaps the best explanation of Sigmund Freud's iceberg analogy and his views of the connection between personality structures and levels of consciousness. High school and college students will find the book interesting.

Smyth, Mary M., et al. *Cognition in Action.* Hillsdale, N.J.: Lawrence Erlbaum, 1987. This very readable presentation of modern cognitive psychology includes a discussion of how automaticity comes about through training and how automaticity is demonstrated experimentally. A number of interesting experiments on dual-task performance are discussed. One of the more readable accounts of automaticity.

Solso, Robert L. *Cognitive Psychology.* 2d ed. Boston: Allyn & Bacon, 1988. Discusses automaticity within the context of resource models of attention. Solso includes several interesting descriptions of automaticity acting in everyday life.

Spanos, Nicholas P., and John F. Chaves, eds. *Hypnosis: The Cognitive-Behavioral Approach.* Buffalo, N.Y.: Prometheus Books, 1989. An extremely thorough review of the cognitive-behavioral approach, which includes the social learning theory of hypnosis. Highly technical; intended to be a review text for professional hypnosis researchers. It may be of some value, however, to serious, advanced college students.

Tart, Charles T. *States of Consciousness.* El Cerrito, Calif.: Psychological Processes, 1983. Tart presents his proposals for "state specific" sciences and develops what he calls the systems approach to the study of states of consciousness. Parts of this book are somewhat technical, but most of it is accessible to the general reader.

Treisman, Anne. "Features and Objects in Visual Processing." *Scientific American* 225 (November, 1971): 114B-125. Treisman provides a clear summary of feature integration theory and includes figures producing readily observable attention effects.

Wallace, Benjamin. *Applied Hypnosis: An Overview.* Chicago: Nelson-Hall, 1979. A nontechnical, introductory book focusing on applications of hypnosis, but not limited exclusively to practical concerns. Highly recommended as a brief overview of hypnosis for junior high and high school students, as well as interested adults.

Wallace, Benjamin, and Leslie E. Fisher. *Consciousness and Behavior.* 3d ed. Boston: Allyn & Bacon, 1991. A general textbook on consciousness containing an excellent, updated chapter on hypnosis. The chapter reviews theories and the history of hypnosis, describes ways of assessing hypnotic susceptibility, reviews research on basic hypnotic phenomena, and discusses practical applications of hypnosis. Highly recommended for high school and college students, as well as interested adults.

Wallace, R. Keith. *The Neurophysiology of Enlightenment.* Fairfield, Iowa: MIU Neuroscience Press, 1986. Presents in nontechnical language the modern scientific exploration of the development of consciousness and enlightenment in persons practicing TM.

Wickens, Christopher D. *Engineering Psychology and Human Performance.* Columbus, Ohio: Charles E. Merrill, 1984. Wickens provides a general survey of engineering psychology, or the application of knowledge from experimental psychology to engineering objects and systems for human use. Treats attention at length, as well as issues of automatic and controlled processing and their implications for the design of systems for human use.

Wolman, Benjamin B., and Montague Ullman, eds. *Handbook of States of Consciousness.* New York: Van Nostrand Reinhold, 1986. This is an excellent sourcebook on psychological theory and research on altered states of consciousness. Discusses trance states, lucid dreams, ultradian rhythms, and many other topics.

Sleep and Dreams

Ahlgren, Andrew, and Franz Halberg. *Cycles of Nature: An Introduction to Biological Rhythms.* Washington, D.C.: National Science Teachers Association, 1990. An easy-to-read introduction to biological rhythms written expressly for the high school student. Contains simple experiments, some of which would make ideal science-fair projects or classroom demonstrations. Very nicely illustrated and well written, this booklet covers most of the fundamental characteristics of circadian rhythms. Highly recommended to students and teachers alike.

Anch, A. Michael, C. P. Browman, M. M. Mitler, and James K. Walsh. *Sleep: A Scientific Perspective.* Englewood Cliffs, N.J.: Prentice-Hall, 1988. The authors cover the entire spectrum of sleep study in this work, integrating the history of sleep studies with more recent knowledge of the field. The book addresses physiological as well as psychological issues and gives sufficient definitions, information, and references for those who wish to study sleep in a more in-depth manner.

Borbely, Alexander. *Secrets of Sleep.* New York: Basic Books, 1986. An excellent book for the student or general reader that thoroughly covers such topics as sleep, sleep deprivation, why sleep is necessary, and sleep as a biological rhythm.

Boss, Medard. *I Dreamt Last Night...* New York: Gardner Press, 1977. Boss forcefully argues for his phenomenological approach to understanding dreams. He describes dreaming as a mode of existing that can be understood as such directly on its own terms, without the need to interpret it symbolically. He clearly demonstrates that position by his analysis of many dreams.

Cohen, David B. *Sleep and Dreaming: Origins, Nature, and Functions.* New York: Pergamon Press, 1979. A comprehensive review of sleep and dreaming research, including sleep stages, functions, development, and disorders. Also includes findings on sex differences in the effects of REM sleep deprivation. Somewhat technical; recommended for advanced college students only.

Coleman, Richard M. *Wide Awake at 3:00 A.M.: By Choice or by Chance?* New York: W. H. Freeman, 1990. A popular account of the applications of circadian rhythms to human physiology and psychology, written by a former director of the Stanford University Sleep Disorders Clinic. Coleman writes for the layperson and covers a variety of topics, including shift work, jet lag, sleep, and dreams. The appendix includes a questionnaire that helps readers determine whether thay are owls or larks. The book explains terms as they are presented and has a glossary.

Craig, P. Erik. "Dreaming, Reality, and Allusion: An Existential-Phenomenological Inquiry." In *Advances in Qualitative Psychology*, edited by Florence Van Zuuren, Frederick J. Wertz, and Bep Mook. Berwyn, Pa.: Swets North American, 1987. Craig provides a masterfully stated argument for the appreciation of the real experience of the dreamer. His careful example also shows the relevance of dreaming to waking life.

Delaney, Gayle. *Living Your Dreams.* New York: Harper & Row, 1979. Delaney has developed and popularized a means of dream interpretation for personal growth, in which dreams are used as sources of insight for solving personal life problems. This book offers an easily accessible manual for applying her approach.

Dement, William C. *Some Must Watch While Some Must Sleep.* San Francisco: San Francisco Book Company, 1976. William Dement, founder of the sleep disorders clinic at Stanford University, provides a nontechnical, personal report of sleep stages, dreams, and sleep disorders. Immensely readable and often humorous. Highly recommended for junior high school, high school, and college students, as well as other interested adults.

Freud, Sigmund. *The Interpretation of Dreams*. Translated by James Strachey. New York: Avon Books, 1965. This challenging book is an English translation of Freud's pioneering study of dreams, which was first published in German in 1900. It revolutionized psychological thought and contains, by Freud's own acknowledgement, his most valuable discoveries.

Halaris, Angelos. *Chronobiology and Psychiatric Disorders*. New York: Elsevier, 1987. A technical review of the diagnosis and treatment of depression and their relationship to circadian rhythms. Not recommended for light reading, but helpful for details when specific information is required. Many of the experts surveyed here present their theoretical models for depression in terms of altered brain chemistry of neurotransmitters.

Hall, Calvin Springer, and Robert L. Van de Castle. *The Content Analysis of Dreams*. New York: Appleton-Century-Crofts, 1966. An extremely comprehensive collection of dreams. It features more than a thousand, collected from college students and sorted for the statistical frequency of contents such as setting, character traits, mood, and relationships.

Hillman, James. *The Dream and the Underworld*. New York; Harper & Row, 1979. The most prominent of the neo-Jungians, Hillman views the dream as an experience of the underworld of traditional mythology.

Hobson, J. Allan. *The Dreaming Brain*. New York: Basic Books, 1988. This highly readable book is an excellent general introduction to the study of dreams from a historical and scientific point of view, with special emphasis on Hobson's own area of study, the biological understanding of the dreaming brain.

_____. *Sleep*. New York: Scientific American Library, 1989. A broad and interdisciplinary view of sleep research, combining knowledge drawn from neurology, psychology, and animal behavior studies. The nontechnical language and lavish illustrations are two major advantages of this book. Highly recommended for high school and college students.

Issa, Faiq G., Paul M. Surrat, and John E. Remmers, eds. *Sleep and Respiration*. New York: John Wiley & Sons, 1990. A compilation of articles and discussions by many of the leading scientists of the field. Especially helpful are the sections after each chapter in which the topic is discussed among specialists. Somewhat advanced, but a basic knowledge of sleep disorders is sufficient for understanding most of the material in this book.

Jung, Carl. *Dreams*. Translated by R. F. C. Hull. Princeton, N.J.: Princeton University Press, 1974. This book assembles some of Jung's basic writings on dreams published earlier (from volumes 4, 8, 12, and 16 in his collected works). It offers a sampling of his views on the relation of dreams and psychoanalysis, psychic energy, alchemy, and the practical use of dream symbols.

Kryger, Meir H., Thomas Roth, and William C. Dement, eds. *Principles and Practice of Sleep Medicine*. Philadelphia: W. B. Saunders, 1989. A very comprehensive work on the subject of sleep disorders. The entire spectrum of sleep and its disorders is covered, with extensive material on treatment practices. A large glossary and numerous references make this book an ideal tool.

LaBerge, Stephen. *Lucid Dreaming*. Los Angeles: J. P. Tarcher, 1985. By experimentally demonstrating lucid dreaming (The awareness, while dreaming, that one is dreaming), LaBerge's research has opened a new wave of theory, research, and applications.

Mahrer, Alvin. *Dream Work in Psychotherapy and Self-Change*. New York: W. W. Norton, 1989. This book is directed both to psychotherapists and laypersons. To the first group, it offers a new experiential approach to dream work. To the second, it offers a complete instructional guide to using dreams to promote self-change.

Mendelson, W. B. *Human Sleep: Research and Clinical Care*. New York: Plenum Medical Book Company, 1987. Provides an overview of research and treatment practices for a number of sleep disorders. Recommended for the college student, but may be understood by those having a basic knowledge of sleep.

Minors, D. S., and J. M. Waterhouse. *Circadian Rhythms and the Human*. Boston: John Wright, 1981. A comprehensive textbook that reviews hundreds of research reports to give an outstanding overview of the field. Written for the college level and above. A classic.

Moore-Ede, Martin C., Frank M. Sulzman, and Charles A. Fuller. *The Clocks That Time Us*. Cambridge, Mass.: Harvard University Press, 1982. A general textbook on circadian rhythms that includes information on animals as well as humans. Some sections are too theoretical for all but the most dedicated of readers. Well illustrated, with an excellent list of references.

Nicholson, Anthony N., and John Marks. *Insomnia: A Guide for Medical Practitioners*. Boston: MTP Press, 1983. Though the title may sound imposing to those who are new to the study of insomnia, this book is quite easily understood by those with a limited knowledge of sleep disorders. The entire work is devoted to insomnia, and it provides information on diagnosis and treatment of various types.

Siffre, Michel. *Beyond Time*. New York: McGraw-Hill, 1964. An enthralling account of the adventures of a cave explorer who stays without a clock alone in caves for months at a time and carefully notes his physiological and psychological changes. Written for the general public, this book generated wide interest in such isolation experiments. Fascinating reading.

Webb, Wilse B. *Sleep: The Gentle Tyrant*. Englewood Cliffs, N.J.: Prentice-Hall, 1975. A nontechnical overview of sleep research, focusing particularly on behavioral components of sleep and sleep disorders. Somewhat dated, but perhaps the most comprehensive introductory book available on sleep that can be easily understood by most high school and college students.

Winfree, Arthur T. *The Timing of Biological Clocks*. New York: Scientific American Library, 1987. A beautifully illustrated book that covers philosophical concepts of time and clocks as well as the nature of circadian and other biological rhythms. Some sections are rather mathematical, but these are well worth the effort to understand and appreciate. Recommended for the college-level or motivated high school student.

MEMORY

Alba, Joseph W., and Lynn Hasher. "Is Memory Schematic?" *Psychological Bulletin* 93, no. 2 (1983): 203-231. This article presents a thorough and detailed evaluation of schema theory and discusses both strengths and weaknesses of schematic explanations. Includes an extensive bibliography of both empirical and theoretical primary source materials.

Allman, William F. *Apprentices of Wonder: Inside the Neural Network Revolution.* New York: Bantam, 1989. This popular book provides easy access to the field of computer modeling and neural networks for the lay reader. It contains one chapter on memory. Both believers' and skeptics' viewpoints on connectionist theory are presented, with illustrations, a general index, selected references, and a bibliography.

Allport, Susan. *Explorers of the Black Box: The Search for the Cellular Basis of Memory.* New York: W. W. Norton, 1986. Chronicles the fascinating search for the cellular basis of memory. The author paints a vivid picture of the personalities and laboratories behind the discoveries and elucidates many of the most important concepts in the field—a treatise on the workings of both brain and science. Written by a scientist and journalist, this easy-to-read 271-page volume contains a modest index but no reference section.

Anderson, J. R. *Cognitive Psychology and Its Implications.* New York: W. H. Freeman, 1990. Although this book generally has an information-processing framework, it is still a thorough reference book on any area concerned with cognitive psychology.

Ashcraft, Mark H. *Human Memory and Cognition.* Glenview, Ill.: Scott, Foresman, 1989. This introductory textbook takes the reader on a delightful journey through the world of memory and cognition. Includes illustrations and suggestions for further reading on memory.

Baddeley, Alan D. *Human Memory: Theory and Practice.* Boston: Allyn & Bacon, 1990. One of the world's leading researchers on memory summarizes the history of research on memory and describes controversies in the field. This comprehensive treatment of memory research includes many practical examples.

_____. *Working Memory*. Oxford, England: Oxford University Press, 1986. Provides a scholarly report of working memory that has been very influential in the memory field. The writing may be too technical for readers who desire only an overview of general concepts, but it is essential for those interested in a deeper understanding of working memory.

_____. *Your Memory: A User's Guide*. New York: Macmillan, 1982. A fully illustrated, easy-to-read book about memory written by one of the top-ranking researchers in the field. Discusses all aspects of research on memory. Recommended as a first book on memory.

Bahrick, H. P. "A Speedy Recovery from Bankruptcy for Ecological Memory Research." *American Psychologist* 46, no. 1 (1991): 76-77. This article addresses the controversy between those who favor naturalistic memory studies and those who favor strict experimental studies; Bahrick favors the naturalistic approach.

Banaji, Mahzarin R., and Robert G. Crowder. "The Bankruptcy of Everyday Memory." *American Psychologist* 44, no. 9 (1989): 1185-1193. This article addresses the controversy between naturalistic and experimental research; the authors favor more controlled experimental approaches.

Bartlett, Frederic Charles. *Remembering: A Study in Experimental and Social Psychology*. Cambridge, England: Cambridge University Press, 1932. A readable accounting of Bartlett's experiments with linguistic and pictorial stimuli, this book includes many interesting examples of how memory for different types of materials changes with the passage of time.

Bellezza, F. S. "Mnemonic Devices: Classification, Characteristics, and Criteria." *Review of Educational Research* 51, no. 2 (1981): 247-275. Presents the case for why mnemonics should be studied, a useful classification scheme for mnemonics, and discussion of criteria for evaluating their effectiveness.

Best, John B. *Cognitive Psychology*. 2d ed. St. Paul, Minn.: West, 1989. One of the most complete texts in human cognition, with chapters on perception, attention, pattern recognition, memory, forgetting, and language. The writing is engaging and encourages readers to think for themselves.

Bransford, John. *Human Cognition: Learning, Understanding, and Remembering.* Belmont, Calif.: Wadsworth, 1979. By a well-respected researcher. Focuses on the role of memory in complex learning. Contains much practical information that would be useful to students in improving performance in school-related activities.

Ceci, S. J., and Urie Bronfenbrenner. "On the Demise of Everyday Memory." *American Psychologist* 46, no. 1 (1991): 27-31. Addresses the naturalistic versus experimental memory study issue, offering a balanced perspective and inviting scientific inquiry regardless of the type of methodology.

Craik, Fergus I., and Robert S. Lockhart. "Levels of Processing: A Framework for Memory Research." *Journal of Verbal Learning and Verbal Behavior* 11, no. 6 (1972): 671-684. This article revolutionized thinking about memory, how it works, and how people process information. Much subsequent work has been based on this perspective.

Crowder, Robert G. *Principles of Learning and Memory.* Hillsdale, N.J.: Lawrence Erlbaum, 1976. Although less information has been gathered on echoic memory than on iconic memory, this book has a more in-depth discussion of echoic memory than is typically found in other texts. A good discussion of the Atkinson and Shiffrin model of human information-processing is presented, as well.

Deutsch, Diana, and J. Anthony Deutsch, eds. *Short-Term Memory.* New York: Academic Press, 1975. This text consists of fifteen papers written by short-term memory researchers. Both the topics and the writing style are rather technical; however, this edition is very useful for anyone needing classical, comprehensive, detailed information about the intricacies of the short-term memory process.

Ellis, Henry C., and R. Reed Hunt. *Fundamentals of Human Memory and Cognition.* 5th ed. Dubuque, Iowa: Wm. C. Brown, 1991. A very readable text composed of numerous examples and illustrations of empirical evidence and practical applications that bring the information to life. Ellis and Hunt employ their expertise in effective, efficient encoding strategies to produce a text that describes complex cognitive processes in a manner that facilitates understanding and recall.

Fiske, Susan T., and Shelley E. Taylor. *Social Cognition.* 2d ed. New York: McGraw-Hill, 1991. Includes several informative chapters on the role of schemata in social interaction, social categories, and self-perception, and looks at information on when various types of schemata are likely to be invoked.

Graham, Kenneth G., and H. Alan Robinson. *Study Skills Handbook.* Newark, Del.: International Reading Association, 1984. A very practical handbook which includes many of the principles set forth by Frank Robinson (who developed the "survey, question, read, recite, and review," or SQ3R, study method). Helps to teach study skills, thereby increasing memory and helping to prevent forgetting.

Graham, R. B. *Physiological Psychology.* Belmont, Calif.: Wadsworth, 1990. A high level undergraduate textbook in physiological psychology that includes illustrations, a glossary, references, and author and subject indexes. Covers the basics of nervous system function from neurons to brain, emphasizing functional systems: sleep, ingestion, sexuality, emotion, sensation, and perception. Contains chapters on the role of the hippocampus in learning and memory, memory per se, and brain dysfunction. The memory chapter provides a more detailed description of cellular memory mechanisms than found in similar introductory texts.

Gregg, Vernon H. *Introduction to Human Memory.* London: Routledge & Kegan Paul, 1986. Explores the cognitive approach to memory, explaining sensory memory, encoding, and retrieval. Includes a very interesting treatment of amnesias. Has an extensive bibliography.

Hall, David, Elizabeth Loftus, and James Tousignant. "Postevent Information and Changes in Recollection for a Natural Event." In *Eyewitness Testimony: Psychological Perspectives*, edited by Gary L. Wells and Elizabeth F. Loftus. Cambridge, England: Cambridge University Press, 1984. Discusses the hypotheses pertaining to the effects of postevent information on original memories, and why these hypotheses cannot be tested. Illustrates how questions about the conditions under which recollections change may be answered.

Hayes, John R. *The Complete Problem Solver.* Philadelphia: Franklin Institute Press, 1981. The title of this book is somewhat deceiving: Although it does discuss problem solving, it emphasizes the role of memory in problem solving, teaches how to use memory effectively, and links memory to learning strategies.

Higbee, Kenneth L. *Your Memory: How It Works and How to Improve It.* 2d ed. New York: Prentice-Hall, 1988. Practical suggestions on how to use research-based principles of memory in daily life. Applies results of laboratory studies to real-life problems. Useful for improving one's study habits and grades.

Kail, Robert V. *The Development of Memory in Children*. 3d ed. New York: W. H. Freeman, 1990. Addresses the development of memory: how children develop memory strategies and the ways memory develops from infancy to childhood to adolescence.

Kintsch, Walter. *The Representation of Meaning in Memory*. Hillsdale, N.J.: Lawrence Erlbaum, 1974. Examines the importance of memory in the area of text comprehension. In particular, Kintsch looks at theoretical and applied issues concerning how people remember what they read and ways that memory for written materials can influence the ability to understand those materials.

Klatzky, Roberta L. *Human Memory: Structures and Processes*. 2d ed. San Francisco: W. H. Freeman, 1980. This popular book examines memory from an information-processing approach. It is divided into three major sections on perception, short-term memory, and long-term memory. The writing style is exceptionally clear.

Kolb, Bryan, and Ian Q. Whishaw. *Fundamentals of Human Neuropsychology*. 3d ed. New York: W. H. Freeman, 1990. An excellent, comprehensive text (almost 1,000 pages, with extensive references, index, and illustrations) aimed at the professional but accessible to the lay reader. Provides essential background in the organization of the nervous system; the biochemical and electrical bases of neural transmission; clinical neurology; and the history, principles, and syndromes of neuropsychology. Includes a chapter on memory, describing the role of the brain and the various amnesiac syndromes. Additional chapters describe clinical methods for assessing memory disorders.

Lachman, Roy, Janet L. Lachman, and Earl C. Butterfield. *Cognitive Psychology and Information Processing: An Introduction*. Hillsdale, N.J.: Lawrence Erlbaum, 1979. A comprehensive book that discusses human memory at length. In addition, it provides an overall view of cognitive psychology and describes how the various subareas fit together. Although somewhat outdated, it is a classic book.

Loftus, Elizabeth F. *Eyewitness Testimony*. Cambridge, Mass.: Harvard University Press, 1979. One of the foremost experts on eyewitness testimony presents a comprehensive overview of the empirical work on such testimony. Also examines the role that eyewitness testimony has played in the American legal system.

_____. *Memory: Surprising New Insights into How We Remember and Why We Forget*. Reading, Mass.: Addison-Wesley, 1988. Loftus discusses the development of the cognitive sciences in seeking greater specificity for human abilities such as thinking and memory.

Loftus, Geoffrey R., and Elizabeth F. Loftus. *Human Memory: The Processing of Information*. Hillsdale, N.J.: Lawrence Erlbaum, 1976. One of the best single books on memory available. Covers learning, remembering and forgetting, and a number of other topics regarding memory.

Lorayne, Harry, and Jerry Lucas. *The Memory Book*. New York: Stein & Day, 1974. A short paperback text designed to help people remember names, faces, dates, and so on; utilizes a variety of techniques and strategies. Well written and easy to read.

Luria, Aleksandr R. *The Mind of a Mnemonist: A Little Book About a Vast Memory*. Pickering, Ontario: Basic Books, 1968. A fascinating case study written by the "father of neuropsychology," who was one of the most significant Russian psychologists. Directed toward a general (nonspecialist) audience. The case study focuses on his subject Shereshevskii (subject "S") and the extraordinary memory he possessed.

McCloskey, Michael, Howard Egeth, and Judith McKenna. "The Experimental Psychologist in Court: The Ethics of Expert Testimony." *Law and Human Behavior* 10, nos. 1-2 (1986): 1-13. This special journal issue contains thirteen articles on issues relating to a psychologist giving expert testimony in court—not highly technical, but written for the reader with a background in the subject.

McDaniel, Mark A., and Michael Pressley, eds. *Imagery and Related Mnemonic Processes, Theories, Individual Differences, and Applications*. New York: Springer-Verlag, 1987. Contributors present theoretical grounding for imagery-based mnemonics, consider individual differences in their use related to age, ethnicity, and sightedness, and describe applications of mnemonics to domains such as special education.

McKoon, Gail, R. Ratcliff, and G. Dell. "A Critical Evaluation of the Semantic-Episodic Distinction." *Journal of Experimental Psychology:*

Learning, Memory, and Cognition 12, no. 2 (1986): 295-306. A systematic review of the evidence against the theory of separate semantic and episodic memory systems. Clear descriptions and analysis of a large number of fairly complicated experiments.

Mandler, Jean Matter. *Stories, Scripts, and Scenes: Aspects of Schema Theory.* Hillsdale, N.J.: Lawrence Erlbaum, 1984. Focuses on how schemata and scripts can account for findings from research on how people understand stories.

Neisser, Ulric. *Cognition and Reality: Principles and Implications of Cognitive Psychology.* San Francisco: W. H. Freeman, 1976. Neisser makes the case for studying real-world memory instead of the artificial memory of the laboratory. Discusses the major goals of cognitive psychology and implications for future research.

_____, ed. *Memory Observed: Remembering in Natural Contexts.* San Francisco: W. H. Freeman, 1982. This collection of brief selections helped to establish the legitimacy of the study of everyday memory. Included are eight fascinating case studies of persons with exceptional visual, verbal, or musical memories.

Norman, Donald A. *Learning and Memory.* San Francisco: W. H. Freeman, 1982. This brief book is an excellent introduction to the topics of learning and memory in the spirit and tradition of the information-processing approach. Uses simple language and includes a number of hands-on experiments that can be easily performed.

_____. *Memory and Attention: An Introduction to Human Information Processing.* 2d ed. New York: John Wiley & Sons, 1976. Concentrates on key research findings in memory, attention, and perception; discusses the acquisition of information, short-term memory, and memory-aiding techniques. Many concrete examples are provided.

_____. *The Psychology of Everyday Things.* New York: Doubleday, 1988. An absolutely delightful book that addresses the use of human cognitive abilities in dealing with daily problems in living. Easily understandable by the general reader; will provoke much discussion.

Parkin, Alan J. *Memory and Amnesia: An Introduction.* Oxford: Basil Blackwell, 1987. An excellent introduction to the causes, assessment, and explanation of memory disorders such as amnesia. Presents some information on the physiology of memory. Can be easily understood without any previous knowledge.

Rubin, David C., ed. *Autobiographical Memory*. Cambridge, England: Cambridge University Press, 1986. An excellent source of theories and research on autobiographical memory. Several chapters focus on memory failures associated with amnesia, considered by some a critical testing ground for the episodic-semantic distinction.

Rumelhart, David E., P. Smolensky, James L. McClelland, and Geoffrey E. Hinton. "Schemata and Sequential Thought Processes in PDP Models." In *Parallel Distributed Processing: Explorations in the Microstructure of Cognition*, by James L. McClelland, David E. Rumelhart, and the PDP Research Group. Vol. 2. Cambridge, Mass.: MIT Press, 1986. Discusses how some of the findings attributable to schemata and scripts can be accounted for within a parallel distributed processing (PDP) approach. Provides a detailed discussion of schemata-like effects in network models, but will be difficult for readers who are not familiar with the parallel distributed processing approach.

Schank, Roger C., and Robert P. Abelson. *Scripts, Plans, Goals, and Understanding*. Hillsdale, N.J.: Lawrence Erlbaum, 1977. The authors discuss their notion of scripts and their work in developing computer programs that utilize scripts as aids in understanding narratives.

Schwartz, Barry, and Dan Reisberg. *Learning and Memory*. New York: W. W. Norton, 1991. This book is a comprehensive outline of all aspects of psychology that pertain to learning and memory. Includes research and historical review. An excellent reference book.

Smith, Frank. *Comprehension and Learning: A Conceptual Framework for Teachers*. New York: Holt, Rinehart and Winston, 1975. This book is a cognitive textbook on the principles of learning in children. It has both an information-processing format and a psycholinguistic perspective, for a comprehensive presentation of research. It is easily read by student and teacher, and it includes comprehension, language, and concept development.

Solso, Robert L. *Cognitive Psychology*. 3d ed. Boston: Allyn & Bacon, 1991. An undergraduate text for courses in cognitive psychology. Solso provides an account of memory that is written on a level appropriate for most high school and college students. Can be used not only to learn more about short-term memory but also to learn about memory processes in general.

Squire, L. R. *Memory and Brain*. New York: Oxford University Press, 1987. Written by one of the foremost memory researchers, this stimulating high-level book attempts to reconcile the divergent views of memory emerging from psychology and neuroscience. Moving from synapse to behavior, it assumes familiarity with both the psychological analysis of memory and basic concepts from neuroscience, including neuroanatomy and neurophysiology. Contains extensive references, both subject and author indexes, and some illustrations. Appropriate for an advanced undergraduate with some background in psychology and biology.

Stern, Leonard. *The Structures and Strategies of Human Memory*. Homewood, Ill.: Dorsey Press, 1985. A fairly sophisticated book that examines various aspects of memory and explores both how to encode and how to retrieve information.

Tulving, Endel. *Elements of Episodic Memory*. Oxford, England: Oxford University Press, 1983. In this book, Tulving intersperses a review of evidence for the episodic-semantic distinction with his personal reflections on the practice of scientific research. An interesting insider's view.

_____. "Episodic and Semantic Memory." In *Organization of Memory*, edited by Endel Tulving and Wayne Donaldson. New York: Academic Press, 1972. Tulving later called this first declaration of the episodic-semantic distinction "not very well thought out . . . impressionistic, incomplete, and somewhat muddled," but it struck a responsive chord and was cited more than five hundred times in psychology literature over the next twelve years.

_____. "How Many Memory Systems Are There?" *American Psychologist* 40, no. 4 (1985): 385-398. In this 1984 address for the Distinguished Scientific Contribution Award from the American Psychological Association, Tulving proposes a "monohierarchical" arrangement of episodic memory embedded in semantic memory and argues for the stochastic independence of episodic and semantic memory phenomena.

Wells, Gary L., and Elizabeth F. Loftus, eds. *Eyewitness Testimony: Psychological Perspectives*. New York: Cambridge University Press,

1984. Fifteen chapters by various authors on topics related to eyewitness testimony. Good source for in-depth coverage on subtopics such as lineups and witness confidence.

Wrightsman, Lawrence S. "Crime Investigation: Eyewitnesses." In *Psychology and the Legal System*. 2d ed. Pacific Grove, Calif.: Brooks/Cole, 1991. Chapter focuses on the application of memory and eyewitness research on the criminal investigation. Uses interesting examples and mentions basics in brief form.

Wyer, Robert S., and Thomas K. Srull. *Memory and Cognition in Its Social Context*. Hillsdale, N.J.: Lawrence Erlbaum, 1989. Wyer and Srull take a social cognition approach to the discussion of short-term memory, using the label "work space" to describe this process. They argue that the social context in which mental processes occur must be considered to provide an accurate and useful model of cognitive processes.

Yarmey, A. Daniel. *The Psychology of Eyewitness Testimony*. New York: Free Press, 1979. An introductory-level book that describes the knowledge of psychological and legal aspects of eyewitness identification and testimony. It is interesting and easily understood.

Yates, Frances Amelia. *The Art of Memory*. Chicago: University of Chicago Press, 1966. The classic survey of memory systems in use from 500 b.c. to the Renaissance, through eras largely devoid of printing, when a trained memory was of critical importance.

Zechmeister, Eugene B., and Stanley E. Nyberg. *Human Memory: An Introduction to Research and Theory*. Monterey, Calif.: Brooks/Cole, 1981. A rigorous introductory textbook. Covers in detail topics such as the stages of memory, consolidation, mnemonics, and constructive processes in memory. The best feature of the book is that it provides the materials and procedures for experiments that one can carry out.

LANGUAGE

Akmajian, Adrian, Richard A. Demers, Ann K. Farmer, and Robert M. Harnish. *Linguistics: An Introduction to Language and Communication*. 3d ed. Cambridge, Mass.: MIT Press, 1990. Chapter 10 of this introductory linguistics text, "Psychology of Language: Speech Production and Comprehension," offers a clear overview of questions and ideas in psycholinguistics. The chapter is very understandable in the context of the book's preceding chapters, which constitute an excellent introduction to the ways linguists study language. Also relevant is chapter 9, "Pragmatics: The Study of Language Use and Communication."

Albert, Martin L., and Loraine K. Obler. *The Bilingual Brain: Neuropsychological and Neurolinguistic Aspects of Bilingualism*. New York: Academic Press, 1978. An excellent, accessible, but somewhat dated account of the theory and research on the structure of bilingual individuals' brains and how they differ from those of monolinguals. Written from both a linguistic and psychological perspective. Good bibliography.

Arnberg, Lenore. *Raising Children Bilingually: The Pre-School Years*. Philadelphia: Multilingual Matters, 1987. An excellent resource for parents interested in rearing bilingual children. Based on the author's experience with her own children in Sweden, this book discusses the issues involved in all types of childhood bilingualism.

Berk-Seligson, Susan. *The Bilingual Courtroom: Court Interpreters in the Judicial Process*. Chicago: University of Chicago Press, 1990. A somewhat specialized application of linguistics research concerning the rules, regulations, and procedures surrounding the use of interpreters in American courtrooms.

Berlitz, Charles. *Native Tongues*. New York: Grosset & Dunlap, 1982. A popular book recounting anecdotes about languages around the world; of special interest is the chapter entitled "There Were Others Before Columbus," which concerns American Indian languages.

Bloomfield, Leonard. *Language*. New York: Henry Holt, 1933. This classic text served in its day as a general introduction to linguistics and remains an invaluable guide to the American structuralist tradition in phonology and morphology. Strongly influenced by behaviorism in psychology, Bloomfield avoids any notion of psychological reality in his discussion of the phoneme, taking a functional perspective instead. Although lengthy (more than 500 pages), the book is engagingly written and may be read by the careful nonspecialist.

Bohannon, John Neil, III, and Amye Warren-Leubecker. "Theoretical Approaches to Language Acquisition." In *The Development of Language*, edited by Jean Berko Gleason. Columbus, Ohio: Charles E. Merrill, 1989. This chapter in a language acquisition textbook provides a comprehensive overview of the theoretical approaches, outlining their general assumptions and evaluating each in terms of supporting and contrary evidence.

Broida, Helen. *Coping with Stroke: Communication Breakdown of Brain Injured Adults*. San Diego: College-Hill Press, 1979. Broida provides a nontechnical introduction to stroke and aphasia. Answers many questions regarding functional deficits, treatment, and prognosis.

Brown, Roger Langham. *Wilhelm von Humboldt's Conception of Linguistic Relativity*. The Hague: Mouton, 1967. This slim but weighty volume is a superb treatment of a phase in the history of linguistic relativity during its Germanic era of the 1700's and 1800's, chronicling various pre-Humboldtian ideas and detailing the grand synthesis that Humboldt performed and passed down to, among others, Sapir and Whorf.

Brown, Roger William. *A First Language: The Early Stages*. Cambridge, Mass.: Harvard University Press, 1973. This account of early language development in English and in several other languages is a classic, and it is accessible to the careful reader interested in the early work which laid the foundation for modern language acquisition research.

Brubaker, Susan Howell. *Sourcebook for Aphasia: A Guide to Family Activities and Community Resources*. Detroit: Wayne State University Press, 1982. Brubaker describes activities that relatives of aphasia patients can use to enhance the recovery process. The absence of an introduction to aphasia and minimal guidance regarding which exercises are appropriate for particular symptom presentations are limiting factors in this text.

Bruner, Jerome S. *Child's Talk: Learning to Use Language*. New York: W. W. Norton, 1983. Looks at the acquisition process from the point of view of pragmatics; investigates how a child comes to use language to accomplish various goals in the world and how, from limited beginnings, the child learns to expand his or her uses of language.

Campbell, Robin, and Roger Wales. "The Study of Language Acquisition." In *New Horizons in Linguistics*, edited by John Lyons. Harmondsworth, Middlesex, England: Penguin Books, 1970. This essay constitutes an early critique of Chomsky and the psychologists he influenced, faulting them for not attending to the communicative function of language.

Carroll, John Bissell. *Language and Thought*. Englewood Cliffs, N.J.: Prentice-Hall, 1964. This slim volume by the editor of Whorf's manuscripts is recommended for its keeping psychology in mind as it teaches fundamentals of linguistics. Of special importance to the topic are the final chapters, "Cognition and Thinking" and "Language and Cognition."

Chomsky, Noam. *Language and Mind*. Enl. ed. New York: Harcourt Brace Jovanovich, 1972. Classic series of lectures Chomsky gave at the University of California, Berkeley, in 1967, along with further chapters elaborating his views. This work, though very technical in parts, is probably the most readable of Chomsky's writings, and it exemplifies the thinking of one of the grand originators of psycholinguistics.

_____. *Syntactic Structures*. The Hague: Mouton, 1971. Chomsky's book put forward the basic ideas of generative grammar, which revolutionized the science of linguistics. Chomsky argues for a universal language acquisition device in humans as well as for the underlying unity of all human language.

Clark, Herbert H. "Language Use and Language Users." In *The Handbook of Social Psychology*, edited by Gardner Lindzey and Elliot Aronson. 3d ed. New York: Lawrence Erlbaum, 1985. This very readable chapter gives an excellent basic outline of language use in social settings. It provides a vocabulary and makes critical distinctions that inform the research of psycholinguists interested in higher-level language processes, including very clear discussions on reference, turn taking, and repair of misunderstandings.

Clark, Herbert H., and Eve V. Clark. *Psychology and Language: An Introduction to Psycholinguistics*. New York: Harcourt Brace Jovanovich, 1977. In its nearly 600 pages, this book summarizes an amazing amount of research. Clark and Clark detail complicated theories, principles, and data in clear and elegant prose, illustrated with excellent examples. A classic in the field of psycholinguistics, and an extremely comprehensive work.

Collins, Michael. *Diagnosis and Treatment of Global Aphasia.* San Diego: College-Hill Press, 1986. Collins focuses on the practical implications of what is known about global aphasia. The text is somewhat technical, but it is valuable for persons who want to learn more about this disorder.

Crystal, David. *What Is Linguistics?* London: Edward Arnold, 1968. A brief, eminently readable introduction to the areas of study covered in linguistics. Assumes no prior knowledge, yet manages to dispel in a lively, engaging style some major misconceptions people tend to have about language and to explain what sorts of inquiries are linguistically relevant. Also discusses the applications of linguistic knowledge to other areas, such as language teaching and speech pathology.

Cummins, Jim. *Bilingualism and Special Education: Issues in Assessment and Pedagogy.* Clevedon, Avon, England: Multilingual Matters, 1984. Written by a leading expert in the field of bilingual education, this small book provides a thorough review of bilingual education programs and their corresponding theories. The author's popular perspective on the education of language-minority children is discussed.

Curlee, Richard F. "Counseling in Speech, Language, and Hearing." *Seminars in Speech and Language* 9, no. 3 (1988). In his introductory article to this issue, Curlee presents a clear and interesting overview of counseling strategies for the speech-language pathologist. Counseling of parents and spouses of persons with speech disorders is detailed.

De Villiers, Peter A., and Jill G. de Villiers. *Early Language.* Cambridge, Mass.: Harvard University Press, 1979. Written specifically for the nonspecialist. Provides a clear and accessible account of children's first sounds, words, and sentences, as well as a discussion of the nature of speech addressed to children and its possible role in facilitating language development.

DeVito, Joseph A., and Michael L. Hecht, eds. *The Nonverbal Communication Reader.* Prospect Heights, Ill.: Waveland Press, 1990. Presents a readable and interesting discussion of nonverbal communication, including several areas that are not generally studied, such as olfactics (smell) and artifactual communication, such as clothing, cars, and jewelry. Applications to interpersonal relationships are discussed extensively. A very useful publication.

Diaz, R. M. "Thought and Two Languages: The Impact of Bilingualism on Cognitive Development." In *Review of Research in Education*, edited by E. W. Gordon. Vol. 10. Washington, D.C.: American Educational Research Association, 1983. An excellent and well-written review of the history and status of the study of bilingualism and intelligence. Discusses problems with research designs and suggests a partial theory for understanding the relationship between intelligence and bilingualism.

Ewing, Susan Adair, and Beth Pfalzgraf. *Pathways: Moving Beyond Stroke and Aphasia*. Detroit: Wayne State University Press, 1990. The authors summarize the experiences of six families that attempt to cope with the aftermath of a stroke. Practical and emotional problems that must be confronted by the patient and the family are discussed.

Fitch, James L. *Clinical Applications of Microcomputers in Communication Disorders*. Orlando, Fla.: Academic Press, 1986. Fitch provides an entry-level introduction to the use of computers in audiology and speech pathology. The text lacks an adequate discussion of the use of computers as adaptive devices, but many potential applications are discussed.

Foss, Donald J., and David T. Hakes. *Psycholinguistics*. Englewood Cliffs, N.J.: Prentice-Hall, 1978. This introduction and summary of the field focuses on questions of modularity. Foss and Hakes are sympathetic to the proposals that the processing stages in both comprehension and production are independent and occur in a strict sequence, and they direct their reviews of the literature to these issues.

Fromkin, Victoria, and Robert Rodman. *An Introduction to Language*. New York: Holt, Rinehart and Winston, 1988. An introductory book that discusses the field of linguistics, including theoretical developments. Demonstrates the manner in which cognitive concepts are being developed in linguistics.

Fudge, E. C. "Phonology." In *New Horizons in Linguistics*, edited by John Lyons. Harmondsworth, Middlesex, England: Penguin Books, 1970. This chapter on phonology in an excellent paperback survey of linguistics is one of the most succinct and readable introductions to the field as a whole, and it provides an excellent summary of the varying definitions of the phoneme that characterized much of the controversy surrounding this unit of analysis in the first half of the twentieth century. Anyone interested in learning more about the phoneme should start with this essay.

Gardner, R. Allen, and Beatrice Gardner. "Teaching Sign Language to a Chimpanzee." *Science* 165 (August 15, 1969): 664-672. The Gardners argue for the continuity of human language with that which preceded it among the higher apes. They indicate that nonhuman primates are not able to achieve verbal language for physiological reasons. They are, however, capable of signing nonverbally and can communicate symbolically with humans.

Gleitman, Lila R. "Biological Dispositions to Learn Language." In *Language Learning and Concept Acquisition*, edited by William Demopolous and Ausonio Marras. Norwood, N.J.: Ablex, 1986. In a highly readable article, Gleitman describes a number of observations which support the notion of the innateness of language-specific faculties.

Grosjean, François. *Life with Two Languages: An Introduction to Bilingualism.* Cambridge, Mass.: Harvard University Press, 1982. A very readable and nontechnical book about bilingualism. Using many examples, it provides a comprehensive and enjoyable review of the topic. Good bibliography.

Hakuta, Kenji. *Mirror of Language: The Debate on Bilingualism.* New York: Basic Books, 1986. A pleasant and easy-to-read book that discusses many important topics in the study of bilingualism. Excellent historical account of bilingualism as a field of study. Other topics covered include bilingualism and intelligence, second language acquisition in adults and children, the bilingual mind, and bilingual education. Good bibliography.

Hall, Robert Anderson. *Linguistics and Your Language.* Garden City, N.Y.: Doubleday, 1960. An introduction to linguistics aimed at the general reader. Clearly explains linguistic terminology. Covers the debate between prescriptivism and descriptivism, and discusses matters of sound, form, meaning, and system in language, as well as historical change and regional differences.

Hamers, Josiane F., and Michel H. A. Blanc. *Bilinguality and Bilingualism.* Rev. ed. New York: Cambridge University Press, 1989. A comprehensive but somewhat technical volume on bilingualism. Good coverage of social, psychological, and cognitive aspects.

Harper, Robert Gale, Arthur N. Wiens, and Joseph D. Matarazzo. *Non-verbal Communication: The State of the Art.* New York: John Wiley & Sons, 1978. Reviews a large number of studies on various areas of nonverbal communication. The material in this book has been organized and presented to give the reader an idea of how the findings were obtained as well as what the findings were. Very thorough and detailed.

Hartstein, Jack, ed. *Current Concepts in Dyslexia.* St. Louis: C. V. Mosby, 1971. Introduces the reader to the terms, specialists, and available treatments of dyslexia. Topical coverage includes dyslexia diagnosis and treatment; roles of reading teachers in educating dyslexics; dimensions of reading and reading disability; the use of therapeutic drugs; and functions of neurologists.

Henley, Nancy M. *Body Politics: Power, Sex, and Nonverbal Communication.* Englewood Cliffs, N.J.: Prentice-Hall, 1977. Focuses on the power aspect of nonverbal communication, both on the interpersonal and on the intergroup level, with particular reference to male dominance. Presents some interesting and well-researched findings.

Hickson, Mark L., and Don W. Stacks. *NVC: Nonverbal Communication Studies and Applications.* Dubuque, Iowa: Wm. C. Brown, 1985. Emphasizes the interaction between biological functions and sociopsychological functions and discusses the influence of sociology on nonverbal communication. The application section discusses nonverbal communication as it occurs in different settings (social situations, the home, and on the job). Provides an extensive discussion of nonverbal research, but the language is not technical and is easily understood. Contains a useful if brief glossary of terms.

Jordan, Dale R. *Dyslexia in the Classroom.* 2d ed. Columbus, Ohio: Charles E. Merrill, 1977. An interesting book aimed at providing useful information to "grassroots professionals" who work with the group of problems the author sees as composing dyslexia. Includes definitions of the three types of dyslexia, their classroom characteristics, methodology for correcting them, methods for distinguishing dyslexia from other learning disabilities, and several useful screening tests.

Just, Marcel Adam, and Patricia A. Carpenter. *The Psychology of Reading and Language Comprehension.* Boston: Allyn & Bacon, 1987. A

review of the literature on language comprehension that focuses especially on reading. A good summary that will expose the reader to the
details of scientific techniques for studying reading.

Kellogg, W. N., and L. A. Kellogg. *The Ape and the Child.* New York:
McGraw-Hill, 1933. The Kelloggs describe the early developmental
period of a chimp raised with their young child. Their argument that
apes are incapable of language stood almost unchallenged until later
research on apes and nonverbal language.

Kessel, Frank S., ed. *The Development of Language and Language
Researchers: Essays in Honor of Roger Brown.* Hillsdale, N.J.: Lawrence Erlbaum, 1988. An anthology of essays written by former
students and colleagues of Roger Brown. Includes overviews of
several of the subfields of language acquisition, as well as autobiographical accounts of several researchers' own development in thinking about language development issues. Of particular interest to the
beginner are the selections by Dan I. Slobin, Melissa Bowerman, and
Jill de Villiers.

Klasen, Edith. *The Syndrome of Specific Dyslexia: With Special Consideration of Its Physiological, Psychological, Testpsychological, and
Social Correlates.* Baltimore: University Park Press, 1972. Klasen's
study of five hundred dyslexic students—containing 153 references—
provides much useful information. Covers many aspects of dyslexia
etiology, associated speech disorders, related organic-sensory and
neuropsychological symptoms, psychopathology, therapy, psychological test results, socioeconomic and family backgrounds, intersibling
relationships, and parental attitudes.

Knapp, Mark L. *Essentials of Nonverbal Communication.* New York:
Holt, Rinehart and Winston, 1980. Knapp provides an excellent, brief
overview of nonverbal communication in easy-to-understand language. Examines the development of nonverbal communication in
children and contains a useful chapter on the ability to send and receive
nonverbal signals and on developing nonverbal skills.

Laird, Charlton Grant. *The Miracle of Language.* Greenwich, Conn.:
Fawcett, 1953. A well-written introduction to the study of language.
Examines word, grammar, and speech from a historical perspective.
Discusses the antecedents of modern English words, sounds, and
structures, and tries to dispel notions of good and "bad" grammar.

Levelt, Willem J. M. *Speaking: From Intention to Articulation.* Cambridge, Mass.: MIT Press, 1989. An excellent comprehensive summary of research on speech planning, production, and articulation. The book's organization reflects actual speech production, moving from the high-level principles of dyadic interaction and message planning to low-level motor control and error-repair principles. Very well written, but in its length and complexity not for the beginner.

Lyons, John. *Noam Chomsky.* New York: Viking Press, 1970. Anyone who wishes to understand the foundations of Chomsky's theory of generative grammar should start with this book. Lyons places Chomsky's work in the context of modern linguistics and provides an introduction to the thought of one of the most influential linguistic thinkers of the twentieth century. Since Chomsky's own books tend to be quite abstract and difficult, Lyons aids the general reader in gaining a foothold in difficult terrain, with the additional advantage that Chomsky read, commented on, and corrected the manuscript. Thus, the book avoids as much as possible any distortion or misinterpretation of Chomsky's work.

McCrone, John. *The Ape That Spoke: Language and the Evolution of the Human Mind.* New York: William Morrow, 1991. While not addressing the cerebral cortex directly, this book for general readers discusses the increased size of the cortex as being associated with the development of language. It gives an interesting outlook on how the mind functions by capturing and holding each thought for a short time only. Bibliographical notes include numerous references.

McNeill, David. "The Creation of Language." In *Language*, edited by R. C. Oldfield and J. C. Marshall. Harmondsworth, Middlesex, England: Penguin Books, 1968. NcNeill provides a succinct, nontechnical discussion of language acquisition from the Chomskyan perspective. Although some particulars of linguistic theory presented here are somewhat dated, the thought which guides the rationalist approach, including a discussion of the language acquisition device, is clearly presented, along with some data supporting the rationalist thesis.

Matthews, Peter Hugoe. *Morphology.* London: Cambridge University Press, 1974. This general text discusses the treatment of morphology in the classical, traditional, structural, and generative schools of thought. Each of the twelve chapters is prefaced with a brief synopsis of the chapter's contents, thus orienting the reader to the subject matter. Although the book is not easy, it is accessible to the interested novice.

Mehrabian, Albert. *Silent Messages: Implicit Communication of Emotions and Attitudes.* 2d ed. Belmont, Calif.: Wadsworth, 1981. Mehrabian discusses how nonverbal communication is used to communicate attitudes, emotions, and preferences implicitly; people are usually unaware of sending or receiving these nonverbal messages. Discusses the use of nonverbal communication in areas such as selling, persuasion, deceit, political campaigns, and advertising.

Miller, George Armitage. *Language and Speech.* San Francisco: W. H. Freeman, 1981. Miller's short book is a good introduction to the data and theories of psycholinguistics, with interesting discussions of language evolution and development in humankind and in the individual. Miller brings up issues of biology and issues of society at large that affect language use. A very good source for the beginner.

Murdoch, B. E. *Acquired Speech and Language Disorders: A Neuroanatomical and Functional Neurological Approach.* London: Chapman and Hall, 1990. Murdoch provides a comprehensive description of the various types of aphasia and dysarthria. Additionally, the author supplies an extended discussion of agnosia and apraxia. Furthermore, the author elucidates how neurological damage and disease processes affect language production and comprehension.

Padilla, Amado M., H. H. Fairchild, and C. M. Valadez, eds. *Bilingual Education: Issues and Strategies.* Newbury Park, Calif.: Sage, 1990. An excellent collection of articles about theories and types of bilingual education. Good discussion of the history of bilingual education in the United States from both a researcher's and teacher's perspective. Examples of model programs are given.

Peal, Elizabeth, and Wallace E. Lambert. "The Relation of Bilingualism to Intelligence." *Psychological Monographs* 76 (1962): 1-23. This is the classic research study that transformed many scholars' and laypersons' negative views of bilingualism into positive ones. An excellent account of the relationship between bilingualism and intelligence.

Piattelli-Palmarini, Massimo, ed. *Language and Learning: The Debate Between Jean Piaget and Noam Chomsky.* Cambridge, Mass.: Harvard University Press, 1980. Represents the proceedings of a conference held in October, 1975, which constituted the only meeting between Piaget and Chomsky. Given that they are the founders of two radically different theories involving the nature of knowledge, this book is required reading for anyone interested in the debate. It is lengthy (more than 400 pages long) and not easy, but the fact that practitioners of different disciplines and methodologies were meeting face-to-face means that the language employed in the book does not become overly technical. Of great value are the discussions at the ends of the presentations and an entire section devoted to commentary on the debate.

Pinker, Steven. *The Language Instinct: How the Mind Creates Language.* New York: William Morrow, 1994. Pinker is a linguist at MIT. The book engagingly presents linguistics as cognitive science. Presents experimental and theoretical advances in the understanding of language in a readable fashion for the college student or educated general reader.

Poyatos, Fernando, ed. *Cross Cultural Perspectives in Nonverbal Communication.* Toronto: C. J. Hofgrefe, 1988. Examines differences and similarities in nonverbal communication across cultures. Contains many tables, charts, and figures, which aid in understanding, as well as an extensive index.

Premack, David. "On the Assessment of Language Competence in the Chimpanzee." In *Behavior of Nonhuman Primates*, edited by Allan M. Schrier and Fred Stollnitz. 2 vols. New York: Academic Press, 1965. Premack outlines the basic lines of the argument on chimpanzee language ability. He is fair in providing space for both sides.

Robins, Robert Henry. *A Short History of Linguistics.* Bloomington: Indiana University Press, 1967. A lively and readable style characterizes this survey of linguistic thought from ancient Greece to twentieth century America. One of the book's major advantages is that it treats linguistic thought developmentally; every idea in linguistics is seen as a product of its era and its antecedents. Robins' prose style is clear and makes the history of linguistics a good story.

Romaine, Suzanne. *Bilingualism.* Oxford, England: Basil Blackwell, 1989. A textbooklike but readable account of the social and linguistic aspects of bilingualism from a community perspective. Topics covered include the bilingual community, the bilingual brain, types of childhood bilinguals, bilingual education, and attitudes toward bilingualism. Extensive bibliography.

Routh, Donald K. "Disorders of Learning." In *The Practical Assessment and Management of Children with Disorders of Development and*

Learning, edited by Mark L. Wolraich. Chicago: Year Book Medical Publishers, 1987. Succinctly summarizes many salient facts about learning disorders, including their etiology, their assessment, their management, and their outcome. The interested reader will also find many useful references to more detailed works.

Samovar, Larry A., and Richard E. Porter. *Communication Between Cultures*. Belmont, Calif.: Wadsworth, 1991. Summary of intercultural communication. Presents information on international cultures and co-cultures within the United States, and translates communication principles and concepts into practical situations.

Sapir, Edward. *Language: An Introduction to the Study of Speech*. New York: Harcourt Brace, 1921. The classic introduction to language. Probably the most eminent linguist of the twentieth century, Sapir provides his own viewpoint on language, drawing from his vast knowledge of many of the world's languages. He demonstrates how all languages share some common features and yet differ markedly in their structures; what can be rendered in a single word in one language may require an entire proposition in another. Much of the foundation for theories of linguistic relativity can be found in this slim volume, along with much of the justification for the universality of language structures. Required reading for all those interested in language study.

_____. *Selected Writings of Edward Sapir in Language, Culture, and Personality*. Edited by David G. Mandelbaum. Berkeley: University of California Press, 1958. Illustrates the broad scope of interests of perhaps the most revered and elegant writer in twentieth century linguistics; provides the earliest linking of language-and-thinking to Einstein's geometry-and-thinking principle of general relativity. While many of his articles are written for various specialists, "The Grammarian and His Language" and "The Status of Linguistics as a Science" are especially recommended for their accessibility and comments on linguistic relativity.

Sarno, Martha Taylor, ed. Acquired Aphasia. 2d ed. San Diego: Academic Press, 1991. Contributions to this volume tend to be technical, but the book contains valuable information concerning neurological and linguistic factors associated with aphasia. The chapters on intelligence, artistry, and social sequelae are unique offerings.

Saussure, Ferdinand de. *Course in General Linguistics*. New York: McGraw-Hill, 1959. This paperback edition is the English translation of a work originally published in French in 1916. It is a compilation and synthesis of notes taken by students from Saussure's courses at the University of Geneva in Switzerland. A number of ideas subsequently of great importance in twentieth century linguistics are presented, including the notion of the phoneme as an operant in a system of contrasts. Accessible to the careful general reader.

Shames, George H., and Elizabeth H. Wiig, eds. *Human Communication Disorders.* Columbus, Ohio: Charles E. Merrill, 1986. This general text covers a wide range of communication disorders. Includes a section on speech-language pathology as a profession. Also includes sections on cleft palate, aphasia, and cerebral palsy.

Snowling, Margaret J. *Dyslexia: A Cognitive Developmental Perspective.* New York: Basil Blackwell, 1987. Covers many aspects of dyslexia, including its identification, associated cognitive defects, the basis for development of language skills, and the importance of phonology. Also contains many references.

The Speech Foundation of America. *Counseling Stutterers.* Memphis, Tenn.: Author, 1989. The Speech Foundation of America is a nonprofit, charitable organization dedicated to the prevention and treatment of stuttering. It provides a variety of low-cost publications about stuttering and stuttering therapy. This publication is written to give clinicians a better understanding of the counseling aspect of therapy and to suggest ways in which it can be used most effectively.

_____. *Therapy for Stutterers.* Memphis, Tenn.: Author, 1989. A general guide to help those who work or plan to work in therapy with adult and older-adolescent stutterers.

Sternberg, Martin L. A. *American Sign Language Concise Dictionary.* New York: HarperPerennial, 1994. A good dictionary of ASL, the language of the deaf. Not a substitute for an ASL class, but a useful reference. Also available on CD-ROM, with video clips.

Tannen, Deborah. *Talking 9 to 5.* New York: William Morrow, 1994. Tannen describes how the different conversational styles of men and women may lead to misunderstandings in the workplace. Tannen is a linguist, and she engagingly combines scientific research with illustrative anecdotes. For the general reader.

_____. *You Just Don't Understand: Women and Men in Conversation*. New York: William Morrow, 1990. An engaging description of the different ways women and men use language. Although Tannen is a linguist, this book is written for a general audience and was a best-seller.

Valett, Robert E. *Dyslexia: A Neuropsychological Approach to Educating Children with Severe Reading Disorders*. Belmont, Calif.: Fearon Pitman, 1980. Contains hundreds of references. Of interest to readers wishing detailed information on dyslexia and on educating dyslexics. There are two main divisions: The first, covering neuropsychological foundations of reading, includes topics such as critical neuropsychological factors, language acquisition, and diagnosis; the second describes a wide variety of special-education topics.

Wagner, Rudolf F. *Dyslexia and Your Child: A Guide for Teachers and Parents*. Rev ed. New York: Harper & Row, 1979. A clear, useful, and simply written book "for teachers and parents concerned with children . . . referred to as dyslexic." Includes careful exposition of dyslexic symptoms, commentary on the problem, ways to treat dyslexia and associated problems, other useful topics, an appendix of recommended reading, and a glossary.

Werner, Heinz, and Bernard Kaplan. *Symbol Formation*. New York: John Wiley & Sons, 1963. Uses information provided by numerous diary studies of language and language acquisition to provide a psychological account of the development of language, connecting changes in expressive language with developmental change in general. The first two parts of this five-part account will be of particular interest to the novice trying to understand the cognitive basis of language acquisition.

Whorf, Benjamin Lee. *Language, Thought, and Reality: Selected Writings of Benjamin Lee Whorf*. Edited by John B. Carroll. Cambridge, Mass.: MIT Press, 1956. Contains many previously unpublished articles written by Whorf from the late 1920's to the very early 1940's. Although some articles may be difficult for nonspecialists, many others, such as "Thinking in Primitive Communities," "Science and Linguistics," and "Languages and Logic," are used almost universally in beginning linguistics classes.

DEVELOPMENTAL PSYCHOLOGY

Theory and Methodology

Gollin, Eugene S., ed. *Developmental Plasticity: Behavioral and Biological Aspects of Variations in Development.* New York: Academic Press, 1981. Excellent coverage of important theoretical issues in modern developmental psychology. Accessible to college or graduate students with some background in psychology and/or biology.

Langer, Jonas. *Theories of Development.* New York: Holt, Rinehart and Winston, 1969. Although somewhat dated, this is an excellent account of theories in development and of their construction and history. Particularly recommended for the treatment of psychodynamic theory. Accessible to college students.

Lerner, Richard M. *On the Nature of Human Plasticity.* New York: Cambridge University Press, 1984. Insightful discussion of modern theory in developmental psychology and some historic antecedents. Emphasis on biological issues. Accessible to advanced students, graduate students, and professionals.

Miller, Patricia H. *Theories of Developmental Psychology.* 2d ed. New York: W. H. Freeman, 1989. Excellent, comprehensive treatment of developmental theory. Describes extant theories in detail and discusses commonalities and dissimilarities. Accessible to the layperson with some background in psychology.

Mussen, Paul Henry, ed. *Handbook of Research Methods in Child Development.* New York: John Wiley & Sons, 1960. Commissioned by the Committee on Child Development of the National Academy of Sciences, this handbook continues to be a classic. Although dated in its applications, it provides conceptual and theoretical underpinnings for a variety of developmental methodologies. Includes many chapters written by eminent developmental psychologists.

Piaget, Jean. *Biology and Knowledge.* Chicago: University of Chicago Press, 1971. This is a seminal summary of Piagetian theory that contains more general information and information concerning theory construction than do Piaget's other, more specific works. Readily accessible to the college student or the advanced high school student.

Sears, Robert R. "Your Ancients Revisited: A History of Child Development." In *Review of Child Development Research*. Vol. 5, edited by E. M. Hetherington. Chicago: University of Chicago Press, 1975. A well-respected developmental psychologist, himself a participant in a longitudinal study from childhood, reviews the founding of the field in a readable and interesting chapter. Places developmental research and methodologies in the context of changes in society's needs and priorities. Discusses influences from other fields of study including anthropology and psychoanalysis.

Shaffer, David Reed. *Developmental Psychology: Childhood and Adolescence*. 2d ed. Pacific Grove, Calif.: Brooks/Cole, 1989. Good general textbook on developmental psychology, with an excellent basic treatment of theoretical issues in development. Accessible to the college or high school student.

Siegler, Robert S. *Children's Thinking*. 2d ed. Englewood Cliffs, N.J.: Prentice-Hall, 1991. Although this book is primarily a technical treatise on a specific area in development, the author discusses modern theory in cognitive development in terms of both Piagetian and information processing perspectives and introduces issues of current theoretical interest in a clear, readable manner.

Triandis, H. C., and A. Heron, eds. *Basic Methods*. Vol. 4 in *Handbook of Cross-Cultural Psychology: Developmental Psychology*. Boston: Allyn & Bacon, 1981. Presents conceptual basis for cross-cultural developmental research and research methodologies. Clearly demonstrates the potentialities and limitations of adapting Western developmental methodologies to the study of non-Western peoples. Presents a variety of research areas including language, memory, Piagetian cognitive structures, and personality development.

Wolman, Benjamin B., ed. *Handbook of Developmental Psychology*. Englewood Cliffs, N.J.: Prentice-Hall, 1982. A comprehensive handbook, the first ten chapters of which focus on research methods and theories. Surveys a variety of developmental methodologies, and demonstrates the relationship between theoretical models and methodologies. Includes a chapter on ethics and regulation of research with children.

Infancy and Childhood: Cognitive Development

Ault, Ruth L. *Children's Cognitive Development: Piaget's Theory and the Process Approach*. New York: Oxford University Press, 1977. This short work both describes and illustrates Piaget's concepts and illuminates the implications of the theory by contrasting them with the non-Piagetian approach of experimental child psychology. Lucid, nontechnical, but thought-provoking.

Coles, Robert. *The Moral Lives of Children*. Boston: Atlantic Monthly Press, 1986. Gives a comprehensive overview of Freudian theory and moral development. Investigates issues such as motion pictures and morality, social classes, psychological events, and personality and moral development. This book is easily read and could generally be enjoyed by high school students.

Duska, Ronald F., and Mariellen Whelan. *Moral Development: A Guide to Piaget and Kohlberg*. New York: Paulist Press, 1975. Presents Piaget's theory and its implications for Kohlberg's expansion into his own theory of moral development. All of the moral stories used by Piaget and Kohlberg in their research are replicated in this book. Also includes research findings and ways in which to apply these theories to everyday situations in teaching children. This book can be easily read by the high school or college student.

Flavell, J. H. *Cognitive Development*. 2d ed. Englewood Cliffs, N.J.: Prentice-Hall, 1985. This classic book, in its second edition, provides a comprehensive overview of the contemporary field of cognitive development. The chapter on social cognition provides interesting examples and descriptions of research evidence on social-cognitive development during infancy.

Gelman, Rochel, and R. Baillargeon. "A Review of Some Piagetian Concepts." In *Handbook of Child Psychology*, edited by Paul H. Mussen. 4th ed. Vol. 3. New York: John Wiley & Sons, 1983. A thorough review, concept by concept, of the developmental research on various types of conservation and classification problems. These authors conclude that the hypothesis of domain-specific changes fits the experimental research better than the idea of global stages does.

Hare-Mustin, Rachel T., and Jeanne Marecek. "The Meaning of Difference: Gender Theory, Post-Modernism, and Psychology." *American*

Psychologist 43 (June, 1988): 455-464. This article is serious reading, but it is not intended for specialists. Presents theories on gender differences developed in the 1980's.

Hyde, Janet Shibley. *Half the Human Experience*. 4th ed. Lexington, Mass.: Heath, 1991. This excellent book reviews research and theory pertaining to all aspects of gender differences. An accessible text for college students that many high school students also could use. Includes many references to other authors and researchers. Particularly valuable as it relates differences in cognitive development to social and biological factors.

Hyde, Janet Shibley, and Marcia C. Linn, eds. *The Psychology of Gender: Advances Through Meta-Analysis*. Baltimore: The Johns Hopkins University Press, 1986. A collection of scholarly articles that reanalyze many research efforts. Should be read by advanced undergraduates.

Jacklin, Carol. "Female and Male: Issues of Gender." *American Psychologist* 44 (February, 1989): 127-133. The coauthor of the pioneering work on sex differences summarizes research between 1974 and 1989.

Maccoby, Eleanor E., and Carol Nagy Jacklin. *The Psychology of Sex Differences*. Stanford, Calif.: Stanford University Press, 1974. Reviews all research on gender differences to the early 1970's. This book is somewhat scholarly but is useful, as it presents the most comprehensive and balanced review of the research up to its publishing date.

Phillips, John L. *The Origins of Intellect: Piaget's Theory*. 2d ed. San Francisco: W. H. Freeman, 1975. This thorough, clearly written text explains Piaget's concepts by providing many examples. An excellent source for the introductory-level student who seeks a comprehensive understanding of Piaget's ideas. Available in paperback.

Piaget, Jean. *The Essential Piaget*. Edited by Howard E. Gruber and J. Jacques Vonéche. New York: Basic Books, 1977. Contains English translations of most of Piaget's writings, from his earliest work (1909), which was heavily biological. Many of these earlier writings were unknown to Americans until translated from the French in the 1950's. Since reading Piaget himself is more difficult than most general works about his theory, the student might consult Piaget's papers selectively on topics of particular interest.

Rest, James R. *Moral Development: Advances in Research and Theory.* New York: Praeger, 1986. This book relates the cultural, educational, religious, and experiential influences on moral development. Shows the results of a moral dilemma test, which is available to the reader, and gives directions for gaining the manual for grading the test. Although generally the reading is too advanced for the beginning student, this book is recommended because of the availability of these tests.

Rich, John Martin, and Joseph L. DeVitis. *Theories of Moral Development.* Springfield, Ill.: Charles C Thomas, 1985. Presents a range of psychologists' theories on moral development, including Freud, Adler, Jung, and Sears. In addition, it places moral development within the framework of higher education and relates it to a life-span perspective. Certain sections of the book would be difficult for a novice student to follow; however, in terms of a summary of theoretical positions, the book is a handy reference.

Shaffer, David Reed. "Moral Development." In *Social and Personality Development.* Monterey, Calif.: Brooks/Cole, 1979. Reviews research and theories of moral development. Each theoretical outlook is examined in depth, including research for and against the findings. This chapter includes the definitions of relevant terms and uses easy-to-read graphs and tables. Highly recommended as an elementary text.

Sigel, Irving E., and Rodney R. Cocking. *Cognitive Development from Childhood to Adolescence: A Constructivist Perspective.* New York: Holt, Rinehart and Winston, 1977. A readable, condensed version of Piaget's theory. A good place for the introductory-level reader to begin.

Infancy and Childhood: Social and Personality Development

Adler, Alfred. *What Life Should Mean to You.* Edited by Alan Porter. New York: Capricorn Books, 1958. Alfred Adler, one of the most important people in establishing birth order as an idea worthy of study, spells out his original views on birth order in this book, originally published in 1931. He believed that the place of the child in the family influences how the parents treat the child, which in turn creates personality differences among the various birth orders. Not all his speculation is necessarily correct, but psychology is grateful to him for saying that birth order is an important concept.

Ainsworth, Mary D. Salter, Mary C. Blehar, Everett Waters, and S. Wall. *Patterns of Attachment*. Hillsdale, N.J.: Lawrence Erlbaum, 1978. Outlines, in general terms, the development of Bowlby's attachment theory. Describes in detail the procedures and scoring techniques for the strange situation and describes the patterns of behavior associated with the secure, avoidant, and resistant attachments. Discusses the research that addresses the antecedents of individual differences in the attachment relationship.

Baumrind, Diana. "Rearing Competent Children." In *Child Development Today and Tomorrow*, edited by William Damon. San Francisco: Jossey-Bass, 1989. Baumrind summarizes her earlier and more recent work on parenting styles. Much of the focus is on the differential effects of demandingness and responsiveness on child development. Provides an excellent overview of the parenting styles research; can be understood by the beginning college student.

_____. "Socialization and Instrumental Competence in Young Children." In *Social and Personality Development: Essays on the Growth of the Child*, edited by William Damon. New York: W. W. Norton, 1983. Looks specifically at Baumrind's parenting-style research with preschoolers. One section is devoted to looking at the development of competence in young girls based on societal views of femininity. Frequent use of headings and italicized main points make this chapter easily understood by the average reader with little or no previous background in psychology.

Bem, Sandra L. "Gender Schema Theory and Its Implications for Child Development: Raising Gender-Aschematic Children in a Gender-Schematic Society." *Signs* 8, no. 4 (1983): 598-616. Introduction to gender-schema for nonpsychologists. Provides an in-depth discussion of this approach to gender-identity formation and compares it to other major psychological theories. Bem also suggests practical applications of her perspective to child rearing.

Blake, Judith. *Family Size and Achievement*. Berkeley: University of California Press, 1989. Discusses the effects of family size on achievement. The author found that only children and children from small families are more able intellectually and gain more education than children who are not the only child or who are from large families.

Bowlby, John. *Attachment and Loss*. 2d ed. New York: Basic Books, 1982. Examines the theoretical foundation of the attachment construct and discusses attachment behavior. Outlines the development, maintenance, and function of attachment in both humans and animals.

Brassard, Marla R., Robert Germain, and Stuart N. Hart, eds. *Psychological Maltreatment of Children and Youth.* New York: Pergamon Press, 1987. An edited collection of articles that considers emotional maltreatment as the "core" component of all other forms of child abuse. Discusses issues of the definition, dynamics, consequences, and treatment of the psychological abuse of children.

Brooks, Jane. "Establishing Close Emotional Relationships with Children." In *The Process of Parenting.* Rev. ed. Toronto: Mayfield, 1991. Explains Dreikurs' view of the democratic family in detail. The focus of his theory, that misbehavior results from faulty goals, is also highlighted. Of particular interest in this chapter is how Dreikurs' views on misbehavior compare with perspectives of other contemporary theorists.

Brooks-Gunn, Jeanne, and Wendy Schempp Matthews. *He and She: How Children Develop Their Sex-Role Identity.* Englewood Cliffs, N.J.: Prentice-Hall, 1979. Provides a clear, thorough description of children's sex-role development for parents, educators, and students. Also provides research evidence and anecdotal examples describing sex-role acquisition from the prenatal period through adolescence. A good, usable reference for high school students.

Christensen, Oscar, and Carroll Thomas. "Dreikurs and the Search for Equality." In *Handbook on Parent Education*, edited by Marvin J. Fine. New York: Academic Press, 1980. Presents the views of Alfred Adler and his impact on the work of Rudolf Dreikurs. Dreikurs' views of the child and parent-child relations dominate the chapter. Dreikurs provides a theoretical basis for understanding children's behavior by examining the social context of this behavior.

Cicchetti, Dante, and Vicki Carlson, eds. *Child Maltreatment: Theory and Research on the Causes and Consequences of Child Abuse and Neglect.* New York: Cambridge University Press, 1989. Edited chapters by leading experts in the field providing a state-of-the-art evaluation of what is known about the causes and consequences of child maltreatment. Describes the history of child maltreatment and intervention strategies designed to prevent or remediate the negative consequences of abuse.

Clark, Robin E., and Judith Freeman Clark. *The Encyclopedia of Child Abuse*. New York: Facts on File, 1989. In encyclopedia form, provides comprehensive information regarding all forms of child maltreatment. Includes discussions of causation, consequences, treatment, and prevention. Entries reflect a range of disciplines including psychology, law, medicine, sociology, economics, history, and education. An extensive bibliography also included.

Coles, Robert. *Erik H. Erikson: The Growth of His Work*. Boston: Little, Brown, 1970. This complete and scholarly work attempts to unify and examine the writings and teachings of Erikson. While the style is somewhat polemic at times, the book is quite valuable as a biography and source.

Coopersmith, Stanley. *The Antecedents of Self Esteem*. San Francisco: W. H. Freeman, 1967. Emphasizes the importance of limits and boundaries of permissible behavior in the development of self-esteem. Discusses the mirror-image idea of humans emulating society as it develops through the parent/child relationship. There are four very helpful measuring devices in the appendix.

Crockenberg, S. B. "Infant Irritability, Mother Responsiveness, and Social Support Influences on the Security of Infant-Mother Attachment." In *Contemporary Readings in Child Psychology*. 3d ed., compiled by E. Mavis Hetherington and Ross D. Parke. New York: McGraw-Hill, 1988. Describes a research project that shows that infant characteristics, such as infant temperament, as well as maternal responsiveness, can influence the development of the mother-infant attachment relationship. Also shows that the availability of social support to the mother can influence the development of attachment.

Damon, William. *Social and Personality Development*. New York: W. W. Norton, 1983. This textbook is an introduction to the social development of the child. Contains an excellent discussion of attachment theory and presents many clear, concise examples of infant and child attachment behaviors. Relates the development of attachment behavior to other important developments in infancy and early childhood.

Dunn, Judy. *Distress and Comfort*. Cambridge, Mass.: Harvard University Press, 1977. Addresses questions commonly asked by parents about infant and child distress. Outlines the development of separation protest and stranger anxiety and discusses the importance of parental behavior in the continuing emotional development of the child.

Eisenman, Russell. *From Crime to Creativity: Psychological and Social Factors in Deviance.* Dubuque, Iowa: Kendall/Hunt, 1991. In addition to detailed discussions of creativity, this book deals with birth order and shows how it can relate to other things. For example, the book discusses birth order and projection, which is the tendency to see things in others that are really in oneself. Firstborns scored higher in the projection of sex and aggression when viewing ambiguous figures.

Erikson, Erik H. *Childhood and Society.* New York: W. W. Norton, 1963. In this classic study, Erikson presents his views and theories on identity and identity crisis—a phrase which he coined—as well as the psychosexual development of the child. The main view is that children grow through a series of progressive crises which should establish a sense of trust, autonomy, initiative, and competence.

_____. *Insight and Responsibility.* New York: W. W. Norton, 1964. This work acts in many ways as a source for Erikson's ideas. It consists of lectures that were given before 1964 and contains his essential ideas concerning psychotherapy, identity crises, the ego, and the beginnings of what later came to be known as psychohistory. A concise yet detailed introduction to Eriksonian theory.

Finkelhor, David. *A Sourcebook on Child Sexual Abuse.* Beverly Hills, Calif.: Sage, 1986. Provides a comprehensive overview of the clinical and research knowledge base regarding child sexual abuse, including its causes, consequences, and treatment.

Garbarino, James, and Gwen Gilliam. *Understanding Abusive Families.* Lexington, Mass.: Lexington Books, 1980. Presents an ecological and developmental perspective on child abuse. Explores the interrelated contributions of child characteristics, parental characteristics, and the community context to the development of an abusive parent-child relationship. Considers the way in which the causes, dynamics, and consequences of abuse may change from infancy through adolescence.

Glenn, H. Stephen, and Jane Nelsen. *Raising Children for Success.* Fair Oaks, Calif.: Sunrise Press, 1987. Provides well-organized and clear suggestions for parents on how to help children develop good intellectual and interpersonal skills through effective parenting practices. Relates parenting to the larger social forces in American culture. Uses many relevant examples; does not require the reader to have any background in psychology.

Hann, Della M., and Howard J. Osofsky. "Psychosocial Factors in the Transition to Parenthood." In *New Perspectives on Prenatal Care*, edited by Irwin R. Merkatz and Joyce E. Thompson. New York: Elsevier, 1990. Hann and Osofsky discuss the problems of being a parent for the first time and give examples of how things can go wrong for first-time parents. They also suggest interventions which can be made to help people be better parents. They cite research showing that depressed parents make their children depressed.

Harris, Judith Rich, and Robert M. Liebert. *The Child: A Contemporary View of Development*. 3d ed. Englewood Cliffs, N.J.: Prentice-Hall, 1991. An excellent summary of social learning theory and its application to the understanding of aggressive behavior. Explains important terms and discusses research focusing on the relation of harsh physical punishment and aggression.

Hetherington, E. M., M. Cox, and R. Cox. "The Aftermath of Divorce." In *Mother-Child, Father-Child Relationships*, edited by Joseph H. Stevens, Jr., and Marilyn Mathews. Washington, D.C.: National Association for the Education of Young Children, 1978. This chapter represents pioneering work that documents how divorce affects children. Reactions of children to the news of divorce and to its aftermath are vividly described.

Hughes, Fergus, and Lloyd Noppe. "Gender Roles and Gender Differences." In *Human Development Across the Life Span*. St. Paul, Minn.: West, 1985. Presents an overview of gender-identity formation across the entire lifespan, including information about gender roles in old age. Provides extensive information about gender from a developmental perspective. Easily accessible to beginning college students.

Huston, A. C. "Sex-typing." In *Handbook of Child Psychology*, edited by Paul H. Mussen. Vol. 4, edited by E. Mavis Hetherington. 4th ed. New York: John Wiley & Sons, 1983. Relatively technical, but provides a masterful organization and in-depth analysis of theory and research relevant to sex typing. Also includes a long and thorough bibliography.

Johnston, Janet R., and Linda E. Cambell. *Impasses of Divorce: The Dynamics and Resolution of Family Conflict*. New York: Free Press, 1988. The authors' project focused on helping parents mediate differences in hostile divorce situations. Issues sustaining conflict and preventing the development of a coparenting relationship are discussed, and methods to achieve a resolution are presented. An excellent source for family counselors.

Kalter, Neil. *Growing Up with Divorce: Helping Your Child Avoid Immediate and Later Emotional Problems*. New York: Free Press, 1989. Presents comprehensive advice on the emotional pitfalls of divorce, warning signs of distress, and methods of preventing and alleviating distress in children from infancy through adolescence. Provides a chapter on communicating with children that parents will find very useful.

Lamb, Michael E., and Joseph J. Campos. *Development in Infancy*. New York: Random House, 1982. A comprehensive textbook on infant development that presents a variety of theories of infant emotional development.

Lott, Bernice E. *Women's Lives: Themes and Variations in Gender Learning*. Monterey, Calif.: Brooks/Cole, 1987. Frequently used textbook for college classes on the psychology of women. Chapters 3 and 4 present an accessible, entertaining account of gender-identity formation from a social-learning perspective, integrating research evidence. Other chapters explore implications of gender-role acquisition for women in adult life. Helpful for those who are interested in gender-related topics in psychology.

Maccoby, Eleanor, and John Martin. "Socialization in the Context of the Family: Parent-Child Interaction." In *Handbook of Child Psychology*, edited by Paul H. Mussen. 4th ed. New York: John Wiley & Sons, 1983. Discusses parenting styles in the larger context of socialization of children within the family. Although sometimes technical in its use of terminology, the chapter provides an excellent comprehensive summary of research findings related to parent-child interactions. Recommended for college students or high school students with some background in psychological terminology.

McNeal, James U. *Children as Consumers*. Lexington, Mass.: Lexington Books, 1986. A multifaceted approach to the entire arena of children and consumption. Addresses issues of education and public policy. Reports interviews with children as well as summaries of data from research studies on children. Informative, thoughtful, and readable.

Mussen, Paul Henry, and Nancy Eisenberg-Berg. *Roots of Caring, Sharing, and Helping*. San Francisco: W. H. Freeman, 1977. Although this book is only partially related to self-esteem, it has a thorough discussion of how situations and other people influence children—influences which certainly cannot be ignored for their impact on self-esteem. Appropriate for most high school and college students.

Roazen, Paul. *Erik H. Erikson: The Power and Limits of a Vision*. New York: Free Press, 1976. While Erikson tried to distance himself from the psychoanalytic approaches of Freud, Roazen shows that Erikson's views still have a basis in that movement. Contains further discussion on the life cycle, normality, and identity.

Ruble, D. N. "Sex-Role Development." In *Developmental Psychology: An Advanced Textbook*, edited by Marc H. Bornstein and Michael E. Lamb. Hillsdale, N.J.: Lawrence Erlbaum, 1984. Presents a comprehensive discussion of gender-identity formation and related issues in developmental psychology. Includes research evidence for sex differences in behavior and biological, social, and cognitive factors in sex-role development. Clearly written, scholarly in tone, and presupposes some prior familiarity with the field.

Schachter, Stanley. *The Psychology of Affiliation*. Stanford, Calif.: Stanford University Press, 1959. This book caused other researchers to begin birth-order studies. Schachter used female subjects and told them they were going to experience painful electric shocks. Firstborns preferred to wait for the alleged shocks with others who were also waiting to receive shocks. Thus, birth order was established as something which made a difference and could be studied.

Spock, Benjamin. *Dr. Spock on Parenting*. New York: Simon & Schuster, 1988. Provides an excellent, accessible, and extremely readable overview of many of the current issues related to parenting, including late parenting, single parenting, fathering, and discipline. Much of the book is written from the perspective of authoritative or democratic parenting. Translates research findings into clear, practical suggestions for parents. Highly recommended for all parents: prospective, new, or experienced.

Straus, Murray Arnold, Richard J. Gelles, and Suzanne K. Steinmetz. *Behind Closed Doors: Violence in the American Family*. Newbury Park, Calif.: Sage, 1981. Reports the results of the first comprehensive national study of violence in the average American family in nontechnical language. The problem of child abuse is discussed within the larger context of other expressions of family violence.

Wallerstein, Judith S., and Joan Berlin Kelly. *Surviving the Breakup: How Parents and Children Cope with Divorce*. New York: Basic Books, 1980. The results of a five-year study investigating how parents and children adjust to divorce. The authors present data on how parents reacted to divorce and how these parental reactions affected their children's adjustment. They also report how children interpreted and reacted to the divorce and how their views solidified or changed over the period of the study.

Wallerstein, Judith S., and Sandra Blakeslee. *Second Chances: Men, Women, and Children a Decade After Divorce*. New York: Ticknor & Fields, 1989. This is a follow-up of Wallerstein's original study. Wallerstein's work presents data on the long-term effects of divorce on both parents and children, and for this reason it is extremely valuable. Useful for those who are anticipating divorce, attempting to cope with divorce, or interested in the long-term consequences of divorce.

Wolfe, David A. *Child Abuse: Implications for Child Development and Psychopathology*. Newbury Park, Calif.: Sage, 1987. Presents a thorough review of facts and issues regarding the abuse of children, emphasizing topics such as sociodemographic risk factors, variations in family socialization practices, factors associated with healthy versus abusive parent-child relationships, psychological characteristics of the abusive parent, and a developmental perspective on the abused child.

Infancy and Childhood: Physical Development

Abel, Ernest L. "Behavioral Teratology of Alcohol." *Psychological Bulletin* 90 (November, 1981): 564-581. Presents a clear definition of teratology as it relates specifically to alcohol and the fetus.

Bower, T. G. R. *Development in Infancy*. 2d ed. New York: W. H. Freeman, 1982. An overview of the developmental milestones during infancy. An excellent introduction to topics in infancy.

_____. *The Perceptual World of the Child.* Cambridge, Mass.: Harvard University Press, 1977. A brief (83-page), basic introduction to issues in infant perception. Includes a thorough discussion of how physical growth from infancy through adulthood provides challenges for perceptual systems. Covers some classic studies of perceptual development. Written for a general audience.

Broome, Marion E., and Charlotte Koehler. "Childbirth Education: A Review of Effects on the Woman and Her Family." *Family and Community Health* 9, no. 1 (1986): 33-44. Describes natural childbirth techniques in birthing. Comparison of effects on parents who participated in prepared childbirth classes versus nonprepared couples are explored as they relate to relationships with newborns. Very easy reading and easily comprehensible. Provides interesting and informative knowledge about prepared childbirth.

Corr, Charles A., Helen Fuller, Carol Ann Barnickol, and Donna M. Corr, eds. *Sudden Infant Death Syndrome: Who Can Help and How.* New York: Springer, 1991. A very useful resource for SIDS family members, professional and lay helpers, and all those wanting to learn about SIDS. Divided into a review of SIDS characteristics and research, effects of SIDS on family members, guidelines for helping them, and resources for such families. Many references are included.

Culbertson, Jan L., Henry F. Krous, and R. Debra Bendell, eds. *Sudden Infant Death Syndrome: Medical Aspects and Psychological Management.* Baltimore: The Johns Hopkins University Press, 1988. This text, with many references, touches many bases. Its chapters—by specialists—deal with the epidemiology, pathology, proposed mechanistics, and possible origins of SIDS. Consideration of the psychological aspects of SIDS loss are also covered, including loss, grieving reactions, family responses, and development of a National SIDS Foundation.

Defrain, John D., Jacque Taylor, and Linda Ernst. *Coping with Sudden Infant Death.* Lexington, Mass.: Lexington Books, 1982. This book is concerned with the responses of families to SIDS—their stress and coping. Deals with parental responses to SIDS, concerns about what to tell other children, fears about the possibility of having another child after SIDS strikes, and identification of support for SIDS parents; provides a parents' questionnaire that helps parents to identify how they are coping with their loss. Well written and educational.

Dworetsky, John P. *Psychology*. St. Paul: West, 1982. This text is designed to be used as an introduction to psychology for undergraduates. Offers a strong, selective research base. Text material is extensive and detailed; helpful running glossaries appear in margins. Appropriate for the undergraduate student and layperson.

Falkner, Frank, and J. M. Tanner. *Human Growth*. 2d ed. New York: Plenum Press, 1986. A three-volume edited set on human growth. The third volume in particular has much work on the genetic, nutritional, and other environmental influences on human growth before and after birth.

Fitzgerald, Hiram E., et al. "The Organization of Lateralized Behavior During Infancy." In *Theory and Research in Behavioral Pediatrics*. Vol. 5, edited by Hiram E. Fitzgerald, B. Lester, and M. Yogman. New York: Plenum Press, 1991. A good overview on the lateralization of motor skills and behaviors in early development. Covers the influence of brain development on lateralized motor skills.

Fogel, Alan. *Infancy: Infant, Family, and Society*. New York: West, 1991. Provides a detailed account of physical, intellectual, and emotional aspects of development, beginning with the prenatal period and proceeding through the first thirty-six months of life. A very comprehensive work that includes cross-cultural information, an extensive bibliography, subject and author indexes, and appendices charting physical growth.

Gallahue, D. L. *Motor Development and Movement Experiences*. New York: John Wiley & Sons, 1976. A well-written resource on the theory, research, and practical applications of motor development and movement from age three to seven years.

Gottlieb, Gilbert, and Norman Krasnegor, eds. *Measurement of Audition and Vision in the First Year of Postnatal Life: A Methodological Overview*. Norwood, N.J.: Ablex, 1985. Detailed chapters cover behavioral, physiological, and psychophysical measures of auditory and visual development. Good resource for information on methods for experiments in perceptual development and for discussion of the inferences drawn from such studies. Written for researchers and students of infant perception.

Harper, Lawrence V. *The Nurture of Human Behavior*. Norwood, N.J.: Ablex, 1989. An excellent review of the biological mechanisms underlying growth and behavioral development. Includes discussions on evolutionary origins of behavioral development, developmental genetics and embryology, and ways in which experience may influence development. Excellent reference section.

Harris, Judith Rich, and Robert M. Liebert. *The Child.* 3d ed. Englewood Cliffs, N.J.: Prentice-Hall, 1991. An excellent review of characteristics of the newborn. Provides a much more thorough view of the baby than other texts in the introductory developmental genre.

Hofer, Myron A. *The Roots of Behavior.* San Francisco: W. H. Freeman, 1981. A good introduction to the biology of early human development and behavior. Has a particularly good section on how development and behavior are influenced by the environment; emphasizes the interplay between biological and environmental forces.

International Research Conference on the Sudden Infant Death Syndrome. *Sudden Infant Death Syndrome.* Edited by J. Tyson Tildon, Lois M. Roeder, and Alfred Steinschneider. New York: Academic Press, 1983. Contains the presentations of more than a hundred contributors at the 1982 International SIDS Conference in Baltimore. Many important areas, including endocrinology, cardiology, respiratory relationships, sleep involvement, airway physiology, and identification of at-risk infants, are included. This technical text provides much information and extensive references.

Kaluger, George, and Meriem Fair Kaluger. *Human Development: The Span of Life.* 3d ed. St. Louis: Times Mirror/Mosby, 1984. The Kalugers offer a strong conceptual approach to human growth and development. A chronological age/stage format is used. Social, developmental, health, and contemporary issues are examined. The authors report on research and substantiate it with other relevant information. Details abound in the chapters on prenatal development, birth, and infancy.

Landy, Frank J. *Psychology: The Science of People.* 2d ed. Englewood Cliffs, N.J.: Prentice-Hall, 1987. Shows the unique relationship between science and the study of human behavior and provides a liberal sprinkling of everyday examples. Research, theory, and practical applications are well balanced. Good information on prenatal development. Material is linked across chapters to connect behavior with a variety of perspectives.

Lipsitt, Lewis. "Critical Conditions in Infancy: A Psychological Perspective." *American Psychologist* 34, no. 10 (1979): 973-980. Discusses SIDS in America. Lipsitt describes his model of sudden infant death syndrome.

Livingston, Martha. "Choice in Childbirth: Power and the Impact of the Modern Childbirth Reform Movement." *Women and Therapy* 6, nos. 1-2 (1987): 239-261. Livingston presents a historical overview of the evolution of birthing practices. Compares the midwife model to modern obstetrics and emphasizes birth as a social and psychological as well as a physiological event. The need for informed choice is emphasized. Very interesting reading and comprehensive coverage of birthing trends.

McAuliffe, Kathleen, and Sharon McAuliffe. "The Gene Trust." *Omni*, March, 1980, 62-66, 120-122. This article examines genetic engineering and the feats it can perform. Interesting discussion of possible future applications to prenatal development.

Maurer, Daphne, and Charles Maurer. *The World of the Newborn*. New York: Basic Books, 1988. An excellent introduction to the infant, from the transitions of birth through early perceptual, cognitive, and social development. Emphasizes findings from scientific research and concludes with an integrated view of infancy. Written for the nonspecialist. Includes pictures and thorough notes with bibliographic information on all cited research.

Naeye, Richard L. "Sudden Infant Death." *Scientific American* 242 (April, 1980): 56-62. This simple but concise article covers considerable ground about SIDS, including possible origins, some epidemiology, pathological aspects, and symptomology. The writing style is informative, geared to the general reader, and replete with useful references.

Oakley, Ann. "Social Consequences of Obstetric Technology: The Importance of Measuring Soft Outcomes." *Birth: Issues in Perinatal Care and Education* 10, no. 2 (1983): 99-108. Examines the responses of mothers to modern technological advances in obstetrics as they relate to Oakley's own experience of birthing. Social and psychological consequences of obstetric interventions for both parents and their relationship with their child are explored. Fluently written in simple, straightforward language.

Payne, V. G., and L. D. Isaacs. *Human Motor Development: A Lifespan Approach*. Mountain View, Calif.: Mayfield, 1987. This book is a comprehensive, in-depth overview of motor development from birth to maturity.

Pick, Anne D., ed. *Perception and Its Development: A Tribute to Eleanor J. Gibson.* Hillsdale, N.J.: Lawrence Erlbaum, 1979. Reviews areas of perceptual development influenced by Gibson's theory of perceptual development, concluding with a chapter by Gibson herself. Covers depth perception, pattern perception, the perception of meaning, and selective attention. Provides detailed examples of the implications of Gibson's theoretical approach for empirical studies of perception.

Rosenblith, Judy F., and Judith E. Sims-Knight. *In the Beginning.* Monterey, Calif.: BrooksCole, 1985. A very readable resource on early development that has excellent chapters on developmental milestones and the influence of the environment on development.

Sameroff, Arnold J., ed. *Organization and Stability of Newborn Behavior: A Commentary on the Brazelton Neonatal Behavior Assessment Scale.* Chicago: University of Chicago Press, 1978. This is vol. 43, no. 177 in the series Monographs for Society for Research in Child Development. Provides a critical overview of the assessment of newborn reflexes by the Brazelton neonatal scale and points to research stimulated by the assessment instrument. An excellent overview of the understanding of newborn behavior, neurological functioning, and capacity for interaction.

Santrock, John W., and Steven R. Yussen. *Child Development.* Dubuque, Iowa: Wm. C. Brown, 1987. A standard book on child development that has an excellent section on physical and motor development. Very readable for the high school or college student.

Scarr, Sandra, Richard A. Weinberg, and Ann Levine. *Understanding Development.* San Diego: Harcourt Brace Jovanovich, 1986. Reviews human development from conception through adolescence. Excellent chapters on genetic and environmental factors in development. Very readable for the high school or college student.

Shaffer, David Reed. *Developmental Psychology: Childhood and Adolescence.* 2d ed. Pacific Grove, Calif.: Brooks/Cole, 1989. A well-written textbook on developmental psychology. The section on infant physical development is a good source about reflexes.

Steinberg, Laurence D., Jay Belsky, and Roberta B. Meyer. *Infancy, Childhood, and Adolescence: Development in Context*. New York: McGraw-Hill, 1991. An introductory child development textbook that presents well-rounded chronological coverage of physical, intellectual, and emotional development from conception through adolescence. Acquaints the reader with basic terminology; includes an extensive bibliography, glossary, and name and subject indexes. Diagrams and charts.

Tomlinson-Keasey, Carol. *Child Development: Psychological, Sociocultural, and Biological Factors*. Homewood, Ill.: Dorsey Press, 1985. A standard book on child development that covers the prenatal through adolescent periods. Has excellent chapters on human behavioral genetics and the brain. Very readable for the high school or college student.

Wagner, Daniel A., and Harold W. Stevenson, eds. *Cultural Perspectives on Child Development*. San Francisco: W. H. Freeman, 1982. This small edited volume provides a variety of chapters on cross-cultural child development written by leading researchers in the field for a nonprofessional audience.

Winchester, Albert McCombs. *The Nature of Human Sexuality*. Columbus, Ohio: Charles E. Merrill, 1973. Presents a nonemotional picture of sexuality. Fact-filled and interesting, it is easy to read.

Adolescence

Belenky, Mary Field, et al. *Women's Ways of Knowing: The Development of Self, Voice, and Mind*. New York: Basic Books, 1986. Describes an intensive series of interviews with more than ninety women and identifies five types of cognitive styles that were used by these women. Individual descriptions and quotations make the book interesting reading. A copy of the interview is included in the book.

Bell, Ruth, et al. *Changing Bodies, Changing Lives: A Book For Teens on Sex and Relationships*. New York: Random House, 1987. A comprehensive book that includes information on various aspects of adolescent sexuality. Written specifically for a teenage audience. Teens from around the United States were surveyed in order to determine the book's contents, and they share their unique perspectives on sexuality. This is perhaps one of the best resources available for teens.

Bervonsky, M. "Formal Reasoning in Adolescence: An Alternate View." *Adolescence* 13 (1978): 280-290. A review of the research on formal thinking. Suggests that formal thinking typically emerges at eleven to fifteen years but that the ability to utilize this thinking varies among individuals.

Bleier, Ruth. *Science and Gender*. New York: Pergamon Press, 1984. Describes the reasons there are more men than women in science and engineering, and reports on other studies concerning male and female abilities.

Bowe-Gutman, Sonia. *Teen Pregnancy*. Minneapolis: Lerner, 1987. An excellent book which discusses values involving sexuality, health issues for adolescent mothers and their babies, contraception, parenting readiness, and the economics of raising a child. The book includes five case studies of pregnant teens, and offers advice for teens who think they may be pregnant.

Buxbaum, Edith. *Troubled Children in a Troubled World*. New York: International Universities Press, 1970. Buxbaum takes a psychoanalytical approach to children's and adolescents' psychological problems. Two chapters, "The Group in Adolescence" and "Problems of Kibbutz Children," are especially relevant to adolescence. The latter looks at kibbutz children generally and at a few particular case studies.

Cote, James E., and Charles Levine. "A Critical Examination of the Ego Identity Status Paradigm." *Developmental Review* 8 (June, 1988): 147-184. Critiques the Marcia identity-status paradigm and notes several areas of divergence from Erikson's conceptualization theory of identity. Advances the argument for an interdisciplinary approach to understanding identity, and identifies several questions about identity crises that need to be considered.

_____. "A Formulation of Erikson's Theory of Ego Identity Formation." *Developmental Review* 7 (December, 1987): 209-218. A comprehensive review of Erikson's theory of ego identity and the role of psychological moratoria in the resolution of identity crises. Discusses Erikson's concepts of value orientation stages and the ego-superego conflict over personality control. Offers criticisms of Erikson's work, and suggests cautions for the researcher.

Eisenman, Russell. *From Crime to Creativity: Psychological and Social Factors in Deviance*. Dubuque, Iowa: Kendall/Hunt, 1991. Discusses causes of crime and makes the important point that most theories of crime are really theories of lower-class crime. The American view of the criminal, juvenile or adult, tends to be that of a person from the lower socioeconomic class, which does not allow an understanding of middle-class and upper-class crime. Both lower-class and white-collar crime are discussed. Juvenile delinquency is explored; the negative family backgrounds of juvenile delinquents are discussed.

Elkind, David. *The Child's Reality: Three Developmental Themes.* Hillsdale, N.J.: Lawrence Erlbaum, 1978. Discusses the ways in which adolescent cognitive skills are reflected in personality and in social behavior. Excellent presentations on egocentrism, ideologies, personal fable, imaginary audience, and pseudostupidity.

Erikson, Erik Homburger. *Childhood and Society.* 2d ed. New York: W. W. Norton, 1963. A presentation of case histories based on Erikson's clinical experiences, as well as a discussion of Erikson's life-cycle model of human development. One section of the book is devoted to an examination of youth and identity. Clinical studies are used to illustrate the problems youth face in identity resolution.

_____. *Identity, Youth, and Crisis.* New York: W. W. Norton, 1968. A theoretical discussion of ego identity formation and identity confusion, with special attention given to issues such as womanhood, and race and identity. Erikson relies heavily on his vast clinical experiences to illustrate the concepts that he discusses. The life cycle as it applies to identity is examined from an epigenetic perspective.

Feldman, S. Shirley, and Glen R. Elliott, eds. *At the Threshold: The Developing Adolescent.* Cambridge, Mass.: Cambridge University Press, 1990. A comprehensive collection of essays on adolescence that presents the findings of a Carnegie Foundation study. Primarily concerned with American society, it does include interesting references to minority adolescents and other cultures as well as historical perspectives. Well-indexed and has an exhaustive list of references.

Flavell, John. *Cognitive Development.* Englewood Cliffs, N.J.: Prentice-Hall, 1985. Presents theory and research on cognitive development from an information-processing approach. Discusses relationship between information-processing and Piagetian theory. An excellent effort to compare and contrast these two perspectives.

Freeman, Derek. *Margaret Mead and Samoa*. Cambridge, Mass.: Harvard University Press, 1983. Freeman's primary purpose is to "right the wrongs" that Mead committed in her *Coming of Age in Samoa*. He presents detailed empirical evidence to advance his arguments and remove readers' doubts about his point of view.

Friedman, Myra. *Buried Alive: The Biography of Janis Joplin*. New York: William Morrow, 1973. A powerful biography of a famous rock singer who died of a heroin overdose. It poignantly describes how insecurity and acute loneliness played a significant role in her death. An interesting and informative book which is appropriate for adolescents and adults. Contains photographs.

Ginsberg, Herbert, and Sylvia Opper. *Piaget's Theory of Intellectual Development*. Englewood Cliffs, N.J.: Prentice-Hall, 1988. In its latest edition, this now classic work contains an updated presentation of Piaget's theory of cognitive development, including a detailed analysis of formal operational thinking.

Glueck, Sheldon, and Eleanor Glueck. *Unraveling Juvenile Delinquency*. Cambridge, Mass.: Harvard University Press, 1951. This book is one of the early classics. The Gluecks, a husband-and-wife team of researchers, use psychological and sociological concepts to try to understand why youth become delinquent. They look at both the personality of the offender and the social background, such as family and neighborhood.

Hunter, Mic, ed. *The Sexually Abused Male*. 2 vols. Lexington, Mass.: D. C. Heath, 1990. Since many juvenile delinquents have suffered sexual abuse, it may be that this abuse helps cause them to become criminals. Some sexually abused children do not become criminals, so this is obviously only a partial explanation. These two volumes deal extremely well with various aspects of abuse, including, but not limited to, how the abused child may go on to become a sex offender.

Hyde, Margaret O., and Elizabeth Held Forsyth. *Suicide: The Hidden Epidemic*. New York: Franklin Watts, 1978. A book written for grades nine through twelve. Discusses the misconceptions of suicide, self-destructive patterns, and motivation theories. Includes a chapter that specifically addresses teenage suicide. Contains a list of suicide prevention centers located across the nation.

Johnson, Eric W. *Love and Sex in Plain Language*. Philadelphia: J. B. Lippincott, 1985. This book was originally written in 1968; this fourth revision remains an excellent resource for the study of human sexuality. It is concise and comprehensive. The author discusses the development of male and female reproductive systems in an understandable manner. Illustrations, a glossary, and an index make the information readily accessible.

Klagsbrun, Francine. *Too Young to Die*. 3d ed. New York: Pocket Books, 1984. An excellent book that combines scientific research with practical examples in a manner that is easy to comprehend. Discusses myths, causes, and prevention of suicide; offers concrete suggestions for talking to a suicidal person. Includes a list of hotlines and suicide prevention centers.

Kroger, Jane. *Identity in Adolescence*. London: Routledge & Kegan Paul, 1989. A presentation of identity development as conceptualized by Erikson and others. Each approach is criticized, and the empirical findings generated by the approach are summarized. The first chapter of the book is devoted to an overview of identity from a developmental and sociocultural perspective. The final chapter presents an integration of what is known about identity.

Lenney, Ellen. "Women's Self-Confidence in Achievement Settings." *Psychological Bulletin* 84, no. 1 (1977): 1-13. Reviews the psychological literature demonstrating that women have lower self-confidence than men, and delineates a number of variables on which this gender difference may depend.

McCoy, Kathy, and Charles Wibbelsman. *The New Teenage Body Book*. Los Angeles: Body Press, 1987. An excellent resource, the book is concerned with the overall health of adolescents. Included is an excellent section on sexually transmitted diseases. Provides addresses of nationwide agencies that assist adolescents with health and sexual concerns. Comprehensive and readable, with illustrations and an index to complement the text.

Madaras, Lynda, with Dane Saavedra. *The What's Happening to My Body? Book for Boys: A Growing Up Guide for Parents and Sons*. 2d rev. ed. New York: Newmarket, 1987. Written by a leading sex educator with the assistance of an adolescent male. The book deals primarily with male puberty, but includes information about sexual feelings and sexual intercourse. A very useful and informative book, written in a conversational style which makes complicated information available to teens. Illustrations and an index are included.

Madaras, Lynda, with Area Madaras. *The What's Happening to My Body? Book for Girls: A Growing Up Guide for Parents and Daughters.* Rev. ed. New York: Newmarket, 1987. Written especially for adolescents and their parents. The author is a leading sex educator, and she is joined by her daughter. The primary focus is on female puberty; however, topics such as sexual feelings and sexual intercourse are also discussed. Well written, with illustrations that enhance the text.

Marcia, James E. "Identity in Adolescence." In *Handbook of Adolescent Psychology,* edited by Joseph Adelson. New York: John Wiley & Sons, 1980. A discussion of the identity statuses developed by Marcia, based on a paradigm derived from Erikson's conceptualization of ego identity. Reviews the research on personality characteristics, patterns of interaction, developmental studies, identity in women, and other directions in identity research. Ends with a discussion of a general ego-developmental approach to identity.

Monahan, John, ed. *Who Is the Client? The Ethics of Psychological Intervention in the Criminal Justice System.* Washington, D.C.: American Psychological Association, 1980. This book contains six chapters which deal with working in the criminal justice system. Ethical dilemmas abound, as the professional may have responsibilities both to the agency and to the client (such as a juvenile delinquent). Specific issues about juvenile delinquency, including theories of causation, are contained in chapter 5, "Ethical Issues for Psychologists in the Juvenile Justice System: Know and Tell," by Julian Rappaport, James T. Lamiell, and Edward Seidman. The authors suggest that community treatment of offenders may be, at times, preferable to incarceration.

Muuss, R. E. "Social Cognition: Robert Selman's Theory of Role Taking." *Adolescence* 17, no. 67 (1982): 499-525. Discusses the relationship between adolescent cognitive skills and the ability to adopt another person's point of view. Includes an overall summary of Robert Selman's model of social cognitive development.

Patterson, Gerald R., and Marion S. Forgatch. *Parents and Adolescents Living Together: Part 1, The Basics.* Eugene, Oreg.: Castilia, 1987. _____. *Parents and Adolescents Living Together: Part 2, Family Problem Solving.* Eugene, Oreg.: Castilia, 1989. This easy-to-read and highly applicable two-volume set addresses many of the effective parenting techniques to use with adolescents based on authoritative parenting. The second volume specifically focuses on improving communication and negotiation skills as well as teaching sexual responsibility, controlling drug and alcohol use, and fostering academic achievement in adolescents. Both books provide clear examples of parents "doing it right" and "doing it wrong," as well as practical homework assignments and practice exercises to help parents try out the suggestions given by the authors.

Peck, Michael L., Norman L. Farberow, and Robert E. Litman, eds. *Youth Suicide*. New York: Springer, 1985. Provides a comprehensive overview of adolescent suicide. Written especially for the individual who is interested in working with suicidal youth, but an excellent resource for all who want to increase their understanding of this topic. Contains information on the psychodynamics of suicide, the impact of social change, the role of the family, and intervention strategies.

Petti, T. A., and C. N. Larson. "Depression and Suicide." In *Handbook of Adolescent Psychology*, edited by Vincent B. Van Hassett and Michel Herson. New York: Pergamon Press, 1987. A well-written chapter that makes the complicated factors involved in depression and a suicide accessible to the general audience. The authors discuss the causes of both depression and suicide, as well as how the two are related. Addresses how to help the suicidal adolescent. Very readable and informative.

_____. *Society and the Adolescent Self-Image*. Princeton, N.J.: Princeton University Press, 1972. Although written in the mid-1960's, this is still one of the best books available on self-esteem. Rosenberg's influence remains strong, and the self-esteem scale he included in this book is still widely used to measure self-esteem. Appropriate for both college and high school students.

Schoenbrun, David. *The New Israelis*. New York: Atheneum, 1973. A thorough probe of Israel as a culture and a people. Explores issues of family expectations of children and the function of military service as they relate to the psychology of adolescence and adulthood.

White, Merry. *The Japanese Educational Challenge*. New York: Free Press, 1987. Clear and compelling investigation of the Japanese educational system. Explores the concept of a system that focuses on parental guidance and the development of strong human relationships outside the home.

Adulthood

Baruch, Grace, and Jeanne Brooks-Gunn, eds. *Women in Midlife*. New York: Plenum Press, 1984. Provides a comprehensive review of a wide range of topics related to women in midlife. Topics include changing roles, psychological well-being, caring for aging parents, motherhood, health care, reproductive issues, sexuality, and cultural differences. Although some of the chapters are fairly technical and research-focused, most are well written and highly informative.

Berglas, Charlotte. *Mid-Life Crisis*. Lancaster, Pa.: Technomic Publishing, 1983. Berglas' short book provides a very readable, nontechnical review of the struggles that many people encounter as they enter middle age. She focuses on issues such as physical, career, and family changes and illustrates her descriptions with examples of people she has encountered through her work as a nurse.

Douglas, Jack D., and Freda Cruse Atwell. *Love, Intimacy, and Sex*. Newbury Park, Calif.: Sage, 1988. In the past several years, there has been a virtual flood of books for the general reader about how to improve intimate relationships. This one is a representative example but perhaps is a bit better than most. It offers many examples rather than superficial techniques, and it is literate and insightful.

Dunnette, Marvin D. *Handbook of Industrial and Organizational Psychology*. Chicago: Rand McNally, 1976. Covers the full range of industrial and organizational psychology through the mid-1970's. Although much of the material is intended for specialists in the field, much also is accessible to the general reader.

Elkind, David. "Erik Erikson's Eight Ages of Man." In *Readings in Human Development: Contemporary Perspectives*, edited by David Elkind and D. C. Hetzel. New York: Harper & Row, 1977. In an easy-to-read, conversational style, Elkind presents the eight stages of Erikson's developmental theory. Intermingles descriptions of Erikson's theory with pieces of his life story in a manner that brings his work to life. An excellent starting point for a basic understanding of Erikson's developmental theory that also provides good insight into Erikson himself.

Erikson, Erik Homburger. *Childhood and Society*. Rev. ed. New York: W. W. Norton, 1964. This revision of a book that first appeared in 1950 is the most widely used basis for understanding Erikson's work. It includes a variety of separately written essays, covering such topics as life history, infantile sexuality, childhood in Native American cultures, play, cultural identity and its exemplification in the personal identities of two historical figures (Adolf Hitler and Maxim Gorky), and Erikson's first detailed presentation of his own psychosocial theory of life-span psychological development.

_____. *Identity and the Life Cycle*. New York: W. W. Norton, 1980. This collection of three previously written papers of Erikson is considered one of the best introductions of his work. The first part consists of clinical notes from field studies with Native Americans and a longitudinal study of children. The second part presents Erikson's stages of life-span psychosocial development in terms of its contributions to the development of a healthy personality. The third part addresses specifically the problem of the accomplishment of ego identity in adolescence.

_____. *The Life Cycle Completed: A Review*. New York: W. W. Norton, 1982. This work presents Erikson's updated outline of his theory of psychosocial development, written when he was already in his eighties. Interestingly, he this time depicts his life-span theory from the final stage—old age—and works backward from it, in order to show "how much sense a re-view of the completed life cycle can make of its whole course."

Evans, Richard I. *Dialogue with Erik Erikson*. New York: Harper & Row, 1967. As the title suggests, this work is the result of several hours of conversation with Erikson, conducted for a film series of discussions with major personality theorists. Has appeal for the novice reader, who will discover Erikson's warmth and humanness in the dialogue. Also has appeal for those familiar with Erikson's theories in that it helps put his ideas into the context of the human condition. Discusses at length the eight stages of development, as well as Erikson's ideas on the application of his theories in the therapeutic environment. Some readers may find the question-and-answer format difficult to follow, but their efforts will be worth the insights they gain from reading the book.

Farrell, Michael P., and Stanley D. Rosenberg. *Men at Midlife*. Boston: Auburn House, 1981. Based on surveys of three hundred men and in-depth interviews with twenty men and their families, the authors have developed an explanatory model for four different types of midlife experience for men. They challenge the notion that the midlife crisis is typical and emphasize the importance of family relationships. The book includes both research data and extensive case histories, which makes it accessible to the scholar and the general public.

Feingold, S. Norman, and Norma Reno Miller. *Emerging Careers: New Occupations for the Year 2000 and Beyond.* Garret Park, Md.: Garret Park Press, 1983. The authors study the professional literature on new, emerging careers and survey more than five hundred colleges and universities as to new courses being offered related to emerging careers. Shows the astounding changes in career choices, with hundreds being eliminated and new ones being added. A futuristic view of emerging career fields and the need to adapt to them.

Gilligan, Carol. *In a Different Voice.* Cambridge, Mass.: Harvard University Press, 1982. Traditional theories of development have tried to impose male thinking and values on female psychology. Gilligan discusses the importance of relationship as well as female conceptions of morality, challenging Freud's views on female superego development.

Goldberg, Dick. *Careers Without Reschooling.* New York: Continuum, 1985. Goldberg is a talk-show host on public radio and television whose consummate interests are business and psychology. At least fifty of these shows addressed the issues of careers and the job hunt. Some were interviews related to the job hunt, which make up the first seven chapters. The remaining fourteen are informational interviews on specific careers.

Gray, J. D., and R. C. Silver. "Opposite Sides of the Same Coin: Former Spouses' Divergent Perspectives in Coping with Their Divorce." *Journal of Personality and Social Psychology* 59, no. 6 (1990): 1180-1191. Canadians rated their former spouses; both agreed that the former wife was more likely to have wanted the divorce. Both saw the other as more desirous of a reconciliation, and the men devalued their former partners to an extent not found in most other groups of people. Gray and Silver interpret these results in terms of cognitive mechanisms for coping with severe chronic stresses.

Green, Michael. *Theories of Human Development: A Comparative Approach.* Englewood Cliffs, N.J.: Prentice-Hall, 1989. For anyone who wants to put Erikson's ideas in the broader context of developmental theories. From the chart comparing seven theorists on sixteen characteristics, to the final chapter on the compatibility of the theories, the author encourages a critical comparison of ideas about development. The eight stages of development are described, as are the influences of culture and history on the development of individuals. The book is a textbook designed for courses in development; most readers will find it well written, easy to read, and complete with summaries and thought-provoking questions about human development. Highly recommended for those contemplating future study of developmental theories.

Hall, Douglas T. *Career Development in Organizations*. San Francisco: Jossey-Bass, 1986. Hall studies the ability of organizations to adjust to the times. He believes that with massive corporate restructuring, demographic changes, value and cultural changes, and turbulent external environments, organizations will find their own adaptabilities increasingly dependent upon the capacity of their employees to change and adapt.

Knowles, Richard T. *Human Development and Human Possibility: Erikson in the Light of Heidegger*. Lanham, Md.: University Press of America, 1986. The philosophical bases of this book will be too difficult in parts for a general reader, but it provides an insightful reinterpretation of Erikson's work. Knowles examines each of Erikson's psychosocial stages of development and adds an additional, existential level of understanding to each.

Knox, David. *Choices in Relationships: An Introduction to Marriage and the Family*. 2d ed. St. Paul.: West, 1988. An excellent source for information about the American family, from its formation through dating and marriage to separation, divorce, and postdivorce adjustment. There is a wealth of relevant statistical information as well as comprehensive reviews of psychological research on the effects of separation, divorce, custody arrangements, and remarriage.

Krannich, Ronald L. *Re-Careering in Turbulent Times: Skills and Strategies for Success in Today's Job Market*. Manassas, Va.: Impact Publications, 1983. Discusses the methodology of career development, redirection, and re-careering. Recognizes the need to prepare for an uncertain future by linking work skills to job search skills. Outlines how one can re-career in the decades ahead.

Landau, Sol, and Joan Thomas. *Turning Points: Self-Renewal at Midlife*. Far Hills, N.J.: New Horizon Press, 1985. Landau, a retired rabbi turned counselor and educator, wrote this book as a guide for the general public for coping with midlife crisis. He discusses his own life history as well as some of the major theoretical explanations of midlife crisis. Uses real-life examples to illustrate midlife changes in areas such as marriage, sexuality, job burn-out, and retirement. His writing is concise and includes many helpful tips for people experiencing a crisis in their own lives.

Levinson, Daniel J., Charlotte Darrow, Edward Klein, Maria Levinson, and Braxton McKee. *The Seasons of a Man's Life.* New York: Alfred A. Knopf, 1978. Summarizes Levinson's influential theoretical approach to adult development, based on in-depth interviews with forty men, ages thirty-five to forty-five. He describes the life cycle from early adulthood through middle adulthood, pointing out the psychological tasks of each stage and transition. Case-study examples are included throughout. Most of the text can be understood without an extensive knowledge of technical terminology or psychological theory.

Lewis, Adele Beatrice, and Bill Lewis, with Steve Radlaver. *How to Choose, Change, Advance Your Career.* Woodbury, N. Y.: Barron's Educational Series, 1983. A book about choosing, changing, and advancing one's career from the vantage point of professionals in the marketplace. The authors emphasize the importance of the career person's participation in the process. Their thirty years in the personnel business affords excellent help to the individual seeking a sense of direction.

McCormick, Ernest James, and Daniel R. Ilgen. *Industrial and Organizational Psychology.* 8th ed. Englewood Cliffs, N.J.: Prentice-Hall, 1985. The text critically investigates a broad field of industrial-organizational psychology. It treats the human condition and the problems generated by the sophistication of a complex technological society. It realistically brings together the concepts of organizational dynamics as they relate to industry, the contributions of industry to organizations, and the policies initiated by personnel which affect both of these areas.

Malone, Thomas Patrick, and Patrick Thomas Malone. *The Art of Intimacy.* New York: Prentice-Hall, 1987. These two psychiatrists draw upon their work with adults having marital difficulties to present the meaning of intimacy and its connection with the growth of the self. The book also offers a careful analysis of ways of being in relationships, along with key distinctions between the "I, me, and self" modes of being with another.

Mathis, Robert L., and John H. Jackson. *Personnel.* 3d ed. St. Paul: West, 1982. Details components of successful and effective organizational behavior. Equal employment opportunity issues and staffing dynamics challenge the reader to compare text information with on-the-job situations. Chapters entitled "Training and Development" and "Appraising and Compensating Human Resources" motivate the reader to search for the most applicable and feasible methods of compensation, incentives, and benefits. Clearly identifies critical areas of organizational behavior.

Miller, Jean Baker. *Toward a New Psychology of Women.* Boston: Beacon Press, 1976. Miller proposes that traditional theories of female development have overlooked a critical ingredient in female behavior— affiliation—which she believes is a cornerstone of female psychology.

Rosenzweig, Mark R., and Lyman W. Porter, eds. *Annual Review of Psychology.* Stanford, Calif.: Annual Reviews. Most volumes of this highly respected series contain a chapter or two on I/O psychology, indexed under "Personnel-Organizational Psychology." Each volume also contains a chapter title index for at least the previous decade, making location of particular topics reasonably easy.

Scarf, Maggie. *Intimate Partners: Patterns in Love and Marriage.* New York: Random House, 1987. A thoughtful analysis of problems in intimate relationships, especially of problems that have long-standing roots. Scarf depicts the essential types of interactions underlying typical problems and shows how they often perpetuate issues from one's parents' marriages.

Schlein, Stephen, ed. *A Way of Looking at Things: Selected Papers from 1930 to 1980, Erik H. Erikson.* New York: W. W. Norton, 1987. The selected papers of Erikson chosen for this work reflect five decades of thought about development and the human condition. Works included are among the best from Erikson's writings and are organized topically, adding to readability. The chapter entitled "The Human Life Cycle" eloquently describes and provides examples of each of Erikson's proposed developmental stages, complete with graphs and charts to assist the reader in comprehending the theory. Difficult reading for the novice, but well worth the effort. Of special interest are the sketches by Erikson distributed throughout the book.

Sheehy, Gail. *Passages: Predictable Crises of Adult Life.* New York: E. B. Dutton, 1976. This widely read book describes the predictable crises of adulthood, including the midlife crisis. Sheehy includes many personal experiences and case examples to illustrate the stages of development. Intended for the general public; Sheehy's engaging writing style and clever chapter titles make the book readable and enjoyable for a wide range of audiences.

Stark, Elizabeth. "Friends Through It All." *Psychology Today* 20 (May, 1986): 54-60. A study of the long-term adjustment of divorced couples who stayed in contact either because of shared parenting or personal reasons. Stark finds that many divorced people develop positive and mutually satisfying relationships but that these often become more distant when one former spouse develops a new romantic involvement. Stark identifies several factors that predict a positive continuing relationship.

Super, Donald Edwin. *The Psychology of Careers: An Introduction to Vocational Development.* New York: Harper, 1957. After Frank Parson's early text *Choosing a Vocation* (1909), this is possibly the next volume incorporating the results of significant research of psychologists, sociologists, and economists during the interim of almost fifty years. It served as a catalyst to launch the important work of researchers in recent decades. Super is still active in structuring his developmental theory to meet contemporary needs.

Wallerstein, Judith S., and Sandra Blakeslee. *Second Chances: Men, Women, and Children a Decade After Divorce.* New York: Ticknor & Fields, 1989. A very important source of information about the long-term effects of separation, divorce, and remarriage. Wallerstein followed a sample of sixty couples and their 131 children for more than fifteen years and produced comprehensive data on changes within the individuals' lives. She identifies factors related to doing well and poorly for both adults and the children of divorce.

Weitzman, Lenore J. *The Divorce Revolution.* New York: Free Press, 1985. The author makes a strong case that changes in divorce laws have caused the feminization of poverty. The work is not without methodological flaws, and the author is a determined advocate of her thesis that no-fault divorce and joint or father custody harm women; however, there is much important information here about an escalating social problem.

Yost, Elizabeth B., and M. Anne Corbishley. *Career Counseling.* San Francisco: Jossey-Bass, 1987. Takes a unique approach to clients' career problems by integrating traditional career counseling techniques with psychological methods of assessment and intervention. Has value for clinical psychologists, social workers, counselors, counseling psychologists, and career specialists such as service counselors, vocational counselors, and college placement counselors.

Aging

Achenbaum, W. A. "Societal Perceptions of Aging and the Aged." In *Handbook of Aging and the Social Sciences*, edited by Robert H. Binstock and Ethel Shanas. 2d ed. New York: Van Nostrand Reinhold, 1985. Examines attitudes toward aging from a historical perspective and assesses the impact of modern innovations such as technology and bureaucratization upon these attitudes. An extensive reference list containing more than one hundred entries is provided.

Atchley, Robert C. *The Social Forces in Later Life*. 3d ed. Belmont, Calif.: Wadsworth, 1980. A basic introduction to many of the issues related to aging. Chapter 8 deals particularly with retirement.

_____. *The Sociology of Retirement*. Cambridge, Mass.: Schenkman, 1976. One of the classic books on retirement, it is based in large part on the author's own research.

Barrow, Georgia M. *Aging, the Individual, and Society*. 4th ed. St. Paul, Minn.: West, 1989. Written in clear, nontechnical language. Examines recent research concerning society's views of the aged. Pictures, graphs, and topical short articles from other sources are incorporated into the cogent writing.

Baum, Martha, and Rainer C. Baum. *Growing Old*. Englewood Cliffs, N.J.: Prentice-Hall, 1980. A unique and excellent book on the many issues related to growing old in American society. Chapter 1, "Theoretical Perspectives," and chapter 4, "Retirement: An Emerging Social Institution," are particularly relevant and stimulating.

Becker, Ernest. *The Denial of Death*. New York: Free Press, 1973. A strong book on the power of death both for the individual and within a culture. Written, to a large extent, from a psychoanalytic standpoint. Not easy to read unless the reader has some background in psychology or anthropology.

Bengston, Vern L., and Joan F. Robertson, eds. *Grandparenthood*. Beverly
  Hills, Calif.: Sage, 1985. The chapters in this volume represent a
  significant effort to pull together much of the available research and
  thinking about grandparenting. Provides much information about and
  insight into intergenerational relations and needs. The authors should
  serve as models for researchers who wish to expand on this aspect of
  family life and American society as a whole.

Binstock, R. "Health Care of the Aging: Trends, Dilemmas and Prospects
  for the Year 2000." In *Aging 2000: Our Health Care Destiny*, edited
  by Charles M. Gaitz. New York: Springer-Verlag, 1985. Binstock
  presents an overview of health care issues, including materials on the
  capacity of older persons to pay for health care and long-term care for
  the elderly. He also outlines long-term policy issues, including the
  prospect of rationing health care on the basis of old-age criteria.

Birren, James E., and K. Warner Schaie, eds. *Handbook of the Psychology of Aging*. 2d ed. New York: Van Nostrand Reinhold, 1985.
  Presents information on the psychology of adult development and
  aging in an edited handbook format. Provides the reader with chapters
  written by experts on a wide range of topics. An authoritative review,
  serving as a definitive reference source for students, researchers, and
  professionals.

Botwinick, Jack. *Aging and Behavior: A Comprehensive Integration of
  Research Findings*. New York: Springer, 1984. A well-written compilation of research concerning aging. The second chapter deals specifically with stereotyping of the elderly.

Butler, Robert N. *Why Survive? Being Old in America*. New York: Harper
  & Row, 1975. This Pulitzer Prize-winning book is written for lay
  readers and provides a comprehensive overview of the prejudices and
  other problems faced by older Americans. Strongly critical of the
  fashion in which physicians, nursing home operators, politicians, and
  others deal with the elderly.

Cherlin, Andrew J., and Frank F. Furstenberg, Jr. *The New American
  Grandparent*. New York: Basic Books, 1986. A groundbreaking book
  based on the first representative nationwide study of American grandparents. Presents a sometimes troubling portrait of grandparenthood
  characterized by strong sentimental ties and loose bonds of obligation.
  Today's grandparents often have the economic resources, vigor, and

mobility to live apart from the family, but at the cost of intimacy, substance, and sentiment.

Cole, Thomas R., and Mary G. Winkler, eds. *The Oxford Book of Aging.* New York: Oxford University Press, 1994. Readings from various cultures and times on the experience of aging. Selections range from Ovid through D. H. Lawrence and Paule Marshall, and they are grouped under the headings of stages/journey, change/metamorphosis, generations, solitude/loneliness, works, eros/thanatos, celebration/ lament, body/spirit, and remembrance. Delightful reading for a general audience.

Coles, Robert. *Erik H. Erikson: The Growth of His Work.* Boston: Little, Brown, 1970. A definitive work on the historical and psychological roots of Erikson's theory and on his writings. Fascinating reading for those who attempt to understand a theory by understanding the person who developed it. Some background in philosophy and some prior exposure to Freud are helpful.

Cox, Harold. *Later Life: The Realities of Aging.* 2d ed. Englewood Cliffs, N.J.: Prentice-Hall, 1988. The writing style is clear and straight-forward. The author has packed the book full of practical information about all aspects of later life, including husband-wife relations, biological and health correlates of aging, theoretical perspectives on aging, work and retirement patterns, and death and dying.

Curtis, Helena. *Biology.* 3d ed. New York: Worth, 1979. An excellent intro-duction to biology for the beginning student. The text is clearly written with numerous illustrations and photographs. Provides an informative study of organismal development and aging that includes a discussion of Leonard Hayflick's experiments, demonstrating that human tissue cells have a definite life span based upon programmed cell divisions.

Darley, John M., Samuel Glucksberg, and Ronald A. Kinchla. *Psychology.* 3d ed. Englewood Cliffs, N.J.: Prentice-Hall, 1986. This introductory text summarizes the findings of studies of cognitive change with aging adults.

Erikson, Erik H., ed. *Adulthood.* New York: W. W. Norton, 1978. The first chapter, written by Erikson, uses the life of the Swedish doctor por-trayed in Ingmar Bergman's film *Wild Strawberries* to highlight the concepts of integrity and despair. Both the film and the chapter are highly recommended. The remainder of the work is also well represented but not as relevant to the concepts of integrity and despair as the first chapter.

_____. *Childhood and Society*. New York: W. W. Norton, 1950. Lays the foundation for and explains Erikson's theory of development. Erikson's psychological training, his artistic background, and his excellent command of the language are evident throughout the book. The clinical method of study is described and then applied to children and to Native Americans. The concept of the ego is developed and explored through biography and literature as well as clinical case histories. Should be read by anyone with an interest in personality or development.

_____. *Identity and the Life Cycle*. New York: International University Press, 1959. Reprint. New York: W. W. Norton, 1980. Expands on the earlier thoughts communicated in *Childhood and Society*. Thoughts about the importance of the historical backdrop in which people develop are more fully expressed than in earlier works. The growth of the individual as reflected in the healthy personality is described in some detail. The writing is dense and may be difficult for the reader who has not had much exposure to Erikson's work.

Erikson, Erik H., Joan M. Erikson, and Helen Q. Kivnick. *Vital Involvement in Old Age*. New York: W. W. Norton, 1986. Published when Erikson was well into his eighties. Describes the stages of the life cycle in reverse chronological order, emphasizing the importance of and dependence on earlier stages of development in successful aging. Clinical examples are abundant and help illustrate the many nuances of Erikson's theory. Not easy to read for those unfamiliar with Erikson's ideas, but a delightful and telling example of Erikson's own generativity and integrity.

Feifel, Herman, ed. *The Meaning of Death*. New York: McGraw-Hill, 1959. One of the original books which stimulated the current interest in death and dying. Contains essays by people such as Carl Jung, Paul Tillich, and Robert Kastenbaum, as well as articles reporting empirical studies. Generally reads well and contains myriad interesting and thoughtful ideas.

_____. *New Meanings of Death*. New York: McGraw-Hill, 1977. Interesting for the general reader. There is an article on hospice and several articles on death and young people.

Ferraro, Kenneth F. "The Gerontological Imagination." In *Gerontology: Perspectives and Issues*. New York: Springer, 1990. Provides an overview of seven themes within research on aging, pointing out that "aging frequently gets a bad name for things it did not cause." Describes a three-year project in which a young female disguises herself as an elderly woman in order to note the ageist reactions of others.

Geist, Harold. *The Psychological Aspects of the Aging Process*. St. Louis: W. H. Green, 1968. Although this book is somewhat dated, it is easy to read and covers a variety of topics, such as a comparison of care of the aged in a variety of countries, sex differences in aging, biological and psychological aspects of aging, and social and cultural aspects of the aging process.

Gelfand, Donald E. *The Aging Network*. 3d ed. New York: Springer, 1988. This four-part book first describes the status of older Americans, then moves on to income-maintenance programs. Most important, the last two sections focus on major programs of aging and service delivery for the elderly. Examines the status of nursing homes.

Goodenough, Ursula. *Genetics*. 2d ed. New York: Holt, Rinehart and Winston, 1978. A comprehensive presentation of genetics for individuals familiar with basic biology. Describes major concepts and mechanisms of genetics in great detail, including classic experiments, molecular genetics, and the role of genes in organismal development. Includes a discussion of the mechanisms by which mutations occur within genes, including aging effects such as those seen in Down syndrome, a condition whose incidence increases with maternal age.

Gross, Francis L., Jr. *Introducing Erik Erikson: An Invitation to His Thinking*. Lanham, Md.: University Press of America, 1987. Introduces the thoughts of Erikson through brief historical excerpts and anecdotes from Erikson's life. Explanations of his theory are also included. Written for the novice and enhanced by frequent examples from classic and popular literature. The writing style is engaging and frequently humorous.

Hayslip, Bert, Jr., and Paul E. Panek. *Adult Development and Aging*. New York: Harper & Row, 1989. An excellent textbook on the adult period of life. Chapter 11 deals with retirement. Has an extensive list of references; particularly good for finding research articles on particular aspects of retirement and other issues.

Karp, Gerald. *Cell Biology*. New York: McGraw-Hill, 1979. An interesting discussion of the structure and biochemistry of the living cell. Describes how the parts of the cell function together, plus how cells function within the context of organismal physiology. Includes an excellent discussion of the causes of both cancer and senescence in living cells, including the role of free radicals and mutation, in chapter 19.

Kausler, Donald H. *Experimental Psychology and Human Aging*. New York: John Wiley & Sons, 1982. Presents a survey of psychological research on human aging. The book summarizes research on gerontology and emphasizes the process of conducting psychological experiments in order to study behavior of the elderly.

Kermis, Marguerite D. *The Psychology of Human Aging: Theory, Research, and Practice*. Boston: Allyn & Bacon, 1984. A textbook that presents a comprehensive picture of diverse topics in aging. Written for students who have no previous background in gerontology. Covers many areas that are not traditionally covered, such as health policies and preventive medicine. Contains numerous case studies of psychological aging as well as practical applications of the research.

Kohut, Sylvester, Jr., Jeraldine J. Kohut, and Joseph J. Fleishman. *Reality Orientation for the Elderly*. Oradell, N.J.: Medical Economics, 1987. Written by an administrator, a nurse, and a clinical psychologist, this book discusses institutionalization of the elderly and treatment methods for older adults. The authors focus on bridging the gap between theory and practice by providing practical guidelines designed to improve the quality of life for older adults. It can be understood by high school and college students.

Kornhaber, Arthur, and Kenneth L. Woodward. *Grandparents/Grandchildren: The Vital Connection*. Garden City, N.Y.: Anchor Press, 1981. The authors explain the "vital connection" that links these generations to each other and expose what they call the "new social contract" that is destroying the emotional bonds between grandparents and grandchildren. For the first time, hundreds of children reveal in their own words and drawings what loving grandparents mean to them and how they suffer when grandparents ignore or abandon them.

Kubler-Ross, Elisabeth. *On Death and Dying*. New York: Macmillan, 1969. A popular book which had a major impact on the general public.

It reads well and is not only interesting but also of practical help to many who are personally dealing with the issue of dying.

Lewin, Benjamin. *Genes.* 3d ed. New York: John Wiley & Sons, 1987. Describes in great detail the major concepts of molecular biology and genetics. Much of the book is devoted to cutting-edge research studies on the identification and isolation of critical developmental genes. Chapter 33 discusses the processes of mutation in genes and how the cellular machinery combats these errors.

Lifton, Robert Jay, and Eric Olson. *Living and Dying.* New York: Praeger, 1974. A short, readable volume which looks at death from a broader perspective than merely as the end of life. Lifton is one of the pioneers in studying and writing about death; all of his many books are worth reading.

Macdonald, Barbara, and Cynthia Rich. *Look Me in the Eye: Old Women, Aging, and Ageism.* San Francisco: Spinsters Ink, 1983. Presents a series of compelling and thought-provoking essays concerning the special problems and issues faced by aging females. Argues that current societal trends may actually be increasing the financial, sexual, and familial difficulties of women.

Mace, Nancy L., and Peter V. Rabins. *The Thirty-Six-Hour Day.* Baltimore: The Johns Hopkins University Press, 1981. A practical and detailed book which helps family members who are caretakers of individuals with memory problems and dementia. Uses a number of examples to demonstrate how impaired family members can be helped and answers practical questions. Can be understood by the general public.

Mitford, Jessica. *The American Way of Death.* New York: Simon & Schuster, 1963. A polemical look at the funeral business. The book made many Americans aware of excesses and shoddy practices, which eventually led to a number of changes—some because of government regulation; however, the reader needs to be aware that it only presents one point of view.

Nuland, Sherwin B. *How We Die.* New York: Alfred A. Knopf, 1994. Nuland, a physician who teaches surgery and the history of medicine at Yale, wrote this book "to demythologize the process of dying" and therefore to make it less forbidding. The processes that accompany common forms of death, including heart disease, cancer, AIDS, and Alzheimer's disease, are described. Not bedtime reading, but an interesting and compassionate treatise on a subject rarely discussed.

Oberleder, Muriel. *Avoid the Aging Trap*. Washington , D.C.: Acropolis Books, 1982. Examines many of the myths concerning aging in the light of research. Offers practical suggestions to attenuate the actual effects of aging. Numerous exercises, such as a test to compute one's "Aging Quotient," maintain reader interest. Especially recommended for the middle-aged reader.

Palmore, Erdman B., et al. *Retirement: Causes and Consequences*. New York: Springer, 1986. A good general overview of retirement by a number of scholars in the field. Some chapters read well; others require more acquaintance with social-science methodology.

Parmelee, P., and P. Lawton. "The Design of Special Environments for the Aged." In *Handbook of the Psychology of Aging*, edited by James E. Birren and K. Warner Schaie. 3d ed. San Diego: Academic Press, 1990. The authors emphasize older people's need for independence even as they move into special housing environments. They discuss security as a primary need for older adults and discuss various types of living arrangements, including continuing care retirement, residential care homes, and nursing homes. They urge more research on the topic of special environments for the aged. Accessible to college students.

Sang, James H. *Genetics and Development*. New York: Longman, 1984. Provides a summary of major research into DNA, genes, and the effects of gene regulation upon organismal development. Aimed at the advanced student. Includes a good discussion of major events in the tissue development of many species and discussions on specialized topics, such as lethal genes.

Stoddard, Sandol. *The Hospice Movement*. New York: Vintage Books, 1978. Written by a layperson for the general public, this is a fascinating account of the author's experiences at St. Christopher's hospice in London and is one of the major sources in introducing the American public to the idea of Hospice.

Troll, Lillian E. "Grandparents: The Family Watchdogs." In *Family Relationships in Later Life*, edited by Timothy H. Brubaker. Beverly Hills, Calif.: Sage, 1983. Troll raises the question, "Why is there heightened interest in grandparenting at this point in time?" Her answers point to the importance of families in the lives of Americans, contrary to the prevailing myths that the family is dying. Her portrayal of grandparents is that of "family watchdogs," ever on the lookout for trouble and ready to provide assistance if a family crisis occurs.

Wass, Hannelore, Felix Berardo, and Robert A. Neimeyer, eds. *Dying: Facing the Facts*. 2d ed. Washington, D.C.: Hemisphere, 1988. Contains chapters on all the major issues about dying. The reading level of the chapters is uneven; some read quite well, others were written with the academic audience primarily in mind.

SOCIAL PSYCHOLOGY

Aggression

Bach, George R., and Herb Goldberg. *Creative Aggression*. New York: Avon Books, 1975. A guidebook for people who cannot confront conflict as well as for those who choose to seek conflict. Helps the reader to assess himself or herself honestly and to approach aggressiveness in new ways.

Bandura, Albert. *Aggression: A Social Learning Analysis*. Englewood Cliffs, N.J.: Prentice-Hall, 1973. Bandura presents a thorough overview of his social learning theory of aggression. He outlines the important antecedents of aggression and the critical factors in the instigation and maintenance of aggressive behavior. He also describes relevant social learning principles and applies them to behavioral change. Accessible to the college-level reader.

Berkowitz, Leonard. *Aggression: A Social-Psychological Analysis*. New York: McGraw-Hill, 1962. This classic volume presents the frustration-aggression hypothesis. Contrasts the frustration-aggression hypothesis with instinct theories of aggression and discusses situational factors implicated in the expression and inhibition of aggression. The role of catharsis in aggression is also discussed.

_____. "Biological Roots: Are Humans Inherently Violent?" In *Psychological Dimensions of War*, edited by Betty Glad. Newbury Park, Calif.: Sage, 1990. This is an excellent, easy-to-read critique of instinct theories of aggression. Berkowitz presents the frustration-aggression hypothesis and applies this theory to an analysis of international conflict. The role of aggression in the human condition and international relations is thoroughly discussed.

_____, ed. *Roots of Aggression*. New York: Atherton Press, 1969. Revisits the frustration-aggression hypothesis. Examines such areas as catharsis, frustration, and conditions facilitating the occurrence of aggression.

Donnerstein, Edward I., Daniel Linz, and Steven Penrod. *The Question of Pornography*. New York: Free Press, 1987. Review of laboratory research on effects of pornography. Distinguishes between the proven antisocial effects of violent pornography and the more speculative claims against nonviolent pornography. Accessible to the general reader.

Geen, Russell G. *Human Aggression*. Pacific Grove, Calif.: Brooks/Cole, 1990. The author, a prominent researcher in the field, provides a solid empirical and theoretical discussion of the concept of aggression. Individual differences in aggression are discussed as well as interpersonal and environmental factors that mediate the expression of aggressive behavior.

Groebel, Jo, and Robert A. Hinde, eds. *Aggression and War: Their Biological and Social Bases*. New York: Cambridge University Press, 1989. This edited volume presents a lively discussion of the biological, psychological, and cultural factors in human aggression. Physiological and individual differences in aggression are presented in addition to social and situational forces that are useful in the control of aggression and the encouragement of prosocial behaviors. Cultural and political issues relevant to aggression are discussed.

Huesmann, L. Rowell, and Neil M. Malamuth. "Media Violence and Antisocial Behavior." *Journal of Social Issues* 42, no. 3 (1986): 125-139. This article is in a special issue of a psychological journal containing eleven articles that summarize the effects of media violence and pornography.

Jacks, Irving, and Steven G. Cox, eds. *Psychological Approaches to Crime and Its Correction*. Chicago: Nelson-Hall, 1984. Covers a wide range of topics related to aggression and positivistic points of view in the face of crime. Examines the modification of aggressive behavior.

Joy, Leslie A., Meredith M. Kimball, and Merle L. Zabrack. "Television and Children's Aggressive Behavior." In *The Impact of Television*, edited by Tannis MacBeth Williams. Orlando, Fla.: Academic Press, 1986. Presents a study of the effects of the introduction of cable television in an isolated community in western Canada on the aggressive behavior of its children.

Liebert, Robert M., and Joyce Sprafkin. *The Early Window: Effects of Television on Children and Youth*. 3d ed. Elmsford, N.Y.: Pergamon Press, 1988. Excellent overview of the socializing effects of television.

Discusses the effects of televised violence and the politics of governmental regulation of television content.

Lorenz, Konrad. *On Aggression.* New York: Methuen, 1966. This easy-to-read classic is a comparative study of aggression in a number of species. Lorenz documents the evolutionary significance of aggression and describes its expression in fish, animals, and humans. He argues that aggression plays an important social role in same-species interactions.

Luschen, Gunther. "Psychological Issues in Sports Aggression." In *Sports Violence*, edited by Jeffrey H. Goldstein. New York: Springer-Verlag, 1983. Describes the cathartic role of sports in both athletes' and spectators' aggressive behaviors. The author summarizes the central role that catharsis plays in several psychological and philosophical perspectives on aggression, then presents the results of empirical studies investigating the links between sports and aggression.

May, Rollo. *Power and Innocence.* New York: W. W. Norton, 1972. Probes the sources of violence. Advances solutions for contemporary society, examining the concept of innocence and challenging traditional views of aggression.

Segall, Marshall H. "Cultural Roots of Aggressive Behavior." In *The Cross-Cultural Challenge to Social Psychology*, edited by Michael Harris Bond. Newbury Park, Calif.: Sage, 1988. Segall presents a summary and critique of important cross-cultural studies of aggression. His presentation focuses on the manner in which gender roles, biology, and cultural forces interact in the socialization of aggression. An intriguing and quite accessible article.

Signorelli, Nancy, and George Gerbner, comps. *Violence and Terror in the Mass Media: An Annotated Bibliography.* New York: Greenwood Press, 1988. Citations and paragraph-length summaries of 784 studies of violent media content and its effects. Very helpful when doing a literature survey.

Zillmann, Dolf, and Jennings Bryant, eds. *Pornography: Research Advances and Policy Considerations.* Hillsdale, N.J.: Lawrence Erlbaum, 1989. Fifteen papers dealing with the content and effects of pornography and the legal debate over pornography regulation. Papers are sometimes difficult but are generally rewarding.

Attitudes and Behavior

Ajzen, Icek, and Martin Fishbein. *Understanding Attitudes and Predicting Social Behavior*. Englewood Cliffs, N.J.: Prentice-Hall, 1980. A very readable introduction to the authors' theory of reasoned action. Applications of the theory to specific areas such as political, consumer, and dieting behavior are also discussed, and more general implications for attitude change and persuasion are addressed.

Allport, Gordon W. "Attitudes." In *Handbook of Social Psychology*, edited by Carl Allanmore Murchison. Worchester, Mass.: Clark University Press, 1935. The first review of the attitude concept. Provides a useful introduction to the historical origins of attitude research.

Aronson, Elliot. *The Social Animal*. New York: W. H. Freeman, 1992. A thorough but basic treatment of social psychological phenomena (self-justification, dissonance, prejudice, conformity), with an emphasis on the cognitive perspective. Includes a name and subject index, as well as a "Notes" section that is a guide to the popular and scientific literatures on topics addressed in the book.

_____. "The Theory of Cognitive Dissonance." In *Advances in Experimental Social Psychology*. Vol. 4, edited by Leonard Berkowitz. New York: Academic Press, 1969. This chapter by one of the leading dissonance researchers critically examines the original theory and offers a revised version of the theory based on empirical findings. Clearly written and easily accessible to nonpsychologists.

Brehm, Jack Williams, and Arthur R. Cohen. *Explorations in Cognitive Dissonance*. New York: John Wiley & Sons, 1962. The sixteen chapters in this volume examine, among other things, the implications of dissonance for decision making, the role of personality factors in the experience of dissonance, and possible physiological factors underlying dissonance. In addition, practical applications of the theory are discussed.

Cialdini, Robert B. *Influence: How and Why People Agree to Things*. New York: William Morrow, 1984. This highly readable account provides a fascinating discussion of six of the most frequently used compliance tactics.

Fazio, Russell. "How Do Attitudes Guide Behavior?" In *Handbook of Motivation and Cognition*, edited by Richard M. Sorrentino and E. Tory

Higgins. New York: Guilford Press, 1986. An excellent introduction to Fazio's initial work on the role of attitude accessibility. Also provides a brief history of the attitude-behavior consistency controversy and attempts to show how issues of attitude accessibility may help resolve parts of the controversy.

Fazio, Russell, and Mark P. Zanna. "Direct Experience and Attitude-Behavior Consistency." In *Advances in Experimental Social Psychology*, edited by Leonard Berkowitz. Vol. 14. New York: Academic Press, 1981. A thorough review of the research and theory on the role that attitude formation plays in the attitude-behavior relationship. Offers examples of both field research and laboratory research. Ideas presented here lay the foundation for Fazio's later work on attitude accessibility.

Festinger, Leon. *A Theory of Cognitive Dissonance*. Stanford, Calif.: Stanford University Press, 1957. Festinger's seminal work represents the formal introduction of the theory. Theory and data on decision making, attitude change, and exposure to attitude-discrepant information are addressed. It is interesting to compare this original work with later versions of the theory.

Gifford, Robert. *Environmental Psychology: Principles and Practice*. Boston: Allyn & Bacon, 1987. An excellent introductory textbook; slightly more sophisticated than its peers. A readable blend of theoretical and empirical work with an emphasis on practical application. An extensive bibliography is also provided. Can be understood by the high school or college student.

Hovland, Carl Iver, Irving L. Janis, and Harold H. Kelley. *Communication and Persuasion*. New Haven, Conn.: Yale University Press, 1953. This first research monograph on persuasion covers issues such as source credibility, fear appeals, and personality and persuasion.

Jacoby, Jacob, and Jerry C. Olson, eds. *Perceived Quality: How Consumers View Stores and Merchandise*. Lexington, Mass.: Lexington Books, 1985. A set of articles contributed by various specialists in perceptions of quality. Presents the views of retailers, manufacturers, and consumers; discusses regulatory and economic perspectives on quality.

Kiesler, Charles A., Barry E. Collins, and Norman Miller. *Attitude Change*. New York: John Wiley & Sons, 1969. Offers a critical analysis of dissonance theory. Also compares and contrasts dissonance theory with other prominent theories of attitude change and persuasion. An excellent general introduction to theory and research on attitude change.

Lewin, Kurt. "Group Decision and Social Change." In *Readings in Social Psychology*, edited by Theodore M. Newcomb and Eugene L. Hartley. New York: Henry Holt, 1947. Describes how Lewin changed food preferences during World War II, providing an excellent example of how to apply field theory to practical problems.

McGuire, W. J. "Attitudes and Attitude Change." In *Handbook of Social Psychology*, edited by Gardner Lindzey and Elliot Aronson. 3d ed. New York: Random House, 1985. One of the most comprehensive reviews of the topic. Covers issues such as the history of persuasion research, the definition of an attitude, and how attitudes are formed, and provides a critical analysis of attitude change theories and a detailed summary of attitude research.

_____. *Communication and Persuasion: Central and Peripheral Routes to Attitude Change.* New York: Springer-Verlag, 1986. Provides a detailed description of the role of elaboration in persuasion and provides a useful summary of recent research in persuasion.

Petty, Richard E., and John T. Cacioppo. *Attitudes and Persuasion: Classic and Contemporary Approaches.* Dubuque, Iowa: Wm. C. Brown, 1981. An excellent textbook that provides a description of major theories of persuasion and supporting research.

Pratkanis, Anthony R., and Elliot Aronson. *The Age of Propaganda: The Everyday Use and Abuse of Persuasion.* New York: W. H. Freeman, 1992. A popular treatment of the role of persuasion in society. Describes numerous persuasion tactics and provides the reader with an in-depth analysis of how they work and what can be done to prevent unwanted propaganda.

Pratkanis, Anthony R., Steven J. Breckler, and Anthony G. Greenwald, eds. *Attitude Structure and Function.* Hillsdale, N.J.: Lawrence Erlbaum, 1989. The papers in this volume summarize how attitudes influence social processes such as cognition and behavior, and update functional theories of attitude.

Proshansky, Harold M., William H. Ittelson, and Leanne G. Rivlin, eds. *Environmental Psychology: People and Their Physical Settings.* 2d ed.

New York: Holt, Rinehart and Winston, 1976. An edited textbook with many outstanding selections from leaders in the field. The editors themselves established the first Ph.D. program in environmental psychology at the City University of New York in 1968; their introduction provides insights into the history and issues of the field.

Saegert, S., and G. H. Winkel. "Environmental Psychology." *Annual Review of Psychology* 41. Stanford, Calif.: Annual Reviews, 1990. Reviews developments in the field, presenting major theories of person-environment relations. Evaluates research with an eye toward future synthesis. Although a good overview, it is slightly technical in spots.

Snyder, Mark. *Public Appearances/Private Realities: The Psychology of Self-Monitoring.* New York: W. H. Freeman, 1987. Very readable review of research and theory about the self-monitoring personality variable. Several chapters devoted exclusively to explaining how self-monitoring relates to issues of attitude-behavior consistency.

Stokols, Daniel, and Irwin Altman, eds. *Handbook of Environmental Psychology.* 2 vols. New York: John Wiley & Sons, 1987. Presents a wide array of chapters on environmental psychology, including theories, history, cross-cultural approaches, the field's relationship to child development, and numerous individual approaches to environmental psychology. A very comprehensive source. A must for anyone in the field; can be understood by the college student.

Wicklund, Robert A., and Jack Williams Brehm. *Perspectives on Cognitive Dissonance.* Hillsdale, N. J.: Lawrence Erlbaum, 1976. Contains seventeen chapters that not only review the evidence for the basic tenets of the theory but also explore implications of the theory for areas such as politics, marketing, and clinical psychology. In addition, alternative explanations for dissonance phenomena are entertained.

Zanna, Mark P., E. Tory Higgins, and C. Peter Herman, eds. *Consistency in Social Behavior: The Ontario Symposium.* Vol. 2. Hillsdale, N.J.: Lawrence Erlbaum, 1982. Perhaps the most important single volume on attitude-behavior relations. The twelve chapters, written by the leading authorities on the topic, raise and discuss all the important issues about not only attitude-behavior relations but personality trait-behavior relations as well. Important for anyone who wishes to understand attitude-behavior relations thoroughly.

Zimbardo, Philip G., and Michael R. Leippe. *The Psychology of Attitude Change and Social Influence*. Philadelphia: Temple University Press, 1991. This textbook presents an engaging review of attitude-change techniques and analyzes their use in various social settings.

Group Processes

Bass, Bernard M. *Bass and Stogdill's Handbook of Leadership*. 3d ed. New York: Free Press, 1990. A complete review of the research of Bass, Stogdill, and others on differences among leaders. Somewhat technical; for advanced students.

_____. *Leadership and Performance Beyond Expectations*. New York: Free Press, 1985. Readable and thorough examination of the work of Bass and others on leadership research and practice. Emphasis on charismatic and transformational leadership.

Brown, Hedy. *People, Groups, and Society*. Philadelphia: Open University Press, 1985. An extremely accessible introduction to group influence and crowd behavior that includes an introduction to general principles of social influence and intergroup relations. The similarities and differences between crowds and other social groups are also discussed.

Brown, Rupert. *Group Processes: Dynamics Within and Between Groups*. New York: Basil Blackwell, 1988. This is a very readable treatment of theories and research on group processes, with a particular emphasis on British and European contributions. A variety of compelling and relevant social issues are covered, such as social conformity, crowd behavior, group productivity, and ethnic prejudice.

Canetti, Elias. *Crowds and Power*. New York: Viking Press, 1962. This is a classic historical discussion of the effects of crowds on individuals and societies. Such avenues of group behavior are described as open and closed crowds, invisible crowds, baiting crowds, and feast crowds.

Davis, James H. "Social Interaction as a Combinatorial Process in Group Decision." In *Group Decision Making*, edited by H. Brandstatter, James H. Davis, and Gisela Stocker-Kreichgauer. London: Academic Press, 1982. Emphasizes models of group process. Good presentation of the social decision scheme approach, particularly as it has been applied in research on jury decision making.

Duffy, Karen Grover, James W. Grosch, and Paul V. Olczak, eds. *Community Mediation: A Handbook for Practitioners and Researchers*. New York: Guilford, 1991. Takes much relevant research and applies it to the topic of community mediation. As the title implies, it is meant for a wide audience, and it is scholarly but not overly technical. Easily readable by the college undergraduate.

Fiedler, Fred E., and Martin M. Chemers. *Improving Leadership Effectiveness: The Leader Match Concept*. New York: John Wiley & Sons, 1984. Discusses field tests of contingency theory and various attempts to implement leader match training. Good emphases on both theory and application.

Fisher, Roger, and William Ury. *Getting to Yes: Negotiating Agreement Without Giving In*. Boston: Houghton Mifflin, 1981. A very practical, short (160-page) paperback. This was a national bestseller for a good reason. The authors review some high-powered research and communicate it in very understandable language; they make a reasonable case for "principled negotiation," though some of their suggestions and examples seem a bit unrealistic.

Forsyth, Donalson R. *An Introduction to Group Dynamics*. Monterey, Calif.: Brooks/Cole, 1983. This thorough volume provides access to a wide-ranging review of evidence regarding all aspects of group processes.

Galanter, Marc. *Cults: Faith, Healing, and Coercion*. New York: Oxford University Press, 1989. A fascinating study of charismatic groups that is particularly appropriate for the general reader. Discusses the unique social factors that characterize such groups and provides three famous case histories (Jonestown, the Unification Church, and Alcoholics Anonymous). A detailed explanation of the social forces that are experienced by members of cults and other extremely cohesive social groups.

Gaskell, George, and Robert Benewick, eds. *The Crowd in Contemporary Britain*. London: Sage, 1987. This edited volume is an excellent collection of studies and observations of crowd behavior. Theories of crowd behavior are introduced, then historical and contemporary examples of crowd behavior are presented. The chapters in this volume are concerned with a range of crowd behaviors, from peaceful to violent actions.

Guzzo, Richard A., ed. *Improving Group Decision Making in Organizations*. New York: Academic Press, 1982. A collection of articles by group decision researchers. It is an exploration of research paradigms that have potential applications to the improvement of decision making by groups. Topics include coalition formation, group remembering, and social judgment analysis.

Hall, Edward Twitchell. *The Hidden Dimension*. Garden City, N.Y.: Doubleday, 1969. One of the best (relatively brief) introductions to the field of proxemics by one of its pioneers. Includes sections on crowding and social behavior, proxemics and culture, and proxemics and the future. Delightfully written and easily understood.

Hastie, Reid. "Experimental Evidence on Group Accuracy." In *Decision Research*, edited by B. Grofman and G. Owen. Vol. 2. Greenwich, Conn.: JAI Press, 1986. A review of research on the quality of decisions made by groups. Strong emphasis on literature pertaining to decision making by juries. Also includes discussion of data on confidence.

Hogan, Robert, Gordon J. Curphy, and Joyce Hogan. "What We Know About Leadership: Effectiveness and Personality." *American Psychologist* 49, no. 6 (1994): 493-504. Describes how the "big 5" dimensions of personality—"surgency," emotional stability, conscientiousness, agreeableness, and "intellectance"—characterize effective leadership. Discusses difficulties in choosing leaders and reasons leaders may fail. Presents implications for the future of the workforce. Published in a professional journal but accessible to high school and college students.

Hogg, Michael A., and Dominic Abrams. *Social Identifications: A Social Psychology of Intergroup Relations and Group Processes*. London: Routledge, 1988. This volume adopts a social-identity perspective on group influence. Two chapters are particularly relevant to the effects of crowd membership on personal identity and behavior. The authors present an excellent summary of the effects of the presence of others on social performance. Another excellent chapter addresses the nature of collective behavior and deindividuation. An accessible review of complex issues.

Holahan, Charles J. *Environmental Psychology*. New York: Random House, 1982. A beginning textbook by a leading researcher in the field. Particularly good coverage of topics such as environmental cognition, environmental stress, crowding, and privacy. The last chapter provides a unifying framework for the field; there is also an extensive bibliography. Can be understood by the high school or college student.

Insel, Paul, and Henry Clay Lindgren. *Too Close for Comfort: The Psychology of Crowding.* Englewood Cliffs, N.J.: Prentice-Hall, 1978. These authors have a background in personality and social psychology, cross-cultural psychology, and social ecology (the study of the relationship between the physical and social aspects of the environment). They bring this relevant experience to bear on the question of the effects of crowding on attitudes, personality, solving problems, and mental and physical health. A very readable paperback that covers the issues in an interesting way.

Jandt, Fred Edmund. *Win-Win Negotiating: Turning Conflict into Agreement.* New York: John Wiley & Sons, 1985. A very readable book designed for anyone involved in negotiation. Many bold claims are unsubstantiated, but the author has considerable experience as a consultant and seminar leader in conflict management and is a good writer. Highly readable at the high school level.

Janis, Irving Lester. *Victims of Groupthink.* Boston: Houghton Mifflin, 1972. An illustration of the factors that can lead groups to make poor decisions with great confidence; includes dramatic examples based on historical incidents. Appropriate for a general audience.

McGrath, Joseph Edward. *Groups: Interaction and Performance.* Englewood Cliffs, N.J.: Prentice-Hall, 1984. Thorough and thoughtful integration of research on group performance. Includes numerous figures and research reports, as well as balanced discussions of ongoing and past debates. Appropriate as a text or reference book.

Milgram, Stanley. *The Individual in a Social World: Essays and Experiments.* Reading, Mass.: Addison-Wesley, 1977. An excellent introduction to group influence and crowd behavior. Milgram, a prominent researcher in the field, describes a number of classic experiments on social influence and crowd behavior. The articles in part 1 ("The Individual in the City") and part 2 ("The Individual and the Group") of this work are particularly relevant to crowd behavior.

Mullen, Brian, and George R. Goethals, eds. *Theories of Group Behavior.* New York: Springer-Verlag, 1987. This comprehensive edited volume considers several theories of group behavior in order to expand fully on this phenomenon. Classic as well as contemporary and controversial theories are described by several of the social psychologists who originally formulated the accounts.

Paulus, Paul B., ed. *Psychology of Group Influence*. 2d ed. Hillsdale, N.J.: Lawrence Erlbaum, 1989. This edited volume contains a selection of articles on many aspects of crowd behavior. Specific topics include the social facilitation effect, deindividuation, and environmental influences on crowds. An excellent source of theoretical perspectives and empirical data relevant to crowd behavior for the college-level reader.

Perry, Joseph B., Jr., and Meredith David Pugh. *Collective Behavior: Response to Social Stress*. St. Paul, Minn.: West, 1978. A general discussion of the crowd and its social influence. The authors first present a theoretical discussion of the crowd, rumor, contagion, and deindividuation, then provide many examples of crowd violence, control, mobilization, and social movements. A very accessible introduction to the topic with specific focus on collective behavior.

Pruitt, Dean G., and Jeffrey Z. Rubin. *Social Conflict: Escalation, Stalemate, and Settlement*. New York: Random House, 1986. Blends good scholarship with practical considerations, though the emphasis is much more on the former. Though not a lengthy book, the authors do a good job of reviewing the literature on conflict.

Rubin, Jeffrey Z., and Bert R. Brown. *The Social Psychology of Bargaining and Negotiation*. New York: Academic Press, 1975. As the title suggests, this book investigates social-psychological issues involved in the negotiation process. Designed for researchers, the book is nevertheless free of unnecessary jargon. The book's biggest drawback is its age, as much research has been conducted since the mid-1970's.

Saks, M. J., and Edward Krupat. "Environment and Behavior." In *Social Psychology and Its Applications*. New York: Harper & Row, 1988. An abbreviated overview of environmental psychology which places crowding in context. Deals with crowding and related issues concisely, so that it provides a good way to cover most of the issues quickly.

Smith, Blanchard B. "The TELOS Program and the Vroom-Yetton Model." In *Crosscurrents in Leadership*, edited by James G. Hunt and Lars L. Larson. Carbondale: Southern Illinois University Press, 1979.

A description of the work of the Kepner Tregoe organization, based in Princeton, New Jersey, on implementation of the Vroom-Yetton theory.

Sniezek, Janet A., and Rebecca A. Henry. "Accuracy and Confidence in Group Judgment." *Organizational Behavior and Human Decision Processes* 43 (February 1, 1989): 1-28. A research article showing how group and individual judgement accuracy and confidence can be compared. Technical, but the figures and main results can be appreciated by the student.

Steiner, Ivan Dale. *Group Process and Productivity.* New York: Academic Press, 1972. A classic work that will remain important in the group decision-making literature. Analyzes the components of successful group performance and the processes required to get there. Scholarly rather than entertaining.

Turner, John C., Michael A. Hogg, et al. *Rediscovering the Social Group: A Self-Categorization Theory.* Oxford, England: Basil Blackwell, 1987. A sophisticated in-depth treatment of a new theory of behavior in groups. This theoretical approach integrates a vast amount of data and sets the stage for further research in group behavior.

Yukl, Gary A. *Leadership in Organizations.* Englewood Cliffs, N.J.: Prentice-Hall, 1989. Textbook approach to leadership in the workplace. Suitable for undergraduate college students.

Zimbardo, Philip G. "The Human Choice: Individuation, Reason, and Order Versus Deindividuation, Impulse, and Chaos." In *Nebraska Symposium on Motivation: 1969*, edited by William J. Arnold and D. Levine. Lincoln: University of Nebraska Press, 1970. An accessible and authoritative discussion of the factors that elicit deindividuation. Presents a number of experiments, anecdotes, and everyday examples of the prosocial and antisocial behavioral effects of increased urbanization and other sociocultural factors that increase anonymity and reduce individual self-awareness and behavioral inhibitions.

Interpersonal Relations

Adler, Ronald B., Lawrence B. Rosenfeld, and Neil Towne. *Interplay: The Process of Interpersonal Communication.* New York: Holt, Rinehart and Winston, 1980. Focuses on the skills and processes at work in effective communication; offers examples and suggestions for improving listening, expressing, and verbal and nonverbal language. The text also reviews the risks and advantages involved in self-disclosure. Very readable and practical.

Altman, Irwin, and Dalmas A. Taylor. *Social Penetration: The Development of Interpersonal Relationships.* New York: Holt, Rinehart and Winston, 1973. This short, very readable book presents the theory of social penetration, describing how self-disclosure varies in breadth and depth over time. Includes helpful illustrations and numerous examples.

Berscheid, Ellen, and Elaine Hatfield Walster. *Interpersonal Attraction.* 2d ed. Reading, Mass.: Addison-Wesley, 1978. Presents a solid overview of the psychology of attraction. Directed toward the reader with no background in social psychology, the book is quite readable; nevertheless, it is highly regarded and frequently cited within the field. Clever illustrations feature many cartoons.

_____. "Physical Attractiveness." In *Advances in Experimental Social Psychology*, edited by Leonard Berkowitz. New York: Academic Press, 1974. A very thorough review of the research examining the role of physical attractiveness in interpersonal attraction. This is a frequently cited and extensively documented chapter that includes interesting discussions of how people judge attractiveness and how attractiveness affects the individual.

Brehm, Sharon S. *Intimate Relationships.* 2d ed. New York: Random House, 1991. Brehm's text reviews the major issues and processes in close relationships: attraction, love, sexuality, social exchange, fairness, commitment, power, jealousy, communication, conflict and dissolution, loneliness, the social network, and therapeutic intervention. Aimed at college students, the book is rich with examples and helpful aids to learning.

Clanton, Gordon, and Lynn G. Smith, eds. *Jealousy.* Englewood Cliffs, N.J: Prentice-Hall, 1977. A short, readable, and interesting edited collection reviewing gender differences, cultural factors, and other issues in jealousy research.

Duck, Steve. *Friends, for Life: The Psychology of Close Relationships.* New York: St. Martin's Press, 1983. Duck, an influential theorist in the field of close relationships, explains the value of friends, the strategies by which friendships are developed, and the ways in which friendships can be assessed and strengthened. Readable and engaging.

_____. *Relating to Others*. Chicago, Ill.: Dorsey Press, 1988. Duck, an important influence in the field of close relationships, discusses the stages in the life cycle of a relationship, from first meeting to maintenance to dissolution. Includes research findings and theoretical context, and suggests additional sources. Extremely readable for the college or high school student.

Duck, Steve, and Robin Gilmour, eds. *Personal Relationships Four: Dissolving Personal Relationships*. New York: Academic Press, 1982. This excellent volume (fourth in a series) by a leading relationships writer features ten chapters on processes of dissolution, different forms of termination, the roles of cognitive processes, attribution, communication, age factors, and family implications.

Festinger, Leon, Stanley Schachter, and Kurt Back. *Social Pressures in Informal Groups*. Stanford, Calif.: Stanford University Press, 1950. This classic work documents the authors' research on housing and friendship preferences and ties work on friendship to theories of group structure and function.

Fromm, Erich. *The Art of Loving*. New York: Harper, 1956. In this classic book, Fromm builds on the theme that immature love is needing to be loved, while mature love is needing to love. The reader learns what qualities must be developed in oneself before one can maturely love another person.

Harvey, John H., Ann L. Weber, and Terri L. Orbuch. *Interpersonal Accounts: Social Psychological Perspectives*. Cambridge, Mass.: Basil Blackwell, 1990. This work reviews the forms and functions of the accounts or stories that people compose about loss, proposing a theory of account-making as a response to stress, and applying the theory to person perception, grief, and literature.

Hatfield, Elaine, and Susan Sprecher. *Mirror, Mirror: The Importance of Looks in Everyday Life*. Albany: State University of New York Press, 1986. An extremely thorough and very readable review of all the different effects of personal appearance—not only on the attraction process but also on the person himself or herself. Explores how judgments of attractiveness are made and addresses the effects of beauty across the entire life span. Nicely supported with photographs and illustrations.

Hendrick, Clyde, and Susan Hendrick. *Liking, Loving, and Relating.* Monterey, Calif.: Brooks/Cole, 1983. The Hendricks provide a thorough review of the processes of affiliation and interpersonal attraction. They include a discussion of issues in contemporary relationships, such as separation and divorce, blended families, changing sex roles, and dual-career couples.

Huston, Ted L., ed. *Foundations of Interpersonal Attraction.* New York: Academic Press, 1974. This edited volume brings together chapters by major researchers in close relationships. Most chapters emphasize theory and are directed at the college student and graduate student.

Knapp, Mark L. *Interpersonal Communication and Human Relationships.* Boston: Allyn & Bacon, 1984. Knapp, a leading communication researcher, explains the nature of interpersonal communication and describes its form in dialogue, ritual, and intimacy. Discusses the important elements in personal communication and how these can be evaluated and developed.

Lauer, Jeanette C., and Robert H. Lauer. *Til Death Do Us Part: How Couples Stay Together.* New York: Haworth Press, 1986. In this valuable book, the Lauers tell couples how to make their relationship last.

Levinger, George, and Oliver C. Moles, eds. *Divorce and Separation: Context, Causes, and Consequences.* New York: Basic Books, 1979. This edited work includes chapters on five aspects of marital termination: historical and cultural perspectives, social and psychological determinants of breakup (including a chapter by Hill, Rubin, and Peplau about their longitudinal study), economic determinants, consequences for former spouses, and consequences for children and families.

Myers, David G. *Social Psychology.* 3d ed. New York: McGraw-Hill, 1990. This very popular social psychology textbook features an unusually good chapter on interpersonal attraction. Offers a solid survey of the research relating to the principles of attraction and provides particularly good coverage of work on love. The author's engaging writing style makes this an excellent starting point for further exploration of the topic.

Phillips, Debora, with Robert Judd. *How to Fall out of Love.* Boston: Houghton Mifflin, 1978. This book reviews a brief, practical, behavior modification approach to coping with terminated or unsatisfactory relationships.

Pines, Ayala M., and Elliot Aronson. "Antecedents, Correlates, and Consequences of Sexual Jealousy." *Journal of Personality* 51 (1983): 108-136. An easy-to-read, clarifying review of the causes, symptoms, and outcomes of jealousy in romantic relationships.

Rubin, Lillian B. *Just Friends: The Role of Friendship in Our Lives.* New York: Harper & Row, 1985. A very accessible popular work examining a much-neglected topic. Considers gender differences in friendships and how friendships coexist with other close relationships in people's lives.

Rubin, Zick. *Liking and Loving.* New York: Holt, Rinehart and Winston, 1973. Rubin discusses how social psychological research answers many questions about love. This book gives hints about what causes two people to be attracted to each other and what may cause them to break up.

Safilios-Rothschild, Constantina. *Love, Sex, and Sex Roles.* Englewood Cliffs, N.J.: Prentice-Hall, 1977. Discusses obstacles to the development of love from a sex roles perspective. The main thesis is that as long as men and women are socially unequal, traditional concepts of masculinity and femininity are often incompatible with mutually fulfilling sexuality and love.

Salovey, Peter, and Judith Rodin. "The Heart of Jealousy." *Psychology Today* 19 (September, 1985): 22-29. This engaging article reviews research findings and suggests practical applications.

Shaver, P., C. Hazan, and D. Bradshaw. "Love as Attachment: The Integration of Three Behavioral Systems." In *The Psychology of Love*, edited by Robert J. Sternberg and Michael L. Barnes. New Haven, Conn.: Yale University Press, 1988. This book contains chapters by all the main social psychologists investigating love. In the chapter by Shaver, Hazan, and Bradshaw, the readers can find out what type of love he or she develops with others—avoidant, anxious-ambivalent, or secure.

Sternberg, Robert, and Catherine Whitney. *Love the Way You Want It.* New York: Bantam Books, 1991. Includes a quick test that allows one to discover which of the three components of love are in one's current relationship. Sternberg also provides guidelines for ways of resolving problems and having a successful relationship.

Vaughan, Diane. *Uncoupling: Turning Points in Intimate Relationships*. New York: Oxford University Press, 1986. Vaughan reviews the noticeable changes and rituals involved in relationship dissolution, illustrating her analysis with real-life examples from survivors of broken relationships.

Walster, Elaine, and G. William Walster. *A New Look at Love*. Reading, Mass.: Addison-Wesley, 1978. This entertaining book answers many questions about love by summarizing psychological research. The section on the male versus the female experience of love is especially enlightening.

Weiss, Robert Stuart. *Marital Separation*. New York: Basic Books, 1975. Weiss recounts the experiences of participants in his series of seminars for the separated, reviewing emotional reactions to separation, practical and philosophical problems. Very readable and helpful to the professional and the layperson.

White, Gregory L., and Paul E. Mullen. *Jealousy: Theory, Research, and Clinical Strategies*. New York: Guilford Press, 1989. This well-written academic book includes chapters on romantic jealousy; the origins of jealousy in sociobiology, personality, and culture; gender effects in jealousy; pathological and violent jealousy; and strategies for assessing and managing jealousy.

Prejudice and Discrimination

Allport, Gordon Willard. *The Nature of Prejudice*. Cambridge, Mass.: Addison-Wesley, 1954. The classic social psychological study of prejudice. While the examples and terminology are dated, theoretical insights and engaging writing are as fresh as ever. Reviews early conceptualization and research on the contact hypothesis as well as theories of how prejudice develops and what techniques can be used to reduce it. Accessible to the novice and expert alike.

Amir, Yehudi. "The Role of Intergroup Contact in Change of Prejudice and Ethnic Relations." In *Towards the Elimination of Racism*, edited by Phyllis A. Katz. New York: Pergamon Press, 1976. Comprehensive review of empirical studies examining the contact hypothesis along with a complete bibliography. Covers research from the 1940's through the early 1970's.

Aronson, Elliot, et al. *The Jigsaw Classroom.* Beverly Hills, Calif.: Sage, 1978. A classic in the field. Discusses the rationale for developing this cooperative learning method, explains the jigsaw technique in detail, and presents the research findings.

Baron, Robert A., and Donn Byrne. *Social Psychology: Understanding Human Interaction.* 4th ed. Boston: Allyn & Bacon, 1989. This popular undergraduate social psychology text contains an excellent chapter titled "Prejudice and Discrimination: The Costs of Hating Without Cause." Explores social categorization, intergroup conflict, cognitive sources of bias, stereotypes, and much more.

Billig, Michael. *Social Psychology and Intergroup Relations.* London: Academic Press, 1976. A critical review of intergroup relations, presented by a leading British social psychologist. Very insightful, but rather heavy reading for most undergraduate students. Extensive bibliography.

British Journal of Social Psychology 23, no. 4 (1984). A special issue of the journal devoted entirely to the topic of intergroup relations. Leading European and North American researchers present both theoretical discussions and empirical papers. Can be read by college students.

Brown, R. "Intergroup Relations." In *Introduction to Social Psychology,* edited by Miles Hewstone, Wolfgang Stroebe, Jean-Paul Codol, and G. Stephenson. New York: Basil Blackwell, 1988. Brown summarizes intergroup relations in this accessible chapter in a social psychology textbook. Locates social identity theory in the broader context of intergroup relations and explains important terms clearly, providing excellent examples; can be understood by the college or high school student.

Deaux, Kay, and M. E. Kite. "Thinking About Gender." In *Analyzing Gender,* edited by Beth B. Hess and Myra Marx Ferree. Newbury Park, Calif.: Sage Publications, 1987. This easy-to-read review article reports research on sex differences, the nature of and attitudes toward men and women, gender stereotypes, and conceptions of masculinity and femininity. Deaux and colleague Laurie Lewis' research on gender stereotypes is reviewed and discussed in terms of gender belief systems held by men and women.

Doise, Willem. *Groups and Individuals: Explanations in Social Psychology.* Cambridge, England: Cambridge University Press, 1978. By a Swiss psychologist who has been in the forefront of intergroup research. Critically discusses intergroup research, particularly the work of Sherif and Tajfel. Translated from the French; reads well and is suitable for college students.

Dovidio, John F., and Samuel L. Gaertner, eds. *Prejudice, Discrimination, and Racism.* Orlando, Fla.: Academic Press, 1986. This rich collection includes one essay apiece on aversive racism and racial ambivalence; three essays on racial stereotyping; a difficult but rewarding chapter by John D. McConahay on the formulation and testing of the symbolic racism concept; an essay by Janet Schofield on the persistence of aversive racism in a recently desegregated school; and a piece by James L. Jones on cultural racism. Most are suitable for upper-level undergraduate psychology majors and graduate students; the introductory and concluding general essays, however, are accessible to the general reader. Includes references, tables, graphs, and subject index.

Freeman, Howard E., and Norman R. Kurtz, eds. *America's Troubles: A Casebook on Social Conflict.* Englewood Cliffs, N.J.: Prentice-Hall, 1969. This well-written book explores many issues of prejudice in American society and presents many first-person essays that bring home to the reader the significant impact of bias on individuals, groups, and society.

Gaines, Stanley O., Jr., and Edward S. Reed. "Prejudice: From Allport to Du Bois." *American Psychologist* 50, no. 2 (1995): 96-103. The authors contrast Gordon Allport's universalist conception of prejudice with that of W. E. B. Du Bois' social-historical approach. They argue that social psychology has neglected the latter and in doing so has missed a significant aspect of the psychology of African Americans. Published in a professional journal but accessible to high school and college students.

Griffin, John Howard. *Black Like Me.* New York: New American Library, 1962. This excellent book is a narrative of the author's experiences traveling around the United States and observing how people react to him after he has taken on the appearance of a black man. This monumental field study, which contributed to the understanding of social prejudice, provides the reader with an excellent example of the significance and need for conducting field research.

Hamilton, David L., ed. *Cognitive Processes in Stereotyping and Inter-group Behavior*. Hillsdale, N.J.: Lawrence Erlbaum, 1981. A rich harvest of the fruits of research. All essays except that of Richard Ashmore (dealing solely with sexual stereotyping) discuss, to a greater or lesser extent, racial stereotyping. The contributions by Shelley E. Taylor (on the salience of the solo black), Myron Rothbart, Mark Snyder, and Terrence E. Rose are especially worth reading. Hamilton provides a summary of the other contributors' work, placing it in the context of earlier research. Includes chapter references and author and subject indexes.

Hewstone, Miles, and Rupert Brown, eds. *Contact and Conflict in Inter-group Encounters*. Oxford, England: Basil Blackwell, 1986. This edited volume brings together scholars from around the world who describe the results of specific contact experiences between particular groups in a wide variety of settings, including Northern Ireland, Israel, Germany, Quebec, and South Africa.

Janssen-Jurreit, Marielouise. *Sexism: The Male Monopoly on History and Thought*. New York: Farrar, Straus & Giroux, 1982. A cultural history of sexism for the sophisticated reader. Describes how sexist attitudes have shaped thought and scientific endeavors in Western culture, and discusses a theory of sexism.

Johnson, David W., and Roger T. Johnson. *Learning Together and Alone*. Englewood Cliffs, N.J.: Prentice-Hall, 1987. Aimed primarily at teachers. Contrasts cooperative, competitive, and individualistic learning methods, and their appropriate uses.

Jones, James M. *Prejudice and Racism*. Reading, Mass.: Addison-Wesley, 1972. This provocative and accessible monograph provides an excellent historical overview of prejudice and racism and an insightful discussion into the effectiveness and ineffectiveness of various strategies for addressing the problems of prejudice and racism.

Kagan, S., et al. "Classroom Structural Bias: Impact of Cooperative and Competitive Classroom Structures on Cooperative and Competitive Individuals and Groups." In *Learning to Cooperate, Cooperating to*

Learn, edited by Robert E. Slavin et al. New York: Plenum Press, 1985. The Riverside project is described, and graphs are interpreted for the reader.

Katz, Irwin. *Stigma: A Social Psychological Analysis.* Hillsdale, N.J.: Lawrence Erlbaum, 1981. A slim but path-breaking study which reports on subjects' reactions to both blacks and the physically handicapped, and develops the notion of ambivalence-induced behavior amplification. A convenient summary of research results is found in the final chapter. Includes tables, references, and author and subject indexes. For upper-level undergraduates.

Katz, Phyllis A., ed. *Towards the Elimination of Racism.* New York: Pergamon Press, 1976. Particularly good essays in this collection include one by the editor on racism in small children; a survey by Richard D. Ashmore and Frances K. Delboca of psychological approaches to intergroup conflict; one of Samuel L. Gaertner's early essays on aversive racism experiments; and an incisive and readable discussion by Myron Rothbart of the reasons of self-interest behind some whites' opposition to racial reform. Includes chapter references and a subject index. For the general reader.

Katz, Phyllis A., and Dalmas A. Taylor, eds. *Eliminating Racism: Profiles in Controversy.* New York: Plenum Press, 1988. Contains an essay by Marilynn Brewer and Norman Miller on the contact hypothesis; several essays on school desegregation; an essay by James L. Jones on three types of racism and possible remedies for each; and a piece by David O. Sears on symbolic racism. Several essays compare and contrast antiblack racism with sexism and with bigotry against Mexican Americans, Japanese Americans, and American Indians. Includes introductory and concluding essays by the editors, chapter references, and author and subject indexes. For the general reader.

Kovel, Joel. *White Racism: A Psychohistory.* New York: Vintage Books, 1970. Reprint. New York: Columbia University Press, 1984. As the title implies, Kovel's approach to antiblack prejudice is psychoanalytic rather than cognitive: No attempt is made to examine stereotyping as a normal human activity. This somewhat turgidly written book is shaped by a left-wing political sensibility that was in vogue in the late 1960's. Nevertheless, the work remains valuable for its paradigmatic distinction between different types of racism. Includes a bibliographical essay, and an index of authors and subjects. For the general reader.

Lewin, Kurt. *Resolving Social Conflicts.* New York: Harper, 1948. Collects Lewin's major papers discussing practical problems of modern society such as prejudice and group conflict. Provides excellent examples of how to apply field theory to social problems.

Lips, Hilary. *Sex and Gender: An Introduction.* Mountain View, Calif.: Mayfield, 1988. Hilary Lips presents a thorough review of myths, theories, and research regarding sex and gender. In addition, the author explores behavior and experiences of males and females comparing similarities and differences. Sex and gender are examined in social relationships, political life, and the workplace.

Messick, David M., and Diane M. Mackie. "Intergroup Relations." In *Annual Review of Psychology* 40. Stanford, Calif.: Annual Reviews, 1989. Reviews intergroup relations theory and research from a cognitive perspective. Categorization, in-group and out-group effects, and intergroup bias are emphasized. Tajfel's social identity theory dominates the section on intergroup bias; his work is examined and critiqued. Variants of social identity theory are discussed.

Miller, Norman, and Marilynn Brewer, eds. *Groups in Contact: The Psychology of Desegregation.* Orlando, Fla.: Academic Press, 1984. This well-written edited volume considers theory and research on the effects of desegregation, particularly in schools in the United States.

Morgan, Robin. *The Demon Lover: On the Sexuality of Terrorism.* New York: W. W. Norton, 1989. A feminist perspective on the influence of certain myths about masculinity and power that pervade cultural manifestations of violence and result in victims of prejudice becoming targets of violence.

Mullen, Brian. "Group Composition, Salience, and Cognitive Representations: The Phenomenology of Being in a Group." *Journal of Experimental Social Psychology* 27, no. 4 (1991): 297-323. This scholarly paper discusses a model of the cognitive mechanisms that seem to drive and maintain stereotyping and prejudice.

Pettigrew, Thomas F. "Prejudice." In *Prejudice*, by Thomas F. Pettigrew, George M. Frederickson, Dale T. Knobel, Nathan Glazer, and Reed Ueda. Cambridge, Mass.: The Belknap Press of Harvard University Press, 1982. Presents a concise and clearly written review of the social psychological literature on prejudice and racism up to 1980. For the high school student and the lower-level undergraduate. Includes a bibliographical essay and an index.

_____. *Racially Separate or Together?* New York: McGraw-Hill, 1971. A collection of reprinted essays, originally written between 1961 and 1969, interspersed with brief summaries of the contents of essays dealing with the same subtopic. Two essays dealing with late-1960's politics are somewhat dated; the essay on social psychology and research on desegregation, however, is useful to the beginning student. Includes chapter endnotes, author index, subject index, tables, and figures. For lower-level undergraduates and the general reader.

Sherif, Muzafer. *Group Conflict and Cooperation.* London: Routledge & Kegan Paul, 1967. Well-written analysis of how intergroup conflict arises and the role of cooperation in reducing conflict. Includes a good description of his classic field experiments using children at summer camps in which intergroup conflict is created and resolved through contact in pursuit of superordinate goals.

Slavin, Robert E. *Cooperative Learning: Theory and Research.* Englewood Cliffs, N.J.: Prentice-Hall, 1990. Reviews various cooperative learning methods, some in detail, and the cognitive, social, and personal benefits associated with cooperative learning.

_____. "Research on Cooperative Learning: Consensus and Controversy." *Educational Leadership* 47, no. 4 (1989/1990): 52-54. A very readable discussion of areas of agreement and disagreement in the field. Only one among a variety of articles in this issue by major theoreticians and teachers of cooperative learning methods.

Stephan, Walter G., and David Rosenfield. "Racial and Ethnic Stereotypes." In *In the Eye of the Beholder: Contemporary Issues in Stereotyping,* edited by Arthur G. Miller. New York: Praeger, 1982. A good critical review of the social psychological literature on whites' and blacks' stereotyping of each other. All technical terms are carefully explained and, when necessary, illustrated by examples. Especially informative on the issue of racism in children, and on the mixed record of school desegregation as a means of breaking down racial stereotypes. Includes figures, chapter references, annotated list of additional readings, author index, subject index, and contributor information at end of book.

Stuck, Mary, ed. *Issues in Diversity: Voices of the Silenced.* Acton, Mass.: Copley, 1990. Presents a series of well-chosen articles that review historical sociological phenomenon related to the "isms" and the problem of oppressed groups in the United States.

Tajfel, Henri, ed. *Differentiation Between Social Groups: Studies in the Social Psychology of Intergroup Relations.* London: Academic Press, 1978. Presents the work of the team of European social psychologists that conceptualized and formalized social identity theory. Thorough and detailed, it is important to those who wish to replicate key experiments or to understand the empirical and theoretical foundations of the theory.

_____. *Human Groups and Social Categories.* Cambridge, England: Cambridge University Press, 1981. An easy-to-read account of Tajfel's conceptualization of intergroup conflict, accessible to college students. This book incorporates his early work on prejudice, essays on social perception and categorization, stereotypes, children's images of insiders and outsiders, and social identity theory. Includes both theory and research, emphasizing descriptions of the former. Tajfel provides an extensive bibliography.

Tajfel, Henri, and John Turner. "The Social Identity Theory of Intergroup Behavior." In *Social Psychology of Intergroup Relations*, edited by Stephen Worchel and William G. Austin. 2d ed. Chicago: Nelson-Hall, 1986. An excellent summary of social identity theory. This chapter focuses on the origin and importance of the theory, including intergroup competition and conflict. It offers examples of the concepts and attempts to answer practical questions.

Tavris, Carol, and Carole Wade. *The Longest War: Sex Differences in Perspective.* 2d ed. New York: Harcourt Brace Jovanovich, 1984. An entertaining and easy-to-read introduction to the psychology of women. Gender differences and similarities are discussed, in addition to the biological and social factors relevant to gender-role socialization.

Taylor, Donald M., and Fathali M. Moghaddam. *Theories of Intergroup Relations: International Social Psychological Perspectives.* New York: Praeger, 1987. Each of the major intergroup theories is presented and discussed in a separate chapter. A schematic chart of each theory is provided as a simple guide to the reader. Includes suggestions for further reading after each chapter. Can be understood by the college or high school student.

Thomas, Gail E., ed. *U.S. Race Relations in the 1980's and 1990's*. New York: Hemisphere, 1990. Explores issues involving racial stratification and education, occupational mobility, economics and cultural pluralism; special attention is paid to the neglect of the problems of the Native American population.

Thorne, Barrie, Cheris Kramarae, and Nancy Henley. *Language, Gender, and Society*. Rowley, Mass.: Newbury House, 1983. Contains an excellent collection of papers that address the nature of sexist language and research findings on gender differences in language use. Draws parallels among gender, power, and social class and their relationship to language and its use. An accessible and valuable source of information.

Turner, John C. *Rediscovering the Social Group: A Self-Categorization Theory*. New York: Basil Blackwell, 1987. Turner's book argues for the group as an important social phenomenon and articulates assumptions made about the relationship between the individual and the group in social identity theory. Provides the reader with a valuable backdrop for understanding many of Tajfel's predictions in a readable blend of theoretical and empirical work.

Walsh, Mary Roth, ed. *The Psychology of Women: Ongoing Debates*. New Haven, Conn.: Yale University Press, 1987. Using a debate format, noted authorities on the psychology of women present their arguments about controversial issues. Topical issues include mental health, psychological characteristics, differences, and social issues. A very accessible yet informative introduction for the general reader.

Williams, John E., and Deborah L. Best. *Sex and Psyche: Gender and Self Viewed Cross-Culturally*. Newbury Park, Calif.: Sage Publications, 1990. The authors have conducted one of the best global studies of stereotypes. Here they present the results of a cross-cultural study of sex-role stereotypes, ideologies, and values in thirty countries. A wealth of statistical data is summarized in a format suitable for the college-level reader.

Worchel, Stephen, and William G. Austin, eds. *Psychology of Intergroup Relations*. Chicago: Nelson-Hall, 1986. Presents the work of leading European and American researchers. Many of the chapters are well written and combine theoretical discussions with empirical evidence. Not all theoretical perspectives are presented, but the bibliography is comprehensive.

Prosocial Behavior

Batson, C. D. "Prosocial Motivation: Is It Ever Truly Altruistic?" In *Advances in Experimental Social Psychology*, edited by Leonard Berkowitz. Vol. 20. San Diego: Academic Press, 1987. A thorough and detailed chapter outlining the empathy-altruism hypothesis and its implications. Reviews the breakthrough research on the effects of empathy on helping, and discusses strategies for determining the nature of the motivation for helping.

Cialdini, Robert B. *Influence: Science and Practice*. 2d ed. Glenview, Ill. Scott, Foresman, 1988. An extremely interesting book dealing generally with the issue of social influence. Contains an excellent chapter analyzing the bystander effect, with emphasis on the role of other people in helping to define a social situation. Cialdini presents some provocative examples and offers advice about how to prevent oneself from becoming a victim.

Cialdini, Robert B., D. J. Baumann, and D. T. Kenrick. "Insights from Sadness: A Three-Step Model of the Development of Altruism as Hedonism." *Developmental Review* 1 (September, 1981): 207-223. A readable account of the development of the ability to self-reward for helping. Describes research showing how helping progresses from being externally determined to being internally motivated. Includes discussion of the negative state relief explanation for helping.

Clark, Margaret S., ed. *Prosocial Behavior*. Newbury Park, Calif.: Sage Publications, 1991. Focuses on the broader area of positive social behaviors and therefore includes discussions of altruism as well as chapters on helping. Two chapters deal with the development of prosocial behavior. Also noteworthy is a chapter that covers aspects of help-seeking behavior. A chapter on moods and one on the arousal cost-reward model are included as well.

Derlega, Valerian J., and Janusz Grzelak, eds. *Cooperation and Helping Behavior: Theories and Research*. New York: Academic Press, 1982. The first chapter provides a nontechnical discussion of the similarities and differences between the related issues of helping and cooperation, while also serving as an introduction to later chapters. Chapters on helping discuss the arousal cost-reward model and extend the model to show how help seekers may be influenced by cost-reward considerations.

Eisenberg, Nancy, and Janet Strayer, eds. *Empathy and Its Development.* Cambridge, England: Cambridge University Press, 1987. Contributions by developmental, clinical, and social psychologists illustrate the multiplicity of approaches to the study of empathy. Many chapters review research on the effects of empathy on helping. Well referenced; an excellent source for those interested in pursuing research on empathy.

Hinde, Robert A., and Jo Groebel, eds. *Cooperation, Prosocial Behaviour, Trust, and Commitment.* Cambridge, England: Cambridge University Press, 1991. Authors from diverse disciplines contribute to this volume, bringing together knowledge about human prosocial activity at the individual, group, and international levels. Chapters are well integrated, relatively free from technical terms, and thought provoking.

Latané, Bibb, and John M. Darley. *The Unresponsive Bystander: Why Doesn't He Help?* New York: Appleton-Century-Crofts, 1970. The classic source on bystander intervention in emergencies, detailing all of Latané and Darley's original research on the problem. The clever methodology of many of their experiments and their engaging writing style make this a fascinating and readable book.

Latané, Bibb, S. A. Nida, and D. W. Wilson. "The Effects of Group Size on Helping Behavior." In *Altruism and Helping Behavior: Social, Personality, and Developmental Perspectives*, edited by J. Phillipe Rushton and Richard M. Sorrentino. Hillsdale, N.J.: Lawrence Erlbaum, 1981. Reviews the research examining the relationship between group size and helping, including a discussion of the methodological problems involved. Contains not only a good summary of Latané and Darley's original theoretical ideas but also some subsequent developments, such as Latané's general model of group behavior known as social impact theory.

Macaulay, Jacqueline, and Leonard Berkowitz, eds. *Altruism and Helping Behavior: Social Psychological Studies of Some Antecedents and Consequences.* New York: Academic Press, 1970. A classic volume reporting much of the earliest work on the social psychology of helping. The book contains two separate chapters by Latané and Darley that provide excellent summaries of much of their original work.

Piliavin, Jane Allyn, John F. Dovidio, Samuel L. Gaertner, and Russell Clark. *Emergency Intervention.* New York: Academic Press, 1981. Explores the processes that lead people to offer help to others. The development of the arousal cost-reward model is traced through the discussion of the particular research on which it is based.

Rushton, J. Philippe, and Richard M. Sorrentino, eds. *Altruism and Helping Behavior: Social, Personality, and Developmental Perspectives.* Hillsdale, N.J.: Lawrence Erlbaum, 1981. Covers, as the title implies, three main areas. Under developmental issues, varied topics such as the influence of television and the role of genetics (sociobiology) are covered. Includes a discussion of moods and a model of how norms may influence helping, and a discussion of bystander intervention.

Staub, Ervin. "Helping a Distressed Person: Social, Personality, and Stimulus Determinants." In *Advances in Experimental Social Psychology,* edited by Leonard Berkowitz. New York: Academic Press, 1974. An important and frequently cited chapter from an earlier point in the history of research in this area. Although social psychologists rarely take issue with Latané and Darley's analysis of bystander intervention, Staub offers a somewhat different perspective, placing more emphasis on personality influences. He also presents some interesting research with children.

Staub, Ervin, Daniel Bar-Tal, Jerzy Karylowki, and Janusz Reykowski, eds. *Development and Maintenance of Prosocial Behavior: International Perspectives on Prosocial Behavior.* New York: Plenum Press, 1984. This set of twenty-four chapters from various researchers focuses not only on helping but also on other positive behaviors such as cooperation, generosity, and kindness. Covers a range of topics, from developmental aspects of prosocial behavior to the effects of help seeking and help receiving to applications of knowledge about helping behavior. A unique aspect of this book is its consideration of research done in many different countries.

Social Perception and Cognition

Allport, Gordon Willard. *The Individual and His Religion.* New York: Macmillan, 1950. This brief and readable book gives a sympathetic look at how religion can influence the many dimensions of a person's life. Allport lays out the theoretical foundation for his internal-external measurement of religiosity.

Batson, C. Daniel, and W. Larry Ventis. *The Religious Experience in a Social Psychological Perspective.* New York: Oxford University Press,

1982. Focuses on the nature and consequences of the religious experience and the difficulties of studying it with the precision of the scientific experiment.

Baumeister, Roy F., ed. *Public Self and Private Self*. New York: Springer-Verlag, 1986. Extends and refines self-presentation theory with individual chapters written by experts in the field. Difficult reading for a layperson, but essential reading for an advanced student of impression management. Its erudite discussion persuasively demonstrates the fundamental importance of self-presentation in social life.

Beck, Aaron T. *Love Is Never Enough*. New York: Harper & Row, 1988. A famous therapist and researcher explains how negative thoughts can interfere in a marriage and teaches the reader how to change unrealistic scripts regarding relationships. Not a typical self-help book; the tone and writing style are serious, although not difficult.

Bem, Daryl J. "Self-Perception Theory." In *Advances in Experimental Social Psychology*. Vol 6, edited by Leonard Berkowitz. New York: Academic Press, 1972. This chapter is the definitive summation of self-perception theory. Includes discussions of the roots of the theory, research relevant to it, and the theory's place within the field of social psychology.

Benner, David G., ed. *Baker Encyclopedia of Psychology*. Grand Rapids, Mich.: Baker Book House, 1985. This encyclopedic reference has a special focus on religious issues and the integration of psychology with the Christian faith, but it includes most other psychological and some theological topics as well. Originally developed for ministers, it is thorough yet very understandable. An excellent 1,200-page resource.

Brehm, Sharon S., and Saul M. Kassin. "Social Perception: Thinking About Ourselves and Others," In *Social Psychology*. Boston: Houghton Mifflin, 1989. This section of Brehm and Kassin's social psychology textbook includes three chapters on person perception and social cognition, including a section on sexism. A clear discussion of self-perception, self-esteem, and self-presentation also is included. The writing is accessible and thought provoking.

Brissett, Dennis, and Charles Edgley, eds. *Life as Theater: A Dramaturgical Sourcebook*. 2d ed. New York: Aldine de Gruyter, 1990. A collection of many short papers that illustrate the uses of self-presentation concepts in sociology, political science, anthropology, and communication studies. Meant as a college text; contains a very useful bibliography.

Burns, David D. *Intimate Connections.* New York: Signet, 1985. This popular self-help book shows how beliefs and expectations can influence people's feelings toward themselves and others. Includes a helpful chapter on how to change such thoughts, and another on how to overcome feelings of inferiority. Also addresses unrealistic relationship scripts.

Buss, Arnold. *Self-consciousness and Social Anxiety.* San Francisco: W. H. Freeman, 1980. Very clearly written, this book tracks the development of internal and external awareness of self as well as some of the developmental causes of shyness and social anxiety.

Carter, John D., and Bruce Narramore. *The Integration of Psychology and Theology: An Introduction.* Grand Rapids, Mich.: Zondervan, 1979. This brief paperback successfully accomplishes its mission of presenting a systematic framework by which the relationship between psychology and theology (particularly conservative Christian theology) can be understood. Reasons for the sometimes tense relationship between psychology and religion are also discussed.

Cialdini, Robert B. *Influence: Science and Practice.* Glenview, Ill.: Scott, Foresman, 1988. Summarizes what has been learned about techniques intended to influence another's attitudes and behavior and how these techniques work. Includes a discussion of the foot-in-the-door technique and other strategies that capitalize on self-perception processes.

Cooley, Charles H. *Human Nature and the Social Order.* New York: Charles Scribner's Sons, 1902. This is an early, but thorough, account of self-concept development. This was the first work to stress clearly that other individuals have a profound impact on the development of the self-concept.

Coopersmith, Stanley. *The Antecedents of Self-Esteem.* Palo Alto, Calif.: Consulting Psychologists Press, 1981. A very well-written and informative look at the background factors that influence the development of self-esteem. Includes statistics and figures but is fairly nontechnical, and the comprehensiveness of the book is well worth the effort.

Deci, E. L., and R. M. Ryan. *Intrinsic Motivation and Self-Determination in Human Behavior.* New York: Plenum Press, 1985. Reviews evidence concerning the overjustification effect and other processes that affect intrinsic motivation. Places this research within the broader context of a general theory concerning internal and external sources of motivation. Offers a compelling account of how people develop or fail to develop a sense of autonomy and discusses the ways in which people who function autonomously differ from people who do not.

Eiser, J. Richard. *Social Judgment*. Pacific Grove, Calif.: Brooks/Cole, 1991. Presents a detailed and broad overview of topics in social judgment, including categorization, the effects of emotion on judgment, causal attribution, and other issues. Describes major theories and research in detail, and provides useful context within which to understand social perception's importance in everyday life.

Fazio, R. H. "Self-Perception Theory: A Current Perspective." In *Social Influence: The Ontario Symposium*. Vol. 5, edited by M. P. Zanna, J. M. Olson, and C. P. Herman. Hillsdale, N.J.: Lawrence Erlbaum, 1987. An overview of self-perception theory that places the theory within the context of recent advances in theory and research in social psychology.

Fischhoff, Baruch, and Ruth Beyth-Marom. "Hypothesis Evaluation from a Bayesian Perspective." *Psychological Review* 90 (July, 1983): 239-260. The authors of this article propose that social psychologists may be overestimating the occurrence of bias by ignoring the possibility that perceivers are using non-Bayesian logic. Their arguments are complex, although this article is clear and follows an orderly sequence of ideas; appropriate for more advanced students of the field.

Fiske, Susan T., and Shelley E. Taylor. *Social Cognition*. New York: McGraw-Hill, 1991. Explains how memory, attitudes, emotions, and motivation combine to affect people's perceptions of others and themselves. Although the writing includes the terminology used by social psychologists, the authors provide many definitions and examples. One of the most comprehensive books available on social cognition.

Gergen, Kenneth J. *The Concept of Self*. New York: Holt, Rinehart and Winston, 1971. An excellent summary of the self-concept written by an important contributor to the field. Presents a historical overview of the study of the self and includes chapters summarizing theoretical issues in conceptualizing the self-concept, psychological processes in self-concept formation and maintenance, and the influence of the self-concept on interpersonal behavior (for example, level of aspiration, self-presentation).

Girodo, Michel. *Shy?* New York: Pocket Books, 1978. A delightful self-help book that is designed to help individuals overcome shyness. Helps the reader understand the connection between shyness and self-esteem. Appropriate for all age-groups, from junior high school on up.

Goffman, Erving. *The Presentation of Self in Everyday Life.* Garden City, N.Y.: Doubleday, 1959. This classic work coined the term "self-presentation" and almost single-handedly created this field of study. Goffman suggested that people stage dramatic performances for their audiences, carefully selecting their lines and props. The book can be easily read by undergraduates and is still full of fresh insights.

Gorsuch, Richard L. "Psychology of Religion." In *Annual Review of Psychology* 39, edited by Mark Rosenzweig and Lyman W. Porter. Stanford, Calif.: Annual Reviews, 1988. This is a good short review of the history of psychology of religion.

Harvey, J. H., and G. Weary. "Current Issues in Attribution Theory and Research." In *Annual Review of Psychology* 35. Stanford, Calif.: Annual Reviews, 1984. Reviews attribution theory and research from 1978 to 1983, a particularly fertile period in the area. Includes a section on the effects of motivation on attribution. Well organized and clear.

Hastie, Reid, Steven D. Penrod, and Nancy Pennington. *Inside the Jury.* Cambridge, Mass.: Harvard University Press, 1983. This book emphasizes how the experimental method within psychology creates an invaluable approach to studying the jury deliberation process. It focuses on how juries make decisions as well as on the product of those deliberations. Provides an extremely detailed and scientific approach to the jury process.

Hayes, Brett, and Beryl Hesketh. "Attribution Theory, Judgmental Biases, and Cognitive Behavior Modification: Prospects and Problems." *Cognitive Therapy and Research* 13 (June, 1989): 211-230. Discusses the use of attributional concepts in therapy. Techniques to reduce biases are presented, along with a discussion of the limits of these attributional retraining or debiasing techniques. For a journal article aimed primarily at professionals, this piece is quite accessible.

Heider, Fritz. *The Psychology of Interpersonal Relations.* New York: John Wiley & Sons, 1958. This classic text presents Heider's attribution and balance theories as well as a number of ideas that were to influence the field for more than twenty years; intended for advanced college students and graduate students.

Hunt, Richard A., and Morton King. "The Intrinsic-Extrinsic Concept: A Review and Evaluation." *Journal for the Scientific Study of Religion* 10, no. 4 (1971): 339-356. This is dated, but it is a comprehensive review of the I-E concept, concluding that more precise and valid measures are needed for a truly scientific study of religion.

Jewell, Linda N., and Marc Siegall. *Contemporary Industrial/Organizational Psychology.* 2d ed. St. Paul, Minn.: West, 1990. A text for an introductory college course offering excellent coverage of the discipline's topics. Written for students majoring in business as much as for those majoring in psychology. A book that almost anyone can understand and enjoy.

Jones, Edward Ellsworth. *Interpersonal Perception.* New York: W. H. Freeman, 1990. Presents a detailed overview and review of topics including impression formation, emotion perception, causal attribution, and attributional biases. Describes major theories and research in detail, and provides useful context within which to understand social perception's importance in everyday life. Available in paperback; engagingly written.

_____, et al. *Social Stigma: The Psychology of Marked Relationships.* New York: W. H. Freeman, 1984. A collection of notable social psychologists collaborated on this book while they were all Fellows at the Center for Advanced Study in the Behavioral Sciences at Stanford University. It presents a broad selection of work (both empirical and theoretical) on stigma and its effects on social perception and judgment.

Jones, E. E., and Thane Pittman. "Toward a General Theory of Strategic Self-Presentation." In *Psychological Perspectives on the Self,* edited by Jerry Suls. Hillsdale, N.J.: Lawrence Erlbaum, 1982. Describes and differentiates the strategies of ingratiation, intimidation, self-promotion, and supplication. Although written for a college audience, its clever analysis will intrigue most readers.

Jones, Warren H., Jonathan M. Cheek, and Stephen R. Briggs. *Shyness: Perspectives on Research and Treatment.* New York: Plenum Press, 1986. Presents a thorough view of the development of shyness and the impact it has on social relationships. Many individuals with low self-esteem suffer from shyness, and it is difficult to understand one without the other. The writing is technical; appropriate for a college audience.

Kahneman, Daniel, et al. *Judgment Under Uncertainty: Heuristics and Biases*. Cambridge, England: Cambridge University Press, 1982. A volume that presents a broad selection of work (both empirical and theoretical) on heuristics and biases in social perception and judgment. It is an advanced book and quite dense, but it is probably the best collection of articles on the topic. Available in paperback.

Kassin, Saul M., and Lawrence S. Wrightsman. *The American Jury on Trial: Psychological Perspectives*. New York: Hemisphere, 1988. An authoritative review of the entire process of trial by jury, from jury selection to verdict. Includes a review of the history of the jury, of jury research, and of highly publicized trials. The presentation of information about specific trials is very interesting and enjoyable to read.

Landy, David, and Elliot Aronson. "The Influence of the Character of the Criminal and His Victim on the Decisions of Simulated Jurors." *Journal of Experimental Social Psychology* 5 (1969): 141-152. One of the earlier experimental articles examining the impact of irrelevant variables on the jury decision-making process. Both defendant character and attractiveness were manipulated and found to have an effect on the determination of guilt or innocence and the number of years of imprisonment.

Leary, Mark R., and Rowland S. Miller. *Social Psychology and Dysfunctional Behavior: Origins, Diagnosis, and Treatment*. New York: Springer-Verlag, 1986. Three chapters of this book use self-presentational concepts to help explain maladaptive behavior ranging from schizophrenia to shyness and stage fright. Accessible to a lay reader. Demonstrates the utility of the self-presentation perspective on problematic behavior.

Lepper, M. R., and David Greene, eds. *The Hidden Costs of Reward*. Hillsdale, N.J.: Lawrence Erlbaum, 1978. A collection of chapters detailing theoretical perspectives and research on the overjustification effect. Also discusses the practical implications of the findings.

Loftus, Elizabeth F. *Eyewitness Testimony*. Cambridge, Mass.: Harvard University Press, 1979. This book provides a comprehensive account of the reliability—or, more appropriately, the unreliability—of remembering people and events from the scene of a crime. Her description of psychological experiments providing evidence for the way people reconstruct memories is both interesting and provocative.

Loftus, Elizabeth F., and Katherine Ketcham. *Witness for the Defense.* New York: St. Martin's Press, 1991. In this book, Loftus explores the fallibility of eyewitness testimony. The presentation of her experiences as a consultant in several court cases, such as those of Ted Bundy and Nazi war criminal Ivan the Terrible, makes this extremely interesting and fascinating reading.

Maloney, H. Newton, ed. *Current Perspectives in the Psychology of Religion.* Grand Rapids, Mich.: Wm. B. Eerdmans, 1977. This edited volume contains several relevant chapters. The one by Capps applauds the qualitative side of James and Allport. The articles by Flakoll, Warren, and Havens review some of the methodological and measurement approaches used in the scholarly study of religion.

Meadow, Mary J., and R. D. Kahoe. *Psychology of Religion: Religion in Individual Lives.* New York: Harper & Row, 1984. This is one of the easiest-reading texts in the field. Nevertheless, its topical coverage is quite broad. The authors explore many different ways of measuring specific facets of religion. Their review of the I-E concept is one of the most comprehensive, and it is certainly one of the most balanced.

Nemeth, C. J. "Jury Trials: Psychology and Law." In *Advances in Experimental Social Psychology*, edited by Leonard Berkowitz. New York: Academic Press, 1981. An extremely complete account of the psychological research completed on a diverse range of topics related to trial by jury. Provides extremely important historical background information on the jury in America, then discusses a number of factors that affect the jury decision process. A fairly technical account of this information.

Paloutzian, Raymond F. *Invitation to the Psychology of Religion.* Glenview, Ill.: Scott, Foresman, 1983. This two-hundred-page paperback textbook is truly an "invitation" to be introduced to the psychology of religion. The author is reasonably successful at reducing a large amount of material into a compact and readable text. This book is a good place to begin one's study.

Peck, M. Scott. *The Road Less Traveled: A New Psychology of Love, Traditional Values, and Spiritual Growth.* New York: Simon & Schuster, 1978. An application-oriented book that takes the reader on a journey through confrontation and resolution of problems toward a higher level of self-understanding. Borrowing from humanistic psychology, this controversial best-seller is surely thought-provoking.

Plotnik, Rodney J. "Social Cognition." In *Introduction to Psychology*. 2d ed. New York: Random House, 1989. Interesting and easy to read. The discussion of social schemata includes good examples, as well as descriptions of original and famous research studies on social schemata. Also included is a discussion of other topics in social cognition, among them attitude formation and change.

Rosenberg, Morris. *Conceiving the Self*. New York: Basic Books, 1979. A thorough review of the principles of self-concept formation and self-esteem maintenance for the general reader. Identifies important motivational factors that influence the self-concept and self-esteem. Summarizes research findings on the relationship of social class, minority status, and group membership to self-esteem.

Ross, M., and G. J. O. Fletcher. "Attribution and Social Perception." In *Handbook of Social Psychology*, edited by Gardner Lindzey and Elliot Aronson. 3d ed. New York: Random House, 1985. This chapter, a comprehensive overview of attribution theory, is clear, engaging, and suitable for readers of all levels. Much of the chapter is devoted to research and the implications of that research on theory; despite this work's status as a review article in a book intended for both academicians and nonspecialists, the authors of this article manage to take a critical stance and ask intriguing questions.

Schachter, Stanley, and Jerome Singer. "Cognitive, Social, and Physiological Determinants of Emotional State." *Psychological Review* 69, no. 5 (1962): 379-399. This experiment is considered a classic by some psychologists. It presents the paradigm that is often utilized in research on the misattribution of arousal. Most general psychology textbooks include this experiment in their chapter on emotions.

Schlenker, Barry R. *Impression Management: The Self-Concept, Social Identity, and Interpersonal Relations*. Monterey, Calif.: Brooks/Cole, 1980. A complete and readable introduction to the study of impression management. An excellent, comprehensive source that collects relevant research and theory; it devotes individual chapters to specific self-presentational behaviors such as self-descriptions, expressed beliefs, and personal appearance.

_____, ed. *The Self and Social Life*. New York: McGraw-Hill, 1985. Contains chapters contributed by eminent researchers who explore various applications of the self-presentation perspective. Topics such as excuse making, self-control, detection of deceit, and social power are covered in a scholarly smorgasbord that shows how pervasive impression management is. College audiences will have no difficulty with this collection.

Schneider, D. J. "Social Cognition." In *Annual Review of Psychology* 42. Stanford, Calif.: Annual Reviews, 1991. Reviews social cognition theories and research with an emphasis on categorization and the formation of trait attributions from behavioral information. Bias is discussed, including a section titled "In Defense of Accuracy." An insightful presentation of research and ideas, this article is an excellent resource for advanced readers.

Schneider, David J., Albert H. Hastorf, and Phoebe C. Ellsworth. *Person Perception*. 2d ed. Reading, Mass.: Addison-Wesley, 1979. Provides a detailed description of person perception research and theory. Available in paperback, this book will appeal to college students and to others with a serious interest in the topic.

Seligman, Martin E. P. *Helplessness: On Depression, Development, and Death*. San Francisco: W. H. Freeman, 1975. Defines helplessness, presents experiments on helplessness, and integrates them into a theory. The experiments utilize a diversity of subjects including dogs and people. Also compares helplessness to depression and proposes a therapeutic strategy for depression. Nicely illustrates how a theory is developed.

Shaver, Kelly G. *An Introduction to Attribution Processes*. Cambridge, Mass.: Winthrop, 1975. Presents attribution theory in detail and with vivid, clear examples. There is some discussion of bias, but since this book was written in the heyday of attribution theory model-building, it is incomplete. This slim paperback is a classic—an excellent in-depth resource for beginners to the field.

Snyder, C. R., Raymond L. Higgins, and Rita J. Stucky. *Excuses: Masquerades in Search of Grace*. New York: John Wiley & Sons, 1983. Presents a theory of excuse making and delineates different types of excuses. A number of research studies are also marshaled to support the theory. Highly readable; includes many examples of adaptive and maladaptive excuses.

Snyder, Mark. *Public Appearances, Private Realities: The Psychology of Self-Monitoring*. New York: W. H. Freeman, 1987. Snyder tracks the development of the self-monitoring construct and systematically tells the reader how an internal or external monitoring of self affects people's behavior. It is easy to understand, clearly written, and thoroughly enjoyable.

Spilka, Bernard, Ralph W. Hood, and Richard L. Gorsuch. *The Psychology of Religion: An Empirical Approach*. Englewood Cliffs, N.J.: Prentice-Hall, 1985. Provides a very comprehensive introduction to the quantitative approach in the scientific study of the dimensions of religion.

Taylor, Shelley E. *Positive Illusions: Creative Self-Deception and the Healthy Mind*. New York: Basic Books, 1989. Summarizes a large number of research studies that investigate the relationship of self-enhancing biases in social psychological processes to mental health and psychological adjustment. Discusses the effects of social psychological processes on the self-concept, coping, and physical health. Accessible to the general reader. Contains a number of everyday examples of important concepts and principles.

Wegner, Daniel M., and Robin R. Vallacher, eds. *The Self in Social Psychology*. New York: Oxford University Press, 1980. Eleven chapters written by eminent social psychologists working within self theory. Provides an introduction to the field for the college-level reader. Specific topics include the self-perception of motivation and emotion, self-presentation, self-disclosure, and prosocial behavior.

White, Gregory L., Sanford Fishbein, and Jeffrey Rustein. "Passionate Love and the Misattribution of Arousal." *Journal of Personality and Social Psychology* 41, no. 1 (1981): 56-62. This experiment nicely illustrates the misattribution-of-arousal paradigm and shows how a hypothesis about the development of passionate love can be tested empirically.

Williams, Robert, and James D. Long. *Manage Your Life*. Boston: Houghton Mifflin, 1991. This book is intended to serve as a guide for personal growth in a variety of areas. The most significant chapters deal with changing the aspects of the self-concept with which a person is dissatisfied. It is a very readable book that uses real-life examples to help convey the main points.

Wilson, T. D., and J. I. Stone. "Limitations of Self-Knowledge: More on Telling More Than We Can Know." In *Self, Situations, and Social Behavior*. Vol. 6 in *Review of Personality and Social Psychology*. Beverly Hills, Calif.: Sage, 1985. Reviews the evidence suggesting that people have limited access to their internal states and the causes of their own behavior. Discusses factors that influence accuracy of self-knowledge.

Worchel, Stephen, and Charles Teddie. "The Experience of Crowding: A Two-Factor Theory." *Journal of Personality and Social Psychology* 34, no. 1 (1976): 30-40. This experiment nicely illustrates the misattribution-of-arousal paradigm. In addition, it was an important experiment in environmental psychology because it showed that population density and crowding are not necessarily the same.

Wulff, David M. *Psychology of Religion: Classic and Contemporary Views*. New York: John Wiley & Sons, 1991. A brilliant blend of various strains of thought and research that is destined to become a classic in the psychology of religion. The author deals evenhandedly with all major religious traditions, something not found in most other books in the psychology of religion. Designed for advanced readers at the undergraduate level.

Yardley, Krysia, and Terry Honess, eds. *Self and Identity: Psychosocial Perspectives*. New York: John Wiley & Sons, 1987. Introduces the college-level reader to the social psychological view of self, from both historical and theoretical perspectives, and its relationship to the social environment. Includes separate sections on the cognitive and affective nature of the self-concept and its formation. Another series of chapters discusses the development of psychological disorders (for example, self-awareness and shyness) and their treatment.

Zebrowitz, L. A. *Social Perception*. Pacific Grove, Calif.: Brooks/Cole, 1990. Presents a detailed and broad overview of topics in social perception, including impression formation, emotion perception, causal attribution, and attributional biases. Describes major theories and research in detail, and provides useful context within which to understand social perception's importance in everyday life. Available in paperback, this book will appeal to college students and those who have a serious interest in the topic.

PSYCHOLOGICAL ASSESSMENT

Intelligence and Intelligence Testing

Aiken, Lewis R. *Assessment of Intellectual Functioning*. Boston: Allyn & Bacon, 1987. An extremely good source, clearly written and comprehensive; with a historical overview, descriptions of crucial tests, many examples, theoretical discussions of concepts of intelligence and useful statistical tables. Includes a glossary of terms, a list of standard tests, a detailed bibliography, and several indexes.

_____. *Psychological Testing and Assessment*. 4th ed. Boston: Allyn & Bacon, 1982. A clearly written introduction to all aspects of psychological testing. The first part of this college-level text deals with the methodology of assessment, the second part with cognitive tests, the third with affective tests, and the fourth with progress in psychological assessment. Includes exercises and suggested readings at the end of each chapter.

Albert, Robert S. "Identity, Experiences, and Career Choice Among the Exceptionally Gifted and Eminent." In *Theories of Creativity*, edited by Mark A. Runco and Robert S. Albert. Newbury Park, Calif.: Sage, 1990. This twelve-chapter book on creativity is a compilation of the expertise of persons who have studied creativity in areas such as anthropology, behavior, cognition, development, and ecology. Topics are varied and include creativity in adolescents, creativity in women, relationships between emotional difficulties and creativity, and social factors that influence creativity.

American Educational Research Association, American Psychological Association, and National Council on Measurement in Education. *Standards for Educational and Psychological Testing*. Washington, D.C.: American Psychological Association, 1985. Although probably not for the casual reader, this brief technical publication describes the standards for testing the experts have established for their own use, and it well illustrates the concern they have that testing must be done responsibly.

American Personnel and Guidance Association. "Responsibilities of Users of Standardized Tests." *Guidepost* 21 (October 5, 1978): 5-8.

Describes ethical concerns in the administration of tests. This article is directed explicitly at users of standardized tests.

American Psychological Association. *Guidelines for Computer Based Tests and Interpretations.* Washington, D.C.: Author, 1986. Describes standards for the ethical use of tests.

Anastasi, Anne. *Psychological Testing.* 6th ed. New York: Macmillan, 1988. Probably the best introduction to the field of psychological testing and to the topics of reliability, validity, and standardization. Written by a psychologist who has been a leader in the profession and who was awarded the National Medal of Science by President Reagan in 1987 for her work.

Ballard, Philip Boswood. *Mental Tests.* London: Hodder & Stoughton, 1920. A fascinating little book, written for schoolteachers, that covers the development of mental tests, the measurement of intelligence, and school-related activities such as reading, spelling, and arithmetic. Gives the English translation of the Binet-Simon test of intelligence, as well as a number of tests the author developed. Should be read for historical context; most of the book's contents are clearly outdated, but certainly give a flavor of what testing was like in the 1920's.

Brown, Frederick Gramm. *Principles of Educational and Psychological Testing.* 3d ed. New York: Holt, Rinehart and Winston, 1983. Covers a wide variety of topics surrounding educational and psychological testing. Specific content areas deal with a wide range of testing instruments along with their usage.

Buros, Oscar Krisen, ed. *The Mental Measurement Yearbooks.* Highland Park, N.J.: Gryphon Press, 1938-1972. One of the most important sources of reviews of tests, this series of yearbooks was originally edited by Oscar K. Buros as a kind of *Consumer Reports* of psychological tests. The volumes cover practically all commercially available educational, psychological, and vocational tests published in the English language. Each yearbook covers tests published during a specified period. Included are critical reviews by test experts, information about publishers, and a thorough list of studies which examine each test.

Cohen, Ronald Jay, et al. *Psychological Testing: An Introduction to Tests and Measurement.* Mountain View, Calif.: Mayfield, 1988. A basic book providing the reader with background information on assessment issues, including intelligence and personality assessment. Also provides the reader with an excellent chapter on the science of technological measurement.

Cronbach, Lee J. *Essentials of Psychological Testing*. 5th ed. New York: Harper & Row, 1990. A sophisticated introduction to testing. Published as a text for college courses in psychological testing, but remarkably accessible, even interesting, to an average reader. Appendix A, "Selected Publishers and Test Distributors," and Appendix B, "Classified List of Tests and Inventories," can serve as first sources to check for the sort of information they list; although brief, they contain much useful information.

_____. "Five Decades of Public Controversy over Mental Testing." *American Psychologist* 30 (January, 1975): 1-30. This classic article is worth pursuing for its excellent review of testing controversies. Clearly illustrates that often they are essentially social and political ones, expressed as dissatisfaction with psychology's efforts.

Crouse, James, and Dale Trusheim. *The Case Against the SAT*. Chicago: University of Chicago Press, 1988. Argues that the SAT is not useful in the admission selection process and is biased against minorities and lower-income individuals. Proposes alternative method of admission selection and the development of new achievement tests.

Daves, Charles W., ed. *The Uses and Misuses of Tests*. San Francisco: Jossey-Bass, 1984. Good discussion of critical issues regarding the use of standardized tests. Topics include the development of standards for test applications, the value of standardized tests for educational decision making, the misuse of standardized tests, and legal issues regarding test use.

Davis, Gary A., and Sylvia B. Rimm. *Education of the Gifted and Talented*. Englewood Cliffs, N.J.: Prentice-Hall, 1985. Presents various skills, behaviors, and characteristics of students who are gifted, talented, and/or creative. The abilities and skills involved in creative problem solving are explained in clear language. An excellent source to gain information on the educational needs of gifted, talented, or creative students.

Fancher, Raymond E. *The Intelligence Men: Makers of the IQ Controversy*. New York: W. W. Norton, 1985. Examines the historical contexts of the IQ controversy. The life experiences of the major hereditarians and environmentalists and how these experiences influenced their perspectives are emphasized. This book is easy to read and does an excellent job of making complex statistics understandable.

Feldman, David Henry, with Lynn T. Goldsmith. *Nature's Gambit: Child Prodigies and the Development of Human Potential.* New York: Basic Books, 1986. Feldman presents a number of case studies of prodigies and their growth and development. One of the best books on the subject.

Gardner, Howard. *Creating Minds.* New York: HarperCollins, 1993. A very readable description and analysis of creative historical figures. Includes discussions of Sigmund Freud, Pablo Picasso, Martha Graham, T. S. Eliot, Albert Einstein, Igor Stravinsky, and Mahatma Gandhi. Analyses focus on characteristics unique to each individual, the symbol system (domain) in which each worked, and how work is evaluated within each domain.

_____. *Frames of Mind: The Theory of Multiple Intelligences.* New York: Basic Books, 1983. Based on a neuropsychological analysis of intelligence, this author rejects the notion of one overall intellectual ability in favor of seven independent intellectual domains: linguistic, logical-mathematical, spatial, musical, bodily-kinesthetic, intrapersonal, and interpersonal.

Garrett, Henry Edward, and Matthew R. Schneck. *Psychological Tests, Methods, and Results.* New York: Harper & Brothers, 1933. A textbook for courses in psychological testing as given in the 1930's. The authors, in their preface, thank Anne Anastasi, who was later to write her own textbook, which became number one in the field. It is interesting to note that the Garrett and Schneck book begins with a chapter on the measurement of physical and sensory capacities such as height, strength of grip, lung capacity, and pulse rate, whereas today's texts would not consider these to be "mental" capacities. A book to be read in its historical context.

Ghiselli, Edwin Ernest, John P. Campbell, and Sheldon Zedeck. *Measurement Theory for the Behavioral Sciences.* San Francisco: W. H. Freeman, 1981. For the reader who wants a more statistical introduction to the concepts of reliability and validity, and who is comfortable with formulas and their derivations. An excellent, brief book, but not one to be read for entertainment value.

Glover, John A. *Becoming a More Creative Person.* Englewood Cliffs, N.J.: Prentice-Hall, 1980. An excellent book on enhancing creativity.

Glover's work is among the most understandable, clear, and concise representations of the field available today.

Glover, John A., and Roger H. Bruning. *Educational Psychology: Principles and Applications.* Boston: Little, Brown, 1987. The chapter on creativity in this book is a succinct and concise review of various aspects of creativity, creative behavior, and creative potential.

Glover, John A., Royce R. Ronning, and Cecil R. Reynolds, eds. *Handbook of Creativity.* New York: Plenum Press, 1989. A comprehensive book on creativity. Excellent source, with chapters by leading authorities in the field. Offers in-depth investigation of salient directions for creativity and creativity research.

Goldsby, Richard. *Race and Races.* New York: Macmillan, 1971. Provides straightforward and accurate information about issues of race, racial differences, and racism. There is a balanced discussion of both the hereditarian and environmentalist perspectives of the IQ controversy. Enjoyable and easy to read for high school and college students alike.

Gordon, W. J. "Some Source Material in Discovery-by-Analogy." *Journal of Creative Behavior* 8, no. 4 (1974): 239-257. Focusing on an associative view of invention, discovery, and learning, Gordon cites thirty-eight examples of associative analogical connections which have triggered famous innovations and breakthroughs. A wide variety of technological fields are included. Interesting reading; gives the foundations of many items used in everyday life.

Gould, Stephen Jay. *The Mismeasure of Man.* New York: W. W. Norton, 1981. A well-written, engaging, and highly critical review of intelligence testing. Gould delineates how tests have repeatedly been misused and abused.

Graham, John Robert, and Roy S. Lilly. *Psychological Testing.* Englewood Cliffs, N.J.: Prentice-Hall, 1984. Provides information pertaining to the history and development of psychological testing, as well as an overview of many of the major tests utilized in the 1980's.

Groth-Marnat, Gary. *Handbook of Psychological Assessment.* New York: Van Nostrand Reinhold, 1984. This book is a digest of psychological tests. It explains the nature of certain tests and candidly weighs their pros and cons; it also offers interpretation procedures in assessing the meanings of IQ scores. Advances the history and development of several of the tests presented. An in-depth work, it is a must for anyone who seriously studies the different specializations of psychology.

Guilford, Joy Paul. *The Nature of Human Intelligence.* New York: McGraw-Hill, 1967. Guilford describes the foundation of his theory of the structure of the intellect and in the process reviews the history of research into and theorizing about intelligence. This volume is an important contribution to the field.

Guthrie, Robert V. *Even the Rat Was White.* New York: Harper & Row, 1976. Provides an excellent historical view of how psychology has dealt with race as an issue. The first section of the book focuses on methods of study, early psychological testing, and the development of racism in the profession of psychology.

Herrnstein, Richard J., and Charles Murray. *The Bell Curve.* New York: Free Press, 1994. The late Richard Herrnstein was a professor of psychology; Charles Murray is a political scientist at the American Enterprise Institute. This best-seller argues that intelligence is biologically determined and that social programs to help disadvantaged groups are relatively unsuccessful and too costly. The book has been strongly criticized by the scientific community for misrepresentation and misinterpretation of data.

Hilgard, Ernest Ropiequet. *Psychology in America: A Historical Survey.* San Diego: Harcourt Brace Jovanovich, 1987. Chapter 13, "Intelligence: Measurement and Controversy," offers an excellent account of the field's development, from mid-1800's attempts to understand individual differences, through testing as a major commercial application of psychology. Material in several other chapters, especially those on industrial/organizational psychology and social psychology, helps place ability testing in the context of its parent discipline.

Hilliard, Asa G., III. "IQ Testing as the Emperor's New Clothes: A Critique of Jensen's *Bias in Mental Testing.*" In *Perspectives on Bias in Mental Testing*, edited by Cecil R. Reynolds and Robert T. Brown. New York: Plenum Press, 1984. Presents a critique both of Jensen's work and of the notion that IQ tests measure intelligence. Hilliard provides a very detailed account of the shortcomings he sees in Jensen's book. References to empirical work that supports his own position are included. Clear and easy to read.

Hoffmann, Banesh. *The Tyranny of Testing.* New York: Crowell-Collier, 1962. Dated but still relevant critique of standardized tests and their use in admission selection. Examines the problem of defective or ambiguous test questions and looks at issues regarding the validity and reliability of standardized tests.

Jensen, Arthur Robert. *Bias in Mental Testing.* New York: Free Press, 1980. An attempt to deal comprehensively with the issues of IQ testing and bias. Jensen challenges the criticisms against IQ tests and offers research to support his view that group differences in IQ test scores are not attributable to bias.

_____. "Test Bias: Concepts and Criticisms." In *Perspectives on Bias in Mental Testing,* edited by Cecil R. Reynolds and Robert T. Brown. New York: Plenum Press, 1984. Responds to the Hilliard critique of his book. Jensen argues against test bias as a reason for the differences between racial groups in IQ test scores. Provides theoretical and research evidence to support his position.

Kamin, Leon J. *The Science and Politics of IQ.* New York: Halsted Press, 1974. Discusses the political nature of the role psychologists have played in support of IQ testing. The role of psychologists in the eugenics movement and in education is discussed. Includes strong critiques of the work done by Burt and Jensen.

Kline, Paul. *Intelligence: The Psychometric View.* New York: Routledge, 1991. Provides a summary of studies focusing on the nature of intelligence and other human abilities. Topics include the history of the concept of intelligence, and ways to measure intelligence. The definitions of statistical and technical terms are presented in a clear and readable fashion.

Lyman, Howard B. *Test Scores and What They Mean.* Englewood Cliffs, N.J.: Prentice-Hall, 1963. A well-written, brief book aimed at readers who may not have a background in testing but need to understand some of the basic issues. As the title indicates, the focus is on the meaning of test scores.

Mansfield, Richard S., Thomas V. Busse, and Ernest J. Krepelka. "The Effectiveness of Creativity Training." *Review of Educational Research* 48, no. 4 (1978): 517-536. An excellent global review of some of the history and the older theories of creativity as well as an examination of the efficacy of the various creativity training programs. An example of scholarly research in the field.

Mitchell, James V., Jr. *The Ninth Mental Measurements Yearbook*. Lincoln: University of Nebraska Press, 1985. A continuation of the famous set of yearbooks published by Oscar K. Buros.

Modgil, Sohan, and Celia Modgil, eds. *Arthur Jensen: Consensus and Controversy*. New York: Falmer Press, 1987. A must for anyone interested in the effects of cultural differences on the science of measurement, with an emphasis on African American experiences. The volume is a collection of essays by outstanding contributors in the field of contemporary intelligence assessment. The last chapter is a competent response to the previous essays by Jensen, an extremely controversial figure in the field.

Montagu, Ashley, ed. *Race and IQ*. New York: Oxford University Press, 1975. Written to challenge the interpretations offered by the hereditarians. Most of the articles were previously published in professional journals or popular magazines. Some of the chapters contain very technical material; however, the authors generally do an effective job translating this into more understandable language.

Nairn, Allan. *The Reign of ETS: The Corporation That Makes Up Minds*. Washington, D.C.: The Ralph Nader Report on the Educational Testing Service, 1980. Presents an excellent discussion of the history of the Educational Testing Service and the development of standardized tests in America. Also provides a detailed critique of the Scholastic Aptitude Test and its use.

OSS Assessment Staff. *Assessment of Men: Selection of Personnel for the Office of Strategic Services*. New York: Rinehart, 1948. A fascinating book that describes the Office of Strategic Services (the OSS, the forerunner of the Central Intelligence Agency) program during World War II to select potential spies and saboteurs.

Rosser, Phyllis. *Sex Bias in College Admissions Tests: Why Women Lose Out*. 3d ed. Cambridge, Mass.: The Center, 1989. Charges that standardized college entrance examinations are biased against women. Discusses the impact of testing bias on admission selection and scholarship allocation.

Runco Mark A., and Robert S. Albert, eds. *Theories of Creativity*. Newbury Park, Calif.: Sage, 1990. Runco and Albert have edited a text with chapters by the leading figures in the field. These twelve chapters are a gold mine for those interested in doing in-depth research in the field of creativity. Runco is also the editor of a major journal on the empirical study of creativity.

Sattler, Jerome M. *Assessment of Children.* 3d ed. San Diego, Calif.: Author, 1988. An outstanding text, including a thorough history of intelligence tests, a survey of issues involved in measurement, specific discussions of many individual tests, considerable scientific and statistical material, many tables, photographs, extensive references, and separate name and subject indexes.

Shaughnessy, Michael F. "Cognitive Structures of the Gifted: Theoretical Perspectives, Factor Analysis, Triarchic Theories of Intelligence, and Insight Issues." *Gifted Education International* 6, no. 3 (1990): 149-151. Presents a perspective on how intellectually gifted people think and discusses research in this area. As psychologists increasingly study gifted children and adults, they must pay more and more attention to the way in which these individuals learn and process information.

_____. "Mentoring the Creative Child, Adult, and Prodigy: Current Knowledge, Systems, and Research." *Gifted Education International* 6, no. 1 (1989): 22-24. Reviews the process of mentoring with various special groups. As mentored people seem to do very well in life, it is important to study this process; this article provides a "how to" overview for the beginner.

_____. "What's New in I.Q.?" *Creative Child and Adult Quarterly* 10, no. 2 (1985): 72-78. This article outlines theories of intelligence. Presents a very good summary of the theories of Gardner, Sternberg, and other theorists in the field.

Sokal, Michael M., ed. *Psychological Testing and American Society, 1890-1930.* New Brunswick, N.J.: Rutgers University Press, 1987. This book had its genesis in a symposium given in 1984 at the 150th national meeting of the American Association for the Advancement of Science. Consists of eight chapters, written by seven different authors, which place testing in a historical perspective.

Sternberg, Robert J. *Beyond I.Q.: A Triarchic Theory of Human Intelligence.* New York: Cambridge University Press, 1985. An excellent book on reconceptualizing intelligence for the 1990's and beyond. It is heavy reading in places but is important for those people genuinely interested in understanding intelligence and Sternberg's theories.

_____. *Intelligence, Information Processing, and Analogical Reasoning: The Componential Analysis of Human Abilities*. Hillsdale, N.J.: Lawrence Erlbaum, 1977. Focuses on a redefinition of human abilities by redescribing intellectual processes with more accuracy than the historical view of intelligence as a static capacity to learn.

_____. *Intelligence Applied: Understanding and Increasing Your Intellectual Skills*. Orlando, Fla.: Harcourt Brace Jovanovich, 1986. A training program based on the triarchic theory of intelligence that Sternberg has developed. Details effective strategies for solving various types of problems, including science insight problems and analogies. Exercises for practice are included.

_____. *The Triarchic Mind*. New York: Viking Press, 1988. This readable and accessible presentation by a highly influential psychologist offers many real-life applications of many different kinds of intelligence, with suggestions for how to improve one's problem-solving skills. Sternberg's information-processing approach argues that there are three distinct types of intelligence: componential (the "school smarts" necessary for effectively processing information); experiential (the insight and ability to think analytically and creatively, and to make routine a new skill); and contextual (practical, "street-smart" intelligence).

Storfer, Miles D. *Intelligence and Giftedness: The Contributions of Heredity and Early Environment*. San Francisco: Jossey-Bass, 1990. Storfer presents information on the effects of nurture on intelligence, focusing on the nature and development of intellectual giftedness and the characteristics of intellectually gifted people. The concept of intelligence in different socioeconomic conditions, in enrichment programs, and in its varying types are highlighted in separate chapters. The factors that influence intelligence and giftedness are examined in detail.

Thorndike, Robert M., and David F. Lohman. *A Century of Ability Testing*. Chicago: Riverside, 1990. Chronicles the development of ability testing in the twentieth century. Provides an in-depth look at ability testing through the eyes of many famous test developers.

Torrance, Ellis Paul. *Creativity in the Classroom*. Washington, D.C.: National Education Association, 1977. This small monograph is one of Torrance's best works and is a frequently cited reference. It describes creativity at different levels, including what teachers can do to foster creativity and the goals that teachers should have in enhancing creativity.

_____. *Education and the Creative Potential*. Minneapolis: University of Minnesota Press, 1963. A compilation of seven papers and six experimental studies conducted by Torrance, who developed a test to measure creative thinking and conducted longitudinal studies on creativity. Information on topics such as developing creative potential in schoolchildren and factors that facilitate or inhibit creativity in children.

_____. *Rewarding Creative Behavior: Experiments in Classroom Creativity*. Englewood Cliffs, N.J.: Prentice-Hall, 1965. Although somewhat dated, Torrance's ideas still influence many teachers and researchers today. This book "covers the waterfront" in terms of the issues relative to creativity and creative thinking.

Tyler, Leona Elizabeth. *Tests and Measurements*. Englewood Cliffs, N.J.: Prentice-Hall, 1963. Another short book that takes a complex topic and tries to simplify it. Part of a series of such booklets aimed at college students taking introductory psychology. Oversimplifies many topics, but still provides a valuable introduction to the topic of psychological testing.

Vernon, Philip Ewart. *Intelligence: Heredity and Environment*. San Francisco: W. H. Freeman, 1979. Presents a thorough and thoughtful review of research on both sides of the "nature-nurture" debate on the development of intelligence. The issue of racial differences in intelligence is also discussed at length.

Walsh, W. Bruce, and Nancy E. Betz. *Tests and Assessment*. Englewood Cliffs, N.J.: Prentice-Hall, 1985. This college textbook is oriented toward students in undergraduate and graduate courses in counseling psychology, industrial psychology, vocational psychology, and educational psychology, and toward disciplines in which assessment is important. Views assessment of a person as incomplete without an assessment of the environment. Chapters 1 and 2, which deal with the history of assessment and test construction, respectively, and chapter 14, which discusses social issues surrounding assessment, may prove of particular value to the assessment novice.

Wechsler, David. *Manual for the Wechsler Intelligence Scale for Children—Revised*. New York: Psychological Corporation, 1974. Contains information about the most widely used contemporary IQ test for children. This test has been revised, however, so many people will encounter the WISC-III.

Weiner, Elliot A., and Barbara J. Stewart. *Assessing Individuals*. Boston: Little, Brown, 1984. A condensed, paperback version (209 pages) of the more standard-length introduction to the field of psychological and educational testing, but it is interestingly written, and the authors' involvement in the topic comes through clearly. Looks at a variety of assessment instruments utilized in testing individuals. Chapters center on instruments designed to assess specific areas.

Weisberg, Robert W. *Creativity: Genius and Other Myths*. New York: W. H. Freeman, 1986. Weisberg discusses the behaviors, activities, and finished products of individuals who have been described as creative. Defines creativity by giving real-life examples and discusses the role that intense knowledge or expertise plays in creative problem solving.

Weiss, John G., Barbara Beckwith, and Bob Schaeffer. *Standing Up to the SAT*. New York: Arco, 1989. Describes the structure of the Scholastic Aptitude Test and presents relevant criticisms of the test and its testing procedures. Also discusses alternatives to standardized college entrance examinations.

Wigdor, Alexandra K., and Wendell R. Garner, eds. *Ability Testing: Uses, Consequences, and Controversies*. Part 1, *Report of the Committee*. Washington, D.C.: National Academy Press, 1982. This first volume of a two-volume report describes the conclusions of a blue-ribbon panel of the U.S. National Research Council on ability testing. Provides a readable, nontechnical overview of ability testing issues, produced by a multicultural, multidisciplinary group which includes a lawyer, an educator, a historian, and a psychologist. Addresses the nature, impact, and incidence of ability testing practices, and the policy questions raised by standardized testing.

Williams, Robert, and Horace Mitchell. "The Testing Game." In *Black Psychology*, edited by Reginald Lanier Jones. 3d ed. Berkeley, Calif.: Cobb & Henry, 1991. Argues that testing is a biased game. The roles of various players (for example, students as pawns) are detailed. The authors' novel approach helps the reader better understand the position of opponents of IQ testing.

Wise, Paula Sachs. *The Use of Assessment Techniques by Applied Psychologists*. Belmont, Calif.: Wadsworth, 1989. Introduces the reader to the ways in which assessments are conducted in real settings by professional psychologists, especially clinical, counseling, organizational, and school psychologists. Well written, with a minimum of technical detail and many examples. Covers assessment in its broad aspects, rather than simply discussing psychological testing.

Wolman, Benjamin B., ed. *Handbook of Intelligence: Theories, Measurement, and Applications*. New York: John Wiley & Sons, 1985. A very good source, containing thirty-five contributions by experts covering the entire field of measurement and assessment. The book was written as a tribute to David Wechsler and honors his pioneering work. The first section covers theories and conceptual issues, and the second addresses measurement issues and specific tests (and their limitations). The conclusion deals with the application of various tests to specific settings.

Personality Testing Techniques

Aiken, Lewis R. *Assessment of Personality*. Boston: Allyn & Bacon, 1989. This textbook is designed to introduce the reader to concepts, methods, and instruments important in personality assessment. It provides a straightforward discussion of psychodynamic theory in the context of projective testing and provides constructive criticisms.

Allport, Gordon W., Philip E. Vernon, and Gardner Lindzey. *Study of Values*. 3d ed. Boston: Houghton Mifflin, 1960. A scale that measures a person's preference for six value orientations: religious, theoretical, economic, aesthetic, social, political values. The personal ordering of these values provides a framework for reflecting upon and understanding the values that make up one's philosophy of life. Language is outdated and gender-biased, but the book represents one application of Allport's work.

American Psychological Association. "Ethical Principles of Psychologists." *American Psychologist* 36 (1981): 633-638. Documents psychologists' ethical responsibilities concerning human rights, particularly pertaining to the right of privacy.

Anastasi, Anne. *Psychological Testing*. 4th ed. New York: Macmillan, 1976. Anastasi clearly evaluates psychological tests and accurately interprets their results; she demonstrates sensitivity to social and ethical implications of test use. Presents a comprehensive picture (in 750 pages) of the nature of testing. Offers significant details about the various tests discussed. A very thorough examination of the scope of testing.

Barrios, B. A. "On the Changing Nature of Behavioral Assessment." In *Behavioral Assessment: A Practical Handbook*, edited by Alan S. Bellack and Michel Hersen. 3d ed. New York: Pergamon Press, 1988. This chapter is a good review of the principles associated with behavioral assessment, which are put in both historical and methodological contexts. The book is a thorough description of behavioral assessment and how it is used in various settings.

Beck, Aaron T., Robert A. Steer, and Margery G. Garbin. "Psychometric Properties of the Beck Depression Inventory: Twenty-five Years of Evaluation." *Clinical Psychology Review* 8, no. 1 (1988): 77-100. Discusses the Beck Depression Inventory and its history, as well as several types of reliability and validity. An excellent example of the research needed to demonstrate the reliability and validity of a psychological test.

Bersoff, Donald N., Laurel P. Malson, and Donald B. Verrilli. "In the Supreme Court of the United States: *Clara Watson v. Fort Worth Bank and Trust.*" *American Psychologist* 43 (December, 1988): 1019-1028. This brief was submitted to inform the Supreme Court of the state of current scientific thought regarding validation of personnel assessment devices.

Bolles, Richard N. *The Three Boxes of Life*. Berkeley, Calif.: Ten Speed Press, 1981. This popular book on life and work planning contains one of the simplest interest inventories devised. Based on Holland's typology, it is called "The Party."

Buros, Oscar Krisen, ed. *Vocational Tests and Reviews*. Highland Park, N.J.: Gryphon Press, 1975. This source consists of the vocational sections selected from *The Seventh Mental Measurements Yearbook* and *Tests in Print II*, and it contains comprehensive reviews of testing materials and comments on the validity and reliability of vocational tests.

Bush, Robert P., Alan J. Bush, David J. Ortinau, and Joseph F. Hair, Jr. "Developing a Behavior-Based Scale to Assess Retail Salesperson

Performance." *Journal of Retailing* 66, no. 1 (1990): 119-136. A good article describing the development of a rating scale of salesperson performance. An example of the scale content is provided.

Campbell, D. T. *Manual for the Strong-Campbell Interest Inventory*. Stanford, Calif.: Stanford University Press, 1977. This manual describes the SCII instrument and its uses. It represents a progression in the use of interest inventories, because it is merged with Holland's vocational themes.

Committee to Develop Standards for Educational and Psychological Testing. *Standards for Educational and Psychological Testing*. Washington, D. C.: American Psychological Association, 1985. This document provides a framework for the evaluation and validation of testing and other assessment devices.

Cormier, William H., and L. Sherilyn Cormier. *Interviewing Strategies for Helpers*. 3d ed. Pacific Grove, Calif.: Brooks/Cole, 1991. The third edition of this book on interviewing represents a major revision and extension of the authors' work. A detailed guide to all facets of interviewing and overcoming obstacles to effective interviews, presented within the context of clinical applications. Includes using the interview to develop and implement intervention strategies. Exercises, worksheets, and other learning activities are provided.

Cottle, William C. *Interest and Personality Inventories*. Boston: Houghton Mifflin, 1968. Part of the publisher's Guidance Monograph series. Geared to the reader seeking a comprehensive overview of interest inventories.

Cronbach, Lee J. *Essentials of Psychological Testing*. 5th ed. New York: Harper & Row, 1990. The measurement of personality traits by projective tests is discussed in chapter 16. Discussion questions are included to assist the reader to understand why projective measures encourage both positive and negative evaluations. This chapter can be understood by high school and college students.

Darley, John M., Samuel Glucksberg, and Ronald A. Kinchla. *Psychology*. 5th ed. Englewood Cliffs, N.J.: Prentice-Hall, 1991. This introductory psychology text discusses the relationship between an aptitude test and the prediction of future performance, providing examples to aid in differentiating aptitude from achievement.

Evans, Larry D., and Sharon Bradley-Johnson. "A Review of Recently Developed Measures of Adaptive Behavior." *Psychology in the Schools* 25, no. 3 (1988): 276-287. A thorough review of six rating scales of adaptive behavior. These are compared to older scales that have been in use for a number of years.

Fogarty, Pat. "Using an Interest Inventory." *Academic Therapy* 22 (November, 1986): 209-212. Focuses on the usefulness of interest assessment in discovering the aspirations of children and in designing appropriate educational experiences for them. Does not require knowledge of technical vocabulary.

Frisbie, G. R. "Measurement of Leisure Interest." *Journal of Career Development* 11 (December, 1984): 101-109. Places the measurement of leisure interests in the overall context of career assessment. Presents the college-level inquirer with the rationale for developing an interest inventory that addresses both work and leisure activities. Examines one such inventory.

Goldfried, Marvin R. "Behavioral Assessment: An Overview." In *International Handbook of Behavior Modification and Therapy*, edited by Alan S. Bellack, Michel Hersen, and Alan E. Kazdin. New York: Plenum Press, 1982. This chapter provides a good introduction to behavioral assessment. It is part of a book that includes many examples of assessment and therapy.

Graham, John R., and Roy S. Lilly. "Measuring Interests, Values, Attitudes, and Personal Orientation." In *Psychological Testing*. Englewood Cliffs, N.J.: Prentice-Hall, 1984. Provides the college-level reader with a concise historical overview of the development of interest inventories. Sample score reports and interpretive information are given for the Strong-Campbell Interest Inventory (Form T325) and the Kuder Occupational Interest Survey (Form DD).

Groth-Marnat, Gary. *Handbook of Psychological Assessment*. 2d ed. New York: John Wiley & Sons, 1990. A presentation of the most widely used psychological tests. Of particular value to the person new to psychological testing is the inclusion of assets and limitations of various tests and discussion of how the various tests were developed. Devotes two chapters to interview strategies, "The Assessment Interview" and "Behavioral Assessment." Recommended readings are included in each chapter.

Herr, Edwin L., and Stanley H. Cramer. "Assessment in Career Guidance and Counseling." In *Career Guidance and Counseling Through the Life Span*. 2d ed. Boston: Little, Brown, 1984. Gives the reader an overview of seventeen of the most commonly used interest inventories. Surveys the kinds of interest scales or categories utilized in each. Allows the reader to compare inventories quickly and easily.

Holland, J. L. *Manual for the Vocational Preference Inventory*. Palo Alto, Calif.: Consulting Psychologists Press, 1975. Describes Holland's vocational classification system, including work activities, general training requirements, and occupational rewards. Holland's theory of vocational choice is basic to a number of tests used for career development.

Kane, Steven T. "A Review of the COPS Interest Inventory." *Journal of Counseling and Development* 67 (February, 1989): 361-363. Examines and evaluates the COPS in a relatively nontechnical manner.

Kanfer, Frederick H., and W. Robert Nay. "Behavioral Assessment." In *Contemporary Behavior Therapy: Conceptual and Empirical Foundations*, edited by G. Terence Wilson and Cyril M. Franks. New York: Guilford Press, 1982. A well-written chapter that provides a detailed description of the procedure of behavioral assessment. A fairly advanced description in the context of a presentation of behavior therapy.

Kaplan, Robert M., and Dennis P. Saccuzzo. *Psychological Testing: Principles, Applications, and Issues*. Pacific Grove, Calif.: Brooks/Cole, 1989. Reviews major issues in psychological testing in a broad range of psychological tests, including selection and personnel decision and tests for choosing careers.

Kerlinger, Fred Nichols. *Foundations of Behavioral Research*. 3d ed. New York: Holt, Rinehart and Winston, 1986. An excellent and thorough presentation of experimental design issues in psychological research. Kerlinger provides a very good chapter on the use of interviews and how to design good interview schedules. The use of interviews in both applied and research settings is discussed. Examples of well-designed interviews are given.

Kleinmuntz, Benjamin. *Personality and Psychological Assessment*. New York: St. Martin's Press, 1982. Kleinmuntz's book is an introductory-level presentation of psychological assessment. He discusses test construction and the statistics involved in developing and using psychological tests as well as various categories of tests. One chapter is devoted to interviewing techniques and applications.

Leiter, E. "The Role of Projective Testing." In *Clinical and Experimental Psychiatry*, edited by Scott Wetzler and Martin M. Katz. New York: Brunner/Mazel, 1989. Leiter discusses projective testing and includes major changes in psychiatry as related to projective techniques. He focuses on changes in current diagnosis and relates them to projective measures.

Morganstern, Kenneth P. "Behavioral Interviewing." In *Behavioral Assessment: A Practical Handbook*, edited by Alan S. Bellack and Michel Hersen. New York: Pergamon Press, 1988. Morganstern describes the full process of the behavioral interview from beginning to end. He includes a discussion of factors which may facilitate or inhibit the interview. Both the conceptual basis and the ethical considerations of the interview are discussed. Interview examples and references are provided.

Morrison, Randall L. "Structured Interviews and Rating Scales." In *Behavioral Assessment: A Practical Handbook*, edited by Alan S. Bellack and Michel Hersen. 3d ed. New York: Pergamon Press, 1988. This chapter is about equally split between describing the use of interviews and the use of rating scales in assessing personality. Clearly written; includes examples of both interviews and rating scales, with references.

Ollendick, Thomas H., and Greta Francis. "Behavioral Assessment and Treatment of Childhood Phobias." *Behavior Modification* 12, no. 2 (1988): 165-204. A very informative review of the normal aspects of fear and the problems associated with abnormal fear. Children's fears and assessment devices for children are the focus of this article.

Phares, E. Jerry. *Clinical Psychology*. 4th ed. Pacific Grove, Calif.: Brooks/ Cole, 1991. Includes a chapter on behavioral assessment within the context of a more comprehensive description of the duties of clinical psychologists.

Reilly, Richard R., Sarah Henry, and James W. Smither. "An Examination of the Effects of Using Behavior Checklists on the Construct Validity of Assessment Center Dimensions." *Personnel Psychology* 43, no. 1 (1990): 71-84. A technical description of a study testing the value of a behavioral assessment procedure in the assessment center.

Stern, Robert Morris, William J. Ray, and Christopher M. Davis. *Psychophysiological Recording*. New York: Oxford University Press, 1980. The authors provide an excellent, readable introduction to basic principles of psychophysiology. Part 2, the main body of the text, covers physiology of and recording procedures for the brain, muscles, eyes, respiratory system, gastrointestinal system, cardiovascular system, and skin. Illustrations depicting typical recordings and a glossary of psychophysiological terms are helpful additions.

Sweetland, R. C., and D. J. Keyser, eds. *Tests: A Comprehensive Reference for Assessments in Psychology, Education, and Business*. Kansas City, Mo.: Test Corporation of America, 1983. A compendium describing more than thirty-five hundred psychological tests and their uses in psychology, education, and business.

Walsh, W. Bruce, and Nancy E. Betz. *Tests and Assessments*. Englewood Cliffs, N.J.: Prentice-Hall, 1985. Of particular interest is the discussion on projective and behavioral assessment, which reviews the concepts behind projective testing and discusses types of projective techniques with specific examples.

Wiggins, Jerry S. *Personality and Prediction: Principles of Personality Assessment*. Reading, Mass.: Addison-Wesley, 1973. A classic book that is a highly technical description of how to use personality assessment instruments correctly. Despite the technicality of the material, this a very worthwhile book for the serious student of personality assessment.

Wise, Paula Sachs. *The Use of Assessment Techniques by Applied Psychologists*. Belmont, Calif.: Wadsworth, 1989. A short book written for the person with a limited background in psychology. The author devotes some space to defining applied psychology and then proceeds to discuss the use of various assessment approaches by clinical, counseling, industrial/organizational, and school psychologists. She gives examples, presents controversies, and suggests additional readings.

Mental Illness Assessment

American Psychiatric Association. *DSM-IV Options Book*. Washington, D.C.: Author, 1991. Presents the diagnostic dilemmas and debates involved in the development of the fourth diagnostic manual of the

American Psychiatric Association. It was prepared by a group of recognized experts on each disorder. DSM-IV promises to be more objective and reliable than its predecessors.

Cohen, R. J., P. Montague, L. S. Nathanson, and M. E. Swerdlik. *Psychological Testing: An Introduction to Tests and Measurement.* Mountain View, Calif.: Mayfield, 1988. A college-level textbook introducing the basic concepts of psychological testing and assessment. Twenty chapters cover all the broad aspects of this field, including historical background, use of statistics, major theories, and a review of personality and mental ability tests and assessments. Discusses computer-based assessment and includes a large list of test publishers. The lack of a glossary, however, makes this less useful for novice readers.

Corcoran, Kevin J., and Joel Fischer. *Measures for Clinical Practice: A Sourcebook.* New York: Free Press, 1987. Reprints more than one hundred self-report assessment instruments. Among them are numerous measures of various emotions and psychological problems in which emotional dysfunction is prominent; there are instruments to measure anxiety, guilt, anger, hostility, depression, stress, and mood. An excellent source for learning how researchers measure emotions, and can be used should one want to conduct a study. Bear in mind, however, that this book does not include some of the most commonly used questionnaires for measuring emotions.

Gould, Stephen Jay. *The Mismeasure of Man.* New York: W. W. Norton, 1981. A historical description of the appraisal of intelligence, starting with the measurement of skulls and proceeding to modern theories of mental ability. By carefully examining and reevaluating original data, Gould concludes that many of these theories, with their contention that intelligence is hereditary, are biased and racist. A detailed and well-documented book for the advanced reader.

Matarazzo, J. D. "Psychological Assessment Versus Psychological Testing." *American Psychologist* 45 (1990): 999-1017. An important article written by one of the best-known specialists in psychological assessment. Provides a brief historical review of psychological assessment and details the differences between psychological testing and assessment. Outlines the framework of psychological assessment and its relevance to courtroom testimony. Written for professional psychologists but comprehensible, for the most part, to college-level readers.

270 *Psychology*

Mischel, Walter. *Personality and Assessment.* New York: John Wiley & Sons, 1968. A somewhat dated but often-cited textbook which helped launch the controversy over whether the environment or personality "traits" are more important in shaping behavior. Does a good job of covering the basic factors involved in measuring psychological constructs. With some important exceptions, remains largely relevant; but should only be used in conjunction with more recent publications.

Nietzel, M. T., D. A. Berstein, and R. Milich. *Introduction to Clinical Psychology.* 3d ed. Englewood Cliffs, N.J.: Prentice-Hall, 1991. An introductory, relatively easy-to-read college-level textbook on clinical psychology. Includes three chapters on testing, interviewing, and observation, and one introductory chapter on psychological assessment. Covers the material well and includes a history of techniques and general procedures. Provides easy-to-follow examples and case studies.

Spitzer, Robert L., M. Gibbon, A. E. Skodol, J. B. W. Williams, and Michael First. *DSM-III-R Casebook: A Learning Companion to the Diagnostic and Statistical Manual of Mental Disorders.* 3d rev. ed. Washington, D.C.: American Psychiatric Press, 1989. This excellent paperback provides many case histories with accompanying diagnoses according to the DSM-III-R. The book, which also includes mental disorders of children and adolescents, discusses fascinating historical cases that were treated by such great therapists as Sigmund Freud, Emil Kraepelin, and Alois Alzheimer. In addition, presents a number of cases from Africa, India, Polynesia, and Russia. DSM-III-R has now been replaced by DSM-IV, but this casebook is still useful.

Spitzer, Robert L., J. B. Williams, and A. E. Skodol, eds. *International Perspectives on DSM-III.* Washington, D.C.: American Psychiatric Press, 1983. Highlights the American diagnostic system from the perspective of different countries. It notes the role that ethnic and cultural differences play in the development of psychological disorders and the problems involved in making a diagnosis in another country. Although DSM-III has now been replaced by DSM-IV, this book is still useful.

Sweetland, R. C., and D. J. Keyser, eds. *Tests: A Comprehensive Reference for Assessments in Psychology, Education, and Business.* 2d ed. Kansas City, Mo.: Test Corporation of America, 1986. A reference book which covers a broad range of assessments in psychology, business, and education. Provides brief descriptions of more than four thousand tests, including age level, details of administration, purpose of test, scoring method, cost, and publisher. Easy to use; provides information in a simple, straightforward format.

World Health Organization. *Manual of the International Statistical Classification of Diseases, Injuries, and Causes of Death.* 9th rev. ed. Geneva, Switzerland: Author, 1977. An internationally recognized diagnostic system established under the auspices of the United Nations. It allows the diagnostician to record and compare disorders from around the world. The mental health section permits nations to compare the incidence of specific psychological disorders in different countries.

PERSONALITY

General Concepts

Barnouw, Victor. *Culture and Personality*. 4th ed. Belmont, Calif.: Wadsworth, 1985. Presents a historical view of various dimensions of culture as they relate to personality. Examines correlational studies, specifically cross-cultural surveys.

Eysenck, Hans J. *The Biological Basis of Personality*. Springfield, Ill.: Charles C Thomas, 1967. This older book provides a thorough, in-depth discussion of Eysenck's theories of the relations between neuroticism, introversion, and extroversion with physiology.

Hall, Calvin Springer, and Gardner Lindzey. *Theories of Personality*. 3d ed. New York: John Wiley & Sons, 1978. A classic textbook describing personality theories. Personality research is mentioned, but not discussed in detail. Includes particularly readable, thorough, and accurate descriptions of psychoanalytic theories. Chapter 1 introduces the topic of personality theories, and describes many dimensions upon which theories can be contrasted.

Hampden-Turner, Charles. *Maps of the Mind*. New York: Macmillan, 1981. Presents brief descriptions and pictorial representations (termed "maps") of basic psychological and philosophical concepts. The organization and presentation are a bit idiosyncratic; the summaries are very good, and the diagrams helpful in synthesizing complex information. Descriptions and maps relevant to the theories of Sigmund Freud, Carl Jung, Erich Fromm, Rollo May, Hans Eysenck, Carl Rogers, Harry Stack Sullivan, and Erik Erikson are particularly relevant to basic issues in personality theory.

Kaplan, Harold I., and Benjamin J. Sadock, eds. *Comprehensive Textbook of Psychiatry*. 4th ed. Baltimore: Williams & Wilkins, 1985. This massive textbook covers every major area of psychiatry in its more than two thousand pages. Brain-behavior relationships, theories of personality, psychological assessment, diagnostic categories, psychotherapy and medication treatments, as well as other specialized applications are presented by the contributors to the volume. Much of what is presented assumes a background in psychology or medicine.

McCrae, Robert R., and Oliver P. John. "An Introduction to the Five-Factor Model and Its Applications." *Journal of Personality* 60 (June, 1992): 175-215. Describes the five-factor model of personality, which asserts that "surgency," emotional stability, conscientiousness, agreeableness, and openness to experience ("intellectance") are basic, underlying dimensions of personality. The five-factor model has gained increasing acceptance by psychologists studying personality, although the research is not without critics. Written for a sophisticated audience.

Mischel, Walter. *Introduction to Personality*. 4th ed. New York: Holt, Rinehart and Winston, 1986. A college-level personality textbook with an emphasis on contemporary issues and research. Each major orientation to personality—psychodynamic, trait, phenomenological (humanistic), and behavioral—is presented with thorough discussions of measurement and research. The reader may find that this text alone is incomplete in its description of personality theories per se, but it makes an excellent companion reading to Hall and Lindzey's *Theories of Personality*. Mischel's own approach to social learning theory is presented.

_____. *Personality and Assessment*. New York: John Wiley & Sons, 1968. The text that inspired debate about the utility of traditional personality theories. Readable but detailed; primarily of historical importance. Contemporary summaries of this issue can be found in Mischel's *Introduction to Personality* and in the *Handbook of Personality: Theory and Research*, edited by Pervin.

Mischel, Harriet N., and Walter Mischel, eds. *Readings in Personality*. New York: Holt, Rinehart and Winston, 1973. Presents a collection of papers by different authors on some of the central topics and viewpoints in personality psychology. Provides in-depth analyses of various trait, state, and social theories of personality. Several chapters by Walter Mischel present his views on social learning, personality, and his empirical work on self-control.

Pervin, Lawrence A., ed. *Handbook of Personality: Theory and Research*. New York: Guilford Press, 1990. A compilation of personality theory and research for the sophisticated reader. Chapters by Walter Mischel ("Personality Dispositions Revisited and Revised: A View after Three Decades"), David Magnusson ("Personality Development from an Interactional Perspective"), and Bernard Weiner ("Attribution in Personality Psychology") may be of particular interest.

Peterson, Christopher. *Personality*. San Diego: Harcourt Brace Jovanovich, 1988. This text on personality contains three chapters that summarize, compare, and evaluate various trait approaches along the
following dimensions: theory, research, and applications. Describes
major criticisms of trait approaches and discusses the practical implications of trait theories.

Weiten, Wayne, Margaret A. Lloyd, and R. L. Lashley. "Theories of
Personality." In *Psychology Applied to Modern Life: Adjustment in the
90's*. Pacific Grove, Calif.: Brooks/Cole, 1991. This text, written for
undergraduate students, provides the reader with a very readable
chapter on personality and theories of personality development. Other
chapters highlight the dynamics of adjustment, interpersonal factors,
developmental transitions, and the impact that personality and styles
of coping can have on psychological and physical health.

Behavioral and Cognitive Models

Bandura, Albert. *Principles of Behavior Modification*. New York: Holt,
Rinehart and Winston, 1969. Presents an overview of basic psychological principles governing human behavior within the conceptual framework of social learning. Reviews theoretical and empirical advances in
the field of social learning, placing special emphasis on self-regulation
and on symbolic and vicarious processes. Applies these principles to
the conceptualization and modification of a number of common behavior disorders such as alcoholism, phobias, and sexual deviancy.

_____. *Social Foundations of Thought and Action: A Social
Cognitive Theory*. Englewood Cliffs, N.J.: Prentice-Hall, 1986. Presents a comprehensive coverage of the tenets of current social cognitive theory. Besides addressing general issues of human nature and
causality, provides an impressive in-depth analysis of all important
aspects of human functioning, including motivational, cognitive, and
self-regulatory processes.

_____. *Social Learning Theory*. Englewood Cliffs, N.J.: Prentice-
Hall, 1977. Lays out Bandura's theory and presents a concise overview of its theoretical and experimental contributions to the field of
social learning. Redefines many of the traditional concepts of learning
theory and emphasizes the importance of cognitive processes in human learning.

Bannister, Donald, and Fay Fransella. *Inquiring Man: The Theory of Personal Constructs*. New York: Penguin Books, 1971. Provides an excellent introduction to Kelly's theory. In addition, a wide range of applications are provided within the overall field of clinical psychology as well as social psychology. It should be noted that the authors are dedicated advocates of Kelly's perspective.

Bannister, Donald, and J. M. M. Mair, eds. *The Evaluation of Personal Constructs*. New York: Academic Press, 1968. This excellent work is unique in that it provides insights into the types of theoretical and research efforts that have been undertaken as a result of Kelly's contributions. Particularly relevant because it was published shortly after Kelley's death and therefore provides an interesting analysis of Kelly's influence at that time.

De Rivera, Joseph, comp. *Field Theory as Human-Science: Contributions of Lewin's Berlin Group*. New York: Gardner Press, 1976. An English translation of research conducted by Lewin and his students when Lewin was at the University of Berlin.

Dollard, John, et al. *Frustration and Aggression*. New Haven, Conn.: Yale University Press, 1939. An early application of S-R theory to complex human behavior. The presentation of the hypothesis that aggression is inevitably caused by frustration is seen here.

Dollard, John, and Neal E. Miller. *Personality and Psychotherapy: An Analysis in Terms of Learning, Thinking, and Culture*. New York: McGraw-Hill, 1950. The best known of the works of Miller and Dollard. Presents a theory of personality and an S-R presentation of psychoanalytic theory and psychoanalytic therapy.

Evans, Richard I. *Albert Bandura, the Man and His Ideas: A Dialogue*. New York: Praeger, 1989. An edited version of an interview with Bandura. Easy to read, presenting Bandura's thoughts on the major aspects of his work in a very accessible form. The spontaneity of the discussion between Evans and Bandura gives a glimpse of Bandura as a person.

Hall, Calvin Springer, and Gardner Lindzey. *Theories of Personality*. 3d ed. New York: John Wiley & Sons, 1978. This book has a chapter on S-R theory and presents a detailed overview of the theory of Miller and Dollard.

Kelly, George Alexander. *Clinical Psychology and Personality: The Selected Papers of George Kelly*. Edited by Brendan Maher. New York: John Wiley & Sons, 1969. This offering is unique in that it contains many of Kelly's last papers. Includes papers that account for the origins of the theory and depicts Kelly's analysis of his work shortly before his death. The presentation is accurate, and it faithfully depicts the essence of Kelly's work.

_____. *The Psychology of Personal Constructs: A Theory of Personality*. New York: W. W. Norton, 1955. This two-volume series provides the essence of Kelly's theory. It provides the theoretical basis for the theory by presenting an analysis of personal constructs, constructive alternativism, and the fundamental postulate. Applications of the theory are also presented, including the Role Construct Repertory Test and fixed role therapy. Kelly's views of the appropriate place of assessment in the therapeutic process are particularly interesting.

Lewin, Kurt. *A Dynamic Theory of Personality*. New York: McGraw-Hill, 1935. Lewin's first major English-language work, consisting of a translation of many of his first papers published in Germany.

Lieber, Robert M., and Michael D. Spiegler. *Personality: Strategies and Issues*. 5th ed. Chicago: Dorsey Press, 1987. Chapter 21 presents a readable synopsis of Mischel's cognitive social-learning theory and reviews the concept of person variables, Walter Mischel's work on delay of gratification, and his position on the interaction of emotion and cognition. Highly recommended as an easy introduction to Mischel's work.

Marrow, Alfred Jay. *The Practical Theorist: The Life and Work of Kurt Lewin*. New York: Basic Books, 1969. This definitive biography of Lewin, written by one of his students, describes the life of Lewin and provides a glimpse of the personality behind field theory.

Miller, Neal E. "Studies of Fear as an Acquirable Drive: I. Fear as a Motivator and Fear-Reduction as Reinforcement in the Learning of New Responses." *Journal of Experimental Psychology* 38 (1948): 89-101. A classic paper that served as the experimental basis for postulating that fear is a secondary drive.

Miller, Neal E., and John Dollard. *Social Learning and Imitation*. New Haven, Conn.: Yale University Press, 1941. Presents an application of S-R theory to social motivation with a special emphasis on imitation.

Mischel, Walter. *Personality and Assessment*. New York: John Wiley & Sons, 1968. Classic exposition of Mischel's early work, containing a compelling critique of traditional trait and state approaches to personality. Discusses issues relevant to the assessment and modification of maladaptive social behavior.

_____. "Toward a Cognitive Social Learning Reconceptualization of Personality." *Psychological Review* 80, no. 4 (1973): 252-283. Written in response to the many reactions Mischel's 1968 book provoked in the research community. Clarifies several common misunderstandings of Mischel's position (for example, the situation-specificity issue) and gives a thorough presentation of his five personality variables. No specialized knowledge in psychology or personality theory is necessary for the reader to be able to follow the author's main arguments.

Mischel, Walter, Yuichi Shoda, and Monica L. Rodriguez. "Delay of Gratification in Children." *Science* 244, no. 4907 (1989): 933-938. Presents an excellent, brief summary of Mischel's work on self-control and delay of gratification spanning almost two decades. Discusses a number of stable individual differences in information-processing and strategic behaviors used by preschool children that were predictive of adult social adjustment.

Modgil, Sohan, and Celia Modgil, eds. *B. F. Skinner: Consensus and Controversy*. New York: Falmer Press, 1987. A collection of essays by psychologists and philosophers. Each topic has a pro and contrary opinion, with replies and rebuttals. Although written at a professional level, this is an excellent volume for a global view of Skinner's ideas and for the clearest understanding of what is "radical" about Skinner's behaviorism.

Neimeyer, Robert A. *The Development of Personal Construct Psychology*. Lincoln: University of Nebraska Press, 1985. Looks at the origins, development, and impact of Kelly's theory. Includes many relevant insights into Kelly's early work, while including applications of the theory in areas such as personality, clinical psychology, and social psychology.

Nye, Robert D. *What Is B. F. Skinner Really Saying?* Englewood Cliffs, N.J.: Prentice-Hall, 1979. The best introductory-level secondary account of Skinner's psychology and philosophy.

Rotgers, Frederick. "Social-Learning Theory, Philosophy of Science, and the Identity of Behavior Therapy." In *Paradigms in Behavior Therapy: Present and Promise*, edited by Daniel B. Fishman, Frederick Rotgers, and Cyril M. Franks. New York: Springer-Verlag, 1988. Places Bandura's social learning theory in the context of contemporary behavior theory and examines its philosophical roots. Difficult because it requires some basic understanding of the philosophy of science, but provides an excellent analysis of the philosophical underpinnings of Bandura's theory.

Schultz, Duane. *Theories of Personality*. 4th ed. Pacific Grove, Calif.: Brooks/Cole, 1990. Chapter 15 of this book contains an excellent summary of Bandura's work. Gives an easy-to-read overview of his philosophical position (reciprocal determinism), discusses his theory (including observational learning and self-regulatory processes), and presents a summary of relevant research conducted within the framework of social cognitive theory. An ideal starting point for anyone who would like to become familiar with Bandura's work.

Skinner, B. F. *About Behaviorism*. New York: Alfred A. Knopf, 1974. In this work, Skinner argues for his radical behaviorism by contrasting it with methodological behaviorism and by illustrating how it treats topics such as perception, memory, verbal behavior, private events, and thinking.

_____. *Particulars of My Life*. New York: Alfred A. Knopf, 1976.
_____. *The Shaping of a Behaviorist*. New York: Alfred A. Knopf, 1979.
_____. *A Matter of Consequences*. New York: Alfred A. Knopf, 1983. Skinner published his autobiography in these three separate volumes. The first describes his life from birth, through his college years as an English major, to his entering Harvard University for graduate study in psychology. *The Shaping of a Behaviorist* presents his years at Harvard and his rise to national prominence. *A Matter of Consequences* begins with his return to Harvard as a professor in the late 1940's.

_____. *Science and Human Behavior*. New York: Macmillan, 1953. A fine introduction to Skinner's thought. The principles of operant psychology are described, with numerous examples of the applicability to an individual's life and the major institutions of society. The chapter on private events illustrates one important way in which Skinner's radical behaviorism differs from methodological behaviorism.

_____. *Walden Two*. New York: Macmillan, 1948. A description of a fictional community based upon experimental practices and behavioral principles. The book was the source of inspiration for several communes and illustrates how all aspects of culture can be submitted to a behavioral analysis. Contains a lengthy criticism of democracy as a form of government.

Smith, B. D., and H. J. Vetter. "Social Learning and Cognition." In *Theories of Personality*. 2d ed. Englewood Cliffs, N.J.: Prentice-Hall, 1991. Covers several cognitive theories of how personality develops. Begins by defining terms used in cognitive psychology, a topic some find dry and some find fascinating. Goes on to cover early theories of how cognitive factors influence personality; this is where Bandura's ideas are introduced. The writing style is serious, not casual. An excellent overview of the field.

Spence, Kenneth Wartenbee. *Behavior Theory and Conditioning*. New Haven, Conn.: Yale University Press, 1956. A succinct and lucid presentation of the Hullian type S-R learning theory which served as the basis for many concepts in Miller and Dollard's S-R theory of personality.

Vargas, Julie S. "B. F. Skinner, Father, Grandfather, Behavior Modifier." In *About Human Nature: Journeys in Psychological Thought*, edited by Terry J. Knapp and Charles T. Rasmussen. Dubuque, Iowa: Kendall/Hunt, 1987. An intimate description of Skinner by his eldest daughter, who is herself a psychologist. Skinner's home, study, and the activities occurring over a Thanksgiving weekend are described.

Psychodynamic and Neoanalytic Models

Adler, Alfred. *The Individual Psychology of Alfred Adler*. Edited by Heinz L. Ansbacher and Rowena Ansbacher. New York: Basic Books, 1956.
_____. *Superiority and Social Interest*. Edited by Heinz L. Ansbacher and Rowena Ansbacher. Evanston, Ill.: Northwestern University Press, 1964. There is no standard edition or comprehensive collection of Adler's writings. He wrote many books, but unlike Sigmund Freud or Carl Jung, he essentially said the same thing over and over (especially after 1913). Any of Adler's later books will give a good sense of his theory. The above two edited works by the Ansbachers take representative excerpts from Adler's numerous books

and, together with editorial comments, give a good picture of the development of Adler's thought.

_____. *Social Interest, a Challenge to Mankind*. New York: Capricorn Books, 1964. An excellent summary of Adler's theories of human nature and social education, incorporating his ideas on lifestyle, inferiority/superiority complex, neurosis, childhood memories, and social feelings. Also contains a chapter on the consultant and patient relationship, and a questionnaire for understanding and treating difficult children.

Appignanesi, Richard. *Freud for Beginners*. Illustrated by Oscar Zarate. New York: Pantheon Press, 1979. The authors describe this book as a "documentary comic book" about the world of Freud. Brief and easy to follow, it very simply reviews the major aspects of Freud's theory, such as the unconscious, sex drives, and dreams, in a picture format. It caricatures Freud's family, friends, and some of his patients. Although it is light and enjoyable, it must be supplemented by other works.

Becker, Ernest. *The Birth and Death of Meaning*. 2d ed. New York: Free Press, 1971. Becker presents a general description of Fromm's ideas embedded in a broad interdisciplinary consideration of human social psychological behavior.

Bettelheim, Bruno. *Freud and Man's Soul*. New York: Alfred A. Knopf, 1983. A brief book written by a man who, like Freud, grew up in Vienna. Bettelheim, who read Freud's books in the original German, maintains that the English translations of Freud's works distort much of what he actually said. He sees this as resulting in a theory of psychoanalysis that is artificial and inhuman. Although Bettelheim attempts to explain what Freud really said, it is not clear that he succeeds. For the serious student of psychoanalysis.

Bottome, Phyllis. *Alfred Adler: A Biography*. New York: G. P. Putnam's Sons, 1939. This classic biography was written only two years after Adler's death. It gives much insight into the man and his theory.

Brome, Vincent. *Jung: Man and Myth*. New York: Atheneum, 1981. This is a sound biography of Jung and discussion of his work. Perhaps its main advantage is that it provides an analysis which is fair to both Jung and his critics.

Campbell, Joseph. *The Hero with a Thousand Faces.* New York: Meridian, 1956. Reviews the many faces of the hero archetype. Considered by many to be a classic in archetypal themes. Folklore, myth, and various rituals are used to explain how the archetypes further individuation. A framework for understanding one's own journey of individuation is provided. Clear, interesting, and written for the general reader.

Coles, Robert. *Erik H. Erikson: The Growth of His Work.* Boston: Little, Brown, 1970. A well-written biography, though Coles has been criticized by some as too friendly toward his subject; some reviewers have gone so far as to accuse him of hero worship.

Combs, Allen L., and Mark Holland. *Synchronicity: Science, Myth, and the Trickster.* New York: Paragon House, 1990. Presents a readable discussion not only of synchronicity but also of the deep structure of the collective unconscious, including archetypes and the concept of the *unus mundus.*

Dreikurs, Rudolf. *Fundamentals of Adlerian Psychology.* New York: Greenberg, 1950. The author was an Adlerian disciple who became the leader of the Adlerian movement in the United States after World War II. His simple style and straightforward advice are very much in keeping with the style of Adler himself. Dreikurs' own expertise was in the area of child development.

Erikson, Erik Homburger. *Childhood and Society.* New York: W. W. Norton, 1950. The first major book that explained the theory Erikson was in the process of developing. Republished in 1963 and again in 1985, this remains one of the most popular, and most frequently recommended, psychology books ever published.

_____. *Gandhi's Truth: On the Origins of Militant Nonviolence.* New York: W. W. Norton, 1969. The better of Erikson's psychohistorical biographies. Erikson examines in detail the historical period in which Gandhi grew up, and the personal experiences that eventually led Gandhi to become one of the world's most influential religious and spiritual leaders. Erikson believes that the writer of a psychohistory should become emotionally involved with the subject; his emotional attachment to Gandhi is apparent. Erikson attributes that attachment to his own lifelong search for the father he had never known.

Evans, Richard Isadore. *The Making of Psychology: Discussions with Creative Contributors.* New York: Alfred A. Knopf, 1976. An excellent compilation of interviews with many of the major forces in the history of psychology. The chapter on Erikson includes not only a discussion of the eight psychosocial stages but also a psychohistorical discussion comparing Adolf Hitler's and Mahatma Gandhi's lives and contributions to the world (Hitler does not fare well in the comparison).

Foulkes, William David. *A Grammar of Dreams*. New York: Basic Books, 1978. While not a general introduction to dream analysis, this formally written book is a landmark study which argues that dream events are essentially grammatical in form.

Freud, Anna. *The Ego and the Mechanisms of Defense*. Rev. ed. New York: International Universities Press, 1966. A short and relatively easy-to-read book written by Freud's daughter. She begins with a brief introduction to psychoanalysis and continues with a comprehensive review of all the ego defense mechanisms, which includes clear examples. Includes a short bibliography. Throughout the book, she notes original sources from her father's writing.

Freud, Sigmund. *Civilization and Its Discontents*. New York: W. W. Norton, 1961. Provides a good, brief overview of the psychosexual stages and places them in the larger context of general living. Written only ten years before Freud's death, this book contains his later ideas. The writing style is excellent.

_____. *Dora: An Analysis of a Case of Hysteria*. New York: Collier Books, 1963. Provides the case history of a woman who suffered from a neurosis. The treatment description of this case provides an excellent practical application of the theory of psychosexual development and its implications for psychopathology and personality development. Very readable.

_____. *A General Introduction to Psychoanalysis*. Translated by Joan Riviere. New York: Garden City Books, 1952. This is a collection of twenty-eight lectures written by Freud for the general public that covers the complete theory of psychoanalysis. It is easy to read and includes extensive material on the psychology of errors (parapraxes), dream interpretation, and the development of symptoms. It is an excellent starting point for those who know very little about psychoanalysis.

_____. *The Interpretation of Dreams*. Translated by James Strachey. New York: Avon Books, 1965. One of the most influential books in Western history, this book describes in detail Freud's original theory of dreams. Those who have not previously read Freud in the original will be delighted to discover that he was a superb writer. This book was first published in German in 1900.

_____. *New Introductory Lectures on Psychoanalysis.* New York: W. W. Norton, 1933. This volume contains seven lectures or papers that Freud wrote toward the end of his career. Among them is "The Psychology of Women," in which Freud attempts to explain some fundamental differences between the sexes. Freud describes female behavior and the Oedipus complex for males and females, and he elaborates on the role of penis envy in female development. The volume also contains lectures on dreams, on the structure of personality, and on anxiety and the instincts.

_____. *An Outline of Psychoanalysis.* Translated by James Strachey. New York: W. W. Norton, 1949. A brief introduction to Freudian theory. Beginning students of Freud may find the tone too didactic and the treatment too abbreviated; however, it is valuable when read in conjunction with a good summary of Freud from a secondary source.

_____. *The Standard Edition of the Complete Psychological Works of Sigmund Freud.* 24 vols. Edited by James Strachey. London: Hogarth Press, 1953-1974. Starting in 1953, all of Freud's written material was published in English in twenty-four volumes. Although these works are more appropriate for advanced readers, all the volumes include an extensive bibliography and comprehensive footnotes which clarify the material very well.

_____. *Three Case Histories.* New York: Collier Books, 1963. Provides three applied examples of psychopathology as an outgrowth of fixation at or regression to early psychosexual stages. Written for the layperson; presented in an interesting manner.

Freud, Sigmund, and William C. Bullitt. *Thomas Woodrow Wilson, Twenty-eighth President of the United States: A Psychological Study.* Boston: Houghton Mifflin, 1967. Written between 1919 and 1932, then revised to the authors' greater satisfaction in 1939, this book was not published until after the death of the late president's wife. To have a "new" book by Freud almost thirty years after his death guaranteed that it would be noticed; not all notice was favorable. As archival research by a major scholar, however, it is unequaled.

Fromm, Erich. *Anatomy of Human Destructiveness*. New York: Holt, Rinehart and Winston, 1973. An in-depth examination of the destructive personality type.

_____. *The Art of Loving*. New York: Harper, 1956. A detailed analysis of how to love and be loved. Distinguishes between genuine love and morbid dependency.

_____. *Escape from Freedom*. New York: Farrar & Rinehart, 1941. Fromm's early seminal work, in which his basic theory about the relationship between political, economic, and religious institutions and personality development was originally articulated. All of Fromm's later books are extensions of ideas expressed here.

_____. *Marx's Concept of Man*. New York: Frederick Ungar, 1961. An introduction to Marx's ideas, including a translation of Marx's economic and philosophical manuscripts of 1844.

_____. *The Revolution of Hope: Toward a Humanized Technology*. New York: Harper & Row, 1968. A detailed discussion of how capital-based economies can be transformed to provide opportunities for productive work without sacrificing productive efficiency, technological advances, or democratic political ideals.

Gay, Peter. *Freud: A Life for Our Time*. New York: W. W. Norton, 1988. A very well-written biography of Freud. Places Freud's work in historical and psychological context. Accessible to the reader who may only have a passing familiarity with Freudian theory.

_____, ed. *The Freud Reader*. New York: W. W. Norton, 1989. A well-edited volume of selections of Freud's work. *The Interpretation of Dreams, Fragment of an Analysis of a Case of Hysteria ("Dora")*, and *Three Essays on the Theory of Sexuality* are particularly important in defining the basics of Freud's theory.

Greenwald, Harold, ed. *Great Cases in Psychoanalysis*. New York: Ballantine, 1959. An outstanding source of case histories written by the theorists themselves. Greenwald uses these case histories to portray the historical context of the psychoanalytic movement. These original case studies provide insight into therapeutic methods used by these great analysts as well as their assessments. Included are Freud, Adler, Jung, Horney, and Sullivan.

Hannah, Barbara. *Jung: His Life and Work.* New York: Putnam, 1976. This positive biographical view of Jung is provided by a Jungian analyst who was a friend and colleague of Jung for three decades. While it may not be as objectively written as other accounts, it has the advantage of being written by a scholar who had firsthand knowledge of many of Jung's ideas.

Horney, Karen. *Feminine Psychology.* Edited by Harold Kelman. New York: W. W. Norton, 1967. A collection of some of Karen Horney's early works in which she describes Freudian ideas on the psychology of women and offers her own observations and conclusions. Horney disputes Freud's notion of penis envy and in later essays explores such topics as distrust between the sexes, premenstrual tension, and female masochism.

_____. *Neurosis and Human Growth: The Struggle Toward Self-Realization.* New York: W. W. Norton, 1950. Presents Horney's theory in its final form. Describes the ways in which various neurotic processes operate, including the tyranny of the should, neurotic claims, self-alienation, and self-contempt. Discusses faulty, neurotic solutions that are developed as a way to relieve internal tensions through domination, dependency, resignation, or self-effacement.

_____. *The Neurotic Personality of Our Time.* New York: W. W. Norton, 1937. This classic work contains Horney's portrayal of the neurotic personality and the relevance of cultural forces in the etiology of psychological disturbances. This post-Freudian document examines Horney's theoretical conceptualizations, including basic anxiety, neurotic trends, methods of adjustment, and the role played by culture. Outlines the manner in which culture influences personality difficulties and describes typical behavior problems that result from the exaggeration of cultural difficulties in one's life.

_____. *New Ways in Psychoanalysis.* New York: W. W. Norton, 1939. Describes major areas of agreement and disagreement with Freud, as well as important elements of her own theory; highly controversial when first published.

_____. *Our Inner Conflicts: A Constructive Theory of Neurosis.* New York: W. W. Norton, 1945. Identifies and describes, through rich detail and examples, the three neurotic trends of moving toward others, moving away from others, and moving against others; highly readable and a good introduction to Horney's main ideas.

_____. *Self-Analysis*. New York: W. W. Norton, 1942. Provides guidance for readers who may wish to engage in informal free association, self-discovery, and personal problem solving.

Jones, Ernest. *The Life and Work of Sigmund Freud*. Edited and abridged by Lionel Trilling and Steven Marcus. New York: Basic Books, 1961. This is an abridged edition of Jones's three-volume biography of Freud. Jones was a confidant of Freud, and his official biographer. Interesting as an "insider's" account of Freud's life.

Jung, Carl Gustav. *The Archetypes and the Collective Unconscious*. 2d ed. Princeton, N.J.: Princeton University Press, 1968. This is volume 9, part 1 of the prestigious Bollingen Series, and Jung's definitive work on the nature and origin of archetypes. Covers the relationship of the archetypes to the collective unconscious. The archetypes of anima, mother, rebirth, child, and individuation are dealt with in considerable depth, with illustrations and clinical examples. For the very serious student of Jung who has already read the basic introductory works.

_____. *Dreams*. Translated by R. F. C. Hull. Princeton, N.J.: Princeton University Press, 1974. This is number 20 in the Bollingen Series; the volume contains papers taken from vols. 4, 8, 12, and 16 of *The Collected Works of C. G. Jung*. Jung discusses his views of dreams as communications of the unconsciousness, as well as the role of archetypes in dreams and dreams as compensation.

_____. *The Essential Jung*. Edited by Anthony Storr. Princeton, N.J.: Princeton University Press, 1983. An excellent collection of Jung's most essential and central ideas; it is organized by topic and includes a readable, high-quality commentary by Storr.

_____. *Man and His Symbols*. Garden City, N. Y.: Doubleday, 1964. The inspiration for this book came to Jung in a dream which depicted the masses gaining knowledge of his theory. Jung consequently set out to write a book that would popularize his ideas without vulgarizing them. Luxuriously illustrated, this volume is available in an oversize edition that maximizes the effect of the many color images that exemplify Jungian archetypes and symbols. The most accessible account of Jung's thought.

_____. *Memories, Dreams, Reflections*. New York: Pantheon Books, 1963. Jung's autobiography. It thoroughly portrays the evolution of Jung's thinking, including all those factors that were critical to his theoretical conceptions. Essential reading for anyone interested in insights into Jung and his work. It should be remembered, however, that Jung's writing is often difficult to follow.

_____. *Modern Man in Search of a Soul*. New York: Harcourt Brace, 1933. This short work covers the basis of Jungian psychology and is recommended by most Jungians as a primer. Jung's approach to psychotherapy, dreams, literature, religion, and the modern crisis are included. Jung puts his ideas into the context of what he sees as the twentieth century bias and its dangers.

_____. *Psychological Types*. Translated by Richard and Clara Winston. New York: Harcourt Brace, 1923. Provides both an overview of the basic principles of Jung's theory and an analysis of the derivation of the attitudes and functions that yield his psychological types. Particularly important to those who are interested in the derivation of Jung's view of typology.

_____. *The Structure and Dynamics of the Psyche*. Translated by R. F. C. Hull. New York: Pantheon Books, 1960. This is volume 8 of Jung's *Collected Works*. A source for writing by Jung concerning archetypes and the collective unconscious.

_____. *Two Essays on Analytical Psychology*. New York: Meridian, 1956. A solid introduction to the bulk of Jung's theories. Covers the core of Jung's personality theory. If read in combination with Jung's *On the Nature of the Psyche*, gives any interested reader an in-depth and comprehensive introduction to Jung's work. Recommended for the serious scholar.

Kardiner, Abram. *My Analysis with Freud*. New York: W. W. Norton, 1977. Kardiner is a well-known analyst. This brief volume is a personal account of his own analysis, with Freud as the therapist. A fascinating "insider's" account of Freudian analysis and the forces that shaped the psychoanalytic movement.

Lerner, Harriet Goldhor. *Women in Therapy*. Northvale, N.J.: Jason Aronson, 1988. Discusses women and their psychotherapists from a psychoanalytic perspective, with references to Horney's theories. Illustrates how Horney's theories apply to many themes and issues in women's psychology.

McGuire, William, ed. *The Freud/Jung Letters*. Princeton, N.J.: Princeton University Press, 1974. Provides a unique analysis of the development of the relationship between Freud and Jung. Accurately portrays the promise of unity and collaboration within the relationship in its early years, beginning around 1907, and exposes the problems that eventually led to the Freud/Jung split, which was complete by 1914. Provides a context for examining the remainder of Jung's work and the personal problems that he was to encounter following his split with Freud.

Miller, Jonathan, ed. *Freud: The Man, His World, His Influence*. Boston: Little, Brown, 1972. Miller has edited a series of essays that put Freud's work in historical, social, and cultural perspective. One essay, by Friedrich Heer, describes the impact of Freud's Jewish background on his life and work in Vienna. Another, by Martin Esslin, describes Vienna, the exciting and culturally rich background for Freud's work.

Mosak, Harold H. *Alfred Adler: His Influence on Psychology Today*. Park Ridge, N.J.: Noyes Press, 1973. This edited volume covers Adlerian applications to understanding education, social issues, and the humanities, as well as discussing the clinical aspects of the theory.

Mosak, Harold H., and Birdie Mosak. *A Bibliography of Adlerian Psychology*. Washington, D.C.: Hemisphere, 1975. This is a very comprehensive bibliography covering Individual Psychology up through the early 1970's. Even articles appearing in newsletters are included. It is organized by author's last name but has a subject index.

Nathanson, S. "Denial, Projection, and the Empathic Wall." In *Denial: A Clarification of Concepts and Research*, edited by E. L. Edelstein, Donald L. Nathanson, and Andrew M. Stone. New York: Plenum Press, 1989. Discusses denial and projection and gives clinical illustrations. The author integrates concepts with other theories and provides relevant examples of research with infants. There is also a discussion of empathy and its relationship to substance abuse.

Quinn, Susan. *A Mind of Her Own: The Life of Karen Horney*. Reading, Mass.: Addison-Wesley, 1988. This biography is an excellent source of information about Horney's personal and professional life. Much of it is devoted to her female psychology. Easy to read; contains photographs, biographical essays, extensive source notes, and a complete list of Horney's work.

Roazen, Paul. *Erik H. Erikson: The Power and Limits of a Vision.* New York: Free Press, 1976. Although Roazen is critical of Erikson, he finds Erikson's approach more likely than Freud's to be helpful in therapeutic encounters.

Rubins, Jack L. *Karen Horney: Gentle Rebel of Psychoanalysis.* New York: Dial Press, 1978. The first biography of Karen Horney. Thorough and well documented; includes detailed discussions of Horney's theories on women. Lengthy but well organized. Can be read by the college or high school student.

Rychlak, Joseph F. *Introduction to Personality and Psychotherapy.* 2d ed. Boston: Houghton Mifflin, 1981. This introductory personality text carefully reviews the work of several leading psychologists and psychotherapists, including Sigmund Freud. Rychlak describes the gradual development of Freud's structural hypothesis, and he reviews Freud's ideas about the instincts, dynamic concepts such as defense mechanisms, and the development of the Oedipus complex for males and females, noting the concerns of modern feminists who have found Freud's work offensive.

Stepansky, Paul E. *In Freud's Shadow: Adler in Context.* New York: Analytic Press, 1983. This is one of the more recent biographies of Adler. It does an excellent job of considering Adler's sociohistorical context and his interpersonal struggles with Freud. True Adlerians will maintain that this book does not do Adler justice.

Storr, Anthony. *Churchill's Black Dog, Kafka's Mice, and Other Phenomena of the Human Mind.* New York: Grove Press, 1988. This fascinating book demonstrates how personality theories can be used to interpret lives. Storr describes the creative process in general, and the lives of Churchill Kafka, and others in particular, from his psychological point of view, primarily psychoanalytic in orientation. The perspectives of Freud, Jung, and Erikson are featured.

Sullivan, Harry Stack. *The Interpersonal Theory of Psychiatry.* New York: W. W. Norton, 1953. A classic work on human development from an interpersonal perspective. Sullivan provides a comprehensive overview of his theory by describing his key concepts and developmental stages. He further illustrates the application of his theory by focusing upon inappropriate interpersonal relationships.

Symonds, Alexandra. "Separation and Loss: Significance for Women." *American Journal of Psychoanalysis* 45, no. 1 (1985): 53-58. Discusses women's feelings about separation and loss. Important illustration of how Horney's theories help explain women's role in interpersonal relationships.

Von Franz, Marie-Luise. *Projection and Re-Collection in Jungian Psychology: Reflections of the Soul.* Translated by William H. Kennedy. La Salle, Ill.: Open Court, 1980. A set of very readable essays by a leading authority on Jung; contains a rare detailed discussion of the origins of the idea of the collective unconscious.

Westkott, Marcia. *The Feminist Legacy of Karen Horney.* New Haven, Conn.: Yale University Press, 1986. This book integrates Karen Horney's earlier papers on the psychology of women with the more complete personality theory that emerged over time.

Whitmont, Edward C. *The Symbolic Quest: Basic Concepts of Analytic Psychology.* Princeton, N.J.: Princeton University Press, 1978. Whitman provides a good general introduction to Jung's theories. A good place for the reader to become more informed about Jung before tackling Jung's own writings.

Humanistic-Phenomenological Models

Allport, Gordon W. "An Autobiography." In *A History of Psychology in Autobiography.* Vol. 5. Edited by Edwin Garrigues Boring and Gardner Lindzey. New York: Appleton-Century-Crofts, 1967. Allport provides an interesting account of his life, including an encounter with Sigmund Freud.

_____. *Becoming: Basic Considerations for a Psychology of Personality.* New Haven, Conn.: Yale University Press, 1955. A short, straightforward, clear statement of Allport's basic assumptions about personality. Allport attempts to provide the basic foundation for a complete personality theory and emphasizes the importance for both open-mindedness and eclecticism in the study of personality.

_____. *Pattern and Growth in Personality.* New York: Holt, Rinehart and Winston, 1961. This textbook is the most complete account of Gordon Allport's personality theory. It includes extensive descriptions of Allport's approach to personality and individuality, personality development, the structure of the personality, the characteristics of the mature personality, and methods of personality assessment.

_____. *Personality and Social Encounter*. Boston: Beacon Press, 1960. A collection of Allport's essays that are scholarly but not overly technical. They are organized into five parts that focus on basic assumptions about personality, personality structure and motivation, personality problems, group tensions associated with prejudice and religion, and social issues and personality.

Anderson, James W. "Henry A. Murray's Early Career: A Psychobiographical Exploration." *Journal of Personality* 56, no. 1 (1988): 139-171. An interesting presentation of the factors that led Murray to become a psychologist and of how his experiences interacted with his theory. An excellent example of how one's life cannot be extricated from one's beliefs about human nature.

Boss, Medard. *Psychoanalysis and Daseinsanalysis*. New York: Da Capo Press, 1982. The book is Boss's most clear and comprehensive presentation of his own approach to existential analysis. It offers a philosophically sophisticated critique of Freudian psychoanalysis with regard to neuroses and therapy and presents an alternative rooted in the existential insights of one's being-in-the-world.

Evans, Richard I. *Gordon Allport: The Man and His Ideas*. New York: E. P. Dutton, 1971. This book is based on a series of dialogues with Allport that focus on his unique contributions and his vision of the future of personality psychology. Also includes a discussion and evaluation of Allport's ideas by three distinguished psychologists who studied under his direction.

Frankl, Viktor Emil. *Man's Search for Meaning*. Boston: Beacon Press, 1963. Includes Frankl's gripping account of his experience as a prisoner in a Nazi concentration camp during World War II and the insights he gained from it. Also presents Frankl's basic formulation of "logotherapy"—his original form of existential therapy, centered on the question of what it is that gives one's life meaning.

Goble, Frank G. *The Third Force: The Psychology of Abraham Maslow*. New York: Grossman, 1970. An accessible, highly readable book. Summarizes in brief, succinct chapters the major concepts and ideas of Maslow, such as basic needs, human potential, psychological growth, values, and synergy. Concludes with a survey of applications in education, mental health, and business and industry.

The Humanistic Psychologist 16, no. 1 (1988). This special issue, "Psychotherapy for Freedom," edited by Erik Craig, focuses on the existential approach to psychotherapy developed by Medard Boss known as daseinsanalysis. It features original articles by Boss and his colleagues at the Daseinsanalytic Institute in Switzerland, as well as pieces by Erik Craig and Martin Heidegger and an annotated bibliography of relevant readings on daseinsanalysis.

Jones, Alvin, and Rick Crandall, eds. "Handbook of Self-Actualization." Special issue. *Journal of Social Behavior and Personality*, no. 5 (1991). A collection of papers on self-actualization and optimal functioning, including theoretical and analytical papers, empirical studies, and examination of issues in assessing self-actualization. The papers, variable in quality and sophistication, cover the field broadly, present interesting implications, and point to future directions.

Laing, Ronald David. *The Divided Self: An Existential Study in Sanity and Madness*. New York: Penguin, 1965. This brilliant study of schizophrenia from an existential approach was a breakthrough for a totally new way of understanding the experience of the psychotic person. Though difficult for a general reader, the profound value of Laing's vision is worth the effort.

Maddi, Salvatore R., and Paul T. Costa. *Humanism in Personology: Allport, Maslow, and Murray*. Chicago: Aldine-Atherton, 1972. This volume compares the work of Allport with the contributions of two other humanistic personality theorists. Although the theories of these three differ substantially, they share an emphasis on human uniqueness, a faith in human capabilities, and a view of people as proactive, complex, and oriented toward the future.

Maslow, Abraham Harold. *Motivation and Personality*. 3d ed. New York: Harper & Row, 1987. Presents Maslow's classic paper describing self-actualizing people and includes major sections on his motivation theory, on normality and abnormality, and on methodology in psychology. Slightly revised by editors, this third edition is more readable than earlier ones. Two additional chapters succinctly describe Maslow's tremendous influence and impact. Includes chronological bibliography of his writings.

_____. *Toward a Psychology of Being.* 2d ed. Princeton, N.J.: Van Nostrand Reinhold, 1968. A major book of Maslow's psychological writings, with significant sections on growth and motivation, self-actualizing cognition, creativeness, and values. The style is rather pedantic.

Masterson, Jenny (Gove), pseudonym. *Letters from Jenny.* Edited and interpreted by Gordon W. Allport. New York: Harcourt, Brace & World, 1965. An example of idiographic or morphogenic study of the personality. After studying 301 letters from an older woman to her son and his wife, Allport grouped her characteristics into eight clusters that correspond to the number of central dispositions that he proposed make up important elements of personality.

May, Rollo. *The Discovery of Being.* New York: W. W. Norton, 1983. This collection of May's essays offers a clear and easily grasped introduction to existential psychology. Though the emphasis is mostly on its relation to psychotherapy, the volume also covers some of the basic principles and background of the existential approach.

_____. *Power and Violence: A Search for the Sources of Violence.* New York: W. W. Norton, 1972. An existential analysis of power, self-affirmation, self-assertion, aggression, and violence. May argues that feelings of impotence, powerlessness, and insignificance underlie aggression and violence, and argues strongly against innocence and for power in terms of psychological and spiritual valuing of self, assuming responsibility, and acknowledging people's potentiality for evil.

May, Rollo, Ernest Angel, and Henri F. Ellenberger, eds. *Existence.* New York: Basic Books, 1958. This famous volume was the first to introduce European existential psychology to American audiences. It includes the first English translations of articles by Binswanger, Minkowski, Straus, and others, as well as a now-classic introductory chapter by May that describes the significance of an existential approach to psychology and psychotherapy.

Review of Existential Psychology and Psychiatry 20, nos. 1-3 (1986-1987). These special issues of this journal, edited by Keith Hoeller and collectively entitled "Readings in Existential Psychology and Psychiatry," feature a collection of classic articles from the 1960's to the 1980's. Included are articles by Van Kaam, Frankl, Boss, Laing, Rogers, May, and others on such topics as existential psychotherapy, anxiety, guilt, freedom, imagination, myth, schizophrenia, suicide, the unconscious, and will.

Rogers, Carl Ransom. *On Becoming a Person*. Boston: Houghton Mifflin, 1961. A highly readable book and an excellent introduction to Rogers' warm, personal, direct style of communicating his ideas. Covers the fully functioning person, Rogers' views on dimensions of the helping relationship and ways people grow in therapy, and applications of his approach in education, the family, and other areas. Provides Rogers' views of person-centered psychotherapy, including its key characteristics and how to research its effectiveness.

_____. *A Way of Being*. Boston: Houghton Mifflin, 1980. A clear presentation of experiences and ideas personally and professionally important to Rogers. Personal chapters deal with experiences in communication, origins of his philosophy, views on reality and his career, and feelings on aging. Other chapters describe foundations, applications, and implications of his person-centered approach, including education, community building, and empathy as a way of life. Includes chronological bibliography of Rogers' works.

Valle, Ronald S., and Steen Halling, eds. *Existential-Phenomenological Perspectives in Psychology*. New York: Plenum Press, 1989. Designed as an introduction to the field, this book examines, from an existential and phenomenological perspective, many of psychology's standard topics, such as learning, perception, psychotherapy, development, and research, as well as areas that traditional psychology overlooks, such as aesthetics, passion, forgiveness, and transpersonal experiences.

Van Kaam, Adrian L. *Existential Foundations of Psychology*. Pittsburgh: Duquesne University Press, 1966. Van Kaam's aim in this book is to provide a dialogue between traditional scientific psychology and the insights of existentialism. He sees psychology as needing to integrate the existential awareness that one's involvement in the world is necessarily from a personal perspective.

Yalom, Irvin D. *Existential Psychotherapy*. New York: Basic Books, 1980. A very well-written presentation of an existential understanding of psychological problems and therapy. Yalom grasps the basic conflicts of psychological life as flowing from "the individual's confrontation with the givens of existence," and he identifies these givens as death, freedom, existential isolation, and meaninglessness. For each theme, he presents the conflict and the way that existential therapy addresses it.

STRESS

Biology

Abram, Harry S., ed. *Psychological Aspects of Stress*. Springfield, Ill. Charles C Thomas, 1970. In this collaboration of chapters on six different stressful situations and how they affect the human being, the different contributors, all medical doctors, examine and discuss the human response to stressful events in life, both pathologically and physiologically. Covers topics from human precognitions to outer-space stressors and intimates that preconceived thought influences future perceptions. Excellent references at the end of each chapter.

Andrewartha, Herbert George. *Introduction to the Study of Animal Populations*. Chicago: University of Chicago Press, 1961. In this classic book by one of the pioneers in animal behavior research, Andrewartha discusses the principal behaviors of many different species, including dominance hierarchies, environmental stress, and displacement activities. The second half of the book is a useful guide to performing animal behavior experiments in the laboratory and the field.

Bloom, Floyd E., and Arlyne Lazerson. *Brain, Mind, and Behavior*. 2d ed. New York: W. H. Freeman, 1988. Written to accompany the Public Broadcasting Service television series *The Brain*. Provides a clear description of the function of the nervous system, with many excellent illustrations. The section on stress describes many of the basic studies which have contributed to an understanding of the relationship between stress and the nervous system.

Cannon, Walter B. *Bodily Changes in Pain, Hunger, Fear, and Rage*. Boston: Charles T. Branford, 1929. The classical formulation of the fight-or-flight response. Cannon's formulations provided the impetus for the study of the interaction between stress and the autonomic nervous system.

_____. *The Wisdom of the Body*. New York: Raven, 1932. This is a classic presentation of the body's physiological adjustments to stress and other situations by one of the most important physiologists of the century. Although parts are technical, the book is worth perusing for its historical interest.

Charlesworth, Edward A., and Ronald G. Nathan. *Stress Management: A Comprehensive Guide to Wellness.* New York: Atheneum, 1984. Begins with an easy-to-understand description of the effects of stress on the nervous system. Most of the book covers assessment of the sources of stress in one's life and suggests how its negative effects can be reduced. Includes Holmes and Rahe's "social readjustment rating scale," as well as excellent and easy-to-follow instructions on relaxation.

Constantinides, P. C., and Niall Carey. "The Alarm Reaction." *Scientific American* 180 (March, 1949): 20-23. A short article by two researchers in Selye's institute that remains of interest. Discusses examples of the research generated by explorations of the General Adaptation Syndrome and notes the work's medical importance. The writing, while not simple, is aimed at the nonspecialist.

Cox, Tom. *Stress.* London: Macmillan, 1978. In two hundred pages, in an easily understood language, explains for the layperson the nature of stress. Discusses the physiological and psychological responses to stress. Contains some line drawings which complement the text, and includes a short index and bibliography.

Curtis, Helena. *Biology.* 3d ed. New York: Worth, 1979. Curtis presents an excellent introduction to biology for the beginning student in this thorough but clear book. In chapter 34, "Integration and Control," she describes the functioning of the mammalian nervous and endocrine systems. Chapters 40, "Brain and Behavior," and 48, "Social Behavior," focus upon neurophysiological responses to the environment and to other organisms.

Goliszek, Andrew G. *Breaking the Stress Habit.* Winston-Salem, N.C.: Carolina Press, 1987. Includes a more detailed description of the physiology of the stress response, questionnaires which allow one to examine one's own problems, and suggestions for the reduction of stress-related problems.

Gray, Jeffrey A. *The Psychology of Fear and Stress.* Cambridge, England: Cambridge University Press, 1987. A thorough discussion of the psychological and physiological factors underlying fear and stress. Gray not only describes the various behavioral and biological processes necessary to understand fear and stress but also discusses their implications for human function.

Levine, Seymour. "Psychoneuroendocrinology of Stress: A Psychobiological Perspective." In *Psychoendocrinology*, edited by F. Robert Brush and Seymour Levine. San Diego, Calif.: Academic Press, 1989. A relatively short chapter which clearly makes the case that hormonal activation during stress is related to psychological processes such as expectancy. A good review of the effects of stress on the release of glucocorticoids (but has limited coverage of other hormones).

Manning, Aubrey. *An Introduction to Animal Behavior*. 3d ed. Reading, Mass.: Addison-Wesley, 1979. Manning's short but thorough book is an excellent introduction to animal behavior research. He describes numerous behavioral models for learning, displacement activities, and stress responses, and cites numerous experimental studies to support these models. Stress and displacement activities are addressed in chapter 5, "Conflict Behavior."

Monat, Alan, and Richard S. Lazarus, eds. *Stress and Coping: An Anthology*. New York: Columbia University Press, 1977. This collection of articles and book excerpts is technical, and includes brief articles by many of the major researchers investigating stress response. Topics range from Selye's theory to examination of social factors in stress to religion and voodoo death.

Ornstein, Robert, and D. S. Sobel. "The Brain as a Health Maintenance Organization." In *The Healing Brain: A Scientific Reader*, edited by Robert Ornstein and Charles Swencionis. New York: Guilford Press, 1990. Discusses the body's responses to stressors from an evolutionary perspective.

Raven, Peter H., and George B. Johnson. *Biology*. 2d ed. St. Louis: Times Mirror/Mosby, 1989. A beautifully illustrated and diagrammed introduction to biology. Major biological topics are presented with great simplicity in this lengthy text, including mammalian anatomy and physiology. Several chapters are devoted to the human nervous and endocrine systems as well as to the mechanisms of animal behavior.

Selye, Hans. *The Stress of Life*. New York: McGraw-Hill, 1956. An introduction to the theory relating stressors to physiological responses. Less complex than some of the more recent books, yet provides a good description of the relationship between stress and the body. Appropriate for a high school or college student with some understanding of basic biology and biological terminology.

Veith-Flanigan, Jane, and Curt A. Sandman. "Neuroendocrine Relationships with Stress." In *Stress: Psychological and Physiological Interactions,* edited by Susan R. Burchfield. Washington, D.C.: Hemisphere Publishing, 1985. A very broad, psychologically based discussion of the interactions of hormones and stress. Suggests multiple levels of interaction among hormones, behavior, and stress. Other chapters in this book also describe related aspects of the biology and psychology of stress.

Wilson, Jean D., and Daniel W. Foster. *Williams Textbook of Endocrinology.* Philadelphia: W. B. Saunders, 1985. A comprehensive textbook of endocrinology. Although very technical, most chapters in the text are clearly written and provide thorough description of the stress-related hormones in individual chapters and a discussion of hormones and stress in chapter 20.

Coping

Allen, Roger J. *Human Stress: Its Nature and Control.* Minneapolis: Burgess, 1983. A well-written account of the broad concept of stress, with good chapters on the general adaptation syndrome and on the psychophysiology of the stress response (that is, the mind-body link). The work is divided into three parts: the nature of stress; the causes and effects of stress; and stress control, which includes the psychophysiological subjects of meditation, relaxation, and biofeedback. Addressed to the general public; includes very good reference lists after each chapter, in addition to an index and illustrations.

Altman, I. *The Environment and Social Behavior: Privacy, Personal Space, Territory, and Crowding.* Monterey, Calif.: Brooks/Cole, 1975. Provides an overview of the social psychological theories of phenomena related to crowding as well as crowding itself. Stresses the relationship of crowding and related phenomena to social behavior rather than individual behavior. Provides a good introduction to the theoretical issues of crowding; the reader may see how more recent data fit into these conceptualizations.

Arnold, Magda B. "Perennial Problems in the Field of Emotion." In *Feelings and Emotions: The Loyola Symposium,* edited by Magda B. Arnold. New York: Academic Press, 1970. Although it is challenging reading for the general reader, this chapter is an excellent short presentation of Arnold's views on appraisal as well as other developments in the field.

Auerbach, Stephen M. "Assumptions of Crisis Theory and Temporal Model of Crisis Intervention." In *Crisis Intervention with Children and Families*, edited by Stephen M. Auerbach and Arnold L. Stolberg. Washington, D.C.: Hemisphere, 1986. This chapter examines some basic issues pertaining to psychological responses to extremely stressful events, including the role of the passage of time, individual differences, and previous success in dealing with stressful events. Crisis intervention and other stress-management programs are also reviewed.

_____. "Temporal Factors in Stress and Coping: Intervention Implications." In *Personal Coping: Theory, Research, and Application*, edited by B. N. Carpenter. Westport, Conn.: Praeger, 1991. Focuses on how behavioral and psychological stress responses differ depending on whether the stressor is anticipated, currently ongoing, or has already occurred. The types of coping strategies that are likely to be most effective for each kind of stressor are described, and many examples are given.

Averill, James R. "Personal Control over Aversive Stimuli and Its Relationship to Stress." *Psychological Bulletin* 80, no. 4 (1973): 286-303. Original presentation of author's descriptive hypothetical scheme for behavioral, cognitive, and decisional control of stressors.

Barber, Joseph, and Cheri Adrian, eds. *Psychological Approaches to the Management of Pain*. New York: Brunner/Mazel, 1982. A compilation of selections, written by authorities from both research and applied areas, concerned with psychology of pain control. Major topics include the use of hypnosis (including self-hypnosis) for the control of pain, the management of acute pain, and the treatments used in interdisciplinary pain clinics.

Bell, P. A., J. D. Fisher, A. Baum, and T. E. Greene. "High Density and Crowding." In *Environmental Psychology*. Fort Worth, Tex.: Holt, Rinehart and Winston, 1990. This textbook chapter covers the entire field of environmental psychology. Other chapters in this book are useful for coverage of phenomena closely related to crowding such as "Personal Space and Territoriality" and "Architecture, Design, and Behavior." A comprehensive book which gives detailed coverage of crowding as well as related topics.

Birbaumer, Niels, and H. D. Kimmel, eds. *Biofeedback and Self-Regulation*. Hillsdale, N.J.: Lawrence Erlbaum, 1979. Reviews the theoretical and clinical issues surrounding biofeedback in particular, as well as relaxation techniques. Clinical examples of headache control, heart rate control, and brain wave control are among the many cases described. Complete indexes, tables, and graphs are included in this excellent book.

Bresler, David E., and Richard Trubo. *Free Yourself from Pain.* New York: Simon & Schuster, 1979. Discusses the nature and control of pain, as well as a number of both traditional and unconventional therapies used in pain management. Numerous self-help forms are included.

Brown, Barbara B. *New Mind, New Body: Biofeedback—New Directions for the Mind.* New York: Harper & Row, 1974. Chapter 8, "Blood Pressure: Blood Vessels and Social Tension," of this classic popular introduction to biofeedback clearly describes how people can make only mildly noxious stimuli into stressors and how psychosomatic illnesses can be learned. Suggests how the power of stressors can be reduced through biofeedback training.

Charlesworth, Edward A., and Ronald G. Nathan. *Stress Management: A Comprehensive Guide to Wellness.* New York: Atheneum, 1985. This book is easy to understand and provides a description of the stress response; it outlines many of the methods used to cope more successfully. Includes questionnaires to help one to assess one's current functioning as well as excellent and easy-to-follow instructions on relaxation. Cognitive techniques for stress reduction are also described. Sources for tapes and related materials are listed.

Elton, Diana, Gordon Stanley, and Graham Burrows. *Psychological Control of Pain.* New York: Grune & Stratton, 1983. Provides an introduction to the neurophysiology and biochemistry of pain and discusses a number of psychosocial variables that influence the experience of pain. Numerous approaches to the control of pain including relaxation, operant conditioning, and group therapy are presented.

Figley, Charles R., ed. *Treating Stress in Families.* New York: Brunner/Mazel, 1989. In today's stress-focused society, this book makes an important contribution. Observations are provided from scientific studies of families regarding how they not only cope with but also produce stress and react to stress. Interventions for prevention are explored.

Fischer, Claude S. "The Individual in the City: States of Mind." In *The Urban Experience.* New York: Harcourt Brace Jovanovich, 1976.

Focuses on crowding as viewed by city dwellers. First reviews the studies of crowding, then focuses on the relationship between urbanism and psychological stress and disorder. Goes on to consider "urban alienation" and, finally, provides evidence and conclusions about whether living in cities makes people unhappy.

Folkman, Susan, Charles E. Schaefer, and Richard S. Lazarus. "Cognitive Processes as Mediators of Stress and Coping." In *Human Stress and Cognition: An Information Processing Approach*, edited by Vernon Hamilton and David M. Warburton. New York: John Wiley & Sons, 1979. Introduces the concepts of primary and secondary appraisal, and includes an interesting discussion of the role of emotion and stress. Assumes some background in psychology, so beginning readers might find this chapter difficult; a good resource for a more advanced reader.

Freedman, J. L. *Crowding and Behavior*. New York: Viking Press, 1975. Describes several of Freedman's studies on the effects of density on human performance and attitudes in a variety of settings. Proposes an original theory to explain these effects. Freedman's density-intensity theory explains how density may have negative effects in some situations and positive effects in others.

Friedman, Meyer, and Diane Ulmer. *Treating Type A Behavior*. New York: Fawcett Crest, 1984. The thesis is that emotional overreactivity is not innate, but is learned and can be changed. The authors describe successful interventions to alter Type A behavior.

Fuller, M. G., and V. L. Goetsch. "Stress and Stress Management." In *Behavior and Medicine*, edited by Danny Wedding. New York: Mosby-Year Book, 1990. Provides an overview of the field, focusing particularly on the physiological response to stress.

Geen, Russell G. "The Psychology of Stress." In *Personality: The Skein of Behavior*. St. Louis: C. V. Mosby, 1976. Survey of research relating to helplessness, uncertainty, stress, and control.

Geen, Russell G., William W. Beatty, and Robert M. Arkin. "Stress and Motivation." In *Human Motivation: Physiological, Behavioral, and Social Approaches*. Boston: Allyn & Bacon, 1984. Addresses stress prediction and control, including principal applications to such phenomena as crowding and learned helplessness.

Girdano, D. A., and G. S. Everly, Jr. *Controlling Stress and Tension: A Holistic Approach.* 2d ed. Englewood Cliffs, N.J.: Prentice-Hall, 1986. This book provides theoretical background along with many self-tests and practical guides to stress management. It is an excellent source for readers who are looking for applications.

Goldberg, Philip. *Executive Health: How to Recognize Health Danger Signals and Manage Stress Successfully.* New York: Business Week, McGraw-Hill, 1978. This book puts stress management into a business context, both for the employee and for management. It provides a good general outline of the problem and suggests possible routes leading to solutions.

Goldberger, Leo, and Shlomo Breznitz, eds. *Handbook of Stress: Theoretical and Clinical Aspects.* New York: Free Press, 1982. Comprehensive compendium of articles by noted researchers of stress processes, stressors, treatment, management, and support. Emphasizes both psychological and physiological aspects of stress. Includes material on coping with stress as well as on treatment approaches to stress and stress-related disorders.

Goliszek, Andrew G. *Breaking the Stress Habit: A Modern Guide to One-Minute Stress Management.* Winston-Salem, N.C.: Carolina Press, 1987. This small but impressive book includes a detailed description of the stress response. Questionnaires are included which allow one to examine one's own problems; a wide variety of suggestions for the reduction of stress-related problems is included. Topics include job burnout, stress and aging, and time management, as well as tension-reduction techniques.

Gould, Stephen Jay. "The Median Isn't the Message." *Discover* 6 (June, 1985): 40-42. A brief critique of cancer survival statistics, written for a general audience. Gould points out that a "median mortality of eight months," which many would read as a death sentence, also means that half the people will live longer, and some much longer.

Greenberg, Jerrold S. *Comprehensive Stress Management.* Dubuque, Iowa: Wm. C. Brown, 1990. An easy-to-read text giving an overview of psychological and physiological stress responses and stress-management techniques. Separate sections on applications to occupational stress, the college student, the family, and the elderly.

Grinker, Roy Richard, and John P. Spiegel. *Men Under Stress.* Philadelphia: Blakiston, 1945. A relatively nontechnical study of psychological trauma resulting from combat stress. A classic of its kind, the book rests on case studies. Reference is made to the importance of emotional and mental determinants of anxiety, the latter determinant expressly being associated with an appraisal process. The general philosophical viewpoint is psychodynamic (that is, Freudian), and the book ends with some historically interesting social speculations.

Gross, Nancy E. *Living with Stress*. New York: McGraw-Hill, 1958. Very easy reading. Relates the story of stress, explains the concept, and gives advice on how to cope with stress in daily life. In a foreword, Hans Selye says that the author succeeds in conveying the essence of what has been learned about stress (although much has been learned since this 1958 book). Lacks references, but includes an index and a glossary.

Hanna, Judith Lynne. *Dance and Stress*. New York: AMS Press, 1988. Comprehensive overview of the relationship between all forms of dance and stress in American and cross-cultural settings. While not written specifically with regard to dance as therapy, this is a very useful book in examining the relationship between stress and dance.

Holmes, Thomas H., and Richard H. Rahe. "The Social Readjustment Rating Scale." *Journal of Psychosomatic Research* 11, no. 2 (1967): 213-218. A now-classic article describing a first attempt to catalog and measure stressors common in American society. The authors' work continues to be cited as an ingenious approach to quantifying stressors.

Jacobson, Edmund. *Modern Treatment of Tense Patients*. Springfield, Ill.: Charles C Thomas, 1970. A complete book on the theory and practice of progressive muscle relaxation, including the step-by-step method, instructions, and case studies. Illustrations of each step are included at the end of the book.

_____. *Tension in Medicine*. Springfield, Ill.: Charles C Thomas, 1967. A wonderful description of progressive muscle relaxation, with a variety of case studies illustrating its application and success. Reports from a number of clinicians are included, with clear graphs illustrating the results.

_____. *You Must Relax*. New York: McGraw-Hill, 1934. A rare classic which may be available in the special collections section of the library. Jacobson is considered the father of modern relaxation training. This book is worth seeking for the pictures of Jacobson's patients after undergoing his relaxation procedure as well as for Jacobson's thoughtful insights.

Kanner, Allen D., James C. Coyne, Catherine Shaefer, and Richard S. Lazarus. "Comparison of Two Modes of Stress Measurement: Daily Hassles and Uplifts Versus Major Life Events." *Journal of Behavioral Medicine* 4, no. 1 (1981): 1-39. Working from different assumptions from those of Holmes and Rahe, the authors focus not on major life events but on the ever-present minor challenges that people face; they look at the frustration that "hassles" produce. They argue that minor events have a cumulative effect that gives them real power.

Kessler, Ronald C., Richard H. Price, and Camille B. Wortman. "Social Factors in Psychopathology: Stress, Social Support, and Coping Processes." In *Annual Review of Psychology* 36. Stanford, Calif.: Annual Reviews, 1985. Reviews the research on life stress and vulnerability, and includes a section on group differences such as sex differences. An excellent starting place for someone interested in stress and health in general. Assumes some background in psychology, but the article is so clear that even relative beginners should find it useful.

Knight, Edwin. *Living with Stress.* Caufield East, Victoria, Australia: Edward Arnold, 1987. In a humorous style, complemented by cartoons, this work describes for the general public the nature of stress and its symptoms. Also discusses stress and physical illness, as well as the management of stress with relaxation techniques. Contains an index and a bibliography.

Kobasa, Suzanne C. "Stressful Life Events, Personality, and Health: An Inquiry into Hardiness." *Journal of Personality and Social Psychology* 37 (January, 1979): 1-11. The original groundbreaking study which attempted to determine why some people develop stress-related illnesses while others do not. It was in this study that Kobasa determined that the key factors which protected some individuals from stress-related illnesses are control, commitment, and challenge. Excellent reading for any audience.

Kubler-Ross, Elisabeth. *On Death and Dying.* New York: Macmillan, 1969. The first in an inspiring series of books helpful to patients, their families and friends, and health care professionals. Five stages of reaction to death are described—denial, anger, bargaining, depression, acceptance. The book suggests ways to assist people to live each day to the fullest and come to terms with mortality.

Kushner, Harold S. *When Bad Things Happen to Good People*. New York: Avon, 1983. A helpful attempt to make sense of personal tragedy and go beyond the initial question of "Why me?" to make renewed connections with meaningful living.

Lazarus, Richard S. "The Costs and Benefits of Denial." In *Stress and Coping: An Anthology*, edited by Alan Monat and Richard S. Lazarus. New York: Columbia University Press, 1977. This excellent article includes a brief discussion of research that can be interpreted using the framework of denial, but it is largely a theoretical piece. After the interesting but slightly tangential section on denial in literature, Lazarus carefully explains the costs and benefits associated with the different forms of denial.

_____. *Psychological Stress and the Coping Process*. New York: McGraw-Hill, 1966. A very important and influential book, perhaps the first to offer a comprehensive treatment of psychological stress and coping. While an excellent critical review of much of the early work on stress and related topics, its coverage of the literature is somewhat selective, and Lazarus' views are forcefully put. Written for a professional audience, but largely accessible to the motivated layperson.

Lazarus, Richard S., and Susan Folkman. *Stress, Appraisal, and Coping*. New York: Springer, 1984. Lazarus and Folkman review the history and development of the concepts of stress and coping. The book, which is organized around their cognitive appraisal theory of emotion, includes sections on coping and health and adaptation, and on approaches to stress management.

Lorenz, Konrad. *On Aggression*. Translated by Marjorie Kerr Wilson. New York: Harcourt, Brace and World, 1966. Lorenz, a Nobel laureate in physiology or medicine for his pioneering animal behavior research, describes animal behavior, especially aggressive behavior, in this exciting, simple book. He addresses one of the key causes of stress in human society and discusses human technological and social evolution within this context.

Marcus, Jay B. *TM and Business*. New York: McGraw-Hill, 1977. Relatively light reading on the applications and benefits of meditation and relaxation skills in the workplace. Descriptions of specific programs in various companies are presented. A bit overstated at points, but a good introduction to a specific application of meditation.

Meichenbaum, Donald. *Stress Inoculation Training.* New York: Pergamon Press, 1985. This short training manual presents a clear, useful overview of stress inoculation training, along with a detailed account of the empirical research completed in testing the approach.

Melzack, Ronald, and Patrick D. Wall. *The Challenge of Pain.* New York: Basic Books, 1982. These authors have made important contributions to the understanding of pain. While some of the material is technical, the general reader will likely find this book interesting and informative. Discusses the puzzle of pain, the physiology of pain, the evolution of the theories of pain (including the "gate control" theory), and the various ways of controlling pain, including drugs, neurosurgery, and psychological approaches.

Monat, Alan, and Richard S. Lazarus, eds. *Stress and Coping: An Anthology.* 3d ed. New York: Columbia University Press, 1991. All three editions of this anthology are useful resources, but this one is particularly good, including articles by Hans Selye and Norman Cousins and an excellent article by Salvatore Maddi and Suzanne Kobasa on how to rear a hardy, stress-resistant child. Most of the articles are free of obscure terms and are appropriate for students of all levels.

National Coalition for Cancer Survivorship. *Charting the Journey: An Almanac of Practical Resources for Cancer Survivors.* Mount Vernon, N.Y.: Consumers Union, 1990. Well-written and thorough presentation of advice and resources for people with cancer and their families. The focus is on survival techniques. Includes sections on treatment options, ways of mobilizing strength, and how to deal with employment and insurance discrimination.

Nessim, Susan, and Judith Ellis. *Cancervive: The Challenge of Life After Cancer.* Boston: Houghton Mifflin, 1991. An excellent reference on all aspects of coping with cancer, including dealing with the diagnosis, treatment, fears of recurrence, and job discrimination. Particularly useful for people who have had active treatment.

Olton, David S., and Aaron R. Noonberg. *Biofeedback: Clinical Application in Behavioral Medicine.* Englewood Cliffs, N.J.: Prentice-Hall, 1980. An excellent review of the theory behind biofeedback and relaxation, along with numerous chapters on clinical applications of coping with stress-related problems. Precise tables and illustrations are provided.

Pirsig, Robert M. *Zen and the Art of Motorcycle Maintenance*. New York: Bantam, 1975. In this brilliant semi-autobiographical bestseller, philosopher Pirsig introduces the reader to value systems in human society. He attacks the stressful, meaningless aspects of daily life and challenges the reader to live life to its fullest. Stresses major concepts such as quality and "selfless climbing" instead of "ego-climbing" in the conduct of one's life.

Powell, Trevor J., and Simon J. Enright. *Anxiety and Stress Management*. New York: Routledge, 1990. This book was written for therapists who must help people deal with anxiety and stress. It is clearly written and can be understood by the layperson. Includes an excellent description of anxiety as a response to stressors and gives the reader an idea of what a therapist might do to help someone suffering from severe problems with stress. Self-help techniques are also explained.

Robbins, Lillian, Barbara Goff, and Lynn Miller. *Cancer and the Workplace: Strategies for Support and Survival*. Newark, N.J.: Rutgers University Press, 1987. An overview of work-related issues that makes suggestions about how colleagues can give constructive support. Discusses the safeguards for which to strive in terms of job security, sick leave, and insurance protection. Reducing the stress of caring for sick family members while working is also considered.

Rodin, Judith. "Managing the Stress of Aging." In *Coping and Health*, edited by Seymour Levine and Holger Ursin. New York: Plenum Press, 1980. In this chapter, Rodin emphasizes that stress produced by the perception of loss of personal control is particularly prevalent among the elderly. She describes interventions and coping-skills training techniques that have been useful in enhancing the sense of control and reducing the stress levels of institutionalized older people.

Sarason, Barbara R., Irwin G. Sarason, and Gregory R. Pierce, eds. *Social Support: An Interactional View*. New York: John Wiley & Sons, 1990. The authors present a well-written, extensive reference tool examining social support from the perspective of personality processes. Results of research looking at individual differences in the impact of social interaction on stress are discussed.

Schaefer, C., J. C. Coyne, and R. S. Lazarus. "The Health-Related Functions of Social Support." *Journal of Behavioral Medicine* 4 (1981): 381-406. Describes the tangible, informational, and emotional categories of social support and the health-protective benefits to be reaped from their use. Useful in helping one understand the different forms of social support available.

Seligman, Martin E. P. *Helplessness: On Depression, Development, and Death.* San Francisco: W. H. Freeman, 1975. A readable and convincing argument for the importance of prediction and control in stressful environments.

_____. *Learned Optimism.* New York: Random House, 1990. The idea here is that if one can learn to be helpless and pessimistic, then one can learn to be optimistic and more adaptive, too. Also contains some interesting information on learned helplessness, including how Seligman came upon the concept.

Selye, Hans. *The Stress of Life.* Rev. ed. New York: McGraw-Hill, 1978. The discoverer of the general adaptation syndrome provides in this work a lucid, comprehensible, nontechnical description of the stress concept and the stress response. The book is divided into five parts, covering the evolution of the stress concept; the means through which the body can defend itself against stress; the diseases of adaptation; the contribution of the study of stress to understanding the theory of life; and the application of the knowledge of stress to medicine to ensure better health. Includes an index and a glossary; the text is complemented by illustrations (photographs and line drawings).

_____. *Stress Without Distress.* New York: New American Library, 1975. A relatively short work in which the father of the stress response advises how to use stress as a positive force to achieve a rewarding lifestyle. The first part of the book covers in layperson's terms the same material as *The Stress of Life,* that is, the general adaptation syndrome; the second part has a more philosophical approach. Includes some line drawings, an index, and a bibliography.

Shaffer, Martin. *Life After Stress.* New York: Plenum Press, 1982. This book is less detailed than others in its discussion of the stress response and self-assessment of stress levels. It provides relaxation instructions (including photographs) and suggestions for time management, managing work stress, nutrition, exercise, and improving communication and reducing stress in family relationships.

Siegel, Bernie. *Love, Medicine, and Miracles.* New York: Harper & Row, 1986. Bestseller by a surgeon describing the importance of psychological factors in cancer recovery and the ability to deal with loss. Emphasizes the impact of love and courage as influences on the course of illness and the healing potential that can help patients become survivors.

Silver, R., and C. Wortman. "Coping with Undesirable Life Events." In *Human Helplessness*, edited by Judy Garber and Martin E. P. Seligman. New York: Academic Press, 1980. This chapter focuses on coping with stress and the resources available through interacting with other people. Social support is shown to be a multidimensional construct which is both productive and counterproductive in helping individuals cope with life events.

Simonton, Carl, Stephanie Matthews-Simonton, and James Creighton. *Getting Well Again*. New York: Bantam, 1980. An important contribution on imagery and visualization as aids in coping with cancer. The book describes techniques that have been successful in helping people use their imagination to conquer serious illness. Critics are concerned that the focus on attitudes may cause those who do not improve or have recurrences to blame themselves.

Smith, W. Lynn, Harold Merskey, and Steven C. Gross. *Pain: Meaning and Management*. New York: SP Medical & Scientific Books, 1980. Includes a number of specific topics—for example, how certain personality variables are predictive of the success of surgery for the relief of chronic pain, treatment approaches to deal with pain experienced by children, and the management of pain among the aged.

Sontag, Susan. *Illness as Metaphor*. Garden City, N.Y.: Doubleday, 1978. A classic work on the stigma of cancer, as contrasted with other illnesses, and how the vocabulary and attitudes of society contaminate treatment. The 1990 paperback reissue adds an informative section on the parallels between AIDS and cancer.

Spielberger, Charles Donald. *Understanding Stress and Anxiety*. New York: Harper & Row, 1979. Stress manual by a stress researcher and specialist. Discusses what stress is, what its sources are, and how to adjust to and live with others.

Suls, Jerry. "Social Support, Interpersonal Relations, and Health: Benefits and Liabilities." In *Social Psychology of Health and Illness*, edited by Glenn S. Sanders and Jerry Suls. Hillsdale, N.J.: Lawrence Erlbaum, 1982. An informative chapter that stresses the need to clarify what is meant by "social support" and suggests a more meaningful approach to understanding the concept. Presents research demonstrating both the benefits and problems arising from various forms of social support.

Taylor, Shelley E. "Adjustment to Threatening Events: A Theory of Cognitive Adaptation." *American Psychologist* 38, no. 11 (1983): 1161-1173. Describes cognitive adaptation theory and the research that was instrumental in its development. Although written for a scientific audience, this article is a wonderful example of how to convey both data and sophisticated insight in clear, simple language that is suitable for students of all levels.

_____. *Health Psychology.* 2d ed. New York: McGraw-Hill, 1991. A moderately high-level college textbook that comprehensively covers the general field of health psychology. As could be expected, many research studies are presented, and not all of them corroborate one another. The general reader should have no particular difficulty handling this material; the writing is reader-friendly.

Tsongas, Paul. *Heading Home.* New York: Random House, 1985. A former senator discusses the impact of lymphoma on his life choices. He describes how the illness served as a catalyst for redefining his goals and increasing his appreciation of family and the need to share.

Vaux, Alan. *Social Support: Theory, Research, and Intervention.* New York: Praeger, 1988. This comprehensive book begins by helping the reader to conceptualize social support, then takes the reader from the theoretical level to the more practical levels of measurement, application, and outcomes. Despite limitations discussed in the book, this work shows the achievements to be made through the utilization of formal and informal social support networks.

Stress and Illness

Antonovsky, Aaron. *Unraveling the Mystery of Health: How People Manage Stress and Stay Well.* San Francisco, Calif.: Jossey-Bass, 1987. This work, which advocates the salutogenic view of health and illness, is written by a medical sociologist. Following up on ideas begun in an earlier book, Antonovsky elaborates on the implications of the "sense of coherence concept," an enduring confidence that events, both within and outside the individual, are predictable and will work out well.

Bammer, Kurt, and Benjamin H. Newberry, eds. *Stress and Cancer.* Toronto: Hogrefe, 1981. This edited group of independently written chapters presents thirteen different perspectives from a variety of professionals working in the field of cancer and stress. Well-written; achieves its goal without imposing editorial constraints. Perception of events is emphasized as a major determinant of healing. Excellent resources.

Brady, Joseph Vincent. "Ulcers in Executive Monkeys." *Scientific American* 199 (October, 1958): 95-98. This article describes a classic series of studies in which monkeys subjected to psychological stress in a laboratory apparatus developed gastrointestinal lesions.

Brown, Barbara B. *Between Health and Illness.* Boston: Houghton Mifflin, 1984. One of many books available for the nonprofessional who simply wants an overview of stress and its consequences. This easy-to-read book is full of accurate information and practical suggestions.

Chesney, Margaret A., and Ray H. Rosenman, eds. *Anger and Hostility in Cardiovascular and Behavior Disorders.* Washington, D.C.: Hemisphere, 1985. Integrating psychology and the Type A behavior pattern, this book provides in-depth information on the technical aspects of behavior. Although some portions of the book are technical, the introductions to each chapter provide historical and nontechnical information related to the broader topic of behavior.

Craig, Kenneth D., and Stephen M. Weiss, eds. *Health Enhancement, Disease Prevention, and Early Intervention: Biobehavioral Perspectives.* New York: Springer, 1990. Includes, among other chapters of interest, an excellent chapter by Neal Miller (the "father of biofeedback") on how the brain affects the health of the body.

Dembroski, T. M., J. M. MacDougall, J. A. Herd, and J. L. Shields. "Perspectives on Coronary-Prone Behavior." In *Cardiovascular Disorders and Behavior*, edited by David S. Krantz, Andrew Baum, and Jerome S. Singer. Vol. 3 in *Handbook of Psychology and Health.* Hillsdale, N.J.: Lawrence Erlbaum, 1983. An extremely thorough work on the status of Type A behavior and its relationship to health in general and heart disease in particular. Includes a look at the history of the concept and ways of establishing the existence of a Type A behavior pattern, and evaluates research in the field.

Dobson, Clifford B. *Stress, The Hidden Adversary*. Lancaster, England: MTP Press, 1982. Addresses a college audience. Covers the physiological and psychological responses to stress, physical and behavioral effects of stress, stress and medical disorders, and the control of stress. Includes a very good index, references after each chapter, and good line drawings which enhance the text.

Feist, Jess, and Linda Brannon. *Health Psychology: An Introduction to Behavior and Health*. Belmont, Calif.: Wadsworth, 1988. Written for undergraduate students. A very readable overview of the field of health psychology. Provides the reader with chapters on stress and health, and various stress-related diseases.

Feuerstein, Michael, Elise E. Labbe, and Andrezej R. Kuczmiercsyk. *Health Psychology: A Psychobiological Perspective*. New York: Plenum Press, 1986. This textbook provides a thorough background and discussion of the effects of stress on health, and it includes discussion of stress management techniques.

Friedman, Meyer, and Diane Ulmer. *Treating Type A Behavior—and Your Heart*. New York: Knopf, 1984. This is an easily read book on preventing heart disease by changing one's lifestyle. Presents the results of a large research project and relates relevant research.

Friedman, Meyer, and Ray H. Rosenman. *Type A Behavior and Your Heart*. New York: Alfred A. Knopf, 1974. Summarizes the history of Type A behavior and presents information as it relates to individuals. Very basic, it is meant to provide an understanding of Type A behavior for the general public. The basics of changing Type A behavior are also presented.

Gatchel, Robert J., Andrew Baum, and David S. Krantz. *An Introduction to Health Psychology*. 2d ed. New York: Random House, 1989. A comprehensive overview of health psychology, giving equal emphasis to both biological and psychological points of view. Includes a chapter on psychological immunology, cancer, and AIDS. Recommended readings are noted at the end of every chapter.

Green, Judith Alyce, and Robert Shellenberger. *The Dynamics of Health and Wellness: A Biopsychosocial Approach*. Fort Worth: Holt, Rinehart and Winston, 1991. A general and very clinically oriented text in health psychology, in which stress occupies an important place. Parts 2 and 3 consist of eight chapters centered on stress and its effects. Less formal and conventional in tone than most texts. Invites the reader to participate actively in measuring and managing stress. Part 3 is especially interesting, as it contains some clinically explicit material on the management of stress.

Holmes, Thomas H., and Minoru Masuda. "Psychosomatic Syndrome: When Mothers-in-Law or Other Disasters Visit, a Person Can Develop a Bad, Bad Cold. Or Worse." *Psychology Today* 5 (April, 1972): 71. An easy-to-understand summary of Holmes's work on the relationship between stress (in the form of life events) and illness.

Houston, B. Kent, and C. R. Snyder, eds. *Type A Behavior Pattern: Research, Theory, and Intervention.* New York: John Wiley & Sons, 1988. Contains thirteen chapters by various authors. The first three chapters nicely introduce the topic in relatively simple terms. Subsequent chapters tend to be more technical and require a better background for understanding. A wealth of references are listed throughout.

Janis, Irving Lester. *Psychological Stress.* New York: John Wiley & Sons, 1958. Describes some of Janis' early investigations evaluating relationships between stress and behavior. The focus is on his pioneering study evaluating the relationship between preoperative stress levels in surgical patients and their ability to adapt to the rigors of the postoperative convalescent period.

Jenkins, C. D., S. J. Zyzanski, and R. H. Rosenman. *The Jenkins Activity Survey.* New York: Psychological Corporation, 1979. Contains the survey used for assessing Type A behavior. Includes the scoring procedure, which is easy to understand and administer.

Kerner, Fred. *Stress and Your Heart.* New York: Hawthorn Books, 1961. Gives a good overview of the effects of stress on the heart; succeeds in outlining, for the layperson, the essentials of the relationship between stress and heart disease. Augmented by an appendix containing an appreciation and a curriculum vitae of Hans Selye, the discoverer of the general adaptation syndrome. Includes an index and a glossary, but no illustrations.

Levi, Lennart. *Stress: Sources, Management, and Prevention.* New York: Liveright, 1967. A relatively short work covering the problems of body and mind, stress as a cause of disease, and psychosomatic treatments.

In a foreword, Selye writes: "[Levi] has attacked some of the cardinal aspects of the relationship between body and psyche. . . . [He has] the talent of combining technical competence with the gift of explaining the findings in an entertaining style." Includes an index, bibliography, glossary, some photographic illustrations, and line drawings.

McQuade, Walter, and Ann Aikman. *Stress: What It Is, What It Can Do to Your Health, How To Fight Back.* New York: E. P. Dutton, 1974. In a nontechnical style, deals with the effects of stress on the cardiovascular, digestive, musculoskeletal, and immune systems. Also discusses the way in which the mind and body handle stress, and the means by which the response to stress can be altered. No illustrations, but the book contains an index and a bibliography.

Managing Stress: From Morning to Evening. Alexandria, Va.: Time-Life Books, 1987. A very good introduction to understanding and managing stress. Written in clear, simple language and widely available, it provides an overview of the sources of stress, the physiological changes associated with stress, the effects of stress on the immune system, the way to assess one's own stress level, and suggestions for numerous approaches to managing stress. Full of illustrations and photographs. A weakness is that the book fails to address adequately the importance of dispositional factors, focusing too heavily on some stress-reduction techniques that few are likely to use.

Monat, Alan, and Richard S. Lazarus, eds. *Stress and Coping.* 2d ed. New York: Columbia University Press, 1985. This anthology consists of twenty-six brief readings under the headings of effects of stress, stress and the environment, coping with the stresses of living, coping with death and dying, and stress management. The selections are readable as well as informative, and the editors give a useful overview prior to each section in which they summarize the relevance and importance of each reading.

Pelletier, Kenneth R. *Mind as Healer, Mind as Slayer.* New York: Dell Books, 1977. This well-known work examines how stress contributes to heart disease, cancer, arthritis, migraine, and respiratory disease. Sources of stress, evaluation of personal stress levels, profiles of unhealthy personality traits, and means of preventing stress-related diseases are addressed.

Pennebaker, James W. *The Psychology of Physical Symptoms.* New York: Springer-Verlag, 1982. Pennebaker discusses his theories about the influence of individual differences in the experience of health and illness. He also provides an overview of some of the research that supports his views.

Peterson, Christopher, and Lisa M. Bossio. *Health and Optimism.* New York: Free Press, 1991. A very readable and enjoyable introduction to recent research on positive thinking and physical health. Optimism is contrasted with pessimism and explored in biological, emotional, behavioral, and interpersonal contexts. Notes at the book's end provide rich detail and further reading. For readers at all levels.

Plotnik, Rod. *Introduction to Psychology.* 2d ed. New York: Random House, 1989. Useful chapter on stress and stress management that shows how thoughts and physiological symptoms influence stress response. Chapter also discusses coping strategies and personality factors that put one at risk for stress and stress-related illnesses.

Price, Virginia Ann. *Type A Behavior Pattern.* New York: Academic Press, 1982. A good technical resource for Type A behavior. Very comprehensive. The introductory chapters provide the nontechnical reader with valuable, understandable information. More than three hundred references are listed at the end of the book.

Rodin, Judith, and P. Salovey. "Health Psychology." In *Annual Review of Psychology* 40. Stanford, Calif.: Annual Reviews, 1989. Summarizes the recent literature in health psychology, with a strong emphasis on health models, and discusses the often complex interactions among relevant variables. The latter include personality traits, cognitive factors, and environmental and cultural influences. Specific behaviors, both health-promoting and damaging, are also discussed.

Selye, Hans. *The Stress of Life.* Rev. ed. New York: McGraw-Hill, 1976. Originally published in 1956, this is the most influential book ever written about stress. It focuses on the relationship between a stressful life and subsequent illness, but it is very technical. Those wanting a less difficult introduction to Selye's writings and work should read his *Stress Without Distress.*

_____. *Stress Without Distress.* New York: New American Library, 1975. Written by the pioneering researcher who discovered and named what is known as the general adaptation syndrome. Describes that syndrome and discusses how to handle stress so as not to suffer the physical declines that so often arise from excessive stress.

Stone, George C., ed. *Health Psychology: A Discipline and a Profession.* Chicago: University of Chicago Press, 1987. A collection of content-specific chapters written to summarize the field's first decade and to set an agenda for the next. Describes the field's history and knowledge base; targets population groups for study, including children, women, minorities, and the elderly; covers training and professional issues.

Taylor, Shelley E. *Health Psychology.* 2d ed. New York: McGraw-Hill, 1991. Written by an active researcher in the field, this engaging text provides substantive coverage of health psychology. A novel quality is its separate chapters on health-enhancing and health-compromising behaviors. Includes detailed sections on stress and coping, patients in treatment settings, and the management of chronic and terminal illnesses.

Wapner, S., and J. Demick. "Development of Experience and Action: Levels of Integration in Human Functioning." In *Theories of the Evolution of Knowing*, edited by Gary Greenberg and Ethel Tobach. Hillsdale, N.J.: Lawrence Erlbaum, 1990. A summary of a holistic/systems, developmental approach to person-in-environment functioning across the life span. Attempts to integrate organismic and transactional worldviews. Illustrates the relations among problem, theory, and method in psychology generally and in environmental psychology specifically. Reviews relevant environmental psychological research on life transitions and provides an extensive bibliography.

Weiten, Wayne. *Psychology: Themes and Variations.* 2d ed. Pacific Grove, Calif.: Brooks/Cole, 1991. Since Selye's work on stress attracted the attention of psychologists, nearly all introductory texts have contained simplified discussions of it and of work by others that preceded and followed it. Weiten's text is one of the best: easy and interesting to read, yet strong in its coverage of scientific psychology. His chapter "Stress, Coping, and Health" is an excellent source of information.

PSYCHOPATHOLOGY

Models of Abnormality

Adams, Henry E. *Abnormal Psychology*. Dubuque, Iowa: Wm. C. Brown, 1981. Typical of many abnormal psychology textbooks which deal in a cursory but thoughtful manner with some of the historical concepts of mental illness. The historical material is related to the various models of psychopathology, which cannot really be separated from a historical understanding. One advantage of this particular text is that it takes the history of mental illness as an important topic and clearly spells out the point of view of the textbook author.

Altrocchi, John. *Abnormal Behavior*. New York: Harcourt Brace Jovanovich, 1980. Practically every textbook of abnormal behavior contains a discussion of the definitional problem. Altrocchi's chapter 1 offers a particularly thorough discussion, put in the historical context of alternative nonmedical approaches to abnormal conditions. Written on the introductory college level.

American Psychiatric Association. *Diagnostic and Statistical Manual of Mental Disorders*. Rev. 3d ed. Washington, D.C.: Author, 1987. This manual summarizes all the psychological and psychiatric disorders and gives the criteria for each classification. Almost all mental health workers are familiar with this volume and use it when diagnoses must be made for insurance companies.

Andreasen, Nancy C. *The Broken Brain: The Biological Revolution in Psychiatry*. New York: Harper & Row, 1984. An excellent introduction to biopsychiatry for the general reader. Andreasen's summary of brain structure and function, and their relationship to mood and behavior, is one of the best in a book of this type. Highly recommended.

Archer, D. "Social Deviance." In *Handbook of Social Psychology*, edited by Gardner Lindzey and Elliot Aronson. 3d ed. Hillsdale, N.J.: Lawrence Erlbaum, 1985. Chapter 26 presents a general review of deviance from the perspective of several sociologists. A discussion of the variety of conditions which are defined as deviant at different times and places, and the negative consequences of labeling. Puts the issue in a socio-logical perspective. Heavy going but worth it.

Bartol, Curt R. *Psychology and the American Law*. Belmont, Calif.: Wadsworth, 1983. Reviews both the criminal law and the civil law as they deal with concepts of competence, dangerousness, and legal responsi-bility. Contains a thorough presentation of the historic origin of the rules pertaining to civil commitment. Written on an introductory level.

Bayer, Ronald. *Homosexuality and American Psychiatry: The Politics of Diagnosis*. New York: Basic Books, 1981. A thorough examination of the politics involved in the removal of homosexuality from the official guide of psychiatric diagnoses (DSM-IV). An important illustration of how political processes become involved in determining what behav-ior, in this case homosexuality, is designated normal or abnormal. Very readable work.

Beck, Aaron T., and Gary Emery. *Anxiety Disorders and Phobias: A Cognitive Perspective*. New York: Basic Books, 1985. This book gives the reader a more in-depth understanding of the specific cognitive aspects that are involved in the development and maintenance of anxiety disorders. There is a focus on phobias, one of the most common types of anxiety disorders experienced by both children and adults in Western society.

Berkow, Robert. *The Merck Manual*. 15th ed. Rahway, N.J.: Merck Sharpe & Dohme Research Laboratories, 1987. Chapter 12 provides information on psychiatric disorders that includes explanation and differentiation of the various types of these disorders, description of their symptoms, and rationales behind therapeutic treatments. Covered are personality disorders, drug dependence, psychosexual problems, neuroses, mood disorders, schizophrenia, and suicidal behavior.

Bootzin, Richard R., and Joan Ross Acocella. *Abnormal Psychology: Current Perspectives*. 5th ed. New York: Random House, 1988. This abnormal psychology text reviews the psychoanalytic perspective in clear, understandable terms with meaningful examples. In the section on psychiatric disorders, the contribution of the psychodynamic model to underlying cause and to treatment of certain disorders is explained.

Braginsky, Benjamin M., D. D. Braginsky, and Kenneth Ring. *Methods of Madness: The Mental Hospital as a Last Resort*. New York: Holt,

Rinehart and Winston, 1969. A major critique of the mental hospital in the United States, with an interesting suggestion for improvement noted by a play on words in the book's title.

Brown, Fredda Herz, ed. *Reweaving the Family Tapestry: A Multigenerational Approach to Families*. New York: W. W. Norton, 1991. Gives an overview of the work done by the Family Institute of Westchester. This approach is important not only from the multigenerational perspective, but also because extremely important issues of race, class, gender, and ethnicity are incorporated into clinical analysis and treatment.

Brumberg, Joan Jacobs. *Fasting Girls: The Emergence of Anorexia Nervosa as a Modern Disease*. Cambridge, Mass.: Harvard University Press, 1988. Brumberg, a historian, presents the history of anorexia nervosa from a sociocultural perspective. This book provides an in-depth examination of how societal values operate to increase the prevalence of a specific psychological disorder. A well-researched and very readable book.

Dollard, John, and Neal E. Miller. *Personality and Psychotherapy: An Analysis in Terms of Learning, Thinking, and Culture*. New York: McGraw-Hill, 1950. This classic work was very influential in bringing behavioral theories into the applied realm of explaining and treating abnormal behaviors. Phenomena such as defense mechanisms, which are concepts from psychoanalytic theory, are examined and explained within a behavioral framework. This book should be read only after the reader has gained a basic knowledge of psychoanalytic and behavioral models of abnormality.

Evans, Richard Isadore. *R. D. Laing: The Man and His Ideas*. New York: E. P. Dutton, 1976. A series of discussions with Laing regarding his views on the concept of mental illness. In this readable work, Laing outlines his objections to the diagnostic and treatment approaches of the mental health establishment.

Frankl, Viktor Emil. *The Doctor and the Soul: From Psychotherapy to Logotherapy*. 2d expanded ed. New York: Alfred A. Knopf, 1965. Highlights how the spiritual and existential domains have been neglected by psychoanalysis and earlier therapeutic systems. Focusing on the "will to meaning," Frankl discusses the meaning of life, death, suffering, work, and love. Examines existential analyses of several types of psychopathology, and presents the therapeutic technique of logotherapy.

_____. *Man's Search for Meaning.* New York: Simon & Schuster, 1962. A powerful book which serves as an example of many publications that emphasize what has been called "moral treatment." Frankl's book is partly autobiographical, based on his experiences as a Jew in a German concentration camp. The book then goes on to develop some ideas related to abnormal behavior. This book has been published in many paperback editions, which have a relatively complete bibliography of writings by and about Frankl and his ideas.

Franks, Violet, and Esther D. Rothblum, eds. *The Stereotyping of Women: Its Effects on Mental Health.* New York: Springer, 1983. Describes ways in which gender-role stereotypes contribute to disorders such as depression, agoraphobia, weight and communication problems, sexual dysfunction, and violence against women.

Freud, Sigmund. *New Introductory Lectures on Psychoanalysis.* Translated by W. J. H. Sprott. New York: W. W. Norton, 1933. Perhaps the most accessible of Freud's writing for the person who is interested in abnormal behavior in general and psychoanalysis in particular. For the most part, an interesting and quite comprehensible elaboration of Freud's general point of view.

Gold, Mark S. *The Good News About Depression: Cures and Treatments in the New Age of Psychiatry.* New York: Random House, 1986. Written in a light, easy-to-read style, this book discusses the myriad biomedical conditions that can lead to depression and describes how they can be diagnosed and treated. Especially valuable for someone who is contemplating psychiatric treatment for depression or who has a loved one who is.

_____. *The Good News About Panic, Anxiety, and Phobias.* New York: Random House, 1989. Written for the nontechnical reader, this book offers a good general summary of anxiety disorders, their diagnosis (and misdiagnosis), and their treatment. The second half deals specifically with the biopsychiatric approach to anxiety. Also includes extensive bibliography and state-by-state listings of experts in the field.

Golding, S. L., and R. Roesch. "The Assessment of Criminal Responsibility: A Historical Approach to a Current Controversy." In *Handbook of Forensic Psychology,* edited by Irving B. Weiner and Allen K. Hess. New York: John Wiley & Sons, 1987. Traces the history of the "guilty mind" requirement for criminal responsibility and finds that recurrent public pressures to restrict the insanity defense follow well-publicized and dramatic cases at widely different historic periods.

Gottesman, Irving I. *Schizophrenia Genesis: The Origins of Madness.* New York: W. H. Freeman, 1991. An excellent, well-written resource on the causes of schizophrenia that can be understood without a technical background. Highly recommended.

Holmes, David S. "Theoretical Perspectives." In *Abnormal Psychology.* New York: HarperCollins, 1991. Holmes reviews the major theoretical perspectives and models that aid in understanding abnormal psychology in this abnormal psychology textbook. Provides a critique of cognitive and other models and gives examples that illustrate the models.

Jahoda, Marie. *Current Concepts of Positive Mental Health.* New York: Basic Books, 1958. Reviews and classifies the many different views of mental health, with an emphasis upon those offered by psychotherapists. Argues for attention to "psychological health," which Jahoda views as a "positive striving," not the mere absence of illness. Good as a review of the early literature on the specific problem of definition. Thorough, but some knowledge of personality theories helps.

Krasner, Leonard, Arthur C. Houts, and Leonard P. Ullmann. *A Psychological Approach to Abnormal Behavior: Invention and Discovery.* Englewood Cliffs, N.J.: Prentice-Hall, 1992. This textbook differs from other abnormal psychology texts in that it examines each category of psychiatric disorders from a sociocultural perspective. Provides an excellent historical overview of the development of the concept of psychological abnormality. Also examines the politics involved in the decision-making process by which behaviors are labeled abnormal.

Meichenbaum, Donald. *Cognitive-Behavior Modification: An Integrative Approach.* New York: Plenum Press, 1977. Explains the process and technique of cognitive-behavioral therapy in an easy-to-understand way. The author presents illustrative examples and is able to bring to life the types of problems that people are likely to have and the corresponding interventions from which they may benefit.

Monahan, J. "The Prediction of Violent Behavior: Developments in Psychology and Law." In *The Master Lecture Series: Psychology and the Law*, edited by C. James Scheirer and Barbara L. Hammonds.

Vol. 2. Washington, D.C.: American Psychological Association, 1983. Reviews the arguments for psychologists to play a role in predicting violence, and the evidence on how well this can be done. The conclusion is that predictions of violent behavior tend to predict a considerable amount of violence that never occurs. Relevant because "dangerousness" is the primary reason for involuntary commitment.

Offer, David, and Melvin Sabshin. "Culture, Values, and Normality." In *Normality and the Life Cycle*. New York: Basic Books, 1984. Provides an excellent sociocultural perspective on abnormality; it gives numerous examples from ancient and modern times regarding the influence of societal standards in dictating which behavior is labeled abnormal. A readable chapter.

Phares, E. Jerry. *Clinical Psychology: Concepts, Methods, and Profession*. 3d ed. Homewood, Ill.: Dorsey Press, 1988. Chapter 4 of this text for college psychology students contains a thorough description of standards for judging normality. These are discussed from the viewpoint of famous psychologists and applied to problems in psychological diagnosis. Cases of the sort found in clinical practice illustrate and help the reader comprehend the issues. Quite readable by the introductory-level student.

Ramsey, Christian N., Jr., ed. *Family Systems in Medicine*. New York: Guilford Press, 1989. A landmark book that expands what is known about family dysfunction and its effects on family members to the field of medicine. Reviews family systems theory, including a family stress model developed by Joan M. Patterson. Family systems research, immunology, endocrinology, biology, health, chronic illness, and behavioral disorders are all covered thoroughly. Suggestions for future directions of research are offered.

Rosenhan, David L. "On Being Sane in Insane Places." *Science* 179 (January 19, 1973): 250-258. More of a "naturalistic illustration" than a scientific experiment, this article raises provocative questions and puts forth some controversial conclusions. Enjoyable reading that does not require much psychological background on the part of the reader.

Rosenhan, David L., and Martin E. P. Seligman. "The Environmentalist Model: Behavioral and Cognitive Approaches." In *Abnormal Psychology*. 2d ed. New York: W. W. Norton, 1989. This chapter provides an easy-to-read introduction to behavioral models of abnormality. The basic assumptions of behavioral models are discussed, and interesting case conceptualizations from a behavioral perspective are given. This is a good source for the reader who is interested in a brief yet informative presentation of behavioral models of abnormality.

Slovenko, R. "Civil Competency." In *Handbook of Forensic Psychology*, edited by Irving B. Weiner and Allen K. Hess. New York: John Wiley & Sons, 1987. Reviews the legal requirement of competency to sign a contract, consent to a medical procedure, make out a will, serve as a witness, and stand trial. As important as competence is in the civil and criminal law, treatments of the topic in a basic work are rare.

Szasz, Thomas Stephen. *Law, Liberty, and Psychiatry.* New York: Macmillan, 1963. A discussion of what Szasz considers the "psychiatrization" of the law. Argues that due process protection and responsibility are eroded by loose "mental illness" standards. Well written, one-sided, somewhat polemical in style. Very readable and informative.

_____. *The Myth of Mental Illness.* New York: Dell Books, 1961. A classic work in which Szasz provides his objections to the concept of "mental illness." An ageless critique of the practice of psychiatric diagnosis; for the advanced reader.

Wechsler, Henry, Leonard Solomon, and Bernard M. Kramer, eds. *Social Psychology and Mental Health.* New York: Holt, Rinehart and Winston, 1970. Each of the first ten papers in this edited volume consists of arguments for one of the alternative definitions of abnormality, each by a leading proponent. The papers, particularly those for and against the medical model, are classics. One would otherwise have to comb many journals to find so many important papers from a variety of perspectives.

Weiner, Irving B., and Allen K. Hess, eds. *Handbook of Forensic Psychology.* New York: John Wiley & Sons, 1987. Twenty-six chapters, each written by an expert in the variety of areas related to psychology and the law. In addition to chapters cited separately here, chapters on the competence of juries, competency to stand trial, diminished responsibility, predicting violence, and psychotherapy with criminal offenders are relevant. Sometimes heavy going, but worth it.

Widiger, T. A., and T. J. Trull. "Diagnosis and Clinical Assessment." In *Annual Review of Psychology* 42. Stanford, Calif.: Annual Reviews,

1991. This article applies a consideration of definitions of abnormality to the continuing problem of specifically what sorts of disabling or distressful conditions should be included in the APA's diagnostic manual. Shows that psychiatrists take the definitional issue seriously.

Willerman, Lee. *Psychopathology.* New York: McGraw-Hill, 1990. Provides a general introduction to psychopathology, with a fairly sophisticated discussion of theoretical facets of abnormality, psychiatric disorders, and their treatments.

Wolpe, Joseph. *Psychotherapy by Reciprocal Inhibition.* Stanford, Calif.: Stanford University Press, 1958. Wolpe's development of a treatment technique called systematic desensitization led to a rapid acceptance of behaviorally based interventions. In this book, Wolpe provides a learning-based explanation for abnormal behaviors. Clinical and experimental support is given for behavioral interventions. The chapters are arranged in such a way that the book can be used as a reference for varying principles in the behavioral model.

Wrightsman, Lawrence S. *Psychology and the Legal System.* Monterey, Calif.: Brooks/Cole, 1987. Contains a review of the legal rules concerning insanity, placed in a historical context, and the rules pertaining to civil commitment. Particularly strong in summarizing a number of court cases in which the insanity defense was employed and in reviewing current arguments for and against this defense. Written on the level of a college introductory text.

Childhood and Adolescent Disorders

American Psychiatric Association. *Diagnostic and Statistical Manual of Mental Disorders.* 3d ed. Washington, D.C.: Author, 1994. This manual (often called DSM-IV) contains diagnostic criteria and many other useful facts about a wide variety of mental disorders. It provides information useful to the categorization of autism and its comparison with other mental diseases with similar symptoms.

Arnold, L. Eugene. *Helping Parents Help Their Children.* New York: Brunner/Mazel, 1978. Outlines general principles of parent guidance. Details are provided about family therapy, including filial therapy (Hornsby and Applebaum's approach). Specific problems of children, such as mental retardation, learning disabilities, hyperactivity, and so on are addressed, as are specific problems of parents, such as the abusing parent, teenage motherhood, adoptive parenthood, and more.

Azrin, Nathan H., and Victoria A. Besalel. *A Parent's Guide to Bedwetting Control.* New York: Simon & Schuster, 1979. A self-help book written for parents with enuretic children in which Nathan Azrin's "dry-bed training" is described. Azrin's treatment is based on behavioral principles; the specific procedures are discussed in terms that most nonprofessionals will understand.

Barkley, Russell A. "Attention-Deficit Hyperactivity Disorder." In *Treatment of Childhood Disorders,* edited by E. J. Mash and R. A. Barkley. New York: Guilford Press, 1989. This chapter provides a thorough discussion of different treatments for ADHD children, including stimulant medication, antidepressant medication, behavior therapy, parent training, teacher training, and cognitive-behavioral therapy. Each treatment modality is discussed in a fair and objective manner, and empirical research is provided to support the conclusions given.

_____. *Attention-Deficit Hyperactivity Disorder: A Handbook for Diagnosis and Treatment.* New York: Guilford Press, 1990. Provides comprehensive discussion of nearly all aspects of ADHD, including assessment, diagnosis, and treatment. Also notable for a thorough discussion of ADHD in older adolescents and adults. This excellent and comprehensive book is written by one of the leading researchers in the investigation of ADHD.

Boskind-White, Marlene, and William C. White, Jr. *Bulimarexia: The Binge/Purge Cycle.* New York: W. W. Norton, 1983. A comprehensible overview of bulimarexia (more commonly referred to as bulimia). Takes a nonpathologizing, empathetic approach in addressing the problems of individuals with bulimia. Filled with illustrative patient histories.

Bruch, Hilde. *The Golden Cage: The Enigma of Anorexia Nervosa.* Cambridge, Mass.: Harvard University Press, 1978. A classic work by a pioneer in the field of eating disorders. Portrays the development of anorexia nervosa as an attempt by a young woman to attain a sense of control and identity. Discusses the etiology and treatment of anorexia from a modified psychoanalytic perspective.

Brumberg, Joan J. *Fasting Girls: The History of Anorexia Nervosa.* Cambridge, Mass.: Harvard University Press, 1988. Outlines the history of anorexia nervosa. Examines the syndrome from multiple perspectives while leaning toward a cultural and feministic perspective. A well-researched and very readable work.

Campbell, Susan B. "The Socialization and Social Development of Hyperactive Children." In *Handbook of Developmental Psychopathology*, edited by M. Lewis and S. M. Miller. New York: Plenum Press, 1990. A succinct overview of the social climate surrounding children with ADHD. This chapter covers such topics as childrearing practices, sibling conflict, family climate, parental psychopathology, and peer relationships of ADHD children.

Carlisle, Jock Alan. *Tangled Tongue: Living with a Stutter*. Toronto: University of Toronto Press, 1985. A comprehensive review of the causes of and treatments for stuttering, written by a stutterer. Besides general information for and identification with the reader, it provides useful appendices on self-help and consumer organizations as well as organizations involved in stuttering therapy and research.

Coleman, Mary, and Christopher Gillberg. *The Biology of the Autistic Syndrome*. New York: Praeger, 1985. Goes into considerable detail at a professional, but readable, level on many aspects of autism. Includes clinical considerations; a review of pertinent literature, disease entities, and treatments within the autistic disorder; and hypotheses concerning its basis. Hundreds of references are included.

Conture, Edward G. *Stuttering*. Englewood Cliffs, N.J.: Prentice-Hall, 1990. A basic text aimed at speech therapy students. Emphasis is on evaluation and treatment, highlighting important treatment differences related to the age of the stutterer. Includes a wealth of clinical examples throughout and a full case study in an appendix.

Dawson, Geraldine, ed. *Autism: Nature, Diagnosis, and Treatment*. New York: Guilford Press, 1989. Contains a wealth of useful information and many useful references. Seventeen chapters cover a broad range of topics, under the general headings perspectives on the nature of autism, neurobiological issues in autism, and new directions in autism diagnosis and treatment.

Glauber, I. Peter. *Stuttering: A Psychoanalytic Understanding*. New York: Human Sciences Press, 1982. Presents the psychoanalytic view of stuttering as the result of unconscious conflicts. Not the dominant view, but one that should be considered for a full understanding of stuttering. The first of two parts presents the basic interpretation. The second part requires more familiarity with psychoanalytic concepts and concerns.

Houts, Arthur C., and Hillel Abramson. "Assessment and Treatment for Functional Childhood Enuresis and Encopresis: Toward a Partnership Between Health Psychologists and Physicians." In *Child and Adolescent Disorders*, edited by Sam B. Morgan and Theresa M. Okwumabua. Hillsdale, N.J.: Lawrence Erlbaum, 1990. Summarizes work in the field of enuresis and encopresis, an elimination disorder involving involuntary soiling. Chapter sections include the assessment, causes, and treatment of enuresis. Reviews types and effectiveness of both behavioral and medical treatments.

Houts, Arthur C., and Richard M. Liebert. *Bedwetting: A Guide for Parents and Children*. Springfield, Ill.: Charles C Thomas, 1984. A self-help book intended for parents that outlines a treatment package for enuresis called the "full spectrum home training" system. This effective treatment approach is described in understandable terms, although the authors advise that the treatment is best conducted under professional supervision.

Johnson, Wendell. *Stuttering: And What You Can Do About It*. Minneapolis: University of Minnesota Press, 1961. Aimed at parents of stutterers; very readable as well as comprehensive. Johnson presents his own research comparing stuttering and nonstuttering children as well as their parents, and he emphasizes the importance of parental expectations as well as the child's self-concept in both the cause and treatment of stuttering.

Kanner, Leo. "Autistic Disturbances of Affective Contact." *Nervous Child* 2 (1943): 217-250. This landmark article began the modern conceptualization of autism. It describes autistic behavior and differentiates autism from "childhood schizophrenia," as others had previously labeled the disorder. Kanner also identifies the good cognitive potential of autistic children, a belief no longer held.

Kendall, Philip C., and Lauren Braswell. *Cognitive-Behavioral Therapy for Impulsive Children*. New York: Guilford Press, 1984. Presents a comprehensive, step-by-step discussion of a popular cognitive-behavioral treatment for ADHD children. The authors provide a thorough rationale for this therapy and provide research data to support the efficacy of the therapy. Practical applications of this therapy are discussed.

Mills, Joyce C., and Richard J. Crowley. *Sammy the Elephant and Mr. Camel*. New York: Magination Press, 1988. An illustrated book for children that presents a metaphorical story regarding enuresis. Designed to promote the self-esteem of enuretic children and to provide a useful way of discussing bed-wetting with children in a nonthreatening way.

Minuchin, Salvador, Bernice L. Rosman, and Lester Baker. *Psychosomatic Families: Anorexia Nervosa in Context*. Cambridge, Mass.: Harvard University Press, 1978. A classic work which outlines the development and treatment of anorexia nervosa from a family systems perspective. Includes a complete description of Salvador Minuchin's famed "family lunch session," in which Minuchin conducts a family assessment and begins treatment of an anorectic patient while eating lunch with the patient and her family.

Mitchell, J. E., and E. D. Eckert. "Scope and Significance of Eating Disorders." *Journal of Consulting and Clinical Psychology* 55 (1987): 37-43. Summarizes relevant research regarding the prevalence, etiology, and treatment of both anorexia and bulimia. The authors' overview of the suggested causes of anorexia and bulimia highlights potential biological factors. Very readable for a scientific piece.

Oppenheim, Rosalind C. *Effective Teaching Methods for Autistic Children*. Foreword by Bernard Rimland. Springfield, Ill.: Charles C Thomas, 1974. This useful book describes educational techniques that Oppenheim, the mother of an autistic son, developed for teaching autistic children. Identifies child-management methods for overcoming autistic children's behavioral difficulties. Includes information on the use of questions and written answers to aid in developing language abilities.

Powers, Michael D., and Jan S. Handleman. "Nature and Needs of Severely Developmentally Disabled Clients." In *Behavioral Assessment of Severe Developmental Disabilities*. Rockville, Md.: Aspen Systems, 1984. This succinct chapter includes useful introductory material, a historical perspective, diagnostic techniques, diagnostic criteria—including comparison of those from DSM-III and from the National Society of Autistic Children—and aspects of patient needs. Contains more than two hundred references.

Rapport, Mark D. "Attention Deficit Disorder with Hyperactivity." In *Child Behavior Therapy Casebook*, edited by M. Hersen and C. G. Last. New York: Plenum Press, 1988. Presents an in-depth case study of an eight-year-old boy who was referred for treatment of ADHD. This chapter provides a thorough discussion of the way in which a child is evaluated and treated for ADHD. In this case study, the boy is treated with stimulant medication and behavior therapy techniques. A comprehensive evaluation of the treatment effects is provided, and special attention is given to continuous monitoring of the boy's behavioral and academic performance.

Schaefer, Charles E. *Childhood Encopresis and Enuresis: Causes and Therapy*. New York: Van Nostrand Reinhold, 1979. Provides an overview of the suggested causes and treatment of enuresis and encopresis. Outlines the physiology of bowel and bladder functioning, examines changes in the suggested causes and treatments of the disorder across time, and reviews present treatment procedures. Useful features include diagrams of important material and a glossary of technical terms.

Schopler, Eric, and Gary B. Mesibov, eds. *Autism in Adolescents and Adults*. New York: Plenum Press, 1983. This edited work distills material presented at a conference attended by national experts in the area. It covers aspects of adult and adolescent autism including perspectives and issues; linguistics; educational, recreational, and vocational issues; medical requirements; and familial coping. Covers many issues that are not often described.

Sheehan, Joseph Green, et al. *Stuttering: Research and Therapy*. New York: Harper & Row, 1970. Contains separately authored chapters from a variety of perspectives, including personality, sociology, physiology, and development. The chapter "Historical Approaches," by Charles Van Riper, is especially interesting, both as a history of ideas about and treatments for stuttering and because Van Riper, himself a former stutterer, is perhaps the most renowned researcher on stuttering.

Shisslak, C. M., Marjorie Crago, M. E. Neal, and B. Swain. "Primary Prevention of Eating Disorders." *Journal of Consulting and Clinical Psychology* 55 (1987): 44-51. Washington, D.C.: American Psychological Association, 1987. Discusses the need for preventive efforts in addressing the rising rate of anorexia and bulimia. Outlines specific prevention strategies that would be appropriate for different age groups. A very readable journal article.

Starkweather, C. Woodruff. *Fluency and Stuttering*. Englewood Cliffs, N.J.: Prentice-Hall, 1987. Aimed at speech therapy students. Presents a readable and thorough summary of current research, with a particular sensitivity to the variability of the problem and to problems in defining stuttering. Coverage of the development of the disorder discusses contributions of both nature and nurture.

Van Bourgondien, Mary E., Gary B. Mesibov, and Geraldine Dawson. "Pervasive Developmental Disorders: Autism." In *The Practical Assessment and Management of Children with Disorders of Development and Learning*, edited by Mark L. Wolraich. Chicago: Year Book Medical Publishers, 1987. Succinctly and clearly describes autism, including its definition, incidence, etiologies and pathophysiologies, assessment and findings, and management. Also included are 133 useful references. Technically written, the article is nevertheless very useful to the beginning reader.

Walker, C. Eugene, Mary Kenning, and Jan Faust-Campanile. "Enuresis and Encopresis." In *Treatment of Childhood Disorders*, edited by Eric J. Mash and Russell A. Barkley. New York: Guilford Press, 1989. Provides an overview of enuresis and encopresis. Presents a case study examining the assessment and treatment of an enuretic child, and provides the addresses of different companies that manufacture urine alarms. Largely written for a professional audience.

Anxiety, Somatoform, and Dissociative Disorders

American Psychiatric Association. *Diagnostic and Statistical Manual of Mental Disorders*. Rev. 3d ed. Washington, D.C.: Author, 1994. The DSM-IV provides specific criteria for making psychiatric diagnoses of obsessive-compulsive disorder and other anxiety disorders. Brief summaries of research findings regarding each condition are also provided.

Barlow, David H. *Anxiety and Its Disorders*. New York: Guilford Press, 1988. The author, one of the leaders in the field of anxiety research, presents his integrative theory of anxiety. The book also describes assessment and treatment of anxiety, and includes a separate chapter on each recognized anxiety disorder. The book's intended audience is graduate students and professionals in psychology, but it is very well written and worth the effort for anyone interested in an up-to-date and comprehensive presentation of anxiety disorders.

Beck, Aaron T., and Gary Emery. *Anxiety Disorders and Phobias: A Cognitive Perspective.* New York: Basic Books, 1985. Though cognitive explanations and treatments for phobias are stressed, this book considers other perspectives as well, and it could serve as an introduction to the topic for the interested high school or college student.

Bliss, Eugene L. "Multiple Personalities: A Report of Fourteen Cases with Implications for Schizophrenia and Hysteria." *Archives of General Psychiatry* 37 (December, 1980): 1388-1397. This journal article is written by a leading scholar in the field of multiple personality. In clear language, the author describes his controversial theory, which suggests that multiple personality disorders develop when children use self-hypnosis as a coping mechanism. Recommended for the reader who is interested in the causes and diagnosis of multiple personality.

Bootzin, Richard R., and Joan Ross Acocella. *Abnormal Psychology: Current Perspectives.* 5th ed. New York: Random House, 1988. This textbook contains an excellent chapter on the dissociative disorders that describes relevant case studies and explains how different psychological theorists view the dissociative diagnoses. The authors' discussion of psychogenic amnesia and psychogenic fugue is particularly informative. Also contains an excellent chapter on the somatoform disorders which describes relevant case studies and explains how different psychological theorists view the somatoform diagnoses. Discussion of hypochondriasis and conversion disorder is particularly informative. Clear, easy to read, and understandable by the high school or college student.

Bourne, Edmund. *The Anxiety and Phobia Workbook.* Oakland, Calif.: New Harbinger Publications, 1990. An excellent self-help book for the general reader who suffers from an anxiety disorder. Also an accessible introduction to the causes and treatments of phobias for high school and college students. Contains self-diagnostic and therapy exercises, as well as other resources for the phobia sufferer.

Breuer, Josef, and Sigmund Freud. *Studies in Hysteria.* Translated and edited by James Strachey, with the collaboration of Anna Freud. New York: Basic Books, 1982. In many ways, this landmark book, first published in 1895, was the genesis of contemporary psychotherapy. Describes the famous case of Anna O., as well as the histories of a number of other conversion patients. A challenging book, useful to the college student who has a serious interest in either conversion disorders or the history of psychology.

Chambless, Dianne L., and Alan J. Goldstein, eds. *Agoraphobia: Multiple Perspectives on Theory and Treatment*. New York: John Wiley & Sons, 1982. Contains several chapters on more specialized topics than are found in other texts on agoraphobia, such as agoraphobia and the marital relationship, and the association between agoraphobia and obsessions. Chambless' chapter, which summarizes the typical characteristics of agoraphobics, and Goldstein's chapter, which includes several detailed case histories, are especially useful.

Davison, Gerald C., and John M. Neale. *Abnormal Psychology*. New York: John Wiley & Sons, 1990. Contains a very readable chapter on somatoform and dissociative disorders. The authors give a well-organized overview of the topic and enhance their discussion with a number of lively examples. Recommended for the high school student, college student, or casual reader.

Delprato, D. J., and F. D. McGlynn. "Behavioral Theories of Anxiety Disorders." In *Behavioral Theories and Treatment of Anxiety*, edited by Samuel M. Turner. New York: Plenum Press, 1984. Behaviorally oriented psychologists have been extremely active in testing and revising theories of anxiety. This chapter of nearly fifty pages describes the obvious and the subtle differences between various behavioral theories. It also compares behavioral to cognitive theories of anxiety.

Emmelkamp, Paul M. G. *Phobic and Obsessive Compulsive Disorders: Theory, Research, and Practice*. New York: Plenum Press, 1982. A somewhat dated but classic work outlining the importance of behavioral strategies in overcoming obsessive-compulsive, as well as phobic, conditions.

Figley, Charles R., ed. *Trauma and Its Wake: The Study and Treatment of Post-traumatic Stress Disorder*. New York: Brunner/Mazel, 1985. This edited book is one of the most often cited references in the field of PTSD and contains some of the most influential papers written on the subject. It is divided into sections on theory, research, and treatment; a second volume with the same title was published in 1986. It is part of the Brunner/Mazel Psychosocial Stress Series, the first volume of which was published in 1978; through 1990, this valuable series had published twenty-one volumes on many aspects of stress and trauma.

Figley, Charles R., and Seymour Leventman, eds. *Strangers at Home: Vietnam Veterans Since the War*. New York: Praeger, 1980. Reprint.

New York: Brunner/Mazel, 1990. This edited book, containing chapters by psychologists, sociologists, political activists, historians, political scientists, and economists, presents a look at the experience of the Vietnam veteran from many different perspectives. Many of the authors were Vietnam veterans themselves, so the book gives a very personal, sometimes stirring view of its subject.

Freud, Sigmund. "Analysis of a Phobia in a Five-Year-Old Boy." In *The Standard Edition of the Complete Psychological Works of Sigmund Freud*, edited by James Strachey. Vol. 10. London: Hogarth Press, 1955. Originally published in 1909, this is Freud's description of the case of Little Hans, the most famous patient in the history of anxiety disorders. Freud is an excellent writer, and he presents many vivid details in this case history, making it interesting to read. One could also look up Joseph Wolpe and Stanley Rachman's behavioral interpretation of Little Hans's phobia, "Psychoanalytic 'Evidence': A Critique Based on Freud's Little Hans," in *Journal of Nervous and Mental Disease* 131, no. 2 (1960): 135-148.

_____. "Inhibition, Symptoms, and Anxiety." In *The Standard Edition of the Complete Psychological Works of Sigmund Freud*, edited by James Strachey. Vol. 20. London: Hogarth Press, 1959. In this paper, originally published in German in 1926, Freud describes his revised theory of anxiety. The paper covers a wide range of topics (including a redescription of Little Hans) and is not as readable as the initial presentation of the case. It is, however, an interesting illustration of the change in Freud's thinking about anxiety.

Gold, Mark S. *The Good News About Panic, Anxiety, and Phobias*. New York: Random House, 1989. For a general audience. Outlines many biological factors which may be associated with phobias. Presents a one-sided approach, heavily promoting a biopsychiatric view of phobias and their treatment.

Goodwin, Donald W., and Samuel B. Guze. "Panic Disorder (Anxiety Neurosis)." In *Psychiatric Diagnosis*. New York: Oxford University Press, 1989. A brief but excellent introduction to the most important psychiatric research on panic disorder. The reader will find a clear discussion of topics such as diagnosis, family studies, and differentiating panic disorder from other conditions. The reference section is a good resource for readers wishing to pursue research on panic disorder in greater depth.

Greaves, G. B. "Multiple Personality: 165 Years After Mary Reynolds." *Journal of Nervous and Mental Disease* 168 (1980): 577-596. This article provides the reader with a solid understanding of the ways in which a history of sexual or physical abuse during one's childhood can lead to the development of multiple personality disorder. Recommended for college students who wish to know more about the causes of multiple personality.

Grinker, Roy Richard, and John P. Spiegel. *Men Under Stress.* Philadelphia: Blakiston, 1945. Long before the term "post-traumatic stress disorder" was coined, this classic book described the stress response to combat in Air Force flyers. It is written in jargon-free language by men who had unusual access to the flight crews.

Horowitz, Mardi Jon. *Stress Response Syndromes.* New York: J. Aronson, 1976. Horowitz is one of the leading psychodynamic theorists in the area of post-traumatic stress. In this readable book, he describes his theory and his approach to treatment.

Jacob, Rolf G., and Samuel M. Turner. "Somatoform Disorders." In *Adult Psychopathology and Diagnosis*, edited by Samuel M. Turner and Michel Hersen. New York: John Wiley & Sons, 1984. Provides the reader with a scholarly overview of somatoform disorders. Relevant diagnostic issues are discussed, in conjunction with a thorough review of the major research studies that have been conducted on somatization disorder, hypochondriasis, and conversion disorder. This chapter is recommended for the college student who seeks a detailed and challenging discussion of somatoform disorders.

Jenike, Michael A., Lee Baer, and William E. Minichiello. *Obsessive-Compulsive Disorders: Theory and Management.* Littleton, Mass.: PSG, 1986. A comprehensive overview of the topic that does not burden the reader with intricate details of analysis. Readable by the layperson. Covers the topic thoroughly.

Keyes, Daniel. *The Minds of Billy Milligan.* New York: Random House, 1981. A journalistic account of a young man's illness with multiple personality disorder. Especially helpful to readers who are interested in the relationship between mental illness and the criminal justice system, since the story's protagonist was convicted of raping several women. An interesting discussion of the insanity defense is included.

Kozak, M. J., E. B. Foa, and P. R. McCarthy. "Obsessive-Compulsive Disorder." In *Handbook of Anxiety Disorders*, edited by Cynthia Last and Michel Hersen. New York: Pergamon Press, 1988. Covers some intriguing research questions that are rarely mentioned elsewhere, those pertaining to cognitive styles and psychophysiological responses of obsessive-compulsive patients. Also presents data pertaining to biological theories of obsessive-compulsive disorder.

Kulka, Richard A. *Trauma and the Vietnam War Generation.* New York: Brunner/Mazel, 1990. Presents the results of the federally funded National Vietnam Veterans Readjustment Study. This book is factual. It contains dozens of tables and figures filled with statistics about the mental and physical health of Vietnam veterans. The same authors published *The National Vietnam Veterans Readjustment Study: Tables of Findings and Technical Appendices* in 1990. This companion volume contains hundreds of tables of detailed results from this comprehensive study.

Marks, Issac Meyer. *Fears, Phobias, and Rituals.* New York: Oxford University Press, 1987. With more than five hundred pages and a bibliography with more than two thousand references, this text provides comprehensive coverage of all aspects of phobias. Written for the professional and researcher, but accessible to college students who are interested in pursuing some aspect of phobias in detail.

_____. *Living with Fear: Understanding and Coping with Anxiety.* New York: McGraw-Hill, 1978. This is a work written for the general public by Britain's foremost authority on fear and anxiety. It is accessible and provides a good introduction to theory and treatment of anxiety.

Mathews, Andrew M., Michael G. Gelder, and Derek W. Johnston. *Agoraphobia: Nature and Treatment.* New York: Guilford Press, 1981. The authors review the literature on the symptomatology, assessment, and pharmacological treatment of agoraphobia, and discuss the behavioral treatment of this syndrome in depth. The appendices, which include a detailed self-help manual for agoraphobics and a brief package of assessment materials, will be of particular interest to many readers.

Mavissakalian, Matig, Samuel M. Turner, and Larry Michelson. *Obsessive-Compulsive Disorders: Psychological and Pharmacological Treatment.* New York: Plenum Press, 1985. An exceptionally well written text based upon a symposium held at the University of Pittsburgh. Issues pertaining to etiology, assessment, diagnosis, and treatment are covered in detail.

Mineka, Susan. "Animal Models of Anxiety-Based Disorders: Their Usefulness and Limitations." In *Anxiety and the Anxiety Disorders*, edited by A. Hussain Tuma and Jack Maser. Hillsdale, N.J.: Lawrence Erlbaum, 1985. The phobia portion of this chapter reviews the major experiments done with animals which demonstrate the many similarities between human phobias and experimental phobias in animals. Clearly illustrates the relevance of animal research to human behavior. Difficult, yet indispensable for a thorough understanding of phobias.

Rachman, S. J. "Obsessional-Compulsive Disorders." In *International Handbook of Behavior Modification and Therapy*, edited by Alan S. Bellack, Michel Hersen, and Alan E. Kazdin. New York: Plenum Press, 1982. Rachman's work using behavioral strategies with obsessive-compulsive patients is unparalleled. No bibliography would be complete without a contribution from Rachman, one of the most respected authorities in the field.

Sackheim, H., and W. Vingiano. "Dissociative Disorders." In *Adult Psychopathology and Diagnosis*, edited by Samuel M. Turner and Michel Hersen. New York: John Wiley & Sons, 1984. Provides the reader with a scholarly overview of the dissociative disorders. Relevant diagnostic issues are discussed, in conjunction with a thorough review of the major research studies that have been conducted on amnesia, fugue, and multiple personality. Ideal for the student who seeks a detailed and challenging discussion of the dissociative disorders.

Sackheim, Harold A., Johanna W. Nordlie, and Ruben C. Gur. "A Model of Hysterical and Hypnotic Blindness: Cognition, Motivation, and Awareness." In *Journal of Abnormal Psychology* 88 (October, 1979): 474-489. Recommended for the college student or serious adult reader who is interested in learning about contemporary research on conversion disorders. In particular, research on hysterical blindness is described in a complete and detailed fashion. The authors attempt to explain why hysterically blind patients believe they have lost their vision, when in reality they are able to see.

Sarason, Irwin G., and Barbara R. Sarason. *Abnormal Psychology: The Problem of Maladaptive Behavior*. 5th ed. Englewood Cliffs, N.J.:

Prentice-Hall, 1987. Includes a very readable chapter on the psychological factors which can produce physical symptoms. A well-organized overview of somatization disorders is enhanced with a number of lively examples. Recommended for the high school student, college student, or casual reader.

Schreiber, Flora Rheta. *Sybil*. New York: Warner Books, 1974. This popular account of a young woman's struggle with multiple personality disorder reads like a well-written novel. The author provides a fascinating description of both the development and treatment of multiple personality. This book will be especially helpful to individuals who are interested in the psychotherapy process.

Tuma, A. Hussain, and Jack D. Maser, eds. *Anxiety and the Anxiety Disorders*. New York: Lawrence Erlbaum, 1985. This thousand-page book contains forty-three chapters of high quality, with most of the leaders in the field of anxiety represented. Every important theoretical approach to anxiety is covered. There are two hundred pages of references, an author index, and a subject index, making it easy to find information on specific topics.

Turner, S. M., and L. Michelson. "Obsessive-Compulsive Disorders." In *Behavioral Theories and Treatment of Anxiety*, edited by Samuel M. Turner. New York: Plenum Press, 1984. Summarizes information regarding diagnostic issues, assessment strategies, and treatment interventions for obsessive-compulsive disorder. Provides an excellent review of intervention efforts employing response prevention and clomipramine.

Waldinger, Robert J. *Psychiatry for Medical Students*. Washington, D.C.: American Psychiatric Press, 1984. An introductory clinical textbook designed for individuals (such as medical students) who are having their first encounters with emotionally disturbed patients. Contains a concise and informative section on the somatoform disorders which explains how to look for and recognize these syndromes.

Walker, John R., G. Ron Norton, and Colin A. Ross, eds. *Panic Disorder and Agoraphobia: A Comprehensive Guide for the Practitioner*. Pacific Grove, Calif.: Brooks/Cole, 1991. This edited volume provides a thorough overview of the literature on the diagnosis, causation, and treatment of panic disorder and agoraphobia. The coverage of material on assessment and on psychotherapeutic and pharmacological interventions is especially complete. Although intended for the clinician, this volume is also a good reference for the layperson.

Wilson, R. Reid. *Breaking the Panic Cycle: Self-Help for People with Phobias*. Rockville, Md.: Anxiety Disorders Association of America, 1987. A publication of a nonprofit organization which is dedicated to disseminating information and providing help to phobia sufferers. The ADAA also publishes the *National Treatment Directory*, which lists treatment programs throughout the country.

Depression

Beach, Stephen R. H., E. E. Sandeen, and K. D. O'Leary. *Depression in Marriage*. New York: Guilford Press, 1990. Summarizes the literature on basic models of depression. Provides the basis for understanding the important role of marriage in the etiology, maintenance, and treatment of depression.

Beck, Aaron T. *Cognitive Therapy and the Emotional Disorders*. New York: International Universities Press, 1976. Clearly lays out the basics of the cognitive model of depression. An important start for those who wish to understand the cognitive approach more thoroughly.

Beck, Aaron T., A. J. Rush, B. F. Shaw, and G. Emery. *Cognitive Therapy of Depression*. New York: Guilford Press, 1979. Summarizes the cognitive theory of depression and describes how this model can be applied in the treatment of depressed clients.

Beckham, Ernest Edward, and William R. Leber, eds. *Handbook of Depression: Treatment, Assessment, and Research*. Homewood, Ill.: Dorsey Press, 1985. Presents a comprehensive overview of depression. Discusses the major approaches to explaining, diagnosing, and treating depression, and presents the research evidence concerning each.

Blehar, Mary C., and Norman E. Rosenthal. "Seasonal Affective Disorders and Phototherapy." *Archives of General Psychiatry* 45, no. 5 (1989): 469-474. Summarizes a National Institute of Mental Health workshop on seasonal affective disorder. The authors discuss issues related to the diagnosis and prevalence of the syndrome. In addition, they present possible mechanisms of action for phototherapy as a treatment and the use of animal models to study seasonal affective disorder. A good summary that avoids being overly technical.

Boyce, Philip, and Gordon Parker. "Seasonal Affective Disorder in the Southern Hemisphere." *American Journal of Psychiatry* 145, no. 1 (1988): 96-99. This study surveyed an Australian sample to determine the extent to which the people experienced symptoms of seasonal affective disorder and to see if the pattern was similar to that of people in the Northern Hemisphere. The results are presented as percentages and are easily understood. Addresses the issue of separating holidays from climatic changes and presents a table of symptoms for seasonal affective disorder.

Burns, David D. *Feeling Good: The New Mood Therapy.* New York: William Morrow, 1980. Provides a very entertaining and accessible presentation of the cognitive approach to depression. Presents basic results and the basics of cognitive theory, as well as a practical set of suggestions for getting out of a depression.

Coyne, James C., ed. *Essential Papers on Depression.* New York: New York University Press, 1985. Includes representatives of every major theoretical position advanced between 1900 and 1985. Each selection is a classic presentation of an important perspective. This source will acquaint the reader with the opinions of major theorists in their own words.

Coyne, James C., and G. Downey. "Social Factors and Psychopathology: Stress, Social Support, and Coping Processes." *Annual Review of Psychology* 42 (1991): 401-426. This influential chapter ties together stress and coping with interpersonal processes to provide a deeper understanding of the nature of depression. Also provides an account of advances in the way both depression and interpersonal processes related to depression may be studied.

Cronkite, Kathy. *On the Edge of Darkness: Conversations About Depression.* New York: Doubleday, 1994. Brief excerpts form interviews with a variety of noteworthy people on the subject of depression. Includes comments of William Styron, Joan Rivers, and John Kenneth Galbraith, along with those of a number of theorists and researchers in the field of depression. Brief appendices list ways to overcome depression, support organizations, and information about medical and drug-induced depression. For the general reader.

Durkheim, Émile. *Suicide*. Reprint. Glencoe, Ill.: Free Press, 1951. In this work, originally published in 1897, Durkheim introduced his classification system of suicide types—altruistic, egoistic, and anomic suicides—and examined the relationship of suicide to isolation and recent loss.

Fieve, Ronald R. *Moodswing: The Third Revolution in Psychiatry*. New York: William Morrow, 1975. This popular book written for the general public offers helpful, informative insight into the many facets of bipolar disorder (manic depression). Accounts of famous people who had the disorder and yet were successful in their lives give hope to those afflicted.

Fremouw, William J., Maria de Perczel, and Thomas E. Ellis. *Suicide Risk: Assessment and Response Guidelines*. New York: Pergamon Press, 1990. This book presents useful guidelines, based on both research and clinical practice, for working with suicidal individuals.

Garvey, Michael J., Robert Wesner, and Michael Godes. "Comparison of Seasonal and Nonseasonal Affective Disorders." *American Journal of Psychiatry* 145, no. 1 (1988): 100-102. These authors present similarities and differences between affective disorders that covary with seasons and those that do not. Despite the inclusion of statistical analyses, the article is understandable to those without a background in statistics.

Goodwin, Frederick K., and Kay Redfield Jamison. *Manic-Depressive Illness*. New York: Oxford University Press, 1990. A comprehensive book on bipolar disorder. Historical events, from diagnosis to treatment, are covered in depth. Issues of treatment and theory are also examined in great detail.

Hawton, Keith. *Suicide and Attempted Suicide Among Children and Adolescents*. Beverly Hills, Calif.: Sage Publications, 1986. This work overviews research results concerning the causes of youth suicide and treatment programs for suicidal youngsters.

Hershman, D. Jablow, and Julian Lieb. *The Key to Genius: Manic-Depression and the Creative Life*. Buffalo, N.Y.: Prometheus Books, 1988. A publication for the general reader. This intriguing book covers some of the phenomena long written about, including facts of great men and women who may have suffered from bipolar illness.

Heston, Leonard L. *Mending Minds: A Guide to the New Psychiatry of Depression, Anxiety, and Other Serious Mental Disorders.* New York: W. H. Freeman, 1992. This leading-edge book, written for the layperson yet useful for the professional, covers many disorders—depression, bipolar disorder, and anxiety, to name a few. The types of treatments available, both biological and psychological, are explained from the viewpoint of the potential consumer of these specialized services. Includes a guide to support groups, more readings, and other resources.

Holinger, Paul C., and J. Sandlow. "Suicide." In *Violent Deaths in the United States*, edited by Paul C. Holinger. New York: Guilford Press, 1987. This chapter presents epidemiological information on suicide in the United States, from 1900 to 1980. It also addresses demographic variables and their relationship to suicide.

Jacobsen, Frederick M., Thomas A. Wehr, Robert A. Skwerer, David A. Sack, and Norman E. Rosenthal. "Morning Versus Midday Phototherapy of Seasonal Affective Disorder." *American Journal of Psychiatry* 144, no. 10 (1987): 1301-1305. Tests the difference in therapeutic effectiveness as a function of when phototherapy is administered. Some statistics are presented, but understanding statistics is not essential, as the accompanying text and figures communicate the findings quite clearly.

Jefferson, James W., and John H. Greist. *Primer of Lithium Therapy.* Baltimore: Williams & Wilkins, 1977. Described as being for the layperson, but contains important information about the usefulness and special precautions of lithium therapy and prophylaxis.

Kasper, Siegfried, Thomas A. Wehr, John J. Bartko, Paul A. Gaist, and Norman E. Rosenthal. "Epidemiological Findings of Seasonal Changes in Mood and Behavior." *Archives of General Psychiatry* 46, no. 9 (1989): 823-833. A thorough description of the major prevalence study on seasonal affective disorder. The statistics are fairly advanced, but the authors' use of figures and tables makes the results understandable. An extensive reference list is provided.

Kasper, Siegfried, Susan L. Rogers, Angela Yancey, Patricia M. Schulz, Robert A. Skwerer, and Norman E. Rosenthal. "Phototherapy in Individuals with and Without Subsyndromal Seasonal Affective Disorder." *Archives of General Psychiatry* 46, no. 9 (1989): 837-844. This study extends research into seasonal variants of affective disorder to people who have less intense forms. Addresses issues of the difficulty of establishing adequate experimental control and practical implications for people with these disorders.

Kleinman, Arthur, and Byron Good. *Culture and Depression*. Berkeley: University of California Press, 1985. This exceptional volume examines the cross-cultural research on depression. Authors from anthropology, psychiatry, and psychology attempt to address the diversity that exists across cultures in the experience and expression of depression. The persevering reader will be rewarded with a journey through time and across many societies.

Lann, Irma S., Eve K. Moscicki, and Ronald Maris, eds. *Strategies for Studying Suicide and Suicidal Behavior*. New York: Guilford Press, 1989. This book examines the various research methods used to study suicide. Considers the relative strengths and weaknesses and offers examples of each method.

Lester, David, ed. *Current Concepts of Suicide*. Philadelphia: Charles Press, 1990. A useful overview of research results on the possible causes of suicide and on programs designed both to prevent suicide and to treat suicidal patients.

Levitt, Eugene E., Bernard Lubin, and James M. Brooks. *Depression: Concepts, Controversies, and Some New Facts*. 2d ed. Hillsdale, N. J.: Lawrence Erlbaum, 1983. Reviews the symptoms, theories, and epidemiology of depression. Also describes the results of a national survey of depression.

Lewinsohn, Peter M., R. F. Munoz, M. A. Youngren, and A. M. Zeiss. *Control Your Depression*. Englewood Cliffs, N.J.: Prentice-Hall, 1978. A self-help book written for a general audience. Describes Lewinsohn's behavioral therapy, which has been found to be an effective treatment for depression.

McGrath, Ellen, ed. *Women and Depression: Risk Factors and Treatment Issues*. Washington, D.C.: American Psychological Association, 1990. Report of the APA Task Force on Women and Depression. Includes discussions of gender differences, women's status, the influence of victimization and poverty, and treatment considerations.

Paykel, Eugene S. *Handbook of Affective Disorders*. New York: Guilford Press, 1982. Provides comprehensive coverage of depression, mania, and anxiety in relation to depression. Includes detailed descriptions of symptoms, assessment procedures, epidemiology, and treatment procedures.

Peck, Michael L., Norman L. Farberow, and Robert E. Litman, eds. *Youth Suicide*. New York: Springer, 1985. A useful overview of the psychological influences on youth suicide and on the treatment and prevention programs that have been used with suicidal youths.

Rehm, Lynn P., ed. *Behavior Therapy for Depression: Present Status and Future Directions*. New York: Academic Press, 1981. An overview of behavioral and cognitive behavioral models of depression.

Rosenthal, Norman E. *Seasons of the Mind*. New York: Bantam Books, 1989. An exceptionally clear and well-written presentation of what is known about seasonal affective disorder by one of the pioneering investigators in the field. The disorder is placed within a historical context and includes a description of symptoms and a self-test. Discusses the risks and benefits of various treatments, including psychotherapy, antidepressant medication, and light therapy. Numerous anecdotes are used to illustrate major points. Includes literary allusions to SAD, suggestions for helping oneself, guidelines for determining when one needs professional help, and a list of resources for more information and help. An excellent book for nonprofessional readers.

Rush, A. John, and Kenneth Z. Altshuler, eds. *Depression: Basic Mechanisms, Diagnosis, and Treatment*. New York: Guilford Press, 1986. Presents research concerning the biological models of the cause and treatment of depression.

Rutter, Michael, Carroll E. Izard, and Peter B. Read, eds. *Depression in Young People: Developmental and Clinical Perspectives*. New York: Guilford Press, 1986. Presents research on many aspects of the problem of depression in children, which had not received much attention from psychologists until the 1970's.

Seligman, Martin E. P. *Helplessness: On Depression, Development, and Death*. San Francisco: W. H. Freeman, 1987. Seligman explains the learned helplessness theory of depression, describing his early research and comparing the symptoms of laboratory-induced helplessness to those of clinical depression.

Shneidman, Edwin S., Norman L. Farberow, and Robert E. Litman. *The Psychology of Suicide.* New York: Science House, 1970. This is a collection of articles, some of which are now regarded as classics in the study of suicide.

Stengel, Erwin. *Suicide and Attempted Suicide.* Rev. ed. Harmondsworth, England: Penguin Books, 1973. This classic work summarizes the demographic and psychological variables that were known at the time to be associated with suicide.

Willner, Paul. *Depression: A Psychobiological Synthesis.* New York: John Wiley & Sons, 1985. This book was written for the specialist in the field but is not beyond the reach of readers with a solid background in science, especially chemistry. The bibliography is very extensive.

Wurtman, Richard J., and Judith J. Wurtman. "Carbohydrates and Depression." *Scientific American* 260 (January, 1989): 68-75. The authors provide a good review of seasonal affective disorder and the relationships that may exist between it and maladaptive behaviors. They also review the more important theories about the cause and treatment of seasonal affective disorder.

Organic Disorders

Bradley, W. "Alzheimer's Disease: Theories of Causation." In *New Directions in Understanding Dementia and Alzheimer's Disease,* edited by Taher Zandi and Richard J. Ham. New York: Plenum Press, 1990. Bradley has investigated the role of genetics in the development of Alzheimer's disease. In this article he discusses the role of chromosome 21 and its possible linkage to Alzheimer's disease.

Chopra, Deepak. *Creating Health.* Boston: Houghton Mifflin, 1987. Chopra is a proponent of meditation, an approach that many American psychologists do not necessarily feel comfortable advocating. Nevertheless, this book is written by a practicing physician for the layperson. He covers a wide variety of psychosomatic disorders, suggests a variety of healthy habits, and presents the viewpoint that "health is our natural state."

Clarfield, A. M. "The Reversible Dementias: Do They Reverse?" *Annals of Internal Medicine* 109 (1988): 476-486. Clarfield reviews a very important question of dementia. His analysis of more than twenty investigations of dementia suggests that the number of reversible dementias may be less than 2 percent.

Miner, Gary D., et al., eds. *Caring for Alzheimer's Patients: A Guide for Family and Healthcare Providers.* New York: Plenum Press, 1989. Presents a considerable amount of useful information in its 292 pages. Includes sections on the biology of the disease and on dealing with the disease (including legal information, caring for the patient, and public policy issues). Good references and helpful appendices.

Oliver, Rose, and Frances A. Bock. *Coping with Alzheimer's: A Caregiver's Emotional Survival Guide.* New York: Dodd, Mead, 1987. The emphasis is on advice for those taking care of a patient with Alzheimer's disease on how to handle the stresses they themselves will experience. Covers common emotional responses such as denial, anger, shame, and self-pity.

Reisner, Morton F., ed. *Organic Disorders and Psychosomatic Disorders.* Vol. 3 in *American Handbook of Psychiatry.* 2d ed., edited by Silvano Arieti. New York: Basic Books, 1975. This is heavy reading. It is, however, an authoritative source of information on the subject of psychosomatic disorders. Chapters 1, 21, 25, and 36 are particularly pertinent overviews of the topic, and several chapters in part 2 focus on specific psychosomatic disorders.

Simonton, O. Carl, Stephanie Matthews-Simonton, and James L. Creighton. *Getting Well Again.* New York: Bantam Books, 1980. Cancer researchers and therapists examine the mind-body connection, effects of beliefs, causes of cancer, effects of stress and personality, and effects of expectations on the development and progress of cancer. They describe a holistic approach to treatment, emphasizing relaxation and visual imagery, that is reported to produce cancer survival rates that are twice the national norm. A very readable book which is readily available in paperback.

Zandi, Taher, and Richard J. Ham, eds. *New Directions in Understanding Dementia and Alzheimer's Disease.* New York: Plenum Press, 1990. Zandi and Ham provide a multidisciplinary look at this disorder. Discusses the fact that Alzheimer's disease, even though a neuropsychiatric disorder, has profound social and political implications that affect family members.

Personality Disorders

Cleckley, Hervey. *The Mask of Sanity*. St. Louis: C. V. Mosby, 1941. In this classic work, Cleckley delineates the primary features of psychopathic personality in considerable detail, and provides a wealth of case history material that vividly illustrates the symptomatology of this disorder. Although many of Cleckley's speculations concerning the causation of this disorder are somewhat outdated, his clinical descriptions remain unparalleled in their depth and richness.

Cooper, Arnold M., Allen J. Frances, and Michael H. Sacks, eds. *The Personality Disorders and Neuroses*. New York: Basic Books, 1986. This edited volume contains chapters on each major personality disorder as well as a discussion of general theoretical and treatment models for the personality disorders and neuroses. Michael H. Stone's chapter on borderline personality, which contains a good overview of different uses of the term, and Otto Kernberg's chapters on narcissistic and histrionic personalities are particularly recommended.

Goldstein, Eda G. *Borderline Disorders: Clinical Models and Techniques*. New York: Guilford Press, 1990. Goldstein lucidly outlines the major clinical features of borderline personality, discusses its development from a variety of theoretical perspectives, and contrasts the major contemporary psychotherapeutic approaches to the disorder. Appropriate for the reader with some background in psychoanalytic theory.

Hare, Robert D. *Psychopathy: Theory and Research*. New York: John Wiley & Sons, 1970. Perhaps the best overview of early research on the psychopathic personality. Reviews the evidence for a number of models of the causation of this disorder, and describes the research literature clearly, thoughtfully, and critically. An excellent primer for the layperson who wishes to learn more about psychopathic and antisocial personalities.

Hare, Robert D., and Daisy Schalling, eds. *Psychopathic Behaviour: Approaches to Research*. New York: John Wiley & Sons, 1978. Contains perhaps the finest collection of chapters on research issues relevant to psychopathic and antisocial personalities. Coverage of research on biological models is particularly impressive. Chapters on the history of the psychopathic personality concept and on assessment issues are also highly recommended.

Lasch, Christopher. *The Culture of Narcissism.* New York: Warner Books, 1979. Lasch outlines the characteristics of "the narcissistic personality of our time," discusses large-scale social changes that he believes are responsible for the increase in narcissism in Western culture, and provides compelling critiques of the awareness movement and other contemporary fads. Although Lasch's tone at times verges on the polemical, his observations are thought-provoking and perceptive.

Reid, William H., ed. *The Psychopath: A Comprehensive Study of Antisocial Disorders and Behaviors.* New York: Brunner/Mazel, 1978. Another edited volume that contains a number of informative chapters on topics such as the neurological bases of antisocial behavior, psychophysiological findings in psychopaths, and the relation between antisocial personality and substance abuse. Nevertheless, the quality of the book is rather uneven; several chapters are marred by unbridled speculation regarding the psychodynamics of the disorder.

Robins, Lee. *Deviant Children Grown Up.* Baltimore: Williams & Wilkins, 1966. Describes Robins' classic study of the long-term outcome of conduct disordered children, and provides a remarkably detailed examination of early risk factors for antisocial personality. Should be required reading for all individuals interested in the development of antisocial and criminal behavior.

Roy, Alec, ed. *Hysteria.* New York: John Wiley & Sons, 1982. Contains chapters dealing with a number of important issues relevant to histrionic personality, somatization disorder, and related conditions. The coverage of historical issues and genetic and biological factors is especially thorough. The chapters on multiple personality and the relation of hysteria to hypnosis may also be of interest.

Vallaint, George E., and J. Christopher Perry. "Personality Disorders." In *Comprehensive Textbook of Psychiatry*, edited by H. I. Kaplan and B. J. Sadock. Baltimore: Williams & Wilkins, 1985. Provides an overview of key conceptual issues relevant to personality disorders (for example, classification models, genetic and environmental factors, treatment approaches) and clearly discusses the clinical features of each disorder. Although this chapter may prove somewhat difficult for readers with little background in psychopathology, it provides one of the most succinct summaries of the personality disorders literature.

Schizophrenia

Bleuler, Eugen. *Dementia Praecox: Or, The Group of Schizophrenias.* Translated by Joseph Zinkin. New York: International Universities Press, 1950. Original German first published in 1911. A classic book in the field, this provides excellent descriptions of the symptoms and very interesting discussions of possible causal factors.

Bowers, Malcolm B. *Retreat from Sanity: The Structure of Emerging Psychosis.* New York: Human Sciences Press, 1974. A fascinating description, often in the words of patients, of the experiences many people have in the very early stages of psychosis. Especially interesting are descriptions of "peak" and "psychedelic" experiences resulting from sensory alterations during the onset of the disorder.

Gottesman, Irving I. *Schizophrenia Genesis: The Origins of Madness.* New York: W. H. Freeman, 1991. Provides a comprehensive overview of the genetic determinants of schizophrenia, written by the foremost authority in the field. Very readable; explains the theory and methods of behavioral genetics research and presents a detailed description of the findings.

Gottesman, Irving I., James Shields, and Daniel R. Hanson. *Schizophrenia: The Epigenetic Puzzle.* Cambridge, England: Cambridge University Press, 1982. Technical but still accessible to anyone with a solid background in genetics of the type obtained in a good general biology course. Concentrates on genetic studies and gives complete references to original technical articles.

Helmchen, Hanfried, and Fritz A. Henn, eds. *Biological Perspectives of Schizophrenia.* Chichester, England: John Wiley & Sons, 1987. A collection of papers by experts in the field, this is a valuable reference source for readers who are interested in the state of knowledge about schizophrenia in the late 1980's. Many of the papers are quite technical.

Herz, Marvin I., Samuel J. Keith, and John P. Docherty. *Psychosocial Treatment of Schizophrenia.* New York: Elsevier, 1990. This book, vol. 4 in the *Handbook of Schizophrenia* series, examines psychosocial causes of schizophrenia and psychosocial treatment approaches. Discusses early intervention. Behavior therapy and supportive living arrangements are covered; results of long-term outcome studies are also reviewed.

Kraepelin, Emil. *Clinical Psychiatry.* Translated by A. Ross Diefendorf. Delmar, N.Y.: Scholars' Facsimiles & Reprints, 1981. A facsimile reprint of the seventh (1907) edition of Kraepelin's classic text. Reveals the origins of contemporary thinking about schizophrenia and other mental disorders.

Lidz, Theodore, Stephen Fleck, and Alice R. Cornelison. *Schizophrenia and the Family.* New York: International Universities Press, 1965. A collection of papers detailing studies of seventeen families that have a schizophrenic member. Selection of subject families was highly biased, and no appropriate matched control families were studied. Nevertheless, this work was extremely influential among mental health workers. The authors' conclusions are not supported, however, by more recent, more carefully controlled studies.

Mednick, Sarnoff A., and Thomas F. McNeil. "Current Methodology in Research on the Etiology of Schizophrenia: Serious Difficulties Which Suggest the Use of the High-Risk Group Method." *Psychological Bulletin* 70, no. 6 (1968): 681-693. This classic paper served to introduce the idea of the high-risk method to researchers in the field of psychopathology. It clearly lays out the rationale behind the approach.

Neale, John M., and Thomas F. Oltmanns. *Schizophrenia.* New York: John Wiley & Sons, 1980. This book provides a comprehensive overview of the illness and examines many of the research methods for exploring its causes.

Snyder, Solomon H. *Madness and the Brain.* New York: McGraw-Hill, 1974. Written in a lively, breezy style, this short volume deals with biomedical factors in many psychological disorders, including schizophrenia. Especially interesting is Snyder's discussion of drug effects, neurotransmitters, and schizophrenia.

Sullivan, Harry Stack. *Schizophrenia as a Human Process.* New York: W. W. Norton, 1962. Perhaps the most available of Sullivan's writings, this book is actually a collection of articles written by him between 1924 and 1935. Once widely popular, Sullivan's theories have not been supported experimentally and are no longer accepted by most psychologists.

Torrey, Edwin Fuller. *Surviving Schizophrenia: A Family Manual.* Rev. ed. New York: Perennial Library, 1988. One of the best books available for the general reader on schizophrenia. Intended primarily for members of families that have a schizophrenic family member, this book should be read by everyone who is interested in the disorder, including every mental health worker. Torrey writes wonderfully and pulls no punches when dealing with outmoded theories and poorly done experiments. Many libraries have only the first edition; read the revised edition if possible.

Vonnegut, Mark. *The Eden Express*. New York: Praeger, 1975. A personal description of the experience of developing schizophrenia. Gives readers insight into the dynamics underlying some cases of the disorder.

Walker, Elaine F., ed. *Schizophrenia: A Life-Course Developmental Perspective*. San Diego: Academic Press, 1991. This book provides an overview of knowledge in the life course of schizophrenia. Chapters are written by experts in the field.

_____. *Schizophrenia: A Life-Span Developmental Perspective*. San Diego: Academic Press, 1991. The entire life-course of schizophrenic patients is addressed in this book, from early childhood precursors to geriatric outcome.

Walker, Elaine F., and Richard J. Lewine. "Prediction of Adult-Onset Schizophrenia from Childhood Home Movies of the Patient." *American Journal of Psychiatry* 147, no. 8 (1990): 1052-1056. Preliminary results from a novel study of the precursors of schizophrenia are presented in this paper. This approach complements the high-risk method in that it holds promise for validating the findings of high-risk research.

Watt, Norman F., et al., eds. *Children at Risk for Schizophrenia*. New York: Cambridge University Press, 1984. This edited volume summarizes the major high-risk projects underway throughout the world at the time it was written. It demonstrates the importance of this work in furthering understanding of the origins of schizophrenia.

Sexual Disorders

Allgeier, E. R., and A. R. Allgeier. *Sexual Interactions*. 3d ed. Lexington, Mass.: D. C. Heath, 1991. A highly readable description of sexual behavior. Contains photographs, charts, and tables which help make the material understandable. Provides a multitude of references. The book itself is an excellent, thorough textbook.

American Psychiatric Association. *Diagnostic and Statistical Manual of Mental Disorders IV*. Washington, D.C.: Author, 1994. In the United States this is the authoritative scheme for classifying psychological disorders. It groups about 230 psychological disorders and conditions into seventeen major categories of mental disorder, including diagnoses for almost every complaint a person could imagine.

Belliveau, Fred, and Lin Richter. *Understanding Human Sexual Inadequacy*. New York: Bantam Books, 1980. A paperback for the lay person that has been officially endorsed by Masters and Johnson. It summarizes the key work of Masters and Johnson on sexual dysfunction and is written in nontechnical language, supplying information that is based on established facts.

Gebhard, P. H., W. B. Pomeroy, B. Wardell, J. H. Gagnon, and C. V. Christenson. *Sex Offenders: An Analysis of Types*. New York: Harper & Row, 1965. Also available in paperback from Bantam Books, 1967, this book provides a detailed analysis of many types of atypical sexual behaviors that are against the law, with excellent information about the psychological and social factors that are involved in the development of these behaviors. The authors are well-respected researchers on other aspects of sexuality, in addition to paraphilias.

Haslam, Michael Trevor. *Psychosexual Disorders: A Review*. Springfield, Ill.: Charles C Thomas, 1979. Written by a psychiatrist, the book provides a perspective from the medical profession. It offers considerable detail and includes anatomical diagrams.

Heiman, Julia R., Joseph LoPiccolo, and Leslie LoPiccolo. *Becoming Orgasmic: A Sexual and Personal Growth Program for Women* Rev. ed. New York: Prentice-Hall, 1988. The book gives step-by-step suggestions to try to help women increase their ability to respond sexually in a variety of positive, growth-promoting ways. The suggestions are practical, creative, and interesting. Although the book is specifically written for women, men will also find it useful. The authors are well-respected sex researchers.

Masters, William H., and Virginia E. Johnson. *Human Sexual Inadequacy*. Boston, Mass.: Little, Brown, 1970. A classic book that is technical and directed toward the professional audience. It is an extremely important book, because Masters and Johnson were the first researchers to use the direct-observation methods that provided a foundation for treating sexual problems.

Rosen, Michael A. *Sexual Magic: The S/M Photographs.* San Francisco: Shaynew Press, 1986. Contains essays written by people who engage in sadomasochistic activities. Includes photographs of the people. In general, provides a personal, honest look into the lives of real people, using a case-study approach.

Stoller, Robert J. "Sexual Deviations." In *Human Sexuality in Four Perspectives*, edited by Frank A. Beach and Milton Diamond. Baltimore: The Johns Hopkins University Press, 1977. Provides a review of several common atypical sexual behaviors, along with several case studies. Concise and readable. Part of an interesting, well-rounded book on sexuality in general.

Szasz, Thomas Stephen. *Sex by Prescription.* Syracuse, N.Y.: Syracuse University Press, 1990. A short book that criticizes a variety of assumptions that guide the practices of some sex therapists. Also examined are the relationships among cultural beliefs about sexuality during several historical periods. Reactions of the medical community to sexual problems and problems in interpersonal relationships are discussed.

Weinberg, Thomas S., and G. W. Levi Kamel, eds. *S and M: Studies in Sadomasochism.* Buffalo, N.Y.: Prometheus Books, 1983. Composed of eighteen articles that provide thought-provoking information on a variety of issues relating to sadism and masochism.

Substance Abuse

Ackerman, Robert J., ed. *Growing in the Shadow: Children of Alcoholics.* Pompano Beach, Fla.: Health Communications, 1986. A collection of brief essays by leaders in the adult children of alcoholics and codependency recovery movements. Includes an outline of the causes and treatments of codependency as well as cross-cultural and family treatment considerations. Valuable to the professional yet readily comprehensible by the lay reader.

Beattie, Melody. *Codependent No More.* New York: Harper/Hazelden, 1987. A comprehensive overview of codependency that is complete with clear examples. A bestseller for many months and probably the most frequently read book in the codependency recovery movement. The majority of the book is devoted to self-help principles for codependents.

Becker, Charles E. "Pharmacotherapy in the Treatment of Alcoholism." In *The Diagnosis and Treatment of Alcoholism*, edited by Jack H. Mendelson and Nancy K. Mello. New York: McGraw-Hill, 1979. This article, with sixty-five references, in a very useful book aimed at effective treatment of alcoholism, describes the uses and pitfalls of the therapeutic drugs utilized. Topics include management of intoxication and alcohol withdrawal syndrome, postwithdrawal assistance, chronic assistance, and alcoholism and depression.

Bennett, Abram Elting. *Alcoholism and the Brain*. New York: Stratton Intercontinental Medical Book, 1977. Deals with relationships between brain function and alcoholism as a brain disease. Coverage includes the concept of alcoholism as a disease, alcohol actions in the brain, testing for alcoholic brain disease, constructive relationships between psychiatry and other aspects of alcoholism treatment, and rehabilitation methodology.

Berger, Gilda. *Addiction: Its Causes, Problems, and Treatments*. New York: Franklin Watts, 1982. Berger, a former special education teacher, writes about the subject of addiction and its problems with sensitivity and depth. She fully explores the idea of compulsive dependency on pleasure-giving substances such as alcohol, illegal drugs, tobacco, caffeine, and food. She also provides insight into causes, treatments, and societal attitudes.

Black, Claudia. *It Will Never Happen to Me!* Denver: M.A.C., 1981. A brief book designed to introduce family members to the dysfunctional rules and roles of the alcoholic family.

Cermak, Timmen L. *Diagnosing and Treating Co-Dependence*. Minneapolis: Johnson Institute Books, 1986. A proposal to have "codependency" declared a diagnostic category by the American Psychiatric Association. Aimed at a professional audience, but may be of interest to the lay reader.

Cox, W. Miles, ed. *The Treatment and Prevention of Alcohol Problems: A Resource Manual*. Orlando, Fla.: Academic Press, 1987. This edited work contains much information on many of the psychiatric, psychological, and behavioral aspects of alcohol. It is also widely useful in many other related alcoholism issues, including Alcoholics Anonymous, marital therapy, family therapy, and alcoholism prevention.

Eskelson, Cleamond D. "Hereditary Predisposition for Alcoholism." In *Diagnosis of Alcohol Abuse*, edited by Ronald Ross Watson. Boca Baton, Fla.: CRC Press, 1989. This article, in a book full of state-of-the-art information, gives considerable useful data on the hereditary aspects of alcoholism, concentrating on alcohol metabolism, animal and human studies, genetic aspects, and genetic markers for the disease. Sixty-five related references are included.

Friel, John. *Adult Children: Secrets of Dysfunctional Families*. Deerfield Beach, Fla.: Health Communications, 1988. A comprehensive overview of dysfunctional family systems and their predictable effects on family members. Clearly written, a valuable resource for both general and professional audiences.

Jaffe, Jerome H. "Drug Addiction and Drug Abuse." In *Goodman and Gilman's the Pharmacological Basis of Therapeutics*, edited by Alfred Goodman Gilman, Louis S. Goodman, et al. 7th ed. New York: Macmillan, 1985. A standard reference for students interested in an overview of the pharmacological aspects of selected addictive drugs. Of greater interest to those interested in pursuing the study of substance abuse from a neurological and physiological perspective.

Julien, Robert M. *A Primer of Drug Action*. 5th ed. New York: W. H. Freeman, 1988. An introductory treatment of types and actions of many abused and therapeutic substances. A useful, quick reference guide for psychoactive effects of drugs used in traditional pharmacological therapy for disorders and of abused substances. Contains good reference lists and appendices that explain some of the anatomy and chemistry required to understand biological mechanisms of substance abuse.

Knott, David H. *Alcohol Problems: Diagnosis and Treatment*. New York: Pergamon Press, 1986. Provides physicians with useful information on diagnosis and treatment of alcoholism. Topics include alcohol use and alcoholism; biochemical factors in alcohol use and abuse; epidemiology, diagnosis, and treatment of the disease; information on special populations affected by alcoholism; and perspectives on its control and prevention.

Leavitt, Fred. *Drugs and Behavior*. 2d ed. New York: John Wiley & Sons, 1982. Inclusive coverage from a psychological perspective of the effects of drugs on many types of behaviors. Includes sections on licit and illicit drugs, theories of drug use and abuse, prevention and treatment, and development of drugs. Important because it considers the effects of drug use on a large range of behaviors and physical states and because it presents a relatively integrated view of biopsychological information on drugs.

May, Rollo. *The Meaning of Anxiety*. New York: Ronald Press, 1950. This classic work by one of the masters of humanism is well-written, clear, and concise. It covers the subject of anxiety, an intricate component of most addictive behaviors, from modern interpretation to management of clinical analysis. Included are self-testing devices in the appendices, an extensive bibliography, and clear and informative notes.

Mecca, Andrew M. *Alcoholism in America: A Modern Perspective*. Belvedere, Calif.: California Health Research Foundation, 1980. This interesting book is useful, entertaining reading, with a wide factual base. It covers the history of alcoholic beverages, the nature of alcoholism, effects of alcoholism on the body, its treatment, community alcoholism prevention, and future perspectives. Included are numerous sources of additional information and a useful glossary.

Mule, S. Joseph, ed. *Behavior in Excess: An Examination of the Volitional Disorders*. New York: Free Press, 1981. This set of nineteen chapters is a must for the beginning student of addictive personalities and behavior. Explains the many drugs of choice available to the addictive person as well as the societal addictions of eating, work, gambling, sports, television, sex, and smoking. Explores the environmental influence on excessive behaviors and psychodynamic and behavioral treatments. An excellent group of writings.

Oxford, Jim. *Excessive Appetites: A Psychological View of Addictions*. New York: John Wiley & Sons, 1985. This internationally focused, easily read book begins by proclaiming that the author himself is an addict in recovery—a workaholic. It is well organized into two parts, one dealing with the topic of the excessive appetite and the other with psychological viewpoints on causes and treatments. The summary at the end draws most of the central themes together in an easily accessible format.

Ray, Oakley Stern, and Charles Ksir. *Drugs, Society, and Human Behavior*. 4th ed. St. Louis: Times Mirror/Mosby, 1987. A good text for the newer student of substance abuse who not only wishes to understand the substances and their biological significance but also is interested in current methods of prevention and treatment. Of special interest are the interspersed history and comments regarding the social aspects of abused substances.

Riley, Diane M., et al. "Behavioral Treatment of Alcohol Problems: A Review and a Comparison of Behavioral and Nonbehavioral Studies." In *The Treatment and Prevention of Alcohol Problems: A Resource Manual*, edited by W. Miles Cox. Orlando, Fla.: Academic Press, 1987. Evaluates behavioral treatment of alcoholism and the efficiency of various treatment methods. Included are sections on behavioral treatment, relaxation training, skills training, marital-family training, contingency management, self-management, comparison with nonbehavioral treatment, future prospects, and conclusions. More than two hundred references are provided.

Rix, Keith J. B., and Elizabeth M. Lumsden Rix. *Alcohol Problems: A Guide for Nurses and Other Health Professionals*. Bristol, England: Wright, 1983. The purpose of this book (with more than two hundred references) is to "provide nurses with information that will contribute to . . . improved education." Contains information on causes of alcoholism, its epidemiology, characteristics of alcohol intoxication and withdrawal, medical treatments, psychosocial aspects, and intervention models and methods.

Schaef, Anne Wilson. *Co-Dependence: Misunderstood-Mistreated*. San Francisco: Harper & Row, 1986. An integration of the principles of the chemical dependency and mental health fields. Covers the history and development of the concept of codependence. Mostly written for a general audience; some chapters are directed toward professionals.

United States Department of Health and Human Services. *Drug Abuse and Drug Abuse Research: The First in a Series of Triennial Reports to Congress*. Rockville, Md.: National Institute on Drug Abuse, 1984. An excellent summary of research on selected substances of abuse. The rest of the series should also be of great interest to the reader interested in substance-abuse research. The strength of this series is the understandable language and style used to convey recent research. Treatment, prevention, and specific drug research are summarized, and a well-selected reference list is provided for each chapter.

_____. *Theories on Drug Abuse: Selected Contemporary Perspectives*. Edited by Dan J. Lettieri, Mollie Sayers, and Helen Wallenstein Pearson. Rockville, Md.: National Institute on Drug Abuse, 1980. An older but good compendium of theoretical positions related to the question of substance abuse. Theories covered include the gamut of empirical and nonempirical thought concerning the predisposition to, development of, maintenance of, and possible termination of abuse disorders. Perspectives are biological, personal, and social. Of interest are a quick guide to theory components and an extensive list of references.

Watson, Ronald Ross, ed. *Diagnosis of Alcohol Abuse*. Boca Raton, Fla.: CRC Press, 1989. This edited work contains fifteen chapters on various aspects of current alcoholism research. They include basic science issues in biochemistry, genetics, enzymology, and nutrition. Other topics covered include diagnosis of alcoholic liver disease, identification of problem drinkers, alcohol testing, and alcoholism screening efforts.

Wilson, Bill. *Alcoholics Anonymous*. 3d ed. New York: Alcoholics Anonymous World Services, 1976. In this compilation of stories, words of wisdom, and insights into the world of the addicted person, the cofounders of Alcoholics Anonymous have been the impetus for an inspiring group of writings. Together with one of their original associates, Sister Ignatia of St. Thomas Hospital in Akron, Ohio, and many others, they have put into words the heart and soul of an addictive person's behavior—physically, emotionally, and spiritually. An essential part of any student's reading in the field of compulsive behavior.

PSYCHOTHERAPY

Historical Approaches

Corsini, Raymond J., comp. *Current Psychotherapies*. 3d ed. Itasca, Ill.: Peacock, 1984. An excellent survey of more than a dozen approaches to psychotherapy, with a brief historical description of the origin of each.

Ehrenwald, Jan. *The History of Psychotherapy: From Healing Magic to Encounter*. New York: Jason Aronson, 1976. A survey introduction to the history of psychotherapy. Contains excerpts from many original sources.

Ellenberger, Henri F. *The Discovery of the Unconscious: The History and Evolution of Dynamic Psychiatry*. New York: Basic Books, 1970. A comprehensive and scholarly history of nonmedical psychiatry. Traces the development of psychotherapy from exorcism to hypnosis to suggestion to the methods of Sigmund Freud and Carl G. Jung.

Janet, Pierre. *Psychological Healing: A Historical and Clinical Study*. 2 vols. New York: Macmillan, 1925. Reflects the biases of its author but provides detailed descriptions of nonmedical treatments from the middle of the nineteenth century to the early part of the twentieth century. Contains material that can be found nowhere else.

Kaplinski, Elizabeth, ed. *Careers in Psychology*. Washington, D.C.: American Psychological Association, 1986. Provides information to students who may be interested in psychology as a career. Defines psychology and describes what psychologists do. Also describes the procedure for preparation to become a psychologist. Single copies of this pamphlet are free upon request from the American Psychological Association.

Masson, Jeffrey Moussaieff. *Against Therapy: Emotional Tyranny and the Myth of Psychological Healing*. New York: Atheneum, 1988. Attacks the very idea of psychotherapy by examining selected historical instances from the nineteenth century onward.

Pande, Sashi K. "The Mystique of 'Western' Psychotherapy: An Eastern Interpretation." In *About Human Nature: Journeys in Psychological*

Thought, edited by Terry J. Knapp and Charles T. Rasmussen. Dubuque, Iowa: Kendall/Hunt, 1989. Argues that psychotherapy appears only in Western cultures and that it serves as an illustration of what these cultures lack.

Saccuzzo, Dennis P., and Robert M. Kaplan. *Clinical Psychology*. Boston: Allyn & Bacon, 1984. A textbook in clinical psychology providing a broad introduction to this field. Covers the historical foundation, the acquisition of clinical skills, theoretical models, psychotherapy, psychological testing, community psychology, and behavioral medicine. A useful introduction to the field of clinical psychology which includes a valuable chapter on the way it relates to other branches of psychology such as learning, motivation, perception, and biological factors.

Torrey, Edwin Fuller. *The Mind Game: Witchdoctors and Psychiatrists*. New York: Bantam Books, 1973. A leading American psychiatrist argues that the cultural and social role of the psychological healer has its origins in the primitive practices of the witch doctor.

Valenstein, Elliot S. *Great and Desperate Cures: The Rise and Decline of Psychosurgery and Other Radical Treatments*. New York: Basic Books, 1986. This is a scholarly and readable account of the history of physical therapies for mental disorders. While it focuses on lobotomy, many other forms of treatment are also described.

Walker, C. Eugene, ed. *Clinical Practice of Psychology: A Guide for Mental Health Professionals*. New York: Pergamon Press, 1981. Intended as an introduction for psychology interns or students who are beginning their work in clinical psychology. Discusses the history of this field and professional issues such as supervision, interviewing skills, ethics, and various forms of treatment. While not intended for the general public, the book will provide a good overview of the field of clinical psychology for someone who is considering entering it.

Behavioral Therapies

Bandura, Albert. *Principles of Behavior Modification*. New York: Holt, Rinehart and Winston, 1969. Provides a detailed description of various behavior therapy approaches, including modeling therapies. Includes case examples as well as summaries of the literature supporting the techniques.

_____. *Psychological Modeling: Conflicting Theories*. Chicago: Aldine-Atherton, 1971. Provides a thorough review of the principles of modeling as well as the research demonstrating its existence. Discusses various theories developed to explain the phenomenon and presents Bandura's explanation for observational learning. Written for those with background knowledge in learning theories.

Bellack, Alan S., and Michel Hersen. *Behavior Modification: An Introductory Textbook*. Baltimore: Williams & Wilkins, 1977. This book, by two of the leaders in the field of behavior therapy, contains extensive chapters describing research and treatment using systematic desensitization, flooding, implosion, and aversion therapy. Since it is a textbook, it places these treatments in the context of other behavior therapy techniques.

Bergin, Allen E., and Sol L. Garfield, eds. *Handbook of Psychotherapy and Behavior Change*. 3d ed. New York: John Wiley & Sons, 1986. A standard reference book for professionals that covers many issues in psychotherapy. Several chapters, including one on modeling therapies written by Albert Bandura, describe various therapeutic approaches.

Dowrick, Peter W., and Simon J. Biggs, eds. *Using Video: Psychological and Social Applications*. New York: John Wiley & Sons, 1983. Provides information on how video equipment can be used to help clients create behavior changes. Included are chapters on self-modeling and self-as-a-model, with detailed descriptions of applications of these techniques.

Foa, Edna B., G. S. Steketee, and L. M. Ascher. "Systematic Desensitization." In *Handbook of Behavioral Interventions: A Clinical Guide*, edited by Alan Goldstein and Edna B. Foa. New York: John Wiley & Sons, 1980. This book was written as a "how-to" guide for the psychotherapist; however, the beginner will also find it readable and engaging. It is very well written and is filled with interesting case material and direct transcripts from therapy sessions. This is the best place to experience what systematic desensitization is actually like for the client and the therapist.

Goldfried, Marvin R. "The Use of Relaxation and Cognitive Relabeling as Coping Skills." In *Behavioral Self-Management: Strategies, Techniques, and Outcomes*, edited by Richard B. Stuart. New York: Brunner/Mazel, 1977. A description of systematic rational restructuring by Marvin Goldfried, who developed the technique; reveals its similarities to and differences from rational-emotive therapy.

Goldfried, Marvin R., and Gerald C. Davison. *Clinical Behavior Therapy.* New York: Holt, Rinehart and Winston, 1976. An elementary, concise description of basic behavioral techniques. Includes clear examples of how these techniques are implemented.

Gordon, Thomas. *Parent Effectiveness Training.* New York: Peter H. Wyden, 1970. Written primarily for parents interested in successfully handling parent-child interactions. The author utilizes behavioral parent training principles to address various topics which primarily relate to improving communication between parents and children as well as handling children's misbehavior.

Karoly, Paul, and Anne Harris. "Operant Methods." In *Helping People Change: A Textbook of Methods*, edited by Frederick H. Kanfer and A. P. Goldstein. New York: Pergamon Press, 1986. A concise and easy-to-follow description of operant methods. Each technique is accompanied by illustrative case studies and recommendations for effective use.

Kazdin, Alan E. *Behavior Modification in Applied Settings.* 4th ed. Pacific Grove, Calif.: Brooks/Cole, 1989. An introduction to behavior modification that can be understood by the high school or college student. Operant techniques are clearly described, with the emphasis on how they are applied in a wide range of settings. Excellent discussion of recent developments in the field.

Krumboltz, John D., and Carl E. Thoresen, eds. *Behavioral Counseling: Cases and Techniques.* New York: Holt, Rinehart and Winston, 1969. Short chapters use case examples to illustrate specific applications of various psychotherapy techniques, including several modeling techniques.

Levis, D. J. "Implementing the Techniques of Implosive Therapy." In *Handbook of Behavioral Interventions: A Clinical Guide*, edited by Alan Goldstein and Edna B. Foa. New York: John Wiley & Sons, 1980. A good discussion of implosive therapy. This book also contains an interesting chapter by Joseph Wolpe on how to gather information to plan treatment and chapters on how to apply exposure therapy to specific disorders such as agoraphobia and obsessive-compulsive disorder.

Martin, Garry, and Joseph Pear. *Behavior Modification: What It Is and How to Do It*. 3d ed. Englewood Cliffs, N.J.: Prentice-Hall, 1988. One of the best introductions to behavior modification. The book offers clear explanations of the principles underlying techniques and detailed guidelines for their effective application. Study questions, practical exercises, and self-modification exercises facilitate mastery of concepts.

Masters, John C., et al. *Behavior Therapy: Techniques and Empirical Findings*. 3d ed. San Diego: Harcourt Brace Jovanovich, 1987. Provides an exhaustive review of behavioral therapies. Theoretical explanations as well as reviews of empirical findings are presented. This text offers an introductory yet complete presentation of behavior therapy. Useful as a reference text for specific behavior therapies.

Matson, Johnny L., and Thomas M. DiLorenzo. *Punishment and Its Alternatives: A New Perspective for Behavior Modification*. New York: Springer, 1984. An excellent and realistic description of the ranges of the punishment techniques available and the conditions under which it might be reasonable to employ them. The criteria for employing punishment when it is deemed to be the best available treatment, its limitations when used exclusively, and the need to employ positive reinforcement in punishment programs are covered. Legal and ethical concerns, empirical analysis, and predictions of future trends are also discussed.

Meichenbaum, Donald. *Cognitive Behavior Modification: An Integrative Approach*. New York: Plenum Press, 1977. Provides detailed descriptions of the use of cognitive approaches in therapy. Brief case descriptions illustrate various techniques including the use of cognitive approaches in modeling. Gives the reader an overview of how a client's self-talk can be used to help create behavior change through a variety of methods.

Paul, Gordon L. *Insight vs. Desensitization in Psychotherapy*. Stanford, Calif.: Stanford University Press, 1966. This short book is a classic. It describes an early and very influential study that showed systematic desensitization to be superior to insight-oriented psychotherapy for treating public speaking anxiety. It was one of the first studies to evaluate therapy effectiveness and is a good illustration of how research to test the effect of therapy is done.

Rusch, Frank R., Terry Rose, and Charles R. Greenwood. *Introduction to Behavior Analysis in Special Education*. Englewood Cliffs, N.J.: Prentice-Hall, 1988. Intended for students contemplating a teaching career, this book provides a readable introduction to the use of operant techniques with individuals who have learning difficulties. Numerous examples illustrate the educational applications of operant technology.

Sansweet, Stephen J. *The Punishment Cure*. New York: Mason/Charter, 1975. An older but very readable book, authored by a professional writer who avoids using jargon yet accurately describes what occurs in aversive therapy situations. A historical perspective of the use of punishment as a means of controlling behavior is offered. Sansweet describes how aversive therapy techniques have been applied to alcoholism, smoking, homosexuality, fetishism, compulsions and phobias, gambling, and bed-wetting in considerable detail.

Sherman, William M. *Behavior Modification*. New York: Harper-Collins, 1990. An accessible introduction in which operant techniques are clearly defined and illustrated with case studies. Includes discussion of cognitive behavior modification and behavioral medicine as well as consideration of problems encountered in the implementation of modification programs.

Watson, David L., and Roland G. Tharp. *Self-Directed Behavior: Self-Modification for Personal Adjustment*. 5th ed. Pacific Grove, Calif.: Brooks/Cole, 1989. This do-it-yourself guide to behavior changes makes extensive use of principles of reinforcement to help the lay reader improve behaviors in areas such as time management, smoking, overeating, assertiveness, insomnia, budgeting, and social behavior.

Wolpe, Joseph. *The Practice of Behavior Therapy*. 3d ed. New York: Pergamon Press, 1982. This book describes the practice of behavior therapy in detail, especially systematic desensitization. It includes chapters on aversion therapy and flooding as well as other therapy techniques, and illustrates how these techniques can be extended to treat problems other than fear and anxiety.

_____. *Psychotherapy by Reciprocal Inhibition*. Stanford, Calif.: Stanford University Press, 1958. The classic book in which Wolpe introduces and advocates systematic desensitization as an alternative to psychoanalytic treatment developed by Sigmund Freud. Describes the basic principles and practice of systematic desensitization for psychiatrists of the late 1950's, who generally had no knowledge of these techniques.

Biological Treatments

American Psychiatric Association. *Electroconvulsive Therapy: Report of the Task Force on Electroconvulsive Therapy of the American Psychiatric Association*. Washington, D.C.: Author, 1978. This report provides the results of a major task force charged with examining the clinical use of ECT. It thoroughly reviews the issues in a very readable format. Extensive recommendations for the use of ECT are provided.

Bloom, Floyd E., and Arlyne Lazerson. *Brain, Mind, and Behavior*. 2d ed. New York: W. H. Freeman, 1988. Beautifully illustrated and artfully written, this popular yet rigorous book probes current understanding of brain processes and their implications. Bloom, one of the world's leading neuropharmacologists, has an exceptional grasp of the diverse fields of neuroscience.

Breggin, Peter R. *Electroshock: Its Brain-Disabling Effects*. New York: Springer, 1979. This book describes many adverse effects of ECT, but severe mental dysfunction in particular. Citing research from both animal and human research, this author makes a strong argument against the use of ECT, stating that it is no more effective than a placebo, but considerably more dangerous.

Endler, N. S., and E. Persad. *Electroconvulsive Therapy: The Myths and the Realities*. Toronto: Hans Huber, 1988. This book is written for a wide audience, from psychiatrists to patients, and therefore it provides a very readable review of the topic. Much space is devoted to exploring nontechnical issues, including the myths about using ECT, the stigma attached to it, and legal and ethical concerns. An extensive bibliography is included.

Fink, Max. *Convulsive Therapy: Theory and Practice*. New York: Raven Press, 1979. Provides a thorough review of numerous issues surrounding the use of ECT. Includes a study of its effectiveness, risks, and legal, economic, and ethical concerns, as well as a comparison of ECT with other treatment methods. Several chapters are committed to a technical review of the mechanisms of ECT.

Freeman, Walter Jackson, and James Winston Watts. *Psychosurgery: Intelligence, Emotion, and Social Behavior Following Prefrontal Lobotomy for Mental Disorders.* Springfield, Ill.: Charles C Thomas, 1942. This book describes the results of eighty lobotomies; it provides case histories, explains the methodology of Freeman and Watts's standard operation, proposes the theory that interconnections between cerebral frontal lobes and the thalamus regulate the intensity of emotions associated with ideas, and virtually provides a "do-it-yourself manual" for doctors wishing to perform psychosurgery.

Friedberg, John. *Shock Treatment Is Not Good for Your Brain.* San Francisco: Glide, 1976. Provides a strong condemnation of ECT. The author believes that mental illness is a myth and that the use of ECT is unnecessary as well as inhumane. This book, which is written in a personal, nontechnical manner, includes interviews with seven individuals who have received ECT and are opposed to its further use.

Fulton, John Farquhar. *Frontal Lobotomy and Affective Behavior: A Neuropsychological Analysis.* New York: W. W. Norton, 1951. This book, by a prominent member of the American medical profession of the time, is dedicated to a description of the work of Egas Moniz and Lima. It discusses both human and animal lobotomy; and it is of historical interest, because Fulton lauds both the achievements and the prospects of lobotomy. Contains many useful references and illustrations.

Gilman, Alfred G., et al., eds. *Goodman and Gilman's The Pharmacological Basis of Therapeutics.* 8th ed. New York: Pergamon Press, 1990. The world's most authoritative treatise on pharmacology, this volume provides comprehensive, technical summaries on all major drug groups, including psychoactive substances. It is almost always the best place to start when researching a drug's activity.

Grahame-Smith, D. G., and P. J. Cowen, eds. *Preclinical Psychopharmacology.* New York: Elsevier, 1985. Offers a technical look at psychopharmacology. In many cases, there is significant overflow into the related area of neuropharmacology. Has individual chapters on major categories of drugs that affect the nervous system.

Julien, Robert M. *A Primer of Drug Action.* 6th ed. New York: W. H. Freeman, 1990. One of the best drug-education texts ever written, this book combines unusual knowledge of drug effects with great insight into psychological and sociological factors. Perfect for scientifically inclined high school and college students.

Katzung, Bertram G., ed. *Basic and Clinical Pharmacology.* 4th ed. Norwalk, Conn.: Appleton & Lange, 1989. Although less technical than some, this book is comprehensive and sophisticated. The chapter by Bourne and Roberts on receptors and pharmacodynamics is superb.

Kleinig, John. *Ethical Issues in Psychosurgery.* London: Allen & Unwin, 1985. This informative book focuses on the bioethical problems raised by psychosurgery. Discusses psychiatric diagnosis, the use of experimental therapies, criteria for success, informed consent, medical priorities, safeguards, and the relation between personality and the brain.

Kolb, Bryan, and Ian Q. Whishaw. *Fundamentals of Human Neuropsychology.* 2d ed. New York: W. H. Freeman, 1985. Quite naturally, the neuroscientist, pharmacologist, and psychologist look at the nervous system and drug action in slightly different ways. This book provides an important psychological perspective on these approaches.

Kramer, Peter D. *Listening to Prozac.* New York: Simon & Schuster, 1994. The author describes the remarkable benefits of the antidepressant drug Prozac, not only for treating depression but also for enhancing normal personality in socially desirable ways. Discusses the implications of such transformations for one's concept of self. Ethical and social ramifications of a biologically based concept of personality are considered. Fascinating reading for a general audience.

Marsh, Frank H., and Janet Katz, eds. *Biology, Crime, and Ethics.* Cincinnati: Anderson, 1984. Explores the relationship between biological factors (genetics, physiology) and criminal and aggressive behavior. Contains a section on psychosurgery and its appropriateness in treating violent and aggressive behavior.

Peck, Robert E. *The Miracle of Shock Treatment.* Jericho, N.Y.: Exposition Press, 1974. This short book provides a nontechnical introduction to ECT. It is written in a very readable style and is intended for the layperson who has little knowledge of the topic. The book includes brief case examples that highlight the usefulness of ECT in certain situations.

Poling, Alan D. *A Primer of Human Behavioral Pharmacology.* New York: Plenum Press, 1986. Psychopharmacology places a special emphasis on drug action in operant-conditioning paradigms. This book provides a fine, relatively nontechnical introduction to this complex, emerging field.

Sackler, Arthur M., et al., eds. *The Great Physiodynamic Therapies in Psychiatry: An Historical Reappraisal.* New York: Hoeber-Harper, 1956. This is a compilation of a number of selected articles on lobotomy and related areas, taken from several important biomedical journals. It includes Egas Moniz's article, "How I Succeeded in Performing Prefrontal Leukotomy." A brief biographical sketch of Egas Moniz is included.

Shuman, Samuel I. *Psychosurgery and the Medical Control of Violence: Autonomy and Deviance.* Detroit: Wayne State University Press, 1977. Covers topics that include the meaning of psychosurgery; its legal, medical, and political implications; aspects of freedom of thought being affected; and the famous "Detroit psychosurgery case." Much useful and interesting information is provided.

Snyder, Solomon H. *Drugs and the Brain.* New York: Scientific American Books, 1986. Snyder, one of the world's leading neuroscientists, provides an authoritative, wonderfully illustrated look at drugs. Excellent reading for the beginner.

Turner, Eric Anderson. *Surgery of the Mind.* Birmingham, England: Carmen Press, 1982. This brief book addresses the ethics of performing psychosurgery, its consequences, and its justifications. Topics include the function and operation of the brain, the selection of lobotomy patients, various types of psychosurgery, and a follow-up of almost five hundred psychosurgical operations.

Valenstein, Elliot S. *Great and Desperate Cures: The Rise and Decline of Psychosurgery and Other Radical Treatments for Mental Illness.* New York: Basic Books, 1986. This well-thought-out book describes the basis for the development, the rise, and the decline of psychosurgery. Its coverage includes the theories of mentation that led to psychosurgery, the endeavors and the methodology of its main proponents, and reasons for both its replacement and its present limited use. Many useful illustrations.

_____, ed. *The Psychosurgery Debate: Scientific, Legal, and Ethical Perspectives.* New York: W. H. Freeman, 1980. This valuable work is edited by Valenstein. Its topical content includes an overview of the history of, rationale for, and extent of psychosurgery; consideration of patient selection; evaluation of various methods used; description of legal and ethical issues involved; and an extensive bibliography.

Cognitive Therapies

Beck, Aaron T. *Cognitive Therapy and the Emotional Disorders*. New York: International Universities Press, 1976. An easy-to-read book that presents a general overview of the cognitive model and illustrates the cognitive model of different psychological disorders.

Beck, Aaron T., and Gary Emery. *Anxiety Disorders and Phobias: A Cognitive Perspective*. New York: Basic Books, 1985. Presents the cognitive theory and model of anxiety disorders, as well as the clinical techniques used with anxious patients.

Beck, Aaron T., A. J. Rush, B. F. Shaw, and Gary Emery. *Cognitive Therapy of Depression*. New York: Guilford Press, 1979. Presents the cognitive theory of depression and actual techniques used with depressed patients. Both makes a theoretical contribution and serves as a clinical handbook on depression.

Berne, Eric. *Games People Play*. New York: Grove Press, 1964. A national best-seller that provides a highly readable introduction to the basic ideas of transactional analysis and games. Provides an interesting catalog of the most common games played in groups of many kinds. The reader will find that he or she can immediately apply the ideas contained here.

_____. *What Do You Say After You Say Hello?* New York: Grove Press, 1972. This is another excellent primary source for the reader who wants to apply transactional analysis to everyday life. Focuses on games and on Berne's final development of his script theory shortly before his death.

Burns, David D. *Feeling Good: The New Mood Therapy*. New York: William Morrow, 1980. Readable introduction to the major concepts and techniques of cognitive therapy; written by one of Beck's students.

Corey, Gerald. *Theory and Practice of Counseling and Psychotherapy*. 3d ed. Pacific Grove, Calif.: Brooks/Cole, 1991. Corey reviews many of the primary schools of psychotherapy and specifically highlights the key concepts, therapeutic techniques, and research associated with RET. Also provides a brief critique of RET.

Dusay, J., and K. Dusay. "Transactional Analysis." In *Current Psychotherapies*, edited by Raymond J. Corsini and Danny Wedding. 4th ed. Itasca, Ill.: Peacock, 1989. This forty-two-page article contains five pages of bibliography and is cowritten by a leading transactional analysis therapist and writer. Thorough and scholarly. The Dusays go into considerable depth in explaining Berne's ideas. A detailed discussion of egograms, the drama triangle, and many more key TA concepts. Recommended for the reader who wants a serious introduction to TA.

Ellis, Albert. "The Evolution of Rational-Emotive Therapy (RET) and Cognitive Behavior Therapy (CBT)." In *The Evolution of Psychotherapy*, edited by Jeffrey K. Zeig. New York: Brunner/Mazel, 1987. This edited book provides an interesting blend of dialogue, debate, and scholarly review of various schools of psychotherapy. Ellis presents thoughtful answers to questions concerning the future of RET, the primary treatment processes, and training procedures.

_____. "Rational-Emotive Therapy." In *Current Psychotherapies*, edited by Raymond J. Corsini and Danny Wedding. 4th ed. Itasca, Ill.: F. E. Peacock, 1989. Provides a review of the basic concepts, history, theory, and treatment approach of RET. Written by Ellis, this chapter provides much insight into his views of RET and presents a transcript of a treatment session that highlights many of the therapeutic processes involved in RET.

Ellis, Albert, and Russell Grieger. *Handbook of Rational-Emotive Therapy*. New York: Springer, 1977. Presents an overview of RET with emphasis on the conceptual foundations and fundamental treatment components. Also highlights procedures for conducting RET with children.

Ellis, Albert, and Robert A. Harper. *A New Guide to Rational Living*. Englewood Cliffs, N.J.: Prentice-Hall, 1975. A self-help book emphasizing RET approaches. A classic RET book in that therapists have suggested this book for their clients for many years. Presents a clear, straightforward approach to RET.

Emery, Gary, Steven D. Hollom, and Richard C. Bedrosian, eds. *New Directions in Cognitive Therapy: A Casebook*. New York: Guilford Press,

1981. Contains cases presented by major cognitive therapists. Focuses on the application of cognitive therapy to a wide range of presenting problems (such as loneliness and agoraphobia), as well as diverse populations (such as adolescents, the elderly, and the psychologically naïve).

Fagan, Joen, and Irma Lee Shepherd, eds. *Gestalt Therapy Now*. Palo Alto, Calif.: Science and Behavior Books, 1970. Contains articles by several leading Gestalt therapists, who discuss the theory of this therapy approach, various Gestalt techniques, and applications. Includes a bibliography of Gestalt books and materials.

Glasser, Naomi, ed. *What Are You Doing? How People Are Helped Through Reality Therapy*. New York: Harper & Row, 1980. Presents twenty-five successful cases of reality therapy. Each case, described in detail, shows how reality therapy is put into practice. The cases range from a patient in a mental hospital to teenage delinquents to problems of aging. An excellent teaching aid in the training of counselors.

Glasser, William. *Control Theory: A New Exploration of How We Control Our Lives*. New York: Harper & Row, 1985. Control theory explains how individuals function. It states that behavior originates from within the individual and is need satisfying. A significant book, easy to read and understand.

_____. "Reality Therapy." In *Current Psychotherapies*, edited by Raymond Corsini. Itasca, Ill.: F. E. Peacock, 1984. In this chapter, Glasser describes in detail the beginnings of reality therapy, his theory of personality, the eight steps of reality therapy, and the processes and mechanisms of psychotherapy. A case example is included to show how the process of reality therapy works.

_____. *Reality Therapy: A New Approach to Psychiatry*. New York: Harper & Row, 1965. Describes Glasser's basic concepts of reality therapy. Glasser also shows how the reality therapist gets involved with the client and how he or she teaches clients more responsible ways to live their lives. This book was a significant contribution to psychotherapy in that it offered an alternative to psychoanalytic therapy.

_____. *Schools Without Failure*. New York: Harper & Row, 1968. Glasser applies the concepts of reality therapy to education, showing that many school practices have promoted a sense of failure in students. He proposes a new program to reduce school failure based on positive involvement, group work, no punishment (but discipline), a different grading system, and individual responsibility.

Goulding, Mary McClure, and Robert L. Goulding. *Redecision Therapy.* New York: Brunner/Mazel, 1979. This three hundred-page book is written by the two therapists who pioneered the integration of transactional analysis with Gestalt therapy. Both Gouldings studied directly with Berne and Fritz Perls. An overview of TA, contracts, and stroking is covered. The clinical use of TA with depression, grieving, and establishing "no suicide contracts" is handled with many case examples and some transcripts of actual sessions. Recommended for the advanced student of TA.

James, Muriel, and Dorothy Jongeward. *Born to Win.* Reading, Mass.: Addison-Wesley, 1971. Another work on transactional analysis that became a best-seller. An optimistic and humanistic version of TA mixed with Gestalt experiments gives the reader a rich firsthand experience of TA. Contains many experiential and written exercises that enable readers to diagnose their own scripts and rackets. A practical program in how to apply the ideas of TA immediately to improve one's life is provided.

Maultsby, Maxie C., Jr. *Rational Behavior Therapy.* Englewood Cliffs, N.J.: Prentice-Hall, 1984. An excellent summary of rational behavior therapy, as developed by Maultsby; discusses self-talk and its emotional and behavioral consequences.

Seligman, Martin E. P. *Learned Optimism.* New York: Alfred A. Knopf, 1991. Chapter 2 provides an especially interesting account of how two young upstart graduate students can blow a hole in one of the most basic assumptions of a well-entrenched viewpoint and promote the development of a new way of looking at things. Chapter 10 describes how explanatory styles might affect health and the mechanism by which this is thought to occur. A test developed to measure explanatory styles is included in chapter 3, and the last chapters focus on how to develop an optimistic orientation. A very readable book which examines a most interesting concept.

Group and Family Therapies

Beck, Aaron T. *Love Is Never Enough.* New York: Harper & Row, 1988. Written for couples everywhere, this text presents a review of cognitive therapy and includes many suggestions for couples wishing to improve their relationship. Through many clinical examples and dialogues with various couples in treatment, Beck highlights some of the key strategies for avoiding difficulties associated with misperceptions and miscommunication.

Bornstein, Philip H., and Marcy T. Bornstein. *Marital Therapy: A Behavioral-Communications Approach.* New York: Pergamon Press, 1986. Highlights some of the key research findings that differentiate distressed and satisfied partners in the areas of communication and conflict resolution. Also presents a clinical guide for counselors and therapists who work with couples to alleviate relationship dysfunction.

Bowen, Murray. *Family Therapy in Clinical Practice.* New York: Jason Aronson, 1978. Bowen is well respected as a family therapist and presenter of workshops. Here he shows his application of family therapy in the clinical setting.

Clark, Lynn. *The Time-Out Solution.* Chicago: Contemporary Books, 1989. Provides the general reader with an excellent overview of the major techniques used in behavioral family therapy. A good resource for parents or others interested in correcting children's misbehaviors through the use of well-tested methods.

Corey, Gerald, and Marianne Schneider Corey. *Groups: Process and Practice.* 2d ed. Monterey, Calif.: Brooks/Cole, 1982. This book is primarily concerned with identifying the main therapeutic stages and assessing the important role that the group leader plays in the process.

Dangel, Richard F., and Richard A. Polster. *Teaching Child Management Skills.* New York: Pergamon Press, 1988. Although child mental health professionals were the intended audience, this book is written in such a way that most nonprofessionals will readily understand it. Chapters 2 and 3 are the most useful because they outline and well illustrate the basic behavioral techniques used in behavioral family therapy.

Donigian, Jeremiah, and Richard Malnati. *Critical Incidents in Group Therapy.* Monterey, Calif.: Brooks/Cole, 1987. Six incidents are chosen by the authors and are presented to therapists from six different therapeutic approaches. Client-centered therapy, Gestalt therapy, individual psychology, reality therapy, rational-emotive therapy, and transactional analysis approaches are then applied to the same incidents.

Falloon, Ian R. H., ed. *Handbook of Behavioral Family Therapy*. New York: Guilford Press, 1988. Provides a thorough review of the applications of behavioral family therapy; written primarily for persons familiar with behavioral therapy. Six chapters are devoted to general issues in behavioral family therapy; twelve chapters illustrate the use of its principles with families whose members have specific clinical problems.

Goldenberg, Irene, and Herbert Goldenberg. *Family Therapy: An Overview*. 3d ed. Pacific Grove, Calif.: Brooks/Cole, 1991. An updated review of the major family therapy approaches, including strategic family therapy. Also provides a background on family development, and highlights issues in family therapy research and training.

Gordon, Thomas. *Parent Effectiveness Training*. New York: P. H. Wyden, 1970. Written primarily for parents interested in successfully handling parent-child interactions. Contains sixteen easily understood chapters that address various topics which primarily relate to improving communication between parents and children as well as handling children's misbehavior.

Gottman, John M., et al. *A Couple's Guide to Communication*. Champaign, Ill.: Research Press, 1976. A very useful guidebook for couples wishing to improve their communication and conflict-resolution skills. Suggestions for practicing improved interactions and increasing daily happiness are included.

Gurman, A. S. *Casebook of Marital Therapy*. New York: Guilford Press, 1985. Reviews some of the various treatment strategies available for dealing with some of the most challenging difficulties in interpersonal relationships (including jealousy, sexual problems, and in-laws). Leaders from a variety of treatment approaches describe various aspects of their therapy approach.

Gurman, A. S., and D. P. Kniskern. *Handbook of Family Therapy*. Vol. 2. New York: Brunner/Mazel, 1991. A significant resource on the various models of treatment for couples and families. Presents a historical overview of marital and family therapy, describes various models and conceptualizations of treatment, and highlights special topics such as sex therapy and divorce interventions.

Haley, Jay. *Leaving Home: The Therapy of Disturbed Young People.* New York: McGraw-Hill, 1980. Presents a treatment program for disturbed young people and their families. Describes the use of intense involvement and rapid disengagement with such families. Haley is one of the foremost theorists and therapists in strategic approaches.

Jacobson, Neil S., and A. S. Gurman. *Clinical Handbook of Marital Therapy.* New York: Guilford Press, 1986. Provides an overview and numerous clinical sections on the major models of relationship therapy and treatment suggestions for selected psychiatric disorders. Designed for clinicians and researchers alike, this edited text presents the views of most of the major figures in marital therapy.

Jacobson, Neil S., and Gayla Margolin. *Marital Therapy: Strategies Based on Social Learning and Behavior Exchange Principles.* New York: Brunner/Mazel, 1979. Presents a description of social learning theory and the methods typically employed in behavioral marital therapy. A landmark book in terms of the history of marital therapy which still offers much candid clinical insight into the most effective methods for alleviating relationship distress.

Madanes, Cloe. *Strategic Family Therapy.* San Francisco: Jossey-Bass, 1981. Provides an overview of strategic family therapy from one of the primary therapists in the field. Describes the philosophy and common approaches employed by strategic therapists in the treatment of a variety of presenting problems.

Minuchin, Salvador. *Families and Family Therapy.* Cambridge, Mass.: Harvard University Press, 1974. A leader in family therapy interventions and techniques writes about his work and experiences treating families at the Philadelphia Child Guidance Center.

Nichols, Michael P. "Behavioral Family Therapy." In *Family Therapy: Concepts and Methods.* New York: Gardner Press, 1984. A very readable, well synthesized chapter. Provides information regarding the leading characters, definitions of important terms, beliefs regarding causes of abnormal behavior, and techniques involved in behavioral family therapy. An excellent piece for the person interested in reading only an article about the topic.

Peterson, Vincent, and Bernard Nisenholz. "Group Work." In *Orientation to Counseling*. 2d ed. Needham Heights, Mass.: Allyn & Bacon, 1990. This chapter gives a very concise yet broad survey of group work as it relates to the general field of counseling and counseling theory. Acts as a good introduction to the field.

Robin, Arthur L., and Sharon L. Foster. *Negotiating Parent-Adolescent Conflict: A Behavioral Family Systems Approach*. New York: Guilford Press, 1989. Illustrates the integration of behavioral family therapy with other types of family therapy. Fifteen chapters are nicely divided between assessment and treatment issues. For the person already familiar with the subject.

Rogers, Carl Ransom. *On Becoming a Person*. Boston: Houghton Mifflin, 1961. Carl Rogers' influence on group work is acknowledged by all in the field. Rogers was mostly involved with encounter groups, but the theories and approaches spoken about in his book form the basis of much of group therapy practice today.

Stanton, M. Duncan. "Strategic Approaches to Family Therapy." In *Handbook of Family Therapy*, edited by Alan S. Gurman and David P. Kniskern. New York: Brunner/Mazel, 1981. Summarizes the strategic family therapy approach and highlights the central components of the MRI group, Milan school, and other notable strategic therapists. Also highlights the dimensions of healthy and dysfunctional families from a strategic model. Finally, briefly outlines some research on the effectiveness of the model in treating a variety of disorders.

Weeks, Gerald R., and Luciano L'Abate. *Paradoxical Psychotherapy: Theory and Practice with Individuals, Couples, and Families*. New York: Brunner/Mazel, 1982. Provides an overview of paradoxical approaches and details a variety of considerations in using paradox in treatment. Presents a compilation of paradoxical methods and describes some of the theories underlying these methods.

Yalom, Irvin D. *The Theory and Practice of Group Psychotherapy*. New York: Basic Books, 1985. Yalom's book is a comprehensive work on group therapy. The entire subject of group therapy, from method to application, is covered both from a theoretical viewpoint as well as from the experiential perspective. Actual cases are used as examples of what happens during a group therapy session, making this work indispensable.

Humanistic Therapies

Axline, Virginia Mae. *Dibs: In Search of Self.* New York: Ballantine Books, 1971. Written for the layperson, this book represents a case-study example of a successful play therapy sequence. Outlines the treatment of a severely disturbed boy, providing an excellent example of what happens in a child therapy room.

_____. *Play Therapy: The Inner Dynamics of Childhood.* Boston: Houghton Mifflin, 1947. Provides a thorough look at play therapy from a very nondirective perspective. Written in the 1940's, but has survived as an important reference for therapists who work with children in play therapy. The writing style is accessible to the layperson.

Bugental, James F. T. *Intimate Journeys: Stories from Life-Changing Therapy.* San Francisco: Jossey-Bass, 1990. A personal tour of the struggles, defeats, and triumphs of one humanistic psychotherapist, Bugental himself.

Davison, G. C., and J. M. Neale. *Abnormal Psychology.* 5th ed. New York: John Wiley & Sons, 1990. A frequently used textbook in the field of abnormal psychology. It gives an interesting overview of Gestalt therapy practice as well as an explanation of how these techniques may be applied to abnormal behaviors. The authors present a balanced critique of Gestalt therapy and of how it fits with the existential-humanistic approach to abnormality.

Dodds, J. B. *A Child Psychotherapy Primer.* New York: Human Sciences, 1985. Provides very practical suggestions and guidelines for persons who are beginning to work with children in a therapy context. Relatively brief (150 pages). A good first resource or overview of the topic.

Greenspan, Miriam. *A New Approach to Women and Therapy.* New York: McGraw-Hill, 1983. A highly readable account of the ways in which mental health systems and mainstream therapies discriminate against women. Describes feminist therapy, compares it to humanistic therapy, and provides case studies.

Ivey, Allen E., and Lynn Simek-Downing. *Counseling and Psychotherapy: Skills, Theories, and Practice.* 2d ed. Englewood Cliffs, N.J.: Prentice-Hall, 1980. This popular textbook on psychotherapy gives a brief overview of Gestalt therapy. It includes examples of Gestalt therapists working with clients and analyzes each statement in terms of type of approach (confrontation, question, or empathy).

Landreth, G. L. *Play Therapy*. Muncie, Ind.: Accelerated Development, 1991. Provides a fairly detailed look at the practical aspects of child psychotherapy from a humanistic, person-centered perspective. Easy to read, even for the layperson, despite having been written primarily for the professional or the student of psychology.

May, Rollo, Ernest Angel, and Henri F. Ellenberger, eds. *Existence: A New Dimension in Psychology and Psychiatry*. New York: Basic Books, 1958. A historically important book that helped initiate existential psychology in America. The first two essays and some case studies are quite readable and rewarding, but some articles may be rather difficult reading.

Nemiroff, M. A., and J. Annunziata. *A Child's First Book About Play Therapy*. Washington, D.C.: American Psychological Association, 1990. Written for children who may be in need of treatment. A great introduction to the principles of play therapy, best used by parents to read to their children before seeing a child therapist. A picture story-book that holds children's attention well.

Perls, Frederick S. *The Gestalt Approach and Eye Witness to Therapy*. Ben Lomond, Calif.: Science & Behavior Books, 1973. Two short books printed in one volume. *The Gestalt Approach* was Perls's last attempt to rework Gestalt therapy and is one of his most complete attempts to do so. *Eye Witness to Therapy* is a collection of verbatim therapy transcripts. They are easily readable and present excellent examples of practical applications of Gestalt theories.

_____. *Gestalt Therapy Verbatim*. Toronto: Bantam Books, 1959. This book is easy to read and contains a good balance of theory and case examples. Many of the examples come from group dream-work seminars and portray the Gestalt approach to dream analysis.

_____. *In and Out the Garbage Pail*. Toronto: Bantam Books, 1969. This is a humorous and free-floating autobiography by the founder of Gestalt therapy. Often entertaining, Perls uses his memories and experiences to illuminate principles of his theory.

Raskin, N. J., and Carl R. Rogers. "Person-Centered Therapy." In *Current Psychotherapies*, edited by Raymond J. Corsini and Danny Wedding. 4th ed. Itasca, Ill.: F. E. Peacock, 1989. One of the last projects that Rogers worked on prior to his death in 1987. Raskin knew Rogers for forty-seven years, and in this chapter he summarizes many of the key principles and concepts associated with person-centered therapy.

Rogers, Carl R. *Client-Centered Therapy.* Boston: Houghton Mifflin, 1951. A landmark text wherein Rogers highlights many of the key components of his evolving approach. The book describes aspects of the therapeutic relationship and the process of therapy.

_____. *Counseling and Psychotherapy: Newer Concepts in Practice.* Boston: Houghton Mifflin, 1942. Rogers' first book-length description of his approach to therapy. This book is of historical significance because it presents a revised version of Rogers' address at the University of Minnesota on December 11, 1940, at which time client-centered therapy was "officially" born.

_____. *On Becoming a Person.* Boston: Houghton Mifflin, 1961. One of Rogers' best-known and most highly regarded books. Presents valuable insight into Rogers, his approach, and the uses of client-centered approaches in education, family life, and elsewhere.

_____. *A Way of Being.* Boston: Houghton Mifflin, 1980. Rogers wrote this book as a follow-up to *On Becoming a Person*, and in it he updates his theory and therapeutic approach. An excellent bibliography is also included.

Schaefer, Charles E., and S. E. Reid. *Game Play.* New York: John Wiley & Sons, 1986. Puts children's games into the context of therapy. While traditional play therapists use toys, these authors introduce the use of games for therapeutic reasons. Written for the professional but also has implications for parents with regard to making choices of games for children; for example, discusses games that can be used to enhance a child's self-esteem. Somewhat long (more than three hundred pages) and perhaps a bit complicated for the layperson.

Skynner, A. C. Robin. *Systems of Family and Marital Psychotherapy.* New York: Brunner/Mazel, 1976. A systems approach to marital and family communication that integrates gender and role as well as relationship and sexuality to complete the picture of the influence of the marital relationship on the family.

Yalom, Irvin D. *Existential Psychotherapy*. New York: Basic Books, 1980. A clinically oriented book that describes abnormality in terms of how one deals with one's own mortality, isolation, lack of fulfilling potential, feelings of meaninglessness, and freedom. Also applies theory to clinical practice and examines implications of the approach.

Psychodynamic Therapies

Adler, Alfred. *The Individual Psychology of Alfred Adler*. Edited by Heinz L. Ansbacher and Rowena R. Ansbacher. New York: Basic Books, 1956.
_____. *Superiority and Social Interest*. Edited by Heinz L. Ansbacher and Rowena R. Ansbacher. Evanston, Ill.: Northwestern University Press, 1964. There is no standard edition or comprehensive collection of Adler's writings; however, the above two edited works by the Ansbachers take representative excerpts from Adler's numerous books and, together with editorial comments, present a good picture of the techniques Adler developed for assessment and therapy.

Axline, Virginia. *Dibs: In Search of Self*. New York: Ballantine Books, 1964. This book, written for a general audience, presents Axline's play therapy, illustrated by the presentation of a clinical case. The two-year treatment process with Dibs, a seriously disturbed child, is described in detail. The book provides an excellent example of child-centered play therapy.

Brink, Terry L. *Geriatric Psychotherapy*. New York: Human Sciences Press, 1979. A how-to manual for counselors who work with the aged. Adlerian theory is used to understand the psychodynamics of later life. Examples of Adlerian assessment techniques (early childhood recollections, dreams) are given, along with ways of cultivating social interest.

Campbell, Joseph. *The Hero with a Thousand Faces*. New York: Pantheon Books, 1949. Campbell was a contemporary theorist who developed Jung's ideas of universal symbols and the power of myth. This book discusses Jung's idea of the hero, and Campbell relates this idea to spiritual leaders such as Moses, Jesus, and Muhammad.

Dinkmeyer, Don C., and W. L. Pew. *Adlerian Counseling and Psychotherapy*. 2d ed. Columbus, Ohio: Charles E. Merrill, 1987. This is a good summary of different Adlerian techniques for psychotherapy. It is written for the practitioner at all levels, from youth guidance counselor to psychiatrist.

Dreikurs, Rudolf. *Fundamentals of Adlerian Psychology*. New York: Greenberg, 1950. The author was an Adlerian disciple who became the leader of the Adlerian movement in the United States after World War II. His simple style and straightforward advice is very much in keeping with the style of Adler himself. Dreikurs' own expertise was in the area of child development.

Engler, Barbara. *Personality Theories: An Introduction*. 3d ed. Boston: Houghton Mifflin, 1991. Engler's chapter on Jung and his psychotherapy is easy to read and contains a good balance between theory and practical application.

Freeman, Lucy. *The Story of Anna O*. New York: Walker, 1972. A popularly written examination of the psychoanalysis of the first analytic patient, with a description of her subsequent life (which was fascinating) and achievements; she became the first social worker in Germany and was responsible for many advances in the care of unwed mothers and their children. A particularly important accompaniment to the Freud and Breuer work.

Freud, Sigmund, and Josef Breuer. *Studies on Hysteria*. 1895. Reprint. New York: Avon Books, 1966. Contains not only the original source for the theory of psychoanalysis ("Anna O.," the only case conducted by Josef Breuer) but also the other analyses Freud conducted and about which he wrote. The germinative work in psychoanalysis.

Goldman, George D., and Donald S. Milman, eds. *Psychoanalytic Psychotherapy*. Reading, Mass.: Addison-Wesley, 1978. A very clear, concise treatment of complicated psychodynamic techniques. Explains difficult concepts in language accessible to the layperson.

Hall, Calvin Springer, and Gardner Lindzey. *Theories of Personality*. 3d ed. New York: John Wiley & Sons, 1978. This is a classic text in personality theory and application, and it gives a detailed description of Jung's theory. Recommended for the serious student of Jung.

Hall, Calvin Springer, and Vernon J. Nordby. *A Primer of Jungian Psychology*. New York: New American Library, 1973. This paperback attempts to provide a comprehensive treatment of Jung's ideas. It is intended for the beginning student of Jung.

Hannah, Barbara. *Jung: His Life and Work.* New York: Putnam, 1976. This is an interesting biographical account of Jung by a psychoanalyst who was his friend for more than thirty years. Gives an insight into how his personal beliefs and experiences shaped his theory.

Landy, Robert J. *Drama Therapy: Concepts and Practices.* Springfield, Ill.: Charles C Thomas, 1986. Particularly valuable in identifying the relationship between drama therapy and other psychotherapies. Contains numerous examples and illustrations of drama therapy as it has been used to address various psychological problems.

Mason, Kathleen Criddle, ed. *Dance Therapy.* Washington, D.C.: American Alliance for Health, Physical Education, and Recreation, 1974. Particularly good in identifying the special groups for which dance therapy is useful. Each chapter explores a special application of dance therapy to a particular audience or treatment population.

Monte, Christopher. "Anna Freud: The Psychoanalytic Heritage and Developments in Ego Psychology." In *Beneath the Mask: An Introduction to Theories of Personality.* 4th ed. Fort Worth, Tex.: Holt, Rinehart and Winston, 1991. In this textbook chapter, Monte describes Anna Freud's contributions to the field of child psychotherapy. The chapter traces Anna Freud's adaptation of her father's psychoanalytic therapy to her work with children. This is a valuable work because it describes Anna Freud's therapy in understandable terms—which is difficult, given the complexity of child psychoanalysis.

Mosak, Harold H., ed. *Alfred Adler: His Influence on Psychology Today.* Park Ridge, N.Y.: Noyes Press, 1973. This edited volume contains a section on clinical applications in education and psychiatry.

Mosak, Harold H., and Birdie Mosak. *A Bibliography of Adlerian Psychology.* Washington, D.C.: Hemisphere, 1975. A very comprehensive bibliography covering Individual Psychology through the early 1970's; even small articles in newsletters are included. There are more than a hundred citations on psychotherapy alone.

Nemiroff, Marc A., and Jane Annunziata. *A Child's First Book About Play Therapy.* Washington, D.C.: American Psychological Association, 1990. Children ages four to seven who are entering play therapy are the intended audience of this book. The book uses frequent illustrations and simple words to communicate to children the purpose and process of children's play therapy. An excellent resource for parents whose children are about to enter play therapy.

Schaefer, Charles E., and Steven E. Reid, eds. *Game Play: Therapeutic Use of Childhood Games.* New York: John Wiley & Sons, 1986. An edited book in which numerous types of games and activities that may be used in play therapy are described. Discusses games which have been specifically designed for play therapy as well as familiar games, such as checkers, whose use may be modified for therapeutic work. The book is largely intended for child therapy professionals of various treatment orientations.

Schneider, Erwin H., ed. *Music Therapy.* Lawrence, Kans.: National Association for Music Therapy, 1959. One of a series of annual publications of the proceedings of the National Association for Music Therapy. While somewhat old, this volume covers a wide variety of applications and settings of music therapy through case studies. It is a classic in the field of music therapy.

Siegel, Elaine V. *Dance-Movement Therapy: Mirror of Our Selves.* New York: Human Sciences Press, 1984. Strong theoretical framework and applied theory of dance and psychotherapy. This is a very scholarly investigation of dance therapy; includes movement as well.

Spotnitz, Hyman. *Modern Psychoanalysis of the Schizophrenic Patient.* 2d ed. New York: Human Sciences Press, 1985. The seminal work in modern psychoanalysis. More comprehensible than the first edition, it is still difficult reading because it requires some familiarity with the theory and (particularly) practice of modern psychoanalytic treatment.

_____. *Psychotherapy of Preoedipal Conditions: Schizophrenia and Severe Character Disorders.* New York: Jason Aronson, 1976. A psychoanalytic approach to psychosis. It presents theory and practice issues clearly and enjoyably.

Spotnitz, Hyman, and Phyllis W. Meadow. *Treatment of the Narcissistic Neuroses.* New York: Manhattan Center for Advanced Psychoanalytic Studies, 1976. A sound and important collaborative effort between the founder of modern psychoanalysis and the person (Phyllis W. Meadow) who spearheaded the movement's appearance and started, with others, the institution founded to advance the philosophy and techniques of modern psychoanalysis.

Wehr, Gerhard. *Portrait of Jung: An Illustrated Biography*. New York: Herder and Herder, 1971. This is an interesting biography of Jung as well as a good introduction to his theory and therapy. Contains numerous fascinating pictures that give insight to the man and his ideas.

Evaluating Psychotherapy

Beutler, Larry E., and Marjorie Crago, eds. *Psychotherapy Research: An International Review of Programmatic Studies*. Washington, D.C.: American Psychological Association, 1991. Reviews a variety of large-scale and small-scale research programs in North America and Europe. Presents a summary of research findings from studies investigating various aspects of psychotherapy including prevention of marital distress, process variables in psychotherapy, treatment of difficult patients, and inpatient hospitalization approaches.

Brodsky, Annette M., and Rachel T. Hare-Mustin. *Women and Psychotherapy*. New York: Guilford Press, 1980. Chapters summarize research issues on gender and gender-role stereotyping, describe disorders of high prevalence in women's lives, and propose a variety of therapeutic approaches for intervening in women's lives.

Chesler, Phyllis. *Women and Madness*. Garden City, N.Y.: Doubleday, 1972. One of the original, classic documentations of the way in which sexism has operated within mental health systems and contributed to unequal treatment of women.

Dutton-Douglas, Mary Ann, and Lenore E. A. Walker. *Feminist Psychotherapies*. Norwood, N.J.: Ablex, 1988. Includes chapters on the integration of feminist philosophy and mainstream therapy systems, feminist psychotherapy with special populations, feminist therapy with men, and future directions.

Frank, Jerome David. *Persuasion and Healing*. Rev ed. Baltimore: The Johns Hopkins University Press, 1973. Provides an overview of Frank's position on psychotherapy. The significance of common treatment components shared by all forms of healing, including psychotherapy, continues to be an important consideration in treatment outcome work.

Garfield, Sol L. *Psychotherapy: An Eclectic Approach*. New York: John Wiley & Sons, 1980. Focuses on the client, the therapist, and their interaction within an eclectic framework. Written for the beginning student of psychotherapy and relatively free of jargon.

Garfield, Sol L., and Allen E. Bergin, eds. *Handbook of Psychotherapy and Behavior Change.* 3d ed. New York: John Wiley & Sons, 1986. Provides a historical overview and synopsis of research studies concerned with the evaluation of psychotherapy. Patient and therapist variables are highlighted in terms of their importance in successful intervention. Additional topics include training therapeutic skills, medications and psychotherapy, and the effectiveness of treatment approaches with children, couples, families, and groups.

Johnson, Karen, and Tom Ferguson. *Trusting Ourselves: The Sourcebook on Psychology for Women.* New York: Atlantic Monthly Press, 1990. Discusses common psychological concerns of women, such as self-esteem, depression, anxiety, sexuality, alcohol, body image, and violence. Highly readable, written for a lay audience. Includes a consumer guide to seeking psychological help.

Kaysen, Susanna. *Girl Interrupted.* New York: Random House, 1993. Kaysen is an author who, as a teenager, spent two years in a private mental hospital after a suicide attempt. This best-selling book is not a chronicle of "mental illness" but a description of life in a psychiatric hospital.

Kazdin, Alan E. *Single-Case Research Designs: Methods for Clinical and Applied Settings.* New York: Oxford University Press, 1982. Provides an overview of various research methods used in psychotherapy research. In particular, this book presents information about case studies and single-case research designs. Single-case research has become increasingly common in psychotherapy research as an alternative approach to group designs.

Phares, E. Jerry. *Clinical Psychology: Concepts, Methods, and Profession.* 3d ed. Chicago: Dorsey Press, 1988. An overview of clinical psychology that includes excellent chapters summarizing psychodynamic, behavioral, humanistic, and other models of psychotherapy. Written as a college-level text.

Rogers, Carl Ransom. *Client-Centered Therapy.* Boston: Houghton Mifflin, 1951. A classic description of the author's humanistic psychotherapy that is still useful as a strong statement of the value of the therapeutic relationship. Written for a professional audience, though quite readable.

Rosewater, Lynne Bravo, and Lenore E. A. Walker, eds. *Handbook of Feminist Therapy: Women's Issues in Psychotherapy.* New York: Springer, 1985. Includes brief chapters dealing with feminist philosophy, techniques, special populations, and ethics. Includes the American Psychological Association's "Principles Concerning the Counseling and Therapy of Women."

Smith, Mary Lee, and Gene V. Glass. "Meta-Analysis of Psychotherapy Outcome Studies." *American Psychologist* 32, no. 9 (1977): 752-760. A classic in the field of psychotherapy research, this journal article represents a significant step in the manner in which knowledge is distilled from the scientific literature. This controversial article concluded that psychotherapy was effective.

Smith, Mary Lee, Gene V. Glass, and Thomas I. Miller. *Benefits of Psychotherapy.* Baltimore: The Johns Hopkins University Press, 1980. Presents many detailed analyses from 475 psychotherapy research studies that were systematically analyzed via meta-analysis.

Stern, E. Mark, ed. *The Other Side of the Couch: What Therapists Believe.* New York: Pilgrim Press, 1981. A fascinating exposé of the private religious beliefs of twenty-four therapists. Each briefly relates his or her own faith, sometimes admitting and other times vehemently denying its influence on his or her psychotherapy. The book can be appreciated by college readers.

Teyber, Edward. *Interpersonal Process in Psychotherapy: A Guide to Clinical Training.* Chicago: Dorsey Press, 1988. An extremely clear and readable guide to modern eclectic therapy. Full of practical examples and written as a training manual for beginning psychotherapy students.

Wolpe, Joseph. *The Practice of Behavior Therapy.* 4th ed. Elmsford, N.Y.: Pergamon Press, 1990. Written by the originator of behavioral psychotherapy. Introduces basic principles, examples of behavioral interventions, and many references to research. Initial chapters are elementary, but later ones tend to be complicated.

Community Mental Health

Bloom, Bernard L. *Community Mental Health: A General Introduction.* 2d ed. Monterey, Calif.: Brooks/Cole, 1984. Although Bloom focuses primarily on community mental health, he provides much information that is relevant to community psychology in general. The discussion of direct service interventions is something that most books on community psychology lack.

Caplan, Gerald. *Principles of Preventive Psychiatry.* New York: Basic Books, 1964. Caplan was a key figure in directing attention to the need to be informed concerning biological, psychological, and sociocultural factors as they influence psychopathology. Furthermore, Caplan's call for an emphasis on primary prevention antedated the origin of community psychology.

Felner, Robert David, et al., eds. *Preventive Psychology: Theory, Research, and Practice.* New York: Pergamon Press, 1983. While its origins may be in community psychology, preventive psychology is presented as a broader enterprise. This volume attempts to provide an integrating framework for preventive psychology with the goal of stimulating applications.

Heller, Kenneth, et al. *Psychology and Community Change: Challenges of the Future.* 2d ed. Homewood, Ill.: Dorsey Press, 1984. Describes how knowledge of groups, organizations, and communities can be applied in addressing social problems. Ecological approaches and prevention-oriented interventions are the primary substance of the text.

Levine, Murray, and David V. Perkins. *Principles of Community Psychology: Perspectives and Applications.* New York: Oxford University Press, 1987. The authors provide an extended discussion of social problems, the conceptual foundations of community psychology, and the application of community-psychology principles to promote effective change. Substantial portions of the text are devoted to labeling theory and the effects of crises.

Mann, Philip A. *Community Psychology: Concepts and Applications.* New York: Free Press, 1978. The origins of community psychology and the relevance of the concept of community are described. Additionally, the assumptions and implications of four models are detailed: the mental health model, organizational model, social-action model, and ecological model.

Nietzel, Michael T., et al. *Behavioral Approaches to Community Psychology.* New York: Pergamon Press, 1977. The authors describe how behavior-modification techniques can be used to solve community problems. Behavior modification is presented as providing both a means to initiate change and a method for evaluating the results.

Rappaport, Julian. *Community Psychology: Values, Research, and Action.* New York: Holt, Rinehart and Winston, 1977. Rappaport provides a comprehensive survey of the paradigms, principles, and practice of community psychology. The book focuses attention on the social roots of pathology and the need for systems-level interventions that are culturally congruent.

AUTHOR INDEX

Abbott, Bruce B., and Kenneth S.
  Bordens 11
Abel, Ernest L. 181
Abelson, Robert P., and Roger C.
  Schank 152
Abram, Harry S., ed. 295
Abrams, Dominic, and Michael A.
  Hogg 219
Abramson, Hillel, and Arthur C. Houts
  327
Achenbaum, W. A. 201
Ackerman, Diane 56
Ackerman, Robert J., ed. 352
Acocella, Joan Ross, and Richard R.
  Bootzin 318, 331
Adams, Henry E. 317
Adelman, George, ed. 31
Adler, Alfred 173, 279-280, 379
Adler, Helmut E., and Robert W. Rieber,
  eds. 3
Adler, Ronald B., Lawrence B.
  Rosenfeld, and Neil Towne 222
Agnew, Neil M., and Sandra W. Pyke
  23
Agranoff, Bernard W., George J. Siegel,
  R. Wayne Albers, and Perry B.
  Molinoff, eds. 42
Ahlgren, Andrew, and Franz Halberg
  140
Aiken, Lewis R. 250, 262
Aikman, Ann, and Walter McQuade
  314
Ainsworth, Mary D. Salter, Mary C.
  Blehar, Everett Waters, and S. Wall
  174
Ajzen, Icek, and Martin Fishbein 213
Akmajian, Adrian, Richard A. Demers,
  Ann K. Farmer, and Robert M.
  Harnish 155
Alba, Joseph W., and Lynn Hasher
  145
Albers, Josef 56
Albers, R. Wayne, George J. Siegel,
  Bernard W. Agranoff, and Perry B.
  Molinoff, eds. 42
Albert, Martin L., and Loraine K.
  Obler 155
Albert, Robert S. 250

Albert, Robert S., and Mark A. Runco,
  eds. 257
Alberts, Bruce, et al. 25
Alcock, John 97
Alexander, Charles N., and Ellen J.
  Langer, eds. 134
Alexander, Charles N., Jayne
  Gackenbach, and Harry Hunt, eds.
  135
Allen, Roger J. 298
Allgeier, E. R., and A. R. Allgeier 350
Allman, William F. 122, 145
Allport, Gordon W. 213, 227, 238,
  290-291
Allport, Gordon W., Philip E. Vernon,
  and Gardner Lindzey 262
Allport, Susan 145
Alschuler, Alfred S., Diane Tabor, and
  James McIntyre 83
Altman, I. 298
Altman, Irwin, and Dalmas A. Taylor
  223
Altman, Irwin, and Daniel Stokols,
  eds. 216
Altner, Helmut, Dietrich Burkhardt, and
  Schleidt Wolfgang 45
Altrocchi, John 317
Altshuler, Kenneth Z., and A. John
  Rush, eds. 343
American Educational Research
  Association, American Psychological
  Association, and National Council on
  Measurement in Education 250
American Personnel and Guidance
  Association 250
American Psychiatric Association 268,
  317, 324, 330, 351, 364
American Psychological Association
  3, 250-251, 262
American Psychological Association
  Council of Representatives 17
Amir, Yehudi 227
Anagnostakos, Nicholas P., and
  Gerard J. Tortora 43
Anastasi, Anne 251, 262
Anch, A. Michael, C. P. Browman,
  M. M. Mitler, and James K. Walsh
  140

Anderson, Barry F., et al.   122
Anderson, James W.   291
Anderson, John F., and Douglas R. Berdie   11
Anderson, John R.   122
Anderson, J. R.   145
Anderson, J. W., and M. B. Smith   82
Andreasen, Nancy C.   317
Andrew, Richard John, and Ernst Huber   67
Andrewartha, Herbert George   97, 295
Andriole, Stephen J.   122
Angel, Ernest, Rollo May, and Henri F. Ellenberger, eds.   293, 377
Angermeier, Wilhelm F.   118
Annunziata, J., and M. A. Nemiroff   377, 381
Antonovsky, Aaron   310
Appignanesi, Richard   280
Applebee, Arthur N.   110
Appley, M. H., and Charles Norval Cofer   78
Apter, Michael J., David Fontana, and Stephen J. Murgatroyd   77
Archer, D.   317
Arenson, Gloria   90
Arkin, Robert M., Russell G. Geen, and William W. Beatty   301
Arnberg, Lenore   155
Arnold, L. Eugene   324
Arnold, Madga B.   67, 298
Aronson, Elliot   213, 228
Aronson, Elliot, and Anthony R. Pratkanis   215
Aronson, Elliot, and Ayala M. Pines   226
Aronson, Elliot, and David Landy   244
Aronson, Eric, and David N. Lee   53
Ascher, L. M., Edna B. Foa, and G. S. Steketee   360
Ashcraft, Mark H.   122, 145
Atchley, Robert C.   201
Atkinson, John William, and D. Birch   84
Atkinson, John William, and Joel O. Raynor, eds.   84
Atkinson, R. L., R. C. Atkinson, E. E. Smith, and D. J. Bem   67
Atwell, Freda Cruse, and Jack D. Douglas   194
Auerbach, Stephen M.   299
Ault, Ruth L.   171

Austin, Colin Russell, and Roger Valentine Short, eds.   90
Austin, George A., Jerome S. Bruner, and Jacqueline J. Goodnow   124
Austin, William G., and Stephen Worchel, eds.   235
Averill, James R.   299
Axline, Virginia Mae   376, 379
Azrin, Nathan H., and Victoria A. Besalel   325

Babbie, Earl R.   18
Babkin, Boris Petrovich   118
Bach, George R., and Herb Goldberg   210
Bach-y-Rita, Paul, ed.   31
Back, Kurt, Leon Festinger, and Stanley Schachter   224
Baddeley, Alan D.   122, 145-146
Baer, Lee, Michael A. Jenike, and William E. Minichiello   334
Bahrick, H. P.   146
Baillargeon, R., and Rochel Gelman   171
Baker, Lester, Salvador Minuchin, and Bernice L. Rosman   328
Baker, Therese L.   11, 18
Baldwin, John D., and Janice I. Baldwin   102, 110, 114
Ballantyne, John Chalmers, and J. A. M. Martin   49
Ballard, Philip Boswood   251
Bammer, Kurt, and Benjamin H. Newberry, eds.   311
Banaji, Mahzarin R., and Robert G. Crowder   146
Bandura, Albert   84, 110, 210, 274, 359-360
Banks, William P., Dale E. Berger, Kathy Pezdek, eds.   123
Bannister, Donald, and Fay Fransella   275
Bannister, Donald, and J. M. M. Mair, eds.   275
Bar-Tal, Daniel, Ervin Staub, Jerzy Karylowski, and Janusz Reykowski, eds.   238
Barber, Joseph, and Cheri Adrian, eds.   299
Barber, Theodore Xenophon   18
Barkley, Russell A.   325
Barlow, David H.   67, 330

Barlow, H. B., and J. D. Mollon, eds. 56

Barnickol, Carol Ann, Charles A. Corr, Helen Fuller, and Donna M. Corr, eds. 182

Barnouw, Victor 272

Baron, Jonathan 122

Baron, Robert A., and D. R. Richardson 84

Baron, Robert A., and Donn Byrne 228

Baron, Robert J. 123

Barrios, B. A. 263

Barrow, Georgia M. 201

Bartholomew, George A., Malcolm S. Gordon, et al. 98

Bartko, John J., Siegfried Kasper, Thomas A. Wehr, Paul A. Gaist, and Norman E. Rosenthal 341

Bartlett, Frederic Charles 146

Bartol, Curt R. 318

Baruch, Grace, and Jeanne Brooks-Gunn, eds. 194

Bass, Bernard M. 217

Bates, David, David Chadwick, and Niall Cartlidge 32

Batson, C. D. 236

Batson, C. Daniel, and W. Larry Ventis 238

Baum, A., P. A. Bell, J. D. Fisher, and T. E. Greene 299

Baum, Andrew, and Robert J. Gatchel, and David S. Krantz 312

Baum, Martha, and Rainer C. Baum 201

Baumann, D. J., Robert B. Cialdini, and D. T. Kenrick 236

Baumeister, Roy F., ed. 239

Baumrind, Diana 174

Bayer, Ronald 318

Baylor, Denis A., and Julie L. Schnapf 64

Beach, Stephen R. H., E. E. Sandeen, and K. D. O'Leary 338

Beale, Ivan L., and Michael C. Corballis 33

Beattie, Melody 352

Beatty, William W., Russell G. Geen, and Robert M. Arkin 301

Beauchamp, A. J., and J. P. Gluck 12

Beauchamp, Tom L., Ruth R. Faden, R. Jay Wallace, Jr., and Le Roy Walters, eds. 18

Beaumont, J. Graham 31

Beck, Aaron T. 239, 338, 368, 371

Beck, Aaron T., and Gary Emery 318, 331, 368

Beck, Aaron T., A. J. Rush, B. F. Shaw, and G. Emery 338, 368

Beck, Aaron T., Robert A. Steer, and Margery G. Garbin 263

Beck, William S., Karel F. Liem, and George Gaylord Simpson 25, 106

Becker, Charles E. 353

Becker, Ernest 201, 280

Beckham, Ernest Edward, and William R. Leber, eds. 338

Beckwith, Barbara, John G. Weiss, and Bob Schaeffer 261

Beecher, Michael D., and Robert C. Bolles, eds. 107

Belenky, Mary Field, et al. 187

Bell, Alan P., and Martin Weinberg 90

Bell, Alan P., Martin S. Weinberg, and Sue Kiefer Hammersmith 90

Bell, P. A., J. D. Fisher, A. Baum, and T. E. Greene 299

Bell, Ruth, et al. 187

Bell-Gredler, Margaret E. 102

Bellack, Alan S., and Michel Hersen 360

Bellezza, F. S. 146

Belliveau, Fred, and Lin Richter 351

Belsky, Jay, Laurence D. Steinberg, and Roberta B. Meyer 187

Bem, Daryl J. 239

Bem, D. J., R. L. Atkinson, R. C. Atkinson, and E. E. Smith 67

Bem, Sandra L. 174

Bendell, R. Debra, Jan L. Cubertson, Henry F. Krous, eds. 182

Benewick, Robert, and George Gaskell, eds. 218

Bengston, Vern L., and Joan F. Robertson, eds. 202

Benjamin, Ludy T., J. Roy Hopkins, and Jack R. Nation 123

Benner, David G., ed. 239

Bennett, Abram Elting 353

Berardo, Felix, Hannelore Wass, and Robert A. Neimeyer, eds. 209

Berdie, Douglas R., and John F. Anderson 11

Berg, Bruce Lawrence 11

Berger, Dale E., Kathy Pezdek, and

William P. Banks, eds. 123
Berger, Gilda 353
Bergin, Allen E., and Sol L. Garfield, eds. 360, 384
Berglas, Charlotte 194
Berk-Seligson, Susan 155
Berkow, Robert 318
Berkowitz, Leonard 210
Berkowitz, Leonard, and Jacqueline Macaulay, eds. 237
Berlitz, Charles 155
Berlyne, D. E. 77
Berne, Eric 368
Berne, Robert M., and Matthew N. Levy, eds. 49, 56
Bernstein, Douglas A., E. Roy, T. Srull, and C. Wickens 67
Bernstein, Ilene L., and Soo Borson 91
Berscheid, Ellen, and Elaine Hatfield Walster 223
Bersoff, Donald N., Laurel P. Malson, and Donald B. Verrilli 263
Berstein, D. A., M. T. Nietzel, and R. Milich 270
Bervonsky, M. 188
Besalel, Victoria A., and Nathan H. Azrin 325
Bess, Fred H., and Larry E. Humes 49
Best, Deborah L., and John E. Williams 235
Best, John B. 146
Bettelheim, Bruno 280
Bettman, James R. 123
Betz, Nancy E., and W. Bruce Walsh 260, 268
Beutler, Larry E., and Marjorie Crago, eds. 383
Beyer, Carlos, ed. 25
Beyth-Marom, Ruth, and Baruch Fischoff 241
Biederman, Irving 123
Biehler, Robert Frederick, and Jack Snowman 102
Biggs, Simon J., and Peter W. Dowrick, eds. 360
Billig, Michael 228
Binstock, R. 202
Birbaumer, Niels, and H. D. Kimmel, eds. 299
Birch, D., and John William Atkinson 84

Birney, Robert Charles, and Richard C. Teevan 77
Birren, James E., and K. Warner Schaie, eds. 202
Black, Claudia 353
Blake, Judith 174
Blake, Robert R., and Robert Sekuler 48
Blakeslee, Sandra, and Judith S. Wallerstein 181, 200
Blalock, Hubert M., Jr. 18
Blanc, Michel H. A., and Josiane F. Hamers 160
Blehar, Mary C., and Norman E. Rosenthal 338
Blehar, Mary C., Mary D. Salter Ainsworth, Everett Waters, and S. Wall 174
Bleier, Ruth 188
Bleuler, Eugen 348
Bliss, Eugene L. 331
Block, J. Richard, and Harold Yuker 57
Bloom, Bernard L. 385
Bloom, Floyd E., and Arlyne Lazerson 31, 67, 295, 364
Bloomer, Carolyn M. 57
Bloomfield, Leonard 155
Blumstein, Philip W., and Pepper Schwartz 91
Boakes, Robert A. 3
Bock, Frances A., and Rose Oliver 345
Boden, Margaret A. 123
Boff, Kenneth R., Lloyd Kaufman, and James P. Thomas, eds. 134
Bohannon, John Neil, III, and Amye Warren-Leubecker 156
Bolles, Richard N. 263
Bolles, Robert C. 77, 107
Bolles, Robert C., and Michael D. Beecher, eds. 107
Bolton, Brian, ed. 49
Bootzin, Richard R., and Joan Ross Acocella 318, 331
Borbely, Alexander 140
Bordens, Kenneth S., and Bruce B. Abbott 11
Boren, Mary Carol Perrot Charles B. Ferster, and Charles B. Ferster 115
Boring, Edwin G., and Gardner Lindzey, eds. 77
Boring, Edwin Garrigues 4, 124
Born, Rainer, ed. 124

Bornstein, M. H.   57
Bornstein, Philip H., and Marcy T. Bornstein   372
Borson, Soo, and Ilene L. Bernstein   91
Boskind-White, Marlene, and William C. White, Jr.   325
Boss, Medard   141, 291
Bossio, Lisa M., and Christopher Peterson   315
Bottome, Phyllis   280
Botwinick, Jack   202
Bourne, Edmund   331
Bourne, Lyle E., Jr.   124
Bourne, Lyle E., Jr., Roger L. Dominowski, and Elizabeth Loftus   124
Bowe-Gutman, Sonia   188
Bowen, Murray   372
Bower, Robert T., and Priscilla de Gasparis   18
Bower, T. G. R.   68, 181-182
Bowers, Kenneth S.   134
Bowers, Malcolm B.   348
Bowlby, John   174
Boyce, Philip, and Gordon Parker   339
Bradford, Larry J., and William G. Hardy   50
Bradley, W.   344
Bradley-Johnson, Sharon, and Larry D. Evans   265
Bradshaw, D., P. Shaver, and C. Hazan   226
Bradshaw, John L., and Norman C. Nettleton   31
Brady, Joseph Vincent   311
Braginsky, Benjamin M., D. D. Braginsky, and Kenneth Ring   318
Brannon, Linda, and Jess Feist   312
Branscombe, Nyla R., and Daniel L. Wann   84
Bransford, John   147
Bransford, John D., and Barry S. Stein   110, 124
Brassard, Marla R., Robert Germain, and Stuart N. Hart, eds.   175
Braswell, Lauren, and Philip C. Kendall   327
Braveman, Norman S., and Paul Bronstein, eds.   107
Brazier, Mary A. B., and J. Allan Hobson, eds.   36

Breckler, Steven J., Anthony R. Pratkanis, and Anthony G. Greenwald, eds.   215
Breggin, Peter R.   364
Brehm, Jack Williams, and Arthur R. Cohen   213
Brehm, Jack Williams, and Robert A. Wicklund   216
Brehm, Sharon S.   223
Brehm, Sharon S., and Saul M. Kassin   68, 239
Breland, Keller, and Marian Breland   77
Brennan, James F.   4
Bresler, David E., and Richard Trubo   300
Breuer, Josef, and Sigmund Freud   331, 380
Brewer, Marilynn, and Norman Miller, eds.   232
Breznitz, Shlomo, and Leo Goldberger, eds.   302
Bridgeman, Bruce   45, 50, 57
Briggs, Stephen R., Warren H. Jones, and Jonathan M. Cheek   243
Bringmann, Wolfgang G., and Ryan D. Tweney, eds.   4
Brink, Terry L.   379
Brissett, Dennis, and Charles Edgley, eds.   239
British Journal of Social Psychology   228
Brodsky, Annette M., and Rachel T. Hare-Mustin   383
Broida, Helen   156
Brome, Vincent   280
Bronfenbrenner, Urie, and S. J. Ceci   147
Bronstein, Paul, and Norman S. Braveman, eds.   107
Brooks, James M., Eugene E. Levitt, and Bernard Lubin   342
Brooks, Jane   175
Brooks-Gunn, Jeanne, and Grace Baruch, eds.   194
Brooks-Gunn, Jeanne, and Wendy Schempp Matthews   175
Broome, Marion E., and Charlotte Koehler   182
Brower, Lincoln Pierson   107
Browman, C. P., A. Michael Anch, M. M. Mitler, and James K. Walsh   140

Brown, Alan G.   32
Brown, Barbara B.   300, 311
Brown, Bert R., and Jeffrey Z. Rubin   221
Brown, Charles H., Charles T. Snowdon, and Michael R. Petersen, eds.   100
Brown, Evan L., and Kenneth Deffenbacher   45
Brown, Fredda Herz, ed.   319
Brown, Frederick Gramm   251
Brown, Hedy   217
Brown, R.   228
Brown, Roger   124
Brown, Roger Langham   156
Brown, Roger William   156
Brown, Rupert   217
Brown, Rupert, and Miles Hewstone, eds.   230
Browning, Ronald A., Gerhard H. Fromm, Carl L. Faingold, and W. M. Burnham, eds.   34
Brubaker, Susan Howell   156
Bruch, Hilde   91, 325
Brugge, John F., and Dennis P. Phillips   54
Brumberg, Joan Jacobs   319, 325
Bruner, Jerome S.   156
Bruner, Jerome S., Jacqueline J. Goodnow, and George A. Austin   124
Bruning, Roger H., and John A. Glover   254
Brush, F. Robert, and J. Bruce Overmier, eds.   118
Bryant, Jennings, and Dolf Zillmann, eds.   212
Bryden, M. P.   32
Buck, Ross   68
Buddenbrock, Wolfgang von   45
Bugental, James F. T.   376
Bullitt, William C., and Sigmund Freud   283
Burgess, Anthony   113
Burgus, Roger, and Roger Guillemin   26
Burkhard, Barbara, and Michael Domjan   102, 118
Burkhardt, Dietrich, Wolfgang Schleidt, and Helmut Altner   45
Burnham, W. M., Gerhard H. Fromm, and Carl L. Faingold, and Ronald A. Browning, eds.   34
Burns, David D.   68, 240, 339, 368
Buros, Oscar Krisen, ed.   251, 263

Burr, David J., and Stephen J. Hanson   127
Bush, Robert P., Alan J. Bush, David J. Ortinau, and Joseph F. Hair, Jr.   263
Buss, Arnold   240
Butler, Charles, and Maureen Caudill   125
Butler, Robert N.   202
Butterfield, Earl C., Roy Lachman, and Janet L. Lachman   129, 149
Buxbaum, Edith   188
Byrne, Donn, and Robert A. Baron   228

Cacioppo, John T., and Richard E. Petty   215
Cain, John, David S. Janowsky, Robert N. Golden, Mark Rapaport, and J. Christian Gillian   28
Cambell, Linda E., and Janet R. Johnston   179
Campbell, Donald T., and Thomas D. Cook   15
Campbell, Donald Thomas, and Julian C. Stanley   15, 19
Campbell, D. T.   264
Campbell, John P., Edwin Ernest Ghiselli, and Sheldon Zedeck   253
Campbell, Joseph   281, 379
Campbell, J. P., and R. D. Pritchard   85
Campbell, Neil A.   32, 57
Campbell, Robin, and Roger Wales   157
Campbell, Susan B.   326
Campos, Joseph J., and Michael E. Lamb   179
Canetti, Elias   217
Cannon, Walter B.   295
Caplan, Gerald   386
Carey, Niall, and P. C. Constantinides   296
Carlisle, Jock Alan   326
Carlson, Neil R.   19, 25, 32, 91
Carlson, Vicki, and Dante Cicchetti, eds.   175
Carpenter, Patricia A., and Marcel Adam Just   161
Carr, Harvey A.   4
Carroll, John Bissell   157
Carter, John D., and Bruce Narramore   240
Cartlidge, Niall, David Chadwick, and David Bates   32

Cash, William B., Jr., and Charles J. Stewart 14

Catania, A. Charles 115

Caudill, Maureen, and Charles Butler 125

Ceci, S. J., and Urie Bronfenbrenner 147

Cermak, Timmen L. 353

Chadwick, David, Niall Cartlidge, and David Bates 32

Chafetz, Michael D. 91

Chambless, Dianne L., and Alan J. Goldstein, eds. 332

Chance, Paul 102

Changeux, Jean-Pierre 33

Chaplin, James Patrick, and T. S. Krawiec 4

Charlesworth, Edward A., and Ronald G. Nathan 296, 300

Chaves, John F., and Nicholas P. Spanos, eds. 139

Cheek, Jonathan, Warren H. Jones, and Stephen R. Briggs 243

Chemers, Martin M., and Fred E. Fiedler 218

Cheng, M. F., Barry R. Komisaruk, H. I. Siegel, and H. H. Feder, eds. 28, 93

Cherlin, Andrew J., and Frank F. Furstenberg, Jr. 202

Chesler, Phyllis 383

Chesney, Margaret A., and Ray H. Rosenman, eds. 311

Chomsky, Noam 111, 157

Chopra, Deepak 344

Christensen, Oscar, and Carroll Thomas 175

Christenson, C. V., P. H. Gebhard, W. B. Pomeroy, B. Wardell, J. H. Gagnon 351

Christianson, Sven-Åke, ed. 68

Cialdini, Robert B. 85, 213, 236, 240

Cialdini, Robert B., D. J. Baumann, and D. T. Kenrick 236

Cicchetti, Dante, and Vicki Carlson, eds. 175

Clanton, Gordon, and Lynn G. Smith, eds. 223

Clarfield, A. M. 344

Clark, Herbert H. 157

Clark, Herbert H., and Eve V. Clark 157

Clark, Judith Freeman, Robin E. Clark 176

Clark, L. V. 85

Clark, Lynn 372

Clark, Margaret S., ed. 236

Clark, Robin E., and Judith Freeman Clark 176

Cleckley, Hervey 346

Cocking, Rodney R., and Irving E. Sigel 173

Cofer, Charles Norval, and M. H. Appley 78

Cohen, Arthur R., and Jack Williams Brehm 213

Cohen, David B. 141

Cohen, R. J., P. Montague, L. S. Nathanson, and M. E. Swerdlik 269

Cohen, Ronald Jay, et al. 251

Cole, Thomas R., and Mary G. Winkler, eds. 203

Coleman, Mary, and Christopher Gillberg 326

Coleman, Richard M. 141

Coles, Robert 171, 176, 203, 281

Collins, Barry E., Charles A. Kiesler, and Norman Miller 214

Collins, Michael 158

Collins, W. Andrew, and S. A. Kuczaj II 69

Combs, Allen L., and Mark Holland 281

Committee on the Use of Animals in Research Staff of the National Academy of Sciences and the Institute of Medicine Staff 19

Committee to Develop Standards for Educational and Psychological Testing 264

Commons, Michael L., John A. Nevin, and Michael C. Davison, eds. 45

Connell, Elizabeth B. 25

Constantinides, P. C., and Niall Carey 296

Conture, Edward G. 326

Converse, Jean M., and Stanley Presser 11

Cook, Thomas D., and Donald T. Campbell 15

Cooley, Charles H. 240

Cooper, Arnold M., Allen J. Frances, and Michael H. Sacks, eds. 346

Cooper, Steven J., and Jeffrey M. Liebman, eds. 80

Coopersmith, Stanley   176, 240

Corballis, Michael C.   33

Corballis, Michael C., and Ivan L. Beale   33

Corbishley, M. Anne, and Elizabeth B. Yost   200

Corbit, J. D., and Richard L. Solomon   82

Corcoran, Kevin J., and Joel Fischer   269

Coren, Stanley   50

Coren, Stanley, and Joan Stern Girgus   57

Corey, Gerald   368

Corey, Gerald, and Marianne Schneider Corey   372

Cormier, William H., and L. Sherilyn Cormier   264

Cornelison, Alice R., Theodore Lidz, and Stephen Fleck   349

Corr, Charles A., Helen Fuller, Carol Ann Barnickol, and Donna M. Corr, eds.   182

Corsini, Raymond J., comp.   358

Costa, Paul T., and Salvatore R. Maddi   292

Cote, James E., and Charles Levine   188

Cotman, Carl W., and James L. McGaugh   26, 33

Cottle, William C.   264

Cotton, M. M., and N. J. Mackintosh   120

Cousins, Norman   69

Cowen, P. J., and D. G. Grahame-Smith, eds.   365

Cowles, M., and C. Davis   19

Cox, Harold   203

Cox, M., E. M. Hetherington, and R. Cox   178

Cox, Richard H.   85

Cox, Steven G., and Irving Jacks, eds.   211

Cox, Tom   296

Cox, W. Miles, ed.   353

Coyne, James C., ed.   339

Coyne, James C., and G. Downey   339

Coyne, James C., Allen D. Kanner, Catherine Shaefer, and Richard S. Lazarus   304

Coyne, J. C., C. Schaefer, and R. S. Lazarus   307

Cozby, Paul C.   12

Crago, Marjorie, and Larry E. Beutler, eds.   383

Crago, Marjorie, C. M. Shisslak, M. E. Neal, and B. Swain   329

Craig, Kenneth D., and Stephen M. Weiss, eds.   311

Craig, P. Erik   141

Craig, Robert L., ed.   85

Craik, Fergus I., and Robert S. Lockhart   147

Crain, William C.   111

Cramer, Stanley H., and Edwin L. Herr   266

Crandall, Rick, and Alvin Jones, eds.   292

Cratty, Bryant J.   85

Creighton, James, Carl Simonton, and Stephanie Matthews-Simonton   309

Crespi, Leo P.   78

Crews, David, ed.   92

Crick, Francis H. C.   125

Crisp, A. H.   92

Crockenberg, S. B.   176

Cronbach, Lee J.   16, 252, 264

Cronkite, Kathy   339

Crooks, Robert L., and Jean Stein   57, 92

Crouse, James, and Dale Trusheim   252

Crowder, Robert G.   147

Crowder, Robert G., and Mahzarin R. Banaji   146

Crowley, Richard J., and Joyce C. Mills   328

Crystal, David   158

Culbertson, Jan L., Henry F. Krous, and R. Debra Bendell, eds.   182

Culbertson, Stuart, Charles B. Ferster, and Mary Carol Perrot Boren   115

Cummins, Jim   158

Curlee, Richard F.   158

Curphy, Gordon J., Robert Hogan, and Joyce Hogan   219

Curtis, Helena   33, 203, 296

Damon, William   176

Dangel, Richard F., and Richard A. Polster   372

Daniloff, Raymond, Gordon Schuckers, and Lawrence Feth   50

Darley, John M., and Bib Latané 237
Darley, John M., Samuel Glucksberg, and Ronald A. Kinchla 203, 264
Darnell, James E., Harvey F. Lodish, and David Baltimore 34
Darrow, Charlotte, Daniel J. Levinson, Edward Klein, Maria Levinson, and Braxton McKee 198
Darwin, Charles 69
Daugherty, Charles, and Linda Maxson 62
Daves, Charles W., ed. 252
Davey, G. C., and I. McKenna 118
David, Edward E., Jr., Willem André Maria Van Bergeijk, and John R. Pierce 56
Davies, D. R., and R. Parasuraman, eds. 137
Davies, N. B., and J. R. Krebs 99
Davis, C., and M. Cowles 19
Davis, Christopher M., Robert Morris Stern, and William J. Ray 268
Davis, Gary A., and Sylvia B. Rimm 252
Davis, James H. 217
Davis, John M., David S. Janowsky, M. Khaled El-Yousef, and H. Joseph Sekerke 27
Davison, G. C., and J. M. Neale 376
Davison, Gerald C., and John M. Neale 332
Davison, Gerald C., and Marvin R. Goldfried 361
Davison, Michael C., Michael L. Commons, and John A. Nevin, eds. 45
Dawes, Robyn M. 125
Dawson, Geraldine, ed. 326
Dawson, Geraldine, Mary E. Van Bourgondien, and Gary B. Mesibov 330
Deaux, Kay, and M. E. Kite 228
DeCharms, Richard 86
Deci, E. L. 86
Deci, E. L., and R. M. Ryan 240
Deffenbacher, Kenneth, and Evan L. Brown 45
Defrain, John D., Jacque Taylor, and Linda Ernst 182
Delaney, Gayle 141
Dell, G., Gail McKoon, and R. Ratcliff 150

Delprato, D. J., and F. D. McGlynn 332
Dembroski, T. M., J. M. MacDougall, J. A. Herd, and J. L. Shields 311
Dement, William C. 141
Dement, William C., Meir H. Kryger, and Thomas Roth, eds. 143
Demers, Richard A., Adrian Akmajian, Ann K. Farmer, and Robert M. Harnish 155
Demick, J., and S. Wapner 316
Dennett, Daniel C. 134
Denton, Derek A. 92
De Rivera, Joseph, comp. 275
Derlega, Valerian J., and Janusz Grzelak, eds. 236
Deutsch, Diana, ed. 50
Deutsch, Diana, and J. Anthony Deutsch, eds. 147
Deutsch, Georg, and Sally P. Springer 42
Deutsch, Morton, Claire Selltiz, Marie Johoda, and S. Cook 14
De Valois, Russell L., and Karen K. De Valois 58
De Villiers, Peter A., and Jill G. de Villiers 158
DeVitis, Joseph L., and John Martin Rich 173
DeVito, Joseph A., and Michael L. Hecht, eds. 158
Diaz, R. M. 159
Dickinson, John 50
DiLorenzo, Thomas M., and Johnny L. Matson 362
Dimberg, Ulf, Arne Öhman, and Lars-Göran Öst 108
Dinkmeyer, Don C., and W. L. Pew 379
Dinsmoor, J. 113
Dobson, Clifford B. 312
Docherty John P., Marvin I. Herz, and Samuel J. Keith 348
Dodds, J. B. 376
Doise, Willem 229
Dollard, John, et al. 275
Dollard, John, and Neal E. Miller 275, 319
Dollard, John, Leonard W. Doob, Neal E. Miller, O. Hobart Mowrer, and Robert R. Sears 86
Dominowski, Roger L., Lyle E. Bourne, and Elizabeth Loftus 124

Domjan, Michael, and Barbara
Burkhard 102, 118
Donigian, Jeremiah, and Richard
Malnati 372
Donnerstein, Edward I., Daniel Linz,
and Steven Penrod 210
Donovan, Bernard T. 26
Donovan, Bernard T., and Joseph
Meites, and Samuel M. McCann,
eds. 29
Donovan, Steven, and Michael
Murphy 137
Doob, Leonard W., John Dollard, Neal
E. Miller, O. Hobart Mowrer, and
Robert R. Sears 86
Douglas, Jack D., and Freda Cruse
Atwell 194
Dovidio, John F., and Samuel L.
Gaertner, eds. 229
Dovidio, John F., Jane Allyn Piliavin,
Samuel L. Gaertner, and Russell
Clark 237
Downey, G., and James C. Coyne
339
Downs, Roger M., and David Stea,
eds. 125
Dowrick, Peter W., and Simon J. Biggs,
eds. 360
Dreikurs, Rudolf 281, 380
Drickamer, Lee C., and Stephen H.
Vessey 98
Driscoll, Marcy Perkins, and Robert
Mills Gagné 103
Duck, Steve 223-224
Duck, Steve, and Robin Gilmour, eds.
224
Dudycha, Arthur L., and Linda W.
Dudycha 12
Duffy, Karen Grover, James W. Grosch,
and Paul V. Olczak, eds. 218
Dunn, Judy 176
Dunnette, Marvin D. 194
Durham, Ross M. 34
Durkheim, Émile 340
Dusay, J., and K. Dusay 369
Duska, Ronald F., and Mariellen
Whelan 171
Dutton-Douglas, Mary Ann, and Lenore
E. A. Walker 383
Dworetsky, John P. 183
D'Zurilla, Thomas J., and Arthur M.
Nezu 125

Eccles, John Carew, and Daniel N.
Robinson 126, 134
Eckert, E. D., and J. E. Mitchell 328
Edgley, Charles, and Dennis Brissett,
eds. 239
Edwards, Allen Louis 16
Egeth, Howard, Michael McCloskey,
and Judith McKenna 150
Ehrenwald, Jan 358
Ehrhardt, Anke A., and John Money
29
Eibl-Eibesfeldt, Irenaus 69
Eimas, Peter D. 51
Eisenberg, Howard M., Harvey S.
Levin, and Jordan Grafman 37
Eisenberg, Nancy, and Janet Strayer,
eds. 237
Eisenberg-Berg, Nancy, and Paul Henry
Mussen 180
Eisenman, Russell 177, 188
Eiser, J. Richard 241
Ekman, Paul 69
Ekman, Paul, Wallace Friesen, and
Phoebe Ellsworth 70
Elkind, David 189, 194
Ellenberger, Henri F. 358
Ellenberger, Henri F., Rollo May, and
Ernest Angel, eds. 293, 377
Elliott, Glen R., and Shirley S. Feldman,
eds. 189
Ellis, Albert 369
Ellis, Albert, and Robert A. Harper 369
Ellis, Albert, and Russell Grieger 369
Ellis, Andrew W., and Andrew W.
Young 34
Ellis, Henry C., and R. Reed Hunt 147
Ellis, Thomas E., William J. Fremouw,
and Maria de Perczel 340
Ellsworth, Phoebe C., David J.
Schneider, and Albert H. Hastorf
88, 247
Ellsworth, Phoebe, Paul Ekman, and
Wallace Friesen 70
Elmes, David G., Barry H. Kantowitz,
and Henry L. Roediger III 16
Elton, Diana, Gordon Stanley, and
Graham Burrows 300
El-Yousef, M. Khaled, David S.
Janowsky, John M. Davis, and H.
Joseph Sekerke 27
Emde, Robert N., T. J. Gaensbauer, and
R. J. Harmon 70

Emery, Gary, Aaron T. Beck, A. J. Rush, and B. F. Shaw 368
Emery, Gary, and Aaron T. Beck 318, 331, 368
Emery, Gary, Steven D. Hollom, and Richard C. Bedrosian, eds. 369
Emmelkamp, Paul M. G. 332
Endler, N. S., and E. Persad 364
Engler, Barbara 380
Enright, Simon J., and Trevor J. Powell 307
Epstein, William, ed. 58
Ericsson, K. A., and H. A. Simon 58
Erikson, Erik H. 177, 189, 194-195, 203-204, 281
Erikson, Erik H., Joan M. Erikson, and Helen Q. Kivnick 204
Ernst, Linda, John D. Defrain, and Jacque Taylor 182
Eskelson, Cleamond D. 354
Estes, W. K. 102
Ettinger, R. H., and J. E. R. Staddon 114
Evans, Jonathan St. B. T. 126
Evans, Larry D., and Sharon Bradley-Johnson 265
Evans, Phil 78
Evans, Rand B., and Robert Irving Watson, Sr. 10
Evans, Richard I. 195, 275, 281, 291, 319
Everly, G. S., Jr., and D. A. Girdano 302
Ewing, Susan Adair, and Beth Pfalzgraf 159
Eysenck, Hans J. 78, 272
Eysenck, Michael W. 126

Faden, Ruth R., Tom L. Beauchamp, R. Jay Wallace, Jr., and Le Roy Walters, eds. 18
Fagan, Joen, and Irma Lee Shepherd, eds. 370
Faingold, Carl L., Gerhard H. Fromm, Ronald A. Browning, and W. M. Burnham, eds. 34
Fairchild, H. H., Amado M. Padilla, and C. M. Valadez, eds. 164
Falkner, Frank, and J. M. Tanner 183
Falloon, Ian R. H., ed. 373
Fancher, Raymond E. 4, 252

Farberow, Norman L., Edwin S. Shneidman, and Robert E. Litman 344
Farberow, Norman L., Michael L. Peck, and Robert E. Litman, eds. 193, 343
Farmer, Ann K. Adrian Akmajian, Richard A. Demers, and Robert M. Harnish 155
Farrell, Michael P., and Stanley D. Rosenberg 195
Faust-Campanile, Jan, C. Eugene Walker, and Mary Kenning 330
Fazio, Russell 213, 241
Fazio, Russell, and Mark P. Zanna 214
Feder, H. H., Barry R. Komisaruk, H. I. Siegel, and M. F. Cheng, eds. 28, 93
Feifel, Herman, ed. 204
Feingold, S. Norman, and Norma Reno Miller 196
Feirtag, Michael, and Walle Nauta 39
Feist, Jess, and Linda Brannon 312
Feldman, Alan S., and Charles T. Grimes, eds. 51
Feldman, David Henry, with Lynn T. Goldsmith 253
Feldman, Robert S. 58, 92
Feldman, Robert Simon, and Linda F. Quenzer 34
Feldman, S. Shirley, and Glen R. Elliott, eds. 189
Felner, Robert David, et al., eds. 386
Fenwick, Ian, and John A. Quelch, eds. 126
Ferguson, Tom, and Karen Johnson 384
Ferl, Robert J., Robert A. Wallace, and Gerald P. Sanders 31, 109
Ferraro, Douglas P., Frank A. Logan 80
Ferraro, Kenneth F. 205
Ferster, Charles B., and B. F. Skinner 115
Ferster, Charles B., Stuart Culbertson, and Mary Carol Perrot Boren 115
Festinger, Leon 214
Festinger, Leon, Stanley Schachter, and Kurt Back 224
Feth, Lawrence, Raymond Daniloff, and Gordon Schuckers 50
Feuerstein, Michael, Elise E. Labbe, and Andrezej R. Kuczmiercsyk 312
Fichtelius, Karl Erik, and Sverre Sjolander 98

Fiedler, Fred E., and Martin M. Chemers 218
Fieve, Ronald R. 340
Figley, Charles R., ed. 300, 332
Figley, Charles R., and Seymour Leventman, eds. 332
Fink, Max 364
Finkelhor, David 177
Fischer, Claude S. 300
Fischer, Joel, and Kevin J. Corcoran 269
Fischhoff, Baruch, and Ruth Beyth-Marom 241
Fischhoff, Baruch, Paul Slovic, and Sarah Lichtenstein 132
Fishbein, Martin, and Icek Ajzen 213
Fishbein, Sanford, Gregory L. White, and Jeffrey Rustein 248
Fisher, Arthur 78
Fisher, J. D., P. A. Bell, A. Baum, and T. E. Greene 299
Fisher, Leslie E., and Benjamin Wallace 139
Fisher, Roger, and William Ury 218
Fiske, Susan T., and Shelley E. Taylor 70, 147, 241
Fitch, James L. 159
Fitzgerald, Hiram E., et al. 183
Flaherty, Charles F. 113
Flanagan, Owen J., Jr. 127, 135
Flavell, John 171, 189
Fleck, Stephen, Theodore Lidz, and Alice R. Cornelison 349
Fleishman, Joseph J., Sylvester Kohut, Jr., and Jeraldine J. Kohut 206
Fletcher, G. J. O., and M. Ross 246
Foa, E. B., M. J. Kozak, and P. R. McCarthy 335
Foa, Edna B., G. S. Steketee, and L. M. Ascher 360
Fodor, Jerry A. 51
Fogarty, Pat 265
Fogel, Alan 183
Folkman, Susan, and Richard S. Lazarus 305
Folkman, Susan, Charles E. Schaefer, and Richard S. Lazarus 301
Fontana, David, Michael J. Apter, and Stephen J. Murgatroyd 77
Forgatch, Marion S., and Gerald R. Patterson 192
Forsyth, Donalson R. 218

Forsyth, Elizabeth Held, and Margaret O. Hyde 190
Foss, Donald J., and David T. Hakes 159
Foster, Daniel W., and Jean D. Wilson 298
Foster, Sharon L., and Arthur L. Robin 375
Foulkes, William David 282
Fox, Michael Allen 19
Fox, Robin, and Jacques Mehler, eds. 62
Fox, Stuart I. 26
Fox, Stuart Ira, and Kent Marshall Van De Graaff 43
Frances, Allen J., Arnold M. Cooper, and Michael H. Sacks, eds. 346
Francis, Greta, and Thomas H. Ollendick 267
Frank, Jerome David 383
Franken, Robert E. 78
Frankl, Viktor Emil 291, 319-320
Franks, Violet, and Esther D. Rothblum, eds. 320
Fransella, Fay, and Donald Bannister 275
Freedman, J. L. 301
Freeman, Derek 190
Freeman, Howard E., and Norman R. Kurtz, eds. 229
Freeman, Lucy 380
Freeman, Walter Jackson, and James Winston Watts 365
Fremouw, William J., Maria de Perczel, and Thomas E. Ellis 340
Freud, Anna 282
Freud, Sigmund 78, 86, 142, 282-283, 320, 333
Freud, Sigmund, and Josef Breuer 331, 380
Freud, Sigmund, and William C. Bullitt 283
Friedberg, John 365
Friedman, Meyer, and Diane Ulmer 301, 312
Friedman, Meyer, and Ray H. Rosenman 312
Friedman, Myra 190
Friel, John 354
Friesen, Wallace, Paul Ekman, and Phoebe Ellsworth 70
Frijda, Nico H. 70

Frisbie, G. R.   265

Frolov, Y. P.   118

Fromkin, Victoria, and Robert Rodman   159

Fromm, Erich   224, 284

Fromm, Gerhard H., Carl L. Faingold, Ronald A. Browning, and W. M. Burnham, eds.   34

Fudge, E. C.   159

Fuller, Charles A., Martin C. Moore-Ede, and Frank M. Sulzman   144

Fuller, Helen, Charles A. Corr, Carol Ann Barnickol, and Donna M. Corr, eds.   182

Fuller, M. G., and V. L. Goetsch   301

Fulton, John Farquhar   365

Furstenberg, Frank F., Jr., and Andrew J. Cherlin   202

Gackenbach, Jayne, Harry Hunt, and Charles N. Alexander, eds.   135

Gaensbauer, T. J., Robert N. Emde, and R. J. Harmon   70

Gaertner, Samuel, and John F. Dovidio, eds.   229

Gaertner, Samuel L., Jane Allyn Piliavin, John F. Dovidio, and Russell Clark   237

Gagné, Robert Mills, and Marcy Perkins Driscoll   103

Gagnon, J. H., P. H. Gebhard, W. B. Pomeroy, B. Wardell, and C. V. Christenson   351

Gaines, Stanley O., Jr., and Edward S. Reed   229

Gaist, Paul A., Siegfried Kasper, Thomas A. Wehr, John J. Bartko, and Norman E. Rosenthal   341

Galanter, Marc   218

Gallahue, D. L.   183

Gantt, W. Horsley   119

Garbarino, James, and Gwen Gilliam   177

Garbin, Margery G., Aaron T. Beck, and Robert A. Steer   263

Garcia, John, and Carl R. Gustavson   107

Gardner, Howard   34, 127, 253

Gardner, R. Allen, and Beatrice Gardner   160

Garfield, Sol L.   383

Garfield, Sol L., and Allen E. Bergin, eds.   360, 384

Garner, Wendell R., and Alexandra K. Wigdor, eds.   261

Garrett, Henry Edward, and Matthew R. Schneck   253

Garvey, Michael J., Robert Wesner, and Michael Godes   340

Gaskell, George, and Robert Benewick, eds.   218

Gasparis, Priscilla de, and Robert T. Bower   18

Gatchel, Robert J., Andrew Baum, and David S. Krantz   312

Gay, Peter   284

Gazzaniga, Michael S.   135

Gebhard, P. H., W. B. Pomeroy, B. Wardell, J. H. Gagnon, and C. V. Christenson   351

Geen, Russell G.   79, 211, 301

Geen, Russell G., William W. Beatty, and Robert M. Arkin   301

Geist, Harold   205

Geldard, Frank Arthur   46

Gelder, Michael G., Andrew M. Mathews, and Derek W. Johnston   335

Gelfand, Donald E.   205

Gelles, Richard J., Murray Arnold Straus, and Suzanne K. Steinmetz   181

Gelman, Rochel, and R. Baillargeon   171

Gennarelli, T. A., and A. K. Ommaya   39

George, F. H.   127

Gerbner, George, and Nancy Signorelli, comps.   212

Gergen, Kenneth J.   241

Germain, Robert, Marla R. Brassard, and Stuart N. Hart, eds.   175

Geschieder, George A.   46

Geschwind, Norman   35

Getting, Peter A.   35

Ghiselli, Edwin Ernest, John P. Campbell, and Sheldon Zedeck   253

Gibbon, M., Robert L. Spitzer, A. E. Skodol, J. B. W. Williams, and Michael First   270

Gibson, Elenor J., and Richard D. Walk   65

Gibson, James Jerome 58
Giere, Ronald N. 20
Gifford, Robert 214
Gigerenzer, Gerd, et al. 20
Gigerenzer, Gerd, and David J. Murray 20
Gilgen, Albert R. 4-5
Gilliam, Gwen, and James Garbarino 177
Gillian, J. Christian, David S. Janowsky, Robert N. Golden, Mark Rapaport, and John Cain 28
Gilligan, Carol 196
Gilman, Alfred G., et al., eds. 365
Gilmour, Robin, and Steve Duck, eds. 224
Ginsberg, Herbert, and Sylvia Opper 190
Giorgi, Amedeo 5
Girdano, D. A., and G. S. Everly, Jr. 302
Girgus, Joan Stern, and Stanley Coren 57
Girodo, Michel 242
Glass, A. L., and K. J. Holyoak 127
Glass, Gene V., and Mary Lee Smith 385
Glass, Gene V., Mary Lee Smith, and Thomas I. Miller 385
Glasser, Naomi, ed. 370
Glasser, William 370
Glauber, I. Peter 326
Gleitman, Lila R. 160
Glenn, H. Stephen, and Jane Nelsen 177
Glover, John A. 253
Glover, John A., and Roger H. Bruning 254
Glover, John A., Royce R. Ronning, and Cecil R. Reynolds, eds. 254
Gluck, J. P., and A. J. Beauchamp 12
Glucksberg, Samuel, John M. Darley, and Ronald A. Kinchla 203, 264
Glueck, Sheldon, and Eleanor Glueck 190
Gobble, Eva Marie R., and Mark Ylvisaker, eds. 44
Goble, Frank G. 291
Godes, Michael, Michael J. Garvey, and Robert Wesner 340
Goedeking, Philipp, Dietmar Todt, and David Symmes, eds. 101

Goethals, George R., and Brian Mullen, eds. 220
Goetsch, V. L., and M. G. Fuller 301
Goffman, Erving 242
Gold, Mark S. 320, 333
Goldberg, Dick 196
Goldberg, Herb, and George R. Bach 210
Goldberg, Jeff 35
Goldberg, Philip 302
Goldberger, Leo, and Shlomo Breznitz, eds. 302
Golden, Robert N., David S. Janowsky, Mark Rapaport, John Cain, and J. Christian Gillian 28
Goldenberg, Irene, and Herbert Goldenberg 373
Goldfried, Marvin R. 265, 360
Goldfried, Marvin R., and Gerald C. Davison 361
Golding, S. L., and R. Roesch 320
Goldman, George D., and Donald S. Milman, eds. 380
Goldsby, Richard 254
Goldsmith, Lynn T., and David Henry Feldman 253
Goldstein, Alan J., and Dianne L. Chambless, eds. 332
Goldstein, E. Bruce 46, 58
Goldstein, Eda G. 346
Goldstein, Martin, and Inge F. Goldstein 20
Goliszek, Andrew G. 296, 302
Gollin, Eugene S., ed. 169
Good, Byron, and Arthur Kleinman 342
Goodall, Jane 98
Goodenough, Ursula 205
Goodnow, Jacqueline J., Jerome S. Bruner, and George A. Austin 124
Goodwin, Donald W., and Samuel B. Guze 333
Goodwin, Frederick K., and Kay Redfield Jamison 340
Gordon, Malcolm S., George A. Bartholomew, et al. 98
Gordon, Thomas 361, 373
Gordon, W. J. 254
Gorsuch, Richard L. 242
Gorsuch, Richard L., Bernard Spilka, and Ralph W. Hood 248
Gottesman, Irving I. 321, 348

Gottesman, Irving I., James Shields, and Daniel R. Hanson 348
Gottleib, Gilbert, ed. 35
Gottlieb, Gilbert, and Norman Krasnegor, eds. 183
Gottman, John M., et al. 373
Gould, James L. 98
Gould, Stephen Jay 254, 269, 302
Goulding, Mary McClure, and Robert L. Goulding 371
Grafman, Jordan, Harvey S. Levin, and Howard M. Eisenberg 37
Graham, Clarence Henry 59
Graham, John Robert, and Roy S. Lilly 254, 265
Graham, Kenneth G., and H. Alan Robinson 148
Graham, Loren R. 119
Graham, Robert B. 26, 51, 148
Grahame-Smith, D. G., and P. J. Cowen, eds. 365
Granrud, C. E., ed. 59
Granrud, C. E., and A. Yonas 66
Gravetter, Frederick J., and Larry B. Wallnau 16
Gray, Henry 35
Gray, J. D., and R. C. Silver 196
Gray, Jeffrey A. 119, 296
Greaves, G. B. 334
Green, David M., and John C. Middlebrooks 54
Green, David Martin, and John A. Swets 46
Green, Judith Alyce, and Robert Shellenberger 312
Green, Michael 196
Greenberg, Jerrold S. 302
Greene, David, and M. R. Lepper, eds. 244
Greene, T. E., P. A. Bell, J. D. Fisher, and A. Baum 299
Greenspan, Miriam 376
Greenwald, Anthony G., Anthony R. Pratkanis, and Steven J. Breckler, eds. 215
Greenwald, Harold, ed. 284
Greenwood, Charles R., Terry Rose, and Frank R. Rusch 363
Gregg, Vernon H. 148
Gregory, Richard Langton 35, 46, 59
Greist, John H., and James W. Jefferson 341

Grieger, Russell, and Albert Ellis 369
Grier, James W. 99, 103
Griffin, Donald Redfield 99
Griffin, John Howard 12, 229
Grimes, Charles T., and Alan S. Feldman, eds. 51
Grinker, Roy Richard, and John P. Spiegel 302, 334
Groebel, Jo, and Robert A. Hinde, eds. 86, 211, 237
Grosch, James W., Karen Grover Duffy, and Paul V. Olczak, eds. 218
Grosjean, François 160
Gross, Charles G., and H. Philip Zeigler, eds. 36
Gross, Francis L., Jr. 205
Gross, Larry P., and Stanley Schachter 95
Gross, Nancy E. 303
Gross, Steven C., W. Lynn Smith, and Harold Merskey 309
Groth-Marnat, Gary 254, 265
Grzelak, Janusz, and Valerian J. Derlega, eds. 236
Guilford, Joy Paul 255
Guillemin, Roger, and Roger Burgus 26
Gulick, W. Lawrence 51
Gur, Ruben C., Harold A. Sackheim, and Johanna W. Nordlie 336
Gurman, A. S. 373
Gurman, A. S., and D. P. Kniskern 373
Gurman, A. S., and Neil S. Jacobson 374
Gustavson, Carl R., and John Garcia 107
Guthrie, Robert V. 255
Guyton, Arthur C. 52, 59
Guze, Samuel B., and Donald W. Goodwin 333
Guzzo, Richard A., ed. 219

Haber, Audrey, and Richard P. Runyon 23
Hager, Joanne L., and Martin E. Seligman, eds. 109
Hailman, Jack P., and Peter H. Klopfer 99
Hair, Joseph F., Jr., Robert P. Bush, and David J. Ortinau 263
Haith, Marshall M. 60
Hakes, David T., and Donald J. Foss 159

Hakuta, Kenji 160
Halaris, Angelos 142
Halberg, Franz, and Andrew Ahlgren 140
Haley, Jay 374
Hall, Calvin Springer, and Gardner Lindzey 79, 272, 275, 380
Hall, Calvin Springer, and Robert L. Van de Castle 142
Hall, Calvin Springer, and Vernon J. Nordby 380
Hall, David, Elizabeth Loftus, and James Tousignant 148
Hall, Douglas T. 197
Hall, Edward Twitchell 46, 86, 219
Hall, Robert Anderson 160
Halliday, T. R., and P. J. Slater 99
Halling, Steen, and Ronald S. Valle, eds. 9, 294
Halpern, Diane F. 127
Ham, Richard J., and Taher Zandi, eds. 345
Hamers, Josiane F., and Michel H. A. Blanc 160
Hamilton, David L., ed. 230
Hamilton, Leonard W., and C. Robin Timmons 52, 114
Hamilton, William J., III, and Peter Marler 100
Hammersmith, Sue Kiefer, Alan P. Bell, and Martin S. Weinberg 90
Hammond, Peter B. 87
Hampden-Turner, Charles 272
Handleman, Jan S., and Michael D. Powers 328
Hann, Della M., and Howard J. Osofsky 178
Hanna, Judith Lynne 303
Hannah, Barbara 285, 381
Hanson, Stephen J., and David J. Burr 127
Hardy, William G., and Larry J. Bradford 50
Hare, Robert D. 346
Hare, Robert D., and Daisy Schalling, eds. 346
Hare-Mustin, Rachel T., and Jeanne Marecek 171
Hare-Mustin, Rachel T., and Annette M. Brodsky 383
Harmon, R. J., Robert N. Emde, and T. J. Gaensbauer 70

Harnish, Robert M., Adrian Akmajian, Richard A. Demers, and Ann K. Farmer 155
Harper, Lawrence V. 183
Harper, Robert A., and Albert Ellis 369
Harper, Robert Gale, Arthur N. Wiens, and Joseph D. Matarazzo 161
Harris, Anne, and Paul Karoly 361
Harris, Judith Rich, and Robert M. Liebert 178, 184
Hart, Stuart N., Marla R. Brassard, and Robert Germain, eds. 175
Hartstein, Jack, ed. 161
Harvey, J. H., and G. Weary 242
Harvey, J. H., W. J. Ickes, and F. F. Kidd, eds. 79
Harvey, John H., Ann L. Weber, and Terri L. Orbuch 224
Hasher, Lynn, and Joseph W. Alba 145
Haslam, Michael Trevor 351
Hastie, Reid 219
Hastie, Reid, Steven D. Penrod, and Nancy Pennington 242
Hastorf, Albert H., David J. Schneider, and Phoebe C. Ellsworth 88, 247
Hatfield, Elaine, and Susan Sprecher 224
Haugeland, John 128
Hawton, Keith 340
Hayes, Brett, and Beryl Hesketh 242
Hayes, John R. 128, 148
Hayes, Steven C., ed. 115
Hayslett, H. T., Jr. 20
Hayslip, Bert, Jr., and Paul E. Panek 205
Hazan, C., P. Shaver, and D. Bradshaw 226
Hearst, Eliot, ed. 5
Hebb, Donald Olding 103
Hecht, Michael L., Joseph A. DeVito, eds. 158
Heidbreder, Edna 5
Heider, Fritz 243
Heiman, Julia R., Joseph LoPiccolo, and Leslie LoPiccolo 351
Heller, Kenneth, et al. 386
Hellriegel, Don, John W. Slocum, Jr., and Richard W. Woodman 79
Helmchen, Hanfried, and Fritz A. Henn, eds. 348
Hendrick, Clyde, and Susan Hendrick 225

Henley, Nancy, and Barrie Thorne, and
  Cheris Kramarae 235
Henley, Nancy M. 161
Henn, Fritz A., and Hanfried Helmchen,
  eds. 348
Henry, Gary T. 20
Henry, Rebecca A., and Janet A.
  Sniezek 222
Henry, Sarah, Richard R. Reilly, and
  James W. Smither 267
Herd, J. A., T. M. Dembroski, J. M.
  MacDougall, and J. L. Shields 311
Hergenhahn, B. R. 103, 119
Herman, C. Peter, Mark P. Zanna, and
  E. Tory Higgins, eds. 216
Heron, A., and H. C. Triandis, eds. 170
Herr, Edwin L., and Stanley H. Cramer
  266
Herrnstein, Richard J. 104
Herrnstein, Richard J., and Charles
  Murray 255
Hersen, Michel, and Alan S. Bellack
  360
Hershman, D. Jablow, and Julian Lieb
  340
Herz, Marvin I., Samuel J. Keith, and
  John P. Docherty 348
Herzberg, Frederick 87
Hesketh, Beryl, and Brett Hayes 242
Hess, Allen K., and Irving B. Weiner,
  eds. 323
Heston, Leonard L. 341
Hetherington, E. M., M. Cox, and
  R. Cox 178
Hewstone, Miles, and Rupert Brown,
  eds. 230
Hickson, Mark L., and Don W. Stacks
  161
Higbee, Kenneth L. 148
Higgins, E. Tory, Mark P. Zanna, and
  C. Peter Herman, eds. 216
Higgins, Raymond L., C. R. Snyder, and
  Rita J. Stucky 247
Highnam, Kenneth Charles, and
  Leonard Hill 26
Hilgard, Ernest Ropiequet 5, 79, 119,
  135, 255
Hilgard, Ernest Ropiequet, and
  Josephine Rohrs Hilgard 135
Hilgard, Josephine Rohrs 135
Hill, Leonard, and Kenneth Charles
  Highnam 26

Hilliard, Asa G., III 255
Hillman, James 142
Hinde, Robert A., and Jo Groebel, eds.
  86, 211, 237
Hinton, Geoffrey E., David E.
  Rumelhart, P. Smolensky, and
  James L. McClelland 152
Hirschmann, Jane R., and Carol H.
  Munter 92
Hobson, J. Allan 142
Hobson, J. Allan, and Mary A. B.
  Brazier, eds. 36
Hochberg, Julian E. 60
Hofer, Myron A. 184
Hoffmann, Banesh 256
Hogan, Robert, Gordon J. Curphy, and
  Joyce Hogan 219
Hogg, Michael A., and Dominic
  Abrams 219
Hogg, Michael A., John C. Turner,
  et al. 222
Holahan, Charles J. 219
Hole, John 27
Holinger, Paul C., and J. Sandlow 341
Holland, J. L. 266
Holland, John H., et al. 128
Hollom, Steven D., Gary Emery, and
  Richard C. Bedrosian, eds. 369
Holmes, Clarissa S., ed. 27
Holmes, David S. 321
Holmes, R. L., and J. N. Ball 27
Holmes, Thomas H., and Minoru
  Masuda 313
Holmes, Thomas H., and Richard H.
  Rahe 303
Holyoak, K. J., and A. L. Glass 127
Honess, Terry, and Krysia Yardley, eds.
  249
Hood, Ralph W., Bernard Spilka, and
  Richard L. Gorsuch 248
Hopkins, Roy, Ludy T. Benjamin, and
  Jack R. Nation 123
Horney, Karen 285-286
Horowitz, Mardi Jon 334
Houston, B. Kent, and C. R. Snyder,
  eds. 313
Houts, Arthur C., and Hillel Abramson
  327
Houts, Arthur C., and Richard M.
  Liebert 327
Houts, Arthur C., Leonard Krasner, and
  Leonard P. Ullmann 321

Hovland, Carl Iver, Irving L. Janis, and Harold H. Kelley 214
Howell, David C. 21
Hrdina, Pavel D., and Radhey L. Singhal, eds. 27
Hubel, David H. 60
Hubel, David H., and Torsten N. Wiesel 60
Huber, Ernst, and Richard John Andrew 67
Hucho, Ferdinand 36
Huesmann, L. Rowell, and Neil M. Malamuth 211
Huffman, Karen, et al. 128
Hughes, Fergus, and Lloyd Noppe 178
Hughes, Jennifer 70
Hughes, Joan C., Dorothy T. Krieger, eds. 28
Hull, Clark Leonard 79
Humes, Larry E., and Fred H. Bess 49
Humphreys, G. W., and M. J. Riddoch 60
Hunt, Earl B. 128
Hunt, Harry, Jayne Gackenbach, and Charles N. Alexander, eds. 135
Hunt, Morton M. 6, 128
Hunt, R. Reed, and Henry C. Ellis 147
Hunt, Richard A., and Morton King 243
Hunter, Mic, ed. 190
Huston, A. C. 178
Huston, Ted L., ed. 225
Hutchison, John Bower, ed. 92
Hyde, Janet Shibley 172
Hyde, Janet Shibley, and Marcia C. Linn, eds. 172
Hyde, Margaret O., and Elizabeth Held Forsyth 190

Ickes, W. J., J. H. Harvey, and F. F. Kidd, eds. 79
Ilgen, Daniel R., and Ernest James McCormick 198
Ilgen, Daniel R., James C. Naylor, and Robert D. Pritchard 81
Insel, Paul, and Henry Clay Lindgren 220
International Research Conference on the Sudden Infant Death Syndrome 184
Isaacs, L. D., and V. G. Payne 185
Ishaq, Waris, ed. 6

Issa, Faiq G., Paul M. Surrat, and John E. Remmers, eds. 143
Ittelson, William H., and Harold M. Proshansky, and Leanne G. Rivlin, eds. 215
Ivey, Allen E., and Lynn Simek-Downing 376
Izard, Carroll E. 70-71
Izard, Carroll E., Michael Rutter, and Peter B. Read, eds. 343

Jacklin, Carol 172
Jacklin, Carol Nagy, and Eleanor E. Maccoby 172
Jacks, Irving, and Steven G. Cox, eds. 211
Jackson, John H., and Robert L. Mathis 199
Jacob, Rolf G., and Samuel M. Turner 334
Jacobsen, Frederick M., Thomas A. Wehr, Robert A. Skwerer, David A. Sack, and Norman E. Rosenthal 341
Jacobson, Edmund 136, 303
Jacobson, Neil S., and A. S. Gurman 374
Jacobson, Neil S., and Gayla Margolin 374
Jacoby, Jacob, and Jerry C. Olson, eds. 214
Jaffe, Jerome H. 354
Jahoda, Marie 321
James, Muriel, and Dorothy Jongeward 371
James, William 6, 71, 136
Jamison, Kay Redfield, and Frederick K. Goodwin 340
Jandt, Fred Edmund 220
Janet, Pierre 358
Janis, Irving L., Carl Iver Hovland, and Harold H. Kelley 214
Janis, Irving Lester 220, 313
Janov, Arthur 36
Janowsky, David S., M. Khaled El-Yousef, John M. Davis, and H. Joseph Sekerke 27
Janowsky, David S., Robert N. Golden, Mark Rapaport, John Cain, and J. Christian Gillian 28
Janssen-Jurreit, Marielouise 230
Jaynes, Julian 136

Jefferson, James W., and John H.
Greist 341
Jenike, Michael A., Lee Baer, and
William E. Minichiello 334
Jenkins, C. D., S. J. Zyzanski, and R. H.
Rosenman 313
Jensen, Arthur Robert 256
Jessen, Raymond James 12
Jewell, Linda N., and Marc Siegall 243
John, Oliver P., and Robert R. McCrae
273
Johnson, David W., and Roger T.
Johnson 230
Johnson, Eric W. 191
Johnson, George B., and Peter H.
Raven 29, 40, 109, 297
Johnson, Karen, and Tom Ferguson 384
Johnson, Roger T., and David W.
Johnson 230
Johnson, Virginia E., and William H.
Masters 351
Johnson, Virginia E., William H.
Masters, and Robert C. Kolodny 94
Johnson, Wendell 327
Johnson-Laird, Philip Nicholas 129
Johnston, Derek W., Andrew M.
Mathews, and Michael G. Gelder
335
Johnston, Janet R., and Linda E.
Cambell 179
Johoda, Marie, Claire Selltiz, Morton
Deutsch, and S. Cook 14
Jones, Alvin, and Rick Crandall, eds.
292
Jones, Edward Ellsworth 79, 243
Jones, E. E., and Thane Pittman 243
Jones, Ernest 286
Jones, James M. 230
Jones, Warren H., Jonathan M. Cheek,
and Stephen R. Briggs 243
Jongeward, Dorothy, and Muriel James
371
Jordan, Dale R. 161
Jorgensen, Caryl Dow, and John E.
Lewis 93
Joy, Leslie A., Meredith M. Kimball,
and Merle L. Zabrack 211
Judd, Charles M., and Louise H.
Kidder 12
Judd, Robert, and Debora Phillips 226
Julesz, Bela 60
Julien, Robert M. 36, 354, 365

Jung, Carl 143, 286-287
Just, Marcel Adam, and Patricia A.
Carpenter 161

Kaczmarek, Leonard K., and Irwin B.
Levitan 38
Kagan, S., et al. 230
Kahneman, Daniel 136, 244
Kahneman, Daniel, and Amos Tversky
133
Kahneman, Daniel, Paul Slovic, and
Amos Tversky, eds. 129
Kahoe, R. D., and Mary J. Meadow
245
Kail, Robert V. 149
Kalat, James 36, 71, 93
Kalat, J. W. 129
Kallert, S., Wolf Dieter Keidel, and
M. Korth 52
Kalter, Neil 179
Kaluger, George, and Meriem Fair
Kaluger 184
Kamel, G. W. Levi, and Thomas S.
Weinberg, eds. 352
Kamin, Leon J. 256
Kane, Steven T. 266
Kanfer, Frederick H., and W. Robert
Nay 266
Kanner, Allen D., James C. Coyne,
Catherine Shaefer, and Richard S.
Lazarus 304
Kanner, Leo 327
Kantowitz, Barry H., David G. Elmes,
and Henry L. Roediger III 16
Kaplan, Harold I., and Benjamin J.
Sadock, eds. 37, 272
Kaplan, Robert M., and Dennis P.
Saccuzzo 266, 359
Kaplinski, Elizabeth, ed. 358
Kardiner, Abram 287
Karoly, Paul, and Anne Harris 361
Karp, Gerald 206
Karylowki, Jerzy, Ervin Staub, Daniel
Bar-Tal, and Janusz Reykowski,
eds. 238
Kasper, Siegfried, Susan L. Rogers,
Angela Yancey, Patricia M. Schulz,
Robert A. Skwerer, and Norman E.
Rosenthal 341
Kasper, Siegfried, Thomas A. Wehr,
John J. Bartko, Paul A. Gaist, and
Norman E. Rosenthal 341

Kassin, Saul M., and Lawrence S. Wrightsman 244
Kassin, Saul M., and Sharon S. Brehm 68, 239
Katchadourian, Herant A. 93
Katz, Irwin 231
Katz, Janet, and Frank H. Marsh, eds. 366
Katz, Jay 21
Katz, Phyllis A., ed. 231
Katz, Phyllis A., and Dalmas A. Taylor, eds. 231
Katzung, Bertram G., ed. 366
Kaufman, Lloyd 61
Kaufman, Lloyd, Kenneth R. Boff, and James P. Thomas, eds. 134
Kausler, Donald H. 206
Kaysen, Susanna 384
Kazdin, Alan E. 361, 384
Keidel, Wolf Dieter, S. Kallert, and M. Korth 52
Keith, Samuel J., Marvin I. Herz, and John P. Docherty 348
Keller, Helen 61
Kellerman, Henry, and Robert Plutchik eds. 73
Kelley, Harold H., Carl Iver Hovland, and Irving L. Janis 214
Kellogg, W. N., and L. A. Kellogg 162
Kelly, D. D. 52
Kelly, George Alexander 276
Kelly, Joan Berlin, and Judith S. Wallerstein 181
Kemper, Theodore D. 71-72
Kendall, Philip C., and Lauren Braswell 327
Kendler, Howard H. 6
Kennedy, Eugene C. 6
Kenning, Mary, C. Eugene Walker, and Jan Faust-Campanile 330
Kenrick, D. T., Robert B. Cialdini, and D. J. Baumann 236
Kent, Raymond D., and William H. Perkins 54
Kerlinger, Fred Nichols 266
Kermis, Marguerite D. 206
Kerner, Fred 313
Kessel, Frank S., ed. 162
Kessler, Ronald C., Richard H. Price, and Camille B. Wortman 304
Ketcham, Katherine, and Elizabeth F. Loftus 245

Keyes, Daniel 334
Keyser, D. J., and R. C. Sweetland, eds. 268, 270
Kidd, F. F., J. H. Harvey, and W. J. Ickes, eds. 79
Kidder, Louise H., and Charles M. Judd 12
Kiesler, Charles A., Barry E. Collins, and Norman Miller 214
Kimball, Meredith M., Leslie A. Joy, and Merle L. Zabrack 211
Kimble, Gregory A. 119
Kimmel, H. D., and Niels Birbaumer, eds. 299
Kinchla, Ronald A., John M. Darley, Samuel Glucksberg 203, 264
King, Morton, and Richard A. Hunt 243
Kinget, G. Marian 6
Kintsch, Walter 149
Kirshner, Howard S. 37
Kish, Leslie 13
Kitayama, Shinobu, and Hazel R. Markus 72
Kite, M. E., and Kay Deaux 228
Kivnick, Helen Q., Erik H. Erikson, and Joan M. Erikson 204
Klagsbrun, Francine 191
Klasen, Edith 162
Klatzky, Roberta L. 149
Klein, David B. 136
Klein, Edward, Daniel J. Levinson, Charlotte Darrow, Maria Levinson, and Braxton McKee 198
Klein, Stephen B. 114
Klein, Stephen B., and Robert R. Mowrer, eds. 107, 120
Kleinig, John 366
Kleinman, Arthur, and Byron Good 342
Kleinmuntz, Benjamin 266
Klemm, W. R., and Robert P. Vertes, eds. 37
Kline, Paul 256
Klopfer, Peter H., and Jack P. Hailman 99
Knapp, Mark L. 162, 225
Knight, Edwin 304
Knight, Kevin, and Elaine Rich 131
Kniskern, D. P., and A. S. Gurman 373
Knott, David H. 354
Knowles, Richard T. 197
Knox, David 197

Kobasa, Suzanne C.   304
Koehler, Charlotte, and Marion E.
    Broome   182
Koertge, Noretta, ed.   93
Koffka, Kurt   61
Köhler, Wolfgang   61
Kohut, Sylvester, Jr., Jeraldine J. Kohut,
    and Joseph J. Fleishman   206
Kolb, Bryan, and Ian Q. Whishaw   37,
    149, 366
Kolodny, Robert C., William H.
    Masters, and Virginia E. Johnson   94
Komisaruk, Barry R., H. I. Siegel, M. F.
    Cheng, and H. H. Feder, eds.   28, 93
Konner, Melvin   80
Kornhaber, Arthur, and Kenneth L.
    Woodward   206
Korth, M., Wolf Dieter Keidel, and
    S. Kallert   52
Kovel, Joel   231
Kozak, M. J., E. B. Foa, and P. R.
    McCarthy   335
Kraepelin, Emil   349
Kramarae, Cheris, and Barrie Thorne,
    and Nancy Henley   235
Kramer, Bernard M. Kramer, Henry
    Wechsler, Leonard Solomon, eds.
    323
Kramer, Peter D.   366
Krannich, Ronald L.   197
Krantz, David S., Robert J. Gatchel, and
    Andrew Baum   312
Krasnegor, Norman, and Gilbert
    Gottlieb, eds.   183
Krasner, Leonard, Arthur C. Houts, and
    Leonard P. Ullmann   321
Krawiec, T. S., and James Patrick
    Chaplin   4
Krebs, Charles J.   99
Krebs, J. R., and N. B. Davies   99
Krieger, Dorothy T., and Joan C.
    Hughes, eds.   28
Kroger, Jane   191
Krous, Henry F., Jan L. Cubertson, and
    R. Debra Bendell, eds.   182
Krumboltz, John D., and Carl E.
    Thoresen, eds.   361
Krupat, Edward, and M. J. Saks   221
Kryger, Meir H., Thomas Roth, and
    William C. Dement, eds.   143
Ksir, Charles, and Oakley Stern Ray
    356

Kubler-Ross, Elisabeth   206, 304
Kuczaj, S. A., II, and W. Andrew
    Collins   69
Kuczmiercsyk, Andrezej R., Michael
    Feuerstein, and Elise E. Labbe   312
Kuffler, Stephen W.   61
Kuffler, Stephen W., John G. Nicholls,
    and A. Robert Martin   37
Kulka, Richard A.   335
Kurtz, Norman R., and Howard E.
    Freeman, eds.   229
Kushner, Harold S.   305

L'Abate, Luciano, and Gerald R.
    Weeks   375
Labbe, Elise E., and Michael Feuerstein,
    and Andrezej R. Kuczmiercsyk   312
LaBerge, Stephen   143
Labov, William   111
Lachman, Roy, Janet L. Lachman, and
    Earl C. Butterfield   129, 149
Laing, Ronald David   292
Laird, Charlton Grant   162
Lake, Max   53
Lamb, Michael E., and Joseph J.
    Campos   179
Lambert, Wallace E., Elizabeth Peal
    164
Landau, Sol, and Joan Thomas   197
Landreth, G. L.   377
Landy, David, and Elliot Aronson   244
Landy, Frank J.   184
Landy, Frank J., and Don A. Trumbo   87
Landy, Robert J.   381
Lane, Harlan   53
Langer, Ellen J.   137
Langer, Ellen J., and Charles N.
    Alexander, eds.   134
Langer, Jonas   169
Langer, Walter Charles   13
Lann, Irma S., Eve K. Moscicki, and
    Ronald Maris, eds.   342
Lapointe, François H.   6
Larson, C. N., and T. A. Petti   193
Larson, David E., ed.   28
Lasch, Christopher   347
Lashley, R. L., Wayne Weiten, and
    Margaret A. Lloyd   274
Latané, Bibb, and John M. Darley   237
Latané, Bibb, S. A. Nida, and D. W.
    Wilson   237
Latham, Gary P.   87

Latham, Gary P., and Edwin A. Locke
  87
Latham, Gary P., and K. N. Wexley
  89
Lauer, Jeanette C., and Robert H.
  Lauer 225
Lawler, Edward E., and Lyman W.
  Porter 88
Lawton, P., and P. Parmelee 208
Lazarus, Richard S. 72, 305
Lazarus, Richard S., and Susan
  Folkman 305
Lazarus, Richard S., and Alan Monat,
  eds. 297, 314
Lazarus, Richard S., Susan Folkman,
  and Charles E. Schaefer 301
Lazarus, Richard S., Allen D. Kanner,
  James C. Coyne, and Catherine
  Shaefer 304
Lazarus, R. S., C. Schaefer, and J. C.
  Coyne 307
Lazerson, Arlyne, and Floyd E. Bloom
  31, 67, 295, 364
Leahey, Thomas H. 7, 13
Leary, Mark R., and Rowland S.
  Miller 244
Leavitt, Fred 355
Leber, William R., and Ernest Edward
  Beckham, eds. 338
LeBow, Michael D. 93
Lee, David N., and Eric Aronson 53
Lee, Vicki L. 7
Lehninger, Albert L. 28
Lehrman, Daniel S. 28, 94
Leiman, Arnold L., and Mark R.
  Rosenzweig 40
Leippe, Michael R., and Philip G.
  Zimbardo 217
Leiter, E. 267
Lenney, Ellen 191
Lepper, M. R., and David Greene, eds
  244
Lerner, Harriet Goldhor 287
Lerner, Richard M. 169
Lester, David, ed. 342
Levelt, Willem J. M. 163
Leventman, Seymour, and Charles R.
  Figley, eds. 332
Levey, A. B., and Irene Martin 120
Levi, Lennart 313
Levin, Harvey S., Jordan Grafman, and
  Howard M. Eisenberg 37

Levine, Ann, Sandra Scarr, and
  Richard A. Weinberg 186
Levine, Carol, and Robert M. Veatch,
  eds. 21
Levine, Charles, and James E. Cote 188
Levine, Michael W., and Jeremy M.
  Shefner 47
Levine, Murray, and David V. Perkins
  386
Levine, Seymour 297
Levinger, George, and Oliver C. Moles,
  eds. 225
Levinson, Daniel J., Charlotte Darrow,
  Edward Klein, Maria Levinson, and
  Braxton McKee 198
Levinthal, Charles F. 61, 94
Levis, D. J. 361
Levitan, Irwin B., and Leonard K.
  Kaczmarek 38
Levitt, Eugene E., Bernard Lubin, and
  James M. Brooks 342
Levy, Matthew N., and Robert M.
  Berne, eds. 49, 56
Lewin, Benjamin 207
Lewin, Kurt 215, 232, 276
Lewine, Richard J., and Elaine F.
  Walker 350
Lewinsohn, Peter M., R. F. Munoz,
  M. A. Youngren, and A. M. Zeiss
  342
Lewis, Adele Beatrice, and Bill Lewis,
  with Steve Radlaver 198
Lewis, John E., and Caryl Dow
  Jorgensen 93
Lewis, Michael, and Leonard A.
  Rosenblum, eds. 72
Lewis, Michael, and Linda Michalson
  72
Liberman, Alvin M. 53
Lichstein, Kenneth L. 137
Lichtenstein, Sarah, Paul Slovic, and
  Baruch Fischhoff 132
Liddell, Howard S. 104
Lidz, Theodore 29
Lidz, Theodore, Stephen Fleck, and
  Alice R. Cornelison 349
Lieb, Julian, and D. Jablow Hershman
  340
Lieber, Robert M., and Michael D.
  Spiegler 276
Liebert, Richard M., and Arthur C.
  Houts 327

Liebert, Robert M., and Joyce Sprafkin 211

Liebert, Robert M., and Judith Rich Harris 178, 184

Liebman, Jeffrey M., and Steven J. Cooper, eds. 80

Liem, Karel F., William S. Beck, and George Gaylord Simpson 25, 106

Lifton, Robert Jay, and Eric Olson 207

Lilly, John C. 129

Lilly, Roy S., and John R. Graham 254, 265

Lindgren, Henry Clay, and Paul Insel 220

Lindzey, Gardner, and Calvin Springer Hall 79, 272, 275, 380

Lindzey, Gardner, and Edwin G. Boring, eds. 77

Linn, Marcia C., Janet Shibley Hyde, eds. 172

Linz, Daniel, Edward I. Donnerstein, and Steven Penrod 210

Lips, Hilary 232

Lipsitt, Lewis 185

Litman, Robert E., Edwin S. Shneidman, and Norman L. Farberow 344

Litman, Robert E., Michael L. Peck, and Norman L. Farberow, eds. 193, 343

Livingston, Martha 185

Locke, Edwin A., and Gary P. Latham 87

Lockhart, Robert S., and Fergus I. Craik 147

Loftus, Elizabeth F. 149-150, 244

Loftus, Elizabeth F., and Camille B. Wortman 76

Loftus, Elizabeth F., and Gary L. Wells, eds. 153

Loftus, Elizabeth F., and Katherine Ketcham 245

Loftus, Elizabeth, David Hall, and James Tousignant 148

Loftus, Elizabeth, Lyle E. Bourne, and Roger L. Dominowski 124

Loftus, Geoffrey R., and Elizabeth F. Loftus 150

Logan, Frank A., and Douglas P. Ferraro 80

Lohman, David F., and Robert M. Thorndike 259

Long, James D., and Robert Williams 248

LoPiccolo, Joseph, Julia R. Heiman, and Leslie LoPiccolo 351

Lorayne, Harry, and Jerry Lucas 150

Lorenz, Konrad 108, 212, 305

Lott, Bernice E. 179

Lowenstein, Otto 47

Lubin, Bernard, Eugene E. Levitt, and James M. Brooks 342

Lucas, Jerry, and Harry Lorayne 150

Luciano, Dorothy S., Arthur J. Vander, and James H. Sherman 44

Ludel, Jacqueline 47

Lundin, Robert William 7

Luria, Aleksandr R. 38, 150

Luschen, Gunther 212

Lyman, Howard B. 256

Lyons, John 163

Macaulay, Jacqueline, and Leonard Berkowitz, eds. 237

McAuliffe, Kathleen, and Sharon McAuliffe 185

McCall, G. J., and J. L. Simmons 13

McCann, Samuel M., Joseph Meites, and Bernard T. Donovan, eds. 29

McCarley, Robert W., and Mircea Steriade 42

McCarthy, P. R., M. J. Kozak, and E. B. Foa 335

McCaul, Kevin D., and Michael D. Storms 74

McClelland, David Clarence 80, 88

McClelland, James L., David E. Rumelhart, P. Smolensky, and Geoffrey E. Hinton 152

McClelland, J. L., and D. E. Rumelhart, eds. 129

McCloskey, Michael, Howard Egeth, and Judith McKenna 150

Maccoby, Eleanor, and John Martin 179

Maccoby, Eleanor E., and Carol Nagy Jacklin 172

McConkey, Kevin M., and Peter W. Sheehan 138

McCormick, Ernest James, and Daniel R. Ilgen 198

McCoy, Kathy, and Charles Wibbelsman 191

McCrae, Robert R., and Oliver P. John 273

McCrone, John 163

McDaniel, Mark A., and Michael Pressley, eds. 150

Macdonald, Barbara, and Cynthia Rich 207

MacDougall, J. M., T. M. Dembroski, J. A. Herd, and J. L. Shields 311

Mace, Nancy L., and Peter V. Rabins 207

McFarland, David, ed. 100, 104

McGaugh, James L., and Carl W. Cotman 26

McGlynn, F. D., and D. J. Delprato 332

McGrath, Ellen, ed. 342

McGrath, Joseph Edward 220

McGuire, William, ed. 288

McGuire, W. J. 215

McIntyre, James, Alfred S. Alschuler, and Diane Tabor 83

MacKay, Donald MacCrimmon 62

McKee, Braxton, Daniel J. Levinson, Charlotte Darrow, Edward Klein, and Maria Levinson 198

McKenna, I., and G. C. Davey 118

McKenna, Judith, Michael McCloskey, and Howard Egeth 150

Mackie, Diane M., and David M. Messick 232

Mackintosh, N. J. 104

Mackintosh, N. J., and M. M. Cotton 120

McKoon, Gail, R. Ratcliff, and G. Dell 150

Mackworth, Jane F. 47

MacLean, P. 38

McNally, Richard 108

McNaught, Brian 94

McNaughton, Neil 73

McNeal, James U. 179

McNeil, Thomas F., and Sarnoff A. Mednick 349

McNeill, David 163

McQuade, Walter, and Ann Aikman 314

Madanes, Cloe 374

Madaras, Lynda, with Area Madaras 192

Madaras, Lynda, with Dane Saavedra 191

Maddi, Salvatore R., and Paul T. Costa 292

Mader, Sylvia S. 94

Mahesh Yogi, Maharishi 137

Mahrer, Alvin 143

Mair, J. M. M., and Donald Bannister, eds. 275

Malamuth, Neil M., and L. Rowell Huesmann 211

Malnati, Richard, and Jeremiah Donigian 372

Malone, Thomas Patrick, and Patrick Thomas Malone 198

Maloney, H. Newton, ed. 245

Malson, Laurel P., Donald N. Bersoff, and Donald B. Verrilli 263

Mandler, Jean Matter 151

Mann, Philip A. 386

Manning, Aubrey 88, 100, 104, 108, 297

Mansfield, Richard S. 256

Marcia, James E. 192

Marcus, Jay B. 305

Marecek, Jeanne, and Rachel T. Hare-Mustin 171

Margolin, Gayla, and Neil S. Jacobson 374

Marin, O. S. M., and Michael I. Posner, eds. 138

Maris, Ronald, Irma S. Lann, Eve K. Moscicki, eds. 342

Marks, Issac Meyer 335

Marks, John, and Anthony N. Nicholson 144

Markus, Hazel R., and Shinobu Kitayama 72

Marler, Peter, and William J. Hamilton III 100

Marmor, Judd, ed. 94

Marr, David 130

Marrow, Alfred Jay 276

Marsh, Frank H., and Janet Katz, eds. 366

Martin, A. Robert, Stephen W. Kuffler, and John G. Nicholls 37

Martin, David W. 16, 21

Martin, Garry, and Joseph Pear 104, 362

Martin, Irene, and A. B. Levey 120

Martin, J. A. M., and John Chalmers Ballantyne 49

Martin, John, and Eleanor Maccoby 179

Martin, Martha B., Cynthia M. Owen, and John M. Morihisa 38
Maser, Jack D., and A. Hussian Tuma, eds. 337
Masland, Richard H. 62
Maslow, Abraham H. 80, 88, 292-293
Mason, Elliott B., and Alexander P. Spence 30
Mason, Kathleen Criddle, ed. 381
Masson, Jeffrey Moussaieff 358
Masters, John C., et al. 362
Masters, William H., and Virginia E. Johnson 351
Masters, William H., Virginia E. Johnson, and Robert C. Kolodny 94
Masterson, Jenny (Gove), pseudonym 293
Masuda, Minoru, and Thomas H. Holmes 313
Matarazzo, J. D. 269
Matarazzo, Joseph D., Robert Gale Harper, and Arthur N. Wiens 161
Mathews, Andrew M., Michael G. Gelder, and Derek W. Johnston 335
Mathis, Robert L., and John H. Jackson 199
Matlin, Margaret W. 47, 62, 130
Matson, Johnny L., and Thomas M. DiLorenzo 362
Matthei, Edward, and Thomas Roeper 53
Matthews, P. B. 53
Matthews, Peter Hugoe 163
Matthews, Wendy Schempp, and Jeanne Brooks-Gunn 175
Matthews-Simonton, Stephanie, Carl Simonton, and James Creighton 309
Maultsby, Maxie C., Jr. 371
Maurer, Daphne, and Charles Maurer 62, 185
Mavissakalian, Matig, Samuel M. Turner, and Larry Michelson 335
Maxson, Linda, and Charles Daugherty 62
May, Rollo 7, 212, 293, 355
May, Rollo, Ernest Angel, and Henri F. Ellenberger, eds. 293, 377
Mayer, Jean 94
Mayer, R. E. 130
Meadow, Mary J., and R. D. Kahoe 245
Meadow, Phyllis W., and Hyman Spotnitz 382

Mecca, Andrew M. 355
Mednick, Sarnoff A., and Thomas F. McNeil 349
Mehler, Jacques, and Robin Fox, eds. 62
Mehrabian, Albert 164
Meichenbaum, Donald 306, 321, 362
Meites, Joseph, Bernard T. Donovan, and Samuel M. McCann, eds. 29
Melzack, Ronald, and Patrick D. Wall 54, 306
Mendelson, W. B. 143
Menzel, Emil W. 111
Merskey, Harold, W. Lynn Smith, and Steven C. Gross 309
Mesibov, Gary B., and Eric Schopler, eds. 329
Mesibov, Gary B., Mary E. Van Bourgondien, and Geraldine Dawson 330
Messick, David M., and Diane M. Mackie 232
Meyer, Glenn E., and Susan Petry 63
Meyer, Roberta B., Laurence D. Steinberg, Jay Belsky 187
Michalson, Linda, and Michael Lewis 72
Michelson, L., and S. M. Turner 337
Middlebrooks, John C., and David M. Green 54
Milgram, Stanley 220
Milgram, Stanley, and Thomas H. Murray 21
Milich, R., M. Nietzel, and D. A. Berstein 270
Miller, Edgar 39
Miller, George Armitage 164
Miller, Jean Baker 199
Miller, Jonathan, ed. 288
Miller, L. Keith 105, 115
Miller, Neal E. 21, 276
Miller, Neal E., and John Dollard 275-276, 319
Miller, Neal E., John Dollard, Leonard W. Doob, O. Hobart Mowrer, and Robert R. Sears 86
Miller, Norma Reno, and S. Norman Feingold 196
Miller, Norman, and Marilynn Brewer, eds. 232
Miller, Norman, Charles A. Kiesler, and Barry E. Collins 214

Miller, Patricia H.   169
Miller, Rowland S., and Mark R. Leary   244
Miller, Thomas I., Mary Lee Smith, and Gene V. Glass   385
Millman, Marcia   95
Mills, Joyce C., and Richard J. Crowley   328
Milman, Donald S., and George D. Goldman, eds.   380
Milne, Lorus Johnson, and Margery Milne   54
Milner, Peter, and James Olds   81
Mineka, Susan   336
Miner, Gary D., et al., eds.   345
Minichiello, William E., Michael A. Jenike, and Lee Baer   334
Minors, D. S., and J. M. Waterhouse   143
Minuchin, Salvador   374
Minuchin, Salvador, Bernice L. Rosman, and Lester Baker   328
Mischel, Harriet N., and Walter Mischel, eds.   273
Mischel, Walter   270, 273, 277
Mischel, Walter, Yuichi Shoda, and Monica L. Rodriguez   277
Mitchell, Horace, and Robert Williams   261
Mitchell, J. E., and E. D. Eckert   328
Mitchell, James V., Jr.   257
Mitford, Jessica   207
Mitler, M. M., A. Michael Anch, and C. P. Browman, and James K. Walsh   140
Modgil, Sohan, and Celia Modgil, eds.   257, 277
Moghaddam, Fathali M., and Donald M. Taylor   234
Moles, Oliver C., and George Levinger, eds.   225
Molinoff, Perry B., George J. Siegel, Bernard W. Agranoff, and R. Wayne Albers, eds.   42
Mollon, J. D., and H. B. Barlow, eds.   56
Monahan, J.   321
Monahan, John, ed.   192
Monat, Alan, and Richard S. Lazarus, eds.   297, 306, 314
Money, John, and Anke A. Ehrhardt   29
Montagu, Ashley, ed.   257

Montague, P., R. J. Cohen, L. S. Nathanson, and M. E. Swerdlik   269
Monte, Christopher   381
Montgomery, Geoffrey   63
Mook, Douglas G.   80
Moore, K. D.   22
Moore-Ede, Martin C., Frank M. Sulzman, and Charles A. Fuller   144
Morgan, Robin   232
Morganstern, Kenneth P.   267
Morihisa, John M., Martha B. Martin, and Cynthia M. Owen   38
Morrison, Randall L.   267
Mosak, Harold H.   288, 381
Mosak, Harold H., and Birdie Mosak   288, 381
Moscicki, Eve K., Irma S. Lann, and Ronald Maris, eds.   342
Mowrer, O. Hobart, John Dollard, Leonard W. Doob, Neal E. Miller, and Robert R. Sears   86
Mowrer, Robert R., and Stephen Klein, eds.   107
Mueller, Conrad George, and Mae Rudolph   63
Mule, S. Joseph, ed.   355
Mullen, Brian   232
Mullen, Brian, and George R. Goethals, eds.   220
Mullen, Paul E., and Gregory L. White   227
Munoz, R. F., Peter M. Lewinsohn, M. A. Youngren, and A. M. Zeiss   342
Munter, Carol H., and Jane R. Hirschmann   92
Murdoch, B. E.   164
Murgatroyd, Stephen J., Michael J. Apter, David Fontana   77
Murphy, Gardner   7
Murphy, Michael, and Steven Donovan   137
Murray, Charles, and Richard J. Hermnstein   255
Murray, David J.   7
Murray, David J., and Gerd Gigerenzer   20
Murray, Thomas H., and Stanley Milgram   21
Mussen, Paul Henry, ed.   169
Mussen, Paul Henry, and Nancy Eisenberg-Berg   180

Muuss, R. E. 192
Myers, D. G. 73, 225
Myers, H. H., and P. S. Siegel 81
Myers, Jerome L. 16

Naeye, Richard L. 185
Nairn, Allan 257
Nathan, Ronald G., and Edward A.
    Charlesworth 296, 300
Nathans, Jeremy 63
Nathanson, S. 288
Nation, Jack R., Ludy T. Benjamin,
    and Roy Hopkins 123
National Coalition for Cancer
    Survivorship 306
Nauta, Walle, and Michael Feirtag
    39
Nay, W. Robert, and Frederick H.
    Kanfer 266
Naylor, James C., Robert D. Pritchard,
    and Daniel R. Ilgen 81
Neal, Helen 54
Neal, M. E., C. M. Shisslak, Marjorie
    Crago, and B. Swain 329
Neale, John M., and Gerald C.
    Davison 332, 376
Neale, John M., and Thomas F.
    Oltmanns 349
Neimeyer, Robert A. 277
Neimeyer, Robert A., Hannelore Wass,
    and Felix Berardo, eds. 209
Neisser, Ulric 63, 130, 151
Nelsen, Jane, and H. Stephen Glenn
    177
Nemeth, C. J. 245
Nemiroff, Marc A., and Jane
    Annunziata 377, 381
Nessim, Susan, and Judith Ellis 306
Nettleton, Norman C., and John L.
    Bradshaw 31
Nevin, John A., Michael L. Commons,
    and Michael C. Davison, eds. 45
Newberry, Benjamin H., and Kurt
    Bammer, eds. 311
Nezu, Arthur M., and Thomas J.
    D'Zurilla 125
Nicholls, John G., Stephen W. Kuffler,
    and A. Robert Martin 37
Nichols, Michael P. 374
Nicholson, Anthony N., and John
    Marks 144
Nickerson, Raymond S. 130

Nida, S. A., and Bibb Latané, and D. W.
    Wilson 237
Nielsen, Joyce McCarl, ed. 22
Nietzel, Michael T., et al. 386
Nietzel, M. T., D. A. Berstein, and
    R. Milich 270
Nisbett, Richard E. 95
Nisbett, Richard E., and Stuart Valins
    75
Nisenholz, Bernard, and Vincent
    Peterson 375
Noppe, Lloyd, and Fergus Hughes
    178
Nordby, Vernon J., and Calvin Springer
    Hall 380
Nordlie, Johanna W., and Harold A.
    Sackheim, and Ruben C. Gur 336
Norman, Donald A. 151
Norton, G. Ron, John R. Walker, and
    Colin A. Ross, eds. 337
Nuland, Sherwin B. 207
Nyberg, Stanley E., and Eugene B.
    Zechmeister 154
Nye, Robert D. 277

Oakley, Ann 185
Oberleder, Muriel 208
Obler, Loraine K., and Martin L.
    Albert 155
Offer, David, and Melvin Sabshin 322
Öhman, Arne, Ulf Dimberg, and
    Lars-Göran Öst 108
Olczak, Paul V., Karen Grover Duffy,
    James W. Grosch, eds. 218
Olds, James, and Peter Milner 81
Oliver, Rose, and Frances A. Bock 345
Ollendick, Thomas H., and Greta
    Francis 267
Olson, Eric, and Robert Jay Lifton 207
Olson, Jerry C., and Jacob Jacoby, eds.
    214
Oltmanns, Thomas F., and John M.
    Neale 349
Olton, David S., and Aaron R.
    Noonberg 306
Olton, David S., and Robert J.
    Samuelson 111
O'Malley, Bert W., and William T.
    Schrader 29
Ommaya, A. K., and T. A. Gennarelli
    39
Oppenheim, Rosalind C. 328

Opper, Sylvia, and Herbert Ginsberg 190

Orbuch, Terri L., John H. Harvey, and Ann L. Weber 224

Ormrod, Jeanne E. 111, 115

Ornstein, Robert, and D. S. Sobel 297

Ornstein, Robert Evan 137

Ornstein, Robert Evan, and Richard F. Thompson 39

Ortinau, David J., Robert P. Bush, and Joseph F. Hair, Jr. 263

Osofsky, Howard J., and Della M. Hann 178

OSS Assessment Staff 257

Öst, Göran, Arne Öhman, and Ulf Dimberg 108

Overmier, J. Bruce, and F. Robert Brush, eds. 118

Owen, Cynthia M., Martha B. Martin, and John M. Morihisa 38

Oxford, Jim 355

Padilla, Amado M., H. H. Fairchild, and C. M. Valadez, eds. 164

Palmer, Frank Robert 130

Palmore, Erdman B., et al. 208

Paloutzian, Raymond F. 245

Pande, Sashi K. 358

Panek, Paul E., and Bert Hayslip, Jr. 205

Parasuraman, R., and D. R. Davies, eds. 137

Parker, Gordon, and Philip Boyce 339

Parker, Rolland S. 39

Parkin, Alan J. 151

Parmelee, P., and P. Lawton 208

Patnoe, Shelley 7

Patterson, Gerald R., and Marion S. Forgatch 192

Paul, Gordon L. 362

Paulus, Paul B., ed. 221

Pavlov, Ivan P. 120

Paykel, Eugene S. 342

Payne, V. G., and L. D. Isaacs 185

Peal, Elizabeth, and Wallace E. Lambert 164

Pear, Joseph, and Garry Martin 104, 362

Peck, M. Scott 245

Peck, Michael L., Norman L. Farberow, and Robert E. Litman, eds. 193, 343

Peck, Robert E. 366

Pelletier, Kenneth R. 138, 314

Pennebaker, James W. 314

Penrod, Steven, Edward I. Donnerstein, and Daniel Linz 210

Penrod, Steven D., Reid Hastie, and Nancy Pennington 242

Penrose, Roger 131

Perczel, Maria de, William J. Fremouw, and Thomas E. Ellis 340

Perkins, David V., and Murray Levine 386

Perkins, William H., and Raymond D. Kent 54

Perls, Frederick S. 377

Perry, J. Christopher, and George E. Vallaint 347

Perry, Joseph B., Jr., and Meredith David Pugh 221

Persad, E., and N. S. Endler 364

Pervin, Lawrence A., ed. 273

Petersen, Michael R., Charles T. Snowdon, and Charles H. Brown, eds. 100

Peterson, Christopher 274

Peterson, Christopher, and Lisa M. Bossio 315

Peterson, Vincent, and Bernard Nisenholz 375

Petri, Herbert L. 81

Petrinovich, Lewis 7

Petry, Susan, and Glenn E. Meyer 63

Petti, T. A., and C. N. Larson 193

Pettigrew, John D. 63

Pettigrew, Thomas F. 232-233

Petty, Richard E., and John T. Cacioppo 215

Pew, W. L., and Don C. Dinkmeyer 379

Pezdek, Kathy, and Dale E. Berger, and William P. Banks, eds. 123

Pfaff, Donald W., ed. 81

Pfalzgraf, Beth, and Susan Adair Ewing 159

Phares, E. Jerry 267, 322, 384

Phillips, Debora, with Robert Judd 226

Phillips, Dennis P., and John F. Brugge 54

Phillips, John L. 13, 22, 172

Piaget, Jean 169, 172

Piattelli-Palmarini, Massimo, ed. 164

Pick, Anne D., ed. 186

Pierce, Gregory R., Barbara R. Sarason, and Irwin G. Sarason, eds. 307

Pierce, John R., Willem André Maria
   Van Bergeijk, and Edward E.
   David, Jr.   56
Piliavin, Jane Allyn, John F. Dovidio,
   Samuel L. Gaertner, and Russell
   Clark   237
Pinder, Craig C.   88
Pinel, John P. J.   29, 95
Pines, Ayala M., and Elliot Aronson
   226
Pinker, Steven   165
Pirsig, Robert M.   307
Pittman, Thane, and E. E. Jones   243
Platt, John R.   22
Plotnik, Rodney J.   246, 315
Plutchik, Robert   22, 73
Plutchik, Robert, and Henry Kellerman,
   eds.   73
Poling, Alan D.   366
Pollio, Howard R.   8
Polster, Richard A., and Richard F.
   Dangel   372
Pomeroy, W. B., P. H. Gebhard,
   B. Wardell, J. H. Gagnon, and C. V.
   Christenson   351
Porter, Lyman W., and Edward E.
   Lawler   88
Porter, Lyman W., and Mark R.
   Rosenzweig, eds.   199
Posner, Michael I., and O. S. M. Marin,
   eds.   138
Powell, Trevor J., and Simon J.
   Enright   307
Powers, Michael D., and Jan S.
   Handleman   328
Poyatos, Fernando, ed.   165
Pratkanis, Anthony R., and Elliot
   Aronson   215
Pratkanis, Anthony R., Steven J.
   Breckler, and Anthony G. Greenwald,
   eds.   215
Premack, David   165
Presser, Stanley, and Jean M. Converse
   11
Pressley, Michael, and Mark A.
   McDaniel, eds.   150
Price, Richard H., Ronald C. Kessler,
   and Camille B. Wortman   304
Price, Virginia Ann   315
Prigatano, George P.   40
Pritchard, R. D., and J. P. Campbell
   85

Pritchard, Robert D., James C. Naylor,
   and Daniel R. Ilgen   81
Proshansky, Harold M., William H.
   Ittelson, and Leanne G. Rivlin, eds.
   215
Pruitt, Dean G., and Jeffrey Z. Rubin
   221
Pugh, Meredith David, and Joseph B.
   Perry, Jr.   221
Pyke, Sandra W., and Neil M. Agnew
   23
Pylyshyn, Z. W.   131
Pyrczak, Fred   23

Quelch, John A., and Ian Fenwick, eds.
   126
Quenzer, Linda F., and Robert Simon
   Feldman   34
Quinn, Susan   288

Rabins, Peter V., and Nancy L. Mace
   207
Rachlin, Howard   8
Rachman, S. J.   336
Radlaver, Steve, Adele Beatrice Lewis,
   and Bill Lewis   198
Rahe, Richard H., and Thomas H.
   Holmes   303
Ramsey, Christian N., Jr., ed.   322
Rapaport, Mark, David S. Janowsky,
   Robert N. Golden, John Cain, and
   J. Christian Gillian   28
Rappaport, Julian   387
Rapport, Mark D.   329
Raskin, N. J., and Carl R. Rogers
   377
Ratcliff, R., Gail McKoon, and G. Dell
   150
Raven, Peter H.   100, 105
Raven, Peter H., and George B.
   Johnson   29, 40, 109, 297
Ray, Oakley Stern, and Charles Ksir
   356
Ray, William J., Robert Morris Stern,
   and Christopher M. Davis   268
Raynor, Joel O., and John William
   Atkinson, eds.   84
Read, Peter B., Michael Rutter,
   Carroll E. Izard, eds.   343
Redican, William   73
Reed, Edward S., and Stanley O.
   Gaines   229

Rehm, Lynn P., ed. 343
Reid, S. E., and Charles E. Schaefer 378
Reid, Steven E., and Charles E. Schaefer, eds. 382
Reid, William H., ed. 347
Reilly, Richard R., Sarah Henry, and James W. Smither 267
Reisberg, Dan, and Barry Schwartz 112, 121, 152
Reisner, Morton F., ed. 345
Remmers, John E., Faiq G. Issa, and Paul M. Surrat, eds. 143
Rescorla, R. A. 121
Rest, James R. 173
Restak, Richard M. 40
Review of Existential Psychology and Psychiatry 293
Reykowski, Janusz, Ervin Staub, Daniel Bar-Tal, and Jerzy Karylowki, eds. 238
Reynolds, Cecil R., John A. Glover, Royce R. Ronning, eds. 254
Reynolds, George Stanley 121
Rich, Cynthia, and Barbara Macdonald 207
Rich, Elaine, and Kevin Knight 131
Rich, John Martin, and Joseph L. DeVitis 173
Richardson, D. R., and Robert A. Baron 84
Richter, Lin, and Fred Belliveau 351
Riddoch, M. J., and G. W. Humphreys 60
Rieber, Robert W., and Helmut E. Adler, eds. 3
Riley, Diane M., et al. 356
Ring, Kenneth, Benjamin M. Braginsky, and D. D. Braginsky 318
Rivlin, Leanne G., Harold Proshansky, and William H. Ittelson, eds. 215
Rix, Elizabeth M. Lumsden, and Keith J. B. Rix 356
Rix, Keith J. B., and Elizabeth M. Lumsden Rix 356
Roazen, Paul 180, 289
Robbins, Lillian, Barbara Goff, and Lynn Miller 307
Roberts, William A., and Nelly Van Veldhuizen 112

Robertson, Joan F., and Vern L. Bengston, eds. 202
Robin, Arthur L., and Sharon L. Foster 375
Robins, Lee 347
Robins, Robert Henry 165
Robinson, Daniel N. 8
Robinson, Daniel N., and John C. Eccles 126, 134
Robinson, H. Alan, and Kenneth G. Graham 148
Rock, Irvin 47, 63-64
Rodin, Judith 307
Rodin, Judith, and Peter Salovey 226, 315
Rodman, Robert, and Victoria Fromkin 159
Rodriguez, Monica L., Walter Mischel, and Yuichi Shoda 277
Roediger, Henry L., III, David G. Elmes, and Barry H. Kantowitz 16
Roeper, Thomas, and Edward Matthel 53
Roesch, R., and S. L. Golding 320
Rogers, Carl R. 294, 375, 378, 384
Rogers, Carl R., and N. J. Raskin 377
Rogers, Susan L., Siegfried Kasper, Angela Yancey, Patricia M. Schulz, Robert A. Skwerer, and Norman E. Rosenthal 341
Romaine, Suzanne 165
Romero-Sierra, C. 40
Ronning, Royce R., John A. Glover, and Cecil R. Reynolds, eds. 254
Rosch, Eleanor H. 131
Rose, Terry, Frank R. Rusch, and Charles R. Greenwood 363
Rosen, Michael A. 352
Rosenberg, Morris 193, 246
Rosenberg, Stanley D., and Michael P. Farrell 195
Rosenblith, Judy F., and Judith E. Sims-Knight 186
Rosenblum, Leonard A. 13, 100
Rosenblum, Leonard A., and Michael Lewis, eds. 72
Rosenfeld, Lawrence B., Ronald B. Adler, and Neil Towne 222
Rosenfield, David, and Walter G. Stephan 233
Rosenhan, David L. 14, 322

Rosenhan, David L., and Martin E. P.
  Seligman 322
Rosenman, Ray H., and Margaret A.
  Chesney, eds. 311
Rosenman, Ray H., and Meyer
  Friedman 312
Rosenman, R. H., C. D. Jenkins, and
  S. J. Zyzanski 313
Rosenthal, Norman E. 343
Rosenthal Norman E., Siegfried Kasper,
  Susan L. Rogers, Angela Yancey,
  Patricia M. Schulz, and Robert A.
  Skwerer 341
Rosenthal, Norman E., and Mary C.
  Blehar 338
Rosenthal, Norman E., Frederick M.
  Jacobsen, Thomas A. Wehr, Robert A.
  Skwerer, and David A. Sack 341
Rosenthal, Norman E., Siegfried Kasper,
  Thomas A. Wehr, John J. Bartko, and
  Paul A. Gaist 341
Rosenzweig, Mark R., and Arnold L.
  Leiman 40
Rosenzweig, Mark R., and Lyman W.
  Porter, eds. 199
Rosewater, Lynne Bravo, and Lenore
  E. A. Walker, eds. 385
Rosman, Bernice L., Salvador
  Minuchin, and Lester Baker 328
Ross, Colin A., John R. Walker, and
  G. Ron Norton, eds. 337
Ross, M., and G. J. O. Fletcher 246
Rosser, Phyllis 257
Rotgers, Frederick 278
Roth, Thomas, Meir H. Kryger, and
  William C. Dement, eds. 143
Rothblum, Esther D., and Violet Franks,
  eds. 320
Routh, Donald K. 165
Rowan, Andrew N. 23
Rowntree, Derek 14, 23
Roy, Alec, ed. 347
Roy, E., Douglas A. Bernstein, T. Srull,
  and C. Wickens 67
Rubin, David C., ed. 152
Rubin, Jeffrey Z., and Bert R. Brown
  221
Rubin, Jeffrey Z., and Dean G. Pruitt
  221
Rubin, Lillian B. 226
Rubin, Zick 226
Rubins, Jack L. 289

Ruble, D. N. 180
Rudolph, Mae, and Conrad George
  Mueller 63
Rumelhart, David E., P. Smolensky,
  James L. McClelland, and
  Geoffrey E. Hinton 152
Rumelhart, D. E., and J. L. McClelland,
  eds. 129
Runco Mark A., and Robert S. Albert,
  eds. 257
Runyon, Richard P., and Audrey Haber
  23
Rusch, Frank R., Terry Rose, and
  Charles R. Greenwood 363
Rush, A. J., Aaron T. Beck, B. F. Shaw,
  and G. Emery 338, 368
Rush, A. John, and Kenneth Z.
  Altshuler, eds. 343
Rushton, J. Philippe, and Richard M.
  Sorrentino, eds. 238
Rushton, William A. H. 64
Russo, J. Edward, and Paul J. H.
  Shoemaker 131
Rustein, Jeffrey, Gregory L. White, and
  Sanford Fishbein 248
Rutter, Michael, Carroll E. Izard, and
  Peter B. Read, eds. 343
Ryan, R. M., and E. L. Deci 240
Rychlak, Joseph F. 289
Ryckman, Richard M. 112

Saavedra, Dane, and Lynda Madaras
  191
Sabshin, Melvin, and David Offer 322
Saccuzzo, Dennis P., and Robert M.
  Kaplan 266, 359
Sack, David A., Frederick M. Jacobsen,
  Thomas A. Wehr, Robert A. Skwerer,
  and Norman E. Rosenthal 341
Sackett, Gene P. 14
Sackheim, H., and W. Vingiano 336
Sackheim, Harold A., Johanna W.
  Nordlie, and Ruben C. Gur 336
Sackler, Arthur M., et al., eds. 367
Sacks, Michael H., Arnold M. Cooper,
  and Allen J. Frances, eds. 346
Sacks, Oliver 40-41, 131
Sadock, Benjamin J., and Harold I.
  Kaplan, eds. 37, 272
Saegert, S., and G. H. Winkel 216
Safilios-Rothschild, Constantina 226
Sagan, Carl 41

Sahakian, William S., ed. 8
Saks, M. J., and Edward Krupat 221
Salovey, Peter, and Judith Rodin 226, 315
Sameroff, Arnold J., ed. 186
Samovar, Larry A., and Richard E. Porter 166
Samuelson, Robert J., and David S. Olton 111
Sandeen, E. E., Stephen R. H. Beach, and K. D. O'Leary 338
Sanders, Gerald P., Robert A. Wallace, and Robert J. Ferl 31, 44, 109
Sandlow, J., and Paul C. Holinger 341
Sandman, Curt A., and Jane Veith-Flanigan 298
Sang, James H. 208
Sansweet, Stephen J. 363
Santrock, John W., and Steven R. Yussen 186
Sapir, Edward 166
Sarason, Barbara R., Irwin G. Sarason, and Gregory R. Pierce, eds. 307
Sarason, Irwin G., and Barbara R. Sarason 336
Sarno, Martha Taylor, ed. 166
Sattler, Jerome M. 258
Saussure, Ferdinand de 166
Scarf, Maggie 199
Scarr, Sandra, Richard A. Weinberg, and Ann Levine 186
Schachter, Stanley 74, 180
Schachter, Stanley, and Jerome Singer 246
Schachter, Stanley, and Larry P. Gross 95
Schachter, Stanley, Leon Festinger, and Kurt Back 224
Schaef, Anne Wilson 356
Schaefer, C., J. C. Coyne, and R. S. Lazarus 307
Schaefer, Charles E. 329
Schaefer, Charles E., and Steven E. Reid, eds. 378, 382
Schaefer, Charles E., Susan Folkman, and Richard S. Lazarus 301
Schaeffer, Bob, John G. Weiss, and Barbara Beckwith 261
Schaie, K. Warner, and James S. Birren, eds. 202
Schalling, Daisy, and Robert D. Hare, eds. 346

Schank, Roger C. 132
Schank, Roger C., and Robert P. Abelson 152
Scharf, Bertram, ed. 48
Scherer, Klaus R. 74
Schiff, William 48
Schiffman, Harvey Richard 55
Schildkraut, Joseph J. 30
Schleidt, Wolfgang, Dietrich Burkhardt, and Helmut Altner 45
Schlein, Stephen, ed. 199
Schlenker, Barry R. 246-247
Schlesinger, Kurt 121
Schmeck, Ronald R., ed. 105
Schmidt-Nielsen, Knut 55
Schnapf, Julie L., and Denis A. Baylor 64
Schneck, Matthew R., and Henry Edward Garrett 253
Schneider, Allen M., and Barry Tarshis 41
Schneider, David J., Albert H. Hastorf, and Phoebe C. Ellsworth 88, 247
Schneider, D. J. 247
Schneider, Erwin H., ed. 382
Schneider, Walter 132, 138
Schoenbrun, David 193
Schoenfeld, William N., ed. 116
Schopler, Eric, and Gary B. Mesibov, eds. 329
Schrader, William T., and Bert W. O'Malley 29
Schreiber, Flora Rheta 337
Schuckers, Gordon, Raymond Daniloff, and Lawrence Feth 50
Schultz, Duane 81, 278
Schultz, Duane P., and Sydney Ellen Schultz 8
Schulz, Patricia M., Siegfried Kasper, Susan L. Rogers, Angela Yancey, Robert A. Skwerer, and Norman E. Rosenthal 341
Schwartz, Barry 105
Schwartz, Barry, and Dan Reisberg 112, 121, 152
Schwartz, Hillel 95
Schwartz, Pepper, and Philip W. Blumstein 91
Schwartz, Robert 95
Scientific American 41
Searle, John R. 132
Sears, Robert R. 170

Sears, Robert R., John Dollard, Leonard W. Doob, Neal E. Miller, and O. Hobart Mowrer   86
Segall, Marshall H.   212
Segalowitz, Sidney J.   41
Sekerke, H. Joseph, David S. Janowsky, M. Khaled El-Yousef, and John M. Davis   27
Sekuler, Robert, and Robert R. Blake   48
Seligman, Martin E. P.   109, 112, 114, 247, 308, 343, 371
Seligman, Martin E. P., and David L. Rosenhan   322
Seligman, Martin E. P., and Joanne L. Hager, eds.   109
Selkoe, Dennis J.   42
Selltiz, Claire, Marie Johoda, Morton Deutsch, and S. Cook   14
Selye, Hans   297, 308, 315
Shaefer, Catherine, Allen D. Kanner, and Richard S. Lazarus   304
Shaffer, David Reed   170, 173, 186
Shaffer, Martin   308
Shames, George H., and Elizabeth H. Wiig, eds.   167
Shapiro, Deane H., Jr., and Roger N. Walsh, eds.   138
Shaughnessy, John J., and Eugene B. Zechmeister   23
Shaughnessy, Michael F.   258
Shaver, Kelly G.   247
Shaver, P., C. Hazan, and D. Bradshaw   226
Shaw, B. F., Aaron T. Beck, A. J. Rush, and G. Emery   338, 368
Sheehan, Joseph Green, et al.   329
Sheehan, Peter W., and Kevin M. McConkey   138
Sheehy, Gail   199
Shefner, Jeremy M., and Michael W. Levine   47
Shellenberger, Robert, and Judith Alyce Green   312
Shepherd, Gordon M.   42, 105
Shepherd, Irma Lee, and Joen Fagan, eds.   370
Sherif, Muzafer   233
Sherman, James H., Arthur J. Vander, and Dorothy S. Luciano   44
Sherman, William M.   363
Shields, James, Irving I. Gottesman, and Daniel R. Hanson   348

Shields, J. L., T. M. Dembroski, J. M. MacDougall, J. A. Herd   311
Shisslak, C. M., Marjorie Crago, M. E. Neal, and B. Swain   329
Shneidman, Edwin S., Norman L. Farberow, and Robert E. Litman   344
Shoda, Yuichi, Walter Mischel, and Monica L. Rodriguez   277
Shoemaker, Paul J. H., and J. Edward Russo   131
Short, Roger Valentine, and Colin Russell Austin, eds.   90
Shuman, Samuel I.   367
Sidel, Joel L., and Herbert Stone   48
Sidman, Murray   17, 114
Siegall, Marc, and Linda N. Jewell   243
Siegel, Bernie   308
Siegel, Elaine V.   382
Siegel, George J., Bernard W. Agranoff, R. Wayne Albers, and Perry B. Molinoff, eds.   42
Siegel, H. I., Barry R. Komisaruk, M. F. Cheng, and H. H. Feder, eds.   28, 93
Siegel, Michael H., and H. Philip Zeigler, eds.   8, 23
Siegel, P. S., and H. H. Myers   81
Siegler, Robert S.   170
Siffre, Michel   144
Sigel, Irving E., and Rodney R. Cocking   173
Signorelli, Nancy, and George Gerbner, comps.   212
Silver, R., and C. Wortman   309
Silver, R. C., and J. D. Gray   196
Simek-Downing, Lynn, and Allen E. Ivey   376
Simmons, J. L., and G. J. McCall   13
Simon, H. A., and K. A. Ericsson   58
Simonton, Carl, Stephanie Matthews-Simonton, and James Creighton   309, 345
Simpson, George Gaylord, William S. Beck, and Karel F. Liem   25, 106
Sims-Knight, Judith E., and Judy F. Rosenblith   186
Singer, Jerome, and Stanley Schachter   246
Singhal, Radhey L., and Pavel Hrdina, eds.   27
Singleton, Royce, Jr., et al.   14
Sjolander, Sverre, and Karl Erik Fichtelius   98

Skinner, B. F.   9, 81, 89, 105-106, 116-117, 278-279

Skinner, B. F., and Charles B. Ferster   115

Skodol, A. E., Robert L. Spitzer, and J. B. Williams, eds.   270

Skodol, A. E., Robert L. Spitzer, M. Gibbon, J. B. W. Williams, and Michael First   270

Skwerer, Robert A., Frederick M. Jacobsen, Thomas A. Wehr, David A. Sack, and Norman E. Rosenthal   341

Skwerer, Robert A., Siegfried Kasper, Susan L. Rogers, Angela Yancey, Patricia M. Schulz, and Norman E. Rosenthal   341

Skynner, A. C. Robin   378

Slavin, Robert E.   106, 233

Sloan, L. R.   89

Slocum, John W., Jr., and Richard W. Woodman   79

Slovenko, R.   323

Slovic, Paul, Daniel Kahneman, and Amos Tversky, eds.   129

Slovic, Paul, Sarah Lichtenstein, and Baruch Fischhoff   132

Smith, Barry D., and Harold J. Vetter   138, 279

Smith, Blanchard B.   221

Smith, Edward E., and Robert J. Sternberg, eds.   132

Smith, E. E., R. L. Atkinson, R. C. Atkinson, and D. J. Bem   67

Smith, Frank   112, 152

Smith, Jillyn   64

Smith, Karl U.   55

Smith, Lynn G., and Gordon Clanton, eds.   223

Smith, Mary Lee, and Gene V. Glass   385

Smith, Mary Lee, Gene V. Glass, and Thomas I. Miller   385

Smith, M. B., and J. W. Anderson   82

Smith, Stanley, Fred Warshofsky, and the editors of Life   48

Smith, W. Lynn, Harold Merskey, and Steven C. Gross   309

Smither, James W., Richard R. Reilly, and Sarah Henry   267

Smolensky, P., David E. Rumelhart, James L. McClelland, and Geoffrey E. Hinton   152

Smyth, Mary M., et al.   138

Sniezek, Janet A., and Rebecca A. Henry   222

Snowdon, Charles T., Charles H. Brown, and Michael R. Petersen, eds.   100

Snowling, Margaret J.   167

Snowman, Jack, and Robert Frederick Biehler   102

Snyder, C. R., and B. Kent Houston, eds.   313

Snyder, C. R., Raymond L. Higgins, and Rita J. Stucky   247

Snyder, Mark   216, 248

Snyder, Solomon H.   349, 367

Sobel, D. S., and Robert Ornstein   297

Sokal, Michael M., ed.   258

Solomon, Leonard, Henry Wechsler, and Bernard M. Kramer, eds.   323

Solomon, Richard L.   82, 114

Solomon, Richard L., and J. D. Corbit   82

Solso, Robert L.   64, 132, 139, 152

Sommer, Barbara B., and Robert Sommer   9

Sontag, Susan   309

Sorrentino, Richard M., and J. Philippe Rushton, eds.   238

Spanos, Nicholas P., and John F. Chaves, eds.   139

Speech Foundation of America, The   167

Spence, Alexander P., and Elliott B. Mason   30

Spence, Janet T., ed.   89

Spence, Kenneth Wartenbee   279

Spencer, Roberta Todd   30

Spiegal, John P., and Roy Richard Grinker   334

Spiegel, John P., and Roy Richard Grinker   302

Spiegler, Michael D., and Robert M. Lieber   276

Spielberger, Charles Donald   309

Spilka, Bernard, Ralph W. Hood, and Richard L. Gorsuch   248

Spitzer, Robert L., J. B. Williams, and A. E. Skodol, eds.   270

Spitzer, Robert L., M. Gibbon, A. E. Skodol, J. B. W. Williams, and Michael First   270

Spock, Benjamin   180

Spotnitz, Hyman   382

Spotnitz, Hyman, and Phyllis W. Meadow   382

Sprafkin, Joyce, and Robert M. Liebert   211

Sprecher, Susan, and Elaine Hatfield   224

Springer, Sally P., and Georg Deutsch   42

Sprinthall, Richard C.   17

Squire, L. R.   153

Srull, T., Douglas A. Bernstein, E. Roy, T. Srull, and C. Wickens   67

Srull, Thomas K., and Robert S. Wyer   154

Staats, A. W.   74

Stacks, Don W., and Mark L. Hickson   161

Staddon, J. E. R., and R. H. Ettinger   114

Staddon, J. R.   106

Stanley, Gordon, Diana Elton, and Graham Burrows   300

Stanley, Julian C., and Donald Thomas Campbell   15, 19

Stanovich, Keith E.   24

Stanton, M. Duncan   375

Stark, Elizabeth   200

Starkweather, C. Woodruff   330

Staub, Ervin   238

Staub, Ervin, Daniel Bar-Tal, Jerzy Karylowki, and Janusz Reykowski, eds.   238

Stea, David, and Roger M. Downs, eds.   125

Stebbins, William C.   55

Steer, Robert A., Aaron T. Beck, and Margery G. Garbin   263

Stein, Barry S., and John Bransford   110, 124

Stein, Donald G.   42

Stein, Jean, and Robert L. Crooks   57, 92

Steinberg, Laurence D., Jay Belsky, and Roberta B. Meyer   187

Steiner, Ivan Dale   222

Steinmetz, Suzanne K., Murray Arnold Straus, and Richard J. Gelles   181

Steketee, G. S., Edna B. Foa, and L. M. Ascher   360

Stellar, James R., and Eliot Stellar   82

Stengel, Erwin   344

Stepansky, Paul E.   289

Stephan, Walter G., and David Rosenfield   233

Steriade, Mircea, and Robert W. McCarley   42

Stern, E. Mark, ed.   385

Stern, Leonard   153

Stern, Paul C.   24

Stern, Robert Morris, William J. Ray, and Christopher M. Davis   268

Sternberg, Martin L. A.   167

Sternberg, Robert, and Catherine Whitney   226

Sternberg, Robert J.   258-259

Sternberg, Robert J., and Edward E. Smith, eds.   132

Stevens, Leonard A.   9, 64

Stevens, Stanley Smith   48

Stevenson, Harold W., and Daniel A. Wagner, eds.   187

Stewart, Barbara J., and Elliot A. Weiner   261

Stewart, Charles J., and William B. Cash, Jr.   14

Stillings, Neil A., et al.   132

Stine, Gerald James   65

Stoddard, Sandol   208

Stokols, Daniel, and Irwin Altman, eds.   216

Stoller, Robert J.   352

Stone, George C., ed.   316

Stone, Herbert, and Joel L. Sidel   48

Stone, J. I., and T. D. Wilson   249

Storfer, Miles D.   259

Storms, Michael D., and Kevin D. McCaul   74

Storr, Anthony   289

Straus, Murray Arnold, Richard J. Gelles, and Suzanne K. Steinmetz   181

Strayer, Janet, and Nancy Eisenberg, eds.   237

Strien, Tatjana van   96

Stryer, Lubert   30, 43, 65

Stuart, Richard B.   96

Stuck, Mary, ed.   234

Stucky, Rita J., C. R. Snyder, and Raymond L. Higgins   247

Sudman, Seymour   24

Sullivan, Harry Stack   289, 349

Suls, Jerry   309

Sulzman, Frank M., Martin C. Moore-Ede, and Charles A. Fuller   144

Super, Donald Edwin 200
Surrat, Paul M., Faiq G. Issa, and John E. Remmers, eds. 143
Surwillo, Walter W. 43
Swain, B., C. M. Shisslak, Marjorie Crago, and M. E. Neal 329
Sweetland, R. C., and D. J. Keyser, eds. 268, 270
Swets, John A., and David Martin Green 46
Symmes, David, Dietmar Todt, and Philipp Goedeking, eds. 101
Symonds, Alexandra 289
Symposium on the Neural Basis of Behavior 43
Szasz, Thomas Stephen 323, 352

Tabor, Diane Tabor, Alfred and James McIntyre 83
Tajfel, Henri 234
Tajfel, Henri, and John Turner 234
Tannen, Deborah 167-168
Tanner, J. M., and Frank Falkner 183
Tarshis, Barry, and Allen M. Schneider 41
Tart, Charles T. 139
Tavris, Carol, and Carole Wade 234
Taylor, Dalmas A., and Irwin Altman 223
Taylor, Dalmas A., and Phyllis A. Katz, eds. 231
Taylor, Donald M., and Fathali M. Moghaddam 234
Taylor, Frederick Winslow 89
Taylor, Jacque, John D. Defrain, and Linda Ernst 182
Taylor, Shelley E. 248, 310, 316
Taylor, Shelley E., and Susan T. Fiske 70, 147, 241
Teddie, Charles, and Stephen Worchel 249
Teevan, Richard C., and Birney, Robert Charles 77
Teyber, Edward 385
Tharp, Roland G., and David L. Watson 363
Thomas, Carroll, and Oscar Christensen 175
Thomas, Gail E., ed. 235
Thomas, James P., Kenneth R. Boff, and Lloyd Kaufman, eds. 134
Thomas, Joan, and Sol Landau 197

Thomas, R. Murray 112
Thompson, Jack George 74
Thompson, Richard F. 43
Thompson, Richard F., and Robert Evan Ornstein 39
Thompson, Travis, and John G. Grabowski 117
Thoresen, Carl E., and John D. Krumboltz, eds. 361
Thorndike, Robert M., and David F. Lohman 259
Thorne, Barrie, Cheris Kramarae, and Nancy Henley 235
Timmons, C. Robin, and Leonard W. Hamilton 52, 114
Titchener, Edward Bradford 9
Tobias, Jerry V., ed. 55
Todt, Dietmar, Philipp Goedeking, and David Symmes, eds. 101
Tolman, Edward Chace 113
Tomkins, Silvan Solomon 75
Tomlinson-Keasey, Carol 187
Torrance, Ellis Paul 259-260
Torrey, Edwin Fuller 349, 359
Tortora, Gerard J., and Nicholas P. Anagnostakos 43
Tousignant, James, David Hall, and Elizabeth Loftus 148
Towne, Neil, Ronald B. Adler, and Lawrence B. Rosenfeld 222
Treisman, Anne 139
Triandis, H. C., and A. Heron, eds. 170
Tripp, C. A. 96
Trochim, William M. K., ed. 17
Troll, Lillian E. 208
Trubo, Richard, and David E. Bresler 300
Trull, T. J., and T. A. Widiger 323
Trumbo, Don A., and Frank J. Landy 87
Tsongas, Paul 310
Tulving, Endel 153
Tuma, A. Hussain, and Jack D. Maser, eds. 337
Turner, Eric Anderson 367
Turner, John, and Henri Tajfel 234
Turner, John C. 235
Turner, John C., Michael A. Hogg, et al. 222
Turner, Samuel M., and Rolf G. Jacob 334

Turner, Samuel M., Matig Mavissakalian, and Larry Michelson 335
Turner, S. M., and L. Michelson 337
Tversky, Amos, and Daniel Kahneman 133
Tversky, Amos, Daniel Kahneman, and Paul Slovic, eds. 129
Tweney, Ryan D., and Wolfgang G. Bringmann, eds. 4
Tyler, Leona Elizabeth 260

Ullman, Montague, and Benjamin B. Wolman, eds. 140
Ullmann, Leonard P., and Leonard Krasner 117
Ullmann, Leonard P., Leonard Krasner, and Arthur C. Houts 321
Ulmer, Diane, and Meyer Friedman 301, 312
Unger, Rhoda Kesler 30
United States Department of Health and Human Services 356-357
Ury, William, and Roger Fisher 218
U.S. Congress Office of Technology Assessment 24

Valadez, C. M., Amado M. Padilla, H. H. Fairchild, eds. 164
Valenstein, Elliot S. 75, 359, 367
Valett, Robert E. 168
Valins, Stuart, and Richard E. Nisbett 75
Vallacher, Robin R., and Daniel M. Wegner, eds. 248
Vallaint, George E., and J. Christopher Perry 347
Valle, Ronald S., and Steen Halling, eds. 9, 294
Valzelli, Luigi 75
Van Bergeijk, Willem André Maria, John R. Pierce, and Edward E. David, Jr. 56
Van Bourgondien, Mary E., Gary B. Mesibov, and Geraldine Dawson 330
Van de Castle, Robert L., and Calvin Springer Hall 142
Van De Graaff, Kent Marshall, and Stuart Ira Fox 43
Van den Berg, Jan Hendrik 9
Vander, Arthur J., James H. Sherman, and Dorothy S. Luciano 44
Van Kaam, Adrian L. 294

Van Toller, C. 44
Van Veldhuizen, Nelly, and William A. Roberts 112
Vargas, Julie S. 279
Vaughan, Diane 227
Vaux, Alan 310
Veatch, Robert M., and Carol Levine, eds. 21
Veith-Flanigan, Jane, and Curt A. Sandman 298
Ventis, W. Larry, and C. Daniel Batson 238
Verhave, Thom 106
Vernon, Philip Ewart 260
Verrilli, Donald B., Donald N. Bersoff, and Laurel P. Malson 263
Vertes, Robert P., W. R. Klemm, eds. 37
Vessey, Stephen H., and Lee C. Drickamer 98
Vetter, Harold J., and Barry D. Smith 138, 279
Villee, Claude Alvin, et al. 44
Vingiano, W., and H. Sackheim 336
Von Franz, Marie-Luise 290
Vonnegut, Mark 350
Vroom, Victor 82
Vucinich, Alexander S. 121
Vygotsky, Lev Semenovich 113

Wade, Carole, and Carol Tavris 234
Wagner, Daniel A., and Harold W. Stevenson, eds. 187
Wagner, Rudolf F. 168
Waldinger, Robert J. 337
Wales, Roger, and Robin Campbell 157
Walk, Richard D., and Elenor J. Gibson 65
Walker, C. Eugene, ed. 359
Walker, C. Eugene, Mary Kenning, and Jan Faust-Campanile 330
Walker, Elaine F., ed. 350
Walker, Elaine F., and Richard J. Lewine 350
Walker, John R., G. Ron Norton, and Colin A. Ross, eds. 337
Walker, Lenore E. A., and Lynne Bravo Rosewater, eds. 385
Walker, Lenore E. A., and Mary Ann Dutton-Douglas 383
Wall, Patrick D., and Ronald Melzack 54

Wall, S., Mary D. Salter Ainsworth, Mary C. Blehar, and Everett Waters 174

Wallace, Benjamin 139

Wallace, Benjamin, and Leslie E. Fisher 139

Wallace, R. Jay, Jr., Tom L. Beauchamp, Ruth R. Faden, and Le Roy Walters, eds. 18

Wallace, R. Keith 140

Wallace, Robert A., Gerald P. Sanders, and Robert J. Ferl 31, 44, 109

Wallerstein, Judith S., and Joan Berlin Kelly 181

Wallerstein, Judith S., and Sandra Blakeslee 181, 200

Wallnau, Larry B., and Frederick J. Gravetter 16

Walsh, James K., A. Michael Anch, C. P. Browman, and M. M. Mitler 140

Walsh, Mary Roth, ed. 235

Walsh, Roger N., and Deane H. Shapiro, Jr., eds. 138

Walsh, W. Bruce, and Nancy E. Betz 260, 268

Walster, Elaine, and G. William Walster 227

Walster, Elaine Hatfield, and Ellen Berscheid 223

Walters, Le Roy, Tom L. Beauchamp, Ruth R. Faden, and R. Jay Wallace, Jr., eds. 18

Waltz, David L. 65

Wann, Daniel L., and Nyla R. Branscombe 84

Wapner, S., and J. Demick 316

Wardell, B., P. H. Gebhard, W. B. Pomeroy, J. H. Gagnon, and C. V. Christenson 351

Warden, Carl John 82

Warren-Leubecker, Amye, and John Neil Bohannon, III 156

Warshofsky, Fred, Stanley Smith, and the editors of *Life* 48

Wass, Hannelore, Felix Berardo, and Robert A. Neimeyer, eds. 209

Waterhouse, J. M., and D. S. Minors 143

Waters, Everett, Mary D. Salter Ainsworth, Mary C. Blehar, and S. Wall 174

Watson, David L., and Roland G. Tharp 117, 363

Watson, John B. 10, 75, 82, 106

Watson, Philip 65

Watson, Robert Irving, Sr., and Rand B. Evans 10

Watson, Ronald Ross, ed. 357

Watt, Norman F., et al., eds. 350

Watts, James Winston, and Walter Jackson Freeman 365

Weary, G., and J. H. Harvey 242

Webb, Wilse B. 144

Weber, Ann L., John H. Harvey, and Terri L. Orbuch 224

Wechsler, David 260

Wechsler, Henry, Leonard Solomon, and Bernard M. Kramer, eds. 323

Weeks, Gerald R., and Luciano L'Abate 375

Wegner, Daniel M., and Robin R. Vallacher, eds. 248

Wehr, Gerhard 383

Wehr, Thomas A., Frederick M. Jacobsen, Robert A. Skwerer, David A. Sack, and Norman E. Rosenthal 341

Wehr, Thomas A., Siegfried Kasper, John J. Bartko, Paul A. Gaist, and Norman E. Rosenthal 341

Weinberg, Martin, and Alan P. Bell 90

Weinberg, Martin S., Alan P. Bell, and Sue Kiefer Hammersmith 90

Weinberg, Richard A., Sandra Scarr, and Ann Levine 186

Weinberg, Thomas S., and G. W. Levi Kamel, eds. 352

Weiner, Bernard 83

Weiner, Elliot A., and Barbara J. Stewart 261

Weiner, Irving B., and Allen K. Hess, eds. 323

Weisberg, Robert W. 261

Weiss, John G., Barbara Beckwith, and Bob Schaeffer 261

Weiss, Robert Stuart 227

Weiss, Stephen M., and Kenneth D. Craig, eds. 311

Weiten, Wayne 83, 316

Weiten, Wayne, Margaret A. Lloyd, and R. L. Lashley 274

Weitzman, Lenore J. 200

Weizenbaum, Joseph 133

Wells, Gary L., and Elizabeth F. Loftus, eds. 153
Werner, Heinz, and Bernard Kaplan 168
Wertheimer, Max 133
Wertheimer, Michael 10, 65
Wesner, Robert, Michael J. Garvey, and Michael Godes 340
Westkott, Marcia 290
Wexley, K. N., and Gary P. Latham 89
Whelan, Mariellen, and Ronald F. Duska 171
Whishaw, Ian Q., and Bryan Kolb 37, 149
White, Gregory L., and Paul E. Mullen 227
White, Gregory L., Sanford Fishbein, and Jeffrey Rustein 248
White, Merry 193
White, William C., Jr., and Marlene Boskind-White 325
Whitham, Frederick L. 96
Whitmont, Edward C. 290
Whitney, Catherine, and Robert Sternberg 226
Whorf, Benjamin Lee 168
Wibbelsman, Charles, and Kathy McCoy 191
Wickens, C., Douglas A. Bernstein, E. Roy, and T. Srull 67
Wickens, Christopher D. 49, 140
Wicklund, Robert A., and Jack Williams Brehm 216
Widiger, T. A., and T. J. Trull 323
Wiens, Arthur N., Robert Gale Harper, and Joseph D. Matarazzo 161
Wiesel, Torsten N., and David H. Hubel 60
Wigdor, Alexandra K., and Wendell R. Garner, eds. 261
Wiggins, Jerry S. 268
Wilkie, William L. 133
Willerman, Lee 324
Williams, J. B., Robert L. Spitzer, and A. E. Skodol, eds. 270
Williams, J. B. W., Robert L. Spitzer, M. Gibbon, A. E. Skodol, and Michael First 270
Williams, John E., and Deborah L. Best 235
Williams, Robert, and Horace Mitchell 261

Williams, Robert, and James D. Long 248
Willner, Paul 344
Wilson, Bill 357
Wilson, Edward O. 83, 89, 109
Wilson, Jean D., and Daniel W. Foster 298
Wilson, Nancy, ed. 96
Wilson, R. Reid 338
Wilson, T. D., and J. I. Stone 249
Winchester, Albert McCombs 187
Winer, B. J. 17
Winfree, Arthur T. 144
Winkel, G. H., and S. Saegert 216
Winkler, Mary G., and Thomas R. Cole, eds. 203
Wise, Jonathan, and Susan Kierr Wise 96
Wise, Paula Sachs 262, 268
Witte, Robert S. 24
Wolfe, David A. 181
Wolfe, Jeremy M., ed. 66
Wolman, Benjamin B., ed. 97, 170, 262
Wolman, Benjamin B., and Montague Ullman, eds. 140
Wolpe, Joseph 324, 363, 385
Woodman, Marion 97
Woodman, Richard W., Don Hellriegel, and John W. Slocum, Jr. 79
Woodward, Kenneth L., and Arthur Kornhaber 206
Worchel, Stephen, and Charles Teddie 249
Worchel, Stephen, and William G. Austin, eds. 235
World Health Organization 271
Wortman, C., and R. Silver 309
Wortman, Camille B., and Elizabeth F. Loftus 76
Wortman, Camille B., Ronald C. Kessler, and Richard H. Price 304
Wright, Robert 101
Wrightsman, Lawrence S. 154, 324
Wrightsman, Lawrence S., and Saul M. Kassin 244
Wulff, David M. 249
Wurtman, Judith 97
Wurtman, Richard J., and Judith J. Wurtman 344
Wyer, Robert S., and Thomas K. Srull 154

Yalom, Irvin D. 294, 375, 379
Yancey, Angela, Siegfried Kasper, Susan L. Rogers, Patricia M. Schulz, Robert A. Skwerer, and Norman E. Rosenthal 341
Yardley, Krysia, and Terry Honess, eds. 249
Yarmey, A. Daniel 154
Yates, Frances Amelia 154
Yates, J. Frank 133
Yin, Robert K. 15
Ylvisaker, Mark, and Eva Marie R. Gobble, eds. 44
Yonas, A., and C. E. Granrud 66
Yost, Elizabeth B., and M. Anne Corbishley 200
Young, Andrew W., and Andrew W. Ellis 34
Youngren, M. A., Peter M. Lewinsohn, R. F. Munoz, and A. M. Zeiss 342
Yuker, Harold, and J. Richard Block 57
Yukl, Gary A. 222
Yussen, Steven R., and John W. Santrock 186

Zabrack, Merle L., Leslie A. Joy, and Meredith M. Kimball 211
Zandi, Taher, and Richard J. Ham, eds. 345

Zanna, Mark P., and Russell Fazio 214
Zanna, Mark P., E. Tory Higgins, and C. Peter Herman, eds. 216
Zebrowitz, L. A. 249
Zechmeister, Eugene B., and Stanley E. Nyberg 154
Zechmeister, Eugene B., and John J. Shaughnessy 23
Zedeck, Sheldon, Edwin Ernest Ghiselli, and John P. Campbell 253
Zeigler, H. Philip, and Michael H. Siegel, eds. 8, 23
Zeigler, H. Philip, and Charles G. Gross eds. 36
Zeiss, A. M., Peter M. Lewinsohn, R. F. Munoz, and M. A. Youngren 342
Zettle, Robert D., and Steven C. Hayes 117
Zillmann, Dolf 76
Zillmann, Dolf, and Jennings Bryant, eds. 212
Zimbardo, Philip G. 90, 222
Zimbardo, Philip G., and Michael R. Leippe 217
Zubay, Geoffrey L. 31
Zyzanski, S. J., C. D. Jenkins, and R. H. Rosenman 313

SUBJECT INDEX

Achievement 80, 88, 174, 191
Achievement motivation 84, 89
Addiction 40, 82, 90, 114, 353-355
ADHD 325-327, 329
Adler, Alfred 173, 279-281, 284, 288-289, 379-381
Aggression 68, 71, 75-76, 84, 86, 98, 101, 108, 111-112, 178, 210-212, 275, 305, 366
Alcoholism 93, 181, 274, 353-357, 363
Allport, Gordon W. 229, 262, 290-293
Alzheimer's disease 39, 42, 44, 208, 344-345
Amnesia 68, 135, 148-149, 151-152, 331, 336
Animal behavior 30-31, 88, 95, 98-100, 103-106, 108-109, 111, 297
Animal communication 99, 101, 129, 160, 162, 165
Anorexia nervosa 27, 91-92, 97, 319, 325-326, 328-329
Anxiety 39, 67, 71, 112, 114, 240, 269, 283, 293, 303, 307, 309, 318, 320, 330-333, 335-337, 341, 355, 368, 384
Aphasia 156, 158-159, 164, 166-167
Artificial intelligence 65, 123-124, 127-128, 130-132, 135
Attachment 174, 176, 226
Attention-deficit hyperactivity disorder. *See* ADHD
Autism 324, 326-330

Bandura, Albert 84, 110-112, 210, 274-275, 278-279, 359-360
Bed-wetting 325, 327-330, 363
Behaviorism 3, 5-10, 74-75, 82, 105-106, 116, 131, 155, 277-278
Bilingualism 155, 158-160, 164-165
Biofeedback 44, 298-300, 306
Bioscience 25
Bipolar affective disorder 340-342
Birth 182, 184-185
Birth order 173, 177, 180
Brain damage 31, 34, 38-40, 42, 44, 156
Brain stem 34, 36-38, 40, 42
Bulimia 325, 328-329
Bystander effect 236-238

Cancer 54, 70, 91, 206, 208, 302, 306-307, 309, 311-312, 314, 345
Career development 196-198, 200, 266
Careers in psychology 3, 6, 358-359
Child abuse 175-177, 181, 193
Chomsky, Noam 111, 157, 163-164
Client-centered therapy 373, 378, 384
Codependency 352-354, 356
Cognitive dissonance 90, 213-216
Cognitive maps 111-113, 125
Color blindness 58, 61-65
Color vision 57-58, 61, 63-64
Community psychology 386
Conformity 83, 217
Consumer behavior 123, 126, 133, 179, 214
Creativity 123, 250, 252-254, 256-261
Cross-cultural psychology 46, 69-70, 87, 96, 155, 165, 170, 183, 187, 190, 193, 212, 216, 220, 235, 238, 272, 303, 342
Crowding 219-221, 249, 298-299, 301
Crowds 217-218, 220
Cults 218

Dance therapy 303, 381-382
Deafness 49-50, 53, 167
Death 112, 114, 201, 203-204, 206-207, 209, 247, 304, 308, 314, 343
Deindividuation 219, 221-222
Depression 27-28, 30, 40, 52, 68, 71, 85, 112, 114-115, 142, 178, 193, 247, 269, 308, 320, 338-344, 353, 366, 368, 384
Desensitization 362
Dieting 92-93, 95-97, 213
Divorce 178-179, 181, 196-197, 200, 224-227
Drama therapy 381
Dreams 140-143, 280, 282-283, 286
Drugs 36, 52, 71, 190, 318, 353-357, 365, 367
Du Bois, W. E. B. 229
Dyslexia 33, 161-162, 166-168

ECT 364-366
Educational psychology 16, 83, 86, 102-103, 106, 112, 115, 117, 123,

147-150, 176, 230-231, 233, 251, 259-261, 268, 370
Electroconvulsive therapy. *See* ECT
Encopresis 327, 329-330
Endorphins 27, 35-36, 40
Enuresis. *See* Bed-wetting
Environmental psychology 125, 214-216, 219, 221, 299, 316
Epilepsy 34, 37
Erikson, Erik H. 176-177, 180, 188, 194-197, 199, 203-205, 272, 281-282, 289
Ethics 17-19, 21, 23-24, 366-368
Ethology 8, 69, 78, 98-100, 103, 105, 107
Existential 197, 291-294, 319, 377, 379

Facial feedback theories 68, 70-71, 75
Family therapy 373-375
Food aversion 91, 107-108
Freud, Sigmund 78, 86, 138, 171, 173, 180, 253, 272, 280, 282-284, 286-289, 320, 333, 380
Friendship 224, 226
Functionalism 4, 6-8, 136

Gender differences. *See* Sex differences
Gender identity 30, 175, 178-180
Genetics 57, 62, 65, 78, 183-184, 186-187, 205, 207-208
Gestalt psychology 58, 60-61, 65, 133
Gestalt therapy 370-371, 373, 376-377
Giftedness 252, 258-259
Grandparents 202, 206, 208
Groupthink 220

Health psychology 310, 312, 315-316
Hearing 46, 48, 50-52, 54-56, 158, 183
Homosexuality 90-91, 93-94, 96, 318, 363
Hormones 25-31, 81, 88, 91, 93-95, 100, 297-298
Horney, Karen 284-286, 288-290
Humanistic 8, 292, 376
Humanistic Psychologist, The 292
Hypnosis 134-135, 138-139, 299
Hypochondriasis 334

Identity 180, 188-189, 191-192, 195
Identity crises 188
Illusions 57, 59, 64
Industrial/organizational psychology 5,

15, 79, 85, 87-89, 194, 197-199, 222, 243, 255, 268, 302
Inferiority complex 280
Interviews 13, 15, 264-267, 270

Jung, Carl G. 143, 173, 204, 272, 284-287, 289-290, 379-380, 383
Juvenile delinquency 189-190, 192

Kelly, George Alexander 275-277

Language 37, 41, 51, 74, 98, 111, 124, 126, 132, 134-135, 146, 152, 155-168, 170
Law 148, 150, 154, 217, 219, 242, 244-245, 269, 318, 320-321, 323-324
Leadership 87, 217-219, 221-222
Lewin, Kurt 7, 83, 215, 232, 275-276
Lobotomy 359, 365, 367
Love 68, 73, 82, 194, 199, 223-227, 239, 248, 284, 309, 371

Marital therapy 372-374
Maslow, Abraham H. 80, 88, 292-293
Media 211-212
Meditation 134-135, 137-138, 140, 298, 305, 344
Memory 37, 39, 41, 46, 51, 63, 68, 91, 99, 103-104, 106, 112, 122, 127, 129-130, 145-154, 170, 241
Moral development 171, 173, 196
Multiple personality disorder 69, 135, 331, 334, 336-337, 347
Murray, Henry A. 77, 79, 82, 291-292
Music 50
Music therapy 382

Neural network 35, 39, 122, 125, 128, 131-133, 145
Neurotransmitters 28, 34-36, 38-40, 42-44, 91, 142, 349
Nonverbal communication 124, 158, 161-162, 164-165, 223

Observational 9, 11, 13-14
Obsessive-compulsive disorder 330, 332, 334-337, 362
Opponent process theory 78-79, 82
Optimism 308, 315

Pain 36, 40, 51-52, 54, 114, 135, 295, 299-300, 306, 309

Parenting 174-180, 193, 324, 361, 372-373
Pavlov, Ivan 74, 103, 118-121
Person-centered therapy 294, 377
Persuasion 164, 214-215
Phenomenological psychology 5, 9-10, 141
Phobias 75, 108-109, 267, 274, 318, 320, 331-333, 335-338, 362, 363, 368
Piaget, Jean 103, 164, 170-173, 189-190
Play therapy 376-377, 379, 381-382
Pornography 76, 211-212
Post-traumatic stress disorder 332, 334-335
Prejudice 12, 213, 217, 202, 227-235, 291
Problem solving 110, 116, 122-125, 127-130, 148, 259, 261
Projective tests 262, 268
Psychoanalysis 143, 170, 231, 280, 282-283, 291, 320, 231, 382
Psychophysics 45-46, 48-49, 55
Psychosurgery 75, 359, 365-368
PTSD. See Post-traumatic stress disorder

Quasi-experimental designs 15-17, 19
Questionnaires 11, 13

Racism 231, 233, 254-255
Rational-emotive therapy. See RET
Reality therapy 370, 373
Relaxation 136-137, 296, 298, 300, 303-306
Religion 238-240, 242-243, 245, 248-249, 291, 385
RET 361, 369, 373
Retirement 201, 203, 205, 208
Rogers, Carl R. 272, 294, 375, 378, 384

SAD. See Seasonal affective disorder
Schizophrenia 27, 39, 244, 292-293, 318, 321, 350, 382
Seasonal affective disorder 338-344
Seeing 48, 51
Self-actualization 80, 88, 292-293
Self-esteem 68, 84-85, 176, 180, 193, 239-240, 242, 244, 246, 384
Self-perception 239-241, 248
Self-presentation 239, 242-244, 246-248

Sex differences 30, 32, 41, 83, 89, 101, 172, 180, 191, 205, 223, 226, 234-235, 342
Sexual behavior 26-29, 92-93, 98, 148, 187-188, 191-192
Shyness 240, 242-244, 249
SIDS. See Sudden infant death syndrome
Skinner, B. F. 7, 9, 82, 89, 103, 105-106, 115-117, 277-279
Sleep 36-37, 42, 51, 140-144, 148
Smell 48-49, 52-53
Social learning theory 84, 110-112, 178, 274, 278
Sociobiology 78, 83, 89, 97, 100-101, 109, 227, 238
Somatoform disorders 331-332, 334, 337, 347
Speech 50-51, 53-54, 158, 163-164, 166-167
Split-brain 32-33, 41, 135
Sport psychology 84-86, 89, 212
Statistics 12-17, 19-24
Stereotypes 228-235
Stress 74, 125, 196, 214, 216, 219-221, 224, 269, 295-316, 332, 339
Stroke 156, 159
Structuralism 4-5, 7-8
Stuttering 33, 167, 326-327, 329-330
Sudden infant death syndrome 182, 184-185
Suicide 68, 190-191, 193, 293, 318, 340-344
Sullivan, Harry S. 272, 284, 289, 349
Systematic desensitization 360

TA. See Transactional analysis
Taste 48-53
Television 211, 238
Thirst 94
Touch 46
Transactional analysis 368-369, 371, 373
Type A behavior 301, 311-313, 315

Vision 39, 46-47, 56-66, 130, 133, 139
Visual development 183

Women, psychology of 22, 172, 174, 179, 187-188, 192, 194, 196, 199, 207, 228, 230, 232, 234-235, 283, 285, 287, 289-290, 320, 342, 376, 383-385